A DOG RUNS

THROUGH IT

A DOG RUNS THROUGH IT

Poems

Linda Pastan

 W. W. NORTON & COMPANY

Independent Publishers Since 1923

New York | London

For information about permission to reproduce selections
from this book, write to Permissions, W. W. Norton & Company, Inc.,
500 Fifth Avenue, New York, NY 10110

For information about special discounts for bulk purchases,
please contact W. W. Norton Special Sales at
specialsales@wwnorton.com or 800-233-4830

Manufacturing by Versa Press
Illustrations by Elsa Senner
Book design by Chris Welch Design
Production manager: Julia Druskin

Library of Congress Cataloging-in-Publication Data

Names: Pastan, Linda, date- author.
Title: A dog runs through it : poems / Linda Pastan.
Description: First edition. | New York : W. W. Norton & Company, [2018]
Identifiers: LCCN 2018002468 | ISBN 9780393651300 (hardcover)
Classification: LCC PS3566.A775 A6 2018 | DDC 811/.54—dc23
LC record available at https://lccn.loc.gov/2018002468

W. W. Norton & Company, Inc., 500 Fifth Avenue, New York, N.Y. 10110
www.wwnorton.com

W. W. Norton & Company Ltd., 15 Carlisle Street, London W1D 3BS

1 2 3 4 5 6 7 8 9 0

for Toby

CONTENTS

PREFACE

My first dog was named Rowdy. I was ten, an only child, and my parents thought a dog would be good company. But I had books for company. I wanted to sit under the shadow of the piano and simply read. Instead I had to walk the dog before I left for school and walk him again when I came home. The Grand Concourse, in the Bronx where we lived, had few trees. Rowdy would pee against apartment houses, against the tires of cars, and when people looked on disapprovingly I would pretend it was not me at the other end of the leash. Why didn't I love Rowdy more? He was a black and white wire-haired terrier with a square face, handsome and well behaved, and I had few other things in my life to love. I have paid dearly for that deficiency by loving the dogs who followed him all too passionately, all too well.

There was the Welsh terrier Rusty, in my teens, also square faced but black and orange. I tried to teach him tricks; I even took him to an obedience class. But my father undid all my careful training by roughhousing with him and repeating the commands I had taught him as if they were jokes. I suffered and suffered more when I had to leave home for college, knowing that my dog would be both neglected and spoiled. When I learned, in my sophomore year, that the boy I was dating also had a dog named Rusty, I married him.

Una was the first dog of our married life, a Bedlington terrier who looked like a lamb. On Halloween we put a sign around the dog's neck: "Wolf in Sheep's Clothing." I named Una for a character in *The Fairie Queen*, though everyone thought I had named her for Charlie Chaplin's wife Oona. But I had young children then, and I fear that though loved, Una was somewhat neglected in the chaos of family life.

Mowgli came next, the dog of my life. I say that in the spirit of a woman saying of a certain man: he was the love of my life. Mowgli was a Rhodesian ridgeback, bred to hunt lions in Africa. He was a large, rust-colored hound with a swordlike ridge of hair growing down his back. Though fierce looking, he was gentle and loving, and he followed me around the house from task to task—from laundry to study to kitchen. Once, when he disappeared for three days, I spent hours searching the woods near our house, shouting his name and weeping copiously. My husband finally found him in a deep hole some builder had dug to test the soil for a septic tank. He borrowed a ladder and carried Mowgli up in his arms. A few years later, though, when we were out of town, Mowgli died of stomach torsion while in a boarding kennel. I have never put a dog in a kennel again.

Caleb was another ridgeback, one with what John Irving called terminal flatulence, modeling a dog after him in *The Hotel New Hampshire*. My daughter Rachel was eleven when we got Caleb, but he was too big to sit on her lap. It was a lap dog she really wanted, so we added a black miniature poodle, Tanya, to our family. He lived with us for twenty-one years, longer than any of our children did.

Annie was our penultimate dog, a Norwich terrier. She looked a little like a large Toto—a cairn terrier.

I had seen one of her brothers at a friend's house, perfectly trained, sitting and lying down and rolling over on command. Perhaps I thought Norwich terriers were born that way. Annie certainly wasn't, but she was an easy and lovable dog, though she would drink water only if someone was petting her. People told me that she would drink if she became thirsty enough, but that was like telling me to let my baby cry himself to sleep, something I had never done.

And now we have Toby, our rescue dog, a gray mini-poodle mix. He is a bit longer than the usual mini-poodle, so perhaps there is some dachshund in his DNA. Our whole family seems to be rescuing dogs recently, a fine trend, and Toby is a delight. But we had been told he was six years old, and when later our vet told us he must be at least ten, it was too late to consider returning him. He might not live for many years, but then neither might we, and in any case, we were hooked.

What is it about dogs anyway, and dog people? We know who we are. We stop strangers on the street who just happen to be walking a dog, and we talk to them. We hang out in dog parks. We cross a street to greet an unknown dog on the other side. And when a dog appears early in a movie, we worry that something will happen to it by the end. In fact, someone has actually made an app where you can put in the name of a movie and it will tell you if the dog is going to die!

Some dog people have a kind of natural authority with dogs; dogs just know to obey them. I am not one of those people. I am more like the substitute teacher who walks into a classroom and every student relaxes and starts to text. My dogs jump on me, bark at me, pull on the leash when we walk. So why am I hooked?

President Truman was supposedly told that if you want to have a friend in Washington, you should get a dog. I live in Washington too, or nearby anyway, but I have lots of friends, so that's not it. Nor is it simply the wish to have company or to be unconditionally loved. It's something much more instinctive, even primal. Perhaps when our ancestors were domesticating dogs by long-ago campfires, a process that took years, we were learning to need them as they would learn to need us.

And so to this book. I knew I had written a

number of poems about dogs over the years, but I was surprised when looking through my work to see how many dogs had sneaked onto a page about something else entirely, making the briefest of appearances. It reminded me of Toby, sneaking onto the forbidden couch when nobody was watching. This book is dedicated to him.

A DOG RUNS

THROUGH IT

The Great Dog of Night

John Wilde, oil on panel

The great dog of night
growls at the windows,
barks at the door.

Soon I must straddle
its sleek back and fly
over the fields

and rooftops
of sleep, above us
a vague moon

loose in the sky,
far ahead of us
morning.

The New Dog

Into the gravity of my life,
the serious ceremonies
of polish and paper and pen, has come

this manic animal
whose innocent disruptions
make nonsense
of my old simplicities

as if I needed him
to prove again that after
all the careful planning
anything can happen.

In the Garden

I tell my dog to sit
and he sits
and I give him
a biscuit.
I tell him to come
and he comes
and sits,
and I give him
a biscuit
again.
I tell my dog Lie Down!
and he sits,
looking up
at me with trust
and adoration.
I pause.
I give him
a biscuit.
This is the beginning
of love and
disobedience.
I was never meant
to be a god.

Departures

My dog barks under an empty tree
long after the squirrel has gone.
He barks and barks, and the squirrel
leaps ten trees away, leaving
the leaf tops trembling like trampolines
after an acrobat is through.
And he stands gazing up at her
who long ago stopped loving him
while that foolish dog still barks.

Heartbeat

The book says:
give the pup
a ticking clock to sleep with,
he'll think
that it's his mother.

When she left
he tried
a different life,
a different lover,
a ticking
clock.

Domestic Animals

The animals in this house
have dream claws and teeth
and shadow the rooms
at night, their furled tails dangerous.
In the morning, all sweet slobber,
the dog may yawn, the cat
make cat sounds deep
in its furred throat.
And who would guess
how they wait for dark
when into the green
jungle of our sleep
they insinuate
themselves, releasing
their terrible hunger.

In the Walled Garden

In the walled garden
where my illusions grow,
the lilac, watered, blooms all winter,
and innocence grows like moss
on the north side of every tree.
No ax or mower resides here—
green multiplies unimpeded—
and every morning all the dogs
of my long life jump up
to lick my face.
My father rests behind a hedge,
bard of my storied childhood,
and in the fading half life of ambition,
wanting and having merge.
Here flowers and flesh don't wither.
Here you will never leave me.
Here poetry will save the world.

Rivermist: for Roland Flint

When the kennel where my ridgeback died
some thirty years ago, wrote
to ask for my business again,
offering us one free night's board
for every three nights paid, I looked
at that name on the envelope: Rivermist,
imagining they were writing to say
that Mowgli was somehow alive,
the swordlike blade of fur still bristling
on his back; that he had waited
all these years for me to pick him up.
And though I've had four dogs since,
a small one at my feet right now, each
running too swiftly through his life and mine,
I could have wept, thinking of rivers and mists—
how in their wavering shadows
they had prefigured and concealed
the losses to come: mother and uncles, friends,
and Roland now, so newly dead, who
on the flyleaf of an early book once wrote,
in his careful, redemptive hand: with love

for Linda and Ira, and for Mowgli.

On Seeing *The Glass Menagerie*: New York, 1946

How did he know about my glass animals,
the way I dusted each one lovingly—the elephant
with its transparent curve of trunk, the blue-eyed hen,
the poodle with its curled, spun-sugar topknot?

How did he know about the awkward boys
who came to the door,
sons of my mother's friends,
coerced into asking me out?

Ah, fragile zoo! Ah, adolescent callers!
I saw that play and knew that someone
understood me, knew that I could hide
in language the rest of my life.

I Am Learning to Abandon the World: for M

I am learning to abandon the world
before it can abandon me.
Already I have given up the moon
and snow, closing my shades
against the claims of white.
And the world has taken
my father, my friend.
I have given up melodic lines of hills,
moving to a flat, tuneless landscape.
And every night I give my body up
limb by limb, working upward
across bone, toward the heart.
But morning comes with small
reprieves of coffee and birdsong.
A tree outside the window
which was simply shadow moments ago
takes back its branches twig
by leafy twig.
And as I take my body back
the sun lays its warm muzzle on my lap
as if to make amends.

Patterns

The way the gulls' tracks in sand—
pattern of bisected triangles—are erased
by the breaking waves;

my mother pinning
the Vogue pattern onto the silky
blue fabric;

the long marching band of numbers: 4
is the square of 2, 16 the square
of 4, and so on;

sex and Samoa—
our adolescent take
on Patterns of Culture;

how history repeats itself:
war, and famine, and quiet
spells of peace;

our fragile days together: toast
and the morning paper, work
and wine and walking the dog

who marks
the usual hydrant, lamppost,
spindly tree.

What mortal patterns wait
in these aromatic tea leaves, in these
indelible lines mapping my palm?

McGuffey's First Eclectic Reader

The sun is up,
the sun is always up.
The silent "e"
keeps watch,
and 26 strong stones
can build a wall of syllables
for Nell and Ned
and Ann.

Rab was such a good dog,
Mother. We left him
under the big tree
by the brook
to take care of the dolls
and the basket.

But Rab has run away.
The basket's gone back to reeds
through which the night wind
blows; and mother was erased;
the dolls are painted harlots
in the Doll's Museum.

Where did it go, Rose?
I don't know;
away off, somewhere.

The fat hen
has left the nest.

I hand my daughter
this dusty book.
Framed in her window
the sky darkens to slate,
a lexicon of wandering stars.
Listen, child—the barking
in the distance
is Rab the dog star
trotting home
for dinner.

Applying to Bellagio

They take husbands,
but they don't take dogs.
Ridiculous!
and all because

they fear that barking
may disturb the muse.
Just ask Calliope.
I'm sure she'd choose

a silky spaniel
with a fluent tail
for inspiration, not
some human male.

I guess I'll have to stay
at home to write,
with dog and husband both
here, in plain sight.

The Art of the Dog

In Mary Cassatt's *Little Blue Armchair*,
it's not the child I look at but the Norwich terrier,
twin to mine, curled up on another armchair.
And in Picasso's *Boy With Dog*, I want
to enter the famous Blue Period to pat it.

There are dogs in the cave paintings in France,
and the hounds in the Bayeux Tapestry
are stitched into the scene by hand, chasing
their embroidered prey right into art history.

It's said that dogs in paintings
domesticate the scene or symbolize love,
that even a still life of flowers and fruit
may have a poodle or dachshund
hidden under the table.

Is a painted dog different
from a dog in a poem—from a dog,
like mine for instance, who follows
me from stanza to stanza as if I'm going
to throw a pencil for him to retrieve
instead of the usual ball?

Velasquez's *Maids of Honor*...
Madame Renoir With a Dog...Van Eyck's
marriage scene, complete with terrier....
At night the museums echo
with the unleashed sound of barking.

Dog in the Manger

As if you'd keep your bones from other dogs
when you were done with them. What nonsense!

In any case, why manger? That Christmas child slept
in the barn with sheep and cows, not dogs.

And doggerel? Your bark
is so expressive

I think you'd choose a sonnet
with beef in it, if you could write.

Dog fight I understand, dog tired too—
you frequent the couch even wide awake.

But raining cats and dogs?
And going to the dogs—where would that be?

Why do I care? Language is where I live.
Besides, I have a dog in this fight.

Pluto

There's the planet, of course
with its icy outcroppings, its moons,

and plutonium, which will light our way
to the future, if it doesn't destroy us.

And plutocrat means wealth,
from the Greek, or power.

But for me it's the dog
with the shiny nose and the stand-up ears

who clowned his way through
my sober childhood.

Argos

Shaggy and incontinent,
I have become the very legend
of fidelity. I am
more famous than the dog star
or those hounds of Charon's
who nip at a man's ankles
on his way to the underworld.
Even Penelope wanted
proof, and Eurykleia
had to see a scar.
But I knew what I knew—
what else are noses for?
Men are such needy creatures
Zeus himself comes to them
as an animal. I'll take
my place gladly
among the bones and fleas
of this fragrant dung heap
and doze my doggy way
through history.

The Animals

When I see a suckling pig turn
on the spit, its mouth around
an apple, or feel the soft
muzzle of a horse
eating a windfall from my hand,
I think about the animals
when Eden closed down,
who stole no fruit themselves.

After feeding so long
from Adam's outstretched hand
and sleeping under the mild stars,
flank to flank,
what did they do on freezing nights?
Still ignorant of nests and lairs
did they try to warm themselves
at the fiery leaves of the first autumn?

And how did they learn to sharpen
fangs and claws? Who taught them
the first lesson: that flesh

had been transformed to meat?
Tiger and Bear, Elk and Dove.
God saved them places on the Ark,
and Christ would honor them with
parables, calling himself the Lamb of God.

We train our dogs in strict obedience
at which we failed ourselves.
But sometimes the sound of barking
fills the night like distant artillery,
a sound as chilling as the bellow
of steers led up the ramps
of cattle cars whose gates swing
shut on them, as Eden's did.

4 A.M.

I was the child until
my mother died;
now I'm the child again

afraid in the night
and sleep as elusive
as the past I cling to.

Old age is all
about saving what's left—
my father's heavy watch,

each tick a heartbeat,
my mother's initialed handkerchiefs
still scenting the drawer.

Buttons without
their buttonholes.
Combs with missing teeth.

I try to keep awake
all day, to sleep at night,
with only the dog

for company—his weight
at my feet holding me
to the earth.

But the sheets are tangled ghosts
waiting to dress me
in their ironed robes.

Marking Time

The dog waits at the door
for someone who is not going to come.
And the door waits
on its rusted hinges, not knowing
whether to open or shut.

Even the path, overgrown
with weeds and brambles, waits
in its own winding purgatory.

See me spending the small change
of my days looking out one window,
then another, for someone
to come and wake me
from this stalled dream of a life,
the way the princess,

in her flowery glass coffin,
was wakened by a kiss. Or the dog,
withholding its serious bark,
could be rescued
by the person it is waiting for,
if only he were coming.

I Sing or Weep

I sing
or weep,
it is the same thing
to the animals,
it is almost
the same thing.
The dog puts his heavy head
in my lap
pretending to know.
His small thunder
brings no rain,
no relief to the leaves
that wait poised
on their stems
for the first sign of wind.
What will their trembling mean?
I feel a mortal weight
that stirs
like some sleeping creature
in my chest.
Song wakens it,

tears waken it.
The nerves follow
their separate paths
to the same shady place
where once simple Adam
named silence,
named speech,
and the animals smiled,
the animals wept,
under their branching horns.

Renunciation

Like flowers
with knife-sharp
petals—

scions
of the sunflower
family—

the bright arrows
of beauty are aimed
at the heart.

So pain hides
in the billowy garments
of pleasure,

wounding
the open eye,
the listening ear.

An end, please, to all
sensation. Close
the museums,

lock the keys of the pianos
in their long, dark
coffins.

I choose an unlit room
and medicinal
sleep. I summon

for company, only my old dog
and, dim and silent as fog,
my old ghosts.

Life and Death on Masterpiece

I want to die an old woman
sun-struck in a garden chair,
my dog at my feet, the way Old Jolyon
in *The Forsyte Saga* did,
the bees around him buzzing

with the sound saws make
in comic strips to mimic sleep.
And just last night, Mountstuart
in *Any Human Heart*
reduced his past

to cinders in a bonfire,
then settled in his chair,
half smiling
with accomplishment,
and was gone.

They both slipped
into death so gracefully,
their shrouds of brilliant sun
half blinding us, their viewers,
in prismatic light.

And the choirs of flowers
in their robes of color,
the gardens sliding into afternoon,
all testified that life itself
could be no better than this.

Old Joke

The children all are grown, the dog has died;
the old joke says that now life can begin,
the creaking door to freedom open wide.
But old age seems my fault, a kind of sin
precluding guilty pleasures—food and drink,
the luxuries of travel, even books.

Depression is the bed in which I sink,
my body primed for pain's insidious hooks:
the swollen fingers and the stiffened back;
the way regret can pierce you with its knife;
the migraines like some medieval rack;
the winnowing of loved ones from my life.

For months I carried that old dog around,
helping her eat and cleaning up her mess.
Though she was deaf, I talked to her—each sound
the rough equivalent of a caress.
If memories are like the poems I wrote
but didn't think quite good enough to save,

and if the final wisdoms I would quote
await that cold anthology: the grave,
then let the sun, at least, become a shawl
keeping me wrapped in warmth until the end;
my lawn a place where children's children sprawl
next to the shy ghost of my canine friend.

Turnabout

The old dog used to herd me through the street
As if the leash were for my benefit,
And when our walk was over he would sit
A friendly jailer, zealous, at my feet.
My children would pretend that they felt fine
When I was anxious at some hurt of theirs
As if they were the parents, for the tears
At their predicaments were often mine.

And now against the whiteness of the sheet
My mother, white faced, comforts with the story
of Brahms, the boy, who couldn't sleep for worry
Until a chord achieved its harmony,
So down the stairs he crept to play the C.
She means her death will make a circle complete.

All Night

The children have gone
through doors so small
we cannot follow
even if we stoop

and the dogs bark all night
hearing calls
in registers too high
for our frail senses.

We follow words instead
but they are only signposts
leading to other words
leaving us lost

in our own landscape.
We struggle merely to see
for the sun too has slipped away
hiding its tracks

in afterlight, to a place of unimagined
reds and golds
a place where children

lounge on grass
calling to dogs whose barking
they can still hear
all these years from home.

Ghosts

We abandon the dead as they
abandoned us. But sometimes
my mother's ghost sits at the foot of the bed

trying to comfort me for all
the other losses: my father longing
to be forgiven, to forgive;

the long line of cousins and aunts
patiently waiting their turns
to be remembered; the dogs

who were my shadows once
whining now at the gates of the afterlife.
My mother smoothes my pillow

as though it were a field of snow
ready to be plowed by dreams where
for brief moments my dead come back:

Jon as a toddler in my uncle's army cap,
Franny with the rosary of days
slipping through her fingers.

At times I wander through
the library of graves, reading
the headstones, remembering a place

where the ashes I scattered once
blew back on the wind, staining
my forehead with their dark alphabet.

In the house where I grew up,
the same sentinel trees
shade the porch

as they shaded the green years
of my childhood when my dead
were alive and full of promise.

The Ordinary

It may happen on a day
of ordinary weather—
the usual assembled flowers,
or fallen leaves disheveling the grass.
You may be feeding the dog,
or sipping a cup of tea,
and then: the telegram;
or the phone call;
or the sharp pain traveling
the length of your left arm, or his.
And as your life is switched
to a different track (the landscape
through grimy windows
almost the same though
entirely different) you wonder
why the wind doesn't
rage and blow as it does
so convincingly
in *Lear*, for instance.
It is pathetic fallacy
you long for—the roses

nothing but their thorns,
the downed leaves
subjects for a body count.
And as you lie in bed
like an effigy of yourself,
it is the ordinary
that comes to save you—
the china teacup waiting
to be washed, the old dog
whining to go out.

This Dog

Maybe I've chosen life—not just
the life of this dog I've rescued
from the shelter, but

my own life, mired in the same
books—Anna, Elizabeth,
Jane, the same

solitary walks—no tugging—
the doctors' offices changed now
to cacophony at the vet's.

I've chosen disruption and broken
sleep and the poetry of barking—
what does each growl mean?

how to parse the hidden syllables
of dogs, this dog? Maybe
it wasn't a choice at all.

Firing the Muse

I am giving up the muse Calliope.
I have told her to pack up her pens and her inks
and to take her lyrical smile,
her coaxing ways, back to Mt. Helicon,
or at least to New York.
I will even write her a reference if she likes
to someone whose head is still fizzy
with iambs and trochees,
someone still hungry for the scent of laurel,
the taste of fame, for the pure astonishment of seeing
her own words blaze up on the page.
Let me lie in this hammock in the fading sun
without guilt or longing, just a glass
of cold white wine in one hand,
not even a book in the other. A dog
will lie at my feet who can't read anyway,
loving me just for myself, and for
the biscuit I keep concealed in my pocket.

Envoi

We're signing up for heartbreak,
We know one day we'll rue it.
But oh the way our life lights up
The years a dog runs through it.

ACKNOWLEDGMENTS

"I Am Learning to Abandon the World" appeared in *PM/AM* (W. W. Norton, 1982); "Argos" appeared in *The Imperfect Paradise* (W. W. Norton, 1988); "Domestic Animals" appeared in *Heroes in Disguise* (W. W. Norton, 1991); "The Animals" and "McGuffey's First Eclectic Reader" first appeared in *Carnival Evening* (W. W. Norton, 1998); "In the Garden" appeared in *The Last Uncle* (W. W. Norton, 2002); "The Great Dog of Night," "Firing the Muse," "Rivermist," and "The Walled Garden" appeared in *Queen of a Rainy Country* (W. W. Norton, 2006); "Old Joke" and "The Ordinary" first appeared in *Traveling Light* (W. W. Norton, 2015).

I'd also like to thank

Catamaran, the *Courtland Review*, *Crysalis*, the *Gettysburg Review*, the *New Republic*, *Plume*, and *Valley Voices*.

"Departures," "Heartbeat," and "I Sing or Weep" appeared in *On the Way to the Zoo* (Dryad Press, 1975).

"All Night" appeared in *Even as We Sleep* (Croissant Press, 1980).

TABLE OF CONTENTS

About Your Adventure

YOU are living in the United States during the 1930s. The Great Depression has gripped the country, causing people to lose their farms, jobs, and homes. How will you survive?

In this book, you'll explore how the choices people made meant the difference between life and death. The events you'll experience happened to real people.

Chapter One sets the scene. Then you choose which path to read. Follow the directions at the bottom of each page. The choices you make will change your outcome. After you finish one path, go back and read the others for new perspectives and more adventures.

YOU CHOOSE the path
you take through history.

In the 1920s, farmers in the Great Plains plowed thousands of acres of land.

From Land to Dust

Long before the first European explorers came, American Indians and the buffalo lived throughout the Great Plains. This wide prairie stretches from Canada all the way south to Texas. It spreads east of the Rocky Mountains to the eastern Dakotas, Nebraska, Kansas, and Oklahoma.

In the mid- to late 1800s, the U.S. government forced American Indians to live on reservations. The government encouraged settlers to farm the fertile land. By the 1920s, farming in the Great Plains was booming. A few years of heavy rainfall produced huge yields of wheat and other crops. Owners of large farms got rich.

7

Turn the page.

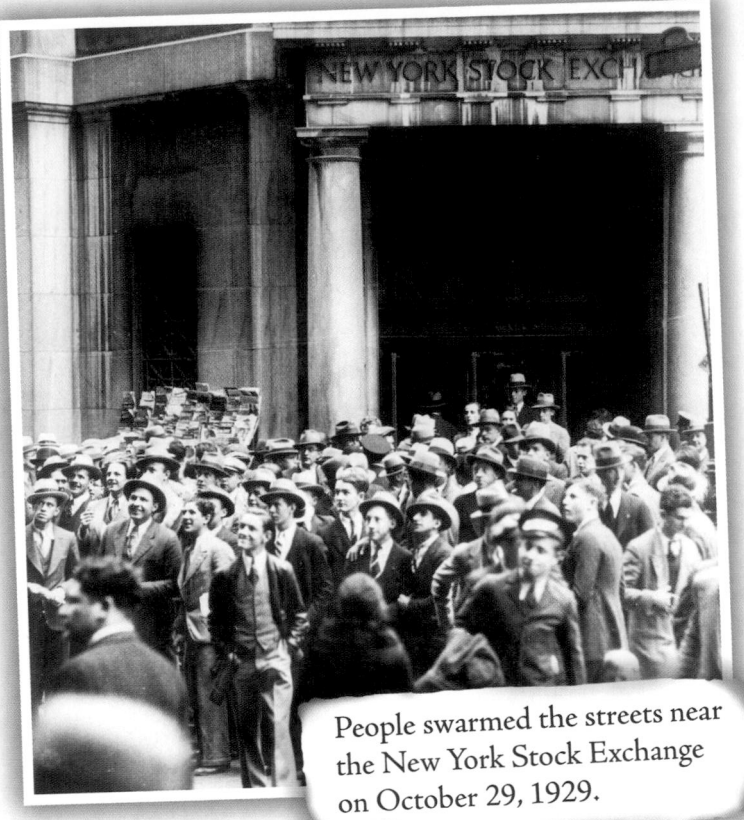

People swarmed the streets near the New York Stock Exchange on October 29, 1929.

Then two things happened that helped create a disaster. In 1929, the stock market crashed. People had been buying shares of companies on the stock market to make money. Prices of stocks kept going higher. Some people made a lot of money.

But on Tuesday, October 29, stock market prices fell about 80 percent. People panicked and tried to sell their shares. The stock market crash caused many companies and banks to go out of business. People were left with no money and no jobs. Crop prices fell. People called it the Great Depression.

In 1931, the second part of the disaster began. Rainfall sharply decreased in parts of the Great Plains. The Plains had experienced droughts before, but the rains had always returned. Not this time. Hot winds blew across the land, taking millions of tons of soil with it.

The southern Great Plains, including parts of Oklahoma, Texas, New Mexico, Kansas, and Colorado, dried up and blew away. A reporter calls the area the Dust Bowl, and the name sticks.

Turn the page.

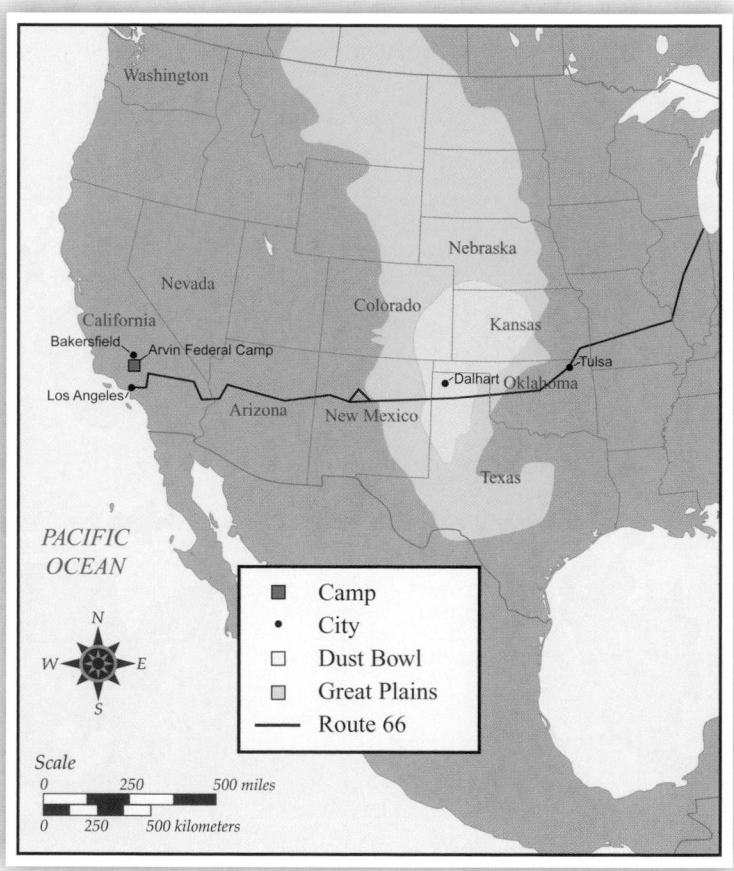

10

You and millions of other people are living with the horror of the Dust Bowl. Some are determined to stay on their farms. Many give up and move to large cities or to California to start a new life. Others travel to the Dust Bowl to write stories and take photos for the rest of the world to see.

➤ To try to stay on your farm, turn to page **13**.

➤ To leave your farm to find work elsewhere, turn to page **43**.

➤ To be a government photographer in the Dust Bowl, turn to page **73**.

A combination of drought and insects killed crops in the Dust Bowl.

A World of Dust

You stand on the porch of your white clapboard house and look out onto the Kansas land. Farm life is all you've ever known. Three years ago, in 1929, you married your girlfriend, Nettie. Your daughter, Ruby, was born the next year. Your father gave you enough land to start a farm of your own.

Last year, 1931, a drought caused crop failures in other parts of Kansas. But it's not just the drought that has you worried. The crash of 1929 hurt everyone. You took your savings out of the bank before it closed. The money is hidden under a loose floorboard in the kitchen.

13

Turn the page.

You had planned to plant wheat this fall. But a neighbor tells you to raise cattle instead. Your farm includes grassy pastures where cattle can graze. "Cattle won't dry up and blow away," your neighbor says, laughing.

➤ *To plant wheat, go to page 15.*

➤ *To buy cattle, turn to page 23.*

Last year was a bumper crop for wheat. You think you can make money with wheat this year too. True, prices did go down a little from last year. But you're sure the drop was temporary. Once the fields are planted, it's time to wait for the rain.

You wait. And wait. The sun beats down onto your fields. The newspaper brings more bad news. Wheat prices continue to fall. Last year's huge wheat crop flooded the market and brought down prices.

One morning, you go to the fields and walk through the drooping wheat. You barely notice as the sky darkens. Then the wind picks up. You see a large, dark cloud coming toward you. It's a dust storm! Should you run for the house or stay where you are?

➤ *To run, turn to page* **16**.

➤ *To stay in the fields, turn to page* **33**.

15

The black cloud barrels across the fields, making a loud, rushing sound. You run to the house as fast as you can. You get inside just as the storm hits. It's black as night inside the house. You hear Nettie and little Ruby crying. You feel in the darkness until you find the kerosene lamp and light it. The light barely makes a dent in the darkness.

The furious wind rattles the windows and doors. Dust pours through the cracks and fills the air, making you cough. After two hours, the terrible howling wind finally stops. Everything in the house is covered with dirt, including you, Nettie, and Ruby. The grit sticks to the roof of your mouth and between your teeth. In a daze, you open the door and go outside.

The wheat field is gone. Everything is covered with dirt and dust. You and Nettie begin shoveling the dirt out of the house.

Huge clouds of dust rolled through the sky, wiping out the sun.

As you are dumping a bucket of dirt in the ditch, an old truck comes wheezing down the road. You don't recognize the man driving it, but he stops and waves.

"My name is Smith," the man says. "I own the land west of here. I'm going to town to see how others fared. You should come too."

➤ To go into town, turn to page **18**.

➤ To stay on the farm, turn to page **20**.

Caddo, Oklahoma, was just one of many bleak Dust Bowl towns.

You get into your old truck and head into town. When the crops were good, the town was a busy place. Now most of the businesses are closed. Wind rattles through broken windows. Tumbleweeds skip down the dusty street.

A small crowd is gathered at the general store. A few people lost cattle in the storm. But several farmers, like you, lost their entire crop.

Smith finds you in the crowd. "Such a shame," he says, shaking his head. Then he clears his throat nervously.

18

"Terrible thing for a family man such as you," he begins. "Me, I don't even live around here. I just come to the farm a few times a year to check on the crops. I'm a banker from Oklahoma City."

"So you're one of those suitcase farmers," you say scornfully. "You buy up land and then plant as much as you can. But you live so far away that you have to pack a suitcase to visit your farm. You don't love the land. You only want to make money from it."

You turn away, but Smith grabs your arm.

"Don't judge me so fast," he says quickly. "I'm here to make you an offer on your land."

19

Your first reaction is to refuse Smith's offer. Then you remember the dead, dry fields.

➤ *To stay on the farm, turn to page **20**.*

➤ *To sell your land, turn to page **31**.*

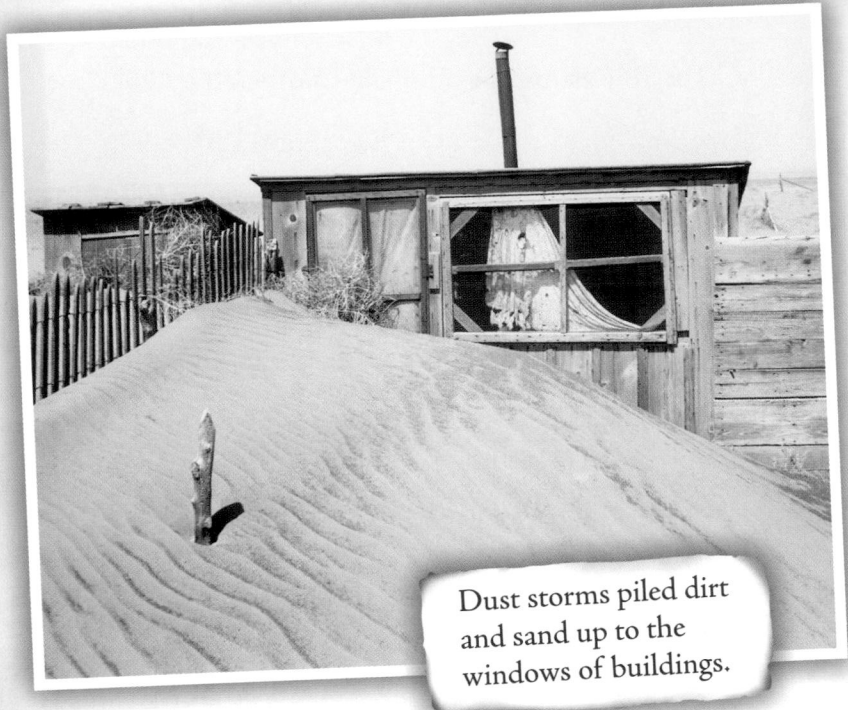

Dust storms piled dirt and sand up to the windows of buildings.

Shaking your head, you return to the farm. It's too late now to replant the wheat crop. Even if you did, the hot, dry wind would kill the wheat before it could grow. You do your best to keep the dairy cow and the chickens alive. Nettie sells eggs, milk, and cheese in town to make a few pennies. She sometimes has to strain the milk several times to remove the dirt.

20

You tack wet sheets and cloths to the windows and doors. Still, you can't keep the dust out of the house. Nettie keeps the plates and cups upside down on the kitchen table. That way, the insides stay clean until you eat.

By 1936, the fifth year of drought, you're worn out. The farm is little more than a desert. The only things that will grow are tumbleweed plants, which you feed to the starving milk cow.

On September 6, you and Nettie listen to President Franklin D. Roosevelt on the radio. He visited the Dust Bowl not long ago. "I shall never forget the fields of wheat so blasted by heat that they cannot be harvested," he says. Then the president begins talking about the Works Progress Administration (WPA). This government program creates jobs for the unemployed, including farmers.

Turn the page.

"I could get a job," you say. "But some of those WPA jobs are far away. I'd hate to leave you and Ruby here alone."

"We could go on drought relief," Nettie says hesitantly. "We'll be able to get help from the government, and you can stay on the farm."

You were raised not to take handouts from anyone, including the government. You're not happy with either choice, but you know you have to do something. The next morning, you drive into town. On one side of the street is the WPA office. Next door, there is a sign that says, "Relief sign-up."

➼ To look for a WPA job, turn to page **34**.

➼ To sign up for government relief, turn to page **36**.

Soon your herd of cattle is grazing in the grassy pasture. They are round and healthy. You hope that in a few years, you'll have a large ranch.

Summer wears on, and no rain comes. The grass dries up in the heat. You're forced to buy expensive cattle feed from town. You're sure the drought can't last too much longer, though.

One morning, you are outside when you see a large black cloud rumbling toward you. At first, your heart leaps with excitement. The rains are coming! Then you look more closely. That is not a rain cloud. It is a huge dust cloud! You can smell the dirt and feel the wind of the storm rushing at you. The barn isn't too far away. But Nettie and the baby are in the house. Where do you go?

➤ *To run for the barn, turn to page* **24**.

➤ *To run for the house, turn to page* **28**.

There's no time to round up the cattle.
You barely make it to the barn before the storm
hits. Dust pours through cracks in the walls.
Soon everything in the barn is covered with dust.
From the pasture, you can hear the cattle hacking
and snorting in panic.

When the wind finally dies down, you rush
to the house. Nettie and Ruby are coughing
from the dust but seem OK. Next, you check the
pasture. The cattle are gray with dust but alive.

Over the next few months, more dust storms
roar across the land. The dirt drifts are so high
that soon your house is almost buried. Some days
you have to climb through the window to get
out. The only thing for your cows to eat is sparse,
dirt-covered grass and hay. They grow sickly and
thin. You're forced to slaughter some of them.
Their stomachs are filled with dirt.

By May 1936, things are looking bleak. There's nothing at all left on the land, not even weeds. You keep losing cattle. The calves that are born are sickly. Many of them die.

One morning, you see an article in the newspaper. "Look here," you say to Nettie. "We can ship our cattle to areas in the middle of the state where there is still grass. They can get fattened up and healthy."

Nettie frowns. "Are you sure it's a good idea?" she says. "How can we be sure that they'll be taken care of there?"

"We sure can't take care of them here," you reply sadly. "They're all going to die if they stay."

➺ *To send the cattle away, turn to page 26.*

➺ *To keep them on the farm, turn to page 39.*

You and several neighbors join together to pay the shipping charges for the cattle. They amount to $46 for your part. When Nettie hears about the cost, she gets angry.

"Forty-six dollars?" she says. "That's almost enough to buy an electric washing machine like the rich people have!"

You try to reason with Nettie. "But if we spend this money now, it's like savings in the bank. The cattle will be healthy, and we'll be able to increase our herd."

Nettie finally agrees to the plan. You send away 50 head of cattle.

In the fall, you go to the train station in town to reclaim your cattle. You are shocked to see their condition. Many of them can barely walk down the ramps. Sending away the cattle was a terrible mistake.

Cattle in the Dust Bowl struggled to find food in the dry pastures.

You spend weeks trying to get the cattle healthy with store-bought feed. The cattle slowly begin to gain weight. But the cost of the feed drains the rest of your money.

Your neighbors who shipped their cattle were just as unlucky. Many of them have sold everything and left. You now have no choice. The farm must be auctioned off.

27

*Turn to page **38**.*

The storm hits before you get inside. The cloud is so black it blocks out the sun completely. You feel around in the dark, coughing and spitting out mouthfuls of dirt. Finally you stumble onto the porch and crawl into the house. Soon the storm is over. The house is filled with dirt. Nettie is crying, and baby Ruby coughs miserably.

As the months drag on, the dust storms keep coming. The dirt piles up so high that it buries the fences, the farm equipment, and even the house. But what worries you most is little Ruby. She struggles to breathe, and her tiny cough breaks your heart. On clear days she seems fine. But there aren't as many clear days as there used to be. One night, you and Nettie have a talk about Ruby's health.

"We need to take her to the doctor," Nettie says. "I've been giving her sugar with a drop of turpentine. But it's not clearing out her lungs as well as it used to."

"We don't have the money," you tell her. "Our savings are gone, and the doctor in town charges a dollar. We only have 75 cents in the money jar, and we need food. If we don't buy food, we'll starve."

"The cow is still giving milk," Nettie replies. "I can get a quarter from selling milk in town. I'm afraid to wait much longer. She's so tiny, and it's so hard for her to breathe."

→ *To take Ruby to the doctor now, turn to page **30**.*

→ *To wait to take Ruby to the doctor, turn to page **40**.*

Red Cross workers taught women to sew masks to keep out the dust.

"You're right, we need to get Ruby to the doctor," you tell Nettie. You have no idea how you will find money for food. But Ruby's health is more important right now.

At the office, the doctor examines Ruby. "It's the dust pneumonia," he says. "You must get this child away from here, or she will die." Breathing in dirt causes dust pneumonia. Your heart sinks as you realize the only way to save Ruby is to leave the farm forever. Everything must be sold.

*Turn to page **38**.*

Smith is right. Your first responsibility is to your family. When Smith tells you his offer, you gasp.

"That's less than half of what the land is worth," you say, startled.

Smith shrugs. "It isn't worth anything now, is it?" he asks. "What are you going to grow on a pile of dust?"

Grudgingly, you agree to Smith's offer. You spend the next two days loading all your furniture onto your creaky old truck. Nettie cries as she packs up the set of china dishes you received as a wedding gift.

31

Turn the page.

On the morning of the third day, Smith shows up. You sign some papers, and he hands you an envelope. Your chest tightens as you shove the money in your pocket. You take one last look at the dry, bare land. You can barely remember the lush green fields and blue skies of your childhood. Sadly, you and your family climb into the truck and drive away. Soon the farm, and your old life, disappear behind you.

THE END

To follow another path, turn to page 11.
To read the conclusion, turn to page 103.

There's no time to make it to safety. Dropping to the ground, you cover your head with your hands. Soon the cloud is upon you. The air around you is so dark that it seems like night. Gasping and coughing, you pull your shirt collar over your mouth. A heavy feeling falls over your legs and feet. You realize that dirt is piling over you in drifts.

You struggle to your feet. You stagger forward, eyes tightly closed against the stinging dirt. Then the wind hits you, and you fall again. It seems like time stands still as you lie there. You gasp for breath and wonder if this is your last day on earth. Sadly, it is. You suffocate in the dust storm.

THE END

To follow another path, turn to page 11.
To read the conclusion, turn to page 103.

33

The WPA gave jobs to about 9 million workers between 1935 and 1943.

USA WORK PROGRAM **WPA**

A tired-looking man is behind a desk in the WPA office. "I need strong backs to build a new city hall in Colby," he says, shoving some papers toward you. "It pays $43 a month."

"How long will I be gone?" you ask.

"Don't know — probably a few months," the man says. "As long as it takes."

34

It's not much money, but it will keep Nettie and Ruby fed. And it means you won't have to sell the farm. You sign the papers. The next day, you kiss Nettie and Ruby good-bye. You then get on the bus headed to the WPA camp. As the bus drives away, you watch the little town you've known all your life disappear into the distance. You tell yourself you'll return as soon as you can.

THE END

To follow another path, turn to page 11.
To read the conclusion, turn to page 103.

When you walk into the relief office, you're surprised to see several farmers you know standing in line. A woman explains that everyone will receive emergency supplies and food. She also tells you about the erosion control programs such as contour plowing. Contour plowing forms curving rows in the soil, which are less likely to blow or wash away.

For the next few years, you and Nettie do whatever you can to stay alive and keep the farm. You work on several local relief projects, mainly repairing buildings in town. You use contour plowing to till your fields. You also plant trees on the farm and between the fields. In the future, these shelterbelts will help keep the soil in place.

Shelterbelts protected fields from wind erosion.

In 1939, a miracle happens — the rains return. In the spring, you plant seeds you received through the relief program. As the wheat grows tall and gentle rains fill the sky, you cry tears of joy. At last, the worst years of your life are over.

37

THE END

To follow another path, turn to page 11.
To read the conclusion, turn to page 103.

The day of the auction, a small crowd gathers near your barn. They are mostly friends and neighbors. You're afraid that they will try to make this a "10-cent auction," where no bid will go over a few pennies. Then they will sell everything back to you for the money they paid for it. But you don't have the money to buy back anything. You just want this to be over. You ask everyone to let the auction happen normally. They want to help you, so they agree. Everything is sold quickly, mostly to owners of large farms.

When it is over, you climb into your old truck where Nettie and Ruby are waiting. Maybe you'll go to Washington or California — somewhere where the dust doesn't kill everything. You drive away, not looking back.

THE END

To follow another path, turn to page 11.
To read the conclusion, turn to page 103.

You decide to keep your cattle. But one by one, the cattle die. Soon they will all be gone.

One hot day, a stranger arrives. "I'm from the Drought Relief Service," he tells you. "The government will buy your cattle. We pay anywhere from $14 to $20 per animal, depending on its condition. We give the meat to the poor."

You agree to sell your cattle. "You're lucky," the man says as he hands you the cash. "All of your animals are well enough to sell. Most cattle are so sick that we have to shoot them on the spot."

You and Nettie agree to use the government money to move to Kansas City. A few days later, you and your family drive away. You leave the farm to be buried in drifts of dry, brown dirt.

THE END

To follow another path, turn to page 11.
To read the conclusion, turn to page 103.

39

"Keeping all of us alive is more important," you insist. Nettie nods and comforts Ruby, who is coughing again. The money buys your family enough beans and bread to live on. You're thankful that your family isn't starving. So many farm families are much worse off.

Two weeks pass. Nettie continues to try home remedies on Ruby, including rubbing her chest with a mixture of lard and kerosene.

Early one morning, Nettie goes to Ruby's room to check on her. Suddenly, Nettie's screams echo through the house.

You race into Ruby's bedroom. The baby is lying lifeless in her crib. You gather her limp body to your chest and sob. Nettie collapses on the floor beside you.

A few days later, you and Nettie stand in the town cemetery, along with your family and friends. It breaks your heart to see Ruby's tiny grave. This hateful dust, you think. How many more innocent people will it kill before it's over?

After the funeral, you and Nettie climb into the truck. You've decided to leave Kansas. There's nothing left for you here. The farm is gone. Ruby is gone. The dust has beaten you. You drive away slowly, never looking back.

THE END

To follow another path, turn to page 11.
To read the conclusion, turn to page 103.

People in the Dust Bowl had little food except for what they managed to grow.

CHAPTER 3

Migrants on the Move

Your family's farm in the Oklahoma Panhandle was once rich and productive. Back in the 1920s, your father took out bank loans to build a new barn and buy a new tractor. Then the dust storms came, and the land dried up.

Mother began doing laundry for other people and selling milk and eggs in town. Dad sold the farm equipment. You and your younger brother, Johnny, do extra chores for your neighbors in exchange for food. But it isn't enough to pay off the loans or to keep you from going hungry.

One day Dad comes in from town. "We can't pay our loans, so the bank is taking the farm," he says sadly. "We have to leave."

43

Turn the page.

"Where are we going?" you ask.

"Well, we could go to Aunt Sally's in Tulsa," Dad replies slowly. "She's offered us a place to stay. But lots of folks are going to California." Dad looks at you. "Where would you like to go?"

44

➤ *To go to Tulsa, go to page* **45**.

➤ *To go to California, turn to page* **50**.

"Let's go to Tulsa," you say. "At least there, we'll have Aunt Sally." Your mother agrees.

"Tulsa it is, then," Dad says. You feel sad about leaving the farm, but you're also excited. Tulsa is about 200 miles east of your farm. It takes your old truck most of the day to get there.

It's the biggest city you've ever seen! The streets are filled with cars, buses, and streetcars. The 11th Street Bridge stretches over the Arkansas River. Beside the bridge, hundreds of homeless people live in ramshackle shanties. Dad tells you this slum is called a "Hooverville," after former President Herbert Hoover. Hoover was president during the beginning of the Great Depression. Many people think he didn't do enough to help them. You turn away, glad that you're going to a real house.

Turn the page.

Once you're settled in at Aunt Sally's, Dad starts looking for work. Over the next few weeks, you and Mother help Aunt Sally with the sewing she does for money.

Dad finds a few odd jobs here and there. The sewing doesn't bring in enough money to feed everyone. Dad sells the truck, but it's not enough. Six months after you arrive, Aunt Sally and your parents have a talk.

"I can't do it anymore," Sally says tearfully. "You're my family, and I love you, but there's no money. I don't know what to do."

46

Dad looks defeated. Mother is crying. "We understand, Sally," Dad says. "We can't ask you to take care of us any longer."

➤ *To move to the Hooverville, go to page* **47**.

➤ *To leave town, turn to page* **64**.

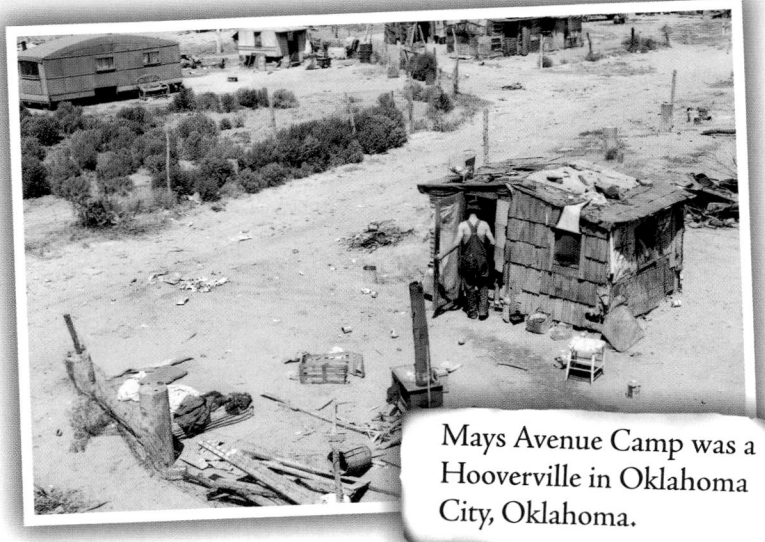

Mays Avenue Camp was a Hooverville in Oklahoma City, Oklahoma.

Your heart sinks as you stare at the crowded Hooverville. You and Johnny search for scraps of wood and metal. Dad uses them to make a tiny hut that rattles in the wind. The only place to wash is a dirty drainage ditch.

There are no jobs. Every day, the family lines up at the soup kitchen downtown. At first, you are ashamed to stand in that line. But your hunger makes you lose your shame. You long to leave. But the truck is gone, and there's no money.

47

Turn the page.

One evening, Dad doesn't come back from looking for work in town. You're not worried. Maybe he found a night job somewhere. Days pass, and he still doesn't return. You're afraid something has happened to him. Then you realize that his clothes are gone as well. He isn't coming back. Mother gathers you and Johnny to her. "It's just us now," she says in a dull voice. "We've got to take care of each other."

You square your shoulders. "I'll go out and find a job," you say, but you're trembling.

Mother hugs you, tears wetting her cheeks. "Bless you," she tells you.

The next morning, you scrub up as best you can and go into the city. The crowds jostle you. The sounds of honking cars fill the air. As you walk down a side street, you pass an old woman huddled on the sidewalk. She grabs your sleeve.

"Please, can you spare a dime?" she asks you.

"I'm sorry, I don't have any money," you say quickly, as you try to pull away from her. She tightens her grip on your arm. "Please," she rasps. "I'm so hungry."

You pull away and run as fast as you can down the street. The shouts of the woman follow you, but she doesn't try to catch you. All you want to do is go back to the shanty, as much as you hate it.

➻ *To return to the shanty, turn to page* **60**.

➻ *To keep looking for a job, turn to page* **61**.

Before you know it, the old truck is piled high with clothes, furniture, mattresses, and boxes. The next morning, you and Johnny climb into the back of the truck. Mother gets in front, and Dad starts the truck and drives away. You can't wait to see the ocean and the California orange groves everyone talks about.

Soon the family is headed west on Route 66, the main road to California. The truck passes a large billboard that reads "NO JOBS IN CALIFORNIA. OKIES KEEP OUT."

"What are Okies?" you ask. Mother frowns. "That's the name that folks in California give to people who move out there from the Dust Bowl," she replies. "It's short for 'Oklahoma.' It's not a nice name, but don't you worry about it."

As it gets dark, the truck veers off the road. "Flat tire," Dad says. "We'll camp here tonight."

Dust Bowl farm families loaded up their cars for the move to California.

Mother cooks beans over a campfire. Dad struggles to change the tire while you and Johnny pitch the tent. Soon a man walks up to the campsite. He has a head of curly hair and an old guitar slung over his shoulder.

"I'll give you a hand with your flat tire if I can have a bite to eat," he says. "Or I can help you with that tent." You're wary of strangers, but this man seems nice. What do you do?

➤ *To refuse the man's help, turn to page* **52**.

➤ *To let the man help, turn to page* **56**.

"No thanks," you reply. The man smiles and continues on his way. After a hot meal of beans and bacon, you and Johnny curl up in the truck. Mother and Dad sleep in the tent. As soon as it is light, Dad finishes changing the tire. You're back on the road to California.

Two days later, you cross the California state line. Dad and Mother decide to celebrate by having lunch at a restaurant. Several other migrant families are in the restaurant. Dad begins chatting with the father of one of the families.

"The San Joaquin Valley is where the work is," the man says. "The big farms are always looking for pickers."

"We were planning on going to Los Angeles," Dad says. He turns to you, Mother, and Johnny. "This decision affects all of us. What do you think we should do?"

Mother thinks there is more opportunity in the San Joaquin Valley.

"Los Angeles! I want to see the ocean!" exclaims Johnny. Dad looks at you. "Guess you're the tiebreaker," he says with a smile. "What do you think we should do?"

➻ *To go to the San Joaquin Valley, turn to page **54**.*

➻ *To go to Los Angeles, turn to page **59**.*

Dust Bowl refugees were tired and hungry when they reached California.

You think hard. Los Angeles sounds exciting. But your family knows farming. "I agree with Mother," you say. Johnny's smile disappears.

Dad smiles. "Don't worry, Johnny-cake," he says. "We'll see the ocean one day, I promise."

After driving through the desert, you arrive at the outskirts of the San Joaquin Valley. You are upset to see a huge sign that says "NO WORK. OKIES GET OUT." Dad keeps driving, but you pass several other signs like it. Finally you see a small sign that reads, "Potato harvesters needed."

The truck bumps down a dirt road. At the end is an enormous field. Many people are already at work. The foreman agrees to hire all four of you. The next day, you use a large metal fork to dig the potatoes out of the ground. You've dug potatoes before, just not this many! But once the potatoes are harvested, the family is out of work again. Dad gathers the family together.

"This isn't what I expected when we came out here," he says. "But we're not starving. There's more work picking fruits and vegetables in the north, if we want it. Or we could go to Los Angeles, like we originally planned. I might be able to find some work there."

You're tired of working in the fields. But you don't know if Dad can find work in Los Angeles.

➤ *To go to Los Angeles, turn to page **59**.*
➤ *To keep working in the fields, turn to page **65**.*

Woody Guthrie wrote many folk songs about his Dust Bowl experiences.

You tell the man to speak to your father. Dad eyes the curly-haired man. Finally he says, "OK, we could use the help."

"Glad to hear it," the man replies, reaching out to shake Dad's hand. "My name's Woody Guthrie." After Woody and Dad change the tire, you all sit down to a meal of beans and bacon. Woody says he grew up in a small Oklahoma town. He tells you about his own kids back in Pampa, Texas. Later, he sings a song he wrote called "Dust Bowl Blues."

When you wake up the next morning, you don't see Woody. "Where is he?" you ask as you help put the cooking supplies in the truck.

"Gone before dawn," Mother replies. "Nice man. I hope things work out for him."

Soon you arrive at the California state line. Several men with rifles block the road. "What's going on here?" Dad asks as the men walk up to the truck.

"You're an Okie, ain't you?" one large man sneers. "There's no room for any more Okies in California."

"You have no right to keep us out," Dad says angrily. The men grip their rifles and step forward. "We're Los Angeles policemen," they say. "We don't want you dirty Okies in California."

Turn the page.

Your family doesn't have enough money to make the trip home. Many people are camping near the state line. Dad decides to join them.

One of the other campers approaches. "We heard of a camp for migrants near Bakersfield," he says, whispering so the guards won't hear him. "There's work there."

"How are you getting there?" Dad asks. "They won't let us pass into California here."

"Got to go north and then into California on Route 15," the man says. "If you want, come with us. We can share food and gas."

➻ To stay at the makeshift camp, turn to page **66**.

➻ To try to get to Bakersfield, turn to page **68**.

"I think Los Angeles sounds wonderful," you say. Johnny whoops with joy.

After another day of travel, you finally arrive in Los Angeles. Dad drives straight to the ocean. You stand on the sandy beach with your toes in the cold ocean foam.

You move into a tiny but clean apartment a few miles from the beach. Dad is lucky enough to find work quickly. He joins a crew digging ditches, which pays $3 a day. Mother gets a job cleaning houses. You and Johnny enroll in school.

At first it's hard. The other kids call you "dirty Okie." Slowly, though, you make friends. Soon Dad and Mother will make enough money to buy a real house. Life in California is good.

THE END

To follow another path, turn to page 11.
To read the conclusion, turn to page 103.

You're too scared to keep looking for a job. Back at the shanty, you curl up under the dirty blanket. You're trapped here, with no money and no way out. You know you're letting your family down, but you don't know what else to do. You pray that somehow you'll all be able to survive until the Great Depression is over.

THE END

To follow another path, turn to page 11.
To read the conclusion, turn to page 103.

"You can do this," you tell yourself, pushing aside your fear as best you can. But you're not sure where to start. As you pass a coffee shop, you spy a rumpled newspaper on the counter. It gives you an idea. You go inside and sit on one of the stools. You rustle through the newspaper until you find the help wanted ads.

"What'll you have?" asks a thin, tired-looking woman behind the counter.

"Oh, nothing, thank you," you say as politely as you can. "I'm not hungry." Then your stomach growls and gives you away. The woman's eyes soften. "How long has it been since you've had a proper meal, child?" she asks kindly.

"I had some soup last night," you lie. You gave your bowl of soup to Johnny when Mother wasn't looking.

Turn the page.

The woman looks you over. "Tell you what," she says finally. "The other waitress is out sick, and I'm all by myself here. I'll give you food if you'll help me with some chores."

You can't believe your luck. Soon you're gobbling down a plate of eggs and toast.

"I'm Betty," the woman says. "Me and my husband own this joint. It ain't much, but it pays the bills."

When you finish breakfast, you scrub dishes, sweep the floors, and take out the trash. By late that afternoon, you're exhausted. You haven't worked this hard since you left the farm. But your stomach is full for the first time in weeks.

"You've got a strong back and you work hard," Betty says approvingly. "How would you like a permanent job?"

Many people in the cities depended on free soup kitchens for food.

You nod. "Now, I can't pay you wages," Betty says quickly. "But I can give you decent food every day. I expect you to be here every morning and work as hard as you did today. Agreed?"

"Agreed!" you say. Betty gives you a greasy paper sack filled with leftovers. You clutch it as if it were a treasure. Maybe one day, you'll be able to earn money. But for now, food is enough.

63

THE END

To follow another path, turn to page 11.
To read the conclusion, turn to page 103.

One night, Dad returns to Sally's house with an old, beat-up car. You don't ask where he got it, and he doesn't tell you. You and your family pack your few belongings and drive out of town.

Every time the money runs out, Dad stops and finds work. You camp in pastures and ditches alongside the road. You and Johnny find scraps of food from restaurant garbage cans.

You finally make it to Washington state. You all find jobs picking apples. As soon as one orchard is done, you move on to the next.

"Don't worry," Dad says to you. "We'll find a place of our own someday." You don't think that day will ever come, though, at least not until the Great Depression and drought are over.

THE END

To follow another path, turn to page 11.
To read the conclusion, turn to page 103.

You don't ever want to be hungry again, so the idea of making money sounds good. Dad agrees. The next day, you pack up and move on. For the rest of the summer, you follow the crops, picking fruit and vegetables. By fall, it's time for cotton to be picked. Cotton pickers make $3 to $4 a day, and all four of you can work. It's backbreaking work, and you hate it. But at the end of the season, the family has a nice bit of money saved.

You live in a small cabin near the cotton fields. The owner lets you stay in the cabin during the winter. It's not much, but it's better than spending the winter in a tent. In the spring, it will be time to move again, following the crops.

You decide you don't mind being a migrant worker. It's not the life you imagined, but it's not bad, either.

THE END

To follow another path, turn to page 11.
To read the conclusion, turn to page 103.

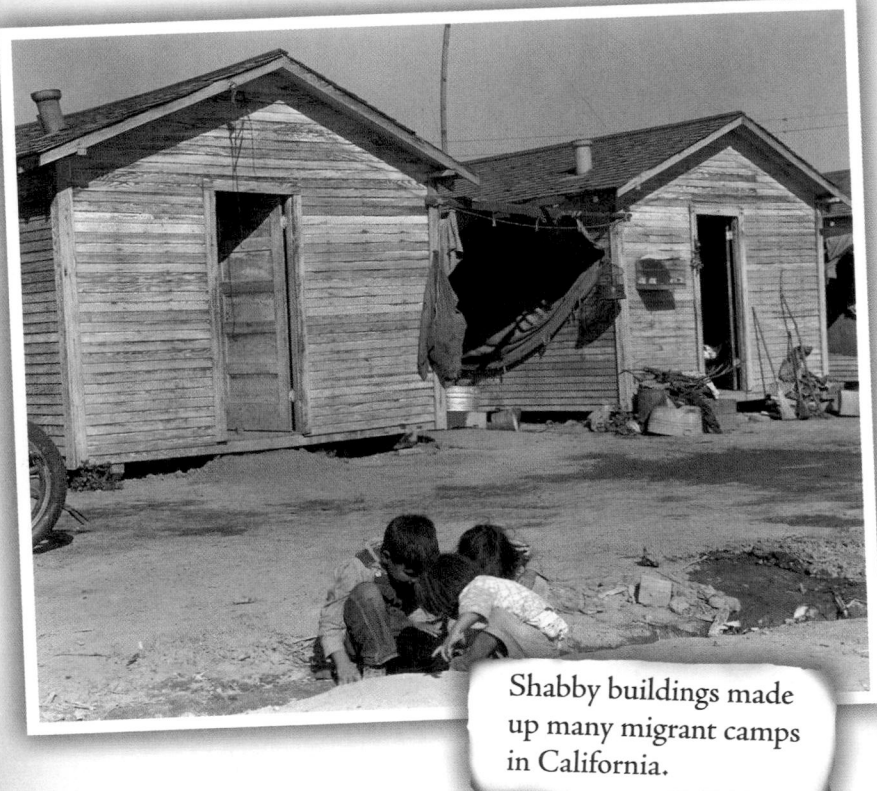

Shabby buildings made up many migrant camps in California.

66 "These men can't keep us out forever," Dad finally says. "We'll stay here until they let us in."

The camp is dirty and crowded. The only water to drink is from an irrigation ditch along the side of the road. The water smells bad and tastes worse.

Every day more people come, and the guards turn them all away. Some leave, but a lot of them set up camp. Soon there are several hundred people camped here. A rumor in the camp says that the guards will be leaving soon. You hope it's true.

One morning, you wake up feeling dizzy. Your stomach hurts terribly. You have bloody diarrhea, which scares you. Mother is worried. She wraps blankets around you. But there's no medicine, and there's nothing more she can do. One of the old women in the camp takes a look at you.

"Dysentery," the woman says, shaking her head. "Must have gotten sick from the water." That night, you die in your sleep.

THE END

To follow another path, turn to page 11.
To read the conclusion, turn to page 103.

67

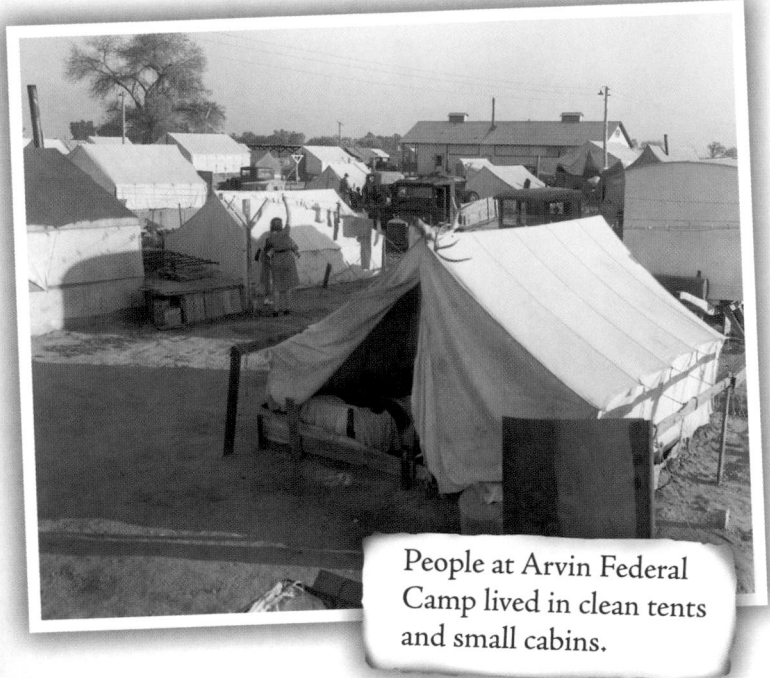

People at Arvin Federal Camp lived in clean tents and small cabins.

It takes you a week to get to Bakersfield. The family you travel with is from Kansas. The Dust Bowl destroyed their farm too.

Finally you reach Arvin Federal Camp on Weedpatch Highway. People call it Weedpatch Camp. The government built the camp just for Dust Bowl refugees. Rows of tidy white tents on wooden platforms fill the camp.

Your family is assigned a tent with its own stove. It costs a dollar a week to live in the camp. Families without money do work around the camp in exchange for their lodging. The DiGiorgio fruit farms are nearby. Your parents get jobs in the fields. You and Johnny go to the local school.

Life in camp is better than anything you remember in Oklahoma. The bathrooms have flush toilets and hot showers. There are dances, potluck dinners, and talent shows. The camp has a library and a medical clinic. Later the camp opens its own school.

One day, you see a man wandering around the camp, writing in a notebook. He sees you and Johnny and smiles. "I'm John Steinbeck," the man says. "I'm writing an article on the camps for *Life* magazine."

Turn the page.

John Steinbeck wrote *The Grapes of Wrath* based on his interviews at Weedpatch Camp.

70

Mr. Steinbeck asks you and Johnny about life in camp. He writes as you talk. Soon Dad, Mother, and a few others join you. They tell Mr. Steinbeck all about their lives in Oklahoma.

"Thank you for telling me your stories," he says when everyone is finished. "You know, I just might write a book about the Dust Bowl."

As Mr. Steinbeck leaves, you feel sorry for him. You doubt that anyone will be interested in reading a book about Okies and the Dust Bowl.

As the sun sets, your family returns to your tent for dinner. Dad says that soon the family will make enough money to buy a house and some land. You look forward to living a good life in California.

THE END

To follow another path, turn to page 11.
To read the conclusion, turn to page 103.

71

Many photographers found jobs with the U.S. government during the Great Depression.

CHAPTER 4

Documenting the Dust Bowl

It's 1935, and photography is your life. You grew up in New York City. When you were a kid, your mother gave you a used camera. You quickly learned to take good pictures. By the time you graduated from high school, you had a job at a small newspaper. But you lost your job a few months ago when the paper went out of business.

You hear about one of President Franklin Roosevelt's New Deal programs called the Resettlement Administration. The people who run the program are hiring photographers to take photos around the country. You sell everything you own except your camera and rickety car and drive to Washington, D.C.

Turn the page.

Roy Stryker was in charge of the photo department of the Resettlement Administration.

Before you know it, you're standing in front of the man who runs the department. "I'm Roy Stryker," the man says, shaking your hand. "So you want to take photos for me?"

You nod as Stryker flips through your folder of photos. He snaps the folder shut and hands it back to you. "Good work. Right now I need photos of the dust storms in Oklahoma and Texas. I could also use some photos of migrant workers in California. I'll pay you $4 a day. Which assignment do you want?"

➔ To go to the Dust Bowl, go to page **75**.

➔ To go to California, turn to page **84**.

"I'll go to the Dust Bowl, sir," you tell Stryker.

Stryker explains that you will send all of your film back to the office to be processed. Soon you're on the road, heading west. Every night, you pitch your tent by the side of the road. By early April, you reach the Texas Panhandle. You have never seen anything like the Dust Bowl. You can drive for hours and never see anything green. The towns are little more than ghost towns.

Several dust storms have hit the area, but you haven't seen one yet. On Sunday, April 14, you decide to hire a pilot to take you over some of the drought-stricken areas. He agrees to take you for the price of gas, which is 19 cents a gallon. It's a beautiful spring morning with clear skies. You get some great pictures of the destroyed farmlands. As the plane turns, you see something large on the horizon.

Turn the page.

"What's that?" you yell above the roar of the engine.

"Dust storm," the pilot yells back. "It's bigger than anything I've ever seen. We should get out of its way." You want to get more photos of the storm, but is it worth the risk?

➤ To tell the pilot to keep flying, go to page 77.

➤ To tell the pilot to land, turn to page 79.

The Black Sunday dust storm covered eastern Colorado, Kansas, Oklahoma, and Texas.

"Let's get closer!" you yell, thinking of the great pictures you could get. The pilot shakes his head but heads straight for the storm.

Leaning out of the cockpit, you snap picture after picture of the oncoming storm. Suddenly a gust of wind hits the plane. It tips crazily to one side. You drop your camera. It falls, disappearing into the black dust cloud.

The engine begins to sputter. "I've got to make an emergency landing!" the pilot yells. The plane dives and hits the ground with a crash.

77

Turn the page.

When you wake up, you are in a hospital. A smiling nurse is beside your bed. "You're lucky," she says. "You only have a broken leg and some bruises." The pilot is all right too. The next day, you call Stryker and tell him what happened.

"You were in a plane on Black Sunday?" he cries.

"Black Sunday?" you say, confused.

"It was a terrible day," Stryker explains. "Huge dust storms struck areas all over the country, sending dust all the way back to Washington, D.C."

"When you're better, you can come back here," he continues. "Or you can stay out on the road and keep taking photos."

→ To go back out on the road, turn to page **81**.

→ To return to Washington, turn to page **101**.

"I think you're right," you yell. The pilot immediately turns back. The black storm gains on you as you race to the landing strip.

"Hang on!" the pilot yells as he lands the plane with several hard bumps. You scramble out of the plane in time to snap several photos of the storm. Then you dash for a small shed.

The storm hits just as you slam the door. Everything goes black, as if a blanket was thrown over the sun. The shed rattles and groans in the wind. Dust fills the air. You can't see the pilot, even though he is standing right beside you.

The storm finally passes. Coughing, you walk out of the shed. The pilot grins at you. "What did you think of your first dust storm?" he asks.

"That was the most frightening thing I've ever seen," you reply.

Turn the page.

"I'm sure it won't be your only one," the pilot says. "They happen all the time these days."

You got your dust storm photos, but you don't want to leave the area yet. The pilot tells you about a struggling farm family nearby. There's also a small town a few miles west that might be a good place to visit. The pilot says some people are filming a movie there.

➤ *To find the farm family, go to page* **81**.
➤ *To go to the small town, turn to page* **83**.

Dust storms made even simple tasks like building a fence a struggle.

You set out on the road. You come to a row of fence posts almost completely buried in the dirt. A man and his son are trying to dig them out. You ask if you can take their picture. The man agrees and tells you he's a wheat farmer. "But we haven't been able to raise a crop here for three years," he adds.

You follow the man and the boy to a small farmhouse. The windows and doors are covered with wet sheets to keep the dust out. A woman and several ragged children greet you. You take several pictures as the woman tells their story.

Turn the page.

"This place was nice once," she says sadly. "Wheat as far as you could see." She leads you to the back of the house, where a small vegetable garden is growing. To your surprise, the plants are green and healthy.

"We water them by hand every day," the woman says proudly. "We carry water from the well. This garden will keep us fed this year." You don't see how those few plants will feed the family, but you don't say anything.

You thank the family and go on your way. There's a small town nearby where you might get some good photos. Or you could move on to the next county. You've heard about some farm auction sales going on there.

➸ *To visit the town, go to page **83**.*

➸ *To go to the next county, turn to page **94**.*

Soon you arrive in Dalhart, Texas. You spend a few days here, taking pictures and talking to the local people.

The big news in town is that a government movie crew is here. They're making a movie about the Dust Bowl called *The Plow That Broke the Plains*. Bam White, a local farmer, is going to be in the movie.

You watch the cameramen film Bam White pretending to plow a field. They pay him $25.

Your assignment is over in a few days. This has been an adventure, but you're tired of being on the road all the time. When you tell Stryker, he begs you not to quit. "I can use you here," he says. "Come back to Washington, D.C."

Turn to page **101**.

You've heard stories about Dust Bowl refugees, penniless and homeless, who follow the harvests in California. These migrant workers travel from farm to farm picking crops.

As you make your way across Route 66, you're surprised at the number of people heading west. Old cars and trucks piled high with furniture fill the roads. Every few miles, you see a car broken down beside the road. Usually you stop and take pictures. Each family has a sad story of their Dust Bowl experience. Most of them hope to find a better life in California.

One afternoon, you stop at a gas station and notice a woman with dark hair and rumpled clothing. She's carrying a camera. Her eyes take in everything, and she often lifts the camera to her face and snaps a picture. As it turns out, she's also a government photographer.

In the 1930s, Dorothea Lange was the most famous government photographer.

"I'm Dorothea Lange," she says as you shake her hand. She's returning from the migrant fields in California. "Be careful," she says as she gets back in her car. "It'll tear your heart out, seeing what those people are going through." She wishes you luck and drives away.

85

Finally you cross the border into California and start to see signs like "pea-pickers' camp," and "migrant camp this way." Which do you follow?

→ *To go to the pea-pickers' camp, turn to page **86**.*

→ *To head to the migrant camp, turn to page **90**.*

Lange's photo "Migrant Mother" showed the world the terrible conditions in the Dust Bowl.

You head down the tiny dirt road to the pea-pickers' camp. At the side of the road is a lone tent, its tattered sides flapping in the breeze. A truck with no tires sits next to the tent.

Inside, a young woman clutches a small baby. Three other children stand near her, staring at you. They are all dirty, with dull eyes. You introduce yourself and ask if you can take their picture. The woman nods, unsmiling.

"Where is everyone?" you ask. "I expected the place to be filled with workers."

"Crops froze," the woman replies. "We're waiting for the next crop to come in. I sold the tires off the truck to buy food, so we're stuck here."

You want to help, but there isn't much you can do. You give each child a penny. They stare at the coins as if they were gold. The mother continues to stare into space. "We're waiting for the next crop to come in," she says again, quietly.

Dorothea was right. It breaks your heart. You can't just leave them there to starve. Maybe you could buy them food. Or you could replace their tires. That might help them move on to find more work.

87

➤ *To look for tires, turn to page* **88**.

➤ *To go to town to buy food, turn to page* **96**.

You pull into the first gas station you see. There's a pile of old tires behind the station. A thin young man with greasy fingernails strolls out to greet you.

"How much for the tires back there?" you ask. "I need four of them."

"Quarter apiece," the man replies. "Pick out what you need."

You find four tires that don't look too worn and give the man a dollar. You load the tires into the car and head back to the camp.

The woman looks stunned when you return. "I don't know why you done this, but thank you," the woman says over and over. When you finish putting the tires on her car, you give the family another dollar. "Good luck," you say. You take several pictures of them, and then drive away.

Where will you go now? You remember the signs you passed earlier. One pointed to a migrant camp. You also remember another one that said something about a fruit-pickers' camp.

➻ *To go to the migrant camp, turn to page **90**.*

➻ *To go to the fruit-pickers' camp, turn to page **97**.*

Poor living conditions were common in most migrant camps.

When you reach the migrant camp, you're surprised at the number of people living there. You pitch your own tent and wander through the camp, taking pictures of people as you go.

"What are you all doing here?" you ask a man repairing a broken-down truck.

"We were blown out of Oklahoma," the man says. "We're waiting for the crops to come in so we can pick them."

As you talk, several other men join you. One is a farmer from Kansas who lost his farm when the town's bank closed. Another is a teacher from Oklahoma City. He couldn't find work because no one can afford to pay teachers. He hopes to get a job at the cannery up north when the crops are harvested.

"You might want to talk to the Ritchie family," one man says. "They came all the way from Arkansas, and they've had some hard times."

"There's the Cooks too," another says. "They've got eight young'uns and no mama."

➥ To try to find the Cook family, turn to page **92**.

➥ To look for the Ritchie family, turn to page **99**.

It's easy to find the Cook camp. You simply follow the sounds of many children playing. As you get to their tent, eight dirty, laughing kids surround you. You introduce yourself and take several pictures of the children. They bombard you with questions.

"How do you make pictures?" "Can I make one?" "Where did you come from?" You laugh and let each child hold the camera. Soon a man in weathered overalls strides up.

"Quit pestering!" he shouts, and the children scatter like mice. "I'm Fred Cook," he says.

As you snap pictures, Mr. Cook tells you that his wife died on the trip out to California. Now he's raising all eight children by himself. To your surprise, he doesn't seem bitter.

"It's not so bad, really," he says. "All but little Jim are old enough to work in the fields. After the harvest, I expect we'll go back home to Kansas for the winter. I've got family there, and the kids can go to school."

You thank Mr. Cook for his time and wander through the camp. As you take pictures, you can't help but think about the lives of these people. They come from many places, but they have all ended up here. All because of the dust.

It's time to move on. Where do you go next?

❧ To head to the fruit-pickers' camp, turn to page **97**.

❧ To go back to Washington, D.C., turn to page **101**.

You continue on, looking for more people to photograph. The things you see break your heart. In one small town, you attend an auction the farmers call a "10-cent sale." To keep a farmer from losing his property, his neighbors bid pennies on everything. Then they sell everything back to the farmer for the same price, free and clear of the bank.

A thin, stooped man is standing off to the side. A boy about 7 or 8 years old is with him.

"Is this your farm?" you ask.

"Yup," the man replies. "Been here most of my life. My daddy farmed this land. I intend to pass it on to my boy here."

The auction starts. No one bids more than a few cents for any item. When the huge tractor comes up, one man bids 50 cents. The auctioneer shakes his head, but he lets the bid win.

You get some great shots of the auction. After the sale, the bidders crowd around the farmer. The farmer gives them money, and they return the items to him. As you drive away, you see the boy climb onto the tractor, a grin on his face. You know the odds are against the man and his son, but you hope they make it.

In Oklahoma, you photograph relief workers passing out shoes and clothes to the poor. You're tired of grit in your food, of drinking dust-filled water, and seeing the tired, hungry people. It's time to go back to Washington, D.C.

95

You're angry that the government isn't doing more to help. You hope your pictures will make them realize the terrible toll of the Dust Bowl.

THE END

To follow another path, turn to page 11.
To read the conclusion, turn to page 103.

"Let me see what I can do," you say as you climb back into your car. There's a small town a few miles down the road. You find the tiny grocery store and go inside.

You pile bread, bologna, beans, and peanut butter on the counter. As you pay for the food, you tell the grocer what you're doing.

"You're feeding those dirty Okies?" he spits. "It was a black day when those folks came to California." You take your bag and leave quickly.

Your car bumps back down the road to the camp. The tent and the truck are still there, but the woman and her children are gone. You set the bag of groceries in the tent. The family will see them when they get back. As you drive away, you wonder what will become of them.

THE END

To follow another path, turn to page 11.
To read the conclusion, turn to page 103.

The fruit-pickers' camp is much nicer than some of the other migrant camps you've seen. The owner of the fields has built several rows of tiny but neat cabins along the edge of the field. Clean laundry hangs on several clotheslines, snapping in the breeze. A few children play around the cabin doorsteps as a group of women watch them.

You strike up a conversation with the women. They are happy to let you take pictures and tell you about the camp.

"We take turns watching the young'uns," one young mother says. "That way, all of us can work some days and make money."

"The owner is good to us," another says. "We come here from Arizona every summer to work. Once the harvest is over, we go back home. We've been doing that for a few years now."

Turn the page.

They tell you about life in the camp. The grower owns several large operations, so there is plenty of work. There is a school where the older children go when they're not in the fields. Sometimes there is a dance or other entertainment. Once a week, a bus comes to take people to town.

"It's a sight better than Kansas," one woman says, tears in her eyes. "The dust killed two of my babies. They came down with dust pneumonia and died on the same day. I'd rather live in a tent here than in my own house in the Dust Bowl."

Your assignment in California is almost over. The pictures you took are back in Washington, and you hope they do some good. Maybe it's time you headed back to Washington too.

Turn to page **101**.

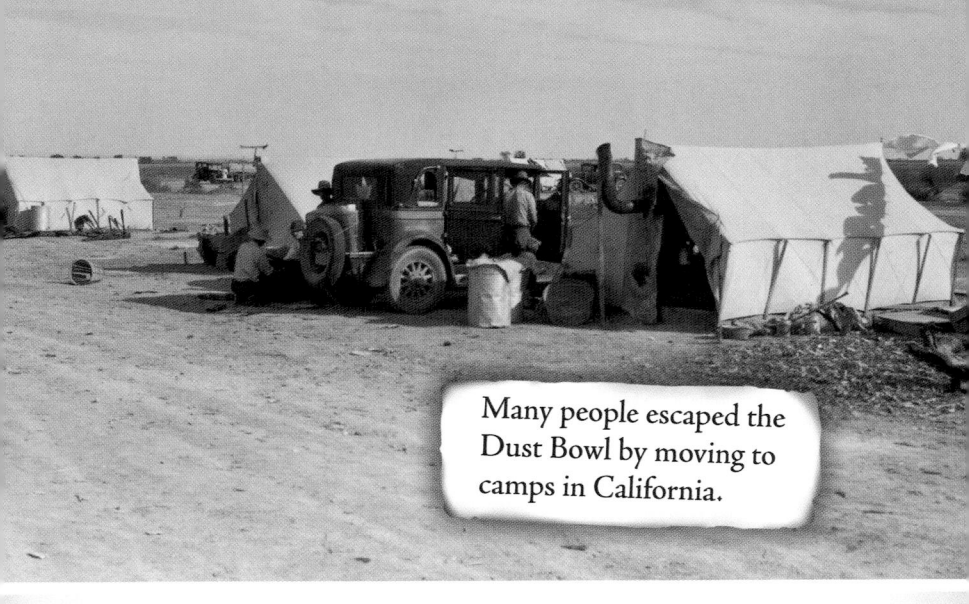

Many people escaped the Dust Bowl by moving to camps in California.

You find the Ritchie family at the edge of camp, near a smelly ditch. A woman in a tattered dress is washing dishes in the brown ditch water. A baby sleeps on an old quilt on the ground.

You introduce yourself and take a few pictures. The woman points to the quilt on the ground. "I made that myself," she says proudly. "It was the one thing I couldn't leave behind when we left our farm in Arkansas."

Turn the page.

"Was it bad there?" you ask.

The woman doesn't answer for a moment. Then she says, "I lost my baby girl, Ethel, to the dust pneumonia. This one was born after we got here last fall." She smiles and strokes the baby's head. "He won't ever have to breathe that terrible dust."

100

You thank her and go on your way. After walking around a bit more, you decide to stay a while. Over the next few days, you take hundreds of pictures. You photograph the outhouses, the tents, and the people. Day by day, families begin to leave, following the ripening crops. Soon it's your turn to leave too. But you'll never forget the migrant camps and the people you met there.

THE END

To follow another path, turn to page 11.
To read the conclusion, turn to page 103.

When you get back to Washington, Mr. Stryker gives you a job cataloging and recording all of the photos that the other Resettlement Administration photographers send in. It's steady work, and you're grateful for it. Someday you might go back out on the road. But for now, you're content to stay in the city.

THE END

To follow another path, turn to page 11.
To read the conclusion, turn to page 103.

Today, much of the land in the Dust Bowl has returned to native grasses.

CHAPTER 5

The Legacy of the Dust Bowl

The Dust Bowl lasted from 1931 to 1939. During that time, millions of people lost their homes and jobs. Thousands died.

At first, no one understood why the Dust Bowl happened. After a while, people figured out that they were partly to blame. Bad farming practices left millions of acres of land open to erosion. Land that was not meant for farming was stripped of its grass, which held the soil in place. When the droughts came, the land dried up and blew away.

103

As the drought continued, the government urged farmers to learn ways to conserve the land. Farmers planted trees and plowed fields in contoured rows. When the rains came in 1939, the Dust Bowl years ended.

In 1941, the United States' entry into World War II (1939–1945) helped end the Great Depression. The war created millions of jobs, and the economy recovered.

The people who lived through the Dust Bowl years never forgot them. Most of the families who left the Dust Bowl never returned. However, not everyone was destroyed by the Dust Bowl. Many families stayed on their farms. When the drought was over, they began farming again. Today there are many successful farms in the area that was once the Dust Bowl.

Some people became famous as a result of their Dust Bowl and Great Depression experiences. Woody Guthrie's songs about life during the Depression made him a star. Dorothea Lange's photographs showed people the horrors of the Dust Bowl. Her photo "Migrant Mother" is one of the most famous pictures in the world. In 1939, John Steinbeck published his book about the Dust Bowl, *The Grapes of Wrath*. It was based on his interviews with people who fled the Dust Bowl for California. The book won the Pulitzer Prize and is still popular today.

During the Dust Bowl years, the government bought millions of acres of land that could not grow crops. Much of this land became parks and national grasslands where the natural vegetation was allowed to grow. Today visitors can see what the Great Plains looked like before the dry, terrible Dust Bowl years.

Time Line

October 29, 1929 — On "Black Tuesday," the stock market crashes. The Great Depression begins.

1931 — Severe drought hits the Midwest. Crops die. "Black blizzards," or dust storms, begin.

1932 — Fourteen dust storms are reported; Franklin D. Roosevelt is elected President of the United States.

1933 — Many of President Roosevelt's "New Deal" programs begin, such as the Agricultural Adjustment Administration.

1934 — The drought worsens and covers more than 75 percent of the United States.

1935 — The government creates the Drought Relief Service to help Dust Bowl families.

The new Soil Conservation Service starts teaching farmers ways to control soil erosion.

The Resettlement Administration begins hiring photographers to document the effects of the Dust Bowl.

On Sunday, April 14, the worst dust storm of the Dust Bowl hits several states and carries dust to the East Coast. People call it "Black Sunday."

1935 — The new Works Progress Administration provides jobs to unemployed Americans.

1936 — Roosevelt is reelected president; Los Angeles sends policemen to patrol the California borders.

1937 — The Resettlement Administration becomes the Farm Security Administration.

1938 — Government conservation programs help keep 65 percent of the soil from blowing away.

1939 — Rains come during the fall, ending the drought; John Steinbeck publishes *The Grapes of Wrath* about the Dust Bowl.

1941 — The United States enters World War II, which helps end the Great Depression.

OTHER PATHS TO EXPLORE

In this book, you've seen how the events surrounding the Dust Bowl look different from three points of view.

Perspectives on history are as varied as the people who lived it. You can explore other paths on your own to learn more about what happened. Seeing history from many points of view is an important part of understanding it.

Here are some ideas for other Dust Bowl points of view to explore:

108

- Not all people in the Dust Bowl lost their money. What would it be like to be a wealthy person during that time?

- The Dust Bowl affected more people than just farmers. What would it be like to be a business or bank owner during the Dust Bowl?

- Many teenagers went out on their own during the Dust Bowl. What would their lives have been like?

READ MORE

Heinrichs, Ann. *The Dust Bowl.* Minneapolis: Compass Point Books, 2005.

Levey, Richard H. *Dust Bowl!: The 1930s Black Blizzards.* New York: Bearport, 2005.

Reis, Ronald A. *The Dust Bowl.* New York: Chelsea House, 2008.

Vander Hook, Sue. *The Dust Bowl.* Edina, Minn.: Abdo, 2009.

INTERNET SITES

FactHound offers a safe, fun way to find educator-approved Internet sites related to this book.

109

Here's what you do:

1. Visit *www.facthound.com*
2. Choose your grade level.
3. Begin your search.

This book's ID number is 9781429623438.

FactHound will fetch the best sites for you!

Glossary

auction (AWK-shuhn) — a sale where goods are sold to the person who bids the most money

drought (DROUT) — a long period of weather with little or no rainfall

dust pneumonia (DUHST noo-MOH-nyuh) — a serious sickness caused by breathing dust

dysentery (DI-sen-tayr-ee) — a serious infection of the intestines that can be deadly; dysentery is often caused by drinking contaminated water.

migrant (MYE-gruhnt) — a laborer who moves from place to place

Okie (OAK-ee) — a negative term for a migrant farm worker from the Dust Bowl

relief (ri-LEEF) — money or other help given to poor people

stock market (STOK MAR-kit) — a place where stocks are bought and sold; someone who owns a share of stock owns part of a company.

suffocate (SUHF-uh-kate) — to die from lack of oxygen

The Good Nazi

The Good Nazi

The Life and Lies
of
Albert Speer

Dan van der Vat

Houghton Mifflin Company
Boston · New York
1997

First U.S. Edition
October 1997

First published in Great Britain in 1997
by Weidenfeld & Nicolson,
an imprint of The Orion Publishing Group, Ltd.

For information about permission to reproduce selections
from this book, write to Permissions,
Houghton Mifflin Company, 215 Park Avenue South,
New York, New York 10003.

CIP data is available.

Printed in the United States of America

QUM 10 9 8 7 6 5 4 3 2 1

CONTENTS

LIST OF ILLUSTRATIONS

Following page 150

'Cathedral of light'[1]
Rudolf Wolters[2]
Karl Hanke[1]
Professor Gall, Hitler and Speer[2]
Speer's designs for the new Berlin[3]
Hitler and Speer examine the plans of their 'Germania'[3]
The Great Hall as seen through the Triumphal Arch[4]
Speer, Hitler and Arno Breker in Paris[1]
A model of the proposed Nuremberg Stadium[4]
Speer with Eva Braun[4]

Following page 246

Hitler and Speer in the Ukraine[3]
Speer with Hermann Göring[3]
Speer 1942[3]
Speer with his family in Berchtesgaden[4]
Speer in Linz, talking to slave-workers from Mauthausen[4]
The hall of Speer's 1938 Reich Chancellery, in 1945[3]
Under arrest: Speer with Dönitz and Keitel in May 1945[3]
Speer at Nuremberg, August 1946[3]
Speer in Spandau prison[5]
Speer with his wife, on his release from prison, 1966[6]
Speer, 1981[3]
Speer's streetlamp, in Berlin[2]

Photographic credits

'Die Tat ist alles, nichts der Ruhm.'
(*'The Deed is all, the glory nil.'*)

Goethe, *Faust II*

'I'll have them wall all Germany with brass.'

Marlowe, *Dr Faustus*

'Wenn Hitler überhaupt Freunde gehabt hätte, wäre ich bestimmt einer seiner engen Freunde gewesen.'
(*'If Hitler had actually had friends, I would certainly have been one of his close friends.'*)

Albert Speer, at Nuremberg, 19 June 1946

A Carnival of Interviews

ALBERT SPEER AND I AGREED to carry out our one and only exercise in mutual exploitation on Shrove Tuesday in 1976. The encounter took place at his comfortable, if architecturally unexciting, family villa in the hills above Heidelberg. I had not the slightest inkling (I seldom suffer from premonitions) that I was to return there sixteen years later in the course of researching this biography – the first book about Speer over which he had no personal influence.

Two rules once governed the classic 'profile' in a serious newspaper of the kind I used to work for. The writer's identity should not be revealed; and the subject should not be contacted. Friends, enemies, relatives and colleagues, however, and of course the archives, were fair game. But personality-cultism is now so rife in the media that the profiler may seek not only an interview with the subject but also personal fame by fleeting association with the profilee. The writer flaunts by-line and photograph while commonly obtruding his or her personality, and even opinions, into an article purportedly about someone else. The biographer, always denied the camouflage of anonymity, is rather more exposed to the same temptation, but has less excuse for succumbing. Unlike most journalism, a serious biography must take the long view if it is not to become a polemic, a hagiography or a 'cuttings job' without depth. Biographers who tackle a living person, or one alive when they start work, can hardly be expected to eschew the chance of assistance from their subject; but that approach gives an arch-manipulator like Speer (his most widely attested characteristic) the chance to exert a decisive influence on the resulting portrayal. Speer was long dead by the time this book was conceived.

A comprehensive list of the books by and about Speer will be found under the heading 'The Speer Corpus' in the Sources section at the end of this volume. Each one was, for better or worse, influenced by the man himself. William Hamsher's approach is betrayed by his title, as is Matthias Schmidt's polemic, unique for taking an openly hostile view even though he consulted his target. Gitta Sereny's exhaustive book on Speer ('whom I knew well and grew to like', as she boldly declares in her opening line) developed out of many consecutive days of interviews with him for a lengthy magazine feature, and was more concerned with questions of guilt and repentance than the facts of his life – what he was rather than what he did. All other contributors to the corpus also acknowledge his assistance, whether by interview, telephone conversation, correspondence or even vetting of the manuscript. Whether this direct help, in the form of the subject's hand on the author's tiller, was an advantage or a disadvantage is not for me to say; whichever it was, this life of Albert Speer lacks it.

A quarter of a century in Fleet Street has left me with the unshakable conviction that objectivity is always in the eye of the beholder (I soon gave up trying to be 'objective' about apartheid, Nazism's first cousin, when reporting from South Africa); truth, too, can be very subjective, as a visit to a court of law will rapidly demonstrate. Honesty therefore remains the best policy for writers: it is entirely possible for them to reveal their standpoint to the reader so that allowances can be made for it. It is no less possible and desirable to be fair to a biographical subject regardless of the writer's likes and dislikes.

The reader is therefore entitled to know that this book arose from a nagging scepticism about Speer's double claim to unique knowledge of Hitler's regime and to contemporaneous ignorance of the extent, if not the very existence, of the genocide that was its driving force. My doubt was aroused by reading his memoirs in 1970, renewed by meeting him in 1976 and reinforced in 1982, when I was asked by my then publishers to read the original German version of Matthias Schmidt's brief polemic, optimistically and prematurely entitled *Albert Speer – the End of a Myth* (I strongly urged them to publish it in English but they decided otherwise). I was not free to take a deeper interest in the subject until 1990, and even then there was one other book to finish and, eventually, three more to be researched and written. But as my bouts of concentration on Speer increased in both frequency and length and finally became continuous, I found myself faced with two main questions: had he told the whole truth at Nuremberg and in his writings; and was the repentance he professed during and after his imprisonment genuine – in short, was he a credible witness for the purposes of both justice and history? These were never rhetorical questions: I soon discovered that such authorities as the legendary 'Nazi hunter' Simon Wiesenthal, the psychologist and analyst of Nazi nihilism Erich Fromm, the historian Joachim Fest and the investigative chronicler of inhumanity Gitta Sereny all felt that Speer had shown sincere contrition.

In 1976, as chief correspondent of *The Times* of London in Germany, I called on Speer, Hitler's erstwhile architect and armaments minister, because his British publisher had offered the paper an exclusive interview with him. My report was not a 'profile' but a straightforward feature about his second volume of memoirs, *Spandau – the Secret Diaries*, describing the contents and interviewing the author. The 'peg' for the feature was the imminent publication of the English translation, which meant that the 'exclusive' was actually an almighty plug for the book, to be published in London ten days later. Speer and his publishers were using me to obtain publicity and I was using him to fill a large space in the paper with my name attached. Such mutual exploitation is a mainstay of journalism. I cannot claim that the resulting meeting was anything more than an interesting diversion for me. I had no sense of interviewing a latter-day Faust about his relations with his personal Mephistopheles, Adolf Hitler. I took away an impression of a patrician old man, arrogant, charming and aloof in equal measure. To this day I remember much more vividly the taxi-driver who brought us together.

My little 'awayday' by train from Bonn to Heidelberg was a welcome distraction from a bizarre time of year in the mainly Catholic Rhineland, the great, bibulous carnival weekend which begins on the Thursday before Lent and ends, amid a cumulative mass hangover, on Shrove Tuesday, the eve of Lent. Political developments are rare over that weekend because many politicians join in the festivities. In the Rhineland proper this appalling manifestation is called *Karneval* and begins with the *Weiberfastnacht* (wives' fast-eve), during which women traditionally cut off the tie of any man foolish enough to be caught wearing one. The rest of Catholic Germany, including the Baden region round Heidelberg, calls the festival *Fasching*. It is taken tremendously seriously, a fact which I did not have in mind as I approached the taxi-rank outside Heidelberg station.

Slipping into the back of the usual buff Mercedes-Benz diesel, I asked the driver to take me up to Schloss-Wolfsbrunnenweg, a long, winding, wooded road in the hills above the Neckar River on which Heidelberg stands. When we reached the gate of the Speer house ten minutes later, after the usual inconsequential conversation, the driver turned round to collect his fare. Up to then I had been addressing the back of his head; now I saw he was wearing a Groucho Marx face-mask with bushy moustache, red nose and glassless spectacles all of a piece, in honour of *Fasching*. He was as full of bonhomie and festiveness as last year's telephone book. I advised him ironically not to overdo things when he went off duty; but that kind of irony seldom registers in Germany, where pleasure is a serious matter.

To my mild surprise Speer himself came to answer the door, escorted by a piebald St Bernard only slightly smaller than a pony. I was half

expecting a butler, or at least a maid, because the house was obviously
designed to sustain such pretensions. It is spacious too, solidly built by
Speer's architect father in 1905, so I had no means of knowing whether
anyone else was at home. Although it was a holiday weekend, I saw
and heard no sign of Frau Margarete Speer or any of the six children,
by then all grown up, or any grandchild – just an elderly man and his
(eventually) quiet and obedient dog. At that time lodgers occupied the
upper storey, and Speer's youngest offspring, Ernst, lived in the con-
verted garage building in the generous garden of the detached villa
with his doctor wife and two children. At the rear edge of the garden
the ridge above and behind Schloss-Wolfsbrunnenweg presents a cliff-
face, against which leans a concrete structure with a door in it,
reminiscent of those on Speer's Atlantic Wall which so indestructibly
disfigured the coastline of my native north Holland. This was the
entrance to the bunker built into the living rock by Albert Speer as an
air-raid shelter for his family in the Second World War. The views over
beautiful Heidelberg and the Neckar valley from the garden are superb.

It was a dazzling winter's day but the inside of the house was
sombre, with drab or dark carpets and curtains and comfortably worn
furniture, of high quality though somewhat ornate in the German
way. Much of this had been replaced with tasteful modern furnishings
when I returned in 1992 to meet Ernst Speer, then in possession of
the house, which now looked much more light and airy.

Speer Senior was courtesy itself. The dog was called Bello, which I
can only assume was a feeble pun of the kind Speer liked so much:
the beast was handsome, but *bellen* means barking in German. It was
friendly and treated me to the odd elephantine nudge before subsiding
to the floor, taking no further part in the interview. The question-and-
answer session lasted about two hours and ranged over the usual
topics covered by any journalist meeting Speer for the first time. I had
read his memoirs, published in English in 1970 as *Inside the Third
Reich*, six years earlier, and had just digested the Spandau volume,
whose German edition had sold a quarter of a million hardbacks in
seven months. Even so, the encounter was a superficial occasion: I was
not sufficiently equipped in those days to challenge Speer's version of
history (although, as stated, I had wondered in 1970 how a man with
a unique vantage-point at Hitler's court – the most compelling reason
for reading his books – could say he had been unaware of the Nazis'
systematic slaughter of the Jews, even as he owned up to his share of
the regime's collective responsibility at his trial while denying personal
involvement in their crimes).

I found it ironic that the man whom Hitler, the frustrated architect,
had admired for his architectural professionalism had himself become
a frustrated architect, unable to bridge the gap opened by more than

twenty years in captivity. But he was pleased by his success as an author and said he had no ambitions left in the twilight of his life. For the rest we discussed such topics as his and Hitler's mutual fascination, life in Spandau and his arm's-length relationship with his children: his greatest regret, he said, was missing their growing up and only getting to know them at an adult distance. The regret did not seem intense; but then Speer had spent the preceding decades regretting his past, a ploy which had saved his neck at Nuremberg and made him a celebrity ever since his release in 1966. The word came to sound like a synonym for ennui as Speer expressed 'regret' that historians oversimplified Hitler as a monster, 'regret' that his 1938 Reich Chancellery had not survived as an Awful Warning against totalitarian architectural bombast, 'regret' that architecture was a closed chapter to him, 'regret' that he had not known at the time about the crimes his fellow-Nazis were committing. I have no reason to doubt these regrets but they were a long way from passionate. Speer's German was mellifluous but also monotonous, so that any topic, be it architecture, armaments, Auschwitz or authorship, tripped off his tongue with the same lack of emphasis or emotional investment as we had devoted to the usual opening remarks about the weather.

The most abiding memory of Speer himself from what was otherwise an unremarkable journalistic exercise was the old man's palpable charm. He was then seventy-one years old but in full possession of his faculties. He stood and sat as straight as a man in the prime of life, over six feet tall and broad to match, neither fat nor thin, with wispy grey hair, bushy black eyebrows, a self-deprecating smile and a courteous, aristocratic manner. He managed to maintain an overall impression of modesty even when telling me how the local 'Juso' (Young Social Democrat) chairman had asked him to address a meeting but withdrew the invitation on meeting him. 'He said I was too charming to be credible as a former high-ranking National Socialist functionary,' Speer remembered. The only revelation I was able to make as a result of the interview was that he had voted Social Democrat since his release from Spandau in 1966. This was undoubtedly because Willy Brandt, the first postwar Social-Democrat Chancellor, had saved Speer from 'denazification' proceedings in 1966 (and, oddly, sent a congratulatory bouquet to his handsome daughter on his release). But the great Hamburg intellectual weekly, *Die Zeit*, found my little disclosure interesting enough to record.

I was back at the house in June 1992 to see Ernst Speer, then in his fiftieth year and running a computer-systems engineering business. Our meeting was in no sense unpleasant – on the contrary – but the youngest of Albert Speer's six children retained the withdrawn trait that his father had admitted to as a young man. As a boy, Ernst had been regarded by friends of the family as the most 'difficult' and least promising of Speer's brood of six (they were wrong on both counts). Eye contact was rare, his eyes were seldom still and he showed signs of nervous irritability. It was a conversation conducted in German and marked by his silences and my attempts to fill them.

Ernst Speer recalled going with his mother and one or other of his siblings to see his father in prison once or twice a year as he grew up. The first time was in 1952, when he was nine. By the time his father got out, Ernst was twenty-three and a student (he got his engineer's diploma in electronics when he was all of thirty years old, not at all untypical of the unworldly German higher-educational system). He had lived at Schloss-Wolfsbrunnenweg since 1968, first in the cottage in the grounds that had once been a garage cum chauffeur's flat, and latterly in the house proper. 'I knew my father only as a stranger,' he said: '*mehr bekannt als verwandt*' (more acquainted than related). 'It is very difficult to describe the relationship ... The uncertainty of having a father and not having one at the same time was a bit of a strain.'

After his release and return to Heidelberg, Albert Speer had been 'unworldly' but immediately asserted himself as master in his own house, his son said. There was a constant stream of visitors seeking interviews, help with books, theses and the like. With all of these, as with his own family, he deployed his *Ausstrahlung* (literally 'radiation' – a powerful aura of charm; Spear had used the same word to describe Hitler's power over people, including himself). When workers came to repair something, he would switch to the local dialect. 'He tuned in to everybody's wavelength.'

I had gone to see Ernst Speer as the current occupant of the ancestral home, to see what, if anything, I could glean from it and him by way of memories and papers. But mixed with this undeniably self-serving motive was another: I felt as a veteran journalist that I ought, in the interests of fairness, to let his family have their say – if they so wished – because they would inevitably feature in my book. On leaving, I had the impression that Ernst Speer was genuinely in two minds about helping me; he said he would think about it.

I therefore made my third and last visit to the house, with permission, about six months later. This time Ernst Speer's wife, Irmhild, was also present. It soon became clear that if she had anything to do with it there would be no help from Schloss-Wolfsbrunnenweg. But we had a most civilised conversation, walking on eggshells but accompanied by an expensive bottle of white wine. My follow-up letter in the New Year, a polite final request for a yea or nay, ended with the assumption that silence presumed dissent. I duly got no reply.

*

Frau Doktor Hilde Schramm, *née* Speer, was almost famous for not giving interviews, especially not about her father Albert Speer, whose quasi-ambassador cum literary agent she had been, woman and girl, while he was in Spandau. I therefore counted myself lucky to be invited to her large apartment in a villa in south-western Berlin in November 1993, even though a blizzard made it hard to find. The invitation, extended over the telephone, was clearly reluctant, and the metaphorical temperature indoors was not much higher than the real one I had half-blindly slithered through outside. If I still thought the two talks with Ernst had been awkward, the brief encounter with Hilde made them seem euphoric. Dr Schramm, an educationist and former eco-political activist in the West Berlin Senate (twice elected to the city parliament on the 'Green'-related Alternative List), was now working for an anti-racist organisation based in Potsdam and targeted on schools.

She was courteous, if decidedly cool and tense, and told me very nearly nothing that I had not already gleaned from her father's books and elsewhere. It was hard work and in the end I made my excuses and left, in the time-honoured, empty-handed fashion of my former profession. These experiences and other futile inquiries led me to give up on the Speer family as sources. They are clearly united in not wishing to help strangers to dig over their notorious father's past: instead, they tend to stand pat on his books and refer inquirers to them. In view of the mountain-range of information on Speer in archives and elsewhere it was the converse of inconvenient for me to be spared extra work and possible extra complications. Nor was their attitude incomprehensible: whenever I go to the Netherlands I am asked whether I am the son of a man with the same name. While I am proud of my late father, a writer famous in Holland (who spent some of the war in hiding to evade working for Speer as a labour conscript), I feel I have been around long enough to be entitled to my own identity. Having also notably failed to persuade Himmler's daughter to go public in another, unrelated context, I found the shyness of the Speers entirely understandable.

More by accident than design, therefore, I eventually found myself in a different position from all the others who have produced books about Albert Speer, his work for Hitler, the quality and/or quantity of his guilt and remorse and his place in history. Aware that Gitta Sereny had been working on him ever since her marathon series of interviews with him in 1978 and unable to catch up, let alone overtake, such a colleague, I decided to await her book and the new insights it would undoubtedly provide, treating it as an extra source and citing it as appropriate. To prove that I had independently, albeit amid other projects, put in a lot of work on Speer, I wrote a 4,000-word feature on him for the *Guardian* six months before her book appeared, pegged to the ninetieth anniversary of his birth in March 1995.

In 1978 Ms Sereny had persuaded Speer to confirm his admission, to *Playboy* magazine in 1971 and again to the Board of Deputies of South African Jews in 1977, that he had known at the time that 'something frightful was happening to the Jews.' He apparently understood that such an 'admission' would alter his public and historical reputation, 'but it would be a relief.' This concession undermined Speer's consistent claim from Nuremberg onwards to have been the blinkered technocrat aware only vaguely if at all of what was going on outside his sphere. But it still did not amount to a confession of *personal* guilt, of crimes committed *by him* against the victims of Nazism, rather than the familiar acceptance of his share of the *general* responsibility of the Hitler regime for war crimes, a stance which had caused such a stir at Nuremberg, again on his release and when his memoirs appeared. Some, such as the American economist J. K. Galbraith, who interviewed him for a week on behalf of the US Strategic Bombing Survey just after the war, needed a fraction of the time to reach the conclusion that Speer was far blacker than he painted himself.

His concern for his reputation led him to show infinite tolerance to serious inquirers, whom he never turned away. I therefore feel I can describe this book as the first on Speer to rely, willy nilly, mainly on external sources. That unique characteristic will outlast at least the next scheduled book on Speer, Joachim Fest's biography: Herr Fest, who was most helpful to me, was Albert Speer's editorial adviser. As such, he spent much time helping him with his memoirs and his diaries, both of which were less than frank – thanks to what was concealed by Speer but is laid bare in the following pages. This biographer had no choice but to stand at a sceptical distance from his subject's version of events: apart from one little interview, I did not get the chance to come under the influence of Albert Speer.

PART ONE

Architect

1

Origins

(1905–18)

BERTHOLD KONRAD HERMANN ALBERT SPEER was born at 11.15 a.m. on 19 March 1905, at number 19, Prinz-Wilhelm-Strasse (later renamed Stresemannstrasse) in the city of Mannheim, at the confluence of the Rhine and the Neckar. The time is shown on his birth certificate[1] and would not be worth mentioning except that Speer rounds it up to noon (as in high noon?) in his memoirs[2] – and also adds other portentous embellishments: 'The thunder of a spring storm drowned out the bells of the nearby Christ Church, as my mother often used to tell me.'

Matthias Schmidt, a doctoral student who did his best to expose Speer as a fraud in 1982, took the trouble to check official weather records and established that there had been no thunder in Mannheim before 3 p.m. that day.[3] Nor could the bells which foretolled the baby's destiny have belonged to the Christ Church because that edifice was not built until 1911, when Albert was six years old. No matter; it was a Sunday, and there were plenty of other churches in Mannheim. Some of them would doubtless have been audible, if they rang the modest quarter-hour, from the Speers' imposing, fourteen-roomed apartment, the entire floor of a grand-bourgeois house built by Albert's father, Albert Friedrich, at the time of his marriage in 1900. This instance of carelessness, not to say self-enhancing prodigality, with the truth at the very start of *Inside the Third Reich* may be taken as an unintentional but useful warning to the reader of the ensuing 522 pages of the English text: *caveat lector*.

The birth certificate also gives the family's religion as Evangelical (which in Germany means Lutheran Protestant). Baden, once a marcher-county of the Holy Roman Empire and today part of the *Land* (federal state) of Baden-Württemberg, was traditionally though not exclusively Catholic, but the Speer family originated in Silesia, a Polish province ruled by Austria until acquired in 1740 by Protestant Prussia. They moved westward via Berlin to Prussian Westphalia in the nineteenth century, in time to prosper in the tidal wave of construction generated by the industrial revolution.

Along the way they acquired lower- and middle-class connections with Swabia (the area round Stuttgart in south-west Germany) and the Westerwald (east of the Rhine and north of Koblenz). Speer had hooded eyes, a physical peculiarity he shared with many Swabians such as Dr Kurt-Georg Kiesinger, West German Chancellor from 1966 to 1969. Via Albert's mother, Luise Mathilde Wilhelmine, *née* Hommel, the family gained a retrospective, bar-sinister connection with the hereditary Marshals of the Empire, the Pappenheims, one of whom sired eight boys with a Hommel ancestor without bothering to make an honest woman of her. Speer's maternal grandfather, Hermann Hommel, rose from the poverty of a Black Forest woodsman's hut to the wealth of owning a precision-engineering company. Speer was particularly fond of his mother's father, one of very few spontaneous and warm members of his extended family: they went shooting together. Frau Hommel, however, was a congenital counter of spoons; and their daughter was a bitterly disappointed young woman who wed Albert Senior only after being jilted by a deceitful army officer. But she was eminently suited in every material and social respect to marry one of the four sons of Berthold Speer, Albert's other grandfather, who practised as an architect in Dortmund in the Ruhr, epicentre of the German industrial revolution. Speer was born too late to know his father's parents but he admitted to Gitta Sereny[4] that his grandfather had not been wealthy, contrary to the impression conveyed in his own memoirs – another significant example of lying about his origins for effect. Speer's father, Albert Friedrich, followed in his own father's footsteps and set up an architectural practice in Mannheim in 1892, when he was twenty-nine. He entered the profession by apprenticeship because the family could not afford to send him to university.

Only when he had firmly established himself was he ready, at the age of thirty-six, to marry the prosperous industrialist's daughter on 5 February 1900 in Mainz, another important Rhineside town to the north of Mannheim. She was not quite twenty-one years old.[5] Love of money played a more important role in the match than love: Albert Speer Senior admitted his overriding interest in money in 1943 to Dr Rudolf Wolters, Speer's wartime assistant, chronicler and agent during the Spandau years.[6] He also looked after his money. Because he had invested heavily in property and land, he was able to overcome the effects, commonly disastrous for the middle classes, of Germany's 'Great Inflation', which peaked in 1923, by judicious property sales for US dollars.[7] Albert Senior also acquired the site in Schloss-Wolfsbrunnenweg, Heidelberg, and built what was originally intended to be a summer home there in 1905. Not surprisingly, the parents preferred this delightful spot to the grime and soot of Mannheim, with its pollution from the sprawling river port and from industries such as chemicals in neighbouring Ludwigshafen. But Speer hated the house because of his unhappy childhood years there. The Speer parents rented out the Mannheim apartment, even though Albert Senior's architectural office was next door, and moved to Schloss-Wolfsbrunnenweg in the summer of 1918. The prosperity of the Speers, who were a two-car family from the outset, would outlast the Kaiser's war, the vicissitudes of the Weimar Republic and, with more than a little help from Albert Junior's Third Reich colleagues, Hitler's war and the ensuing reconstruction as well.

Albert, as he was always known despite his imposing array of forenames, was the middle son of three. The elder brother, Hermann, the mother's favourite, born in December 1902, turned into a wastrel and the younger, Ernst, the father's favourite, born in December 1906, was killed in the Second World War. There was no sister. The young Albert was something of a weakling, subject to fainting fits; according to his memoirs, 'weakness of the vascular nerves' was diagnosed.[8] This sounds suspiciously like one of those ill-defined, circulatory ailments to which German hypochondriacs, of whom there is no shortage, seem to be peculiarly vulnerable. But later events show that Speer did have a real circulatory weakness: eventually it killed him. He may once have had unusually low blood pressure, rife in the Rhine valley and surrounding areas. At any rate, if we are to believe his self-analysis in later life, his weakness and his 'piggy in the middle' status between his stronger, bullying brothers, combined with an absence of parental affection, turned him into a withdrawn youth, largely reliant on the boys' French-Jewish governess, a Mademoiselle Blum, for such personal warmth as was shown to him in early childhood.[9]

His mother was not only bitter but also a snob. Having brought more money than her husband to their marriage, she was free to indulge her taste for all things French and for such fripperies as servants' livery, embellished with a coat of arms, to which the Speers were not entitled.[10]

It is only too easy to accept Speer's description of a loveless boyhood and home life as authentic. It is altogether typical of the experiences of many another product of the stiff German *grande bourgeoisie* of the time, more Victorian than the Victorians (whose queen and prince-consort were German after all). Speer's account rings true psychologically. These middle-class households, where displays of emotion were discouraged even as decorous sentimentality was encouraged, proved a rich breeding ground for emotional cripples such as Speer. So when he wrote that his ability to manipulate people and cope with difficulties derived from his boyhood weakness,[11] that was probably only half the story. His parents' loveless marriage – they had separate suites of rooms at Mannheim – and his own emotional starvation must also have led him to use his considerable wits to get what he could in a domestic setting which he describes as artificial and uncomfortable.

It is a truism nowadays that a loveless childhood may well produce a loveless adult. But many Germans from stable and loving families fell for Hitler just as Speer did; and not a few of the plotters against Hitler came from high-class families just as stiff and unloving as Speer's. It is therefore facile to argue that Speer's undoubtedly miserable early years made him especially likely to become a Nazi war criminal; as with so many other criminals, opportunity was the overriding factor. And Speer, coldly romantic sentimentalist though he was, turned out in the end to be capable of passion after all, as the extraordinary circumstances of his death would illustrate more dramatically than anything else.

The kind of household originally occupied by his parents is still to be found intact in modern Germany, though ever more rarely. Such an apartment typically occupies an entire floor of a very large, five-storey building which forms one side of an enormous block enclosing a communal courtyard or *Hof*. I have visited apartments like this in Germany still occupied by one family, and others converted into a multiplicity of small flats or even into a hotel with dozens of rooms – all this on just one floor. Before the First World War, in a wealthy district like Mannheim's Oststadt, the apartment would have been maintained by a full array of servants, who in the Speer family's case usually numbered seven and shared the back entrance with the children. Visitors arrived in state in the courtyard and progressed up the external staircase to the family's separate front entrance at first-floor level. By definition there could be no horizontal 'upstairs-downstairs' division in this colossal flat, but there was a distinct vertical one between front and back at the Speers' Mannheim home.

A large hall with a dummy fireplace faced with real Delft tiles opened on to a spacious reception room with tasteful French furniture and a massive crystal chandelier. There was a conservatory for breakfast, furnished with items from several eastern countries, which Albert Senior had bought at the World Exposition in Paris in 1900 in readiness for an opulent married life. Other reception rooms included a living room and a dining room big enough for a table for more than twenty people.[12] Albert Junior placed his family among the top twenty or thirty of Mannheim society. Germany was and remains strongly regional (the disparaging say 'provincial'), so this status implies a higher social standing than may be apparent to English or French (but not American or Dutch) eyes.

Behind the divide were a large kitchen, the children's bedrooms and quarters for those servants who lived in. All this lavish living space was served by a nanny, Berta, a cook, a liveried butler, a chauffeur (Bachmann) and three maids. But amid all this material wealth, young Albert's best, indeed only, pre-school friend by his own account was Frieda Allmendinger, daughter of the building's concierge, with whom he played in the grimy *Hof*. She, Mademoiselle Blum, grandfather Hommel, the staff of Albert Senior's office and one or two Heidelberg schoolfriends all brought significant relief to an otherwise lonely childhood not after all totally devoid of warmth.

But what of the country into which he was born – the second German Reich? As a unified state it was five years younger than Speer's father. It was essentially the creation of Bismarck, the Iron Chancellor, an achievement tactlessly crowned at the Palace of Versailles in January 1871 after the crushing Prussian victory over the French in the war of 1870. This Bismarckian settlement of the perennial 'German Question' – and of Europe – paved the way for the new Reich to become the Continent's dominant military, political and finally economic power. Historians date the decline of Britain as well as of France from the foundation of the Second Reich.

Bismarck's shrewd forecast that if there was to be a general war in Europe, it would be triggered by 'some damned foolish thing in the Balkans' was entirely correct but only a part of the truth. He sowed the most fertile seed of the Second Reich's destruction himself, by seizing Alsace-Lorraine, French since the Thirty Years' War (1618–48). Over and above this unforgivable humiliation, he exacted enough reparations from France to fund the German industrial revolution. The sequestration of Alsace-Lorraine was a constant reminder of France's military and political decline, arousing a thirst for revenge which was the most important root-cause of the First World War.

Bismarck's sovereign, Kaiser Wilhelm I, died in 1888 and was succeeded by his son Friedrich. Tragically for Germany, Europe and the world, he was already terminally ill and ruled for just ninety-nine days. Had this liberal and humane prince with his British wife, Queen Victoria's daughter, survived, the brakes might well have been kept on German nationalism and militarism. But his son became Kaiser Wilhelm II at the age of twenty-nine and Europe soon discovered that a cuckoo had taken up noisy residence in its nest. The erratic 'Kaiser Bill' forced the restraining Bismarck's resignation within two years.

Bismarck, as part of his arrangements for confining the French to their newly reduced circumstances, had taken good care to nurture relations with St Petersburg. But only one year after his retirement the Russians agreed an *entente* with a resurgent France, ending its long, postwar diplomatic quarantine (the Soviet Union was to perform the same service for a defeated Germany a generation later). In 1892 Franco-Russian relations expanded to include a defensive, reciprocal military assistance pact. Thus, exactly ten years after Bismarck converted the three-year-old German-Austrian understanding of 1879 into the Triple Alliance including (for the time being) Italy, Europe acquired the rival power bloc which, when Britain joined it, became the Triple Entente and was to fight Germany in the First World War.

As an island nation Britain maintained a small army to police its colonies and relied on the world's greatest fleet for the strategic protection of itself and its empire. Germany, a continental power with a narrow coastline and a deep hinterland, had built upon the Prussian military system a formidably modern, conscript army capable of swift mobilisation by rail against its main rivals, France and Russia. But in 1898, on the urging of Admiral Alfred von Tirpitz, Wilhelm and a compliant Reichstag decided on massive naval expansion in an undisguised challenge to British maritime supremacy. The British eventually responded with the startling initiative of an alliance with Japan in 1902, securing that rising power's cover for their Far Eastern possessions so that the Royal Navy could concentrate closer to home. Having ditched splendid isolation because of the German threat to their naval supremacy, the British quickly moved on to the *Entente cordiale* with France in 1904 and rapprochement with Russia in 1907.

Thus to Bismarck's fateful legacy, French revanchism over Alsace-Lorraine, was added a disastrous contribution from the Kaiser: British fear of a fast-growing German battlefleet, ship for ship the most advanced in the world. The third main component of the growing tension in Europe which would explode in 1914 was Russian jealousy: of Austrian influence in the largely Slav Balkans and of German influence in Turkey.

Wilhelm II, a pompous and mercurial autocrat, believed imperious behaviour was synonymous with imperial power. United Germany had inherited the essentially feudal Prussian social order, a monarchy sustained and constrained by the Prussian *Junker* landowning class such as Bismarck. Wilhelm saw himself as an absolute ruler. The Reichstag was elected by universal male suffrage but enjoyed strictly limited powers, which did not include electing the Chancellor, the Kaiser's personal appointee, as was each member of the imperial cabinet. With its erratic emperor and its well-rewarded, well-educated official class both enjoying tenure for life, Wilhelm II's Reich was 'the best run but worst ruled' state in Europe, according to a contemporary German Socialist.

The Kaiser's aggressive opportunism in foreign affairs rapidly destabilised Europe. Blackmail was the only means whereby he could now add to German colonial possessions since the rival European powers had long ago carved up the best prizes among themselves. As Germany stepped up the unwinnable naval arms race, the Kaiser clumsily tried to separate France and Russia, but lost interest when the latter was roundly defeated by Japan in 1905. The British were now committed to their decisive naval margin over Germany and built accordingly: 'We want eight and we won't wait,' said the British jingoists as they successfully campaigned for eight extra 'dreadnought' battleships. German attempts at rapprochement with each other major power in turn failed because Wilhelm could see an alliance only as a master-servant relationship. Thus the British, the French and the Germans rather surprised one another with their successful cooperation in forcing an end to the Balkan wars of 1912–13, involving Serbia, Montenegro, Bulgaria and Greece on the one hand and Turkey on the other. But the rapport, prompted by fear of a generalised war, did not last. Bismarck's 'damned foolish thing in the Balkans' – the assassination at hapless Sarajevo – duly sparked off that very conflict, first drawing in Austria and Serbia, then Germany and Russia, then Belgium, France and Britain.

The German general staff launched its Schlieffen Plan in a bid to knock France quickly out of the war, as in 1870. The German army would then have been free to concentrate against the perceived main enemy, Russia. The strategy required a sweep through neutral Belgium by a hugely swollen German right wing which aimed to encircle Paris. But the rape of Belgium drew in Britain; the French, the British and the Belgians managed to halt the mighty but clumsy advance, and the two sides dug in on Germany's Western Front. On their Eastern Front, the Germans at first retreated and then hammered the pursuing Russians, whose vast numbers alone denied the Reich a quick final victory. The Reich therefore became bogged down in a titanic struggle on two fronts, exposing the false assumptions behind the Kaiser's disastrous strategy. Britain reigned supreme on the surface of the sea and, as the French held out, built up its army on the Western Front to become their equal partner in the deadlocked trenches.

At sea the British applied their traditional tactic against a continental enemy: naval blockade. The Germans were unable to break out of this war-winning naval stranglehold with their white elephant of a High Seas Fleet. Instead they developed the U-boat as the instrument of a counter-blockade, which came within a week or two of bringing Britain to its knees in spring 1917 by almost severing the transatlantic lifeline from North America, littering the North Atlantic and the Mediterranean with shipwrecks.

The surface blockade which slowly starved the Germans out was all but invisible and led to only a few naval engagements and losses. The 'frightfulness' of the U-boats destroyed more than eleven million tons of Allied shipping and tens of thousands of sailors, provoking a reluctant United States to tilt the balance against Germany and Austria with its fresh manpower and huge industrial potential. Congress declared war in April 1917, the month when the British drew back from the brink of disaster by at last ordering their merchant ships to sail in convoy.

In the east, however, the Germans were trouncing the Russians, who succumbed to revolution later in the year; the Bolsheviks signed the harsh Treaty of Brest-Litovsk in March 1918. The Kaiser had at last achieved his objective (albeit in reverse order) of closing down one front so as to be able to concentrate on the other. In that same March the last German 'big push' in the west began, to the consternation of the Allies. It eventually petered out for lack of supplies and morale in the ranks; some army units up to divisional strength refused orders. The even more demoralised High Seas Fleet, virtually confined to port since its tactical victory but strategic defeat at the Battle of Jutland in May–June 1916, the one great fleet action of the war, mutinied *en masse* in October 1918. The general staff, which now ruled Germany *de facto*, sought an armistice. Thus, contrary to the pernicious postwar legend fostered by Hitler and the Nazis, the German army was not stabbed in the back by war-weary politicians at home but gave up the struggle on its own account. Hostilities ended at 11 a.m. on the 11th day of the 11th month of 1918.

The fate of Germany, Austria and their allies was sealed when the Americans decided to fight; but the defeat was far from total. Germany had thoroughly beaten Russia on the Eastern Front and had not been overrun on the Western, having come very close to a victory there also. Overall, though the population was racked by hunger, damage to German territory was minuscule whereas much of Belgium and northern France had been devastated. The Allied armies did not march on Berlin as in 1945 but limited themselves to occupying the Rhineland, preferring to intervene (alongside the Germans) in the post-revolutionary civil war in the new Soviet Union. The defeat in the west was in itself therefore less traumatic for Germany than its aftermath, the peace settlement.

Talks dragged on for more than seven months in Paris before a new government under the Social Democrat (SPD) Chancellor Gustav Bauer responded to an Allied ultimatum by reluctantly signing the Treaty of Versailles with the consent of the Reichstag on 26 June 1919. By that time the Kaiser had abdicated and gone into exile in the Netherlands, while the High Seas Fleet had scuttled itself in internment in Scapa Flow, the main wartime base of the Royal Navy. Germany escaped a generalised, Soviet-style revolution, attempted by the sailors and their supporters in the north and later by Communists in Berlin and Bavaria. The moderate Social Democrats remained shakily dominant in government from 1919 until 1930, an extraordinarily unsettled and uniquely fascinating period which saw the rise and fall of the Weimar Republic (named after the city where its constituent assembly sat).

But just as the incorporation of Alsace-Lorraine into an expanded Germany in the triumphalist ceremony at Versailles in 1871 had been the main cause of the Great War, so the Treaty of Versailles, forced on a defeated Germany in 1919, was the root of the Second World War in Europe. The Reich, as it was still called despite the departure of Wilhelm II and his Crown Prince in November 1918 (the word means state rather than empire), lost all its overseas territories. Poland had emerged from the Russian Revolution and Versailles as an independent state and was awarded a swathe of territory conferring access to the Baltic via the 'Polish Corridor', which cut off East Prussia from the rest of a truncated Germany. The main city and port in the corridor, Danzig, was hived off as a demilitarised 'free city' despite its mostly German population. The south-eastern part of Upper Silesia round Katowice also eventually went to Poland. The East Prussian outpost and port of Memel (now Klaipèda) was apportioned to a newly reconstituted Lithuania. In the west, the North Schleswig region was detached, pending a plebiscite to decide whether it should be German or Danish (it chose the latter. South Schleswig stayed German.).

Not surprisingly, the main territorial adjustment favoured a vengeful France, which not only recovered Alsace-Lorraine but also took over the neighbouring German industrial province of the Saar for fifteen years as compensation for the Lorraine coal and steel industries exploited and then ruined by the Germans (the Saar later reverted to Germany by plebiscite). The south-western Rhineland was to be occupied by French and British troops for up to fifteen years. The German armed forces were limited to a total of 100,000 men, who were forbidden to acquire aircraft or U-boats.

Hindsight shows that the most important provision of the Versailles pact, essentially a stricter and expanded version of the Armistice terms, was Article 231. This placed the entire blame for the war of 1914–18 on Germany and its allies, exacting reparations to be specified at a later date. Understandably it was a devastated France which, mindful of when the shoe had been on the other foot in 1870, pressed hardest for financial compensation, but on an impossible scale. The justification for it, Germany's alleged monopoly of war guilt, was at best simplistic, a victors' judgment.

This verdict and the sentence, the crushing burden of reparations, were rejected on principle by very nearly every German adult, left, right and centre or of no political persuasion at all. Undermining Versailles by any means available became something of a national sport, a matter of honour for many – as well as a great spur to dishonesty in public life and general amorality at every level of society. The importance of this attitude for the Weimar years and the rise of the Nazis cannot be overstated. German nationality had become a new form of original sin. If everyone generally was guilty, then nobody was particularly guilty. Hitler was preaching to the converted when he began to parlay the imputed stigma of German nationality into a renewed and defiant German nationalism.[13] Speer later fully identified himself with the overwhelming majority who rejected Versailles:

> Through a clause in the Versailles peace treaty even I, who was still a child at the time, was declared guilty of having started the First World War. Through this paragraph, dictated by hatred of the Germans, the German nation was instantly burdened for all time with a heavy guilt, which was also accepted in this form by a weak German government through its signature on the treaty. I joined Hitler's movement because Hitler promised to free the German nation and thus every single German from this guilt.[14]

2

Enter Hitler

(1918–31)

ALBERT SPEER WAS THIRTEEN YEARS OLD at the Armistice. None of his immediate family had been caught up in the fighting or suffered notably in the war, although nobody could entirely evade the general shortages of food and other supplies. He always remembered the hunger of 1918. Frau Speer proved remarkably ingenious with the turnips which became a staple towards the end, but a turnip was still a turnip, no matter how one sliced it. Great wealth in money and property was of little use to a family without rural connections. Mannheim was lightly bombed about thirty times from Allied airfields in nearby France, and sometimes the rumble of the guns, especially from Verdun, could be heard in the city at night. As an unprecedented manifestation of war the air-raids were frightening enough but did little damage and were not comparable with what was to happen twenty-five years later. One small bomb hit a house in the Speers' neighbourhood. In his memoirs Speer describes his awe at the age of ten on being allowed to explore with his brothers a locally based Zeppelin airship used for bombing London in 1916, after its officers had been entertained at the Speer home. Fantasising as young boys will, he would get out of bed in the night and sleep on the floor in sympathy with the soldiers at the front. No less typical of his age in wartime, he followed the war reports closely.[1]

His formal education had begun at the usual age of six in a private elementary school which existed to extract the maximum *Leistung* (performance) from its pupils. From there he moved to a state high school (*Oberrealschule*, roughly equivalent to an English grammar school) at the age of eleven. This less privileged, more robust environment only encouraged his already marked tendency towards reserve and withdrawal, but Speer mentions acquiring a friend called Quenzer, from a humble background, who introduced him to such innocent but less refined boyhood delights as kicking a football. Then, as now, even the wealthiest German parents sent their children to local state schools as a matter of course (there was no extra tier of fee-paying schools for the privileged to compare with England's divisive 'public' school system; boarding schools were rare and generally reserved for boys destined for the military, the offspring of Germans living abroad, orphans or 'difficult' children). The boys transferred to Helmholtz *Oberrealschule* when the family moved to the Heidelberg house in the last summer of the war. Now they could at least grow vegetables in the garden and find wood for heating.

Albert came to loathe the house because he was so unhappy there as a teenager. He returned to it perforce on his release from Spandau but he eventually retreated to a remote farmhouse he bought in Upper Bavaria for long periods, especially when writing. His brothers Hermann, more than two years older, and Ernst, less than two years younger, helped to make life in Heidelberg a misery for the weak, withdrawn middle son for whom nobody had much time. His father was a progressive liberal but also had a mean streak inherited from his own mother. Speer Senior had been brought up to suppress such feelings as he was left with after a childhood no warmer than the one he afforded his son. The parents however loved the house in Heidelberg and lived in it to the end of their days (apart from a period after the war when the US army occupied it). Albert's mother Mathilde (the name by which she was known to her few intimates) regarded the house as her 'life's work', into which she put her heart and soul. On the edge of a forest, it reminded her (doubtless in a romantically sanitised, sentimental sort of way) of her father's humble childhood home in the Black Forest. Originally it had two reception rooms, a conservatory, kitchen, three rooms for servants, two bedrooms for the boys, a master bedroom with balcony and en-suite bathroom and a guest bedroom. Extensions were added after it became the main family home in 1918 and a garage with flat was built separately (itself converted and extended after 1945).

Looking back, newly widowed, in 1947 (presumably with rose-tinted spectacles firmly in place), Mathilde Speer recalled the house in glowing terms as a place where, 'overflowing with mother-love', she would sing lullabies to her babies and fondly watch the boys disporting themselves naked in the garden in the summer heat.[2] The Speers were able to buy the adjacent property, a piece of land with a small cottage on it. This came in handy for Mathilde when the US army requisitioned the main house, and again when Margarete Speer had to take in lodgers during the early years of her husband's imprisonment. Speer's mother died in 1952, five years after his father.

Having had a sound educational start, Albert proved eventually to be a first-class student with a scientific bent but also very good at German – an accomplished all-rounder. He learned to give the impression of effortless ability to soak up knowledge on most subjects as if by osmosis, but also worked very hard before examinations, which he never failed.[3] These talents remained latent until his last two years at school, until which time he was a no more than average performer. But he was not without the rebellious spirit usually shown by bright schoolboys, even if his habit of copying the bad marks awarded to him and fellow-pupils from the class register into his school diary seems a little obsessive. Never reluctant to indulge in self-analysis, he cited this as an early portent of his later taste for statistics.[4] Religion did not interest him as a boy.

Forced in spartan, postwar conditions to walk up hill and down dale to school for three-quarters of an hour, Albert's frail, gangling physique began to strengthen. But, though tall, he was light enough to cox a boat, at a rowing club he happened to pass on the way to school, for the two years until he reached sixteen. His mother disapproved of this 'plebeian' sport, but he became friends with a boy called Ehret, the best oarsman in the school, who naturally encouraged him to persist. He grew strong enough to row and eventually became stroke of his boat, setting the pace for the seven oarsmen behind him – an early taste of power and leadership, perhaps. But he soon came to prefer canoeing, an activity more suitable for a loner like him or for chastely romantic outings with the one and only female he knew intimately from youth until old age. He became a better than average, all-round sportsman, taking up not only skiing and mountaineering (local opportunities abounded) but also rugby football, a rare pastime in Germany but on offer at his Heidelberg school. When it came to more private pleasures, the young Speer was something of a prig. He loftily dismissed the experiments of his peers with alcohol, cigarettes and even dancing; and when it came to girls there seems only ever to have been the one.

When he was seventeen he met Margarete Weber (Margret to her family and friends, Gretel to Speer) one morning on the way to school. Born on 8 September 1905, the daughter of a cabinet-maker, she was just six months his junior. Snobbery led the Speers to look down on the Webers, but Herr Weber was a considerable figure in the town, a member of the city council and owner of a prosperous business. He was a *Meister*, a master-craftsman, a rank which still enjoys special prestige in Germany. Although a crucial part of his daughter's attraction for Speer was the spontaneous warmth of the Weber family environment, so different from his own, the friendship developed intellectually rather than emotionally. The two young people shared an effusive interest in classical music and concerts as well as poetry, drama and novels.

Gretel, intelligent but lacking intellectual training, would defer to

Albert in these and most other matters. Within a year the couple had romantically resolved to ignore the class-based disapproval of both families and get married. The Webers sent their stubbornly fixated daughter to a boarding school at Freiburg in the Black Forest in the hope that the attachment would blow over. But the relationship was precisely of the kind least likely to wither on a rarefied diet of passion-free letters about culture. The correspondence was, on his side at least, as long-winded as Speer's mature prose – a writing style for which the word 'prosaic' might have been coined and which had to be professionally leavened before his memoirs could be published. According to Gitta Sereny, who was allowed to see them in 1978, the letters lacked sentimentality and sensuality alike or any reference to his inner life, thoughts or feelings, or indeed to the momentous events, such as political unrest and the occupation of the Ruhr, going on in Germany at the time.[5]

No German with an iota of intelligence could possibly have been unaware of the general political and diplomatic upheavals of the Weimar period. The young swain's failure to mention them cannot therefore be construed as ignorance or even indifference: he may well have regarded them as distasteful, irrelevant in the context or best ignored for the sake of peace of mind. This ability to compartmentalise (to put it no more strongly) stayed with him for life, enabling him later to plead unawareness of major events in his immediate vicinity with a straight face.

More than six years of separation, first when she was away and then when he was at university, only increased their rarefied rapture and determination to marry. Any inclination on the youth's part to indulge in distractions at school was now suppressed as he solemnly applied himself to preparing for work and marriage. He duly came top of his class in German, physics and mathematics and achieved a high average in the *Abitur* (matriculation) examination, which he sat in summer 1923 at eighteen, a year early.

Speer very much wished to study mathematics but his parents wanted him to become an architect like his father and his grandfather before him (and eventually his eldest son, Albert). He was able to take this new frustration in his stride, just as he had coped with the enforced separation from Gretel; there is no evidence that either caused him any real pain. He seems to have had the even temper of a man with no temper to lose. It was she who encouraged and doubtless helped him to make the best of this Hobson's choice. He swallowed all parental restrictions with aplomb; architecture, unfortunately we may think, became his grand, indeed for many years his only, 'passion' (just as, one suspects, mathematics would have done had he been allowed to take that road). He always devoted himself equally but totally to the job in hand, quite capable of seeing the wood and the trees at the same time and of delegating dull tasks to others.

Times temporarily became hard for the Speer family in autumn 1923 as the German government recklessly printed money to meet the impossible reparations and the resulting inflation got completely out of hand. At the peak of the crisis in November, the US dollar (£1 then equalled a little less than $5) was worth four thousand, two hundred million Reichsmarks; one new 'Rentenmark' after the currency reform of that month was worth a billion old marks or one British shilling (5p). Albert was obliged to begin his architectural studies modestly, at the Technical University in Karlsruhe, only twenty-three miles south of Heidelberg, rather than at one of the great universities further afield. Albert's maternal grandfather Hommel had died and his father raised dollars by selling the dead man's business interests for a lot less than they were worth.[6]

Albert now received an allowance of $16 a month. Since one could survive on a dollar a week before reform, this would have represented luxury for the majority of German families. Speer was usually better off than almost all his student contemporaries. My own modestly funded father vividly remembered his schooldays on the Dutch-German frontier at that time, when one guilder was more than enough for a profligate day out across the border; as the train took them back in the evening, the Dutch boys hurled great wads of unwanted marks out of the windows. A bitter contemporary German joke told of the thief who dogged a man taking his wages home in a laundry basket and stole the basket – after tipping the money into the gutter.

With the customary easy-money supply restored to the Speers, Albert completed the semester at Karlsruhe and transferred in spring 1924 to the distinguished Technical University in Munich, the splendid capital of the south German state of Bavaria, for the second half of his first academic year. The German undergraduate's right to change universities was and is one compensation for the inordinate length of the study period.

Munich is south Germany's most handsome city. It has all the majesty of a capital, thanks to the sense of grandeur of the Wittelsbachs, the Bavarian royal house from the twelfth century whose throne vanished with so much else in 1918. The centre retains its medieval configuration with sections of city wall and two fourteenth-century gates still in place. No doubt such stone glories as the vast Old Pinakothek art gallery, built in the style of the Venetian Renaissance by Leo van Klenze in the early nineteenth century, were more inspiring for a student of architecture than the provincial buildings of Karlsruhe. But in Speer's case we can only surmise, because even in his writings on architecture he passes over his time in both cities, which suggests he attached little importance to his early experiences in either. Another Munich throwback to the Italian Renaissance, if rather more ornate, is St Michael's Church, built by the Jesuits in the sixteenth century and the repository of many Wittelsbach memorials, including the tomb of the deranged Ludwig II. But the prime symbol of the city is Gothic (apart from the onion domes on its twin towers, a south German manifestation of Turkish influence): the surprisingly austere Frauen-kirche, the church of Our Lady, the Catholic city's protector, with its unadorned brick exterior and pure white interior, free of the rococo fungus which pollutes so many other south German churches, baroque or not.

Speer's most significant discernible benefit from his time in Munich was meeting Rudolf Wolters, who was to be his most enduring and loyal friend, and for twenty years the most important man in his life.

Wolters, a fellow-student in the school of architecture, was nineteen months older than Speer, having passed his *Abitur* at the normal age of nineteen and gone to Munich Technical University. He was born on 2 August 1903 to middle-class parents at Coesfeld, Westphalia, a small town on the North German Plain some twenty miles north of the Ruhr conurbation and halfway between Münster and the Dutch border. Like Speer's, his father was an architect and his mother came from the master-artisan class (her father was a carpenter in the shipbuilding industry). Wolters attended the local 'humanistic' *Gymnasium*, a grammar school specialising in classical and language studies. His artistic and mathematical talents, which opened the way to studying architecture, were accompanied by a facility in German (if in no other modern language) which far surpassed Speer's own and extended to a keen interest in writing as well as in German literature.

One characteristic of Wolters, a compulsive scribbler, which was to be of outstanding importance in the later years of both men, to say nothing of the historical record, was keeping a diary, supplemented by carefully preserved letters and papers.[7] Wolters Senior gave his son a diary on 1 August 1914, the day Germany declared war on Russia, inspiring a lifelong habit. Personally modest, Wolters was a natural conservative with the nationalist outlook shared by so many Germans, reinforced and distorted as it was by Versailles. He suffered from malnutrition in 1918 as his family struggled to scrape together enough money and food to survive; but he was able to go to Munich at the very height of the inflation crisis to study architecture. He and Speer seem to have overlapped for one semester before Wolters went to Berlin – to be followed by Speer early in 1925.

The two young hopefuls were lucky enough to be students during the brief heyday of the Weimar Republic, between the triumph over the Great Inflation in 1923 and the onset of the Great Depression and accompanying swing to the right in 1930. The time they shared in Munich from spring 1924 was less politically dramatic for the city than the preceding five years, especially 1923, but neither took much interest in such matters, concentrating instead on competing for the best mark in essays and exercises.

Munich had become the mother city not only of Bavaria but also of one of many small groups on the political fringe: the National-Socialist German Workers' Party (Nazional-sozialistische deutsche Arbeiterpartei, NSDAP). Bavarian morale had cracked earlier than that of the rest of Germany in 1918. It was Bavarian units that took the lead in defying orders in the trenches of the Western Front, to the disgust of at least one member of the 1st Company, 16th Bavarian Infantry Regiment of the Reserve, 6th Bavarian Division, VII Corps, 6th Army – Lance-Corporal Adolf Hitler. Personal knowledge of Bavarian disloyalty to his adopted cause of German supremacy (he was born and raised in the Linz area of Austria) did not prevent him from spreading the myth that the politicians had stabbed his beloved army in the back in 1918. Hitler had the right to complain, having won the Iron Cross, Second Class, in 1914 (when it counted for something; later an Austrian officer was to remark that the only way to avoid this medal was by committing suicide), and earning the First Class in 1918, always an exceptional award for a common soldier.

He spent the war as a company runner delivering messages under fire. Unfortunately none of the many bullets he dodged in this highly dangerous work proved fatal, although he was wounded in the leg on the Somme and was gassed by the British in the last German offensive, succumbing to temporary blindness south of Ypres in Belgium in October 1918. A moody loner, regarded by his comrades as boring and by his officers as too eccentric for promotion, Hitler was a totally committed soldier who was personally devastated by defeat – for which someone, somewhere, or if possible everyone, everywhere, was going to have to pay. Nobody took Germany's humiliation more personally than this displaced Austrian and adoptive Bavarian.

The dangerous offensive, launched by General Erich Ludendorff in March 1918, got to within forty miles of Paris but was finally overcome after six months of hard fighting. It was the civil government of Germany, denied a say in running the war throughout, that was left by the generals to negotiate peace. Although the first post-imperial Chancellor was a prince, Max of Baden, it was the Social Democrats (SPD) who grasped the nettle and reluctantly settled at Versailles, after eight months of frequently bitter, unreciprocated concessions to the vengeful Allies.

Following a spell at a special military hospital in faraway Pomerania, Hitler found his way back to Munich at the end of 1918, serving as a guard at a prisoner-of-war camp until it was closed in January. Munich soon became the target of a chaotic Communist bid for power. At the other end of Germany the naval mutiny which foreshadowed the Armistice had already inspired a would-be 'Republic of Oldenburg' where 'Workers' and Soldiers' Councils' tried to take over power. Now anarchists and Communists attempted to install a similar system of soviets, on the recent Russian model, in Bavaria.[8] Munich succumbed to political uproar well before Berlin was affected. A month or so of Communist 'rule' was forcefully terminated on the night of 13–14 March 1920 by Bavarian elements of the new Reichswehr (national defence force) set up under Versailles. A right-wing coalition took power in Bavaria under Gustav Ritter von Kahr as 'State Commissioner-General'; leftists and moderates were excluded without reference to the ballot-box.

As ferment affected Berlin and elsewhere and agitation mounted against the SPD, Munich became a magnet for right-wing agitators from all over the country. These included violent extremists and members of the Freikorps (freebooting paramilitary units made up of malcontents and nationalist veterans), which flowered briefly and dangerously in the early 1920s. They often deployed in secret ad-hoc alliance with the Reichswehr, whose maximum permitted strength of 100,000 was deemed inadequate by the authorities for containing unrest across the country. The far left was up in arms to sweep away the institutions of the old regime, such as the Reichstag (now dominated by the moderate SPD), which had led Germany into a disastrous war; the far right was up in arms to recover for Germany what it had lost in an unjust settlement, signed by the SPD, of a war which had ended with its army 'unbeaten in the field' (it had however dispersed in the face of the enemy and would hardly have been able to resist an invasion). Ominously, extremists of left and right were united in hatred of the SPD and of Versailles.

Hitler's interest in politics got him a post at the press and information office in the Political Department of the Reichswehr's VII District Army Command in spring 1919. As such he was told in autumn to investigate a possible source of trouble, a 'German Workers' Party' (Deutsche Arbeiterpartei), founded by Anton Drexler, a fitter, in the previous March. Although it could muster an audience of only two dozen or so for the meeting Hitler attended on 12 September, it was already an amalgamation of two earlier grouplets. The meeting took place in one of Munich's enormous beer-cellars, which still come into their own in autumn for Munich's notorious *Oktoberfest* beer festival, but which in the 1920s and 1930s acquired an extra claim to fame as venues for political meetings. Hitler got up and made a short but impassioned speech from the floor against detaching Bavaria from tumultuous Germany into a union with neighbouring Austria. Subsequent events reflected his belief in the very opposite – absorption of his native Austria into a greater Germany. Meanwhile he was promptly invited to join not just the DAP but its committee, as member number seven, alongside Captain Ernst Röhm, an army and Freikorps veteran impressed by his oratory.

Hitler soon hijacked the organisation, addressing a meeting of 111 people in fiery, nationalist terms in a corner of one of the biggest beer-halls, the Hofbräuhaus, in October. Before the end of the war Austria had acquired its own DAP, which in May 1918 restyled itself the Deutsche National-sozialistische Arbeiterpartei (DNSAP) and adopted the swastika, an ancient eastern symbol for the sun, as its emblem. The DNSAP enjoyed an informal alliance with the DAP, which on Hitler's urging renamed itself the NSDAP in April 1920, when he left the Reichswehr to go into full-time politics as the party's political organiser. Karl Harrer, DAP chairman, resigned in protest as Hitler moved in.

Hitler was in charge of party propaganda when he addressed more than 2,000 people, assembled in the Hofbräuhaus on 24 February 1920, at the first 'Nazi' rally (Nazi is an acronym, an ever-popular device in German and a useful antidote for the huge compound words of the language. Nazi is analogous to 'Sozi', for Socialist; another pertinent example is Gestapo, from GEheime STAatsPOlizei). Röhm proved his worth to the infant party by persuading VII District's sympathetic infantry commander, Major-General Franz-Xaver Ritter von Epp, to provide physical protection, and even secret support from army funds, for the Nazis, without which they would probably have gone under – the root of an always ambivalent connection.

As in other Fascist parties, the NSDAP's ideology was an eclectic ragbag. Hitler's twenty-five-point party programme was both national-ist and socialist, as befitted the party's title. It was above all anti-Versailles and anti-Semitic, as well as opposed to the boss class, the bourgeoisie, Christians, Communists, foreigners, intellectuals, land-owners, rentiers, modernism in art, monopoly, Prussians, Russians, other Slavs and Social Democrats. It was in favour, *inter alia*, of autarky, a Greater Germany, Fascism in Italy and later Spain, Japanese expansionism (but not Japanese people), land reform, law and order, *Lebensraum* ('living space', a euphemism for eastern conquest), mother-hood and racial purity. The roots of the Nazis' main doctrine of anti-Semitism were complex. Suffice it to say here that the Jews had been the scapegoats of Europe for centuries because they were regarded as (a) alien and anti-Christian, (b) undeservedly rich, and (c) accessible. The Nazis were boosting party funds as early as 1920 with a brand of tobacco called Anti-Semit.

Hitler was obsessed with Jewry since his impoverished youth in Linz and Vienna, where many readily identifiable, orthodox Jews lived. He was most sincere in agreeing with those, all too numerous at all levels inside and outside Germany, who categorised 'the Jews' as traitors with foreign connections, war profiteers, bloodsucking capitalists or, at another level, unclean competitors for work and housing or else small-scale traders exploiting the poor. Atavistic condemnation of the Jews as the 'murderers of Christ', encouraged by generations of bigoted priests, was also an important element in anti-Semitism. Despite owing his prized Iron Cross, first class, which he always wore on his austere uniform, to a Jew (Captain Hugo Guttmann, adjutant of his regiment, who recommended him several times), Hitler told a journalist, on the record, in 1922, three years before *Mein Kampf* was written: 'Once I really am in power, my first and foremost task will be the annihilation of the Jews.'[9]

Such ambition must have seemed a sick joke at the time, coming from the bumptious leader of one grudge-based faction among many, and even more so after events in Munich on 8 and 9 November 1923. By then the NSDAP had its own militia, the Sturmabteilung (a reference to trench warfare: 'storm section' or SA) under Ernst Röhm, whose role was to protect the party's meetings and leaders and to go on the rampage against its opponents. Hitler recognised that political violence was double-edged but drew from this commonplace insight a conclusion precisely the opposite of the rational person's: that it was therefore desirable, because it showed the party meant business, because all publicity was good publicity and because in a period when government was weak and authority appeared to have abdicated, direct action seemed understandable, even attractive. In the most literal sense the SA made the Nazis a force to be reckoned with by ensuring that Hitler's voice was heard, despite the competing political clamour.

Some 600 brown-shirted 'stormtroopers' surrounded the Bürger-bräukeller, another huge beer-hall, on the evening of 8 November. A crowd of 3,000 had come to hear a speech by Commissioner-General Kahr, who was flanked by the military and police commanders of the state of Bavaria. Hitler consciously imitated the abortive 'Kapp Putsch' of March 1920, when ex-naval Captain Hermann Ehrhardt's Freikorps brigade with its swastika badge, having helped suppress the Munich soviets, had tried to oust the SPD government in Berlin but was foiled by a general strike. He fired his pistol in the air and announced a 'national revolution' as Kahr and his retinue were detained by SA men. Hitler proclaimed that he would form a new government with General Ludendorff, whom he had impudently (and imprudently) failed to consult in advance. The angry old warhorse nevertheless decided to stand with Hitler and 3,000 Nazi supporters in the ensuing confrontation with 100 police on the Marienplatz at the heart of Munich. The police opened fire, killing sixteen demonstrators. Ludendorff marched through the police line unscathed while Hitler fled in a waiting car.

It was a fiasco; but it made Hitler famous. Tried with nine others, including Ludendorff, still a national hero, for treason on 24 February 1924, Hitler wore his Iron Cross, first class, and dominated the proceedings, seizing the chance to make his debut on the world stage before 100 reporters. 'There is no such thing as treason against the traitors of 1918,' he declared: 'I feel myself the best of Germans, who wished the best for the German nation.' These were just two pearls in an address which lasted four hours. He accused the SPD of destroying a nation of seventy millions. Condemning the 'stab in the back' and Communism, Hitler blamed the SPD, not only for the unrest to which the Nazis were making such an egregious contribution but also for everything else, from artistic decadence in Berlin to the recent hyperinflation (that at least was a valid charge). He declared war on Marxism and proclaimed that his, and Germany's, hour would come. It was an electrifying performance from a political upstart who, with his natural instinct for mass communication, seized this golden opportunity and never looked back. He was convicted of treason on 1 April, but instead of life imprisonment he received the minimum sentence of five years, which merely made him a martyr. In the nine months before a lenient authority released him from the fortress prison at Landsberg Castle he dictated *Mein Kampf* (my struggle) to his fellow-prisoner, secretary and later deputy, Rudolf Hess, who edited and embellished it as he typed.

This ranting jumble of a book, unfortunately if understandably the least-read bestseller ever written, set out Hitler's racial views and programme in detail, as well as his designs on the Marxist Soviet Union and his hatred of Jews, democrats, liberals, Socialists, the Roman Catholic Church and France. *Mein Kampf* encapsulated the prejudices and fears of millions, dissatisfied with their lot in a Germany reeling from the 1918 defeat, the 1919 humiliation at Versailles and the 1923 currency collapse; the coming slump would only compound the anxiety and encourage the yearning for scapegoats and certainties across the country. The message got through in spite, rather than because, of the indigestible text that contained it. There were more than enough sympathetic commentators to simplify, summarise and sanitise the Nazi bible and to sugar the pill of revanchist nihilism which lay at its heart. The NSDAP had already found its propaganda genius in the twisted shape of Joseph Goebbels, doctor of philosophy of the University of Heidelberg and highest intellect in the Nazi leadership, which he joined in 1924. Hitler was no writer, but he was an artist of the spoken word, tailoring his message to suit the many different audiences – statesmen, students, steelworkers – to whom he would personally peddle it. Meanwhile whole cohorts of eager harbingers, by no means only Nazis, did much of his groundwork for him as he set out to sell himself as all things to all Germans.

There is no evidence that Speer took any notice of all the ferment occasioned by the 'beer-hall putsch' and the consequent court case, which became a show trial – for the defendants. This cannot logically be taken as proof that he did not notice but only that, as one of nature's instinctive compartmentalisers, he did not note it in his letters to Gretel. Arriving in Munich in time for the second semester, which started in spring, he studied dutifully for a year and then decided to complete his studies at the *Technische Hochschule* (university) in Berlin, to which he moved in 1925. As with his letters to Gretel, so with his memoirs, which whisk us from school in Heidelberg through Karlsruhe and Munich to Berlin in little more than a page.[10] He wrote that he paid no attention to Hitler's doings because he was too busy working and planning for marriage three or four years ahead. He presents himself at this stage of his life as completely apolitical, concentrating on the job in hand and taking little interest in the wider world. This of course dovetails neatly with his self-image as presented at Nuremberg and in his books: the man who was always too busy to be anything but an apolitical and, yes, even amoral, technocrat.

In the vacations Speer and Gretel found no difficulty in getting together and sometimes joining other young people for the lengthy treks into the forests or the Alps which were so much in vogue in Germany before and after the Great War. The land of Goethe and Beethoven was also more inclined in the aftermath of defeat to listen to the Teutonic trumpetings of Wagner and his son-in-law, Houston Stewart Chamberlain, the English-born, naturalised German philosopher of Aryan supremacy. This dangerous rubbish featured all too prominently in the youthfully idealistic discussions that accompanied such expeditions between the wars: more groundwork for Hitler.

The naïve young participants in such earnest exchanges – and in Germany they would be specially earnest because there solemnity is commonly held to be synonymous with seriousness – had never dreamed of questioning authority or been made aware of social issues at school or at home. After 1918 the 'back to nature' idea was taken up by any number of student groups, youth clubs and even national 'leagues', a tendency that the Nazis, with their slogan *Blut und Boden* ('blood and soil', shorthand for racial purity and back to the land), were well placed – and especially keen – to exploit. Eventually millions of young people were to be swept into the Hitler Youth for boys or the Bund deutscher Mädel (German girls' league). Similar mobilisations were favoured no less keenly in Communist and other totalitarian states. The German movements began spontaneously but soon became highly organised, politicised and imbued with Teutonic pseudo-mysticism, thus both open and conducive to a totalitarian takeover. The British by contrast developed their Ramblers' and Youth Hostel associations and the uniforms, mottoes and muscular Christianity of their Scouting movement became the butt of a fond nation's comedians rather than the basis of a cod ideology. The very idea of a Ramblers' Association group advancing in step to the shouted refrain of a marching song or discussing philosophy under the spreading chestnut tree is unsustainable: here surely is where German abstractionism and British pragmatism go their very separate ways.

Speer, his fiancée and their friends were not card-carrying members of any such formal organisation; rather they organised their own bouts of mountaineering, canoeing, cycling, camping, hiking or skiing. For them as for most other participants such retreats to the wilderness were undoubtedly a way of escaping from the stresses of the intermittent, and ultimately incomplete, national postwar convalescence. As a student, the reserved Speer did not join anything much, whether clubs or student fraternities, and eschewed the team sports which had occupied so much of his time as a schoolboy. But he remained assiduous in his dedication to Gretel, to the great outdoors, to music and the theatre. Nor was he averse to company in his leisure hours, facilitated as they were by the rare ownership of a car.

After another such summer of intensive *Kultur*, Speer and several fellow-students from Munich, including Rudolf Wolters, began to arrive in Berlin for the new academic year. Both he and Speer wanted to study architectural drawing under Professor Hans Poelzig, designer of Berlin's circular Grosses Schauspielhaus (grand theatre), which had caused a sensation with its interior like an ice cave in 1919.[11] But demand was high, space was limited and Speer's draughtsmanship was not good enough. He was later able to circumvent this deficiency, rather fundamental in an architect, by paying other students to do drawing exercises for him; but meanwhile he seems to have cooled his heels to some extent in his first semester in the capital before signing up with another professor. Students from Anglo-Saxon universities, accustomed to highly structured degree courses, limited qualifying time and packaged options have always found it amazing that their German counterparts determine their study programme largely for themselves, bureaucratic modalities permitting, just as they used to do in the Middle Ages. Speer does not tell us how he spent the 'lost' semester, if such it was, academically; he would have been free to attend any lecture with a seat to spare.

But he does say he studied the history of architecture under Professor Daniel Krenkler, an Alsatian who was more German than the Germans but who seems to have slipped out of sight between the lines of the reference books. He is of most interest in the present context for having prompted Speer to write another passion-free letter to Gretel, this time about the value of miscegenation as a factor that had strengthened, rather than weakened, the German race, which he saw as tired out by recent history – a thesis not likely to appeal to Nazis but of obvious interest to a Franco-German from an area where the two rival nations overlap. The question of race thus clearly played a role in the thought and conversation of the couple and their contemporaries, as it did for so many other, older Germans in all walks of life, before and after the First World War. In that respect at least they were far from abnormal; and if they discussed one burning socio-political topic of the day, they can hardly have avoided all mention of the rest.

Rejected by Poelzig, Speer and Wolters jumped at the chance to sign up for a course given by Professor Heinrich Tessenow, who was appointed to the chair of design and buildings at Berlin in time for the spring semester of 1926. Tessenow leaned away from the classical towards the naturalistic (and nationalistic) in architecture, favouring simple, pared-down designs with regional references but without superfluous adornments. He disapproved of the Nazis, who therefore reciprocated; but the puritan sentimentalism of his architecture appealed to them all the same, and several joined his seminar ('Reds' gravitated towards Poelzig's). The Nazis were inconsistent and ignorant in artistic matters, wrongly classifying Tessenow as a modernist but freely plagiarising his ideas when it suited them.

Speer was full of enthusiasm for his new teacher, showing a degree of veneration for Tessenow surpassed only by his admiration for Hitler.[12] Speer's two architectural mentors could hardly have been more different except in one respect: each had a strong will and commanded exceptional loyalty. Meanwhile relations between the *Kommilitonen* (fellow-students) Speer and Wolters were moving closer as they competed with each other for class prizes in Tessenow's department: Speer usually won, with Wolters as runner-up.[13] Wolters however saw himself as the more intellectually inclined of the two and less interested in sport, taking a broad, historically derived view of the world while Speer's outlook was governed by pragmatism.[14]

Wolters thus put his finger on a seminal characteristic of Albert Speer. Not only was he, like many another reserved individual, specially susceptible to a stronger personality such as Tessenow's: he was also an opportunist. Further, he cultivated a most un-German, casual air, dressing like some caricature of the chaotic student – crumpled clothes with tie askew and all the more noticeable for being tall and gawky. He seemed to be a minimalist when it came to work, cheerfully farming out his drawing chores to others for a few marks and often cutting lectures. Yet his results were consistently sound, and since he was not the architectural genius that Wolters, in early moments of uncritical admiration, took him to be, Speer must have worked when nobody was looking, probably late at night. The consequent, carefully cultivated impression of easy success will not have endeared him to his colleagues. He availed himself enthusiastically of the myriad musical and theatrical opportunities, including revues, offered by Weimar Berlin in its brief and brittle flowering, albeit against a background of increasing political uncertainty and unrest. Speer may have been virtually oblivious of events in Munich but he did notice the poverty and 'decay' all around him in Berlin. He would have had to be a complete recluse to avoid them.

One other quality which stood out then and later was generosity. Speer may have been studiously relaxed, coolly courteous, detached if not withdrawn and never the life and soul of the party, but he could be relied upon to help a fellow-student down on his luck. He was much better off than most students but he was always good for a touch. Nor could he be accused of buying popularity, which did not interest him (esteem was another matter). Never ostentatious or spendthrift, he simply possessed means that others lacked and, provided he had enough for his own modest requirements, was as indifferent about money as about many another aspect of life that others found important. Wolters went through a difficult period financially and remembered how Speer would unfailingly lend him money towards the end of each month, to be repaid when the hard-pressed Westphalian's next cheque arrived – a favour he was to return in full measure.

The two men completed their studies and passed their examinations in summer 1927. Speer formally graduated in February 1928, earning the right to style himself *Diplom-Ingenieur* (*Dipl.-Ing.*) thenceforward. Wolters decided to stay on and study for his doctorate; Speer had the same idea but in the spring semester Tessenow, still his hero (for the time being), took him on as his academic assistant, complete with modest salary, a rare honour for a new graduate. The gilded youth had done extraordinarily well, acquiring his diploma with high marks after a mere nine semesters and then easing himself into an academic post under one of the country's leading professors. All this took place when Germany was in the forefront of modern architecture, thanks to such masters as Walter Gropius, Ludwig Mies van der Rohe and the remarkable concentrations of talent in the Werkbund and Bauhaus schools.

For a freshly qualified, socially advantaged young man of twenty-three the auspices looked very good indeed. Speer however had not proved himself to be a budding architect of great promise, but only an expert at smoothly passing tests and examinations in the subject (with a little help from his friends to cover his weakness in drawing). His admiration for Tessenow was clearly reciprocated: the professor would hardly have given him a job otherwise. Taking the poorly paid post was undoubtedly a sound career move. Money was not a problem because Speer's proud father continued to pay him an allowance.

Speer's childhood and education had trained him for indifference in every sense. His feelings had been stifled, if not extinguished altogether, by lack of affection at home, a background which left him emotionally indifferent most of the time. There was also a new generalised amorality, encouraged by the 'all Germans are guilty' verdict of Versailles; the great inflation, one of its indirect results, rewarded the dishonest while ruining decent people, including much of the bourgeoisie. The social, economic and cultural effects were radical. *Angst*, that untranslatable Germanic unease somewhere between anxiety-neurosis and clinical depression, reached tidal-wave proportions. Finally, any architectural inspiration Speer was to show was quantitative rather than qualitative, as we shall see in the next chapter. He had impressed, and been impressed by, his professor; but, whatever Tessenow's qualities as a teacher, he was an indifferent architect of spartan cum folksy tastes, overshadowed by many compatriots in a country full of outstanding practitioners. Speer had received a no more than average education in his reluctantly adopted subject and emerged fully trained by, in and for indifference.

Tessenow's first student intake included not only Speer and Wolters but also several other young men who would serve under Speer after he caught Hitler's eye and began his rapid rise to power. He had no other friends to draw upon. One of these was Willie Schelkes, the son of an Austrian ropemaker, born in Freiburg on the edge of the Black Forest in 1904. He studied landscape gardening and then landscape architecture in Munich until 1929, when he too made the move to Berlin and joined the Tessenow seminar, benefiting from the hospitality of the professor's charming, easy-going young assistant.[15]

Six months after landing his first job Speer completed part two of his eight-year-old programme of preparation for life by eloping across town with his childhood sweetheart. She came to Berlin and they married, without forewarning their families, on 28 August 1928 in the city's Memorial Church (now a memorial twice over: originally commemorating Kaiser Wilhelm I, it was heavily bombed in the Second World War and its remaining tower stands as a reminder of that conflict). Back in Heidelberg the Speers and the Webers were therefore startled to receive identical telegrams saying, 'Married today. In love. Albert and Gretel.' The Speers had never even met the bride of their second but already most successful son, or her family. Like most other events in his private sphere, Speer gives his wedding exceedingly short shrift in his memoirs.

For Germany at large the period between the currency reform of late 1923 and the Wall Street crash of October 1929 was not without hope: on the contrary. The fledgling Soviet Union had ended the Weimar Republic's diplomatic isolation by concluding the bilateral Treaty of Rapallo in 1922, even if others saw it as no more than a mutual recognition of pariah states, formalising their relations. The French occupation of the Ruhr in 1923 because of overdue reparations ended in 1925, when the multilateral Locarno Agreement, confirming Germany's borders, was signed, clearing the way for German membership of the League of Nations. The triumphs of Gustav Stresemann, the outstanding Foreign Minister of the Weimar era, even extended to reparations. They were eased, thanks also to American initiatives in 1929; sadly the benefits were soon undermined by the slump. The Versailles Treaty remained in force, but for Germans of goodwill its sting had been drawn. Hindenburg, erstwhile symbol of German militarism, was elected President in 1925 and committed himself to Weimar. Hitler came out of prison with the manuscript of part I of *Mein Kampf* (published in 1925) and reorganised a Nazi Party riven by conflict between its 'national' and 'socialist' wings. He had deliberately left his rivals to fall out among themselves while he was unavoidably detained, so that he could sweep back to take command on his own terms.

In a period when aviation commanded constant headlines, the airship *Graf Zeppelin* did its bit for Germany's prestige by wafting across the Atlantic and round the world. But as the New York Stock Exchange went down in October, the Maginot Line went up just inside France's border with Germany. In 1930, however, the French army finally marched out of the Rhineland, ending the postwar occupation. The liner *Europa* struck another blow for German glory by wresting the Blue Riband for fastest North Atlantic crossing from the British veteran *Mauretania*. But as Germany succumbed more heavily than any other industrial power to the economic depression triggered off by Wall Street, the Nazis advanced in the September election from twelve to 107 seats in the Reichstag (the Communists won seventy-seven). The SPD was at last ousted and Heinrich Brüning, Catholic Centrist

Chancellor since March, was faced with triumphantly unruly, extremist minorities of left and right in parliament. Unable to assemble a reliable majority, Brüning fatefully sought and won President Hindenburg's consent to rule by decree under Article 48 of the Weimar Constitution, which paradoxically supplied the means of undermining every demo- cratic safeguard which that generally admirable document contained.

Henceforward German politics took to the streets with a vengeance. The big-city universities became hotbeds of intrigue, demonstrations, fights, even riots. Speer glosses over this ferment on the classroom doorstep (and sometimes within) in his memoirs but can hardly have been unaware of the fact that the Nazi German Student League made huge gains in student-union elections in 1929 (thirty-eight per cent) and 1930 (sixty-six). His own students, such as Peter Koller, a fresh recruit to Nazism, changed the subject in tutorials from architecture to politics.[16] Speer obviously listened with interest because on 4 December 1930 he was persuaded to join some of his pro-Nazi students and 5,000 other spectators in the Neue Welt beer-hall at Hasenheide in the Berlin inner-city district of Neukölln for a Nazi rally, part of yet another student election campaign. Speer and his students were allo- cated places on the platform in the huge hall alongside other academics.

As was his wont, Adolf Hitler kept his audience waiting while minions raised the tension in the hall. A Nazi student leader reported in emotive terms the alleged murder of two SA men by Communists. But the main attraction of the evening spoke calmly and reasonably, tailoring his address to his young and enthusiastic but also intelligent and educated listeners, many of them from cultivated backgrounds. He played up to their ideals, calling for a return to traditional national values of valour and honour, an end to division, conflict and the standards of the second-rate. He called for the consignment of a corrupt and selfish republic of weaklings and cowards to the oblivion it deserved. He was rewarded with a standing ovation.[17]

Afterwards, Speer went for a walk on his own, to clear his head. He failed. In the New Year he applied for membership of the Nazi Party.

3

Pillars of Light

(1931–33)

ALBERT SPEER WAS ACCEPTED as a member of the National Socialist Party with effect from 1 March 1931.[1] While waiting for his application to go through, he was briefly repelled, though not sufficiently to change his mind, by a more typical Nazi manifestation: a frothing, raving but calculated demonstration of rabble-rousing at the Sports Palace by Joseph Goebbels, Nazi Gauleiter (regional party chief) of Berlin and the party's official head of propaganda since 1929. Speer's suppression of his own repugnance was made easier by the routine police response of indiscriminate, mounted baton attacks on the crowd. This was fortunate because Goebbels, who played John the Baptist to Hitler's Messiah, contributed greatly to the rapid rise of the Führer's future architect.

Speer's voluntary registration preceded Hitler's appointment as Chancellor by twenty-two months. It is therefore undeniable that conviction rather than expediency was his motive for joining. Those who applied after 30 January 1933, when Hitler achieved power, were regarded within the party, especially by the old guard, as second-class members, mere bandwagon-jumpers who had waited until the political wind changed before committing themselves. Goebbels and others of the old guard felt the same disdain towards the 'Septemberlings' – those who came in after the party's electoral success in September 1930. The Nazi *crème de la crème*, certainly in Hitler's eyes, were the 'old fighters' of the 1920s, about whom he was wont to become maudlin (except when having such as Ernst Röhm, the SA leader, killed for allegedly betraying him). Speer could not have failed to see that the Nazi tide was rising (he must have noticed the ferment at the university even if he went round Berlin with his eyes shut) and decided in good time to ride the crest of the new political wave, like the opportunist he was. Membership numbers were allocated in strict order of joining: Speer's was 474,481, out of an eventual total of some seven million, or one in ten of the German population (one in seven adults). And having freely chosen to join, he inevitably enlisted in some of the hundreds of 'front' organisations the Nazis founded to gain influence over every aspect of national life, in conscious imitation of Soviet Communism.

One such was the brand-new NSKK (Kraftfahrer-Korps) or motoring corps, formed under the aegis of the SA. Speer became head (and for the time being, sole motorised member) of the NSKK in the south-west Berlin suburb of Wannsee where he and Gretel then had a flat.[2] His main qualification was owning a car. The NSKK was soon to become paramilitary, preparing young men to drive armoured vehicles in the same way as the NS-Fliegerkorps trained aircrew before Hitler drove squadrons of tanks and planes through the remnants of Versailles; by that time Speer had more important things to do than driving his car on party errands, or even driving a tank.

As an architect he was already a member of the Bund (league of) deutscher Architekten but he immediately joined the Nazi 'fighting group' Kampfbund deutscher Architekten und Ingenieure. Wound up in May 1934, when it was subsumed into Goebbels's Reichskulturkammer (RKK, chamber of culture, founded in September 1933), the KDAI had a membership of about 2,000 in 1932, or less than one per cent of the professions it sought to embrace. But from the inception of the RKK any practitioner of any artistic profession had to be a member of the appropriate section in order to be allowed to work. Expulsion was professional death, a threat calculated to keep people under control, which was the overt aim of the Nazi social strategy of Gleichschaltung, forcing individuals and organisations into line. Speer also became a member of the Deutsche Arbeitsfront (labour front, set up to absorb the entire German workforce, including trade and white-collar unions plus management associations); the NS-Volkswohlfahrt (welfare organisation for party members' families); and even the Reichsluft-schutzverband (national air-defence association).

Speer advanced three main reasons for joining the Nazi Party as he did and when he did. In his memoirs (1969) and elsewhere he said he was motivated by fear of Communism, the only apparent alternative in a country where social and economic pressures had led to extreme political polarisation. Although he always said he had not taken much interest in politics in his youth and was too busy to do so when working for the Hitler regime, he had at least found the time to reach the not unimportant or unpolitical conclusion that Marxism was a real threat which he personally had to oppose. However superficial the thought process he devoted to this widespread contemporary fear, it was hardly consistent with his use of the adjective 'frivolous' to describe his decision to apply.[3]

Second, he was undoubtedly, indeed avowedly, 'fascinated' by Hitler himself and his tailor-made display of sweet reason at the Hasenheide meeting: by the man rather than his programme, of which Speer professed to know very little. We shall have to return to the conundrum of Hitler's charisma, a quality attested by countless contemporaries but invisible to non-Germans (especially non-speakers of German) and even to modern Germans, all of whom are left cold by films and recordings of the dictator in full oratorical flight. Finally, as we saw above, in 1979 Speer belatedly added another reason: rejection of German guilt as defined at Versailles, which Hitler promised to expunge.

Opportunist or no, Speer cannot be accused of joining the party, three years before it came to power, in the hope of professional advancement. There is no evidence of this kind of ulterior motive – far from it – and no reason to doubt his version: he simply went to a meeting, like so many before him, was duly impressed by Hitler, again like many other Germans, and made his application without having met any Nazi official above the level of student organiser, let alone any of the party's national figures. But he was bemused to discover that his mother, inspired by a Nazi march-past, had been converted at about the same time, joining the Heidelberg branch without even going to a meeting or telling her family. Speer also kept his membership secret from his parents until after the Nazis came to power. Albert Senior never joined, regarding Hitler as a 'criminal upstart'. The old man met him just once at a Berlin theatre in 1938 in the company of his son and almost fainted with shock. They never discussed the event.[4]

Speer unwittingly chose a bad time to seek his fortune as an architect. His not yet intimate friend Wolters had on the face of it made a wiser move by deciding to stay on and read for his doctorate. The post with Tessenow had cachet and paid about 300 Reichsmarks (£15 or $70 in 1928) per month – enough for a childless couple to live frugally in Berlin – but filled less than half his time. With five months of vacation and two days per week free, it was not a job for a grown man. Speer therefore tried simultaneously to build up a private architectural practice. Before taking the assistantship in 1928 he had applied for a post in, of all places, Kabul, Afghanistan, where Amanollah Khan, the first post-independence ruler, had ambitious plans for modernisation. But the dominant conservative element in that ungovernable country stoked up tribal revolt in 1928 and the Khan was forced to abdicate in 1929. So instead of becoming a Himalayan town-planner, architect and teacher, Speer returned the few library books on Afghanistan that he and Gretel had unearthed and settled down to life in the febrile capital, commuting from Wannsee to Charlottenburg, the inner suburb surrounding the Technical University.

After 'seeing the light' at the Hasenheide meeting, Speer was persuaded to attend a session of yet another Nazi front organisation, the Kampfbund deutscher Kultur (Campaign for German Culture), at which

Tessenow's architectural outlook was specifically attacked (significantly, even the assault on his mentor failed to deflect Speer from membership). His professor's taste for regionalism and simplicity was, whether deliberately or out of ignorance, confused with the modernism of the rest of the *Ring*, the group of architects which included such leading figures as Gropius, Mies van der Rohe, Poelzig and Tessenow himself. Speer tells the story[5] of how a student of his and Tessenow's sturdily wrote to Hitler in defence of the professor, generating a reply from the party formally confirming Nazi respect for his work. After the Nazis came to power, however, Tessenow fell out of favour and was banned from teaching. Speer notes that, once he had acquired some influence in Nazi circles, he was able to have his old chief reinstated until the war was over. After 1945 Tessenow's stock reached new heights, helping him to rise to rector of the Technical University in a few years. According to Speer, the professor was anything but a hard taskmaster, giving no lectures but only showing up for a few hours a week to set and mark essays. He left it to his young assistant to teach the students the basics of architecture.[6]

With his introvert tendencies Speer obviously found such instruction as he was required to give more stressful than it had seemed when he was on the receiving end, a common experience for new recruits to teaching. Meanwhile the private practice he tried to set up in his birthplace of Mannheim and also in Berlin refused to get off the ground. His parents-in-law, the Webers, generously did their best to help, giving him one of his first commissions: their new but imposing family house, built on a site in the Ackerweg at Heidelberg in 1930. In Berlin he managed to win commissions for garage extensions at two houses in Wannsee where he was living, as well as the rather more original task of designing a headquarters for the German Academic Exchange Service in Berlin.

Among the other crumbs of work he was able to glean as the depression deepened in an especially susceptible because still convalescent Germany, Speer won lesser prizes (never better than third) in competitions for such small-scale projects as interior-design work for a church at Rheinfelden on the Swiss border near Basle and a parish hall in Mannheim, both in 1931. In 1932 he was commissioned to redesign a Mannheim shop and in the following year was retained for the conversion of a country house at Perleberg in the Prignitz area, in the north-west of Brandenburg state. The property belonged to Dr Robert Frank, general manager of Prussian Electricity until sacked by the Nazis, whom Speer was able to protect later; Frank reciprocated by sheltering his family in north Germany in 1945.[7]

As head of the Wannsee sub-branch of the Nazi Corps of Motorists, Parteigenosse (Party Comrade) Speer was required, in keeping with the strictly vertical leadership structure of the party, to report to Kreis-leitung (district command) Berlin-West. In charge was a personable young man by the name of Karl Hanke, who had served an apprenticeship as a miller but had gone on to graduate as an engineering teacher, joining the Nazis in 1928. As part of the party's administrative expansion after the big gains in the election of 14 September 1930 (which the Speers missed because they were enjoying a canoeing holiday on the Danube in Austria) Hanke leased a villa in Grunewald, a wooded suburb, for his headquarters. He invited an enthusiastic Speer to refurbish it.[8]

Such was Albert Speer's modest first assignment for the National Socialist Party. As a volunteer he did not even receive a fee for the complete interior redesign. Speer says he advised a willing Hanke to choose the latest Bauhaus wallpapers, despite their 'Communist' associations (everything 'modern' in art was held by Nazi ideologists to be decadent, un-German, Bolshevik and/or Jewish). A chord was struck; Speer was to hear from him again often. Hanke became a crucial early contact for Speer in his dealings with the party.

As the depression in Germany deepened into the slump, Speer was told at the beginning of 1932 that Prussian state finances were so reduced by the collapse in revenue caused by low economic activity that he would have to accept a cut in his salary after three years working for Tessenow. Speer consulted Gretel and resigned. They decided to move to Mannheim, where he hoped to support himself by managing the Speer family's considerable property interests in the area while working harder to obtain architectural commissions. But pickings were lean indeed, as we saw above. Even the humble shop-refurbishment job came his way only through family connections: the business was situated in one of the Speer family's buildings. Speer, still dependent on his father's financial support, nevertheless offered Willie Schelkes, who had graduated without prospects in 1931, a monthly salary of 150 marks – perhaps the earliest example of his gift for picking outstanding colleagues and subordinates. Schelkes would remain one of his most valued and effective architectural aides. The Speers lived in a flatlet in the house where he had been born and were allowed to weekend with his parents at Heidelberg.

The NSKK did not boast a branch in faraway Mannheim, so Speer was 'assigned' by the party administration in Berlin to the SS motorised section as a strictly temporary 'guest' member. According to his memoirs, he was not enrolled as a member of the SS, which at this stage was still a small, if growing, internal party police cum personal bodyguard for Hitler, very much overshadowed by Röhm's bloated SA.[9] There is no evidence to refute Speer's claim that he never sought SS membership. Later he would decline an honorary high rank, whereupon SS chief Heinrich Himmler had Speer listed as his honorary adviser, without consultation.

With little enough to distract him at work, Speer took Gretel back to Berlin at the end of July 1932, leaving Schelkes to mind the almost empty store at Mannheim for the time being. The young man had clearly overcome his indifference to politics by now. He and Gretel returned specifically to participate in the last few days of campaigning, in an election battle seen at the time as no less crucial than hindsight proves it was. It made the Nazis the largest single party in the Reichstag with 270 seats. This was short of a majority; but under the constitution the leader of the largest party had the right to be asked by the President to form a government.

As a loyal member of the NSKK, Speer placed his car at the disposal of the party. On the 27th he drove to Berlin's Staaken airfield to collect a Nazi courier and take him to Brandenburg town stadium, west of Berlin, where Hitler was due to address his second rally of the day. Speer saw from a distance that the party leader was already at the airport, fuming and lashing his jackboots with a riding-crop because his motorcade had not yet arrived. Speer's passenger was in party uniform, which drew abuse from some pedestrians at the climax of a shrill campaign as they drove into town. Hitler, now just behind Speer with his motorcade, stood up in his big Mercedes as it swept through the outskirts of Brandenburg until slowed to a crawl by left-wing demonstrators. Hitler exhibited rather more physical courage than in Munich after the Beer-hall Putsch: as the driver inched forward through the hostile mob he stayed on his feet and faced down the crowd. Hitler was now at the height of his demagogic powers, and a stadium filled to overflowing cheered him to the echo. A similar scene on a rather larger scale greeted him on his heavily delayed arrival at the next electoral rally, his third of the day, at a stadium in Berlin. Once again Nazi officials had to hold the crowd's interest and attention for hours on end while awaiting Hitler.[10]

Party activists knew how to whip up indignation against the left, the Jews, the western powers and the capitalists in order to create a suitably fervid atmosphere before he arrived. When the Führer was on his way a series of announcements would be made that he was drawing ever nearer and finally that he had arrived outside the venue. His appearance on the platform drew a storm of applause and Hitler would proceed to 'play' the spectators as if he were the conductor and they the orchestra. He made them wait and wait until he felt instinctively that he had teased them into their most receptive state. He would, if there was space on the platform, walk up and down, his chin cupped in his hand, deep in thought and gazing at the floor. He began by speaking quite softly so that the audience would have to concentrate to hear him, which of course reduced it to silence. The ensuing political congress was as sexual as it was rhetorical, complete with stimulating foreplay, tender beginning, increasing excitement and orgasmic crescendo. Watching the extraordinary film footage of Hitler at the podium, one does not have to be a Freudian to recognise that when he and a crowd came together, they did so in more than one sense.

Somewhere in this context is to be found the secret of Hitler's charisma, which has mystified so many since his death: the attraction was clearly parasexual, and lust is notoriously irrational. If we have ever asked ourselves how anyone could desire an individual we ourselves find repugnant and concluded that there is no accounting for taste, we have come as close as we ever will to solving the mystery of Hitler's attraction for one of the most gifted nations on earth, made vulnerable by a series of exhausting collective traumas: war, defeat, social chaos, hyperinflation, slump. The 'mystery' merely derives from largely academic discussion of the phenomenon at the wrong level, that of the intellect. For millions of Germans it was love; and love is blind, however it may come to be rationalised. Unfortunately they fell for a cynical seducer rather than a sincere suitor. So did Speer, whose infatuation lasted not quite fourteen years.

Speer and Gretel had arranged to go off to the Masurian Lakes in East Prussia for one of the boating holidays they liked so much, instead of waiting until polling day on Sunday 31 July. They had bought their tickets and deposited their collapsible canoes and bags in the left-luggage office at the station, planning to take the overnight train from Berlin on Thursday the 28th. At lunchtime Karl Hanke, now head of party organisation under Goebbels for the whole of Berlin as well as a Reichstag deputy, located them at their lodgings by telephone and asked Speer to join him at the Nazis' new Gau (district) headquarters in the Voss-Strasse, unadventurously renamed 'Adolf Hitler House'. The street, in the administrative heart of the city on the south-eastern edge of the Tiergarten park, was then lined with buildings of Second-Reich vintage, about fifty years old and imposing within as well as without (the area was destroyed in the Second World War). There he was invited to refurbish the whole of the interior as soon as ever possible. With work so hard to find, Speer was delighted. The holiday was called off.

Speer looked back on this fairly modest if timely offer as the great turning-point in his career.[11] With the best will in the world, the student of his life and times will find it hard to understand why. His decision to join the Nazi Party eighteen months earlier looks no less important; his first major commission from Goebbels and his lunch with Hitler, both described below, seem rather more so. The party had beggared itself with its expenditure on the endless electioneering of the time, never mind acquiring a prestige property in the middle of the city so as to be close to the seat of power. Speer laboured round the clock and so did the building tradesmen, also loyal party members; they all had to wait for their pay. What was to be Germany's last democratic election for seventeen years, scheduled for 6 November 1932, had diverted overstretched Nazi funds to more immediate requirements. The attention of Goebbels was also focused on more pressing matters, although Hitler found a moment to inspect the gleaming premises named after him and express himself well satisfied. Speer was not there at the time; he had returned to Mannheim to glean more work in his home area if he could.

The Centrist Chancellor Heinrich Brüning had been ruling Germany by decree since the election of September 1930, which he called when the Reichstag refused to pass his budget in July. Unemployment rose and rose again to pass six million (in a country of seventy million) early in 1932, compared with 1.3 million just before the Wall Street crash in October 1929; the figures cover only those registered as unemployed, not the rather larger total of those in need or search of work. Brüning improved upon the 1929 Young Plan for the easement of the reparations burden (fixed at 132 billion gold marks at Versailles) by paving the way for their cancellation in talks with the major powers at Lausanne in spring 1932. This remarkable coup was however completely overshadowed by the slump and its appalling social consequences throughout the industrialised world.

After the sclerotic President Hindenburg won his second term, defeating Hitler by six million votes (they scored fifty-three and thirty-seven per cent of the turnout respectively) in April 1932, he allowed himself to become the political prisoner of the nationalist, militarist right wing. Brüning had plans to tackle the burgeoning 'aid for the east' scandal in which funds intended to help preserve the big *Junker* estates in East Prussia, all but cut off by the Polish Corridor from the rest of the ailing German economy, had vanished into private pockets. Hindenburg, and even more his son, owners of a huge estate at Neudeck, felt threatened by the scandal; the old President demanded Brüning's resignation on 30 May. The whole affair was another prime example of the moral laxity of the day.

The news was received with delight by the 'Harzburg Front' alliance of the far right, set up in 1931 to oust Brüning and form a 'truly national government'. It comprised military and industrial figures, Pan-Germans, some of the *Junkers*, the Stahlhelm nationalist veterans' group, the Nazis, and the German Nationalists led by Alfred Hugenberg, an industrial, press and film magnate who also chaired the front.

Hitler, having acquired a useful certificate of respectability by rubbing shoulders with these socially acceptable arch-conservatives, decided to break ranks. Having also gained the ascendancy, with the machiavellian assistance of Goebbels, for the 'national' over the 'socialist' tendency in the party as represented by the brothers Gregor and Otto Strasser, and encouraged by recent electoral trends, Hitler was resolved to abolish democracy democratically and become Chancellor constitutionally. Although always ready to form ad-hoc alliances as means towards this end, he was not willing to compromise his ambition of absolute power by committing himself to a formal coalition. He would not let himself be used by others: precisely the reverse.

Brüning was succeeded by Franz von Papen, a Westphalian aristocrat and former staff officer – a medieval throwback with ultra-Catholic, monarchist, nationalist, agrarian and anti-democratic convictions. This wealthy and personally charming political lightweight had no ministerial experience and was supported by the Minister of Defence, Kurt von Schleicher, who as a general wielded decisive influence over the doddering Hindenburg in these dying days of Weimar. Schleicher, having helped to bring about, and then terminate, the brief tenure of Brüning, now wanted Papen as a stalking-horse for his own designs on the Chancellery. Schleicher was also trying to manipulate the Nazis for his own ends and persuaded Papen to endorse lifting the ban on Hitler's SA, the Nazis' brownshirt army, which was thus out in force on the streets for the November 1932 election. Papen's one success was to follow the trail blazed by his predecessor and formally secure the abolition of war reparations. He also summarily dismissed the democratically elected SPD state government of Prussia by decree, appointing himself Reich Commissioner for Germany's overwhelmingly largest constituent state. This was too reactionary even for Schleicher, who used his influence on Hindenburg one more time to get Papen sacked on 3 December and himself appointed instead – the last Chancellor of the Weimar Republic.

But Papen's role in its destruction was not finished yet. Determined to exact revenge on Schleicher, he turned to Hitler with the offer of an alliance. As the Nazi chief was leader of the largest party in the Reichstag, once they came to terms he rather than Papen had to be awarded the Chancellorship, an offer Hindenburg was at last persuaded by Papen to make on 30 January 1933. Papen, appointed Vice-Chancellor, thought he and his ultra-nationalist allies would be able comfortably to keep the *parvenu* under control while they ran the government. They were soon disabused.

In a remarkable display of courage or stupidity, Papen stood up at Marburg University in Bavaria in June 1934, eighteen months into the Third Reich, and condemned Nazi excesses, calling for a return to constitutional propriety. Unlike Schleicher, he escaped assassination

during the 'Night of the Long Knives' on 30 June, in which Hitler
purged the SA in general and its chief, Röhm, in particular. The Nazis'
principal bully-boy, small, fat but battle-hardened, had been calling for
a 'second revolution' to give expression to the 'socialist' strand in
National Socialism. Gregor Strasser was assassinated for good measure,
among the 200 or so victims of the purge. So was Gustav Ritter von
Kahr, who had put down the Beer-hall Putsch in 1923 (Hitler was an
enthusiast for revenge). Ex-Chancellor Schleicher and his wife were
shot dead at their home, probably at the behest of Göring, who saw
him as a potential rival and who, with Goebbels and Himmler, had
organised the 'Blood Purge' on Hitler's behalf. Speer was in Berlin,
noticing the tension but otherwise an ignorant bystander.[12]

By this time however his stock in the party was rising fast. His last private
commission was the 1933 conversion of the Perleberg country house
mentioned above. His first for the Hitler government came from Goebbels,
who by that stage had presumably had ample time to review Speer's
work in the building occupied by Hanke as business manager of the Berlin
Gau headquarters. 'The Doctor', as Goebbels was known in the party
(the only Ph.D. of topmost rank) was appointed Minister for National
Enlightenment and Propaganda on 5 March 1933, after the only election
in the history of the Reich (Communists were excluded on the convenient
excuse of the Reichstag fire). As such he was principal executant of the
Nazi socio-cultural policy of Gleichschaltung or forcing into line. He
wanted a ministerial base worthy of his new role and had Hanke, now his
adjutant and personal assistant at the Ministry as well as administrator of
his Gauleitung, telephone Speer in Mannheim. He and Gretel threw a few
essentials into their little BMW and drove overnight to Berlin: fortunately
Speer was as keen as ever on cars.
    The task this time was worthy of a real architect: the internal
reconstruction of an imposing building in the Wilhelmplatz designed
inside and out by Karl Friedrich Schinkel, leading nineteenth-century
architect responsible for many important German public edifices, mainly
in Berlin and Potsdam. Speer drove straight to the building, arriving
at the same time as the new master of the house, who had not yet
been shown round it. The tall, thin, rumpled architect and the short,
wiry arch-demagogue with the limp toured the building discussing
alterations until Goebbels told Speer to start work at once, money no
object. Ironically, Goebbels was not impressed by the results, according
to Speer, because a few months later he had the rooms redone regardless
of Schinkel's original design – in 'ocean-liner style'.[13]
    It was a different story when Speer happened to see plans for an
open-air rally to be held after dark on May Day 1933, at Tempelhof
aerodrome close to the centre of Berlin (unique for its huge canopy

under which aircraft loaded and unloaded their passengers at the doors to the terminal building). Speer seized the chance to propose an innovation for which he is probably best remembered still: the towering, lit-up backdrop for a massive public rally. The black, white and red horizontal tricolour of the old Reich was still in use, and he had two made to hang hoist-side uppermost so that the stripes were vertical. Each was ten storeys high; between them hung a similarly lengthy Nazi standard, red with a black swastika on a white ground, the whole brilliantly lit up. This formed the huge backdrop for a platform, high and wide, from which the salute was taken and the speeches made. Some 150 searchlight beams – the entire contemporary stock of the Luftwaffe – shone ten miles high round the airfield to form a 'cathedral of light': the Nazi rally as it was to be remembered by history was born. Tessenow, who saw the plans, was unimpressed.

The Nazis – Hanke, Goebbels, Hitler himself – loved it. Speer became 'Commissioner for the Artistic and Technical Presentation of Party Rallies and Demonstrations', his first official post under the Nazi regime, albeit a party rather than a government one. Here indeed was a great turning-point in his career: a central role in the party's projection of its image to the German people and the world. It was also undoubtedly what he was best at and in no sense derived from Hitler's ideas, even though the concept could hardly have fitted them better. The key element was hugeness, the impression of infinite space which dwarfed the groundlings compelled to look up in their thousands to where the Führer stood overlooking and dominating them, bathed in light against a background of red and black, blood and iron. Here all the world was indeed a stage, and all the men and women merely players, their many imperfections concealed by the darkness of the rally field, made all the darker by the surrounding columns of light. It was a stunning effect.

So far, however, the untried architect Albert Speer had not been called upon to design a real building, or at any rate nothing larger or more challenging than a suburban house for his in-laws. Goebbels cannot have been as dissatisfied with Speer's work as his rejection of the young man's respectful refurbishment of the propaganda ministry suggested. Like many another Nazi official, the worst offender being Hermann Göring, 'the Doctor' collected titles and functions from state and party like a hungry shoplifter let loose in a supermarket with an outsize trolley. Hugenberg had fallen out with the Nazis and on 26 June 1933 was ousted from the Ministry of Nutrition, allocated to his Nationalists under the terms of the moribund coalition which had brought Hitler to power. Goebbels gobbled it up – and called in Speer again to remodel and extend the ministerial residence that went with the job.[14] He promised to do it in two months, provoking scepticism from both Goebbels and Hitler himself. Speer managed it to the day by working the tradesmen in three shifts round the clock (which is more than could be said of most German industries even after 1939, no matter how vital they were to the war effort, as will be seen) and deploying a huge fan to dry the plaster, the paint and the wallpaper before the furniture was hurriedly moved in and paintings hung.

In this final detail Speer made a serious error of taste and sinned against Hitler's puritanical cultural code. He innocently chose a few pictures from the National Gallery in Berlin, which boasted a collection of expressionist paintings by Emil Nolde. Goebbels and his put-upon wife Magda loved them – until Hitler came calling and anathematised them. Therein lay a rich irony, because Nolde was as right-wing as anyone could wish, having joined the Nazis at the same time as Hitler himself in 1920. Of Danish descent (his real name was Hansen and he was born in Nolde, Schleswig-Holstein, by the Danish border), the controversial artist used very bright colours and distorted shapes outlined in thick black paint, depicting mystical and supernatural themes. Imagine his perplexity as a good Nazi when 1,000 of his paintings, much the greatest number of works by any of the 112 German and foreign artists targeted, were expropriated during the Nazi campaign against 'degenerate art' which Hitler finally unleashed in 1936. Their creator was proscribed and forbidden to work.

The Führer, a frustrated architect and artist who in his youth touched up monochrome postcards with colour for a *Groschen* or two on the streets of Vienna, demanded realism in art and loathed all modern manifestations such as expressionism, cubism, dadaism and even comparatively gentle works by impressionists. Nolde's paintings are even more stark than those of the Fascist Norwegian artist, Edvard Munch, and make the works of such as van Gogh and Gauguin look insipid (although they too were banned). Goebbels immediately toned his enthusiasm down to zero, summoned Speer for a ticking-off and ordered him to have the nasty Noldes returned to the gallery. But the redesign of the ministerial residence itself, complete with grand new hall built on, met with the doctor's approval.

Having made such an impression with his May Day banners and pillars of light, Speer was invited to Nuremberg in July to work the same magic for the party rally, the first to be held by the Nazis as ruling party. It was to be a gigantic, triumphal celebration of the constitutional revolution which had brought them to power. The local Gau office lacked the moral courage to approve the main innovation in Speer's backdrop design, a golden Nazi spreadeagle thirty metres wide on a wooden frame, to be placed above the podium on the Zeppelin Field at Dutzendteich, a huge park south-east of the ancient city which was to be consecrated in 1935 as the permanent seat of the Nazi *Parteitag* (party congress). Rallies had already been held there by the Nazis in 1923, 1927 and 1929 (when 150,000 turned up). The city was historic and Bavarian; it was also a railway junction at which no fewer than seven lines converged, capable of bringing hundreds of thousands of participants from all over Germany.

Speer and his folder of sketches were referred to party HQ in Munich, some ninety miles to the south-east. Speer's 'to whom it may concern' letter from Berlin party headquarters got him into the office of Rudolf Hess, co-author of *Mein Kampf*, Hitler's secretary and erstwhile fellow-prisoner of only eight years before, recently promoted to the party office of Deputy Führer. Hess said that only the Führer himself could pronounce on something so important and sent Speer in a party car to Hitler's first-floor apartment at Prinzregentenplatz 16, near the Prince-Regent Theatre.[15] The new Chancellor of Germany was cleaning a dismantled pistol and told the tall visitor to put the drawings on the table. Pushing the gun parts to one side, he leafed silently but attentively through the drawings and said the one word, 'Agreed', before turning his attention back to the automatic. There was no eye contact. Speer withdrew, returned to Nuremberg and ordered local party officials to execute his design to the letter. They were astounded that he had managed to obtain approval from Hitler himself and in person; but the rally was of crucial importance to Hitler, who always provided its high point with one of his marathon rants. So was architecture, as Speer was beginning to discover (so indeed was the theatre, which represented the fusion of Hitler's two passions, mass manipulation and architectural design).

The rally lasted from 31 August to 3 September under the slogan 'Congress of Victory'. Half a million supporters attended, sleeping in tents like an army on the march, or else in requisitioned public and commercial buildings such as warehouses, churches, halls and factories. The feeding of the 500,000 (not to mention their watering and sanitation) was a miracle of thorough organisation, a German talent much more significant than the much-vaunted 'efficiency' so often glibly ascribed to them. Not least in the context of Nazism, this characteristic helps to explain why when they are good they are very, very good, and when they are bad they are horrid – dangerous though such generalisations are.

A temporary grandstand on the Luitpoldhain, another large open space close to the Zeppelin Field, was built virtually overnight to take some 60,000. On 1 September the party banners were 'consecrated' at a ceremony in which a solitary, black-clad SS man mounted the platform and unfurled the 'blood flag' of the party. Then the faecally brownshirted Ernst Röhm recited the list of the party's glorious brawl-dead (such as Horst Wessel, an SA stormtrooper who was squalidly if not undeservedly murdered, allegedly by a Communist, after writing the party's eponymous anthem: Goebbels made him the party's main martyr). Little did the beer-bellied SA leader know that this was his last Nuremberg Rally; not even his name was mentioned the following year.[16] September 2 was dedicated to daylight and torchlight parades by party organisations in formation, followed by fireworks. On the last day the fireworks were rhetorical as the rally climaxed in a tirade from Hitler against the Nazis' enemies at home and abroad, the Jews as always awarded pride of place. Once again the masses were dwarfed by Speer's bannered stage-set with its innumerable, and endless, columns of light. This was stage-design rather than architecture, but it shared the hallmark of bullying bigness, of sheer crushing size, with the building plans for Berlin soon to be sketched out by Hitler and drafted in detail by Speer.

The architect was called in again to set the scene for another major Nazi *Fest*, the autumn harvest festival at Bückeburg, west of Hanover in Lower Saxony. He also helped to design a national broadcasting exhibition in an increasingly busy 1933. Speer was summoned by Hitler himself next, to help with the refurbishment of the Chancellor's apartments in Berlin. The design had been assigned to Professor Paul Ludwig Troost, the Munich-based, Westphalian architect who built the 'Brown House' (a reference to the colour of the party uniform, not the building's), the Nazi national headquarters on Briennerstrasse in the 'Party capital', and the matching 'Führer Building' opposite, on Arcisstrasse (both now used by Munich University). Troost's building supervisor came from Munich and did not know Berlin, so Speer was assigned to help him.

The Berlin residence, on the corner of Wilhelmstrasse at the Wilhelmplatz, bequeathed by the late Weimar Republic to its principal assassin, was thoroughly shabby, neglected and primitively equipped. Hitler was living on the top floor, in the flat previously occupied by the State Secretary to the Chancellery. Like all projects he initiated, he wanted the internal reconstruction done immediately. Hitler, Speer and a couple of acolytes went on a three-hour tour of the building, noting in detail what needed changing. They were amazed to learn that there was a passage from the adjacent Foreign Office through the attic to the Hotel Adlon on the other side, so that the Chancellor could escape the demonstrators who had so often besieged the buildings during Weimar. As work got under way at a feverish pace, Hitler acquired the habit of coming down to make an inspection tour almost every day, taking mental note of every altered detail and giving his opinion. He was in a tearing hurry to see the work completed so as to have an official residence with which to impress visitors.

After a couple of dozen such inspections, Hitler turned to his youthful assistant architect and asked, almost diffidently, 'Will you come to lunch with me today?'

4

Supping with the Devil

(1933–37)

THERE IS NO FIRST-HAND DESCRIPTION of Speer's first appearance at Hitler's table other than the page or so Speer devotes to it in chapter three of *Inside the Third Reich*. It is a pedestrian account which has a flavour of unspontaneously added colour, despite the fact that the well-known German journalist, author and historian Joachim Fest, a leading analyst of the Nazi period, helped Speer considerably to enliven and polish his memoirs. It is clear that Speer was advised to add as much human interest as possible to what was originally in all probability a dry-as-dust description of a crucial event in the young man's life. The result is not art.

Speer writes that he was in particularly noticeable sartorial disarray because some wet plaster had fallen on him. Hitler therefore promised to lend him a jacket, which he did, complete with the gold party badge unique to the Führer. To the chagrin of Goebbels, who noticed the badge, Speer sat at Hitler's right hand in the guest-of-honour position. He was thus well placed to remind Hitler that he had been responsible for the much-admired May Day and Nuremberg rally settings. Speer goes on to say Hitler told him years later that he had earmarked Speer during the work on the Chancellor's residence as someone to whom he could entrust his most cherished plans. 'After years of frustrated efforts I was wild to accomplish things – and twenty-eight years old. For the commission to do a great building, I would have sold my soul like Faust. Now I had found my Mephistopheles. He seemed no less engaging than Goethe's.'

In writing (rather more elegantly) about this encounter, Fest himself deduces that the two men 'fell in love at first sight'; later he imputes, not at all unreasonably, an element of homo-erotic (as distinct from homosexual) attraction in the first real meeting between the two indifferent architects.[1] The more modern psychobabble for this unremarkable phenomenon is 'male bonding'. It was the participants, not their 'relationship' or its wellsprings, that were extraordinary.

*

Speer also described Hitler as his catalyst. Before we consider how he gave Speer his first major building project, it is necessary to shift our focus briefly to the architectural background.

The eighteenth century saw a reaction in the western world to baroque architecture and its over-elaborate rococo offshoot. The American and French revolutions and Palladio were other influences leading to a classical revival, complete with Greek pillars and Roman arches. The reaction to this reaction was the neo-Gothic revival of the early nineteenth century. But the industrial revolution, with its advances in engineering, manufacturing techniques and materials, led to the first experiments in industrial building methods, such as the mid-century Crystal Palace in London, made of glass and iron, and later the Eiffel Tower, of steel. At this time also the bourgeois proto-Socialist William Morris, architect and painter, started a revolution in interior decoration and furniture design. He and his sympathisers led a reaction to industrial mass production, standardisation and the capitalism which inspired them both. His mixture of rationalism and romanticism with national references was taken up all over Europe and is recognised as an inspiration for modern architecture.

German unification in 1871 was the zenith of the *Gründerzeit* (foundation period), when a rash of new building, some outstanding but much of it shoddy (hence the term 'Jerry-built'), erupted across the Second Reich. Countless new factories and workers' estates shot up, the expanding middle class built villas and apartment houses, railway stations sprouted and purpose-built office blocks made their appearance in the cities. The architect Peter Behrens founded the *Werkbund* (work alliance) and was joined by Walter Gropius, Ludwig Mies van der Rohe and the Franco-Swiss Le Corbusier. The underlying philosophy of this modern movement was the fusion of architecture and the machine into the 'machine aesthetic'. Gropius regarded the practice of hiding the new technique of building on a steel frame as dishonest and, closely followed by Mies van der Rohe, designed the abstractly functional, naked steel and glass structures so familiar today. Expressionism was one reaction to the hard lines of the *Werkbund*, favouring a more romantic, individualistic approach.

Among the most important of a profusion of trends was Functionalism, which in German terms meant a fusion of the new machine aesthetic with Prussian neo-classicism. A prime exponent was Mies van der Rohe. Favoured features included reinforced concrete, glass, flat roofs, white stucco walls and unusual shapes. Flat roofs sprang leaks in wet weather unless construction was of the highest standard; they also meant less work for thatchers and tilers, while prefabrication increased unemployment among other building workers.

Shortly after the First World War Gropius founded one of the most important and influential schools of architecture of modern times, the Bauhaus. Its doctrine was a new rationality in architecture, interior design and furniture – the application of science and the latest technology to design. Originally based in Weimar, spiritual home of the eponymous republic, the Bauhaus was forced to move out of Thuringia in 1924 after the state government fell to ultra-rightwingers. The school transferred to Dessau in Saxony-Anhalt and built itself a striking yet essentially functional, white-stuccoed headquarters not overly high, with a flat roof, curved corners and huge, oblong windows of many panes framed in black steel. One of the most spectacular achievements of Walter Gropius, it triumphantly survived the war and forty years of Communist rule in eastern Germany.

The influence of this 'international style' can be seen all over Europe, from houses on the coast of Northumberland to railway stations all over Italy and in so many hotels, factories, apartments and office-blocks. Similarly pervasive is the Bauhaus influence on furniture: any visitor to Dessau will find most of the furniture on view there instantly familiar. It is hard to believe that the 'modern' low-slung, armless chair, of square, steel tubing with oblong, studded leather cushions identical on seat and back, was designed by Ludwig Mies van der Rohe for the Barcelona International Exposition of 1929. He was director of the Bauhaus from 1930 until the Nazis forced its closure in 1933, shortly after it had moved again, to Berlin. In 1937 he emigrated to the United States in protest, not against the Nazis but against their refusal to give him any work, despite his importunate requests.

The ferment of ideas in architecture and design between the wars reflected the unstable, uncertain conditions of Weimar Germany and helped to explain why that country remained in the forefront of modern art in most of its forms from the apotheosis of the Hohenzollern monarchy in 1870 until the advent of Hitler in 1933. The Nazis faced all ways on architecture as they did in so many other areas, often vilifying the 'modern' as alien, Jewish, Marxist or just decadent. They preferred modified Romanesque for public buildings (such as party HQ in Munich) and the Bavarian rural style for the Hitler Youth headquarters; yet they happily went functionalist for Göring's Ministry of Aviation and any number of other public buildings, precisely because the style was orderly, practical, efficient and endowed with many other German virtues. Nazi 'policy' on architecture can best be summarised as follows: if it was useful they used it.[2]

But as with so many other aspects of Nazi ideology, it was the Führer's opinion, or others' sometimes mistaken or overzealous interpretation of it, that mattered. Hitler's appreciation of architecture was limited to romanesque, neo-classical, heavy neo-baroque but above all over-bearing, nineteenth-century buildings. Self-appointed 'master-builder of the Third Reich', he liked to be photographed beside the large-scale models of his Berlin building projects as developed by Speer, as if to remind posterity that he was even greater than they were or would be. The Ring, the street which encircles the heart of Vienna, was his favourite architectural inspiration, no doubt because he knew it well at first hand; a close second was central Paris as rebuilt by Haussmann for Napoleon III, including such mighty structures as the Arc de Triomphe, the Pantheon and the great dome of the Invalides above Napoleon's tomb. His private library was dominated by books on war and on architecture. Hitler's knowledge of both was encyclopaedic if also typical of the enthusiastic autodidact.

His intimate acquaintance with a large number of individual trees did not make him an expert on the forest as a whole, but his sketchbooks were full of rough drawings of colossal battleships and immense domed buildings. His knowledge was less than the sum of its parts; yet he amazed Speer and others with his grasp of every structural detail of the Paris Opéra and other great theatres, even though he visited almost none of them. Apparently he could rattle off the dimensions of their proscenium arches to the last centimetre. 'Modern art', whatever that meant, was by definition degenerate, as we have seen, because the Führer, self-styled first artist of the nation, said so. True German art, however, enjoyed an unbroken descent from Aryan cultures and was therefore inherently superior in exactly the same way and for the same reasons as German bloodstock. It must be said that this alleged purity of descent from Aryan antecedents (which for the sake of this argument included not only ancient Greek and Roman but also Egyptian, Indian and Middle-Eastern monuments) was an idea much older than Hitler, deriving from the early days of German nationalism. His views on art (and his interest in giant battleships) were remarkably similar to those of Kaiser Wilhelm II.

All that being so, modern German art could be good because it was German or bad because it was modern, depending on which way the wind was blowing. This whimsical attitude explains the often self-contradictory Nazi posture on such matters, founded as it was on bigotry and totalitarianism. Xenophobia, a natural corollary of anti-Semitism and resentment of Versailles, put any identifiably foreign, modernistic trend beyond the pale. Abstract art, because it had to be explained, lent itself to élitism and appeared to embody and portend chaos and revolution. Flat roofs were seen as 'oriental' and modern painting and sculpture as soulless, whereas what Germany needed, the Nazis proclaimed, was to turn its back on modernism for its own sake and get back to nature. In other words, the Philistines were the masters now: the Austro-Bavarian, Alpine German provincials showed the hated Prussian intellectuals the door. The Prussian Academy was purged of the likes of Emil Nolde; among the fifty or so replacements were such architects as Hermann Giesler (whom we shall meet again) – and Albert Speer.

The Nazis meanwhile did not hesitate to steal the ideas of the Bauhaus without acknowledgment or permission. Functional principles were freely applied to industrial plants, to Fritz Todt's autobahn network with its road-bridges – the great progressive symbol of the new Germany – and to the bold Tempelhof terminal with canopy by Ernst Sagebiel (who also designed the aviation ministry). Architects such as Tessenow and Behrens were criticised but allowed to carry on designing buildings. The National Socialist architectural style evolved into a pared-down neo-classicism with the emphasis on size. As in other countries, including the leading democracies, the neo-classical was chosen for public buildings because it was impressive. In Germany and Fascist Italy such structures were an instrument for imposing the will of the dictator upon the people. Their disproportionate, inhuman scale expressed not the pomp and majesty of a benign, established authority but the desire of an authoritarian regime to intimidate. The same intent lay behind the stark, regimented construction of industrial plant and housing at Salzgitter with its giant steelworks and Wolfsburg with its huge Volkswagen factory, both Nazi 'new towns': no folksy, rural references here.

The Bavarian Paul Ludwig Troost, Hitler's first architect, an implacable enemy of modernism, had joined the Nazis in 1924. After masterminding the twin party buildings in Munich under the direct supervision of Hitler (the Brown House was erected on the foundations of the Palais Barlow, donated by Fritz Thyssen, the steel magnate and early Nazi enthusiast) he built two temples of honour for the party martyrs of the Beer-hall Putsch nearby. He next designed the city's heavily neo-classical House of German Art. It boasted a high 'Greek' portico all of 185 metres long and was a mere parody of the great Karl Friedrich Schinkel's museums in Berlin. Troost did not live to see it finished. Another of his Munich tasks in which Hitler took a close personal interest was a further, even uglier memorial to the Beer-hall dead inside the Feldherrnhalle (hall of the generals).

Troost's special responsibility for Munich, Germany's new artistic and party capital, passed to Hermann Giesler. It was to be one of a handful of cities to be specially favoured with giant building projects which were never to be realised; few were even begun. To the original three, Berlin, Nuremberg and Munich, were eventually added twenty-seven others, including Linz in Austria, near Hitler's birthplace at Braunau-am-Inn; Hamburg, Cologne, even Dresden with its unique collection of *Lumpenbarock* buildings and Semper's famous opera house.[3] In 1941 the Norwegian city of Trondheim was selected for vast expansion as Greater Germany's principal northern port. Even in the last catastrophic weeks of the war, Hitler would spend hours studying reconstruction plans and models for cities long since bombed to rubble.

Hitler's passion for architecture was such that Professor Troost was one of the very few people he looked up to, just as Speer was one of the tiny handful he liked. Speer was surely right to see this trio as a vertical one, with Hitler in the middle regarding Troost as his master and Speer as his own pupil, to be moulded to his will. Close contact when accompanying Hitler on many a trip to Munich to inspect the new party buildings meant that the tall, thin, shaven-headed Troost, with his taste for stripped neo-classicism, came to exert as much influence over Speer as Tessenow. This became clear when Troost died in January 1934 after a short illness. Accurately if in poor taste, Walter Funk, the ex-journalist who was then Goebbels's state secretary in the propaganda ministry, remarked to Speer: 'Congratulations! Now you are the first.'[4]

Troost had also been working on the plans for a permanent site for the party congress at Nuremberg. What had originally been a sports field was extended to an area five times as large, a total of twenty-eight square kilometres. Speer was invited, on the strength of his great success with the light and banner shows, to continue the colossal development of the permanent site at Dutzendteich. Hitler revised the sketches he had drawn while in prison in 1925, demanded ten million marks from the city council and ordered Speer to start work on enlarging the existing Luitpold arena as the first stage, soon after he took Troost's place as principal architect to the Führer. But it was capable of accommodating 'only' 200,000 people.

Speer therefore designed another arena for the adjacent Zeppelin Field – capacity 340,000. A square of stone terraces with curved corners enclosing a flat grassed space, the stadium was so huge that the postwar, full-size field for amateur athletics which now occupies its south-east section (spectators stand or sit on a mere corner of the terracing, the rest of which is overgrown with grass) takes up less than one-eighth of Speer's ground plan. The field was named after the airship pioneer Count Zeppelin because he had borrowed it for experimental flights in 1909.

The tribune took up the north-eastern side (it was stripped of its vast, crowning party spreadeagle and the pylon at each end by the Americans in 1945). Speer put a row of high pillars at the rear of the tribune (they were demolished by the city authorities in 1967). The small podium with its steel railing from which Hitler orated can still be visited, however, jutting out from the centre of the high stone platform. He and his entourage would enter the stadium from the north-east via the stairs leading up to the tribune and pass through a high vestibule on to the platform. From the rear the tribune looked liked a fortress; within it was the 'Hall of Honour' and a memorial 'chapel' with no religious connotations. It is hard when standing where Hitler stood and surveying the remains to envisage the sheer vastness of the torchlit scene over which Hitler gazed from his podium.

But there is a highly effective aid to the imagination in the form of a superb and chilling record of the scenes at Nuremberg: *Triumph of the Will*, the technically brilliant propaganda film made by Leni Riefenstahl. The music of Wagner, Hitler's fellow anti-Semite and favourite composer, accompanies the dictator's descent on Nuremberg by air, reminding the viewer that the Nazi regime was the first to exploit modern technology to the limit. The hundreds of thousands of onlookers and goose-stepping participants (50,000 uniformed members from the German Labour Front alone, marching with glistening spades on their shoulders instead of rifles), the myriad flags, the endless streams of torches passing in the night were all filmed in 1934, when the proceedings took up an entire week for the first time.

The 1935 rally, for which the Zeppelin Field stadium was completed, was even bigger. On each occasion Speer borrowed the Luftwaffe's searchlights to make his 'cathedral of ice'.[5] But no sooner had the Zeppelin arena been completed and used for the first time than it too was held to be inadequate. Speer was told to build one even bigger on the adjacent Märzfeld or March field. Its official capacity was to have been half a million. Work started in 1938 but the project was halted for ever by the war; there were no more Nuremberg rallies after September 1938. By that time the parades had become overwhelmingly military, with immensely broad lines of tanks and troops on the march as 'Stukas' (*Sturzkampfflugzeuge*, diving combat-aircraft) screamed overhead, frightening the spectators both on the spot and round the world by newsreel.

Another monstrosity planned for the rally complex was the granite 'German Stadium' with seating for 400,000 people – so enormous that binoculars would have been supplied to enable the spectators to follow the proceedings. By this time the Nazis' building megalomania was out of control: the stadium would have featured several stone towers 100 metres high (twice as tall as the Arc de Triomphe) topped with the party eagle. The insanity of the Nuremberg construction programme is illustrated by a file in city records dealing exhaustively with the acquisition of a stallion called Rheinfried for the sculptor Josef Thorak, professor at the Munich School for Graphic Arts, for 1,715 marks.[6] The purchase was ordered by Hitler himself who, always very sharp in money matters, demanded reimbursement from the rally organisation. The purpose of this extravagance was to assist the professor to produce equestrian statues no less than twenty-five metres high for the stadium. The idea that he might spend an hour with his sketchbook at a stud farm or a cavalry barracks obviously did not occur to the spendthrifts in charge of the construction programme. In the end Thorak fell out with Speer because the rally authority was very slow to pay his fees for two bronze horses with riders and eight figures. The bill was 660,000 marks and the last instalment was paid only in October 1942; the statuary was never installed because the stadium was never built.

One of the chief characteristics of Nazi leaders, as we have noted, was to accumulate offices, titles and functions. The result was administrative chaos as well as often deadly demarcation disputes between the satraps. Hitler encouraged this trend because it helped him to divide and rule. A major economic project might involve, for example, Hermann Göring as Plenipotentiary for the Four-Year Plan, Robert Ley as chief of the German Labour Front, Walter Funk as Minister of Economics, Fritz Sauckel as Commissioner for Labour Deployment, Alfred Rosenberg as Minister for the Occupied Eastern Territories – and Heinrich Himmler as SS-Reichsführer (C-in-C), because the SS ran a parallel economy inside and outside the camps and liked to have a hand in everything. So did Martin Bormann as chief of party organisation and thus boss of the Gauleiters; even with him the foregoing list of rival authorities who might want a stake in a project is not exhaustive. After Speer's elevation to the munitions ministry in 1942, he too would become involved in these endless battles about competence and might have to defer, or pay lip-service, to any or several of these rivals to get his way. It was a game at which he was to become a master: always keen to present himself as apolitical, Albert Speer proved to be a 'natural' at the office politics associated with inter- and intra-departmental in-fighting, as ruthless as any opponent.

The deliberate fudging and overlapping of responsibilities and the empire-building that both led to and resulted from it was not confined to the highest echelons but reached all the way down the spatchcocked Nazi power structure. Thus at the outset of his Third Reich career Speer soon added the role of chief of rally presentation to that of court architect. In January 1934 he acquired two more posts.

Hitler liked his entourage to wear uniform on public occasions; the tall and untidy civilian Speer rather stood out among the dignitaries in party brown, army grey and SS black. Hitler therefore appointed him to what was effectively a sinecure: head of the chief office for construction on the staff of his deputy, Hess. He was now entitled to wear black jackboots, light brown shirt, tunic and breeches with matching high-fronted cap and greatcoat featuring a leather belt sixty millimetres wide, complete with holster containing a small Walther

PPK 7.2mm automatic pistol.[7] In spring Goebbels gave Speer a post of similar rank in his ministry, in recognition of his work as chief rally designer. Handing out such semi-honorific offices was also a way of exerting influence over the recipients and staking a claim to their allegiance.

On 30 January 1934, the first anniversary of the Nazis' accession, Speer was given charge of a section of Robert Ley's Labour Front called Schönheit der Arbeit (SdA) – beauty of labour – a concept that sounds no less odd in German than it does in English. This was no sinecure, however, and was an idea entirely in line with the social policies of Bismarck. As the better-known and often ridiculed Kraft durch Freude (KdF, strength through joy) organisation set out to organise the leisure time of the labour force, so SdA set about its working conditions. The motive behind both programmes was the same: to get more labour and less trouble from the workers by keeping them amused, diverted and occupied. Bismarck had his anti-Socialist law but by way of a *quid pro quo* founded the German welfare state as a very substantial, paternalistic recompense. The Nazis abolished trade unionism but copied Mussolini's Fascists in Italy with KdF, which included an elaborate programme of organised holidays by train and even ocean liner (two ships were built specially). Dr Ley of the Labour Front was in overall charge of the programme, which he saw as a major blow against the class system: this was the never quite extinguished 'Socialist' side of National Socialism in action.

The Volkswagen 'Beetle' was originally styled the *KdF-Wagen*. Professor Ferdinand Porsche's immortal 1936 design was subsidised by the Nazi regime and offered to workers prepared to pay a small weekly sum towards eventual delivery of a car which would confer the freedom of the new autobahns on its owners. But the Wolfsburg plant switched to war production in 1939 and no private car was ever delivered. Nor was the money refunded. KdF also offered organised sports and hiking (a craze at the time, as we saw), visits to concerts and theatres, folk dancing and evening classes, all heavily subsidised by the state when not free of charge. Such organised leisure was also promoted by the Soviet and allied Communist regimes for the same reasons and was part of the totalitarian scheme of things for controlling the masses. It was also in broad terms good for the workers' health and therefore the economy as a whole, an example of enlightened self-interest on the part of the 'nanny state'.

Another example of social engineering was the Nazis' vast programme of job creation through public works, such as roads, that had the hugely beneficial side-effect of modernising the infrastructure, not just facilitating the movement of troops as the cynics suggested. It was not only in its architecture that the Third Reich consciously harked

back to the Roman Empire. Nor were public-works employment pro-
grammes the monopoly of totalitarian governments, although they are
better placed to regiment society by decree. The early 1930s also saw
the birth of the New Deal in the first administration of Franklin D.
Roosevelt, who did not shrink from extending his job-creating largesse
to rearmament, in the shape of a timely expansion of his beloved United
States navy, to the huge benefit of the labour-intensive shipbuilding and
associated industries.

SdA improved the workplace itself. Robert Ley had been impressed
by Dutch examples and flowerbeds began to appear outside German
factories. Derelict land was cleaned up and put to use, if only as a
lawn for the workers' lunchbreak in good weather. Indoors, offices and
canteens were refurbished with more windows, modern ventilation,
illumination and fresh, light paintwork. Cheap and cheerful but robust
furniture was designed and mass produced by SdA for industry. Much
of it might have been lifted from a Bauhaus catalogue. Speer in a
footnote in his memoirs proudly notes the warm approval of Sir Nevile
Henderson, British Ambassador to Berlin from 1937 until the outbreak
of war.[8] Hitler, he adds, was not interested in such matters. SdA may
have been the most beneficial aspect and most benign achievement of
Speer's dozen years as a senior Nazi functionary.

But Hitler did take an interest in the wellbeing of the workers
building the autobahns, ordering Speer to design model barracks with
high-quality basic facilities. One senses that it was the buildings rather
than their occupants that interested Speer's all-powerful client, but
Hitler did ask for a report on the navvies' reaction. As work at the
Chancellery progressed, Speer, still based at his private office (just
moved to the nearby Behrensstrasse) became a habitué of Hitler's table,
which could cope with a maximum of ten for lunch or dinner in the
apartment he had commandeered from the State Secretary (later
Minister) to the Chancellery, Hans Lammers, while his own was being
remodelled. He had a balcony built on to the latter, the better to bask
in the adulation of the crowds which would gather under his window
in his early days in power.

Hitler, a personally abstemious, teetotal, non-smoking vegetarian,
would unwind at table, from which officials were excluded for fear of
gossip. Göring and Goebbels, who understood the importance of being
present at court whenever possible, were the most senior paladins
regularly on hand. The other diners tended to be either from Hitler's
personal entourage or else middle-ranking, 'old guard' Nazi Party
functionaries with whom, for about the first year of his rule only, he
would talk of the good old days in Munich. In later years they
embarrassed him and were kept at a distance; but the personal
retinue of adjutants, drivers, secretaries, 'court photographer' Heinrich

Hoffmann and a few others, not forgetting Eva Braun, the mistress for whom Hitler showed not one whit of affection in public, remained almost exactly the same. In the evenings he would sit with his cronies watching newsreels and one or even two films, laid on by Goebbels in the apartment.

One evening Göring, never slow when it came to self-aggrandisement, asked Hitler for permission to employ Speer, still technically an architect in private practice, to redesign his new residence as Presiding Minister of Prussia, only recently redecorated: as heir-presumptive he wanted it to be second only to the Führer's. The already bloated former air-ace had noted Speer's influence at court and wanted to latch on to it himself. Speer was not consulted in advance about the request, which was granted.

On another occasion, an official reception in spring 1934, Hitler was startled to be introduced to Frau Margarete Speer. Not only had he never met her before; he had not even known that Speer was married. Hitler, always the social gallant, kissed her hand and murmured arch compliments. He asked whether the couple had any children; as if inspired, Gretel gave birth to six in the ensuing nine years. Since the first was born about three months after the introduction, the Speers cannot be accused of producing him, at least, by command of the Führer, even if one is moved to speculate about the rest.

A similar circle of intimates would gather round Hitler in the early days of power at the Osteria Bavaria, an artists' restaurant in Munich, or at one café or another in the city, when he was visiting. Back in Berlin, there were many more formal invitations to public receptions and dinners at the Chancellery, to which Gretel was now also invited.

Speer was hard at work on the Zeppelin Field, drawing inspiration from the Pergamon Altar, the ancient Greek edifice stolen from northwest Turkey for a museum specially built by Schinkel in Berlin. The main Nuremberg tram-sheds had already been blown up to make way for the latest grand folly. It was at this time that Hitler and Speer formulated their so-called 'law of ruins' whereby they built with distant posterity in mind. The remains of the Reich were to show the greatness of those who produced them, even when overgrown and worn 1,000 years hence. This morbid romanticism was inspired by the relics of ancient civilisations, such as the Pergamon Altar, the Pyramids and the monuments left all over Europe by the Romans. Speer, never much of a draughtsman, had someone else draw his vision of the Zeppelinfeld ruins as they might look after a millennium of neglect (in fact only a dozen years were needed for them to attain this state, with a little help from high explosive). Hitler approved, thus providing the psychologist Erich Fromm with another powerful piece of evidence of the Führer's necrophiliac tendencies.[9]

More down to earth was the calculation behind Speer's idea of the torchlit evening rally: by confining the participants to an ill-lit field he concealed their beer-bellies and unheroic stature. Geography decreed that many of them were Bavarians, the least likely of all Germans to match the spurious ideal of the tall, blond Nordic exemplar of the master race.

Immediately after the Blood Purge of the SA leadership at the end of June 1934, Speer was commissioned to rebuild the Borsig Palace, where Vice-Chancellor Papen had his offices, as the new headquarters for the residual SA leadership, which Hitler wanted under his eye in Berlin in future rather than out of sight in Munich. Papen wisely made himself scarce as his staff were summarily evicted on Hitler's orders (Speer found the blood of Papen's assistant on the floor of an office, his first direct brush with the brutality of the regime).

Speer's talent for stage design was invoked again in August 1934, when President Hindenburg faded away at the age of eighty-seven. His remains were reverently deposited by the memorial to his greatest triumph over the Russians at Tannenberg in East Prussia in 1914. Speer had long black banners hung from the towers of the huge monument. There were no swastikas this time; this was not a party occasion and the emblem had not yet displaced the black, white and red tricolour as the national flag. Hitler publicly eulogised the field marshal whose death so conveniently removed the last restraint on his total power over the most dynamic nation in Europe. He promptly made himself head of state as well as of government and party.

Speer was more interested in Greek models, especially Doric, the simplest classical style, than Roman when developing the Nuremberg rally complex. He and Gretel toured Greece on their first trip abroad in May 1935, studying the ruins. Speer adopted the horseshoe shape of the Greek stadium rather than the oval of the Roman arena for his projected German Stadium at Nuremberg. It is very difficult to imagine how anyone could gaze on the ruins of Epidaurus and Delphi and claim to have 'derived' such monstrous parodies from them. The attribution might be literally true but aesthetically the complete disregard of the Greeks' sense of proportion led to grotesque results in twentieth-century Germany.

More modest in scale, the Speers' new house in the wooded 'lake district' of south-west Berlin was ready for them on their return. The area lies at the south end of the 'AVUS' (*Auto-Verkehr und Übung-Strasse* – car traffic and practice road), a four-mile stretch of urban motorway straight as an arrow which was sometimes closed to the public for motor-racing. Some would say the public treated it as a racetrack all year round (they still do); a dedicated driver of fast sports cars, Speer was well placed to get to the office at remarkable speed.

By this time their first child, inevitably named Albert, born on 29 July 1934, was approaching his first birthday. Living in rented flats had lost its appeal, so Speer spent 70,000 marks on his modest new home, which he unexcitingly designed himself (the postwar sale of the site did wonders for his family finances). It had a modest 135 square metres of living space, and Speer borrowed 30,000 marks from his father. Albert Senior took out a mortgage which his son paid off, along with his own, by the end of the war.[10]

The house awaiting the Speers on their return from their first trip abroad had two reception rooms and three bedrooms, in marked contrast (as Speer pointed out in his memoirs) with the palatial residences acquired as soon as possible after they came to power by other Nazi leaders, of whom the most acquisitive was Göring. At this stage in his career, of course, Speer was still the semi-detached architect with a confirmed place at Hitler's court but without any senior state or party post: an *arriviste* who had not yet arrived. But from 1936 his work began to reach beyond the frontiers of the Reich: he was given representational commissions, including refurbishing the German Embassy in London's Belgravia that summer. In the same year he salvaged the design of Otto March for the Berlin Olympic Stadium in Spandau. Its modernist, glass and concrete outline had infuriated Hitler, who threatened to call off the Games. Speer drew up a plan to clad the already erected steel skeleton in stone and suppress the glass walls; the Games were thus saved for another deployment of Leni Riefenstahl's triumphalist cameras (and for the embarrassing personal triumph of the 'racially inferior' Jesse Owens, the black American quadruple gold medallist). The stadium is still in use.

In an extremely rare reference to his private life, Speer confesses in his memoirs that he neglected his family at this period for the sake of his work, which left him too tired at the end of a long day to devote any energy to Gretel and the baby. This wilful neglect, followed by the enforced and irreparable separation for twenty years after Nuremberg, meant that Speer enjoyed almost no close contact with any of his children before they had grown up and away from him – a remarkable fact for a father of six and a classic instance of sacrificing the present for the sake of the future. He was thus even more remote from his own children than he had been from his parents in his own childhood. This all too familiar tendency of the young man on the make was doubtless reinforced by Speer's workaholic and opportunistic traits: he felt he could not turn down any commission from Germany's new masters. And although he often expressed regret for missing out on a father's relationship with his young children, there is not a shred of evidence that he would have enjoyed it, or taken the chance of spending more time with his family had it arisen or been made to.

At first he refused fees for his work on state buildings, to the astonishment and derision of Göring, although he graciously, and no doubt gratefully, accepted payment from Nuremberg for his rally work. He eventually received a single fee of 30,000 marks for all his labours there prior to 1 January 1935 and a handsome 40,000 a year thenceforward (plus 54,000 for basic expenses such as staff and office costs). He also accepted a bonus on completion of each stage, plus a 0.2 per cent commission on the total cost. He recalled his Nuremberg income as 1,000 marks per month; but the city archive reveals this rather grander remuneration for the rallies.[11] He admits to having accumulated a personal fortune from his architecture of 1.5 million marks by the end of the war, when another million was outstanding in unpaid fees.[12]

Too tired to talk to his wife after an exhausting day's work, often followed by supper with the Führer, Speer none the less found the residual energy to father three more children before the war (and two during it). Hilde was born on 17 April 1936, Friedrich on 6 May 1937 and Margret on 19 June 1938. Neither his wife nor any of his children (nor his parents) rate an entry in the index of *Inside the Third Reich*, his autobiography, and are only fleetingly mentioned in the text. References to the author's emotional and spiritual life are perfunctory to non-existent in this book, although *Spandau – the Secret Diaries* makes some amends in this area. Indeed if it had not been for the suggestions of his original publisher, Wolf Jobst Siedler, and his editorial adviser, the journalist and historian Joachim Fest, he would also have left out crucial contemporary events which he witnessed, such as the notorious *Reichskristallnacht* pogrom of 9 November 1938, also absent from the index.[13]

The development of the Nuremberg Rally site as planned in 1935 would have cost up to 800 million marks, of which the stadium, whose foundation stone was laid by Hitler in 1937, would have taken between a quarter and a third. The scale of the uncompleted enterprise – only the Zeppelinfeld and the granite shell of a 50,000-seat Congress Hall, semicircular in the manner of a Roman theatre, were finished – dwarfed the grandest monuments of the ancient and modern worlds, from the Pyramid of Cheops to the Statue of Liberty. Speer had a model built and put it on display in the German pavilion at the Paris World's Fair of 1937, where to his own amazement and the delight of Hitler it won a gold medal.

The Paris event was thus a double triumph for Speer, because he also designed the pavilion itself. The French organisers had offered the rival totalitarian powers, Hitler's Reich and Stalin's Soviet Union, two prime sites opposite each other on the right bank of the Seine in front of the Palais de Chaillot. Hitler was highly annoyed by this juxtaposition until Speer, on a reconnaissance visit to Paris, 'stumbled' into a room and saw a drawing of the Soviet pavilion, which included a pair of 'Socialist-realist' figures ten metres high on a tall stone platform, portrayed as striding towards the German pavilion.

Speer's response was simply to build much higher, to seventy metres. An oblong structure showing four square columns on either side and three at the front, with the proportions (and at least some of the elegance) of a telephone box was built on the forward end of the pavilion. It was crowned by a heavy pediment bearing an eagle with hunched wings and a swastika in its talons, poised to swoop down on the Soviet pair, the whole lit from within at night to show columns of light *à la manière de* Nuremberg. At the foot of this vulgar and boastful edifice stood a rough-hewn bronze, seven and a half metres high, of a family of three Aryans by Josef Thorak. No expense was spared; contemporary reports state that 100,000 tons of stone were brought to Paris for the pavilion by 1,000 railway wagons. The French were carefully even-handed: B. M. Iofan, the designer of the overborne Soviet pavilion, was also awarded a gold medal. Thus did the great powers of the earth compete like schoolboys to make an impression.[14]

The international firmament was darkening as rapidly as the German scene while Speer was establishing himself as the leading architect of the Nazi regime. One edifice Speer was not asked to redesign was the blackened Reichstag building, gutted in 1933 just four weeks after the Nazis came to power, allegedly by a retarded Dutch Communist but probably instigated by Göring, one of whose many jobs was President–speaker – of the German parliament. Only four weeks later the Reichstag, sitting elsewhere, passed the 'Enabling Act' which gave Hitler his dictatorial powers. By July Germany was a one-party state and by October it had walked out of the League of Nations. One month after the June 'Night of the Long Knives', the first Nazi attempt to take over Austria failed, despite the murder of Chancellor Dollfuss. In March 1935, conscription was imposed; in September the anti-Semitic 'Nuremberg Race Laws' were promulgated. The democracies, afraid of war and resolved to appease, acquiesced in Hitler's march into the Rhineland in 1936 as the Spanish Civil War broke out and the Italians embarked on their Abyssinian adventure. The great game of call-my-bluff for the future of Europe had begun.

5

Redesigning Berlin

(1937–38)

THE REOCCUPATION OF THE RHINELAND was a bluff by Hitler, deploying a parade-ground army which would have been pushed to field three divisions and could not have withstood a determined riposte by the French. It was also a turning point for the Third Reich because Hitler had for the first time defied the victors of 1918 on a major issue by military means and got away with it. It was no coincidence that at this very moment of risky triumph, his first territorial *tour de force*, the Führer's thoughts turned to the realisation of his architectural dreams for Berlin. His first victory on the world stage intensified his triumphalist ambitions: he was absorbed in designing his own monument long before he had begun to 'earn' it, like a gambler who boasts how he will spend his winnings before the game has even begun. Many people proclaim what they would do if they won the lottery – or became dictator. Hitler was one such. But he did become dictator, by sheer willpower; and when he did, he unfortunately proved to be a man of his word.

It is easy to lapse into hindsight and conclude that here, in the Rhineland in March 1936, was the moment when a determined stand by the democracies would have stopped the Nazis in their tracks. But that would be to overlook the fact that Hitler in his early years of power was as adept at reading the mood of foreign leaders as at manipulating his domestic audience. France and Britain had lost a generation of young men less than twenty years before (so indeed had Germany, but without the consolation of victory, however pyrrhic). It was not at all irrational of western leaders, some of whom regarded Versailles as unduly harsh anyway, to reflect domestic public opinion by placing the avoidance of another general war in Europe above all other considerations (including Abyssinian independence, raped by Italy, and Spanish republicanism, killed by Franco with Nazi and Fascist support). Appeasement was by no means unpopular, however ignoble it may now seem after filtration through the Germanophobia of such as Winston Churchill, vindicated *ex post facto*.

The Americans too were still in strongly isolationist mood (unlike their President), a different sentiment whose practical results were indistinguishable in Europe. But appeasement regrettably only inspired Hitler to more and bigger demands and made him look invincible at home and abroad. Appeasement may well have seemed the prudent course to its practitioners (who often made the mistake of trying to claim the moral high ground at the same time as they gave in) but it set a bad example, giving comfort to aggressors. Nor on this occasion did a soft answer turn away wrath. Compromise was a concept as alien to the Nazis as to their contemporaries in the Japanese military junta.

Hitler was a 'pro-active' Micawber. He had aims – exterminating Jewry, acquiring *Lebensraum* in the east, restoring and expanding German power – and he had the intransigent will to achieve them no matter how. Instead of 'waiting for something to turn up' to get him out of a difficulty, he let his opponents' weaknesses lead them into difficulty and then ruthlessly exploited their discomfiture. Once he had gained the ascendancy in Germany only a coup, a disabling disease, death or superior external force could have stopped him. The left might have done so before 1933 had Stalin and the German Communists not joined the Nazis in opposing the SPD; the Wehrmacht could have spiked his guns afterwards but let itself be seduced by the prospect of massive expansion and rearmament. If the French had been prepared to go to war over the Rhineland, Hitler would have anticipated it and switched to another item on his immutable agenda: he was, after all, foiled in Austria in 1934 but returned to the charge in 1938, absorbing his native land in the *Anschluss*. A master of bluff himself, he knew instinctively when others were bluffing or blustering. The other secret of his early success was the utter implacability he shared with his Japanese allies.

Meanwhile the completion of the Zeppelinfeld in 1934 had at last given Albert Speer a large, complete structure in stone to show for his work as Hitler's architect, even if most of its area was the vast empty space in the middle, as devoid of substance as any of his 'cathedrals of light'.

But for all its vastness, the Nuremberg plan was an architectural sideshow compared with Hitler's designs on and for Berlin, which he had been sketching since his time in Landsberg prison in 1925. The central idea was a great hall with a dome (diameter 250 metres) to dwarf St Peter's and a triumphal arch (height 120 metres) to make the Arc de Triomphe (a mere forty-eight metres) look like a portico, linked by a north-south avenue two and a half times as long as the two-kilometre Champs Elysées (and of course rather wider, at 120 metres compared with 100). The great hall would take 150,000 people on a floor space of 38,000 square metres. The arch would carry all 1.8 million names of Germany's dead from 1914 to 1918.

When Speer got to work on Hitler's ideas and developed a plan affecting the entire city, Berlin's dozen railway termini were scheduled for demolition in cooperation with the rail and transport authorities, to be replaced by just two, north and south, considerably facilitating reconstruction. It cannot be emphasised too strongly that Speer, granted the closest approximation to a *carte blanche* ever given to anyone by Hitler, *expanded* on his patron's plans, increasing the dimensions of the great dome and other features. Megalomania was undoubtedly the driving force; but the explosion that had quintupled Berlin's population in two-thirds of a century of German union from 800,000 in 1871 led to intractable traffic problems in the motor age. Successive national and city governments had been fretting over solutions since 1910.

The Chief Burgomaster (lord mayor) of Berlin was Dr Julius Lippert, an 'old guard' Nazi aged forty-one in 1937 and sufficiently committed to his city to be chary of seeing its budget swallowed up by uncontrollably ambitious Nazi building plans. A lawyer, journalist and protégé of Goebbels (still Gauleiter of Berlin), Lippert was also, in typical Nazi hat-collecting manner, editor of *Der Angriff*, the Nazi weekly for Berlin. He proved incapable of thinking as big as Hitler or Speer. Invited to submit plans for a grand avenue 120 metres wide, he made it 100 metres; asked a second time, he did it again, to Hitler's fury. Speer was not alone in his astonishment that Hitler tolerated this defiance for four years.[1]

The dictator left Lippert to his own devices for the time being but, in a classic display of Nazi power politics, simply bypassed the city government and told Speer he was in charge of the entire Berlin plan. He gave his young architect two postcards on which he had drawn his dome and his arch a good decade before. 'We must surpass Paris and Vienna,' Hitler said. To put pressure on the recalcitrant Berlin authorities, he let it be known that he might build a new capital from scratch, as the Americans had done in Washington.[2]

Speer was formally appointed Generalbauinspektor für die Reichshauptstadt (Inspector-General of Construction for the Reich Capital, or GBI) with the rank of state secretary (not to be confused with an American or British secretary of state), the highest grade in the German civil service and equivalent to a junior minister. But the relevant decree of 30 January 1937, the fourth anniversary of Hitler's accession, made Speer, not yet thirty-two, directly answerable to Hitler and nobody else, whether Mayor Lippert or Gauleiter Goebbels. At his own wish, Speer remained in private practice, a constitutional anomaly fudged by classifying his new office as a research institute. Today it would be called a quango (quasi-autonomous, non-governmental organisation), unelected and unaccountable to anyone except central government. He was paid 1,500 marks per month (comparable with Lippert's salary) plus expenses and cars, a fraction of his continuing earnings as a private architect. Hitler left it to his state secretary in the Chancellery, Hans Lammers, to work out the details with Speer, who now matched Fritz Todt, the Inspector-General for Roads, in rank.

Speer soon revealed the remarkable talent for organisation which was to stand him in such good stead when he assumed the much wider responsibilities of minister in charge of the entire war economy. His new department was an administrative *tabula rasa* but he seems to have needed no lessons in how to set it up. This ability to organise was undoubtedly one of the secrets of his rise to power and was obviously brought out by the need to arrange speedy fulfilment of contracts awarded on the whim of a dictator who demanded instant gratification.

Everything seemed to need doing in the most desperate rush, whether Goebbels's office, Hitler's official apartments, the Zeppelin stadium or the Paris pavilion. Huge quantities of material, transport and labour had to be organised on the turn. The fact that Speer had Hitler's personal authority for his tasks was not enough to explain his ability to orchestrate the timely completion of complicated projects; important men such as Göring and Todt could lay claim to a priority no less urgent. Hitler gave Speer a good start by summarily evicting the Academy of Arts from its premises at number 4, Pariserplatz. Next door at number 3 was Todt's office; the Chancellery stood to the south, just across an enclosed garden, all in the eastern shadow of the Brandenburg Gate, symbol of Berlin.

Speer built his new department round three core sections: Main Office (for administration and budget), Planning Bureau and General Construction Management. The latter was assigned to Walter Brugmann, a senior civil servant from Nuremberg, while the Main Office was headed by Professor Karl Maria Hettlage, a financial expert and a Catholic with no enthusiasm for Nazism (he once exclaimed to Speer, 'You are Hitler's unrequited love,' after seeing the pair together). For the Planning Bureau Speer recruited two erstwhile fellow-students turned colleagues: Rudolf Wolters and Willi Schelkes who, doubtless with alacrity, deserted Mannheim for Berlin. Wolters had acquired useful experience in urban planning in Siberia and more recently working for the railways in Berlin. Both men became heads of department in the Planning Bureau; so did Hans Stephan, architect and city administrator, and Gerhard Fränk, an administrative lawyer. Wolters, tipped off by Speer of the latter's impending promotion, resigned from the railway to be ready to start work with the 'GBI' in January 1937.

These gifted cronies all drew salaries above the going rate, thanks to Speer's successful demand to Lammers that he should be able to attract the best men available. By 1938 the annual salary bill for thirty-seven such GBI recruits amounted to 425,000 marks.[3] Speer also recruited Annemarie Wittenberg, a young employee of the Goebbels ministry who had been seconded to him when he worked there, as his principal personal secretary, a move that shaped the rest of her life.

The former exhibition suites in the ex-academy were used to display models and a large-scale map of Berlin, all laid out on a collection of tables at waist height. Models of projected buildings were made on the premises, ensuring that there was always something new to divert Hitler on his frequent visits. Speer's team worked morning, noon and night and evaded the attentions of the bureaucracies of both state and party, knowing they were engaged on plans to change the face of Germany which were of special interest to Hitler. The average age of 'Speer's Kindergarten' was a little more than his own, in the early thirties. The war saw to it that they were never absorbed into the regular bureaucracy.

It was a good place to work – provided only that one lived for one's job. The hours were long but the atmosphere was informal and the boss especially so. Speer preferred his people not to be card-carrying Nazis because party duties tended to interfere with working time. He got Hitler's permission to hire talented non-Nazis, for several of whom the GBI office thus became a political sanctuary. Wolters by his own admission was in broad sympathy with the Nazis but felt no need to join the party. This was to his advantage after the war, for which he was duly grateful to Speer, at any rate until they fell out many years later.[4]

Speer's young men felt they belonged to an elite and soon developed their own *esprit de corps*: Stephan, a gifted amateur cartoonist, drew caricatures of his colleagues which were commonly captioned by Speer himself and put on the office noticeboard. The GBI's men were highly privileged, well placed to take little or no notice of the increasingly unpleasant happenings outside their closed world of urban planning. It is only too plausible to trace back to this refuge from the excesses of the regime Speer's claim at Nuremberg that he never knew of them at the time: it is not however what went on at his office that counted in this context but his time at Hitler's court and his constant contact with the Nazi leadership. Hitler's renowned passion for architecture and construction usually protected the GBI office from outside inter-ference by anyone, no matter how powerful. One beneficiary was Marion Riesser, Wolters's long-serving secretary, who was half Jewish. Later she was able to return Speer's favour.

As respite from the long and busy hours at GBI Speer would send and sometimes accompany a key colleague or two on trips abroad in

1937. Wolters went to America to study advanced transport systems. Speer and Schelkes lodged at the German Embassy in London for a few days' tourism; Schelkes also accompanied Speer and Gretel to Italy. Schelkes, Wolters and Stephan led a group that went to Paris for the World's Fair. Wolters took charge of organising German architectural exhibitions abroad for the GBI, whose head office had expanded to ninety-one employees, including twenty-eight architects, when Germany went to war in 1939.

The GBI was also free to hire any working architect for specific projects in Berlin. The Berlin redevelopment plan envisaged large numbers of symbolic public buildings. Speer retained respected older architects such as Peter Behrens, Paul Bonatz and Wilhelm Kreis and also gave major works to men of his own age, including former fellow-students such as Friedrich Tamms. These and others worked on new ministries, military headquarters, offices for leading companies and other projects that were to take over the whole of the new centre of Berlin. There was to be an east–west axis to cross the main north–south one; both were to extend to the autobahn ring round the city. The axes were to be lined with office blocks, each slightly lower than the last as one moved away from the centre. There was to be an airport at the end of each of the four 'spokes'. The futuristic Tempelhof close to the centre was to become a park, to banish aircraft noise from the city centre.

Hitler's morbid interest in seeing his own outsize memorial built in his lifetime and to his detailed instructions, like a latter-day King Mausollus, was the impetus behind Speer's sweeping plan for the entire city. The domed hall in the north obviously had to be linked by a monumental avenue to the arch in the south, celebrating victories yet to be won by recording those killed in Germany's Great War defeat (incontrovertible evidence of Hitler's will to reverse it). The matchingly vast 'Grand Square' – capacity one million people – on the north side of which the domed hall would stand, was to be free of traffic; the east–west axis already existed, running from the Frankfurterallee in the east via Unter den Linden in the centre to Heerstrasse in the west, crossing the line of the north–south axis just to the south of the square. The north–south avenue was to continue to the southerly main rail terminus.

To line the north–south axis with public buildings to scale, it was necessary to clear a huge area of the city centre. Speer's unbridled extrapolation of Hitler's grand avenue with its monster monuments was on such a scale that about 50,000 apartments near the city centre had to be demolished. Hitler doubtless lost no sleep over the social consequences of Speer's pursuit of his 'client's' orders *à l'outrance*, but it is clear that Speer rather than Hitler was directly and personally responsible for the bulk of the suffering thus caused. It was Speer who signed the eviction and demolition orders.

Under a dictatorship there was no need to spend years on planning permissions, public inquiries, appeals and counter-appeals: it was all done by decree. It so happened that nearly half of the apartments to be torn down were occupied by Jews, which meant there was even less need to worry about the present plight or future fate of those evicted to make way for the granite megaliths of Hitler and Speer. Speer was not 'obeying orders' so much as issuing them on his own initiative. As will become clear, Speer used his powers as GBI to order the eviction of tens of thousands of Jews, an action which turned out to be only the first stage of a journey to horrors of which Speer persistently denied contemporary knowledge. These mass evictions are also the first landmark on a trail of evidence which proves he was a fraud.

North of the superdome Speer planned an oblong lake, aligned to north-north-west, in which the great hall would be mirrored on such precedents as Versailles, Hampton Court Palace and the Washington Monument. The big northerly railway station was to be sited at the northern end of this sheet of water. A new naval headquarters would overlook the lake from the east and the city hall and police headquarters from the west. On the south side of Speer's grand square, facing the domed hall, was the Führer's Palace (150 times more voluminous than Bismarck's) and to the south-west a new Chancellery (not to be confused with the one actually built by Speer in 1938 and described below). The High Command of the Wehrmacht took the south-east. These ridiculously overblown buildings were designed by Speer; the only intrusion he permitted on his intended masterpiece was the extension to the Reichstag planned for the north-east corner, on which Woldemar Brinckmann worked with him.

All these edifices would tower over the Brandenburg Gate on the east–west axis to the south-east of the square. Even without its recently acquired scorch-marks, the Reichstag proper, which manages to look quite imposing in its present-day, partly rebuilt, freestanding condition, would have appeared similarly overborne and secondary on the eastern side of the square, an accurate representation of its role in the Third Reich. Ironically it was Speer who suggested pulling it down and Hitler who forbade it: he wanted to keep it as a social facility for deputies of a physically much enlarged (if politically much reduced) Reichstag in its enormous new building. The extant Reichstag enclosed one-fiftieth of the volume of the proposed great hall. Apartment complexes were to be built to the north of the grand square, capable of accommodating many more people than those razed to make way for the new capital, to be restyled 'Germania'. We can be certain that there would have been no place for Jews in the new residential area.[5]

His musical idol and friend, Wilhelm Furtwängler, observed admiringly to Speer, at the time his overweening plan became known, how wonderful it must be to be free to realise his building ideas in such grand style. The conductor of the Berlin Philharmonic elicited a reply which is noteworthy for two reasons: it shows that Speer, even at the moment of his own architectural apotheosis, fully understood the enormity as well as the enormousness of his scheme; and it is his only known self-deprecating wisecrack: 'Imagine someone saying to you, it is my unshakable will that the Ninth [symphony by Beethoven] may only be played on the mouth-organ from now on.'

But Germania, due for completion in 1950, was aborted by Hitler's war before anything was built. The one visible part of the mad plan that was implemented was the bodily removal, westward to its present position, of the Victory Column celebrating the defeat of France in 1870, because it obstructed the designated crossing of the two axes. The only other visible relic of Speer's role as architect and GBI is a row of cast-iron double streetlamps on Strasse des 17. Juni, the westward extension of the famous Unter den Linden avenue which was and remains the German capital's broadest. The house Speer built for himself and Gretel among Berlin's lakes in 1935 was destroyed by bombs although photographs and plans of it survive.[6]

The US army blew up the other residence he designed for himself – his chalet cum studio at Hitler's refuge on the Obersalzberg, an enclave of south-eastern Bavaria surrounded by the territory of Hitler's native Austria. Speer had found a small hunting lodge in the Ostertal, also in the Bavarian Alps, in 1935 – somewhere he could take his expanding family and also work without office distractions. Hitler heard of this and made Speer an offer which, as usual, he could not refuse: the use of a house near his own retreat, the Berghof (named after an inn which was on the spot until Hitler acquired it).

The house in question was a villa which had belonged to the Bechstein family (the piano-makers who were among the first of Hitler's supporters from the upper classes) until they made him a gift of it. Speer designed a building more suited to his professional needs in 1936 and Hitler ordered Bormann to have it built. Bormann and Göring were the only others apart from Speer who were allowed a house inside the three-kilometre inner security fence at the Berghof, an estate 1,940 metres above sea-level which eventually encompassed seven square kilometres. This was another unmistakable indication of Speer's status.

Hitler had designed his own house in detail, building it round the chalet he had originally acquired. It included a vast picture window that could be lowered through the floor to give an unencumbered view on a clear day of Berchtesgaden and distant Salzburg in Austria.

Speer sneers in his memoirs that Hitler had, like some fourth-rate architectural student, built this over his garage, so that in a north wind the living room stank of petrol.[7] The massively expanded cottage also offered views of the Untersberg Mountain, where Charlemagne, founder of the first greater German Reich, is said to sleep, awaiting recall to restore the full glory of the German nation. Hitler found this myth irresistible.

The attraction of his company as a host during his frequent retreats to Obersalzberg was less so. Speer is not the only historical witness to the titanic tedium at Hitler's court, but was the one best placed to attempt a detailed description.[8] The seldom changing cast of characters included the hangers-on from late nights in Berlin and long lunches in Munich; but the Berghof was a holiday home, so at least women were present. They included Eva Braun, Hitler's mistress, and a few secretaries. The odious Bormann, originally secretary and chief of staff to the Deputy Führer, Rudolf Hess, then private secretary to Hitler himself and master of his privy purse, finally Reichsleiter (national chief) of the party and head of the 'Party Chancellery' after the defection of Hess in 1941, was in charge of the Berghof, its construction, expansion and maintenance. It was one of his many ways of making himself indispensable, a strategy which made him (never Speer) the most powerful man in the Reich after Hitler himself, largely because he came to control access to the Führer. Where Hitler was, morning noon and night, there was Bormann. The refined architect frankly loathed the vulgarian peasant, a feeling which was reciprocated. Bormann was also the one leading Nazi whom Speer completely failed to manipulate, suborn or otherwise win over.

Hitler rose late, briefed himself and presided over a protracted and late lunch served by tough SS bodyguards bursting out of their waiters' uniforms. There would follow a half-hour stroll along a narrow path to the teahouse, perched on a cliff overlooking Berchtesgaden. Here in particular, apparently, Hitler liked to indulge his propensity for endless monologues so boring that on occasion he even sent himself to sleep. At about 6 p.m. the party rose and made its way to the car park twenty minutes away, to be driven back to Hitler's house by a motorcade which wound its way up Bormann's intricate and expensive mountain roads. There was a two-hour interlude before the usual suspects assembled for a protracted supper in the dining room, followed by a film show in the 'salon', as was Hitler's post-prandial habit in Berlin also. He seldom went to bed before 2.30 a.m., whereupon the exhausted survivors of the evening got down to some serious drinking before staggering off to their own beds. Those with vital work to do went to the Berghof as rarely as possible.

Speer wrote that Hitler, ever the petty bourgeois, ordered Eva Braun to keep herself out of sight when German or foreign dignitaries were visiting; Speer would go and keep the self-effacing schoolmaster's daughter company in her private sitting room if he could get away. At the head of the Third Reich there was thus an intellectual empty space. The subdued atmosphere was only rarely relieved by levity among the inner entourage – Eva and his personal staff were the only people Hitler allowed to take even the slightest conversational liberty, presumably because it would not affect his total control over their lives; from anyone else it would have been unthinkable *lèse majesté*. Hitler unsurprisingly liked to dominate, which among other adverse consequences meant he would not tolerate overtly intelligent women around him, a preference which compounded the banality and boredom of his court.

A modicum of relief from this tedium was provided by the personal friendships that developed among some members of the entourage. The Speers were close to SS-General Dr Karl Brandt, a personal physician to Hitler and overlord of the euthanasia programme and low-temperature experiments on prisoners. Gretel Speer and Anni Brandt became closest friends; doubtless they did not dwell on Brandt's special contributions to the appalling history of the German medical profession, which got him hanged after the trial of the SS doctors at Nuremberg. Speer's own closest friend at court was Hitler's aristocratic Luftwaffe adjutant, Lieutenant-Colonel Nicolaus von Below.

Hitler never lowered his guard, and there were barely half a dozen people with whom he was on 'Du' terms – permitted to use the informal second-person pronoun reserved by the German language for a child, one's spouse, a close relative, an intimate friend, a pet and God. Speer was not among Hitler's *Dutzfreunde:* he and the rest of the world were referred to as 'Sie', a mode of address so distant that it takes the third-person plural form of the verb – even if only one person is being spoken to.[9] But these conventions, unknown in English which only has 'you' for singular or plural, intimate or remote, are very useful for keeping people at arm's length in a country which even today is cautious about using first names. In the Obsersalzberg chapter of his memoirs, Speer reasonably concludes that he never broke through the final barrier which would have made him truly Hitler's friend, as such a connection is commonly understood.

Almost nothing is known about the nature of Hitler's intimacy with Eva Braun when they were alone together, although there has been much prurient speculation. Speer merely notes that this surprisingly spirited woman had enough humour to refer to herself ironically as 'mother of the country' whereas Hitler called her his *Tschapperl*, Austrian dialect for dimwit.

With one or more young children to look after constantly from 1934, Gretel Speer had little time to fritter away at the Berghof. The same applied to her workaholic husband, who wrote how much he resented the huge waste of time and energy involved: he complained that he was frequently summoned to the Berghof by Hitler's overzealous aides, who were prone to interpret a casual, 'Where is Speer?' as a *Führerbefehl* (order) to have him flown in at once from wherever he might be. On his breathless arrival, Hitler was often surprised to see him and might well have nothing to discuss.

Speer's time was especially short after the first anniversary of his elevation to GBI for Berlin, the fifth of his master's accession. At the end of January 1938 Hitler invited Speer – it was not couched as a command – to build him a huge new Chancellery by 10 January 1939, the date of the New Year reception for the diplomatic corps. Speer was bowled over; there had been no hint of such a plan, and the deadline was a formidable challenge. None the less, after a few hours' reflection, Speer inevitably took it on, promising to have it ready for use on 9 January. He was given the entire length of the Voss-strasse as the southerly side of an oblong site of sixteen hectares, including an enclosed garden on the northerly side. Its position was a little to the south and east of the proposed grand square and the long, relatively low building was the only part of the Speer/Hitler grand design for Berlin that was actually built and put to use (although it would have been employed for lesser purposes once Germania was complete, as Speer intended to build an even larger Chancellery on his big square). It was demolished after the war, leaving only a grassed-over mound.

Only three storeys high at the front on Voss-strasse, the new Reich Chancellery nevertheless was entirely in keeping with the untrammelled gigantism favoured by Speer and his client. Its frontage was 400 metres long, stretching from the Wilhelmplatz at the junction with the Wilhelmstrasse in the east to the edge of the Tiergarten park in the west. There were to be 420 rooms in a straggling building that boasted an internal volume of 360,000 cubic metres.

The ceremonial entrance on the Wilhelmplatz at the eastern end led into an open 'court of honour' where distinguished guests were received. The outsize features of the building included a south-facing marble gallery which, size being everything, was twice as long as the Hall of Mirrors at Versailles, though perhaps a shade less understated. Behind the central expanse of this gallery, on its northern side, was Hitler's vast study, twenty-seven metres by fourteen and a half, two storeys high – featuring five pairs of tall French windows opening on to a patio looking north over the garden. The patio boasted a pair of outsize bronze horses by Josef Thorak, who thus appears to have found another use for Hitler's gift, the overpriced stallion Rheinfried.

Externally, the Chancellery was in the pared-down neo-classical style. The south-eastern corner, including the façade on the Wilhelmplatz, was the only part of the edifice that was not built from scratch. Speer incorporated the outside of a building designed by the Wilhelmine architect Eduard Jobst Siedler, which boasted windows with tops like Roman arches and pilastered casements with Greek-style pediments over the top (in every sense). He drove the double entrance doors through the Wilhelmplatz side and also added a balcony at first-floor level, so that Hitler could come straight out of his apartment to greet a crowd.

The bronze door into the building proper, reached by crossing the court of honour eastwards, was attained via a flight of ten steps and a portico with four unornamented pillars. The entrance was flanked by a pair of crude, glowering bronzes more than twice as large as life, each of a barrel-chested, thick-necked, nude male in a rather camp posture, with outer arm holding out a torch and inner arm wafting ineffectually at waist level. In photographs these totalitarian statues look ill at ease with their own nakedness, with every good reason. Above the door they guarded was a bas-relief stone eagle, its wings half open. The portico and the pillared recesses on the long walls of the court of honour were lit up at night from within by concealed lamps, as in Speer's Paris pavilion a year earlier. The floor of the court was paved in square flagstones of light dolomite limestone, picked out by a grid of darker lines lengthwise and crosswise, making a pattern of squares within squares, just like Speer's windows.

Speer was also in complete charge of the interior design of this, his most ambitious completed project. The decor was suitably elaborate but is most interesting for harking back, unexpectedly perhaps, to the work of his father. Albert Speer Senior had been commissioned more than thirty years earlier to design a new building for the Rheinische Creditbank in Mannheim. According to an illustrated article in a 1917 issue of a Berlin design periodical, *Wohnungskunst* (housing-art), the bank had French windows and chandeliers clearly influenced by Versailles, ornate ceilings, pilasters and romanesque features. The overall effect, though obviously on a comparatively modest scale, clearly foreshadowed the son's heavily ornate Chancellery (but when Albert Senior saw the Berlin reconstruction plans his only recorded comment was, 'You've all gone completely crazy!'). Speer chose panelled bronze doors with ornamental surrounds vaguely reminiscent of classical or ancient Egyptian models. Lavish use was made of the most expensive marbles for floors and walls.[10]

He devoted special attention to the windows, all of which were strictly rectilinear, divided and subdivided into squares by bronzed metal frames (Speer had done some work on a doctoral thesis on the history of the window, which he would take up again in prison before abandoning it altogether). If Speer needed a stylistic trademark, these oblong windows with their square panels might have served: he used them in almost every building he designed, including his Berlin and Berghof houses, the orangerie at the Chancellery and elsewhere (the Bauhaus preferred horizontal oblong subdivisions for windows but also used metal frames).

Many photographs survive, some in colour, of the 1938 Chancellery.[11] The influence of Versailles (perhaps as seen through a glass darkly) is clear throughout the interior, especially in the inordinately long marble gallery. It had a shiny green floor and a long row of deeply recessed French windows framed in pink and green marble, as were the doors; there were tight bunches of rigidly vertical electric 'candles' standing to attention on the walls between them. Despite the many windows, the reflective floor and the light stucco of the plain ceiling and walls (lined with large tapestries rather than mirrors), the overall effect, even with sunlight coming in, is crushingly heavy. The adjacent mosaic hall, designed and supervised by Hermann Kaspar, was even more gloomy; the opaque, backlit glass ceiling could not compensate for the complete absence of windows. A colour photograph of the interior of the nearby rotunda looks as though it was taken through rose-tinted spectacles: the lavish use of dark pink marble gives an overwhelming impression of diluted blood running down the walls, like a chapel converted into an abattoir.

Hitler's study is no less overpowering, with its walls lined by dark red marble from Limburg and its coffered ceiling of light rosewood panels framed in darker palisander. The main door was to the south, and the visitor was made to trek a dozen metres before arriving in front of the desk in the north-west corner (a form of tyrannical grandiosity superbly parodied by Charles Chaplin in *The Great Dictator*). This unhomely item of furniture faced west and was four metres wide. A high-backed, padded leather chair that might have been filched from the Bauhaus stood behind it; two or three brocaded armchairs stood in front; a large brass lamp stood on top; a bucolic arras hung behind; a geometric-pattern carpet lay beneath.

Desk and matching sideboard with outsize ormolu carriage-clock recall the French Imperial style except for their distorted proportions (they are inevitably too long for their height, or too low for their length; had their heights been proportionate, Hitler might have been able to look over them, but not if he was sitting down at the time).

In front of the centre of the north wall, interestingly for 1938, was a marble map-table five metres wide which undoubtedly came in handy when Hitler began to swallow up Europe shortly after moving in. To the right was a conference area in front of a gigantic fireplace; a sofa as wide as the map-table faced the fire, with an arc of matching chairs to either side. A huge globe stood in the north-east corner of the room, awaiting the time when Hitler would make his bid to dominate it. One may assume that he personally ordered this item of equipment; there was no reason why Speer should have thought of supplying such an aid to aggression. The tabletop was a single slab of marble fourteen centimetres thick, measuring 5 by 1.65 metres and resting on five bulky trestles and a single support at each end, all made of elaborately inlaid, darker marble. The map-table stood in front of the centre window looking towards the orangerie.

Hitler frequently appeared unannounced to inspect his new working environment but hardly ever proposed an alteration. Speer wrote[12] that one reason behind his chief's unbridled impatience to have the building finished was hypochondria. What sounds remarkably like a 'nervous stomach' or a chronic digestive disorder led Hitler to believe that he would not live long. He rejected the advice of his young physician, Dr Brandt, that he should undergo a thorough internal investigation by specialists. Instead he turned to eccentric, self-prescribed vegetarian diets and then to Dr Theodor Morrell, a friend of Heinrich Hoffmann, Hitler's personal photographer, who swore by him after a possibly coincidental recovery from a grave illness for which he prescribed. Morrell was no more than a quack bacteriologist who gave Hitler a series of nostrums, administered by tablet and injection, which at first seemed to assuage the Führer's symptoms. Göring, himself no stranger to pills and hypodermics, dubbed Morrell Reichspritzmeister (jab-master). Morrell joined the inner circle round Hitler for the duration, probably making a major contribution to Germany's eventual defeat. Speer himself went to see Morrell in this period at his smart, Kurfürstendamm consulting rooms because he was run down by overwork. He was duly prescribed a cocktail of pills and vitamins but prudently sought a second opinion from Professor Gostav von Bergmann, an internal specialist, who simply prescribed a reduced workload. The youthful Speer made a rapid recovery, which he sycophantically ascribed to the unswallowed pills of Dr Morrell, who thus rose even higher in Hitler's esteem. Eva Braun thought Morrell was just a dirty old man.[13]

Hitler's own recovery proved shortlived and he constantly predicted an early death for himself, which fear instilled an even greater sense of urgency in him, whether about the completion of the Chancellery or of the planned conquests. He had sought to commit his eventual successor to a programme for world domination in a political testament drawn up as early as November 1937; he drafted his will in May 1938. The state of the Führer's mind, as influenced by his internal organs at this time, cannot have been unconnected with the gravity and gathering pace of political events at home and abroad, to which we shall return shortly.

Speer had a force of 8,000 craftsmen and labourers working in two shifts, 4,500 on the site and the rest working on materials, fixtures and fittings elsewhere, to fulfil his promise that the new Chancellery would be ready by 9 January 1939. The job was completed on the 7th, Speer having allowed himself the two days of the weekend as a reserve to cope with any last-minute hitches. There were none, although Speer's taste for portents (as identified by 20:20 hindsight) led him to describe in his memoirs how workers broke Bismarck's neck while transporting his bust through the new building. Speer suppressed the 'omen' and quietly commissioned the leading German sculptor of the day, Arno Breker, to make a replica which was 'aged' by soaking in tea.[14]

Hitler flew up from Munich on the 7th to take possession and was delighted by Speer's miraculous punctuality, objecting only that the reception hall should be three times the size (this was done within a year). Always prone to *Schadenfreude*, he was very amused by Speer's worry that foreign dignitaries, on their long march to be officially received, might slip on the polished, bare floors of the ceremonial rooms, taking the view that diplomats should be able to negotiate slippery surfaces (Hitler alone knew that he himself would soon ensure they had the greatest difficulty in maintaining their mental equilibrium). He also liked the inlaid half-drawn sword motif on his desk, which would surely scare any diplomat who had managed to keep his feet: Speer does not explain how this aggressive symbol got there, even as he takes credit for including, however vainly, representations of Wisdom, Prudence, Fortitude and Justice in the panelling over the study doors.

The scarcely less luxurious (though markedly smaller) cabinet room was also much admired, but never used for its official purpose. Cabinet government was dead in Germany. The momentarily contented client rewarded his architect with a celebratory dinner, the Nazi Party's Golden Badge and one of his own watercolours painted in Vienna in 1909 (Speer later described it ungraciously as characterless). Hitler formally opened the building on 10 January and later in the day held his New Year diplomatic reception in the marbled caverns of his new headquarters, which incorporated an air-raid shelter installed as the foundations were dug: the bombing of Guernica in Spain by the Luftwaffe in April 1937, an early instance of indiscriminate urban aerial bombardment, had been prudently recognised as a portent.

6

Evicting the Jews

(1938–41)

THE REMILITARISATION OF THE RHINELAND in March 1936 was followed by the formation of the pariah alliance which was to play the role of aggressor in the Second World War. Mussolini's Fascist Italy turned its back on the national tradition of Anglophilia to form the 'Rome-Berlin Axis' with the Nazis, formalised in October 1936. Exactly one month later, on 25 November, Germany and Japan signed the 'Anti-Comintern Pact', a political alliance against the Soviet Union and international Communism. This triangle was cemented by rampant expansionism, alarming and eventually uniting nearly all the other major powers against the Axis.

Having entrenched his dictatorship at home by extending the Enabling Act of 1934 in January 1937, Hitler spent the rest of the year preparing for war. In September he denounced the Treaty of Versailles and removed all restraint on rearmament. Having already disposed of the fatally divided left as the Nazis' only political rival for power, Hitler rounded on the military, the only institution capable of ending his control. Field Marshal Werner von Blomberg, Minister of Defence and Commander-in-Chief of the Wehrmacht, and General Werner von Fritsch, C-in-C of the army, were both dismissed in February 1938, the one for marrying an alleged prostitute and the other for falsely imputed homosexuality. Hitler assumed personal command of the Wehrmacht that month. Its members had been swearing loyalty to Hitler himself rather than the state since Hindenburg's death in 1934.

It was in the same year that Hitler had made his first bid for Austria, an idea specifically forbidden by the postwar settlement. When the Austro-Hungarian Empire was wound up in 1919, the majority of Austrians (i.e. the contemporary inhabitants of what is now the Federal Republic of Austria) favoured eventual union with Germany. The idea of *Anschluss* was an issue long before Hitler came to power. The

Weimar Republic and the Vienna government got as far in March 1931 as agreeing on a customs union (precursor of unification, whether German in the nineteenth century or European in the late twentieth). The French objected, as did such former components of the Habsburg Empire as Czechoslovakia, Romania and Yugoslavia ('the Little Entente'). The International Court at The Hague declared the plan contrary to international law because of Versailles – by a majority of eight judges to seven.

Unfazed by this tepid rebuff, Hitler took up *Anschluss* as soon as he assumed power. Thus encouraged, local Nazis assassinated the Austrian Chancellor, Engelbert Dollfuss, in his office on 25 July 1934. The ensuing coup was foiled by the police. Hitler continued to back the Austrian Nazis even as he signed a treaty recognising Austrian independence in 1936. In February 1938 the successor to Dollfuss, Kurt von Schuschnigg, invited to Berchtesgaden, was browbeaten by his erstwhile compatriot, who wanted political concessions for the Nazis. Appeasement was at its inglorious nadir and Schuschnigg, knowing there was no hope of support from Britain or France, yielded; but then he went home and spiritedly called a referendum on national independence.

Hitler sent troops to the border and on 11 March issued an ultimatum demanding Schuschnigg's resignation in favour of the Austrian Nazi leader, Arthur Seyss-Inquart. Schuschnigg, having cancelled the plebiscite in an attempt to buy off the relentless Hitler, resigned. On Göring's suggestion the Austrians invited the Wehrmacht to 'restore order'. The crude annexation was retrospectively 'legitimised' by a plebiscite of a different sort: over ninety-nine per cent of the electorate purportedly voted *Ja* to a single question approving both the *Anschluss* and the Nazi Party's list of Austrian candidates for the Greater German Reichstag.

Having regained sovereignty in the Rhineland by acting with boldness and vigour while others vacillated, so Hitler acquired it over Austria. Huge crowds turned out to welcome the German army (giving rise to the barb that Austrians could not decide whether they were conquered or liberated in 1945; there was certainly no keener Nazi than an Austrian one).

Hitler's step-by-step programme for the expansion of Greater Germany now envisaged mopping up those parts of other countries which had been German or had significant German minorities which he could use as stalking horses. The next item on this quite logical if also bullying agenda was the Sudetenland, the largely German-speaking arc of western Bohemia in Czechoslovakia. Over three million Germanophones lived there, nearly a quarter of the Czechoslovak population, more than enough to lend enthusiastic support to the local Nazi Party led by Konrad Henlein. The region was rich in minerals and, by judicious manipulation of the map, could also be shown to contain Czechoslovakia's equivalent of the Maginot Line, a massive network of concrete fortifications in the Bohemian highlands, to be manned by thirty-five divisions – a formidable commitment by a small but efficient state. The Prague government of President Eduard Beneš also tried appeasement, but the more concessions it made to the Sudeteners and their German supporters, the more they demanded. Unlike Austria, Czechoslovakia's borders were guaranteed by both France and the Soviet Union.

Even before he had snapped up Austria, Hitler was telling the Reichstag of the 'dreadful conditions' of the Germans in Bohemia, whom he openly promised to 'defend'. A frontier incident in which several Germans were killed gave him an excuse to send troops to the border. The fine Czechoslovak army resolutely mobilised 400,000 troops and manned its bunkers. The French and the Russians made diplomatic protests while the British distanced themselves from a physically impossible intervention in a faraway country of which they knew little. Hitler backed off – for the moment. He left it to Henlein to raise the temperature still further by declaring Sudeten home rule in April 1938. Prague agreed to federalise the country on Swiss lines to give the Sudeteners autonomy, but nothing would appease Hitler now. He had told his generals secretly on 30 May that he would move against Czechoslovakia on 1 October.

By mid-September Hitler had ostentatiously ordered work to be stepped up on the Siegfried Line, opposite Maginot in the west, and promised to go to the aid of the Sudeten Germans. Neville Chamberlain, the British Prime Minister, flew to Berchtesgaden to 'reason' with Hitler. On his return, pausing only to consult Edouard Daladier, his French opposite number, and his own cabinet, Chamberlain on 20 September asked the Czechoslovaks to give in, for the sake of Europe. President Beneš, constitutional head of one of the best-equipped armies in the world, tragically agreed; his cabinet resigned. But Hitler was not satisfied when Chamberlain rejoined him on the Rhine at Bad Godesberg. Producing a map with the Sudetenland most generously drawn to include the fortifications, he said he would march in on 1 October unless granted all the lands marked. Beneš now refused. Mussolini called a conference for 29 September to 'mediate'. Hitler however made a honeyed speech on the 26th at the Sports Palace in Berlin. Having got Chamberlain's measure he promised that the Sudetenland was his last European territorial demand.

The hapless premier begged for mercy once more, this time in Munich, coming away on the 29th with the piece of paper promising 'peace in our time'. The rump of Czechoslovakia was defenceless and the Germans dominated central Europe. Nobody was surprised when the Wehrmacht on 15 March 1939 incorporated Bohemia and Moravia into a German 'protectorate'. Speer was inspecting the classical ruins of southern Italy at the time, in the company of some of his architects, Dr Brandt and the unhappy Magda Goebbels, routinely betrayed by her priapic cripple of a husband and comforting herself with Karl Hanke, Speer's first Nazi patron.

Czechoslovakia was erased from the map of Europe after twenty years as the most prosperous and progressive successor-state of the Austrian Empire. Eight days later the Wehrmacht marched from East Prussia into Memel, German until ceded to Lithuania in 1919. The occupation of Prague, however, put an end to appeasement in Britain. Rearmament, began reluctantly in 1936, now proceeded at an accelerating pace.

The next item on Hitler's agenda was crystal clear; indeed, he had obligingly announced it. He was unmistakably set on reversing the results of 1918, the most spectacular aspect of which was the loss of the Danzig–Posen (Gdansk–Poznan) region, giving Poland, independent of Russia since 1917, access to the Baltic. On 24 October 1938, less than a month after his 'final' territorial claim, Hitler demanded the return of the great Baltic 'free' city of Danzig on the Baltic coast with its majority at that time of ethnic Germans, plus land for an autobahn and railway to link East Prussia with Germany proper – a German corridor across the Polish Corridor. Shamed by Munich, Chamberlain offered the Poles a guarantee of their borders, thus also reviving the faltering French commitment to eastern Europe.

Diplomacy did not work with Hitler because he was not amenable to compromise. The British and French, compromisers to a fault, were unable to help Poland directly for reasons of geography, or indirectly (such as by attacking Germany from the west) for reasons of politics and psychology. They had no answer to Nazi aggression, simply refusing to understand that Hitler was totally ruthless and would never let up unless stopped in his tracks. When thwarted, as happened in Austria and Czechoslovakia, he would bide his time and return to the charge as soon as possible, supremely confident that his opponents would back down.

The German people did not want war and were hugely relieved when it did not come, a celebration easily transmogrified by Goebbels into triumphalism over the absorption of Czechoslovakia. Before sending his troops into Prague, Hitler summoned President Emil Hacha of 'Czechia' to his overbearing study in Speer's new Chancellery and so bullied him that he had a heart attack; Dr Morrell's intervention revived him to such effect that Hitler had to browbeat him all over again into 'allowing' the Wehrmacht in. 'Czechia' was wound up and the rump of Slovakia became an 'independent' puppet after part of it and ex-Czechoslovakia's easternmost province of Ruthenia were given to Hungary, whose fealty was thus bought by the Nazis.

This in turn put them in a position to 'influence' neighbouring Romania, whose government not unwillingly soon allowed the country, with its rich reserves of oil and grain, to become part of the new Greater German sphere of influence. Hitler had now gained control of an area nearly as large as that held by the Central Powers (Germany and the Austro-Hungarian Empire) in 1914 – without firing a shot. The abdication by the democracies at Munich was another powerful incentive to generalised amorality in Germany.

Shocks and upheavals abroad were matched by no less ominous developments within Germany. To his abiding credit, General Ludwig Beck, the new C-in-C of the German army, resigned over Czechoslovakia on 18 August 1938. No other general supported his attempt to halt Hitler's programme of calculated aggression; the last possible internal restraining factor was thus removed (Beck was to shoot himself when the belated officers' plot of 20 July 1944 failed to make him head of state).

When a German Jew shot one of Foreign Minister Joachim von Ribbentrop's diplomats in Paris in November 1938, it took Goebbels just two days to organise one of the most dramatic and sinister events in Germany's prewar history: the national pogrom untranslatably known as *Reichskristallnacht*, a chill reference to the showers of glass on urban streets all over Germany after Nazi-led thugs smashed and burned synagogues, Jewish businesses and even homes, killing at least 100 Jews.

All this apparently passed Speer by as he worked day and night to complete his Chancellery. He made no mention in his draft memoirs of this turning-point in the history of the Third Reich. It was only when prompted to do so by Joachim Fest, his editorial mentor, that he included a short passage on the events of 9 November 1938 in his final draft.[1] Even so, the passage is short and unexciting and Speer's description of his own reaction, limited to distress over the 'disorder' of it all, is banal and explicitly indifferent.[2] In scale, scope and significance the pogrom far outstripped the earlier horrors of 1934, such as Goebbels's public book-burning of liberal and/or 'Jewish' literature and the 'Night of the Long Knives', in which the Nazis attacked their own dissidents (to widespread non-Nazi applause). Speer wrote that Hitler washed his hands of the orgy of destruction and accused Goebbels, one of the most fanatical Nazi anti-Semites, of presenting him with a *fait accompli*. Speer exploits the atrocity as one of many chances to remind us of his 'apolitical' approach to his work: 'The task

I have to fulfil is an unpolitical one,' as he reminded Hitler in a memorandum as late as 1944.

The relevant passage in chapter eight of *Inside the Third Reich* merits close analysis as a preparation for the real record of Albert Speer's personal involvement in the persecution of the Jews later in this book. He writes that he reluctantly accepted Hitler's anti-Semitism as part of his character, par for the course and something the Führer himself seldom referred to when eating and talking with his entourage (a claim destroyed by the Goebbels diaries). Speer's ability to compartmentalise enabled him to separate the nature of the regime from the work he was doing for it and the character of the man who led it. We can take him at his word when he says he was quite capable of separating out the 'vulgar business', the distasteful anti-Jewish graffiti (and official notices, slogans and banners), the destruction of Jewish premises, the burnt-out shells of synagogues, from his 'idealised picture' of Hitler. He goes on: 'During the years after my release from Spandau I have been repeatedly asked ... what I actually knew of the persecution, the deportation and the annihilation of the Jews; what I should have known and what conclusions I ought to have drawn.' Yes indeed; this is the nub of the issue of Speer's credibility:

> I no longer give the answer with which I tried for so long to soothe the questioners but chiefly myself: that in Hitler's system, as in every total-itarian regime, when a man's position rises, his isolation increases and he is therefore more sheltered from harsh reality; that with the application of technology to the process of murder the number of murderers is reduced and therefore the possibility of ignorance grows; that the craze for secrecy built into the system creates different degrees of awareness, so it is easy to escape observing inhuman cruelties.

All this was no more than 'legalistic exculpation'. He was not to know that the pogrom would lead to Auschwitz – but he accepted that he had sidestepped the implications. 'Whether I knew or did not know, or how much or how little I knew, is totally unimportant when I consider what horrors I ought to have known about and what conclusions would have been the natural ones to draw from the little I did know.'[3]

This train of thought, triggered by the hint that he ought at least to refer to an event as seminal as *Reichskristallnacht*, is the quintessence of the image of himself that Speer presented to the world from the moment of his arrest in May 1945, as we shall see in due course. That he needed prompting to mention it at all is significant in itself. He could hardly have failed to notice that the murder of the diplomat which led to the pogrom was soon used to justify another batch of anti-Semitic statutes to add to the Nuremberg laws of 1935.

Abroad, Hitler continued to apply stick and carrot in order to keep the world off balance, wondering which way he would jump next. In December 1938 he had concluded a non-aggression pact with France, renouncing any claim to Alsace-Lorraine; three months later he contemptuously completed the dismantling of France's erstwhile client, Czechoslovakia. In April 1939, six months after demanding the return of Danzig, Hitler gave notice of termination of the German-Polish non-aggression treaty he had concluded, amid cynicism on either side and surprise elsewhere, in January 1934: both parties had known it was a postponement rather than a cancellation of the showdown over the corridor.

Responding to the sea-change in the public mood away from appeasement, Chamberlain offered guarantees not only to Poland but also to Romania and Greece. Hitler, understandably, did not take his co-signatory of the abject Munich agreement seriously. The party press whipped up a storm about alleged persecution by the Poles of their German minority; the Poles went so far as a partial mobilisation in response. Hitler ordered the Wehrmacht to draw up 'Plan White' for an invasion of his eastern neighbour and in May concluded the military 'Pact of Steel' with Mussolini.

There was to be one more bilateral deal which shines through the intervening decades as the most cynical of them all. On 23 August 1939, even as the Anglo-French were seeking to reach an accommodation with the Soviet Union, Hitler and Stalin concluded the Nazi-Soviet non-aggression pact, in the full understanding that it too was a postponement rather than a cancellation of an inevitable confrontation. Germany's ally in the anti-Comintern pact, Japan, was staggered; when Tokyo retaliated in April 1941 by making a similar arrangement with Moscow without consulting Berlin, Hitler's fate would be sealed. But his pact with Stalin was supplemented by a simultaneous secret protocol agreeing to carve up Poland and giving Stalin a free hand in the trio of little Baltic states (Estonia, Latvia, Lithuania) which had, like Poland and Finland, broken away when the tsar was usurped by the revolution. Polish resistance, immortalised in hopelessly gallant pictures of cavalry charging German tanks, collapsed one calendar month after the Wehrmacht used a faked border incident as its excuse for invasion on 1 September 1939.

Hitler was genuinely surprised, even stunned into silence, according to Speer, when Britain and France declared war over Poland on the 3rd. Poland was however dismembered, part reclaimed by the Reich, part by the Soviet Union and the rump formed into the Nazis' puppet 'General Government' zone. To crown their strangulation of just twenty years of Polish independence, Hitler and Stalin concluded a third pact, a friendship and frontier treaty, on 28 September. On this basis, Stalin

felt free to attack Finland on 30 November, only to see the Finns make
fools of the Red Army in a brilliant defence that endured for three and
a half months before they were forced to give in. Neutral Finland (the
western democracies sent volunteers to help resist Hitler's then 'friend'
Stalin) tragically lost its eastern territories to Russia and perforce
became Hitler's ally (on the principle that 'my enemy's enemy is my
friend') when he invaded the Soviet Union in June 1941.

In the west, a small British Expeditionary Force took its place on the
left of the French army facing Germany, just as in 1914. For seven
months there was a 'Phoney War'; then Hitler launched another
Blitzkrieg on his Polish model by attacking Denmark and Norway in
April 1940. The Anglo-French response was ineffectual and chaotic.
Chamberlain, humiliated by Norway and his own ineffectiveness
against a fiendish enemy, was replaced by Winston Churchill, a man
of an altogether sterner stamp, on 10 May – the very day that Hitler
hurled the Wehrmacht at the Netherlands, Belgium and Luxembourg,
all neutral, and France itself in a third round of *Blitzkrieg*.

The strategy was – as in 1914 – to seize a quick victory in the west
before preparing for the main event, the invasion of the Soviet Union,
to gain access to all the *Lebensraum* and Jews Germany could handle.
The conquest of Poland had already cleared the way, not only to
Soviet-held territory but also to a large proportion of the Jews he
planned to exterminate: the first move against them outside Germany
was the creation of the compulsory, enclosed ghetto at Lodz in April
1940. France fell on 22 June, giving Hitler his chance to reverse the
shame of 1918 by requiring the armistice with the French to be signed
in the same railway carriage at the same place as in 1918: the forest
of Compiègne, north of Paris. Britain, despite the retreat of its disarmed
army across the Channel, rejected all Nazi blandishments and stood
alone for exactly a year, until Hitler repeated the Kaiser's mistake by
opening a second front without closing the first.

Meanwhile Professor Albert Speer (the title was conferred by Hitler
personally as another mark of esteem in 1936) was flexing his muscles,
an increasingly important player in the dangerous game of power
politics in Berlin. As an 'apolitical technocrat', he was taking to the
new role of high state functionary as if born to it, to the awe of the
coterie of architects and others he had drawn round himself since
becoming Hitler's favourite architect. That he was no slouch at the
political in-fighting encouraged by Hitler's calculated distribution of
overlapping or opposed areas of responsibility is shown by Speer's
ruination of the lord mayor of Berlin, Dr Lippert, for resisting Speer's
grandiose plans for the capital. It was a classic Third Reich demarcation
dispute caused by the deliberately vague boundaries of rival fiefs.

The confrontation erupted in the middle of 1938 when Speer's office announced its intention of demolishing the building of the Berlin Association of Architects and Engineers to make way for new construction. A senior civil servant and engineer, Dr Konrad Nonn, on hearing of this from Dr Lippert, protested to the Minister of the Interior, Wilhelm Frick. An appeal to Speer himself naturally fell on deaf ears. Goebbels, Lippert's patron, noted disapprovingly in his diary on New Year's Day 1939: 'Hanke [now state secretary in the propaganda ministry] ... gives me an account of a disgraceful attack that Speer is planning against Lippert in the newspapers. I did not mince my words when I gave my opinion. Wonderful: too cowardly to attack him openly, so he stabs him in the back. Very nice. Nobody can get away with that kind of thing where I am concerned.'[4]

Speer wrote to Lippert on 1 June 1940, arrogantly informing him that, as they could not agree on the postwar reconstruction of Berlin, he would settle the matter by decree. The importance of the work, Speer claimed, gave him absolute priority and his office as GBI gave him supreme authority for the task; there was no room for compromise, negotiation or deals. Lippert replied that he was fully prepared to cooperate but the building plans imposed impossible strains on the city budget. Further, the law imposed unity of administration and clear lines of responsibility in municipal government; yet here was an outside authority effectively imposing its will on a city department. Four days later, on 28 June, Speer cited Hitler's 1937 decree making him GBI for Berlin as his authority for a decree of his own. This simply stated that he was entitled to give orders to the mayor about the north–south and east–west axes, the new residential areas and university campus as well as several residential districts.

A ruthlessly determined Speer took the opportunity of his next visit to the Obersalzberg on 16 July to complain to Hitler about Lippert's alleged obstructionism and stubbornness. Hitler ordered Bormann, as his secretary, to tell Lammers, promoted to Minister in the Chancellery, to dismiss Lippert. The mayor was duly sacked, putting Goebbels's nose severely out of joint.

As Paul Ludwig Troost's successor in the role of Hitler's personal architect, Speer had as his main responsibility the city of Nuremberg, locus of the party congress and rallies, until he became GBI, which brought him the even more important, ideologically central task of converting Berlin into Germania. All this gave him much more power and influence than Troost had ever enjoyed. Yet Munich, second only to Berlin in its designated role as capital of the Nazi movement and originally Troost's special responsibility, had been entrusted, not to Speer as his successor but to Hermann Giesler, self-taught architect and brother of the Gauleiter of Munich. Speer however took the view that Munich should be his because it had been Troost's.

But Giesler, aged forty-five, was formally confirmed by a Führer decree as 'Counsellor-General for Construction for the Capital of the Movement' in December 1938, directly answerable to Hitler for rebuilding Munich, just as a jealous Speer was for Berlin as GBI. It was another demonstration of Hitler's predilection for 'divide and rule', setting one office-holder against another. Even his favourite architect was not spared such encouragement to jealousy. On the Führer's orders, Munich too was to have its grand axis, lined with overbearing buildings such as a new KdF (Strength through Joy) headquarters and a party publishing house, plus monuments at each end and a new station with huge dome; existing rail tracks were to be displaced to make room for reconstruction. A party 'victory monument' 250 metres high and an autobahn ring were also to be imposed on the Bavarian metropole, which was to be a 'centre of European culture' as well. The details were left to Giesler. The special significance of Munich had already been literally cast in stone by Troost's work in the area round the Königsplatz, including the party and Führer buildings, party shrines and the House of Art.[5]

Giesler had won Hitler's favour by designing the party training college at Sonthofen in Bavaria and other party facilities at the Gau capitals of Augsburg in Bavaria and Weimar in Thuringia. When Giesler was entrusted by Hitler in autumn 1940 with the principal role in the replanning of Linz, the dictator's favourite Austrian provincial city, to which he planned to retire and donate a vast gallery full of plundered art, Speer was positively alarmed. He came to regard the Bavarian architect as a dangerous rival who needed to be put in his place. He therefore drafted a decree conferring upon himself the power to supervise all major planning projects throughout the Reich as 'Führer's Commissioner for Architectural Art and City Planning', transcending party authority in urban construction.

At this point Bormann, himself jealous of Speer's swift rise to power and esteem, took a hand behind the scenes, sympathising with Giesler to such an extent that he was moved to make a written protest against Speer's blatant empire-building. The latter thereupon realised that he had been pushing his luck and withdrew, settling for an 'overview' of major works planned for the forty-one Gau capitals (which included all the towns ultimately designated 'reconstruction cities') and limiting his direct supervisory role to Nuremberg and Berlin. He had found the limit of his authority and influence in the Byzantine world of Nazi intrigue, and its name was Bormann.

Speer rationalised his retreat in a *démarche* to Hitler at the Berghof on the Obersalzberg in January 1941, after a slow recovery from a kidney infection.[6] He now officially took the view that it would be inappropriate for him to take responsibility for the party's urban projects in detail. A successfully completed plan would redound to the credit of the relevant architect, whereas a failure would undoubtedly be laid at his door (not the argument of a naïve, apolitical technocrat). 'It would thus be a thankless task.' What was more, such direct supervision was becoming a major burden; a formal commission extending this role would merely make things worse. It would be better both for the wellbeing of the relevant tasks and for himself 'if I could broadly stand back from these duties'. Speer could then concentrate on his 'life's work', the Berlin and Nuremberg projects. In the official record of his *Führerbesprechungen* (conferences with Hitler) Speer notes that the Führer emphatically and heartily agreed with this distancing move, saying that it would be a pity if Speer were to lose himself in such matters, even if he 'would not be able to avoid giving advice from time to time'. But Hitler ruled that it would be left to Speer, at his own request, to decide when and how. Speer also gave up his party posts at 'Beauty of Labour' and as 'Commissioner for Construction of Party and Labour-Front Buildings' at this point.[7]

Speer and Giesler however remained close enemies, as is shown by a request from Bormann to Speer a whole year later, at the end of January 1942, that he should make it up with the Bavarian.[8] In March Speer finally agreed it was absurd that the two architects should still be ignoring each other on public occasions; it would be good if collegial relations could be restored. He formally withdrew his allegation that Giesler had indulged in plotting against him behind his back (a case of the pot calling the kettle black) and protested that he had never questioned his rival's professional reputation. But Speer ordered his team of architects not to work on a Giesler project without his permission.

Giesler (his name is misspelled in Speer's memoirs, which make only a passing reference to the dispute) never became a threat to Speer's position as chief court architect, although his planning workload was not significantly lighter. In addition to such pet projects of Hitler's as Munich and Linz, Giesler was in charge of major construction work in Weimar, Goethe's chosen home and thus Germany's equivalent to Stratford-on-Avon (Hitler also wanted to impose his will on the city which had produced the constitution of the lost republic: the jewel of Thuringia was thus awarded its very own Adolf-Hitler-Platz). Speer was cunning and petty enough to use his control over allocations of such materials as steel to hamper Giesler's work in Munich in 1939.[9]

Giesler and Speer were obliged to make the best of each other's enforced company for a unique occasion at the end of June 1940. At that time

Hitler's temporary headquarters were in a village outside the northern French town of Sedan, scene of so many Franco-German clashes; the armistice of 22 June was due to come into effect in the early hours of the 25th. Like Giesler, Speer was summoned to HQ on the 24th so that he could accompany Hitler on a private tour of surrendered Paris. Speer asked if Germany's leading contemporary sculptor, Arno Breker, could come too as an expert guide, a request which was granted. This turned out to be a rare chance for Speer to indulge his taste for both *Schadenfreude* and practical jokes, although the anecdote is missing from his memoirs.[10] Speer mischievously asked the Gestapo to go and fetch Breker. They refused to say where he was being taken on security grounds, which must have given the Nazi hammer- and chisel-smith a nasty few hours. Speer found this cruel jape highly amusing.

His own account of the short trip to France mentions dining with Hitler and his generals on the preceding evening in a commandeered peasant cottage. It must have been an unusually vivid memory, even for someone as close to the centre of power in the Third Reich and as unemotional as Speer. Moments before the armistice was due to go into effect at 1.35 a.m. on the 25th, Hitler ordered the lights turned off and the windows opened. A bugler outside blew the ceasefire. Sheet lightning flashed somewhere in the distance, though no thunder could be heard in the room.[11] Speer's taste for omens had been no less well served at the time of the signature of the Nazi-Soviet pact, when the Northern Lights had been seen over the Berghof, unusually far south. While waiting to accompany Hitler to Paris, Speer seized the chance of making a flying visit to Rheims, where the French kings were crowned and buried and where they kept the *oriflamme*, the national battle-standard.

At last, at 3 a.m. on the 28th, Hitler and his three-man artistic entourage left in a small motorcade for a local military airfield, from which they flew to Le Bourget airport on the outskirts of Paris. The trio were dressed as army officers because Hitler would allow no civilians to be seen with him on conquered territory. They were driven into the heart of the city in three Mercedes-Benz limousines. Paris was already illuminated by the early daylight of midsummer but was totally silent. The little group of jackbooted Germans thus joined the exiguous ranks of those who have seen the Place de la Concorde devoid of traffic and Parisians.

Hitler's first stop on a three-hour tour was at the over-ornate Paris Opéra, where he performed a feat of memory. Although he had never set foot in Paris before, he knew every nook and cranny of the theatre and, of course, every measurement of Charles Garnier's neo-baroque extravaganza. Hitler loved it and was highly excited by a long-anticipated experience. To his everlasting honour, the French usher who accompanied the *Herrenvolk* round the building politely refused Hitler's proffered fifty-mark tip – twice. The next stop was the Eiffel Tower, doubtless irresistible for being the largest metal structure in the world. Then came Les Invalides, where Hitler stood in silence for a long moment before the tomb of his predecessor and only modern rival in the business of uniting Europe by force. Worshippers studiously took no notice when Hitler and his entourage looked briefly into the Sacré Coeur basilica, the nineteenth-century medieval pastiche in Montmartre and the last stop on Hitler's only visit to Paris.

Back in the requisitioned cottage that night, Hitler, once again swollen with conquest, ordered Speer to draft a decree to resume reconstruction of Berlin. He had decided, he said loftily, to outbuild Haussmann in Berlin rather than destroy his Paris. The decree was backdated to 25 June, the official date of France's humiliation at his hands. The whole experience of defeating the French and personally taking symbolic possession of their beautiful capital had clearly produced ecstasy in the conqueror. The war was specifically not to be allowed to delay the Berlin plans. Speer decided to concentrate on what he defined as 'the Führer's immediate programme', the core buildings round the Adolf-Hitler-Platz. Göring secretly diverted 84,000 tons of steel from the war effort, pretending it was required for rail and waterway purposes. None the less, serious work never began and Allied bombers would soon swamp the preparatory demolitions in a wider sea of rubble.

Three months later Germany, Italy and Japan concluded their 'Three-Power Pact', a political statement rather than a military alliance (never concluded between Japan and its European allies, an omission that was a great relief for the Allies in the Middle East and India). At this period the fighting was concentrated in and around the Mediterranean as Hitler prepared his greatest gamble and mightiest round of *Blitzkrieg*, the attack on the Soviet Union.

Towards the end of 1940 Rudolf Wolters suggested to Speer that he start a 'Chronicle' of the GBI. Speer agreed, instructing heads of departments and sections to supply Wolters with raw material for this semi-official diary of the 'Speer *Dienststellen* [offices]'. It is thus a rather more important, because more reliable, historical source for Speer's governmental career than his memoirs. It was compiled by someone else, albeit an admirer (at the time), from his own and others' first-hand contributions and it was not intended for public consumption. This is not to say that the Chronicle was written without posterity in mind – on the contrary. But it included risqué material that would never have found its way into official records in the Third Reich,

with its informer culture and its brusque way with dissidents. Before
exploring Speer's main work for Hitler, the three years when he ran
the heart of the war economy (after all, the architecture was indifferent
or else unbuilt castles in the air), we may pause to consider the
Chronicle itself, at the moment in our story when it becomes a key
source. There are at least three reasons for doing so.

Unlike the other main sources – the vast body of papers from
Speer's department, the protocols of his meetings with Hitler, other
administration and party sources and Speer's writings – the Chronicle
was not intended for external eyes when it was written. Second, it was
compiled by a man at the centre of the events it describes, from reports
by those who made them happen and as an informal counterpoint to
the official record, checked not only by contributors but also by Speer.
Finally the Chronicle, and the abortive effort by Wolters and Speer to
'sanitise' it, together make the complete version the principal (though
not the only) testimony to Speer's hypocrisy as self-appointed 'scapegoat
of the nation' at Nuremberg and 'duty national penitent' on his release
from Spandau (both terms were coined by Wolters). The unexpurgated
Chronicle is the centrepiece of the Wolters Bequest which, in its totality,
proves Speer's 'penitence' was false and shows he lied when he insisted
at his trial and in his memoirs that he bore no *personal* responsibility
for the Hitler regime's crimes against humanity but only his share of
collective responsibility as a Nazi leader of highest rank: *nostra* but
definitely not *mea culpa*.

Here, for example, is what was erased from the Chronicle entry for
April 1941 by Wolters on behalf of Speer, who let the passage stand
at the time it was written but later endorsed the excision by handing
over the cut version to the German Federal Archive. The damning
paragraph, the first of many omissions, describes the work of the GBI's
Resettlement Department, formed in spring 1939 and led by Dietrich
Clahes, former presiding minister of the state of Brunswick. It is
translated by the present author and is quoted here in full:

> The rate of clearance of the demolition areas and the resettling of local
> tenants in Jew-flats was increased from the beginning of the year. The
> Jew-flats rented from local landlords were cleared and the Jewish tenants
> were packed into Jewish living space on Jewish-owned land. The purpose
> of this clearance of the areas, vital for the war effort, was to make the
> cleared areas of flats in the Reich capital available for catastrophe purposes
> (air-raid damage). In the period from 1.1 to 15.4.41 a total of 366
> tenants in areas 4, 9, 12, 14 and 25 were required to resettle. Further,
> in the same period, about 1,000 rooms were allocated to some fifty offices
> and plants for purposes vital to the war effort.

*

Meanwhile, in North Africa, the British had the beating of the Italians well in hand until the Germans irrupted into the theatre, sending Rommel's Afrika Korps to Libya to shore up a collapsing Italian army in February 1941. British defeats in Greece and Crete as well as serious setbacks in North Africa ensued.

At the same time Speer's most dangerous opponent in the Nazi hierarchy, Martin Bormann, established himself at the centre of power: to be precise, in May 1941, when the unbalanced Deputy Führer, Rudolf Hess, flew himself to Britain on an abortive 'peace mission'. This attempt at an accommodation with Britain on the eve of the invasion of Russia may have been the product of an unbalanced mind but was entirely in keeping with the oft-expressed wish of Hitler, who none the less promptly disowned Hess. Having succeeded him as Hitler's private secretary, Bormann now also became the second man in the party, though with a different title: Head of the Party Chancellery, with the top party rank of Reichsleiter, all of which left him in command of the forty-one Gauleiters and, even more important, of Hitler's appointments diary. Nobody, with the possible exception of Speer carrying a roll of architectural drawings, could now get to see Hitler without seeing Bormann first, a fact which made him the most powerful man at court until the end of the Third Reich.

By the beginning of 1941 a substantial Speer *Transportstandarte* (regiment) and a Speer *Transportflotte* (flotilla) had been formed and was already rapidly expanding. The former disposed of many hundreds, later thousands, of heavy trucks; the latter acquired 280 barges originally earmarked for the invasion of Britain to carry stone, marble and other building materials to Berlin; plans already existed to expand this fleet to 1,000. There was also a *Baustab Speer*, a building staff which was able to divert 6,000 workers to repairing bomb damage in Berlin as the RAF got into its destructive stride (the Chronicle wryly noted after a heavy night in April 1941: 'The English thus carried out valuable preliminary work for reconstruction purposes'). Chronicler Wolters was given the extra task by Speer in June 1941 of overseeing a special section of a state publishing house which was to produce architectural books and engravings under GBI auspices.

Will Nagel, once Speer's first party superior as head of the Nazi Driver Corps in Berlin-West, was now his chief of staff cum commander of the 'Speer Transport Brigade'. By mid-1941 the brigade comprised three uniformed 'regiments' run on paramilitary lines and manned largely by recruits considered to be on national service. All three units were sent to the Eastern Front soon after the massive onslaught on Russia. A fourth regiment was being formed to serve in North Africa and a fifth would see service in Crete and Sicily. The brigade operated close to the front and worked harmoniously with the Luftwaffe, which provided most of its equipment in exchange for deliveries of ammunition and fuel.

By August 1941, again in cooperation with Göring's air ministry, the GBI had added 30,000 air-raid shelters to Berlin's stock, raising capacity to about 1,887,000 people or getting on for half the population. Speer was now commissioned by Field Marshal Erhard Milch, Inspector-General of the Luftwaffe and already a close ally of Speer's, to build 83,800 more shelters so that 2.5 million of the four million inhabitants could take cover against the steadily increasing air-raids.

In the same month Speer opened a campaign within his own department against the spread of 'strolling bureaucratism', obviously the deadliest enemy of his own penchant for improvised organisation, his most important administrative gift. His three topmost department heads, Hettlage, Brugmann and Fränk, and one or two other senior officials accompanied him to Horchers Restaurant, Göring's favourite and the most exclusive in Berlin, for a curious little ceremony. Beforehand, Speer laid out his plans to delegate all but the most important decisions to his various departments. They and major outside projects would become all but autonomous. The half-dozen chiefs then repaired to the restaurant for a 'funeral' dinner: Hettlage produced a small coffin containing 'Bureaucracy' wrapped in a shroud of administrative paper. It later went on permanent display in his office as a reminder of good intentions.[12]

But the GBI's machinery for evicting Jews unashamedly bucked the anti-bureaucratic trend at this very period, as these passages from the Chronicle prove:[13]

In accordance with Speer's order, a further action was started to clear about 5,000 Jew-flats. The existing apparatus was appropriately enlarged so that the Jew-flats, despite the universal problems resulting from the war situation, could be made ready at top speed and filled with demolition tenants from the areas to be cleared most urgently. By these measures the Jew-flats were brought into use for their predetermined purpose and on the other hand further empty flats were made ready for catastrophe purposes [August 1941].

In the period from 18 October to 2 November in Berlin about 4,500 Jews were evacuated. Thus 1,000 more flats were cleared for bomb-damage victims and made available by the GBI. The flats were later readied for the accommodation of demolition tenants.

The third major action for the de-renting of Jew-flats was inaugurated at the end of November. After negotiations with participating authorities the GBI made available another 3,000 Jew-flats for the accommodation of possible bomb-damage victims [both passages from the entry for November 1941].

On 22 June 1941 Operation Barbarossa hurled the main strength of the German army at the Soviet Union, which was as roundly drubbed in the opening phase as Russia had been in 1914. Within months the Germans were at the gates of Moscow. But the Japanese had obtained revenge for the now shattered Nazi-Soviet rapprochement of 1939 on 13 April 1941, when Foreign Minister Matsuoka Yosuke concluded with panache a non-aggression pact between Moscow and Tokyo. He was able to do so because the Russians feared war with Germany and the Japanese feared there would not be one (which would have left Stalin free to intervene in the Far East once Japan had gone to war against western interests in the Pacific). Hitler was not informed and was duly furious, but did not even consider delaying or abandoning his surprise attack on the Russians. Yet Stalin's Japanese deal enabled him to pull Marshal Zhukov's tanks and artillery out of the Far East to save Moscow and impose a harsh winter on the Germans, giving the Russians a desperately needed breather.

Less than six weeks after Barbarossa, as if to confirm the close link between *Lebensraum* and anti-Semitism laid out in *Mein Kampf*, Göring ordered the SS to supervise the 'evacuation' of Europe's Jews (the first experiments with mass gassing took place at Auschwitz-Birkenau in September). In November 1941 Speer declined to take charge of construction of new cities in the occupied eastern territories, despite a request for his services from Alfred Rosenberg, the crazed Nazi 'philosopher' who had been appointed minister for the new *Lebensraum*. Instead, Speer made his last artistic tour abroad for a quarter of a century in that month, visiting neutral Portugal and Spain in conjunction with German architectural exhibitions mounted by Wolters.

As if to foreshadow his future ministerial role in war production, of which he could have had not the slightest inkling at this time, Albert Speer made two moves which arose from, but lay outside, his expanding brief as GBI. In December 1941 he visited General Friedrich Fromm, C-in-C of the Home (reserve) Army, to offer the services of his department, its engineers and workers to the general war effort. The GBI department had inevitably become involved in construction for the Wehrmacht in the Berlin area, retaining 26,000 workers for the purpose by the end of 1941. Repairing bomb damage and building air-raid shelters also fell to the GBI, who garnered a new title, Chief of Defence Construction, late in 1941.

Designers from the Speer office worked on three plants for building the twin-engined Junkers Ju 88 dive-bomber at Brno in Moravia, Vienna and Graz in Austria. The office also took charge at this stage of construction at the experimental rocket station at Peenemünde in Pomerania, a typical example of the Nazis' chaotic, hand-to-mouth method of allocating tasks which, in these cases, logically belonged to Fritz Todt. In November 1941 Hitler ordered increased aircraft production, with a view to reversing the result of the Battle of Britain the year before, as soon as victory was secured in Russia. Todt, worried by the plight of the troops in the frozen mud of Russia, wanted priority for the army. Even so, when Speer sounded him out on stopping all non-essential construction at the end of July 1941, Todt had refused, as did Hitler. It was while visiting an aircraft plant at Dessau at this time that Speer got a sight of intelligence projections of British and American aircraft production, which he found staggering; but nobody else in the Nazi leadership took this daunting forecast seriously or bothered Hitler with it.

In January 1942, Speer's office became involved in repairing and extending the railways in Nazi-occupied Russia, to facilitate the movement of troops and supplies. Speer, whose office employed a total of 65,000 workers at this time, offered 30,000 men for this task. GBI technicians were diverted into the 'Speer Construction Staff' and put to work on repairing the facilities destroyed by the retreating Russians, the world's leading experts on 'scorched earth' tactics. An appreciative Todt asked Speer to take charge of restoring the railways throughout the Ukraine.

Speer therefore hitched a lift in the official aircraft of Sepp Dietrich, the Waffen-SS general, for an inspection tour of work going on in the area round Dniepropetrovsk, only to be caught in a week-long snowstorm after his arrival. Finally, having failed to get out by train, Speer accepted another lift from Dietrich's pilot when the weather cleared, back to Rastenburg in East Prussia, Hitler's 'Wolf's Lair' headquarters for the eastern campaign, whence he intended to fly on to Berlin. He could not get to see the Führer, closeted all evening with Todt, whose principal post was Minister of Armament and Munitions. Todt eventually emerged very late, looking exhausted, for a nightcap with Speer. As he went off to bed, the Reich's chief engineer offered its chief architect a lift back to Berlin in his personal aircraft. Speer accepted – only to be summoned to Hitler's presence moments later to report on what he had seen in southern Russia. The session began at 1 and ended at 3 a.m. An exhausted Speer decided to sleep in for a few hours and find another means, later in the day, of getting back to Berlin.[14]

Nevertheless he was awakened at 8.30 a.m. by the insistent telephone at his bedside. It was Dr Brandt – bearing the shocking news that Fritz Todt was dead.

The machine at his disposal that day, an adapted Heinkel He 111 twin-engined bomber, was on loan from Luftwaffe Field Marshal Hugo Sperrle because his own aircraft was under repair. The plane took off at about 8 a.m., turned in the air as if to land again and crashed in flames after a mid-air explosion. The official inquiry, ordered by Hitler and arranged by Field Marshal Erhard Milch, state secretary at the air ministry, failed to determine the cause but suggested pilot error and iced-up wings as possibilities. Rumours abounded, as ever after such a trauma: it was Göring, who wanted Todt's empire; it was Speer, ditto; it was Bormann stopping Todt from 'doing a Hess'; it was an enemy agent; it was the SS, punishing Todt's doubt of victory (the most appealing conspiracy theory). The crash has never been explained.

The name of the man whose early demise propelled Speer to prominence as Hitler's chief architect, Troost, means consolation. Todt means death; and for the second time another man's sudden death would now transform the life of Albert Speer, even more radically.

PART TWO

Minister

7

In Todt's Footsteps

(1942)

HITLER, SLEEPING LATE AS USUAL, seemed stunned when he was told of Todt's death an hour or so after Brandt called Speer. At noon on the same day, 8 February 1942, the latter was summoned to the Führer's office. It was Speer's turn to be astounded when Hitler told him he was to take on all Todt's responsibilities, not just the construction tasks. The apolitical Speer had the wit to ask for a written order to take over, which Hitler promptly dictated. He was sworn in at Rastenburg (now Ketrzyn in Poland) on the 15th, at which moment he was formally vested with all the offices and titles of the late Dr Todt. The appointment was gazetted five days later. When Göring arrived at Rastenburg in haste on the afternoon of the 8th to see what pickings he could glean from the Todt empire, he was left speechless on being told that Speer, still only thirty-six years old, was to be given everything, thus becoming the youngest minister of the Third Reich.

Like Speer, Fritz Todt was a Swabian from Baden and one of a tiny handful of convinced Nazis who was also a born improviser and administrative genius. Todt was born in Pforzheim, the son of a manufacturer, and studied civil engineering at the technical universities of Munich before the First World War and Karlsruhe after it, obtaining his doctorate in 1920. During the war he fought on the Western Front, eventually joining the Air Corps as a flying observer; he was wounded in action. After 1920 he worked successfully as a building engineer with a private company but was attracted to the 'Socialist' side of National Socialism, joining the party with his wife in January 1923 and helping to establish its local organisation in Swabia. Soon appointed the equivalent of honorary colonel in Ernst Röhm's SA, Todt headed the construction-engineering section of the Nazi association for architects and engineers as well as several party technical organisations and offices in the gift of Deputy Führer Rudolf Hess, labour chief Robert Ley and others. He became a leading advocate of creating jobs by public works, one of the Nazis' few positive achievements and akin to Roosevelt's New Deal.

On 30 June 1933 Todt was named Inspector-General for German Roads, including the colossal autobahn network programme, and got the chance to put his employment theories into practice all over the country. Fifteen regional offices supervised a staggering roadbuilding campaign; Todt's first stretch of autobahn from Frankfurt to Heidelberg via Darmstadt was ready before the end of September 1933. Three years later 125,000 men were at work on the new concrete highways and another 120,000 in ancillary work such as quarrying. In September 1939, when the war broke out, 3,065 kilometres of autobahn had been completed and another 1,689 were under construction. The sweeping, landscaped dual carriageways had become a powerful symbol of the new Germany.

Todt, the world's principal user of concrete, moved seamlessly into other major construction projects such as the West Wall, begun in May 1938 as the Czechoslovak crisis mounted. This was the Wehrmacht's response to the Maginot Line on the other side of the French border. Impatient with the slow progress, Hitler ordered Todt to take over; by October 1938 1,000 companies and 430,000 men working a thirteen-hour day had built 5,000 concrete installations on the Siegfried Line, as it became known. Göring, overlord of the economic Four-Year Plan, made Todt its 'Plenipotentiary for Construction' – a classic Nazi overlapping appointment which did nothing to impede Todt's plans to revolutionise the construction industry.

His responsibilities rapidly spread from roads to embrace fortifications, docks and harbours, waterways and related installations, then armaments factories and finally housing for the workers. Productivity rose and material waste fell. It was Hitler himself who coined the term 'Todt Organisation' in May 1938 for the personally modest engineer's mighty construction empire with its great armies of uniformed workers, deemed to be on national service. Hordes of them followed hard on the heels of the Wehrmacht's *Blitzkrieg* conquests to repair roads and railways and to build airfields and strongpoints. The Todt Organisation had 800,000 men in Russia by the end of 1941 – and, as we have seen, even that was not nearly enough. A quarter of a million men were simultaneously at work on the Atlantic Wall opposite Britain, pouring 800,000 tons of concrete per month along the Channel coast into gun emplacements, blockhouses, U-boat pens and the like.

On 7 March 1940 another decree promoted Fritz Todt to Minister for Weaponry and Munitions (Bewaffnung und Munition), an additional, not an alternative, responsibility for the most productive individual in the Nazi leadership. Todt was not enthusiastic about this new post because he felt he lacked the technical expertise: he was a civil engineer, not a gunsmith. There was a cautious welcome from the relevant industries, which had observed how he created huge new opportunities for construction firms and material suppliers by means of fundamental reorganisation of working practices, affecting management at least as much as workers. Even this heavy additional responsibility for Todt was not enough for his master, who made him Inspector-General for Water and Energy (including power stations and fuel plants) in another decree on 29 July 1941 – his last appointment. But this one was welcome because it was a rational extension of existing Todt Organisation responsibilities and suited to his engineering skills, although even he could not make much of it in the six months he was to hold the title.

Todt's approach to the armaments industry alarmed the Wehrmacht because he began to impose a pragmatic compromise between military specifications and industrial capacity and potential, instead of allowing Wehrmacht requirements to dictate the production of an endless proliferation of short-run items, models, types or marks. He also set up quasi-autonomous working groups of companies and committees to coordinate supply and production in the main sectors of the armaments industry. The underlying principle was industrial 'self-responsibility' – *Selbstverantwortung* – the autonomous responsibility of industry for how it executed its assigned tasks. So long as a given industrial sector met its targets, it was left to itself and insulated from interference by generals, bureaucrats and even party bosses. There were two main difficulties that prevented Todt from perfecting this fundamentally sound scheme within the short time available to him. The first was Hitler's never-ending interference in weapons procurement: his extraordinary command of detail led him to regard himself as the ultimate expert and he was already the ultimate court of appeal in disputes between overlapping authorities. Second, there was the never-ending disruption of the skilled labour force caused by the conscription of irreplaceable workers who should have been permanently exempt.

Unlike Speer, Todt was no courtier or manipulator but first and foremost a technician. He was not equipped to deflect the dictator's whims or outmanoeuvre powerful competitors for manpower, materials and plant. His modesty and reserve worked both for and against him; Hitler did not regard him as a threat and held him in the highest personal esteem, making him the first recipient of the 'German Order' for outstanding non-military services to Volk and Reich, but that did not mean he would always or even customarily prefer Todt's view over others'. Speer constantly described himself as the 'apolitical technocrat' but his predecessor had a much better claim to this disarming description. Todt was a loyal party man but took no part in Nazi in-fighting:

he saw it as highly inimical to the efficiency he knew was essential for a German victory.[1]

His pragmatism, his organising ability, his personal expertise and experience all led Todt to lose faith in such an outcome for Hitler's adventurism earlier than any other Nazi satrap. His misgivings mounted as the Wehrmacht slowed in the mud and stalled in the snow and savage cold of deepest Russia, and probably peaked when Hitler rashly declared war on the United States within days of the Japanese attack on Pearl Harbor in December 1941. Todt understood that Germany had no answer to American industrial potential, even if it were to overcome the Soviet Union's daunting demographic and geographic advantages. He was upset by the maltreatment of Russian prisoners of war, unprotected by the Geneva Convention (not ratified by Moscow) and classified as subhuman by Nazi ideology; he could not convince Hitler that Soviet tanks were better than German; he could not persuade him to concentrate all resources on the welfare of the frozen German army. He had tried on at least two occasions before the evening of 7 February 1942 to persuade Hitler that the war was unwinnable.[2]

Hitler had an irrepressible respect for real experts such as Todt (which is why he usually avoided their company and did not seek their advice) but he also had an eerie ability to sap the will of even the most independent-minded interlocutors, who therefore avoided a *tête-à-tête* with him whenever they could.[3] The German expression for such a meeting is *unter vier Augen* (under four eyes, i.e. with just two people present), the terms on which Hitler received Todt for the last time on that bitter February evening. Todt, dogged rather than histrionic, armed himself with a paper unfavourably comparing German with Allied industrial capacity in some detail. The unrecorded meeting lasted some six hours and must have been stormy because aides heard raised voices through the closed doors. When he came out he was drained and depressed as he joined Speer for a drink before turning in at about 1 a.m. Less than twelve hours later Speer was once again called upon to step up into a dead man's shoes.

His official responsibilities were already a bustling administrative conglomerate by the end of 1941, as the Wolters Chronicle makes clear. He had moved on with impressive smoothness from architecture to town planning, and from planning to a rapidly increasing role in construction once the war began. The latter expansion was not only a logical extension of his function as GBI for Berlin but also a useful relief for Todt, whose colossal construction empire, like the Wehrmacht it was supporting, reached the absolute limits of its capacity in the Russian winter of 1941–42. Giesler's building gangs were diverted to the northern and central sectors of the Eastern Front as Speer's were sent to the Ukraine or southern sector, strategically the most important.

Hitler's decision to choose Speer as Todt's replacement in all his responsibilities was thus not as outlandish as commonly presented. In spring 1939, when he accompanied Hitler on a tour of the Siegfried Line (on which British troops more or less tunefully threatened to hang out their washing) Hitler told Speer that he would have to take over Todt's construction role should the need ever arise. In summer 1940 Speer managed to talk Hitler out of shifting a large part of Todt's mounting burden, including the newly conceived Atlantic Wall facing Britain, on to his shoulders forthwith. Speer knew that Todt, whom he genuinely admired and respected, did not feel he had reached the end of his tether – far from it – and would therefore be offended by what seems to have been a genuine attempt by Hitler to make life easier for him. So when Todt died, it was never a case of an architect becoming with one bound (and without relevant organisational experience) construction and munitions supremo. Speer all but *expected* to succeed Todt in his civil-engineering capacities, which were at least as important as his ministerial portfolio of armament production and rather more time-consuming. Hitler clearly took the view that Speer might as well finish the job and take on Todt's ministerial fief also. The surprise lay in the speed and tidiness of Hitler's decision (encouraging conspiracy theorists to conclude that he must have made it in advance – and therefore in foreknowledge – of Todt's death). The move, indisputably one of Hitler's best administrative strokes, deprived such incorrigible empire-builders as Göring and Himmler of the chance to snatch parts of the dead man's legacy.[4]

Todt might have been shy and retiring as an individual (if only too firm in his views) but he was a public figure. His indisputably great engineering achievements were highly visible all over the country and were thus trumpeted at home and abroad by the Nazi propaganda machine as among the new regime's most outstanding achievements. Countless German workers owed the heroic engineer their liberation from unemployment and their families the very food on their tables. His would have been a hard act for anyone to follow. Speer, although he had a great deal in common with Todt – region of origin, prosperous background, technical education, ability to organise and inspire despite personal reserve – was not a public figure, hated making speeches and had no interest in fame. Power was another matter altogether, and the new minister moved swiftly to consolidate his hugely enhanced position.

The German economy, in which Albert Speer was about to become the key figure, had been devastated by the First World War. Ten years of struggle, enormously exacerbated by reparations and the great inflation, brought production back up to the 1914 level by 1928. But Wall Street crashed within a year, and the economy reached a new low in 1932, when six million Germans were out of work. The Nazis came to power in 1933 with an employment programme, which they pursued as energetically as those for eradicating the Jews and acquiring new land in the east. Unemployment declined to relatively manageable levels by 1936 (about 1.7 million), thanks to a strong American revival under the New Deal and also the rapid expansion of the Wehrmacht. In the last days of peace in Europe joblessness in the Third Reich was effectively unknown. This transformation had begun with the huge public works instituted by Todt and also Göring, Speer and others on behalf of the Nazis, and had been rounded off by increased armaments production.

The main lesson the Nazis chose to learn from 1914–18 was the need for economic self-sufficiency – autarky – in any future war. Hitler was fully aware that the required *Lebensraum* could not be acquired without conflict, even though he achieved the restitution and con-solidation of much lost German territory by threats alone, knowing he lacked the means of realising them by force at the time he made them. But in the longer term he was not bluffing: he merely got his timing wrong by underestimating latent British resolve – witness his promise to Admiral Raeder as late as 1939 that there would be no war with Britain before 1944–45, which must have meant he knew and accepted it would come.[5]

Memories of the effects on food and other supplies of the strategically decisive British naval blockade remained vivid, and the driving force behind *Lebensraum* was the determination to acquire food and raw materials, especially iron and other minerals, which could not be artificially replaced, and oil and rubber, which could be synthesised, albeit not at an economic price. The lesson of autarky as derived from 1918 was highly selective and was understood, or misunderstood, in exactly the same way by the Japanese military junta, already embarked on a programme of acquiring self-sufficiency by conquests on the east Asian mainland. It ignored, for example, such overriding lessons as not fighting a war on two fronts, not taking on a greatly superior combination of enemies and not ignoring other laws of war (and logic). The great paradox of autarky as a policy was that Germany, like Japan, became even more dependent on foreign suppliers to build up the forces it needed to acquire the resources for ceasing to depend on them.[6] Germany was dependent on foreign sources for well over half its strategic raw materials, and by the time war broke out in Europe it had only managed to reduce this dependence to forty-five per cent. Stockpiling was by definition a strictly temporary expedient, and poor harvests in 1934 and 1935 presented severe competition for the limited supply of foreign exchange.

Hitler's reoccupation of the Rhineland in 1936 was thus economically motivated as well as political: he wanted total control of the Ruhr with its coal and huge industrial resources. Foreign sources of raw materials, fearful of German rearmament, were already dragging their feet in delivering essential supplies. The Reichswehr, the defence forces of the Weimar Republic, had started consulting German industry as early as 1926 about the problem of vital materials such as oil and rubber. Plans to produce synthetic substitutes were already far advanced, as were programmes for producing tanks, aircraft, heavy warships and submarines in defiance of Versailles, well before the Nazis took over. As noted in Part I, the will to circumvent, undermine or nullify the treaty was all but universal in pre-Hitler Germany. And, thanks to the Rapallo Pact between Germany and the Russians in 1922, the Germans practised tank and air warfare secretly for years before and after 1933 in the Soviet Union, which was still supplying Hitler with food and raw materials in the last hours before he invaded it.

The Nazis were fortunate in inheriting the considerable services of Dr Hjalmar Horace Greeley Schacht, economist, banker and convinced nationalist, who masterminded the currency reform that ended the great inflation of 1923, whereupon he became President of the Reichsbank, Germany's central bank. He resigned in 1930 in protest against continuing reparations payments and the Weimar Republic's mounting overseas debts. Thrown into unaccustomed idleness, he read *Mein Kampf* and was impressed by Hitler's will to overcome Germany's problems (yet more evidence, if such is needed, that economists are no wiser or less gullible than anyone else). Schacht introduced Hitler to some leading Rhineland industrialists in 1930, at a crucial moment in the party's fortunes. It was thus a matter of course that Schacht was given back to his old job at the Reichsbank when Hitler came to power.

From August 1934 he also served as Reich Minister of Economics, enabling him to fund rearmament with full deployment of the Reichsbank's resources and influence (which is why its contemporary successor, the Bundesbank, is constitutionally independent of the German government today). In typical Nazi manner the financial and economic overlord of the new Germany was given the specially created post of General Plenipotentiary for the War Economy – no sinecure or empty title, since he put German rearmament on a strong footing under a secret Reich defence statute of March 1935. The title came without specific powers or even responsibilities, so he had to descend into the jungle of competing Nazi spheres of influence like all the other paladins. Unlike Göring, Bormann or Himmler, he did not enjoy it.

But the brilliant Schacht was also a firm believer in sound economic practice, as then understood. He had no fundamental objection to such Keynesian ideas as deficit-financing, the only major means available for funding vast public-works and armament programmes. But the conqueror of hyperinflation was also committed to sound money at home and minimal foreign debt to reduce dependency abroad. Printing money as a means of financing public debt was anathema to him, as was recklessly increasing imports to ease poor harvests or stockpile vital materials. An impatient Hitler ordered Göring to take charge of procuring foreign exchange and raw materials abroad, another and most blatant instance of the Nazi habit of fudging areas of responsibility. The fat bully, still energetic in those early days of power, lost no time in shouldering the expert aside.

Schacht resigned as Minister of Economics and war-economy chief in November 1937, but his prestige was such that he was invited to stay on as Minister without Portfolio; and when his five-year term as Reichsbank President expired in March 1938, Hitler even reappointed him. Walter Funk succeeded him at Economics and as Plenipotentiary. Schacht parted company with Hitler when the Nazis went to war, apparently drawing the line at putting to use the weaponry his own financial wizardry had helped to produce (he was eventually sent to a concentration camp in 1944 on suspicion of involvement in the July Plot; after the war he was acquitted of war crimes at Nuremberg and in the West German courts).

In summer 1936 Hitler drew up a memorandum to Göring and Blomberg, the Minister of Defence, on a Four-Year Plan for the German economy, the stated goal of which was autarky in 1940. It predictably favoured more *Lebensraum* as the 'final solution' (*sic*) to Germany's food and raw-material problems (which could only be seen as such, be it noted, by those intent on war; in peacetime, Germany was experiencing no serious difficulty in obtaining what it needed on world markets, at least in quantities reconcilable with prudent housekeeping principles). But Hitler also saw no need to stockpile for a protracted war, unachievable in any case; conveniently, he envisaged seizing an unassailable position for Germany by *Blitzkrieg* against its neighbours one by one; so did the Wehrmacht, which had taken up the new armoured and aerial tactics with enthusiasm and practised them on the real testing ground provided by the Spanish Civil War. What was needed was a defence industry capable of producing fast but short runs of munitions, which was not an economic problem but only a question of will.[7]

Hitler therefore announced the 'second Four-Year Plan' at the 1936 Nuremberg Rally in September (the first, though never styled as such at the time, was deemed to have been the programme for jobs which the Nazis announced on taking office in 1933). Göring was appointed Plenipotentiary for the Plan, with powers to coordinate the work of all relevant authorities in party, state and nation. It was a typically bombastic, sweeping Hitlerian appointment, a dictator's wand-waving exercise which awarded a brief so vast as to be unmanageable by anyone to a man totally unsuited to the command of anything more complex than a squadron of biplanes (which he had done with great gallantry at the end of the First World War, succeeding the 'Red Baron' von Richthofen in command of Germany's finest fighter squadron). The result was a shambles which even an Albert Speer could not wholly rationalise, a major contribution to Germany's ultimate defeat.

The plan was not comparable with the Soviet Union's five-year plans, which were rigid exercises in command economics; Hitler's was a rolling programme for economic self-sufficiency, to be achieved by all available means. The defence and economics ministries were soon sidelined by the Reich Marshal's new fief (he was already overlord of aviation as well as of the new Luftwaffe). German industry was not enthusiastic, partly because it rightly feared gross Nazi interference and partly because Göring became an unpredictable source of competition. In summer 1937 he set up the Hermann Göring Works at Salzgitter, an ore-processing and steelmaking complex which swiftly became one of the biggest companies in the world and had to be divided into three to remain manageable. Even so, Germany could not achieve self-sufficiency in steel (or aluminium) by the outbreak of war; Göring, the Wehrmacht and industry alike resorted to stockpiling willy-nilly (not an efficient practice, as will be seen) and managed to accumulate a six-month reserve of chromium and tungsten, ten months of iron ore and a year and a half's manganese – all essential for the manufacture of sophisticated modern munitions – by autumn 1939. Germany was completely self-reliant for coal and nitrogen.[8]

To make confusion worse confounded, the Supreme Command of the Wehrmacht (headed by Hitler himself) was awarded control of all armaments factories in another defence law of September 1938, leaving Funk in charge of non-military economic affairs only (which did not prevent him from securing the nation's food supply in time for the war, a remarkable performance in the circumstances). On 29 August 1939, three days before the invasion of Poland, the War-Economy Regulations came into force; by the end of the year, Funk's residual powers over the economy passed to Göring, making him the complete master (on paper) of the entire German industrial war effort. But there was no total mobilisation of industry to match or support that of the Wehrmacht in 1939–41. The country's production capacity had breadth but no depth, stockpiles but no long- or even medium-term plan for sustained mass production of anything. Shift work was virtually unknown.

Each arm of the Wehrmacht had its own Weapons Office and the Supreme Command had a separate Economics and Armament Office, led by General Georg Thomas (a man who, like Dr Todt, bore out the old Russian saying that a pessimist is a well-informed optimist and duly incurred Hitler's displeasure). General Thomas said on the eve of the invasion of Russia that the autarky programme had distorted the war economy; synthetic processes could not produce anything like enough oil and rubber and conquests so far made had not solved other shortfalls. The *Anschluss* of Austria and the occupation of Czechoslovakia had made important contributions to the Reich's war effort, such as Austrian iron ore and Czechoslovak raw materials, arms and vehicle plants. Polish industry, less advanced anyway, was being demolished for ideological reasons. The conquest of Denmark and Norway secured the safety of the vital supply-route for Swedish iron ore, on which German arms production was heavily reliant. More matériel and minerals were seized in the Low Countries but French munitions were of little more use than the equipment abandoned by the British army at Dunkirk – incompatible, primitive or just antiquated. Coal and steel facilities in these countries were of obvious value.

As a result of these conquests and deals with neutral countries for other raw-material supplies, the Reich's resources in these and primary industry grew by a third between 1938 and summer 1941; but its needs had grown even faster and were about to become insatiable as the Wehrmacht raced into Russia. One more quick victory was all that was needed to make Germany unassailable; Britain, with its disarmed little army, had not given in but the Luftwaffe would surely cripple its ability to wage war by knocking out its key industries and its shipping. By February 1941 Hitler had abandoned the last vestige of any plan to invade: since the end of 1940 his mind had been concentrating more and more on the last and largest target. The Soviet Union had all the resources Germany could possibly need for long-term survival: land, corn, oil, chrome, minerals of all kinds, even gold. So confident was Hitler of a quick victory that he actually disbanded forty divisions on the eve of Operation Barbarossa. Even so, on the day of invasion, 22 June 1941, the Wehrmacht deployment on the Eastern Front outnumbered the Soviet Western Front forces of three million troops by a quarter of a million.

The proliferation of military supply authorities was, like Hitler himself, principally concerned with the technical aspects and quality of weaponry and neither knew nor cared about the industrial implications of equipment orders. The results, exacerbated by constant interference and changes of priority by Hitler, included shortages, bottlenecks, duplication, waste, delay, lack of standardisation and a bewildering array of types of aircraft, vehicles and other items. Hitler's solution was to appoint yet another arms overlord: none other than Fritz Todt, made Minister for Weaponry and Munitions on 17 March 1940.

As such, he acquired full responsibility for the Atlantic Wall (its armament as well as its installations) and the construction of fortified U-boat pens on the French Atlantic coast, notably at Brest (still used by the modern French navy for its nuclear submarines). But his ministerial title was exaggerated: his role as munitions supremo was confined to the weapons of the army, admittedly the dominant user. Göring's Luftwaffe and Raeder's Kriegsmarine still went their separate ways, their arms-procurement bureaux headed by Field Marshal Erhard Milch and Admiral Karl Witzell respectively. All Todt could do was work towards enlisting their cooperation. The head of the army's Weapons Office, General Karl Becker, who had concentrated on technical specifications without regard to production problems, found his role reduced to research and development; Todt also had the power to interfere in these areas if production considerations seemed to require it. Becker took his diminished role as a reflection on his honour and, depressed also by family troubles, committed suicide. He was succeeded by General Wilhelm von Leeb.

As supreme technocrat of the Hitler regime, Todt was also head of the Nazi Party Main Office for Technology and a major-general in the Luftwaffe as well as rising to the equivalent of full general in the SA (but held no honorary SS rank). Todt was the immediate founder of the system of industrial autonomy which helped Germany to raise production for a long war, as Speer, who built hugely upon it, properly acknowledged.

But the true originator of 'self-responsibility' was Walter Rathenau, industrialist and head of the electrical giant AEG (founded by his father). Placed in charge of a new War Raw-Materials Department in 1914, he rationalised production in such a way that productivity doubled with no increase in equipment or labour costs. In June 1922, having just left the postwar Ministry of Reconstruction to become Foreign Minister, Rathenau was shot dead by right-wing extremists in Berlin because he was a Jew and because he had been in charge of reparation payments (ironically, in 1916 he had supported the conscription of 700,000 Belgians for German factories, unprecedented in modern times but another example to the Nazis in general and Speer in particular).[9] In the twenty-two months of his ministry, Todt resolutely held bureaucracy at bay, relying on a dozen expert advisers and comfortably managing without the formal and cumbersome civil-service apparatus to be found in other departments. He had as little time or space for placemen and time-servers as Speer, whose entourage was more numerous only because his accumulation of responsibilities was rather larger.

Hitler flatly told Göring that Speer was taking over all Todt's offices. These included the pompous title of 'Plenipotentiary-General for Control of the Construction Industry in the Four-Year Plan', which Todt had held. The spectacular growth of the Todt Organisation had aroused jealousy in the Reich Marshal, and the two men had often clashed, partly for reasons of personality and partly because their vaguely defined areas of responsibility overlapped.

But in his prewar, architectural and GBI days Speer had been the recipient of Göring's sometimes effusive admiration – so effusive that Wolters was moved to excise one such piece of flattery from his Chronicle.[10] And on this occasion Hitler made it clear from the start that he would back Speer. Indeed the Führer, having been craftily persuaded by Speer to *order* him into Todt's job, had no choice but to support him. Göring was unsackable as an 'old guard' Nazi who knew where all the skeletons were buried, but Hitler's disenchantment with the Reich Marshal started with his failures against Britain in 1940, if not sooner. The Führer knew his official heir-apparent was a broken reed. Speer had also cultivated good relations, which had become a genuine friendship, with Göring's own number two in the Luftwaffe, Erhard Milch, a connection which would soon pay great dividends. This link arose from the close cooperation between the Luftwaffe and Speer's Construction Staff and Transport Brigade in Berlin and on the Russian Front. The field marshal was as ready to get round Göring as Speer.

The new minister was jealous of the dignity as well as the powers of his office from the start. He made no secret of his annoyance when a man called Konrad Haasemann arrived at Rastenburg on 9 February to brief him on the workings of his new department. The hapless Haasemann had been Todt's personal assistant and rose no higher than head of personnel at the ministry. Speer read this as a provocation by Todt's leading aides and took the overnight train to Berlin that evening to take command. The morning papers, bought at the station, had been orchestrated by the propaganda ministry to hail Speer's appointment (Goebbels wrote in his diary that Speer was 'probably the only man able to run [Todt's] great legacy in keeping with its purpose'). The party daily, *Völkischer Beobachter*, and the regional papers ran remarkably similar reports cum profiles.

A tired Speer toured the ministry's main building at number 3, Pariserplatz, conveniently next door to his GBI office, and called on the heads of the main departments. This unstuffy procedure, typical of

Speer at work, spared him the necessity of summoning them one by one in order of rank – and denied them the chance to snub, evade or unitedly confront him that day. Todt's key men were devoted to their late boss and a few of them proved unable to transfer their loyalty. Chief among the intransigents were Xaver Dorsch, Todt's head of construction, and Karl Otto Saur, his technical chief. All three of the ministry's most important officials were hostile; the third, Dr Walther Schieber, head of armament delivery with the rank of state secretary, said after meeting Speer: 'He lacks Todt's human warmth. Even his heart is cool.'

Speer had the sense not to upset the ministry by instant reorganisation and mass dismissals (he even left Todt's inelegant office exactly as it was) but soon brought two of his GBI cronies into the top level: Hettlage as head of finance and Willy Liebel, Lord Mayor of Nuremberg, in charge of the administrative Central Office. Speer removed only one senior official: Günter Schulze-Fielitz, just promoted to state secretary by Todt, sending him to Munich to head the Water and Energy Inspectorate inherited from the dead man. At the same time, Speer gave his trusted friend Wolters posts in the ministry and Todt Organisation press offices, analogous to one of his roles at the GBI. This was undoubtedly useful for a semi-official chronicler; it was also useful for Speer to have a trusted observer, not to say spy, in such strategic positions.

Todt's mangled remains arrived by train in Berlin on 11 February and Speer was at the head of the official party that went to the station to take delivery of the coffin. A tearful Hitler was the chief mourner at the state commemoration, held in the Mosaic Hall at the Chancellery the next day. Disingenuously, Xaver Dorsch quietly assured Speer of his loyalty during the burial ceremony at the Invaliden cemetery.[11] Shortly afterwards, Speer was sitting in Göring's office on the latter's invitation. His ill grace when told of Speer's appointment by Hitler had given way to the breezy, gimlet-eyed bonhomie the calculating airman usually displayed. He produced a document for Speer to sign, saying it was similar to the written agreement between himself and Todt (which had subordinated the latter to Göring as head of the Four-Year Plan and thus led to much conflict).

Speer took it away with him unsigned as the two men parted with smiles and handshakes. His mind was focused on the meeting at the air ministry to which he had been invited by Milch (acting for Göring) the very next day – Friday, 13 February – to talk about munitions with top-level service and industry representatives. Speer took the precaution of visiting Hitler on the eve of this baptismal conference and enlisting his support as promised. The Führer told him that if he experienced any problems in asserting his new authority, he should simply invite the entire meeting to follow him to the seldom-used Cabinet Room and Hitler would back him up.

Among the thirty present were Milch, in the chair, Walter Funk, Minister of Economics, Generals Fromm (Reserve Army), Thomas (Wehrmacht Economic and Armament Office) and Leeb (Army Weapons Office) plus Admiral Witzell, together with leaders of industry. The main item on the agenda was how to eliminate conflict between the different requirements of the various services. The mood of the meeting was in favour of unified supervision of this aspect of the war economy by a single authority – one man. Funk proposed Milch, who judiciously declined; Speer then announced that Hitler was waiting in the Cabinet Room to speak about Speer's role. Hitler was deliberately vague about this but told the participants to 'be decent to Speer'. Milch promised an end to destructive competition from the Luftwaffe, still independent in arms procurement, while the Wehrmacht and army representatives offered full cooperation. The meeting was adjourned to 18 February, in Speer's ministry; when it reconvened, he got his way. He took the unusual step of passing round a document confirming his mandate to take a supervisory role in arms manufacture. The most reluctant signatory was Admiral Witzell; but he signed. The route to standardised and rationalised munitions production was open, although much hard work remained to be done.

The message was clear: Speer was in charge. And as a bonus, after Hitler's hour-long address to the meeting on the 13th, Speer had found himself talking to Bormann in the presence of the Führer and, like the opportunist he was, sought the blessing then and there of both men to recruit the best industrial experts regardless of whether they were in the party, on the grounds that technical prowess was more important than overt political commitment. Since Hitler had just advised Speer to rely absolutely on the best industry had to offer rather than the bureaucrats they both hated, Bormann could hardly refuse. There is no evidence that Speer did so, but he had every reason to relish this early victory over the boss of the party machine as requital for his defeat at Bormann's hands in the dispute with Giesler: if so, the feeling did not last long.

But thus encouraged, the new Reich minister addressed ministry staff on the morning of Saturday the 14th. It was his first public speech, and it consisted of flat platitudes, praise for his predecessor and an appeal for cooperation. Dorsch warned openly and rudely in his reply as most senior official: 'Trust does not come by itself; it has to be earned.' This early test had gone badly, in marked contrast with Speer's first foray into Nazi politicking (thanks to help from Hitler and Milch). Speer also had a message sent to the Todt Organisation (TO) units at the front, telling them he was fusing his own Construction Staff into the TO as a mark of respect for his predecessor (happily this tactful move served the interests of efficiency).

The next milestone in the fraught settling-in period of the young minister was passed on 19 February: his maiden Führer conference, the first of a long series of meetings whose records form one of the major sources for the history of the German war effort as well as Speer's role in it.[12] The meeting took place at Rastenburg and Speer was accompanied by Milch and two generals: from the very inception of these conferences the custom was established that Speer would bring with him specialists in the various agenda items. This saved Speer, a natural delegator (but no slouch at absorbing and digesting information), much homework and also took advantage of Hitler's wariness of true experts: it was possible to blind him with science despite his extraordinary capacity for absorbing detail. Hemming in Hitler was Speer's consciously adopted method of manipulating him.

The record of the first conference shows how quickly and radically Speer would tackle the daunting task of reorganising munitions production by making the most efficient use of existing resources. He took with him the draft of a draconian decree for punishing arms manufacturers who made false claims for labour, parts, equipment or raw materials. Penalties ranged from penal servitude to death. Speer's ministry alone would decide on prosecutions, which would take place before the infamous Volksgericht ('people's court'), best known for turning political trials into travesties. It was in force by the end of 1942 and, as a classic example of Nazi government by terror, must have had a frightening influence across all armament and related industries.[13] The draft aroused strong objections from Otto Thierack, Minister of Justice and President of the People's Court, as an intrusion on his sphere; from Hans Lammers, Minister at the Chancellery, because he had not been consulted; and from Göring because the decree affected parts of the economy covered by his Four-Year Plan. When the amended but still harsh text was agreed by all parties, it was quickly extended by Speer to cover construction.

He glosses over his self-damning decree in his memoirs and makes no mention at all of his first move against this kind of corruption: the dispatch without trial to a concentration camp of two managers who had used skilled workers exempt from conscription as domestic servants. Even in Nazi Germany such high-handed action by an unempowered authority was illegal; it also constituted Speer's second crime against humanity after his eviction of Berlin's Jews, and thus ultimately a second reason for rejecting his claim to innocence of specific crimes. The ruthlessness of the 'Decree for the Protection of the Armaments Industry' and of Speer's thrust for control of that area of the economy had been unmistakably foreshadowed by his handling of the dispute with the unfortunate Mayor Lippert of Berlin over building plans. As in his previous post, so in this one: woe betide anyone who tried to infringe his authority as he understood it. Speer instinctively grasped the workings of the Nazi power system and used it with relish. There is no need to consider further his absurd claim to have been apolitical; more examples of his authoritarian approach to power will appear in due course.

Other topics covered at his first ministerial meeting with Hitler (who usually conducted business with his key subordinates separately, thus preserving the compartmentalisation of power essential to the *Führerprinzip*) included roadbuilding in Russia, the Luftwaffe's increasing demand for labour, energy supplies, tank production in Poland, rationing, prizes for good workers and a dozen other topics relating to the war effort, the use and rewards of labour, abandonment of unnecessary construction and postwar planning. Apparently Speer had mastered this bewildering array of briefs to the satisfaction of his master, whose manner was however distinctly more distant towards his protégé than it had been during their cosy chats about architecture. Since the character of their encounters had altered commensurately with Speer's change of role and since there would now always be others present at their meetings, this atmospheric cooling seems entirely logical and there is no evidence that it worried Speer at the time. But then he had so much else to worry about and to do. Unaccustomed though he might be to public speaking, Speer did not lack an instinct for public relations. Within a week of his appointment, the mechanophile Speer had happily taken the controls of a tank and driven a half-track at top speed to demonstrate that he was serious about his key role in the conduct of the war. Goebbels made the most of such propaganda opportunities.

Speer had already substantially extended Todt's system of production committees. There would soon be thirteen 'Main Committees' for the various types of weaponry (Todt had set up three, for tanks, munitions and arms), each controlling special committees responsible for specific end-products. There would also be 'Rings' (four by April 1942) for the principal categories of supplies, whether of parts or raw materials; these too supervised a plethora of specialised working groups, as Speer explained to Hitler.[14] There was inevitably some overlapping between sub-rings and subcommittees because one group's end-product might well be another's component. The committees and rings became 'executive organs' of the Speer ministry, run by technical managers and empowered to issue directives and orders to industry. Key figures in the autonomous system who had passed the age of fifty-five were required to nominate a deputy under forty.

By the time the system was fully established, more than 10,000 industrialists and technical experts were working for Speer as unpaid volunteers, whereas the staff of the ministry proper, soon a much more powerful empire than Todt's, peaked at just 218 in 1944. The volunteers played a role very similar to Roosevelt's 'dollar-a-year men', roped in to administer American war production. The areas of responsibility and agenda of the committees and rings were laid out in a ministerial decree (the Nazis' favourite statutory instrument) signed by Speer as early as 20 April. Speer himself stood at the top of the system, with about thirty leading industrialists chairing the main committees and rings and ten heads of main ministry departments (expanded from Todt's three) all reporting directly to him, rather than going through a state secretary. This put him in close and constant touch with the key men in the war economy and enabled him to fine-tune production informally and very quickly.

Karl Saur supervised the production of armaments while Dr Schieber was his opposite number for the supply of materials and parts. Mayor Willy Liebel's Central Office added planning to its administrative role in the ministry while Liebel himself left the governance of Nuremberg to his deputy and moved to Berlin to work for Speer full-time.

Arms users were to state their needs to the ministry, which would then forward them to industry for fulfilment, taking responsibility for delivery. The new system gave the ministry an overview of requirements for end-products and supplies alike, and enabled it to adjust military specifications to industrial capacity as well as tuning manufacturing methods, including specialised plants, standardisation and mass pro-duction, to military needs. The committees and rings also acted as a network for the exchange of technical information. Development commissions were added to the structure in September 1942, bringing officers and industrial designers together to improve equipment and produce new ideas. There was one for tanks, led by Professor Ferdinand Porsche, genius of the motor industry; others covered weaponry, ammunition, artillery and military transport. These commissions played a central role in coordinating military needs with research and develop-ment, taking new equipment to and through the testing stage and deciding what should go into mass production.

The committees and rings had their own regional sections and Speer's ministry soon appointed regional officials in the Defence Districts (not to be confused with the parallel party organisation in this sphere described below). But the Wehrmacht, in the shape of General Thomas, head of its Economics and Armament Office, controlled a national network of armaments inspectorates and commands. Speer and Thomas drew up a system of cooperation in March 1942; yet Speer soon displaced the realistic general, regarded by Speer as calculating to a fault. The latter acquired control of the inspection system in May, when Hitler promulgated a decree to this effect drafted by Speer. The role of the Wehrmacht in armament provision shrank rapidly; General Thomas, now an official of the ministry, was dismissed by Speer in November 1942 and soon found himself in the concentration camps (there is no evidence that Speer was responsible for his fate). His health ruined, he never forgave Speer for his sacking and its consequences, dying in an American prisoner-of-war camp just after the German surrender. His successor was the colourless Major-General Waeger, a sop to the Wehrmacht High Command. Speer was clearly not a man to cross, but his threats against hoarders and fiddlers, apart from his two admitted instances of sending people to concentration camps, are known to have led to only three People's Court prosecutions, of which one was dropped while the outcome of the other two is unknown.[15]

Hitler wholly supported Speer's proposal of 19 February 1942 for an immediate ban on all industrial plans for postwar production, on pain of stringent penalties (Göring issued a decree on these lines in April 1942 in his capacity as overlord of the Four-Year Plan, but it was Speer's idea). At the same opening Führer conference, Speer began a long and frustrating campaign to reserve key workers for armaments production rather than letting the Wehrmacht conscript them. Hitler at this stage required the TO to release 10,000 younger men to the forces but allowed it to recruit an equivalent number of older men from the construction industry, now devoted exclusively to war work and effectively under Speer's control.

One month later Speer won Hitler's overall agreement to extending the 'self-responsibility' system to naval armaments. The Hamburg shipbuilder Hermann Blohm, of Blohm und Voss, was appointed chairman of the Main Committee for Naval Construction; Grand-Admiral Raeder, the naval C-in-C, agreed in principle to the extension of the system to U-boat construction – but not immediately. Thus when it came to the Wehrmacht, Speer in 1942 controlled army munitions, worked closely with the navy and cooperated more loosely (but not ineffectively, thanks to his good relations with Milch, who was already running a broadly comparable system) with the Luftwaffe. His control over raw materials from stone to steel gave him direct influence over the work of many other organisations such as Giesler's construction operations and even the SS, which had begun to develop an economic empire of its own, using concentration-camp labour and handing out honorary ranks to its industrial contacts.

One of the earliest successes of the new arms-production regime under Speer was standardisation of ammunition. In an interview with the British historian, Lord Bullock, in 1979, Speer said the position before he came had been 'like a baker's shop' with the army ordering one type and then suddenly another, without planning or consideration of outside factors.[16] Many plants were just ticking over instead of being worked hard. Another early improvement, which had an enormously beneficial effect on munitions production without significant extra expenditure, was a general release of stockpiled materials. The savage punishments threatened for hoarding, misreporting, concealing, diverting or misusing materials and production equipment and the help of the honorary and part-time expert advisers working for Speer winkled out vast reserves which made a dramatic increase in productivity possible.

Within six months, Speer boasts in his memoirs, ammunition output rose by ninety-seven per cent, production of cannon was up by twenty-seven and tanks, badly needed in Russia, by twenty-five (the highly effective Main Committee on Tanks was led by Dr Walter Rohland, a steel magnate and technical expert recruited by Todt who became one of Speer's most important aides). Overall, arms productivity was up sixty per cent. It was only during this period, whose main achievements would soon be handsomely surpassed, that Germany caught up with the annual production rates it achieved in the First World War, which had not been matched in 1940 or 1941. But, as noted earlier, the war effort had been geared to *Blitzkrieg* until the Wehrmacht stalled in Russia, and in 1940 Hitler had banned research and development on any projects that would take longer than one year to complete.

Another important element of Speer's frenetic settling-in period – it could hardly be called a honeymoon – was his attempt to win over the party leadership. His first presentation to them took place in Munich on 24 February 1942. Present were Reichsleiters (the highest party rank, held by such as Bormann, the most senior, and Robert Ley, head of the Labour Front) and Gauleiters, the party's regional bosses. The latter included a few friends and admirers of Speer such as Goebbels (Berlin), Karl Hanke (Lower Silesia) and Karl Kaufman (Hamburg) but were overwhelmingly opposed, like the Reichsleiters, to Speer's burgeoning authority over industry, which most of them saw as grazing ground for the party (a main source of graft, influence and power). Each Gauleiter answered to Bormann in party matters but to the Ministry of the Interior in his other capacity as Reich Commissioner for (civil) Defence in his Gau – another typical overlap of responsibilities and potential cause of conflict with Speer's industrial role. The Gauleiters derived much of their power from control of local labour and were making pleas for special exemptions almost before the ink was dry on the Führer decree forbidding inessential projects. Bormann himself carried on building at the Obersalzberg, Hitler's mountain retreat, while Fritz Sauckel, Gauleiter of Thuringia, planned to continue redeveloping Weimar.

If Speer had been pedestrian in his maiden speech to his new staff, he was in bullish mood when he stood up in front of the party satraps. Local construction projects, he told them, even those dearest to their hearts, would have to make way for the war effort. Peacetime building of all kinds would be suspended. He urged his audience not even to ask for approval of special projects of any kind, unless they were a direct contribution to the war effort; Speer himself had shelved vast but now irrelevant plans, he said. He appealed for help in finding more labour for armaments, construction and the TO. He outlined his 'self-responsibility' system, which applied to major construction projects such as strengthening the West Wall as well as to armament production. The party could help by raising awareness and morale among German workers.

Speer underlined the imminent new penalties for hoarding manpower and matériel. Now fully into his stride, he said the Soviet Communists were ahead of the Germans in one important respect: they showed no hesitation in punishing crimes against the state, and Germany should do no less in the drive for armaments. There was much applause for the dynamic young minister (as Goebbels portrayed him in the party-controlled press) at this crucial meeting; but any sympathy he won would wane soon enough, though not before his second presentation to the same audience on 18 April, just two days before his elaborate but straightforward system of industrial autonomy officially came into effect.

In what seems to have been a euphoric mood, or at least a feeling that he could carry all before him, Speer paid a call that February evening on Todt's widow, who lived in Munich; there he met Hermann Giesler (whose brother Paul was the local Gauleiter) for the first time in several months. In such a restricted context, at least, the two rival architects showed collegial civility. Speer was already making arrangements to hand over his GBI responsibilities (although, like a true Nazi, he kept the title) to his closest and most senior colleagues there, including Schelkes and Wolters. The senior men of the inspectorate joined Speer for a 'farewell' dinner at Horchers Restaurant on 2 March.

Earlier that day Speer had revealed to General Thomas, the Wehrmacht procurement chief, his plan for a new supreme economic authority for armaments, to be styled Central Planning. The day before, he had outflanked Göring by having himself appointed General Plenipotentiary for Armament Tasks under the Four-Year Plan. This voluntary piece of kowtowing to some extent eased the Reich Marshal's irritation and jealousy over the young minister's huge encroachments on 'his' economic territory, which he none the less continued to neglect. Behind the Central Planning ploy lay Speer's conviction that control of raw materials was the *sine qua non* of centralisation of munitions production. As usual, his brief as arms supremo was so vaguely defined that it sounded awesome but impressed few of his rivals in other ministries and authorities. He therefore set up a committee of three: himself, Milch (Göring's Luftwaffe procurement chief) and, despite initial misgivings, Wilhelm Körner, the Reich Marshal's state secretary. His calculation was that Göring would be satisfied to have two of his senior men on Central Planning, while Speer could rely on his good relations with Milch for a permanent *de facto* majority there. Other senior officials were to be coopted as required.

On 3 March Speer and a few officials, including Milch, went to see Göring at his stupendously vulgar 'hunting lodge' at Karinhall, an hour's drive north of Berlin. The minister presented the marshal with a *fait accompli* by announcing that Hitler had instructed him to organise a Central Planning office. There is no record of any such order in the voluminous records of Speer's many Führer conferences, which does not mean it was an invention; but such a decision seems rather too important to have been simply forgotten. Put like that, however, Speer's announcement could elicit only one response: Göring's consent. He insisted that Körner should be on the triumvirate; Milch persuaded Speer that he would not be a threat but rather a useful channel of communication with Göring, who had been completely outmanoeuvred and sidelined by Speer. Hitler confirmed the arrangement a few days later by decree, describing Central Planning as a super-ministerial rather than a representative authority, supreme over the various overlapping supremos whose rivalry Speer was determined to ride over – roughshod if necessary. The navy was upset not to be included, but Hitler backed Speer's refusal to expand the tiny group.

Central Planning, dominated by Speer from the outset, decided how to cut the cake yet was not meant to concern itself with providing the ingredients. But it reduced still further the importance of Funk's Ministry of Economics, now clearly doomed as an effective institution; and its existence also enabled Speer in autumn 1942 to abolish the office of the Plenipotentiary for Iron and Steel under the Four-Year Plan, held by General Hermann von Hanneken, a Göring appointee.

It was clear to Speer, as it had been to Todt, that an efficient armament effort required coordination of raw-material supply, munitions production, transport – and labour. The horizontally organised rings took care of supplying and distributing materials and parts while the vertically operating committees oversaw production. The very success of these arrangements soon made the coordinating Armament Council set up at once by Speer (and the aviation ministry's already extant and analogous Industry Council) superfluous, because its technical expert members were working together in any case on the main committees and rings. In this respect, as in others, Germany was over-organised, the national tradition of intricate bureaucracy being compounded by the Nazi taste for overlapping Führers, Leiters and assorted grand panjandra such as Reich Marshal Göring, the world's only six-star general: they spent much of their time getting in each other's way and intriguing against one another.

The key to the Speer system for arms production was improvisation, for which flexibility, initiative and minimal bureaucracy were required – along with freedom of action, which was asking a lot, not to say the ultimate, in a totalitarian state. Hitler however, as we have seen, respected technical experts (usually in spite of himself) and had a special personal regard for Speer, to whom he therefore allowed a unique degree of room for manoeuvre, at least so long as his protégé was successful. It is surely one of the great ironies of history that improvisation now became the key to over-organised Germany's ability to stay in the fight against a growing and already far larger army of enemies, whereas the bumbling democracies, especially Britain, had adopted an unprecedented measure of command economics for their war efforts. Curiously enough, Stalin's Soviet Union also developed a remarkable talent for improvisation and headlong expansion of indus-trial productivity, even before the prospect of defeat by the Nazis concentrated Russian minds.

None the less it was not until 1944 that 'efficient' Germany (population seventy million) passed 'laissez-faire' Britain (population forty-five million) in aircraft production. But, compared with the Germans, the British had taken the long view from the beginning. The Munich crisis of autumn 1938 prompted them to begin repairing twenty years of neglect in defence procurement; and in some areas, such as reserved occupations, important precautions were taken well before the war. Speer by contrast faced, two and a half years into the war, the formidable task of forcing a heavily outnumbered Germany to adjust from the instant gratification of *Blitzkrieg* to the long haul, in which returns would be much smaller for much greater effort and sacrifice. Hindsight enables us to recognise the wisdom and courage of the doubting General Thomas and the pessimistic Dr Todt in seeing, and saying, that the war had become unwinnable for Germany when the Wehrmacht faltered at the gates of Moscow and Hitler precipitously declared war on the United States.

Labour, Speer saw, was crucial. To secure enough of it, which is to say skilled Germans and unskilled foreigners, for an integrated armaments programme, the goodwill of the Gauleiters with their powers over regional labour was rightly recognised by Speer as essential, Hence his early wooing of the party bosses described above. But the master of the party's system of controlling the grassroots through the Gauleiters was Martin Bormann, head of the party machine. Speer already knew to his cost that Bormann, nicknamed 'the brown eminence' for his backroom power and machinations, was not only no pushover but also Hitler's most influential courtier and power-broker: he alone knew the Führer's innermost secrets and was also extremely jealous of Speer's rising star.

The once-bitten Speer, instinctive manipulator as he was, did all the right things by mastering Nazi browbeating language overnight and ostentatiously appearing to take the Gauleiters into his confidence, explaining his plans to them before going public. But his attempt to get round Bormann in the same way as he had got round Göring – by choosing from the man's own subordinates an aide well disposed towards himself – soon went awry. Speer proposed to Hitler the appointment of a Commissioner-General for the Deployment of Labour, and in the same breath suggested a Gauleiter in good standing as his candidate: Karl Hanke of Lower Silesia. But Hanke was known to be a friend of Speer's, who had played an important role in his career by getting him his first architectural work for the party. Bormann immediately saw through Speer's manoeuvre, which must have been obvious to a man like him, and put forward another candidate: Fritz Sauckel, his own successor as Gauleiter of Thuringia and like himself a member of the Nazi Old Guard (membership number 1,395). Hitler and even Göring, the latter doubtless flattered to be asked, had gone along with Speer's proposal – until Bormann intervened.

There was of course a Reich Ministry of Labour, headed by Robert Ley. This former Gauleiter of Cologne had become a Reichsleiter and head of the German Labour Front, the organisation which dealt with all labour problems by taking over trade unions and trade associations – worker and boss organisations – alike. The head of the Reich Labour Office, directly answerable to Dr Ley, was Dr Friedrich Syrup, who fell ill in 1941 and was succeeded by a Dr Mansfeld. Once again bedazzled by their *Blitzkrieg* successes, the Nazis had taken a relaxed view of the efficient use of labour until the first setback in Russia. They had come to power with a job-creation programme which relied heavily on labour-intensive public works and had deliberately avoided the kind of industrial 'rationalisation' that kills jobs. By the outbreak of war rearmament had helped to make unemployment a thing of the past.

A 1938 statute gave Göring powers to recruit workers for tasks important to state policy, but even in more effective hands than those of the head of the Four-Year Plan this was nowhere near enough to bring about efficient use of the labour force. At the time of the invasion of Russia Germany had 1.5 million foreign workers – prisoners of war (the Geneva conventions allowed rank-and-file enemy captives to be put to work in non-military industries) and genuine volunteers (many workers had migrated to Germany from Poland, Holland and France from 1935 as rearmament got under way). Some six million Germans had meanwhile been conscripted into the Wehrmacht. War industries made up for these manpower losses by recruiting from less vital areas of the economy, including commerce (especially after Allied 'area bombing' of cities from summer 1942 made serious inroads into office blocks, stores and the like).

As the new overlord of army munitions, the most demanding sector of the war economy, Speer was looking for tight but flexible control of the requisite sectors of the labour force through a commissioner with appropriate powers; his idea was that he should technically come under the aegis of the Four-Year Plan, to appease Göring and deflect charges that Speer was becoming too powerful, but should take his main orders for labour from Speer's department. Dr Ley put himself forward for the post but Speer rejected him on grounds of conflict of interest: he was already meant to represent workers, bosses and state in the labour market. Besides, Ley was ineffectual and Bormann opposed any transfer of power to him at the expense of his Gauleiters.

8

Hard Labour

(1942–43)

HITLER CHOSE FRITZ SAUCKEL as Commissioner-General for the Deployment of Labour on 19 March 1942. Not knowing the man, Speer was prepared to make the best of the appointment. But Bormann's blocking of Hanke was compounded by a no less jealous Lammers, head of the Reich Chancellery, who vetoed the idea of placing the new commissioner under Speer's orders. Bormann agreed with this constitutional objection, a second setback for Speer. The third was Hitler's decision to make Sauckel responsible for labour deployment throughout the economy rather than in munitions alone. Speer had to settle for 'collegial cooperation' with the new labour supremo, still answerable to Bormann as a serving Gauleiter and technically also to Göring as a 'plenipotentiary under the Four-Year Plan', but in no sense to Speer. Hitler however so broadened his brief later in 1942 that Sauckel could do what he liked to get labour; he was obliged only to consult Hitler and keep him informed, becoming a supreme Reich authority answerable only and directly to the Führer. Göring promptly wound up his own labour-deployment section in a rare example of a Nazi leader taking spontaneous action against duplication at the expense of his own power.[1]

Thus Sauckel was appointed to a strategic task suggested by Speer, whose brief was extended by Hitler over the entire economy, yet was in no sense answerable to Speer, soon to be Germany's prime employer of labour. That this was so was surely proved by Hitler's words when, in the presence of Speer on 21 March 1942, he handed Sauckel his commission, adjuring him to 'do whatever you can for the Minister of Armament'.[2] This can only have meant that Hitler was appointing Sauckel to take on much more than providing labour for military munitions production, and also that he was expressly not at Speer's beck and call.

Ernst Friedrich (Fritz) Christoph Sauckel was born at Hassfurt-am-Main in northern Bavaria in October 1894. His father was a postman (a civil service appointment in Germany, conferring tenure until retirement) and his mother a seamstress. He was clever enough to earn a place in a *Gymnasium*, the most academic category of German secondary school, but left at fifteen to go to sea in Scandinavian ships. Interned in France as an enemy alien for the duration of the First World War, which broke out when his ship was in a French port, he trained as a fitter and worked in industry afterwards, joining the Nazis in 1923. He was elected to the Thuringian legislature for them in 1927, the year he was appointed Gauleiter for the province in succession to Bormann. He led the Nazi parliamentary party in the regional diet; when the Nazis, on the crest of their wave nationally, won the Thuringian election in 1932 he became Presiding Minister (state premier). After such democratic posts were abolished in 1933, he was appointed Reich Lieutenant (Statthalter) for both Thuringia and Brunswick and also got a seat in the Reichstag, from 1933 a sinecure with no power (Speer had one also). An honorary general in the SS, Sauckel was also Reich Defence Commissioner for the Kassel Defence District. Like his admired party chief, Bormann, Sauckel was a devoted father of ten children.

As ever, Sauckel's 'blank cheque' for the recruitment and allocation of labour turned out to be covered with small print imposing manifold restrictions. One of Speer's most persistent complaints against his Nazi colleagues was their stubborn refusal to recruit German women for war work. In vain did the arms minister point to the examples of Britain, the Soviet Union and the United States in this area, citing the fact that the number of females in domestic service in Germany hardly altered throughout the war, remaining around the 1.4 million mark. In Britain two-thirds of female domestics were diverted to war work, leaving just 400,000. More women worked in German industry during the First World War than the Second. Hitler, Göring, Bormann, the generals and many others objected to the conscription of female labour, for two main reasons: they did not wish to antagonise the population as a whole, and they believed in the 'three Ks' – *Kinder, Küche, Kirche* (kids, kitchen, kirk) – as a woman's proper concerns, the latter optional, the former especially encouraged and the kitchen taken as read. Eventually some half a million German women were taken out of domestic work and into the factories, only to be replaced by a similar number of women shipped in from the occupied Ukraine.

There the Speer Construction Staff, which had been working on the railways in the southern sector of the Russian Front, took on roads and general construction as well, even as it was subsumed into the Todt Organisation. Under Speer the TO expanded to seven great 'Deployment Groups' (*Einsatzgruppen*): three behind the main sectors of the German Front in the USSR (north, central and south), a fourth working in the front line there, one in the far north (Norway, Finland and northern Russia), one in western and the seventh in south-eastern Europe. Each group had its own small logistical staff in Berlin, working independently but answerable to Speer through Dorsch, his construction chief. Speer himself headed a TO command staff of five men including Dorsch to supervise the sprawling organisation, the most formidable military construction force ever known, rivalled in speed and efficiency, if not at all in scale, only by the US navy's 'Seabees' (CBs, construction battalions) in the Pacific theatre. The legacy of this colossal embodiment of the Nazis' 'bunker mentality', which surely derived from the experiences of their leaders, especially Hitler, in the trenches of the First World War, can stupefy to this day. Frontier defences, gun emplacements, blockhouses and bombproof shelters, built for the TO by hordes of Germans and their slaves, are still to be seen in many parts of modern Europe, from Alderney in the British Channel Islands to the Alps and beyond, too big and strong to be blown up or completely demolished.

One of Speer's first meetings was with General Jacob, commander of pioneers (fortification troops), and General Friedrich Fromm, C-in-C of the Home Army and already an ally of Speer's, to ensure that TO and Wehrmacht construction work did not overlap. The TO already dwarfed the military's work in this area, which was rapidly reduced to local and ad-hoc tasks only. Hitler always favoured the TO, approving its remorseless expansion as a top priority; he was, after all, the greatest personal consumer of concrete in the history of the world, demanding stupendous bunkers for himself in Berlin and Berchtesgaden, Rastenburg and several other transient or longer-term headquarters. Even after non-essential work was banned in April 1942, the TO grew and grew.

Although Speer had the thoroughly reliable and energetic Walter Rohland from the Ruhr steel industry, a Todt appointee, working for him as head of the Main Committee for Tanks, he decided to make himself thoroughly expert in these most important weapons systems of a modern army.[3] He told Wolters in March 1942 that he felt a broad grasp of everything could only be acquired if he completely understood one major weapon. He chose tanks, not only because he loved machines, especially when he was in the driving seat, but also, it is fair to deduce, because Hitler was particularly interested in them and possessed enormously detailed knowledge on the subject. Speer was quite content to delegate the work to the experts in this field as in all others; he merely ensured by personal visits to training and testing grounds as well as manufacturing plants, engine works, gun suppliers and army engineering workshops that his knowledge of tanks was first-hand and thorough. We have seen how one of his very earliest official acts was to take the controls of a tank; within a week he was doing it again, and on 5 March he was closeted with Hitler, discussing tank production as if born to it.

The Chronicle of Speer's office for spring 1942 presents a scarcely credible picture of frenetic activity as Speer plunged into his new and vast responsibilities; that he covered the ground is borne out by other, more formal sources, such as the records of his ministry and his meetings with Hitler. But on 10 April, the day after his first press conference as minister, he found time to preside over an informal session for senior colleagues old and new at the Engineers' Club in Wannsee, south-west Berlin. Fears that there might be tension between Speer's old coterie and Todt's men proved groundless and a good time was had by all. The chief's pronounced taste for practical jokes and *Schadenfreude* was shown by the cruel laughter which attended a confidential psychiatrist's report on Walter Brugmann, Speer's construction chief in the Ukraine, as it was passed round the table: not surprisingly, the engineer's huge new responsibilities had caused nervous strain.

As the budget for essential, non-war construction was capped at two billion marks for the rest of 1942, Speer signed a decree on 14 April linking material allocations directly to their availability. Total allocation would depend on total supply; individual allocations must not exceed the production capacity of recipients for the given period (usually one month). On the 17th, Speer told the assembled economic advisers to the Gauleiters that armaments took precedence over the whole of the rest of industry, and that he now identified transport and labour as the biggest problems for the medium term. Funds for new construction of armament plant were slashed from eleven to three billion marks as Speer pointed out that it was much more efficient to introduce or extend shift working at existing plants than to build new ones.

It still seems extraordinary that it should have been necessary to point this out in Germany two and a half years into the war. Speer found two shifts working at factories that could and should have three; and single-shift working, even in the most vital war industries, was still commonplace – while the troops in Russia complained of shortages. Speer concluded that arms production could be doubled with only 80,000 extra workers, provided all labour was put to work efficiently. Shortages of locomotives and rolling stock could and would be resolved in the same way.

Back at the engineers' club on the 18th, Speer had a heavy bet with Dr Rohland – specifically two hundredweight of fruit – that the munitions workforce would, thanks to his productivity reforms, increase by 300,000 in six months, by which time there would be a total of six million engaged in industrial and Wehrmacht armament plants, chemical manufacture and railway vehicles – the Speer industrial empire as it then stood. He won. None the less, as late as February 1943 he would still be pressing for the closure of non-essential industry and the diversion of yet more labour to munitions. At the same time he had a rubber stamp made for his office with his signature under the message, 'Return to sender – irrelevant to war-effort'; he also ordered the GBI office to abandon the last vestiges of work on Germania, even abstract planning and architectural drawings. As a lover of music, Speer must have had mixed feelings when he attended the reopening of the Berlin State Opera on 12 December 1942, repaired on Göring's insistence after bomb damage.

Speer's birthday present to Hitler on 20 April 1942 had been a pair of tanks – the first production Tigers designed by Professor Porsche, who was awarded a high decoration for his efforts. Six days later Speer made a rare speech in the Reichstag, urging total mobilisation of the economy, by now a favourite theme of his as he came to understand the problem (Goebbels was still vainly urging the same course on 18 February 1943 at the Sport Palace, in the approving presence of Speer; both ministers were made to wait for more than a year).

Speer's first major intervention in the transport field took place on 30 May 1942, when he had talks at Karinhall with Göring about increasing locomotive production to make denser use of the railway system. Two days later he called on Julius Dorpmüller, the septuagenarian Reich Minister of Transport, to discuss the same topic as well as the creation of a Main Committee for Locomotives, signs of the importance he attached to the movement of goods. When Mayor Liebel took up residence in Berlin in mid-April 1942, he also took charge of a new section of the ministry to supervise transport, coal and energy.

The ministry's takeover of the Wehrmacht's role in munitions inspection was formally ordered in a Hitler decree of 7 May 1942 and effected at a meeting of all military arms inspectors and General Thomas at the Wehrmacht Supreme Command (OKW) in the presence of its chief, Field Marshal Wilhelm Keitel. Thomas stayed on for the time being, but he now passed officially from Keitel's to Speer's control. Keitel was one of Hitler's closest advisers and looked the very model of a Prussian general; but his inability to say No to the Führer, spectacular even by Nazi standards of sycophancy, earned him the nickname 'Lakeitel' in the German army – a pun on the word *Lakai*, lackey. Although he was a member of the triumvirate with Hans Lammers and Martin Bormann which served as Hitler's executive for Wehrmacht, government and party respectively, he was less important in terms of military influence and advice than General Alfred Jodl, the OKW chief of staff (operations). Hitler himself was supreme commander of the Wehrmacht, just as he was of state and party.

In June 1942 Speer inspected the army's experimental rocket range at Peenemünde on Germany's eastern Baltic coast, where General Walter Dornberger and Dr Wernher von Braun were hard at work on the world's first ballistic missile, codenamed A4, which would become notorious as the V2, and other missile projects. The latter included ground-to-air anti-aircraft missiles, which would have been of much greater value to the Luftwaffe in its struggle against Allied bombing, now becoming a significant disruptive force, and to the navy, whose U-boats were faced with mounting Allied air attacks. That the notion of unified command represented by the Wehrmacht was a charade is surely shown as much by the fact that neither airmen nor sailors knew much about what the army's brilliant team was doing at Peenemünde as it is by Speer's constant battle against inter-service rivalry. But this fundamental inefficiency was to be found among all the main belligerents, especially America and Japan.

The V1 'flying bomb', meanwhile, the first cruise missile, was being developed separately by the Luftwaffe. Both V-weapons (the V stood for *Vergeltung* – vengeance) but particularly the V2, consumed resources and manpower out of all proportion to their value to the war effort. Himmler's SS, ever on the lookout for chances to expand its quasi-autonomous, military-industrial complex, managed to 'horn in' on Peenemünde by offering to build extra facilities there with slave labour from the concentration camps. Speer cannot have failed to be aware of this by August 1943 (at the very latest), by which time his office had thoroughly familiarised itself with the work, and working practices, of SS-General Hans Kammler, the SS construction chief, on the Baltic and elsewhere.[4]

Only one personal visit by the minister to a concentration camp is on record: to Mauthausen, near Linz, on 30 March 1943. It was by all accounts a bizarre occasion. The busy day-trip to the 'Ostmark' (post-Anschluss Austria) began with tours of the Hermann Göring and the Nibelungen steelworks in Linz and St Valentin and ended with calls at the monastery of St Florian and the Steyr rifle factory. Mid-point of the programme was Mauthausen, a name which probably first crossed Speer's consciousness as a source of labour for one of the quarries supplying stone for some of his grand building projects.[5] Described in the Chronicle as an 'SS factory', Mauthausen, when shown to the armaments minister in under an hour, made such a positive impression that he complained shortly afterwards in a letter dated 5 April 1943 to Himmler about the 'luxurious' construction standards he had seen there. He proposed that a small delegation of his own and SS representatives should tour the concentration camps to see what savings could be made. The SS should switch to 'primitive' construction methods involving 'minimal material and labour', he chided, having issued a decree that very month that all wartime construction had to be temporary and of the most basic materials.

This outburst had the richly ironic result of a furious written response from SS-General Oswald Pohl, Himmler's dim and brutal chief of administration and economics and ex-officio head of industrial production at the camps. All construction had been carried out in line with current regulations, and Speer himself had approved the prevailing standards as recently as 2 February 1943, Pohl fumed in a letter to Himmler's assistant, Dr Rudolf Brandt: 'Reich Minister Speer does not seem to know that we have over 160,000 prisoners now and are constantly fighting epidemics *and a high mortality [rate]* [author's italics], because the lodging for the inmates, including the sanitary facilities, are totally inadequate.'[6]

The spectacle of SS-Obergruppenführer Pohl (belatedly hanged for war crimes in 1951) opposing unclad wooden walls in concentration-camp huts, on the grounds that they would kill even more 'social undesirables' than prevailing SS hospitality standards were doing already, is enough to give crocodile tears a bad name. Two of Speer's staff called Desch and Sandler, and Kammler himself, embarked on a tour of the camps soon after the exchange and 'a highly positive picture' of conditions duly emerged. There was one very serious exception: 'At Auschwitz they uncovered catastrophic sanitary conditions,' Speer wrote in his book on the economic empire of the SS. He did not say which Auschwitz; there were three separate camps, one for administration, one for mass executions (the infamous death camp at Auschwitz-Birkenau) and a labour camp for war production. It is to be assumed that he meant the latter. On 30 May 1943 he raised the steel ration for construction at concentration camps in general and made a special, much higher allocation of 2,400 tons of various steel items specifically for Auschwitz. It is only fair to deduce that in thus promoting his improvement of standards at Auschwitz he was not claiming to have bettered conditions at the death camp; but it is very hard to believe that Speer did not know of the existence of the mass-murder facility by then.

Staying with the subject of Speer's guilty knowledge, we may note here that the Chronicle contains an innocuous-looking entry for 28 April 1942, in the form of an increasingly rare reference to the work of the GBI's department, which was still part of the Speer's empire: 'The programme of distribution of flats to holders of the Knight's Cross in Berlin was inaugurated by Herr Clahes. By the beginning of May flats were assigned to thirteen Berlin holders of the Knight's Cross, including three with Oak-Leaf and Swords.'

Readers of the sanitised copy might be puzzled by this apparent aside, but all is made clear by an earlier entry in the unexpurgated version, dated 21 January 1942: 'The GBI ordered that the circle of [those] entitled to Jew-flats becoming free (demolition tenants, bomb-damage victims) shall be extended to severely war-wounded, soldiers and NCOs with the Iron Cross First Class and officers who are decorated with the Knight's Cross. The resettlement programme in progress was therefore halted.'[7] Without this passage, the cut version gives the impression that Speer, quoted as complaining to Lammers of the Chancellery about the change of use of much housing to offices, cared deeply about the plight of the homeless, whereas his main concern at that stage was to make sure that Germans with medals got first refusal of apartments from which Berlin's Jews had been forcibly ejected. The 'resettlement' theme seldom recurs, even in the uncut Chronicle, until the last entry of all on the subject, appended to the entry for 25 October 1942, a convenient summary of Albert Speer's direct involvement in the persecution of Berlin's Jews:

> After the GBI gave up resettlement affairs, Vice-President Clahes made a concluding report on the labours of the Main Department [for] Resettlement for the period 1 February 1939 to 15 November 1942. This report included the following: the task of the Resettlement Department was to identify all Jew-flats in the territory of the Reich capital, to clear them and assign them to tenants who had lost their flats through reconstruction measures. In all 23,765 Jewish flats were identified. The circle of [those] to be provided was, on the GBI's proposal, extended by decree of the Führer to war-wounded soldiers, Knight's-Cross holders, and NCOs and men awarded the Iron Cross First Class. Of the identified Jew-flats 9,000 were distributed. The number of resettled persons comprised 75,000. In the process 2,600 flats were completely refurbished. For the accommodation of possible bomb-damage victims 3,700 part-furnished flats were made ready.[8]

The Jews had also been driven out of Germany's formidable scientific establishment, thereby reducing in advance the country's ability to wage war: under the Nuremberg race laws of 1935 a quarter of all German physicists lost their posts for being Jewish. The generality of German scientists was conservative and nationalistic, a fact which hardly made them unique in Germany after Versailles but was also no advertisement for their freedom of thought. Their colleagues in Allied countries tended to boycott them because of the 'manifesto to the civilised world' signed by such as Max Planck, of quantum-theory fame, and Röntgen, the discoverer of X-rays, disputing allegations of German atrocities in Belgium early in the First World War. Werner Heisenberg, who coined the 'uncertainty principle' in particle physics in 1925, was a volunteer after the war in the fascistic Freikorps which enthusiastically crushed the Communist bid for power in Bavaria. He was also distantly related to Heinrich Himmler (hardly his fault but it probably helped to save his career).

Albert Einstein was thus notable among German scientists, not at all for being Jewish nor yet only for his revolutionary relativity theories, but also for being one of the few scientists who supported the Weimar Republic before he found it necessary to emigrate to the United States on the rise of Hitler in 1933. Fortunately for civilisation, particle physics, including atomic research, was dismissed as 'Jewish science' by the German scientific establishment and the Nazis alike.

The Kaiser Wilhelm Society for the Advancement of Science (KWS), founded in 1911, oversaw the completion of the new premises of the Kaiser Wilhelm Institute for Physics (KWIP) in 1937 (Einstein had been director of the institute from 1914 to 1933). But Planck, whose dearest wish had been such an institute, had resigned as President of the KWS in 1936 over its lack of independence from the Nazis. The KWIP was requisitioned by the army in October 1939. Its director then was Peter Debye, from (still uninvaded and neutral) Holland, who was told to take German citizenship or be dismissed. True to the enterprising spirit of his countrymen, Debye in a judicious career-move took leave of absence and went to Cornell University in the United States – as a visiting professor on full pay! Kurt Diebner, head of an atomic research programme backed by Army Ordnance, succeeded him. He appointed Otto Hahn (discoverer with Strassmann in 1938 of nuclear fission, the effect of bombarding uranium with neutrons) and Professor Heisenberg, head of the Institute for Theoretical Physics at Leipzig University and 1932 Nobel prizewinner, to run the KWIP nuclear research programme.

Secret research into the potential of uranium isotope 235 was under way by the end of 1939 in America, Britain, France, Japan and Russia as well as Germany, where the Uranium Association of scientists involved in such research was founded in April. Fear that the Nazis would develop nuclear weapons prompted Einstein to issue two warnings to the US administration, which with its limitless resources (and help from Jewish exiles) won the race to develop the atomic bomb and the nuclear reactor alike.

As munitions minister Speer acquired control of the modest German atomic programme as one of his many new responsibilities. The Germans took an active interest in both applications of the newly discovered nuclear chain-reaction. Before a means of enriching uranium – enhancing isotope 235 to 238 – was discovered, enabling ordinary water to be used as a coolant, a 'moderator' was needed to slow down the chain reaction for the reactor application: either graphite, which was very costly to purify, or heavy water, which Germany imported from Norway until it occupied the country and was able to help itself to the tiny output of the Norsk Hydro company. It also availed itself in summer 1940 of Belgium's stock of uranium oxide from the Congo (hitherto only tiny quantities had been extracted by the Germans in Czechoslovakia) and exploited the Paris cyclotron. Progress was slow; to the loss of brilliant minds to anti-Semitism was added Wehrmacht conscription of young scientists and technicians, always a headache for Speer. Another restraint on the programme was Hitler's 1940 ban on research not expected to yield results within a year. All this changed just as Speer took over, when the army handed responsibility for nuclear research back to the KWS; the army had already in effect decided to put its money on the V2.

German interest in nuclear research declined with the funds and number of scientists engaged in it (seventy mostly part-time, down to forty-four in 1942), but the reduced programme still enjoyed the classification *kriegswichtig* (important for the war-effort) if not *kriegsentscheidend* (decisive). The KWIP held a secret nuclear research conference at the end of February 1942. But physics as a whole was still frowned upon for ideological reasons, and there were almost no graduates in the subject in Germany from 1940. The Nazis advocated 'German physics' and disowned 'Jewish physics' (quantum and relativity theories). The emphasis at the conference was on nuclear energy and enough interest was aroused for Göring's Reich Research Council to take notice and snatch control of the project from the KWS and the Ministry of Education. Heisenberg became head of the KWIP (and physics professor at Berlin University) at this point as the Nazis, in a typical fudge, belatedly recognised the importance of the new physics – provided Einstein was never mentioned. The few scientists involved, including Heisenberg, recently rejected for a chair at Munich because of his enthusiasm for particle, and his distaste for 'German', physics, were now able to find work, notably at the new Reich University in Strasbourg, capital of the re-annexed Alsace.

In 1942 the scientists clearly saw Albert Speer as their great hope. General Fromm, who headed the army's pre-Speer interests in armament production as C-in-C of the Reserve Army, and Albert Vögler, president of the KWS, went to see him in April. As a thoroughly modern technocrat, Speer was genuinely interested in nuclear energy but decided early on that it was unlikely to be *kriegsentscheidend* for Germany, or indeed any other belligerent. Heisenberg extolled the possibilities of nuclear energy as a substitute for fossil fuels in a private reprise, for Speer's benefit, of his conference speech, discounting nuclear explosives, however, as unachievable in the current war. As indeed they were, as far as the European theatre was concerned; Germany had surrendered over two months before the first experimental nuclear explosion.

Heisenberg after the war tried to parlay his own and his colleagues' advice to Speer to abandon the atomic bomb and go for nuclear energy into a manifestation of scientific resistance to Hitler. The scientists had underestimated the United States and been deterred by the cost and scale of the industrial effort needed to make a bomb in time for it to make a difference to Germany's growing plight. The fact that Heisenberg, when he had recovered from the shock of the news from Hiroshima, was able in a matter of days to guess accurately the structure of the first bombs does indicate that the Germans, who had after all discovered fission, had the necessary knowledge. What is certain is that he was no resistance hero; like Ludwig Mies van der Rohe, he was hurt by Nazi rejections but ready, even desperate, to accept work from them. Unlike the architect he was given some. Germany was his country, right or wrong. The truth about Heisenberg's attitude looks likely to remain as uncertain as his famous principle.[9]

Speer wrote in his memoirs that Heisenberg poured cold, rather than heavy, water on the idea of the atomic bomb, even when Speer ordered a German cyclotron from Krupp and offered to find money and materials for the research. He was taken aback when the scientists produced a modest list of requirements – in the knowledge that they would have to start from small beginnings, for technological rather than financial reasons. Hitler, the master of detail, was out of his depth in advanced scientific theory and was put off by the possibility of a chain reaction that might run out of control and burn up the earth or its atmosphere, a fear shared by some of the US 'Manhattan Project' scientists. It is inconceivable that he would have hesitated on moral grounds to build and use an atomic bomb had he thought it practicable.

The bomb was briefly discussed at a Führer conference towards the end of June 1942, and the idea appears to have been abandoned by Speer in the ensuing autumn, even though interest in 'miracle weapons' was mounting amid Germany's worsening military situation. The German cyclotron at Heidelberg split its first atom only in May 1944, when Speer visited it. Nuclear research was awarded three million marks in 1943 and slightly more in 1944, the emphasis firmly placed on a reactor, which Heisenberg rightly foresaw as a means of powering ships. But the Allies disrupted the modest programme by attacking the Norsk Hydro facility and research centres at Hamburg and Kiel in Germany. Speer wrote that wolfram (tungsten ore) imports expired with Portuguese neutrality in summer 1943, whereupon he ordered that the German stock of uranium should be used to make cores for the armour-piercing shells fired by anti-tank guns. His contention that this proved Germany had abandoned the bomb in unanswerable. Those at whom the shells were fired apparently did not notice the new, ultra-heavy filling, which was probably used only experimentally.

Of course there can never be any real reason to be thankful for Nazi German anti-Semitism (or any other form of racialism). None the less the ideologically based, doctrinaire contempt for anyone and anything Jewish, including particle physics, of the Hitler regime does appear to have saved Britain, Russia and the world at large from a nuclear catastrophe that might even have surpassed the massacres of Jews and others for which Nazism will for ever be execrated.

The aerial pounding of Germany by high explosive and incendiary bombs became a serious nuisance within months of Speer's appointment. The poverty of intellect behind Allied (especially British) bombing strategy saw to it that German output not only remained buoyant but also expanded surprisingly in many areas until September 1944, when production peaked – just as the bombing began to cripple transport. But it was an increasingly important factor in German economic and civilian life from 30 May 1942, when the RAF scraped the barrel to assemble the first '1,000-bomber raid' (in fact 1,046 aircraft, some of which would have been rather better employed protecting the constantly endangered Atlantic convoys). It scattered bombs in the general direction of the Rhineland city of Cologne, managing to miss the city's magnificent Gothic cathedral. The raid was a propaganda coup for the obsessive Air Chief Marshal Sir Arthur 'Bomber' Harris, C-in-C of Bomber Command, and it caused ructions in the Nazi High Command, especially for Göring, who as Luftwaffe chief was responsible for air and ground defence against bombing. He once boasted that if the enemy ever managed to bomb Germany, 'you can call me Meyer' (usually a Jewish name, it need hardly be said). Not long after the RAF began its raids, Göring, who unlike Hitler was not afraid to visit bombed areas, was touring the streets of a damaged town when someone in the crowd shouted, 'Meyer!'

The effect of Allied bombing on German civilians was similar to that of the Luftwaffe's earlier campaign against British cities (or quite possibly less), another attestation of the intellectual bankruptcy of the Harris school of thought, which closely resembled that of Haig, the British C-in-C on the Western Front in the First World War. Bomber Command had the highest casualty rate of any major arm of British forces in the Second World War. A very high proportion of the losses was among officers, the country's best-educated young men (personally they were no more important than sailors or soldiers but they represented an especially high individual investment by the state, just as infantry subalterns had done in the earlier war, only to be thrown away by the thousand). Since the Americans would not share their relatively precise Norden bombsight with their Allies, RAF standards of accuracy left much to be desired.

Making a virtue of necessity, the RAF officially adopted a policy of 'area-bombing' of cities and also regarded any bomb that fell within *five miles* of its target as a hit. Rationalising their own inability to hit anything much smaller than a city on most days, and even less so at night, which the British favoured because they lacked long-range fighters to cover their bombers by day, the strategists took comfort in the theory that if you could not hit the factory, you could at least destroy the workers' homes (and probably the workers, if truth be told) and disrupt production that way. The almost laughable delicacy with which the British had begun the war, dropping leaflets rather than bombs and refraining from raiding the Norwegian airfields in case civilians were accidentally hurt, had turned to ruthless brutality, driven by British determination to hit back at an enemy mostly out of reach of their navy and much too strong for their army.

The Americans, when they started bombing, and even Portal, Chief of Air Staff, and some of his air marshals, preferred the concept of precision or pinpoint bombing of specific, strategic targets such as key factories. The mistake usually made by adherents of this rather more thoughtful tendency was to overestimate their own success and underestimate German ingenuity, which largely meant Speer's, in getting damaged plants back to work at high speed, often time and again, and building barracks for homeless workers virtually overnight. The Americans would bomb by day such promising targets as the ball-bearing factory at Schweinfurt (17 August 1943), the main source of these crucial components in every major movable item of equipment. They used B17 'Flying Fortress' and other heavily armed bombers, protected by fighters as far as possible, and took heavy casualties until the long-range Mustang fighter came on stream.

Reconnaissance would show spectacular damage, but the Germans would quickly return to work in the ruins and the first raid would not be followed up by frequent repeat attacks to make sure the plant never got back on its feet. It was only in winter 1943–44 that raids were renewed on the ball-bearing factories; and even then the Americans desisted prematurely. Speer told the RAF in 1946 that unrelenting attack on the industry would have brought the Wehrmacht to a halt in four months. His reaction was a typical piece of improvisation on the run: he appointed a particularly vigorous Special Commissioner for Ball-Bearings, Philip Kessler, a general manager from the industry, to restore and sustain production.

Attacks on one plant in a given industry were seldom accompanied by simultaneous bombing of other factories in the same specialised sector of the economy to increase the pressure. The Americans thus had half a strategy where the British had virtually none, assembling great swarms of bombers in the dark to stage horrific but strategically ineffectual attacks such as the bombing of Hamburg in July 1943. Even that was an isolated event not followed up by the RAF, so that the Germans could concentrate massive aid on the shattered Hanseatic city, whose industries (as distinct from the housing stock and commercial buildings) were working again in a remarkably short time. Peenemünde naturally came under attack but was able to carry on functioning almost to the end of the war.

Even what is generally regarded in Britain as Bomber Command's most daring and spectacular mission, the Dambuster Raid on the night of 16–17 May 1943, was far less effective than it seemed. Nineteen Lancasters of 617 Squadron, equipped with a specially designed 'bouncing bomb' to be dropped at treetop height so as to skip towards a dam across its lake while the aircraft climbed and turned steeply away, were sent to attack the five principal dams of the Ruhr region under Wing Commander Guy Gibson, VC. The largest dam, the Möhne, broke and unleashed a terrifying tidal wave down the Ruhr valley. The dam with the largest reservoir behind it, the Sorpe, was hit but held: had it broken, Ruhr industry would have been crippled for the summer. But the British, who sustained nearly forty per cent losses, erroneously divided their force and sent some bombers to attack the Eder valley dam, which was irrelevant to the Ruhr industrial water supply: it existed to maintain navigable levels in local waterways. Thus the RAF's most daring precision raid came very close to a strategic success with a handful of planes but was largely wasted for being only slightly misjudged. Damage and civilian casualties were astounding; but the objective of knocking out the Ruhr was not achieved, as Speer discovered to his relief on a tour of inspection on the morning after the raid.

Another piece of Speer improvisation prompted by the increasing level of bombing was the establishment in July 1943 of the 'Ruhr Staff', based in Kettwig, a task-force whose job was to organise the restitution of damaged plant and workers' accommodation in Germany's most important industrial zone, now constantly subject to carpet-bombing (the British alone launched more than forty raids in their 'Battle of the Ruhr'). Speer would have liked another 39,000 men to keep the area going, but the Ruhr Staff formed 'flying squads' of workers to plug the gaps. Further disruption was caused by persistent rumours, spread by British and resistance propaganda, that men working in the area and/or on the Atlantic Wall were to be sent into

Russia to work for the TO: French, Belgian and Dutch workers melted away, causing a new shortfall of 60,000 men. The cities, towns, coal mines, steelworks and other installations in the densely populated and built-up area near the Dutch border were so close to one another that the RAF was quite likely in missing one target to hit another contributor to German strategic production. In all, some half-million mostly German workers were transferred at this period from civil to munitions production.

Increasingly worried by the rapid build-up of transport blockages, Speer called on Reich Minister Dorpmüller, who seemed to be overwhelmed by the problems. The Deutsche Reichsbahn, the German state railway system, was effectively bankrupt, he had told Speer on 21 May 1942, inviting his dynamic young colleague to take charge. Speer, about to set up the Reich Iron Association the next day to rationalise the production and distribution of steel, refused; but four days later Hitler appointed him and Milch as 'co-dictators' of transport. The two increasingly close colleagues immediately set in hand a rush programme to accelerate repairs of damaged rolling stock and locomotives. By the 29th Speer had traced Professor Thiesen, the man who had organised German internal transport during the First World War, and asked him to do it again. At the same time Speer appointed one of his few friends among the Gauleiter fraternity, Karl Otto Kaufmann of Hamburg, Commissioner for Shipping. Dr Theodor Ganzenmüller, one of Hitler's inspirational appointments – after his Herculean performance restoring wrecked railways in Russia, Hitler had without consultation bumped him up to state secretary in Dorpmüller's ministry – was told to take charge of the entire Deutsche Reichsbahn. The railways in the occupied eastern territories were taken out of the hands of Wehrmacht area commanders and transferred to the Reichsbahn.

In like spirit, Speer was given charge of the same economic areas in the occupied east as came under his aegis in Germany as minister and inspector-general of construction, roads, water and energy. Inside Germany a national grid was formed to even out distribution of electricity; rationing was imposed by power cuts. Meanwhile the Opel company was ordered to step up manufacture of heavy trucks; on 22 June the Main Committee for Trucks set in motion Speer's orders to build just one type of each of three categories of light lorry (1.5, 3, and 4.5 tonners). A programme to develop and produce non-petrol-powered propulsion units for cars was started at this period, even as Speer issued a stream of orders simplifying the structure of the Todt Organisation: Xaver Dorsch now became head of a streamlined TO Central Office, with Dr Gerhard Fränk, a Speer crony, as his administrative deputy.

The suspension of the road programme inside Germany for the duration enabled Speer to send the labour thus released to build roads for the army in the Soviet Union, a dictatorial decision which not unnaturally distressed many of those affected and led workers elsewhere to fear a similar fate, as we saw. The Speer transport brigades led by Will Nagel were amalgamated with the Todt brigades to form a single Todt Transport Group under Nagel, promoted to Gruppenführer (major-general). Also in July 1942, 50,000 Russian prisoners were assigned to the TO, which was desperate for manpower in the Soviet Union. A 'Speer Legion' of Russian lorry drivers was formed a few weeks later to work in the west of the Reich, where there was a serious shortage of truckers. At the same time Speer called for a plan to simplify the paperwork in his mushrooming empire.

Speer and Milch officially functioned as co-chairmen of the Transport Command in Central Planning, with no fewer than four state secretaries, including Ganzenmüller of the Reichsbahn, under them, as well as Gauleiter Kaufmann (shipping) and Mayor Liebel (administration). All forms of transport lay in their purview. Nothing was too trivial to escape Speer's reorganising eye. On a train journey to Rastenburg at the end of 1942, he personally unscrewed an amazing array of unnecessary metal fittings in his first-class compartment: clothes-hangers fixed to the wall, reading lamps, pocket-watch holders, wash-stand grips and the like. The train crew took a dim view of this apparent vandalism, but Speer kept his booty and sent it all to Ganzenmüller with a request to strip trains of such items and give them to the scrap-metal collection. This unexpected crop was a result of Hitler's concern that Speer should not undertake unnecessary risks: he forbade his minister from flying by Kondor bomber in case he was shot down, and also forbade him from visiting TO units in northern Finland, Lapland and Russia at Christmas 1942. He went to western France instead, to see the men working on the Atlantic Wall and the naval bases before going to the Obersalzberg to see 1943 in.

Speer was still not officially in charge of naval armaments at this fourth New Year of the war, although the spread of his power over raw materials and components gave him more and more influence over their production. He had visited the U-boat chief, Karl Dönitz, in Paris in June 1942, where the admiral had a spartan apartment (his headquarters were at Lorient on the French Atlantic coast) and they had fruitful discussions of such common interests as the massively fortified U-boat pens building at Brest and elsewhere and Germany's backwardness in radar technology. Further meetings took place later in 1942. By the time the RAF took its mind off area raids long enough to notice maritime bunkers, they had sand-filled concrete roofs five metres thick and were bombproof.

The naval C-in-C, Grand-Admiral Erich Raeder, was chary of Speer's growing power over munitions and frowned on his most successful subordinate's contacts with the minister, forbidding the chief submariner from discussing technical matters with him. Dönitz commanded the only arm of the Wehrmacht capable of delivering a strategic victory (by cutting the Anglo-American transatlantic lifeline) once the army became bogged down in Russia. But the Naval High Command lost its chief on 30 January 1943, when Raeder was subjected to one of Hitler's calculated, screaming rages and sacked. The reason was the defensive victory by a much inferior British force over two German heavy cruisers and escorts in the icy Barents Sea at the end of December. Hitler demanded that all surface ships be stripped of their guns, which should be sent to the defence of Norway, and broken up. Raeder vainly pointed out that this would be tantamount to presenting the Royal Navy with a massive strategic victory over the Kriegsmarine, whose remaining capital ships, by their mere presence in northern waters, tied down the British Home Fleet and menaced the Russian convoy route.

As so often happens on such occasions, the new man – freshly promoted Grand-Admiral Dönitz – succeeded in reversing the decision which had led to his predecessor's dismissal. He persuaded Hitler that if all the big naval guns were to go to Norway, let them at least remain attached to their hulls. He retained direct command of the U-boats, his and Germany's most formidable weapon, promoting their brilliant operational chief, Admiral Eberhard Godt, and leaving him in day-to-day charge.

Dönitz fully understood the advantages to be derived from linking naval munitions production to military and quickly came to an understanding with Speer. The result was what amounted to a contract between the two men. In return for entrusting control of naval armament production to Speer, the new C-in-C could look forward to a doubling of U-boat production from twenty submarines to forty, including more of the larger types, in all a tripling of monthly tonnage. At the end of June 1943, Speer chose Otto Merker of Magirus Deutz, a specialised-vehicle builder, to relieve the flagging Hermann Blohm on the Main Committee for Shipbuilding.

Merker copied the US shipbuilding example and organised a new production system for two revolutionary submarines designed by Professor Hellmuth Walter: the Type XXI ocean-going boat, displacing 1,600 tons surfaced, and the Type XXIII coastal submarine (234 tons). Their hydrodynamic shapes, based on those of large sea-mammals, and advanced battery packs enabled them to travel submerged twice as fast as earlier boats, and faster underwater than surfaced. They were a deadly new threat to Allied convoys, whose sufferings had eased markedly in spring 1943 when long-range and carrier-borne airpower gave the escorts the edge over the U-boats for the first time – victory in the 'Battle of the Atlantic'.

The new boats and their main components were built inland at widely dispersed plants and transported by waterway, rail and road to Germany's Baltic coast for rapid assembly and launching, a new procedure designed to evade some of the increasing effects of Allied bombing. Production began without pause for prototypes in November 1943, after Speer and Dönitz signed a decree in July giving the go-ahead. Fortunately the bombers caused such serious disruption to transport as well as to manufacturing and assembly facilities in the latter part of the war that the 'electroboat' programme was delayed by a crucial six months. One-third of the new boats completed were destroyed in the assembly yards; many more were never completed. Had it been possible to adhere to Merker's timetable, the new boats would have outrun most escorts and wrought renewed havoc among shipping, disrupting the invasion of the European mainland. Rather than develop a new generation of expensive, high-speed escorts (thousands would have been needed), the Americans might well have deployed the first atomic bombs against the U-boat bases with their thick concrete carapaces, proof against conventional explosive. The Germans had no reason to be grateful for the relentless bombardment of their country at the time; this ironic but alarming piece of hindsight offers another view.[10]

Speer's stewardship of the TO often took him to the coast, principally to check progress on the Atlantic Wall. Nothing like as dense as the West Wall or Siegfried Line inside Germany's borders with Belgium and France, completed in 1940, the coastal defence line involved about half as much work – but in a quarter of the time available for the West Wall. The TO needed 80,000 more men to complete the task, to be recruited from France, both occupied and unoccupied (the latter was brusquely taken over in November 1942 when the Americans landed in North Africa) and from Algeria, governed by the French collaborationist Vichy regime. Speer went on inspection tours at the end of July and again in August 1942. At the end of that month he was back on the coast at Dieppe to examine the scene of the Anglo-Canadian commando raid which had been a disaster for the attackers and also led to a reinforcement of Atlantic Wall defences and garrisons. Speer took the opportunity of driving a captured British Churchill tank, finding it markedly inferior to the latest German Panthers and Tigers.

At the end of the year he was back in France with Wolters and a troupe of artistes to entertain his TO men at Christmas. He told them the Atlantic Wall had to be complete by spring 1943. Its purpose, he said, was the same as that of the West Wall at the beginning of the war: to hold back the western Allies while concentrated on the Eastern Front.

Despite his profound natural reserve and dislike of speechmaking, Speer seemed, according to Wolters's Chronicle for the period, to enjoy being the centre of rank-and-file attention on such visits. The unfortunate performers tended to be ignored as workers crowded round Speer with their ideas and complaints. On one of his earlier visits to the wall in the Pas de Calais area, the giant guns at Cape Gris Nez were fired at Dover twice in his honour and he was mobbed by TO men in the canteen. Speer fully understood the importance of boosting morale in this way, however distasteful such close contact with large groups of men might be to him. The same laid-back charm which had brought him admirers at university easily won over his subordinates at all levels, except for the handful who remained loyal to the memory of Dr Todt.

In a rare display of emotion, excised from the sanitised Chronicle for its treacle content, Speer publicly mourned the death in Berlin of Hans-Peter Klinke from head wounds suffered at Stalingrad while serving as a sergeant in the Waffen-SS. Klinke, born in 1908, had been a student with Speer and Tessenow, an exceptionally gifted one whom Speer was happy to recruit as an architect in 1932, and who worked as closely as anyone with him on the grand plans for Nuremberg and Berlin. It is not unreasonable to connect Klinke's decision to join up with the suspension of architectural work for the duration. This left a gifted and dedicated young practitioner with nothing to do in 1942, when he joined Hitler's bodyguard regiment, the most élite unit in the Waffen-SS, soon winning the Iron Cross. Speer clearly thought highly (or had a guilty conscience) about his 'first colleague' Klinke, persuading Hitler to award him the title of professor on his death-bed and sentimentally acknowledging his debt to the young man with whom he had hoped to resume architectural work after the war.

Hitler sent a wreath; Speer the music-lover persuaded his friend, Wilhelm Furtwängler, musical director of the Berlin Philharmonic, to send part of the orchestra to play Bach in the model room at the GBI offices on the Pariserplatz, where the coffin stood on a bier. The funeral panegyric, in which the intimate second-person pronoun *Du* embellishes a leaden text of patriotic officialese, does not bear repeating (it represents the biggest single cut from the original Chronicle, fully merited on stylistic grounds). It may fairly be added here that Speer, while he could never be accused of false modesty, openly acknowledged the help he had from others. He undoubtedly had the gift of choosing, inspiring and leading first-class colleagues, who often exhibited a lasting loyalty (reciprocated as long as they were of use to him).

A more personal loss in the Stalingrad débâcle, which sealed the fate of the Third Reich, was Speer's younger brother, Ernst, serving as a private soldier in the front line with the doomed Sixth Army. They had last seen each other when Ernst visited his exalted brother at his office while on leave just before the abortive German pincer assault on the city dominating the Volga region in August 1942. Speer managed to exchange a few sentences between appointments and telephone calls and promised to get his brother a posting to a TO unit in the west at the end of the campaign. 'I had not even shaken his hand.'[11] But it was not as if they had ever been close.

The Russians counter-attacked in November, encircling the Sixth Army and cutting it off (Hitler forbade it to retreat). Letters from Ernst to his parents in Heidelberg revealed he had 'Sixth Army disease' – jaundice – and was starving and freezing in a front-line casualty station. The Speers appealed to Albert to exploit his personal influence – something he virtually never did. Ernst meanwhile, though still seriously ill, stole back to his unit. Field Marshal Milch tried personally to find him while leading a last attempt to relieve the encircled Germans by air, flying in a few supplies and lifting out badly wounded men such as Klinke. Ernst Speer was declared missing in action and, like more than 200,000 comrades in arms, never returned from Stalingrad, where 94,000 survivors surrendered in February 1943. More than one-tenth of the peak front-line strength of the Wehrmacht was lost in this single, climactic battle – a blow from which it never recovered. The losses in arms, munitions, matériel, vehicles and aircraft were astronomical, requiring even greater feats of productivity from the German war economy and the man who was rapidly acquiring control of it.

As Minister of Armament and Munitions, Albert Speer had many problems. The list of his responsibilities in the Chronicle after exactly one year in office (February 1943) is enormous. Despite manful attempts to simplify and streamline the organisation of his swelling empire, made possible by constant vigilance against bureaucracy, the air was thick with paper to such an extent that when enemy bombers destroyed a ministry building its staff gave a silent cheer because piles of paperwork had gone up with it. But the most frequently recurring and intractable problem throughout his first year and a half as a minister (before he became overlord of the entire war economy, including non-military production) was labour, exacerbated as it was by constantly shifting priorities – Hitler's unpredictable whims, changing fortunes on the battlefields, the haphazard effects of the bombing and conflicting demands in east and west.

Speer had met the newly appointed Commissioner-General for Labour Deployment, Fritz Sauckel, on 5 May 1942 for a working session on labour requirements for the quarter April–June. Speer listed his needs and Sauckel said he would look for the bulk of the additional workers in the occupied eastern territories. On 22 May he announced the recruitment of 350,000 skilled workers in France for the German munitions industry. This made Speer uneasy, and in the first days of June he began to investigate the possibility of assigning specific tasks for the German war effort to workers in their own occupied countries, especially France: to take the work to the labour rather than vice versa.

He realised as early as anyone that extending wholesale labour conscription to the occupied countries was bound to be a most effective recruiting sergeant for Soviet and Polish partisans, French, Dutch and other resistance movements. My own father spent much of the war in hiding in Holland to escape forced labour in Germany (while he lay low elsewhere, a male lodger hastily squeezed between ground-floor ceiling and upper-storey floor of our house as soldiers with fixed bayonets burst in to prod the plaster and tap the walls). Loudspeaker vans would go round ordering all men between eighteen and forty to assemble at the end of their streets with a blanket, a change of clothing and enough food for three days. Standards of obedience outside Germany being rather less slavish than inside it, the village-idiot tendency was the most strongly represented among the few respondents after the first occasion. None the less, hundreds of thousands were rounded up, of whom large numbers never returned home.

We have seen how tens of thousands of men were moved about the map of Europe, whether from Germany to roadbuilding in Russia or from the Atlantic Wall to urgent reconstruction in the Ruhr. But the Reich itself constantly sucked in extra labour, compounding its problems by allowing skilled workers to be taken by the Wehrmacht, whose non-combatant 'tail' was more than three times the size of its frontline 'teeth'; more than ten million Germans were conscripted into the Wehrmacht. In 1942 the GBI in under six months built a vast reception and transit camp outside Berlin for men (and half a million women) brought from the east to work there. It boasted Germany's largest delousing station, with a capacity of 1,500 people a day. In August, when Sauckel cheerily took on more demands for such labour, Speer promised him a night at the opera when he delivered his two-millionth Russian worker. Sauckel does not seem like the kind of man who would have got much out of such a treat; on the other hand he needed no encouragement of this or any other kind. Complaining of the increasing difficulties of finding workers in the east, Sauckel remarked to Speer that 'rigorous measures have had to be taken'.[12] Speer responded by asking Hitler for even more sweeping powers to be given to the commissioner on whom he so heavily depended.

He also had talks with Obergruppenführer Oswald Pohl and Brigadeführer Dr Hans Kammler, the SS economic and labour chiefs, resulting in an agreement that 'inmates of the concentration camps will be made available for armaments factories'. Meanwhile 100,000 extra Algerians were to be recruited for the Atlantic Wall. Prisoners of war were being detached from the TO in the east to work in the Reich itself and, insufficiently supplied by Sauckel in the west, the TO was finding labour on its own account in France. Some 450 firms were told to produce a total of 20,000 men by mid-November.[13]

At another session with Sauckel at the beginning of October, Speer was firmly promised another two million foreign workers by 1 May 1943 (as it happened, Labour Day in Europe). He simply could not get enough and had plenty of work for any number of men who could be lured or dragooned into the arms industry. The day after seeing Sauckel, Speer persuaded Hitler to agree to a block on recruitment of key workers for the Wehrmacht, a promise that was once again soon forgotten. The conscription, release and re-conscription of such skilled men caused enormous disruption. Later in October 1942 there were more talks with the SS Economic Office about deploying camp labour in arms factories. Then, too, Speer clearly still believed that Sauckel would fulfil his promises, underestimating his difficulties as the commissioner himself did: Sauckel was soon juggling with statistics to conceal the shortfall in his grand programme.

Shortages of labour were dealt with according to local circumstances: an entry in the uncensored Chronicle for the end of July 1943 briskly remarked: 'At [TO] Group Southeast [Russia] it was possible to stabilise labour deployment at the Bor building project by allocation of 3,000 Hungarian Jews. Another 3,000 Hebrews are expected for a new deployment in Bor.' This was also the first use of the word 'Jews' in the sanitised Chronicle (although the word 'Hebrews' was of course cut out). In the unsanitised version for March 1943, there is an earlier reference to deploying the Hungarian Jews after negotiations between the German Foreign Office and the Budapest government: the TO, it reveals, had organised 6,000 of them into construction companies, of whom 4,000 would be released for the copper-mine project at Bor – 'in exchange for the simultaneous handover of 100 tons of washed copper ore per month'. Later Adolf Eichmann would exchange Hungarian Jews for Allied trucks.

*

Rudolf Wolters, Speer's oldest friend and nemesis of his reputation.

Karl Hanke, Speer's friend, first Party boss and patron, Gauleiter of Lower Silesia.

'Cathedral of light': Albert Speer invented this intimidating form of public display, here seen at the Nazi Party Rally at Nuremberg in 1937.

Three architects inspect progress on the House of German Art in Munich, 1935: (left to right) Professor Gall, Hitler, Speer.

(*left*) Speer's extrapolation of Hitler's ideas for the main north-south axis at the heart of 'Germania' (rebuilt Berlin). The model looks north from the South Station towards the Triumphal Arch and Great Hall with dome.

Hitler and Speer examine the plans of their Germania.

The Great Hall as seen through the Triumphal Arch.

Tourists in Paris, June 1940: (left to right) Speer, Hitler and the sculptor Arno Breker.

A model of the proposed 400,000-seater German Stadium at Nuremberg.

Speer got on well with Eva Braun, Hitler's future wife, seen here at Berchtesgaden in 1941.

Speer left no stone unturned in looking for more sources of labour, but his attempts to recruit German women were, as noted above, consistently frustrated. Sauckel resisted the idea once more at a meeting in the office of Dr Lammers of the Chancellery in January 1943. The meeting made slow progress and was adjourned to the Engineers' Club on the Wannsee lake for a second day of talks. The subject of recruiting women was discussed again in the same circle at the end of the month. Employment problems also occupied much of the time of Central Planning, and early in April 1943 Göring himself took the chair at a meeting to discuss what to do about a labour shortfall now officially estimated at 2.1 million, most of them skilled vacancies. Speer, Lammers, Goebbels, Funk (economics minister), Himmler, Bormann, Milch and Sauckel were present. Once again there was no question of seriously mobilising German womanhood: 211,000 men awaiting conscription were temporarily assigned to armaments. Over a quarter of a million men were now working on the Atlantic Wall.

By June 1943, however, Sauckel had increased the munitions labour force by twenty-three per cent, according to a publicly grateful Speer in a speech to armaments workers at the Berlin Sport Palace. Since he became minister, Speer added, the munitions workforce had risen by half and raw material supplies by 132 per cent, monthly artillery production had increased fourfold and tank deliveries to the front line by more than twelve times. More tanks had been made in May 1943 than in the whole of 1941, and they were also better, Speer boasted, thanking Todt for laying the foundations of the leap in production. On 23 June time was found for a high-level meeting of officials to arrange an improvement in the diet of workers in the Ruhr, foreigners in arms factories and even Russian prisoners of war, whose treatment was usually indistinguishable from that meted out to concentration-camp inmates. Speer made much of this type of action, of which there were several instances, at Nuremberg, yet conceded that the motive was not mercy but enlightened self-interest: a malnourished worker was much less efficient than a properly fed one. At the end of June he scraped together 100,000 extra men for Ruhr damage control, half from the Atlantic Wall, 30,000 from construction and the rest from the Reich Labour Service.

Also in June, monthly concrete production passed the one million cubic metres mark and 170 kilometres of wire was recovered from the abandoned French Maginot Line. But on 13 July French workers were denied Bastille Day leave for the next day by Sauckel, who rightly feared that they would not bother to return. Speer now changed his mind about the wisdom of importing French labour, telling Sauckel on the 23rd that he wanted to declare French war-production factories out of bounds, to keep the French workers in them and to guarantee that they would no longer be made to come to Germany. The workers would thus actually be drawn to working for Germany at home instead of deserting their posts in Germany. The plants were called *Sperrbetriebe* (off-limits factories) which prompted a rather obvious pun. They became a pet project of Speer's, and they had the desired effect. Officials met a few days later at Speer's house to arrange deep cuts in civilian production so as to release half a million extra workers for munitions.

A reading of the Chronicle and the voluminous records of Speer's conferences with Hitler covering his first year and a half as a minister yields a detailed picture of scarcely imaginable hyperactivity in a profusion of fields. His importance to the maintenance of the war effort was clear to a growing number in the leadership of an embattled Reich. Albert Speer was now working flat out, sixteen hours a day, as the most important 'crisis manager' in the German war effort. Keeping the Wehrmacht going with weapons, keeping industry supplied with men and material, keeping up supplies of raw materials, keeping transport on the move amid mounting difficulties – it was a constant, ever-expanding crisis. This did not prevent Hitler from deciding, at the end of the summer 1943, to ask even more of him.

9

Pinnacle of Power

(1943)

SELDOM TEMPTED BY FALSE MODESTY, Albert Speer headed the nineteenth chapter of his memoirs with the words: 'Second Man in the State', a reference to his good self. His strongest opponent at Hitler's court, Martin Bormann, was jealously telling his cronies in summer 1943 that Speer wanted to succeed Hitler:

> He was not entirely wrong in this assumption. I recall having had several conversations with Milch about the matter.
>
> At the time Hitler must have been wondering whom he should select for his successor ... Hitler probably thought he recognised kindred features in me ... Possibly he regarded me as an artistic genius who had successfully switched to politics, so that I thus indirectly served as a confirmation of his own career.[1]

Nuremberg's future apolitical technocrat, an instinctive master of office politics, had been drawn into full-blown power politics from the moment he succeeded Fritz Todt. Speer had outmanoeuvred Göring, his first challenger, with ease, not to say relish, and had even found a way round Hitler by swamping him with experts in each main agenda item at their armament conferences. The size of the Speer delegation assembled outside Hitler's door on these frequent occasions – a dozen, fifteen or even more – had become a byword, not to say a standing joke, at Führer headquarters.[2] Among the highest Nazi leaders only Bormann proved immune to Speer's manipulative charm.

The frustration of the Wehrmacht before Moscow in winter 1941–42 and its decisive defeat at Stalingrad a year later raised fundamental questions about Hitler's leadership, even in the absolute dictatorship of Nazi Germany. He was after all not only the Commander-in-Chief of the Wehrmacht, a title reconcilable with his role as head of state and government, but also C-in-C of the German army – its operational head in the most literal sense. The Luftwaffe and the navy retained their quasi-autonomous C-in-Cs and staffs, but the army supreme command was headed all too actively by Hitler himself. The two senior army generals at his headquarters, Keitel and Jodl, were no more than chiefs of staff, whose job was least of all to reason why but rather to transmit the Führer's orders to the frontline commanders. Field marshals often had as little room for initiative as subalterns, with no say in strategy and not much more in tactics, especially when things were going badly, as at Stalingrad.

Goebbels was a master of manipulation, the original 'spin doctor' of the modern age unprecedented in his exploitation of the mass media; but he did not succumb to his own propaganda. Hitler's most fanatical supporter was also a profound cynic; the plangent prophet of final victory was a hard-nosed realist who was the first to call publicly for total war. Increasingly prone to praise Speer in his assiduously kept diary, Goebbels discerned not just a *Führungskrise* but a *Führerkrise* in the Russian disaster: it was not merely a question of bad leadership but of Hitler himself. Hitler's most loyal disciple saw Stalingrad as Germany's Dunkirk, the moment when the war had been palpably transformed into a struggle for national survival. It is possible that he carried on believing his own continuing forecasts of final victory but it is certain that he knew Germany would have to try rather harder to achieve it. Goebbels did not aspire to unseat, still less to supplant, his idol Hitler in the perceived crisis; his target was the triumvirate that decided not only who got to see Hitler but also what ideas and advice got through to him: Lammers of the Chancellery, Keitel of the Wehrmacht and Bormann of the party, the greatest of these being the last.

Goebbels turned for support in his campaign for total mobilisation to the intellectual élite of the regime, by definition a small minority – most notably Speer, Walter Funk, Minister of Economics, and Robert Ley, Minister of Labour. Like Goebbels and no others at the topmost level, they had academic training and qualifications. These four decided to press in the highest councils of the Reich for austerity in the economy, administration, consumption and culture. Goebbels's call for 'total war' at the Sport Palace on 18 February 1943 was followed by the closure of luxury restaurants and social facilities for the duration, as an example to the population.[3] Goebbels also had personal designs on the portfolio of Joachim von Ribbentrop, the over-promoted Foreign Minister.

After Stalingrad, brandy and champagne, if not other forms of alcohol, were banned at the Führer's headquarters (Hitler was teetotal anyway and rarely seen 'front officers' making their way to the bunker so far behind the lines were not deeply moved by this modest sacrifice). Goebbels wanted to galvanise and redeploy Göring with his panoply of neglected powers over the economy and so many other areas of German life, including his notional status as heir-apparent to Hitler. He alone of the old guard offered a potential counterweight to the triumvirate, given the right kind of support and motivation. He had lost power and influence to such as Bormann (to say nothing of Speer) out of sheer laziness, but was undoubtedly a man of great gifts who needed only to reassert the enormous powers Hitler had vested in him years before. Hitler was fully aware of his shortcomings and not infrequently commented on them; but his abiding soft spot for the 'old fighters' preserved Göring's place at court, diminished even further as it now was by the increasing penetration of Allied air-raids and such horrifying strokes as the raids on Hamburg, the Ruhr dams and Schweinfurt. A meeting at Goebbels's official residence was particularly interested in exploiting Göring's title of Chairman of the Ministerial Council for Reich Defence, in order to push through an austerity programme. Speer, Milch and Körner, the members of Central Planning nominally under Göring's tutelage, were present, as well as Funk, Ley and a handful of other senior administrators.

The fat Reich Marshal took a dim view of Goebbels ever since he closed Horchers, Göring's (and Speer's) favourite Berlin restaurant, but was mollified when it was allowed to reopen as a Luftwaffe officers' club. Even so, the intellectual tendency assembled by Goebbels thought it best that Speer should represent them and call on Göring at the Obersalzberg late in February 1943:

> This was the first time I emerged from my reserve as a specialist to plunge into political manoeuvring. I had always carefully avoided such a step ... I had decided that it was wrong to imagine I could concentrate exclusively upon my specialised work. In an authoritarian system anyone who wants to remain part of the leadership inevitably stumbles into fields of force where political battles are in progress.

In other words, Speer knew then and later that he was *ex officio* a major participant in the politicking of the Nazi regime (and had to be if he wanted to stay in office). The power-play on which he was now embarked, against Bormann's antechamber mafia, was too important for him to be deterred by the apparition in a green velvet gown that greeted him on the Reich Marshal's doorstep. Göring was wont to explain these manifestations by remarking that such attire was on anatomical grounds more appropriate for a man than a woman, and even more so for a man who had been shot in the groin during the Beer-hall Putsch in 1923 (a kilted Scot might sympathise with this view, if not with the red nail-varnish, rouged cheeks and outsize jewels that accompanied the uninhibiting outfit). The discussion went so well that Goebbels was invited to come down from Berlin the next day and join in. The Reich Marshal, egged on by the eggheads, was seized with an excess of energy and enthusiasm seldom seen in him since 1940. It was soon clear to the plotters, if such they can be called, that he would need to be carefully restrained if he was not to blow everything by an ill-timed or miscalculated outburst in Hitler's presence.

Speer engineered a cosy supper *à trois* with Hitler at Rastenburg on 8 March 1943. Goebbels put on a bravura conversational performance, elegantly sugaring the pill of a revived Reich Defence Council which he was about to feed to the Führer – when news came of a heavy raid on Nuremberg. Hitler's mood changed abruptly as he ordered General Karl Bodenschatz, Göring's chief adjutant, to be woken up for a surrogate bawling out: no point now in speaking up for Göring. None the less the 'conspirators' through Göring persuaded Lammers to chair a meeting at Berchtesgaden on 12 April, at which the issue was to be the now persistent discrepancy between Sauckel's recruitment figures and the rather more modest supplies of new labour. The gap had reached about a million and was the result of statistical sleight of hand whereby, for example, any worker moved from one job or place of work to another was counted as an addition to the labour force. Taking up this genuine complaint was a way of confronting the Bormann camp, to which both Lammers and Sauckel belonged.

Göring, Speer and Milch turned up, among others; but so, unexpectedly, did Bormann himself as well as Keitel and Himmler. Bormann was in bullish mood, having been formally named that very day official secretary to the Führer – acknowledgment of his central importance to Hitler since the flight of Hess. Meanwhile Goebbels, his sensitive antennae alert to any shift in the balance of power inside the regime, reported from afar that he had been 'taken ill' with recurrent kidney trouble and would not be able to attend – undoubtedly a diplomatic illness.

The loose cannon Göring proceeded to diverge so far from the prearranged script that he sided with Sauckel and attacked Milch (a softer target than Speer) for doubting him. The demand from Speer and his allies for 2.1 million extra workers was dismissed as outrageously uncalled for by a confident Sauckel, and the half-baked scheme to use Göring as a guided missile against the triumvirate collapsed for lack of a workable control system. All this is recounted in chapter 18 of *Inside the Third Reich* and is borne out, to a degree, by Goebbels's diary and the Chronicle (signed by Speer as each entry was added); but the principal source for the story as a whole is Speer himself.[4] Heinz Höhne, a leading German historian of the period, noted that Speer asked senior subordinates whether he was *führerfähig* – capable of being Führer – and they daringly replied Yes; but that was in summer 1943, months after the alleged Goebbels-Speer flank attack on the antechamber trio had failed. Speer owned up to his ambition, which he naturally denied in his own interests at Nuremberg, to Gitta Sereny in 1978.[5] We need not doubt the ambition, but the manoeuvring with Goebbels against Bormann was surely no more than that: a political power-play which Bormann won with ease, convincing Goebbels by 12 April that it was better to join the party chief than try to beat him at his own game.

Speer nowhere misrepresented his ploy with Goebbels against Bormann as the first step in a coup against Hitler himself, despite the propaganda minister's alleged talk of a Führer crisis after Stalingrad. The account of it that Speer wrote at Nuremberg has him taking the initiative, whereas Goebbels gets more credit in the memoirs. Even so Speer's descriptions of it may be seen as inflationary in conspiratorial terms, an attempt to present a mere manoeuvre as a serious plot. Since Speer will be shown later in this book as claiming that he himself plotted to assassinate Hitler, it is pertinent to refer here to an item in the record of Speer's Führer conferences from the very time of the academic alliance against the Bormann brigade. The 'protocol' (conference record) was taken on Speer's behalf by one of his secretaries, both as insurance against misinterpretation, distortion, error or omission and as a reminder to pass on relevant points to others, whose names are noted in the margins. The context on this occasion is Hitler's approval of plans for the great Führer bunker underneath the Chancellery in Berlin, and his wish to have the air-raid shelter already in place reinforced in the meantime. The relevance of the passage will become clear: 'The Führer concurs with the proposal of Colonel Claus so to develop the design of the ventilation fittings that war-agents injected [into them will] run out again downwards.' 'War-agents' stands for *Kampfstoffe*, a generic term for chemical and biological weapons – such as poison gas. The entry proves that Speer knew in February 1943 of this precaution against a gas attack on the Berlin bunker.[6]

Far away from the claustrophobic world of bunkers, of Nazi in-fighting and Speer's unceasing search for allies in building up his economic empire (soon to be hugely enlarged by Hitler himself), the war was going from bad to worse for the Reich. At the Casablanca Conference in January 1943, as the Russians were expelling the Wehrmacht from the Caucasus, Roosevelt announced that the Allies would settle for nothing less than unconditional surrender by the Axis powers. The Stalingrad débâcle in February was followed by a series of Soviet counter-attacks and victories. The savage Nazi suppression of the uprising in the Warsaw Ghetto in May was scant consolation for the surrender of the Afrika Korps (no longer led by Rommel) a few days earlier, on the 12th. The world's largest tank battle, a prolonged struggle in the Kursk region of Russia over July and August, ended in defeat for the Wehrmacht's last major counter-attack on the advancing Red Army. Mussolini fell at the end of July and had to be rescued by SS commandos in September, when the Anglo-Americans were well established in Sicily and about to land on the Italian mainland.

Most ministers, with the obvious exception of Speer, were of little significance in the governance of the Third Reich. The cabinet as such never met; instead Dr Lammers would chair meetings of groups of ministers at the Chancellery on Hitler's behalf to deal with a given issue. Speer made allies of the 'non-political' or 'technical' ministers, such as Dorpmüller (transport), Funk (economics) and Schwerin von Krosigk (finance); to exert any influence at all, they could go to Speer rather than Bormann for access to Hitler's ear. Göring, as we have seen, was a broken reed; his grandiose role as head of the Four-Year Plan was undermined by the growth of Speer's power and largely usurped by Central Planning's control of supply. Speer and his governmental allies, as he was to tell Allied interrogators, were

> an association of sufferers in a common cause who would discuss their administrative difficulties and occasionally help each other. For example, if I discovered that a Gauleiter was being difficult about food-supply matters, I could bring pressure to bear upon him by threatening to cut coal deliveries to his Gau. We thus attempted to make up for the lack of Reich authority by using primitive measures of blackmail. It was not an easy task being a *Fachminister* [specialist minister] in this war; bombed by the enemy, not respected by the 'big shots' of the Reich, without any backing and bitterly denounced for every mistake. However, relatively speaking, I was better off than the others.[7]

The last member of the Speer-centred specialist ministers' group was the Minister of Food, Richard-Walter Darré, who was also the Reich Farmers' Leader and head of the SS Main Office for Race and Resettlement. As a party hack with inchoate theories on race, blood and soil, Darré was as intellectually impressive and politically significant as his ministerial successor from 1944, Herbert Backe, which is to say not at all; but Speer made such use of them as he could. He was among many other things an accomplished 'people-user'.

Rather more important to him was his carefully cultivated and growing influence among the general staff of the army. His allies there, united in their loathing of Bormann's ally, Keitel, an impressive-looking field marshal whose feet of clay extended to the top of his cropped head, included Generals Kurt Zeitzler, Friedrich Fromm and Heinz Guderian. Zeitzler was army chief of staff from 1942; Fromm headed the Reserve Army and was especially important to Speer because of his role in army procurement. Guderian, the greatest tank commander and armoured-warfare strategist in any army, had triumphantly ridden point for *Blitzkrieg* until his tanks faltered twenty miles short of Moscow through no fault of his and he was demoted to head Panzer training in December 1941. But in a rare reversal, Hitler recalled him in February 1943 as inspector-general of Panzer Forces, in an attempt to revive German armoured prowess after Stalingrad. Guderian's opposition to the ill-conceived imbroglio at Kursk in the ensuing summer was ignored, leading him to ask Speer to organise a meeting with Zeitzler. Mediation was necessary because the Panzer genius had fallen out with the chief of staff in a demarcation dispute.

The two men quickly buried the hatchet in the interests of filling the vacuum at the top of the struggling German army. Hitler was C-in-C, as noted above, but had so many other things to do that he neglected the detailed responsibilities of a post normally too much on its own for one man to manage competently in wartime. Yet he would not allow anyone else to take operational command. Guderian, and now Zeitzler, wanted to see a new, full-time C-in-C appointed from among the profusion of first-class field commanders available. The army had nobody at court, they felt, to fight its particular corner, whether against the other services and the SS, which had their own C-in-Cs or equivalent and suffered less interference, or other institutions.

Neither Keitel nor Jodl, though from the army, represented its particular interests. Speer and Guderian sounded out Hitler separately about relieving him of the burden of active and direct, if intermittently and erratically exercised, command of the army – only to be rebuffed in short order by a Führer for whom the question had already become a vexed one. Unbeknown to their military juniors, two field marshals had already individually raised it: Kluge, the indifferent and usually subservient commander of Army Group Centre in Russia (who had once, to Hitler's fury, challenged Guderian to a duel); and Manstein, of Army Group South, probably the best general of his generation, whose scepticism was to lead to his dismissal in March 1944.

As we have seen, Speer was much better off in his relations with the Luftwaffe, thanks to Milch (but no thanks to Göring); and with the navy, once Dönitz relieved Raeder of supreme command at the end of January 1943, on the tenth anniversary of Hitler's accession. On the strength of having acquired control over naval munitions and unfazed by the failures to neutralise Bormann or persuade Hitler to make way for a real general, Speer in July 1943 coolly asked Hitler for powers over all industrial production, so as to be able to rationalise the entire manufacturing economy in the interests of maximum efficiency in arms output. Speer was confident such an arrangement would produce half a million extra arms workers almost painlessly. Such a rationalisation was also in line with his and Goebbels's abiding belief in total mobilisation (the two men perforce remained on collegial terms, even though Goebbels was now flattering Bormann by making his submissions to Hitler in writing through Bormann's office, while Speer, like Himmler but nobody else among the Nazi leadership, continued to rely on his own direct access to the Führer). Many factories could be quickly adapted, with their managements and workforces, to munitions-related production, Speer pointed out. It was not a new idea; Funk at economics had long had something similar in mind, but collided with the Gauleiters and their powerful regional vested interests. A clash with the Gauleiters inevitably brought Bormann into play on their behalf, as Speer was soon reminded.[8]

A memorandum made the rounds, inviting objections and comments in the month before Lammers was to chair a meeting to settle the matter in the Cabinet Room at the Chancellery on 26 August 1943. Funk was ready, not to say eager, to stand aside for Speer to take over his ministry's powers over non-military production, and all others present concurred. Lammers reported the result to Hitler and a few days later Speer went to see him for confirmation of his new powers.

But Bormann had got there first, according to Speer's recollections, to tell Hitler in effect that Speer was working another ploy behind the back of Lammers and Göring. In vain did Speer protest that Lammers had been in the chair at the relevant meeting while he (Speer) had gone through the proper channels and consulted everybody who needed consulting. Körner as Göring's state secretary had also been involved. Speer now enlisted Funk to help him smooth Göring's ruffled feathers and the draft decree was amended to include a clause stating that his powers as head of the Four-Year Plan were unaffected (this made no real difference as Central Planning had all but hijacked the plan). Mollified, Göring solemnly signed the paper, which was handed over to Lammers, who was then able to advise Hitler that there were no further obstacles. On 2 September 1943, therefore, Hitler signed the decree which promoted Speer to Reich Minister of Armaments and War Production. He did so willingly; what is more, he ordered Speer to use his newly extended powers in Italy as well, as the Wehrmacht dug in very effectively against Allied assaults there. The jealous Bormann had been frustrated this time but was unlikely to forget it. The two rivals for Hitler's attention had arrived at an uncomfortable stalemate.

That Speer had gone up in the world and in Hitler's estimation overall was made clear by the reaction of those courtiers not in

Bormann's pocket. General Rudolf Schmundt, as OKW representative Hitler's most senior adjutant, told Speer the army was right behind him. Army chief of staff Zeitzler, Speer's ally, quoted Hitler as saying that Speer was 'a new sun to replace Göring'. Hitler himself addressed Speer and Himmler together at a daily situation conference at this time as 'you two peers'. Speer lists all these flattering reactions to the extension of his empire, requested by him and granted in more than full measure by Hitler, in the context of his own admission that the whole business had inspired him to consider whether the succession to Hitler was within reach. Meanwhile Himmler added another portfolio to his own collection: he was made Minister of the Interior at the end of August 1943, a logical progression for Hitler's chief policeman, jailer, torturer and mass executioner. Himmler profoundly mistrusted Bormann, which fact could only have pleased Speer (no less suspect to the SS chief, who had recently warned him explicitly not to repeat his attempt to suborn Göring).

Despite the mounting bomb damage, productivity in almost all war industries was still increasing. So long as this was the case, Speer was fairly safe, even from the machinations of a Martin Bormann. Prompted by the disproportionate damage caused by the Dambusters' raid and the knowledge that it could have been strategically catastrophic, Speer on his own initiative took on yet another responsibility in June 1943: the selection of enemy strategic targets for the Luftwaffe to destroy, setting up a commission in his ministry under a power-industry executive specially recalled from army service (ironically Rudolf Wolters was to take charge of another committee, elsewhere in Speer's empire, whose task was to make administrative preparations for the reconstruction of bombed German cities after the war).

The Luftwaffe was no longer up to the job of effective aerial bombardment of Britain, even on a small scale, as the air defences there were so strong (only days before setting up the target commission Speer had ordered an increase in V2 rocket production; Hitler was increasingly obsessed with revenge on Britain for the bombing, diverting resources from much-needed anti-aircraft defences and other requirements). Besides, the British had a national grid served by many small-scale power plants to protect their electricity supply, a fact which made it difficult to shut down their well-dispersed industries. The turnaround in the U-boat campaign in spring 1943, putting the submarines on the defensive for the first time, meant that the British were ever freer to build up their supplies from North America with impunity, whether of finished munitions for themselves and the American forces in Britain or of raw material for manufacture at home.

The Russians on the other hand relied unduly on a handful of vast power stations in the Urals and elsewhere, and some of their vital war industries were over-concentrated, while their anti-aircraft defences were patchy at best. Speer took a personal interest in the discussion and planning of air attacks on the stations; Göring ordered an extra wing of long-range bombers for the Luftwaffe group in Russia earmarked for the project. But once again it was too little, too late. The Wehrmacht was on the retreat and the distances to the targets from German-controlled airfields were therefore growing rapidly, while the Russians were becoming stronger in the air. The Luftwaffe faced a war of attrition on two fronts, east and west, and its demand for anti-aircraft guns correspondingly reduced the supply of anti-tank cannon (basically the same weapon) to the Eastern Front, where the long, high-velocity barrels were as desperately needed as in the Ruhr, Berlin and so many other bomb-battered areas of Germany. The air group was diverted to bombing Russian railway lines late in 1943, a waste of energy as well as resources on frosted ground.

Here at least was one area where Speer's much-vaunted 'miraculous' increases in production could not begin to cope with the need. Hitler constantly demanded more and bigger tanks. Experiments were in hand with a 100-tonner, nicknamed 'Mouse' but well beyond contemporary technology, and preliminary work was even ordered on 'Mousekin', the codename for a 1,000-ton monstrosity that would have needed a swarm of smaller vehicles as escorts, just as a battleship needed destroyers. In the face of all this, Speer could not find or create the capacity to make tens of thousands of extra cannon. Mountains of weaponry of all sizes had been and continued to be lost in the Soviet Union. The transport system could not get replacements and ammunition to the front where they were needed, while troops in Germany had all the latest gear. Production figures for the period, of which Speer was inordinately proud, always impress, and we shall examine some of them later; but distribution was just as important, and Speer was in effective charge of that also, with less evident success.

Autumn 1943 brought a second transport crisis. It was greater by far than that of spring 1942, when Speer and Milch had been able to clear most of the blockages by summer, a success followed up by reorganisation of rolling-stock production and the railways themselves. The main committees and rings were each given a transport commission to facilitate distribution of materials and finished goods. But late 1943 produced a disastrous combination of crises for German transport: the Italian surrender, necessitating a huge movement of troops and supplies through the Alps; mounting damage and disruption (especially of coal and steel supplies) from bombing; sabotage by partisans; industrial dispersal and reorganisation made necessary by the bombing; and the vitally important harvest. Occupied territory was looted for rolling stock (the Netherlands finished the war without a single operable locomotive). The transport crisis was never to ease until the war was lost; attacks on the infrastructure mounted as a prelude to the Normandy landings in June 1944, and after that the damage was done not only from the air but increasingly by the artillery of advancing armies in east and west. The chronic oil shortage was compounded by increasing difficulties in distributing it.[9]

Part of Speer's rationalisation of manufacturing was well in hand before his ministry increased its scope and changed its name. We noted the protected-factory scheme for France, soon extended to Belgium and the Netherlands, in which workers would make goods in their own countries for the German war effort, while Germans (and their forced and slave labourers from the camps and occupied lands) concentrated on munitions at home. The Vichy-French Minister of Production, Professor Jean Bichelonne, was treated like the honoured representative of a friendly government rather than a vassal from a conquered territory when he came to Berlin as Speer's guest within days of the latter's promotion. This was clearly the most efficient means of employing French workers in aid of the Reich war economy; protected from deportation yet not obliged to turn out weaponry for their conquerors, the French would not be driven into the arms of the Resistance in such numbers.

Bichelonne offered wholehearted cooperation in the proposed German-French Production Commission, which was to be extended to other parts of Europe. The two youthful ministers even saw this as something of a trial run for European economic integration (Napoleon never understood either why his ideas on European integration were not embraced outside France). The astounding result was soon to be a total of 10,000 French factories, large and small, working away at producing civilian goods for Germany under the protection of Speer, leaving Sauckel with no business in France, and soon the Low Countries.

As he did when he succeeded Todt, Speer addressed himself to the Gauleiters as soon as he possibly could after his powers were increased. Coincidentally, Heinrich Himmler had arranged to make the principal speech at a conference of Gau- and Reichleiters at Posen in Silesia (today Polish Poznan), on 6 October 1943. Invitations went out from Bormann's office a week earlier; the only ministers invited were Rosenberg (Occupied Eastern Territories) and Speer, who planned to seize the opportunity to try to instil a little realism into these constant obstacles to his rationalisation plans. The Gauleiters were Bormann's creatures as regional party bosses but now also came under Himmler, the new Minister of the Interior, as local Defence Commissioners.

The Nazi satraps were expected to endure a long day's speechmaking from 9 a.m. to 7.30 p.m., with a break for lunch and a party in the evening. The morning session was monopolised by Speer's team of six speakers (culminating with himself), including Dr Walter Rohland, his honorary steel and tank supremo, who gave the one and only speech he ever made to such an audience. Speer's five harbingers informed the party bosses of various aspects of the war economy, warts and all, presenting a bleak picture of growing problems in raw materials, supply, labour and distribution. Because the Gauleiters in particular were the greatest obstacle to nationwide reorganisation of industry and labour, Speer's fifty-minute address just before the lunchbreak boiled down to a hard-hitting demand for total commitment to the total national interest with commensurate sacrifices by sectional interests: total war. The entire German economy would have to go over to war priority so that another million and a half workers could be switched from civil production to munitions, leaving the French workforce to make consumer goods for Germany. Goebbels was there as Gauleiter of Berlin and approved heartily. Speer ended with a clear threat to obstructive Gauleiters:

> The manner in which the various *Gaue* have hitherto obstructed the shutdown of consumer goods production can no longer be tolerated. Henceforth, if the *Gaue* do not respond to my requests within two weeks, I shall myself order the shutdowns. And I can assure you that I am prepared to apply the authority of the Reich Government at any cost. I have spoken with Reichsführer-SS Himmler, and from now on I shall deal firmly with the *Gaue* that do not carry out these measures.[10]

Himmler had a different agenda: on 4 October, also at Posen, he had inducted the most senior officers of his SS into the deepest and darkest secret of the Third Reich: the Final Solution, the bureaucratised mass-murder programme which was well on the way to destroying some twelve million human beings, about half of them Jews. He would make similarly grisly presentations to groups of Wehrmacht generals on several occasions in 1944. These uncompromising revelations to the top leadership of the Reich would make it very difficult for the Nuremberg defendants to claim ignorance of the Final Solution. Speer nevertheless made the attempt and got away with it.

Hitler's reaction to the Allies' announcement of their principal war aim, the unconditional surrender of the Axis powers, at Casablanca in January 1943 was to remark: 'We have burned our bridges.' For Germany it was a case of total victory over a massively superior coalition of hostile powers or else cataclysmic defeat. There could be no compromise, no negotiated armistice, no question of voluntary or conditional surrender. The reason for this dire 'choice' was the genocide programme, whose existence (if not extent) was known to the Allies and now increasingly referred to in their propaganda. They had already threatened before Casablanca to put the war criminals involved on trial.

> Q: What do you want to do to the Jews once you have full discretionary powers?
> A: Once I really am in power, my first and foremost task will be the annihilation of the Jews.

The questioner was a journalist called Josef Hell; the respondent was Adolf Hitler. The date was 1922, the year before the Beer-hall Putsch made Hitler a national figure.[11] Anyone who read this part of an interview in an obscure journal might well have dismissed it as the raving of a racist megalomaniac, as indeed it was. Many people said the same when the first part of *Mein Kampf* appeared in 1925, expanding at enormous length on this murderous sentiment. Despite these clearest possible declarations of intent, many Germans, on hearing whispers of the persecution and worse of Jews and others or even witnessing one or other of the excesses of the Hitler regime from 1933 onwards, preferred to discount them (as indeed did most of the outside world). Germans were wont to remark: 'If only the Führer knew ...' as their children came home with stories of how little Isaac or Miriam had 'disappeared' from their class, or as they themselves noticed that the Jewish family across the hall had 'disappeared' from their flat. Later, troops home on leave would tell dark stories of special SS units, special trains and special areas that were out of bounds to soldiers.

The fiends who ran the Final Solution to the Jewish Question did not advertise, any more than Hitler had his orders on the subject written down for the record. Those who transmitted such orders were wont to preface them with the phrase, 'The Führer wishes.' The Führer's wish was universally regarded as synonymous with a Führer order because Hitler's name was not lightly taken in vain. The Nazi system depended on compartmentalisation and relied no less heavily on the 'need to know' rule. It was a truism of the time that to stay out of trouble, it was prudent to concern oneself exclusively with one's own assigned sphere. Thus, when many Germans claimed after the war not to have known about the worst excesses of the regime, they were telling the truth, strictly speaking, though not necessarily or always the whole truth: many had guessed from what they did know that terrible things were happening beyond their limited horizons. They had kept their heads down and preferred not to know; they had 'obeyed orders' because they were fully aware of the alternative. These are reasonable mitigating arguments for rank-and-file individuals so long as they do not pretend they acted otherwise. Indeed those never subjected to dictatorship or foreign occupation have been over-eager to demand moral courage, a rare quality, of such people, sometimes retrospectively. The same lack of understanding was displayed by the West Germans towards the East Germans after the fall of Communism in 1989.

But these reservations could not apply to the main Nuremberg defendants such as Speer, who gave orders on Hitler's behalf yet had influence over him and were capable on occasion (when it suited them) of undermining, subverting or disobeying his orders, a fact to which we shall return. To aid the will to ignorance, the death camps were on the eastern fringe of the Reich; Speer never visited one (although he was explicitly warned against going to Auschwitz, as will be seen); he did have direct personal knowledge of concentration and slave-labour camps, sometimes barely distinguishable from one another. Speer also disingenuously admitted that he could have found out more but chose not to. Exactly how much he knew at the time will never be known; the circumstantial evidence for his having lied at Nuremberg about the extent of his knowledge is overwhelming, and the Posen meeting of 6 October 1943 is central to such a conclusion. But first a little more background on the Nazi genocide programme is necessary.

On 31 July 1941 Göring, one of whose many titles under a Hitler decree of October 1936 was 'Commissioner for the Final Solution of the European Jewish Question', wrote to Reinhard Heydrich, SS security chief, ordering him to draw up a plan for the 'final solution of the Jewish question'. For its implementation, in another Nazi administrative convolution, both Göring and Heydrich were answerable to Himmler. A meeting on how to carry out this instruction was held in a villa at Wannsee, the lakeside south-western suburb of Berlin, on 29 January 1942. Heydrich and fourteen other prominent administrators, including SS leaders, state secretaries, Gestapo chief Heinrich Müller and his subordinate, Adolf Eichmann, Heydrich's adviser on Jewish affairs, were present. Unlike Hitler's orders to Himmler to slaughter the Jews and other 'inferior' people such as gypsies and the handicapped, the meeting was recorded, if only in summary form; thirty copies were typed. No representative of Todt's (later Speer's) ministry was there. Heydrich stated that Hitler had approved the 'evacuation' of all Jews to the east in huge labour columns. The majority were expected to die on the journey; the survivors, by definition the most dangerous, would be 'treated accordingly' – worked to death or simply exterminated. After an arcane and detached discussion about half-castes and Jews married to Aryans, the meeting adjourned for a light lunch.[12]

Four SS *Einsatzgruppen* (task groups) had gone into Russia on the heels of the Wehrmacht in 1941 to kill Jews. In December 1941 *Aktion Reinhard* (as in Heydrich) began in earnest on the opening of the first of four death-camps in Poland at Chelmno (Belsec, Sobibor and Treblinka, where genocide was also done by carbon monoxide from engine exhausts, soon followed; mass-extermination facilities were then added to Auschwitz and Majdanek, where cyanide gas was the principal murder weapon). It is often forgotten that as many non-combatants were massacred by bullet in occupied Europe, mostly in the east, as died in the camps; and as many non-Jews were killed as Jews, who were however the declared main target of Nazi genocide.

The purpose of rehearsing these facts is to recall the scale of the phenomenon of which Albert Speer persistently denied knowledge; despite his admitted personal responsibility for the abuse of slave labour all over Europe; despite his frequent contacts with Himmler and his economic minions; despite the extra work of his railway subordinate, Theodor Ganzenmüller, in organising the cattle-truck trains even though they disrupted troop and supply movements; despite Gretel Speer's best-friendship with Anni Brandt, wife of the 'euthanasia' supremo who also ran the unspeakable experiments on prisoners; and despite his proven presence at the Posen meeting, where Himmler spelled out what the Final Solution meant. This is part of what the SS-chief said:

> With its few words, the sentence, 'The Jews must be eradicated,' is easily said, gentlemen. For him who must carry out what it requires, it is the very hardest and gravest that exists...
>
> I ask you truly just to listen to what I say to you in this circle, and never to talk about it. We were confronted with the question: what about the wives and children? I resolved to find a completely clear solution for this as well. I did not regard myself as entitled to eradicate – i.e. to kill or cause to be killed – the men, and to allow the avengers, in the shape of the children, to grow up for our sons and grandsons [to deal with]. The grave decision had to be taken to cause this people to vanish from the earth...
>
> I felt it was my duty to speak quite openly for once, and to tell you, as the highest agents and highest dignitaries of the party, of this political order, of this political instrument of the Führer, how it has been. In the lands we occupy, the Jewish question will be dealt with by the end of the year...
>
> You will believe me [when I say] that I had great difficulties with certain economic institutions. I have cleared out large Jewish ghettoes in the staging areas [of Poland]. In a Jewish ghetto in Warsaw we had four weeks of street fighting. Four weeks! We dug out about 700 bunkers

there. So this ghetto made fur coats, clothes and suchlike. When we wanted to get at it earlier, it was said: Halt – you are disrupting the war economy! Halt – arms factory! Of course that has absolutely nothing to do with party-comrade Speer, you [Speer] can [do] nothing about it. It is the ... so-called arms-plants that party-comrade Speer and I will clean up in the next [few] weeks and months. We shall do it unsentimentally, as all things have to be done in the fifth year of war – without sentiment, but with great heart for Germany.

With that, I should like to have done with the Jewish question. Now you know the truth, and you [will] keep it to yourselves ... I believe it was better for us – all of us – to take on this responsibility (for a deed, not just an idea) on behalf of our people, and then to carry the secret with us to the grave.[13]

Despite the fact that Himmler addressed Speer directly (with the formal second-person pronoun *Sie*) in the coda of this ghastly address (which none the less gave no details of precisely how the Jews were being murdered), Speer always insisted he was not present when it was delivered. Professor Erich Goldhagen of Harvard University disinterred the speech and used it as the basis of a devastating attack on Speer in a 1971 magazine review entitled 'Albert Speer, Himmler and the Secret of the Final Solution'.[14] Unfortunately the magazine piled Pelion upon Ossa by attributing these further words to Himmler in the same speech: 'Speer is not cut from the same cloth as a [typical] Jew-loving political obstructionist of the Final Solution. He and I will tear the last living Jew on Polish soil out of the hands of the Wehrmacht generals, send him to his death and thereby close the last chapter of the Polish Jews.'

No such words, or any section with this meaning, are to be found in the speech as preserved in the Federal German archives at Koblenz. Challenged on this by Speer himself, Goldhagen confessed that the passage was intended as a clarifying extrapolation of Himmler's real meaning. It should never have been printed in quotation marks; he had intended to remove them but never got round to it.[15] Leaving aside the questions raised by such standards of scholarship, we can nevertheless believe Goldhagen, simply because he would hardly have consigned such a devastating knockout of a 'quotation' to a mere footnote under what was meant to be a demolition job on Speer's memoirs.

Speer made no reference in those memoirs to Himmler's Posen speech but only to his own earlier the same day. The Goldhagen review, especially the cod quotation cited above, sent him scurrying to Koblenz, where he spent much of the ensuing year and a half looking for proof that he had not been there when Himmler referred to him.

The short answer was, as ever when someone is trying to prove a negative proposition, that there was no proof of his absence at the material time. Unfortunately (for their author) his memoirs give the opposite impression. Speer wrote of the ensuing evening as if he had still been in Posen, describing the way many Gauleiters had got so drunk 'that they needed help to get to the special train taking them to the Führer's headquarters that night' – a distasteful display of which he vainly complained to Hitler the next day. Would he have complained had he not witnessed the scene? Would he have been offended enough to protest to the Führer himself had he merely heard about it the next morning? Had the Gauleiters never got drunk before?

The final part of this book gives details of how he dealt with this and other even graver instances when the truth came back to haunt him after he had committed himself in print. We may note here that Speer, supported by three 'witnesses', insisted thirty-five years after the event that he had left with Rohland by road for Rastenburg, 430 kilometres away, for supper with Hitler, long before Himmler got up to make the last speech of the day at about 5.30 p.m.[16] The controversy over the Himmler speech with its reference to 'you, party-comrade Speer', the naïve argument that Himmler had bad eyesight (but presumably he wore his spectacles to see better), the calculation of the time needed to drive from Posen to the Wolf's Lair in 1943 and so on and so forth, all begged the real question. Did Speer actually *need* to be present for Himmler's shocking speech, or would he not in any event have learned of its grisly contents from contacts who would have heard his name mentioned during it, such as his few friends among the Gauleiters – Hanke (Lower Silesia), Kaufmann (Hamburg) and Schirach (Vienna)? Or did everyone present at such a momentous meeting truly never mention it privately afterwards? And would those who stayed on long enough to hear the SS chief and witness the Gauleiters' binge have mentioned the lager louts without referring to the mass murderer? It is simply impossible to believe that Speer was unaware of the Final Solution after Posen in October 1943, if not considerably earlier.

Interviewed by the British historian Lord Bullock in 1979, Speer was asked whether Hitler personally ordered the genocide programme. He replied that it was impossible to believe he had not. He added that Himmler had made it clear at Posen on 6 October 1943, in the presence of Hitler's oldest cronies, that 'the Jews and the women and the children were being murdered'. Had Hitler not known of the Final Solution, Himmler could not have revealed it to such a group, some of whom would have ensured that it got back to the Führer at once: 'indeed he said that it was a secret which we had to take with us to the grave; we dared not say anything of it to anyone.'[17] Note the double 'we'. It is impossible to deny that the answer reads as if the speaker was there when the cited words were uttered. If the above was a slip by Speer, it was surely a Freudian one.

Before Himmler revealed his ultimate secret to the Gauleiters, Speer revealed a dramatic one of his own to them as they thirsted for their lunchbreak. It was all to do with vengeance against England, home of the hated bombers:

> We have a national secret, a secret which has been kept from the entire German people ... But I should like to emphasise that there are important undecided factors here which do not allow [me] to speak too soon of a definite deployment of these new weapons. I should like to compare our experiments ... with the successful trials of a racing car. We now have to transfer the performance of this racing car, which was achieved with individual models [made by] high-grade experts, to the production-run of a normal car – and then achieve the same performance as before. You can imagine that this transition from top-quality work to mass production will probably cause some difficulties which must be overcome, and made up for at first, by a relatively strong delivery of quantity [on our part].

German arms were of superior quality but greater quantities were also needed – hence the importance of labour recruitment. Italian workers (conscripted after the fall of Mussolini) had filled the gap for a while, but many young men were still being drafted from munitions plants into the army. As German workers were recruited, foreign workers replaced them, but somehow quality had to be maintained. Means had to be found to extract that extra ten per cent reserve of effort that German workers could still provide by keeping the workforce in place to reduce retraining time, and by confronting slackers and malingerers. Workers who stayed away after their homes were bombed could be lured back by extra ration coupons, to be issued only at the factory, forcing them to report for work. Bonus incentives for ideas from the workforce should be increased.

He made it clear that it was not only obstructive Gauleiters and slack workers he wanted the SS to root out but also corrupt managers manufacturing banned consumer goods 'on the side' for favoured customers: 'I have asked Reichsführer-SS Himmler to make the SD available to me for rooting out that kind of manufacture, and I have reached an agreement with the SD whereby it has access to all arms factories and can discover the necessary evidence in them.' The SD would also seek out consumer-goods factories in munition towns and raid them, so that they could be taken over for arms manufacture or closed down and their workers redirected to the war effort. Munitions industry 'hellhounds' would pounce on useless or illicit production.

Speer vented his frustration over the extraordinarily large amount of 'luxuries' still being made in Germany. They included typewriters, copying machines, radios, heating pads, refrigerators and other domestic appliances. The Wehrmacht still enjoyed ludicrous luxuries such as high-quality clocks and watches or leather jackboots for officers; the forces also swallowed up eleven out of every twelve kilograms of office materials produced. A single factory had used eighty tons of paper to wrap sugar cubes (the cubes by themselves represented a waste of effort). The norm should be equality of standards between the home and battle fronts. Eliminating waste could be worth an extra twenty divisions.[18] The thin applause Speer got at Posen for this ringing indictment of lack of commitment in a total war was 'in keeping with the most difficult audience in Germany' – the Gauleiters.

Five days after he thus indirectly but unmistakably rebuked them, Speer was formally given, by Hitler's decree, yet another brief of acute interest to them: planning the postwar reconstruction of the cities, a task which, as we saw, he gave to Rudolf Wolters. Just one week after Posen, reports reached Speer of Gauleiter resistance to the closure of inessential factories as he issued a decree against hoarding by the Wehrmacht. He also launched a drive against unnecessary printed matter, hoping to release more skilled men for armament work.

10

Production Peaks

(1943–44)

THE EXPANSION AND CONCOMITANT reorganisation of Speer's own department made a considerable addition to the paper mountain at this point, the end of October 1943, when the reshuffle of economic responsibilities for the war effort was at last formalised into a statutory text on the 29th – a document so long that it was dubbed 'the tapeworm decree' by his staff. In the Chronicle Wolters hailed its completion, on agreement of the new demarcation from the diminished Ministry of Economics, as 'a historic day'. Speer's empire was now divided vertically into seven main departments: Central Office; raw materials; arms delivery; consumer production; technical office for arms production; construction; and energy. Six 'horizontal' sections handled functions and responsibilities affecting all seven offices: production planning; armaments; technology; supply; economics and finance; and culture (including press and information). The key men in the new structure included the trusty Mayor Liebel (Central Office); Hans Kehrl (raw-materials department and planning section); Karl Saur of the Todt Organisation (both technical office and technical section); and Karl Hettlage (economics and finance).

Part two of 'tapeworm' refined the roles of main committees (production) and rings (supply), economic and specialist groups, including commissions, into the final version of the 'self-responsibility' system for manufacturing industry in the war economy. Part three covered internal relations between the various industrial institutions set up at all levels by the Speer ministry on the one hand, and, on the other, external relations between them, collectively and severally, and other authorities, including the Gauleiters cum defence commissioners and any other external organ with a role in the war economy.

Before this decree was issued, Speer had gone to the Baltic coast for a meeting of armaments inspectors to discuss the implications of the next military call-up. The conference took place in a train at a siding at the eastern Baltic port of Stettin as a precaution against bombing;

so many were present that there were two for every seat and the temperature inside the dining cars became unbearable. Speer seized the chance to escape to nearby Peenemünde inspecting the rockets and to the Gotenhafen area visiting the U-boats and dining with some highly decorated skippers. On the day the decree came out, the absurdly busy Speer attended a fashion parade of men's suits: he was interested in gleaning skilled men for the arms industry by simplifying production of such fripperies. He noted wryly that the most upstanding models wore the suits the industry wanted to produce, while men too old for war service displayed the rest.

There seemed to be no limit to Speer's economic powers, interests or responsibilities. In the first week of November he was busy drafting a decree to engender a better use of manpower by the Wehrmacht to release more men already in uniform for service at the front. Hitler signed it, to take effect on the 27th. One gloomy November evening, Speer viewed a display of household items such as saucepans, buckets and cutlery; once again he was amazed by the unnecessary quality, complex design and variety of these basic goods. His Berlin construction inspectorate completed a new bunker for Goebbels as Gauleiter and ex-officio defence commissioner for Berlin; he was well pleased. So doubtless were the 3.7 million Berliners (out of four million) who had access to bomb shelters from 1 November. Speer received a progress report on the V2 rocket on the 8th (his experts pointed out that the research and development men always exaggerated, and advised a large pinch of salt); and on the 16th, SS-General Kammler reported on progress in the construction of the V2 factory inside the Harz Mountains by forced labour. Two days later Speer was involved in arranging the transfer of workers from shipbuilding to the steel industry to facilitate the dispersed, sectional prefabrication of U-boats.

On 22 November 1943 Berlin experienced its heaviest night raid yet by RAF Bomber Command. It cost Speer a ministerial headquarters, his official flat and almost his life, because he insisted on watching the deadly display from a central Berlin flak tower (a concrete structure topped with anti-aircraft guns and searchlights for more effective air defence amid tall buildings). The tower rocked to severe blasts as the ministry's block in the area burned down, destroying masses of records (Speer hailed this as another blow against bureaucracy, the eternal enemy within). He sheltered under a railway arch as high winds disrupted the work of the overstretched firemen. Speer was forced to return to his old office at number 4, Pariserplatz, after a hair-raising night in which about 3,500 Berliners were killed and 400,000 made homeless. As officeless ministry staff dispersed to undamaged buildings, Speer temporarily instituted a daily noon meeting of department heads for coordination purposes, as many telephone connections had also been destroyed in the bombing. Massive damage to city railway tracks and rolling stock led Speer to order a new bypass route that would take east–west trains round rather then through Berlin if they did not need to stop in the city. On 1 December, the various temporary outstations of the ministry were reunited in new quarters at three adjacent buildings on the Potsdamerplatz in the heart of Berlin.

Eight days later the ever mobile Speer found himself, by arrangement, in the Harz Mountains in the middle of Germany, a long way indeed from the sea. He was visiting the office in Blankenberg where the new-generation Walter U-boats were being planned. Otto Merker, the new and dynamic head of the Shipbuilding Main Committee, had accelerated the blueprints just by gathering all the shipwrights working on the project in the one office, saving six months of toing and froing. It was thus possible to present to Speer and Dönitz a wooden mock-up of one of the 'electroboat' types that afternoon, before a festive 'comradeship evening' took over the town cinema. The Chronicle waxes enthusiastic about this jollification, but any party at which Speer and (especially) Dönitz were guests of honour may have needed some time to warm up (although the corporate enthusiasm of a group of German officials with permission to let their hair down should not be underestimated). Speer was not the only observer to note the prevalence of drunkenness at all levels of the Nazi regime, including the highest (despite Hitler's teetotalism).

Speer was naturally abstemious in such matters and would not have had a hangover on the morning of 10 December, which was probably fortunate. His next port of call was the V2 factory at Nordhausen in the Harz Mountains. The plant, called the Central Works, was an elaboration of a network of caves dug before the war for the safe storage of military chemicals. Speer freely acknowledged his comprehensive horror on first seeing the human hell which this factory, served by the slaves of 'Camp Dora', had become.

Production of the V2 had been driven underground in August 1943 by the RAF, which also targeted Peenemünde, at the limit of the effective range of its bombers. The island rocket-station, inaugurated in 1936, was a rare example of a facility shared by the always squabbling armed forces. The Luftwaffe used the western firing range for the V1 (manufactured mainly at Volkswagen's Fallersleben plant) while the army used the eastern for the V2. The RAF completely destroyed the original V1 factory at Friedrichshafen in summer 1943. The two weapons systems had their fiercely competitive champions in Karl Saur, Speer's grudging subordinate and master technician (V2), and Erhard Milch, Göring's procurement chief and Speer's friend and ally (VI).

Himmler, ever ready to expand his economic empire, offered, at a meeting with Hitler and Speer on 22 August 1943, to provide the labour for the V2 from the concentration camps, leaving the details to the chill Kammler, blond, blue-eyed clone of the assassinated SD commander, Reinhard Heydrich. Speer was by this time accustomed to doing business with Kammler and his superior, Oswald Pohl, the SS economic chief. On 15 September 1942, for example, this trio had met to discuss the expansion of Auschwitz which, as we have noted, was a three-tier establishment: base camp, death camp and slave-labour camp. While the SS ran all three, Speer was responsible for the output of the last-named which included *Buna* or synthetic rubber, manufactured by an IG Farben process. Germany's lack of access to real rubber made this plant more and more important as the war went on. That did not prevent the SS from working up to 30,000 slave workers to death at Auschwitz III, over and above the millions exterminated at Auschwitz II (both had been constructed by Kammler). At this meeting, Speer authorised extra materials for the construction of 300 new barrack blocks for 132,000 prisoners at III. He came to regret this after his visit to Mauthausen camp in spring 1943, where he concluded that SS construction methods were too lavish, as we saw; but in Speer's defence it should also be mentioned that in his correspondence with the SS leaders he complained of the inefficiency of the slave-labour system as seen at first hand by him at the V2 plant.

Overall responsibility for the V2 however remained with Speer's ministry through its technical chief, Karl Saur, as well as specific responsibility for materials and funding. It was at this time that Himmler offered Speer the exalted honorary rank of SS-Oberstgruppenführer (equivalent to full general), which was politely declined; Himmler none the less had Speer formally listed as an adviser on his personal staff, without the minister's contemporary knowledge or consent. One result of the Speer-Kammler accord was Camp Dora (Dora stands for D in the German phonetic alphabet), also underground and alongside the factory. The workers were drawn mainly from the concentration camp at Buchenwald outside Weimar, near the Harz area. Conditions at Buchenwald however were measurably better. Concentration-camp prisoners from elsewhere had also been doing the heavy work at Peenemünde from May 1942.

Dr A. Poschmann, chief medical officer of the Todt Organisation, was not quite the living mockery of his profession represented by so many other Third Reich doctors, including Speer's friend Karl Brandt, for all of whom a special hypocritic oath should have been devised. The relatively good doctor had been to Dora a few days before his minister and warned Speer that the 'camp' – in fact a few tunnels with four levels of sleeping bays cut into them – put him in mind of Dante's *Inferno*. The director of the complex was Gerhard Degenkolb, one of

Kammler's henchmen and Speer's choice to head Special Committee A4 (codename for the V2). Major-General Walter Dornberger and Dr Wernher von Braun, those future masterminds and heroes of the United States ballistic-missile and space programmes, were on hand to supervise the complicated technical side of the manufacturing process; they had been working on the V2 since 1932. The prisoners, from a dozen countries, toiled up to eighteen hours a day and slept underground. There was no heating, ventilation or running water (except down the walls). Half-barrels were provided for 'sanitation' and dysentery was rife, the food was loathsome (Speer tried it) and the men saw the sky once a week at the Sunday roll-call.

Speer's horrified reaction was immediate. The Chronicle records that some of his accompanying subordinates had to be sent on leave to get over the shock. He ordered the construction of barracks above ground for the workforce, releasing the necessary materials and supplies, and imposed a better diet. He forestalled the planned introduction of summary execution by the SS to discourage sabotage by the skeletal, stinking workers. Speer freely conceded in later life that his motive was no more than enlightened self-interest: if the work was to be done, the workers needed to be in a condition to do it properly. The same motive led him earlier in the war to seek better rations for foreign labour, including Russians, elsewhere, a subject over which he quarrelled with Sauckel and others. Poschmann's demands, after his and Speer's visits, for basic sanitation, medical and dental attention were met. Sewage trucks were to remove the excrement which had informed the atmosphere of Dora. Speer even asked Dr Brandt to use his influence with SS colleagues to ensure the workers were better treated; the white-over-black-coated poisoner made a special exception for his friend and obliged.

But Kammler's SS guards remained in charge; and the order for more humane treatment of the slaves was only grudgingly honoured. There were 11,000 men working at Dora when Speer visited it; by the end of the war 60,000 had passed through this hell on earth, of whom half sooner or later died of the experience. In the month of December 1943, 5.7 per cent of the workforce on hand died; in August 1944, the death rate had declined to 0.8 per cent per month. Speer told the Nuremberg court that he had never visited a labour camp; perhaps in his recollection he classed Dora, which he admitted visiting, as a concentration camp like Mauthausen. The distinction was a fine one, of little interest to the inmates.[1]

The irony in this labour-intensive as well as materially and financially draining V2 programme was that it was a waste of effort, particularly for the overburdened chemicals industry. Each thirteen-ton rocket carried a warhead of 1,650 pounds of explosive and could of course be used only once. An American Flying Fortress heavy bomber cost six times as much but was easier to manufacture and could deliver three times as much explosive over a greater distance many times over; RAF Lancasters could double that. Even when the Germans managed to impose more than twenty per cent casualties on the raiders (although many Allied planes were shot down only after they had dropped their loads), heavy bombers remained a far better investment. Germany neglected this type of weapon: its main effort in this area went into the Heinkel He 177, the so-called 'America-bomber' (it never did). But that was a botched design whose faults were modified much too late in the war to affect its course. The brunt of the Luftwaffe's bombing offensives was therefore borne by medium bombers.

Some 5,000 V2s delivering 3,680 tons of explosive were fired at London, Antwerp and Liège in seven months. Many were duds. Berlin, smaller than the British capital, was hit, at an accelerating rate, by 50,000 tons of bombs in five years. Even the wildly inaccurate V1 flying bomb was a better investment than the silent, invisible V2, not least for psychological reasons: the buzz of the 'Doodlebug' was followed by an even more frightening silence as the engine cut out and the bomb plunged to earth, to explode at an unpredictable spot. The V1 also cost far less and carried a larger, one-ton warhead. Some 9,500 were fired at southern England (of which nearly half were intercepted) and 6,500 at Antwerp, but the Allies expended 36,000 tons of bombs in attacks on the launch sites alone.

Speer acknowledged in his memoirs and many subsequent interviews that the V2 in particular was one of the biggest blunders of the German war machine, diverting attention and productive effort from such more obviously useful contemporary developments as the 1942 'Waterfall' ground-to-air missile, which would have been a much more expedient application of Germany's decisive lead in propulsion; so conceivably might a rocket-powered aircraft developed from the experimental Messerschmitt Me 163, which like Waterfall was being worked up at Peenemünde despite constant technical problems with both.

Speer goes further, accepting that the V2 mistake was above all his own, even if Hitler, as ever concerned first with attack and then with revenge but never with the protection of the people, was personally responsible for the decisions to build the Vengeance weapons. Speer's unrestrained enthusiasm for the V2 compounded the error, just as he had compounded the grossness of Hitler's architecture. His commitment helped to produce a crisis of expectation as Goebbels trumpeted Germany's 'secret weapons' that would soon, he promised again and again, reverse the trend at the front. Hitler had the faith of desperation; Goebbels was probably too cynical to believe in 'miracle weapons' at this late stage; Speer appears to have been overly credulous.[2]

Unrealised plans existed for a super-V2 against the United States, and for a V3 and a V4. The V3 was a hugely long-barrelled 'supergun' (in the same league as the gun President Saddam Hussein of Iraq tried to build in the 1980s) which was meant to fire enormous projectiles at Britain at a rate of 600 an hour from a site at Mimoyecques in the Pas de Calais; the muzzle velocity of what was effectively a giant air-gun was to have been increased by booster injections of air as the missile passed up the 130-metre barrel. The V4 was to have used a smooth-bore barrel and a similar propulsion method to fire a long, thin projectile with wings or fins that would open after launch to confer stability and accuracy. This arrow-bomb was designed to have a high trajectory and great penetrative power against fortified installations such as Gibraltar. But, like the poison and nerve gases developed by the Germans, the easily imitable V4 was not deployed for fear of retaliation in kind. The V3, of which three examples were built, simply did not work and was abandoned.

What might have been achieved but for such unrealistic diversions of resources was shown by the increases in production of the main conventional weapons under Speer's tutelage. Combat aircraft production more than trebled from the 1941 annual level of 11,030 (20,100 in Britain) to 14,700 (23,600) in 1942, 25,220 (26,200) in 1943 and 37,950 (26,500 in Britain but 110,752 in the United States) in 1944. Within the German figures, fighter production increased more than fifteen-fold from 1941 to 1944, even though no effective replacement for the formidable Me 109 and Fw 190 fighters was produced in sufficient numbers to affect the course of the war, thanks to a crippling row over the role of the world's first operational jet aircraft. Speer could legitimately claim a large part of the credit for aircraft production even though he did not acquire control of it until well into the latter year. He and Milch, Göring's deputy for production, worked ever more closely together in Central Planning on allocating priorities and materials for all armament requirements, including those of the Luftwaffe, regardless of any differences over V1 and V2.

Germany increased its production of medium and heavyweight battle-tanks sixfold from 1941 to 1944, delivering 2,875 in 1941, 5,673 in 1942, 11,897 in 1943 and 17,328 in 1944 – a result directly attributable to the special efforts of Speer, Rohland and such high-powered advisers as Porsche, urged on by an avid Hitler.

U-boat production experienced a modest rate of increase: total 1941 construction, expressed in displacement tonnage, of 161,719 rose by a modest nineteen per cent to 193,000 in 1942, less than fifteen per cent to 221,093 in 1943 and under six per cent to 233,551 tons in 1944, the year in which the emphasis was switched to the new Walter types.

Ammunition production also increased sixfold over the period 1941–44 but it is worth mentioning the 1940 figure as well here, as an illustration of the 'short-termism' behind German war planning until the setback in Russia at the end of 1941. In 1940, 865,000 tons of German ammunition sufficed for the conquest of Denmark, Norway, Belgium, Luxembourg, the Netherlands and France. In 1941, preparations for Operation Barbarossa notwithstanding, only 540,000 tons were manufactured. The figure for 1942, 1,270,000 tons, seems modest given the size and depth of Wehrmacht penetration of the Soviet Union and the increasingly desperate struggles there. Production understandably more than doubled in 1943 to 2,558,000; and when Germany was on the defensive on all fronts in 1944, ammunition output peaked at 3,350,000 tons, a total which nevertheless fell well short of all needs in such insatiable areas as anti-aircraft shells.

All the foregoing figures for 1944 seem even more remarkable when it is borne in mind that Allied bombing *reduced* planned output by a third or more in all main areas of munitions production. The last quarter of the year saw the beginning of the steep and final plunge in manufacture as the converging Allies crushed the German economy and stifled the nation's material ability to resist. Even so, in 1944 as a whole, Speer's war machine produced enough equipment for the army alone fully to equip or re-equip 225 infantry and forty-five armoured divisions – when it had no more than 150 in the field.[3] Some of this equipment however was of dubious quality: Speer copied and mass-produced for the German Home Guard the British Sten gun, Churchill's 'cheap and nasty' machine-pistol of dramatic unreliability. But Hitler had been so determined to build up German heavy-weapon stocks that a serious shortage of light infantry weapons made itself felt at the end of 1943, requiring yet another upheaval in arms production as some factories were forced to switch over to such basic items as rifles.

It was at the turn of this fateful year that the Allied bombing began to dictate the performance of the German war economy, even as the latter began to rise to its greatest heights of productivity. The *New York Times* confidently reported on 10 April 1943 that German coal and steel production had been halved by the Anglo-American raids, whereas the true reductions were far less. Hitler ordered no response to this wildly over-optimistic claim in the hope that the Allies would choke on their own propaganda. Morale remained surprisingly buoyant among the German population under the bombardment, except in Berlin which was now under constant attack. American bombing by day was more accurate and concentrated; but British night bombing was more deadly with its cocktail of high explosive and incendiary devices. The German civilians and their leaders referred to it as 'terror bombing'. They were not exaggerating, whether they meant the effects on themselves – or the motives of the British Air Staff.

Hitler was not indifferent to the escalating aerial bombardment: on the contrary, his passion for ever-thicker and more numerous bunkers grew commensurately. But he seemed so completely impervious to the consequences for the German in the street that even the emotionally withdrawn Speer noticed it at the time. The Führer had not allowed himself to be seen by the public, and had only occasionally spoken on the radio, since before the Stalingrad disaster and the surrenders in North Africa and by Italy. We have noted his total refusal to visit the scenes of bombing in Berlin, in such marked contrast with the conduct of King George VI and Queen Elizabeth (and Prime Minister Churchill) in London, where a few minutes of 'walkabout' by a national leader could so easily turn private citizens' personal tragedy into a morale-boosting occasion for public solidarity, patriotism and even pride, as an envious Goebbels was the first to recognise. The Berliners could 'take it' as staunchly as any Londoner; but their leader, for all that he was a veteran of the slaughter in the trenches of 1914–18, manifestly could not. As he was driven swiftly through the ruins he would avert his eyes. At the same time, according to Speer in chapter twenty-one of his memoirs, Hitler's outward confidence in victory seemed to grow, although he simultaneously made himself more and more unreachable.

Speer put his hero's change in attitude, also towards himself, down to mounting stress: a dilettante accustomed to bursts of inspired activity separated by long intervals of idleness was being forced to work harder and harder to stay afloat in a rising sea of problems, which ran against his nature. Any tendency he might have had to delegate was now extinct and his innate indecisiveness was accentuated by constant exhaustion, which led to irritability, torpor and periods when he seemed catatonic, except perhaps with his Alsatian dog, Blondi. Never by nature a man for small talk, 'to me and others he spoke in an impersonal, rather aloof manner.'[4] He had in effect turned himself into a prisoner. Teatime with Hitler became even more tedious, and might begin as late as 2 a.m. and end at 4 – one of the few times he achieved a kind of relaxation. More and more he would ruminate about the reconstruction of Linz, his chosen retirement home in Austria; Hermann Giesler, the architect allocated the task of rebuilding it, would be sent for rather than Speer, the anointed planner of the new Berlin. But when the daily bombing report was brought to him, Hitler gave no thought to the casualties; instead he might order the immediate restoration of the local theatre. Having cut himself off, 'Hitler continued to make all decisions himself, in total disregard of any technical basis ... in a total vacuum.'[5]

Inevitably the relationship between Hitler and his architectural friend

Speer suffered in this gloomy, suspicious and edgy atmosphere.

> Until the summer of 1943, Hitler used to telephone me at the beginning of every month to ask for the latest production figures ... I gave him the figures in the customary order, and Hitler usually received them with exclamations such as: 'Very good! ... Well then, nice to talk to you. My regards to your wife' ...
>
> The telephone calls gradually ceased ... From the autumn of 1943 on ... Hitler fell into the habit of calling [Karl] Saur to ask for the monthly reports.

Paranoia can be catching. Speer, with justice, as will be shown, concluded that Saur, his technical lieutenant inherited from Todt, was disloyal and even acting as Bormann's spy in his ministry, just as Walter Schieber, Speer's supply chief and an honorary brigadier-general in the SS, was known to be Himmler's.

Tired out by this constant intrigue, by Hitler's endless changes of mind over production priorities and doubtless by his own colossal burden of work, Speer made his third annual attempt to get away to the far north for the turn of the year. Hitler, as we saw, refused him leave to visit Todt Organisation units and Wehrmacht bases in northern Norway, Finland and Russia at the end of 1942 out of fear for his personal safety (the same had happened in 1941). But in 1943 there was no objection. The risky yet entirely voluntary (indeed eagerly sought) Christmas excursion thus undertaken by a father of six children under ten (Ernst, the last, had been born only in September 1943), in the middle of a war when time at home was reduced to an absolute minimum, seems odd in general terms if not so much for a cold fish like Speer. On the other hand, bawling babies were perhaps the last thing Hitler's overstressed armourer needed at this stage; even so, the workaholic Speer now threw away the last predictable chance he would ever have to spend more than a fleeting hour or two with his family before his children grew up. It is not mere hindsight to point this out, for the war was manifestly going badly and any committed family man would surely have seized the chance to spend a few Christmas days at home when the future looked so dark. If absence for Christmas was unavoidable (which it was not), then a New Year break was surely possible; or vice versa. When he undertook his third-time-lucky flight to the north Speer was as much Hitler's loyal acolyte as ever. But his excursion precipitated a chain of events which radically altered this unquestioning attitude.

Preparing for his break, Speer summoned about 100 of his most senior subordinates to thank them for their work in the expanded ministry, warning them that the burdens could only increase as Germany's difficulties continued. Unrelieved tension between the ministry and the TO command under Xaver Dorsch was reflected in Speer's decision to relocate the men he had planted in the TO main office back to his own Central Office: Dr Gerhard Fränk, Erwin Bohr and Dr Rudolf Wolters. Several other cronies such as Professor Karl Hettlage, the financial expert (and future state secretary in the West German finance ministry), Dietrich Clahes, evictor of the Berlin Jews, and transport chief Will Nagel were also given desks in the Central Office to enlarge and strengthen it in its consolidated role of supervising the TO, roads, water and energy. A prolonged drought had lowered water levels across the country, crippling the ever more important waterway network (less vulnerable than railways and roads to air attack) and hydro-electric power stations. The Chronicle noted growing pessimism and passivity among ministry officials as they reported these problems.[6] On the evening of the 21st, Speer took supper with his *Vorzimmerdamen* (anteroom ladies), traditional protectors of the German boss-figure to this day; they included the ever-faithful Annemarie Kempf, née Wittenberg, once of Goebbels's office, and Edith Magira, who had wholeheartedly transferred her loyalty from Fritz Todt to Albert Speer.

On the morning of 22 December he flew out of Berlin in his new official aircraft, a converted Focke-Wulf 200 Kondor long-range bomber commanded by ex-Lufthansa Captain Hermann Nein, his personal pilot. Speer was accompanied by a small suite (including chronicler Wolters and secretary Kempf) and two entertainers – Sigfried Borries, a leading classical violinist, and the conjuror Helmut Schreiber (known after the war by the stage-name Kalanag) for the diversion of the fighting and construction battalions in the frozen north. Spirits and cigars were among the luxuries taken aboard for the same purpose. The first stop was at a TO site in East Prussia and the next in the depths of Estonia, where a none too successful attempt was being made to extract viable quantities of shale-oil from the local limestone strata. No stone was being left unturned, quite literally, to tackle Germany's worsening oil shortage, the weakness most likely to cost it the war: for this reason the Nazis had encouraged the conversion of coal to oil by hydrogenation from 1933. Their hopes of extracting all the real oil they needed from the conquered Caucasus began to wither on the stalemate in the southern sector of the Eastern Front in 1943.

From Estonia the Kondor continued its low-level flight over the Gulf of Bothnia, northbound across Finland, where Nein landed safely in the all-day darkness on an improvised runway lit by paraffin lamps at Rovaniemi, on the Arctic Circle in the north of the country. The next day they flew onward 300 miles to Petsamo (now Pechenga in Russia) to visit the local bases, including Linakhamari on the coast of the

Barents Sea, a short step from the fortified outposts on the Fisher Peninsula (today Russian Poluostrov Ribachiy). This was the northern extremity of the German Eastern Front, barely fifty miles from Murmansk, the only northern Soviet seaport open in winter and therefore the terminus of the frightful Anglo-Russian convoy route, which the Red Army had barely managed to retain in 1941. It need hardly be said that the Todt Organisation and the German army had industriously turned this most unpromising and bitterly inhospitable area into an elaborate network of bases with social facilities and row upon row of barracks. German engineers had constructed bridges and thousands of kilometres of roads in the Petsamo area, which the Finns were forced to surrender to the Russians as a result of being unwillingly trapped on the German side in the war by the Soviet invasion of 1939; the Germans had taken it over but the Russians regained it in 1945.

Speer delighted in driving himself over the forbidding terrain, taking to skis for the last stretch to the front-line outposts in the company of General Hengl, the local Wehrmacht commander. German artillerymen fired a 5.9-inch howitzer from their gun emplacement and demolished a Soviet dugout opposite – the first time Speer had seen a shot fired in anger (the huge shells expended in his honour on the French Channel coast earlier in the war had really been aimed at the sea rather than Dover, which might have answered back). Immediately afterwards Speer witnessed his first death in action when the lance-corporal standing next to him at the observation slit was felled by a sniper. The chief complaint from the frontline troops was the shortage of light infantry weapons, especially submachine-guns, for which they were largely reliant on captures from the Russians. Speer made notes with a view to corrective action on his return.

The main 'business' purpose of Speer's Christmas trip was to inspect the mining complex on the Kolossjoki River – the Third Reich's only source of nickel, a vital constituent of high-grade steels. He found a healthy and growing stockpile of ore – too healthy, because there was not enough transport to take it southward, thanks to the priority afforded to a bombproof power station being built locally. Speer intervened and the flow of nickel to German industry soon regained the required level.

Meanwhile there were comradeship evenings to be had in the snowy wasteland. Returning inland from Petsamo to Lake Inari, the largest in Finnish Lapland, the Speer party was entertained in a forest clearing, where a great bonfire had been lit. German TO workers and Finnish lumberjacks warmed themselves inside and out with schnapps and flames as Borries played Bach, Mozart and Paganini on his violin, followed by Schreiber's magic tricks. Speer's party left by skis to spend the night in a vast Lapp tent with a fire in the middle under a hole in the roof; they arranged themselves like the spokes of a wheel, their boots towards the flames (a major's breeches caught fire and had to be doused). The wind got up and made it almost impossible to sleep as thick smoke was blown about the tent and people's faces turned black with soot. Would-be sleepers repeatedly went outside for breathable air and at 3 a.m. Speer was driven out altogether by the fumes, electing to spend the rest of the night outside in a reindeer-skin sleeping bag. When he got up he noticed shooting pains in his left knee.

The next night was more comfortable, in the personal blockhouse of the German C-in-C, Ice- (i.e. Barents) Sea Front, Colonel-General Dietl. For Christmas Eve the party made for the TO base at Kirkenes, the north-easternmost settlement in occupied Norway, just west of the borders of the Soviet Union and Finland. Speer, in his element at the wheel of a powerful car on an empty though difficult road, drove the 500 kilometres from Rovaniemi, whither the party had returned briefly, to the base on the 'Ice-Sea Highway'. Some 500 TO men came in from outlying posts to join the surprise party in the headquarters hangar of the TO's 'Viking' district. Speer made a short, seasonal speech, starting with an obligatory, 'Heil Hitler, TO-men', which elicited a perfunctory echo. A military band stoked up a more convivial atmosphere by leading the men in carols and songs and a TO draughtswoman of twenty-one, who had been working in the area for two years, donned a Father Christmas costume and handed out presents to the visitors from Germany. They reciprocated with Christmas parcels containing wine, chocolate, cake, cigarettes and a seasonal candle.

Speer and his assistants left the now thriving party to its own devices at eleven, to see in Christmas Day with the fliers at Kirkenes airfield, from which they had bombarded Murmansk and attacked the Allied Arctic convoys to such devastating effect. They spent the night at the airbase and toured more local TO and military installations to deliver their seasonal greetings over the next few days. Speer spent his last Lapland night in Skoganvarra before boarding the Kondor on the morning of New Year's Eve to return to Germany. Even now his young family were not to see him: Captain Nein landed at the Rastenburg airstrip because Speer was due to confer with Hitler at a series of meetings starting on New Year's Day 1944.[7]

This multiple conference, organised by Bormann, began with a review of the progress of the armaments programme of February 1942, drawn up when Speer took ministerial office; he reported it fulfilled in every respect and was not challenged. On the 2nd, the topics included electricity output, shipbuilding and naval armaments. Speer met Göring and Dönitz the next day to talk about research and development plans, followed by a meeting on the labour situation in France, all before lunch with Hitler. Afterwards the same trio called on General Zeitzler, army chief of staff, and then Himmler, still on the subject of removal of labour from France to Germany. The Chronicle is curt on this series of meetings; Speer's 'no-go' factories might be in full swing in France and the Low Countries by now, but it seems clear from reading between the lines of the January entries that Frenchmen were still being forced to work in Germany, thus undoubtedly encouraging recruitment to the Maquis. The main subject of the first Führer conference of the year was Germany's labour requirements for 1944, the fifth full year of the war. The Chronicle's reticence contrasts with Speer's memoirs (chapter twenty-two), where he described how he was at odds with everyone from Labour Commissioner Sauckel to Hitler himself.

The Führer, no less, produced pencil and paper at the climactic conference, jotting down and totting up the quantity of labour each economic satrap would like to have allocated to him in 1944. Hitler then asked Sauckel whether he could lay his hands on four million workers.

Yes, was the boastful reply, provided he once again got a free hand in occupied Europe. Keitel and Himmler were ordered to cooperate; Speer objected but was brusquely overruled, yet he exacted an airy promise from Sauckel that his no-go factories would be given priority before workers were dragooned into jobs in Germany. Speer claimed to have worked against the new drive for forced labour through his own representatives in occupied territory and his friends in the army, but the adverse current of the war itself saw to it that Sauckel's promised programme collapsed. As few as 100,000 people may have been uprooted for work in Germany in the year the Allies began their overland advance from the east, the south and finally the west. Speer was undoubtedly right to take the view that on this vexed issue of labour he had lost the argument to Gauleiter Sauckel and his powerful ally, Bormann. The customary conspicuous over-consumption, with ludicrously lavish presents making a mockery of fashionably frugal refreshments, at Göring's birthday party in Karinhall, his hunting lodge, on 12 January 1944, the last gala event in the history of the Third Reich, did nothing for Speer's depressive mood. The sharp pains in a left knee weakened in childhood, which had first shown themselves again in the Lapland snow, were now constant and accompanied by an ominous swelling. Dr Brandt insisted he went to hospital. On the 18th an exhausted Speer reluctantly reported to the clinic at Hohenlychen, north of Berlin, owned by the Red Cross but run by the SS.[8]

Dr Karl Gebhardt had saved the careers of sports stars and the mobility of not a few others, including the King of the Belgians, in his capacity as a specialist in knee injuries. He was also a close confidant of Himmler and a Gruppenführer in the SS, in which capacity he had become a specialist in experimenting on concentration-camp prisoners (not that this was known to Speer at the time, of course). The illness was undoubtedly a crisis for Speer, but he succeeded in later life in making more of a drama out of it than the attestable facts justify.

To retain Hitler's favour and influence at his court, as in any other dictatorship from Alexander the Great's to Saddam Hussein's, it was necessary to be on hand. Bormann understood this principle and profited from it more than anyone; but it was no less clearly appreciated by such as Himmler, Goebbels and Speer himself, who spent more time with Hitler than any other leading Nazi with a job in the real world outside the bunker; only Bormann and the Führer's personal retinue – Eva Braun, his adjutants, secretaries and servants – saw more of him. If he could no longer be present because confined to bed, Speer could at least actively hang on to the reins of his power and promptly turned his sickroom in Ward I into an office, working the same breakfast-to-midnight hours as ever and keeping his staff in two adjacent rooms fully occupied.

His health had never been robust. Childhood fainting fits and vague 'circulation disturbances' so commonplace, not to say popular, in Germany were followed in adulthood by claustrophobia or panic attacks which were surely psychosomatic, brought on by stress or anxiety as his responsibilities grew exponentially. No physical cause was found for all this and usually nothing stronger than common-sense advice was dispensed by his doctors. In 1936 Speer took his current crop of circulatory and gastric disorders to Dr Theo(dor) Morrell, a fashionable Berlin general practitioner specialising in bacteriology, urology and venereal diseases, who had saved the life of Heinrich Hoffmann, Hitler's court photographer, in 1935. Hoffmann proclaimed his virtues to the vegetarian Hitler, who consulted the doctor about his own gastric and intestinal problems (endemic, it seems, in higher Nazi circles: Himmler and Göring were among the other sufferers). Morrell's vitamin and mineral injections restored Hitler's appetite and made him feel so much better, before he became a compulsive pill-popper, that he made Morrell his personal physician (Dr Brandt, the other court doctor, travelled with Hitler whereas Morrell did not).

Speer took Morrell's advice to slow down, if not the pills prescribed, and recovered, acquiring enough faith in the pill-pusher to wish to turn to him again in 1941, when he developed new dyspeptic symptoms. Morrell's absence however forced him to go to Professor Henri Chaoul, a radiologist, who X-rayed his gastro-intestinal tract and reported the results to Dr Morrell without a recommendation. Morrell diagnosed inflammation and a possible grumbling appendix but prescribed nothing more drastic than a strict diet and tablets against worms. Once again the patient made a full recovery; he did not hesitate to send his elder daughter, Hilde, to Morrell in February 1943.[9]

As soon as Speer was on his back the Nazi vultures gathered. One of the party's secret 'liaison men' (spies) in the ministry, Xaver Dorsch, the TO construction chief and devotee of the late Dr Todt's memory, tried to spirit a locked filing cabinet out of the personnel office. Dorsch officially represented within the ministry the German Civil Servants' Association, controlled by the party like every other representative body, of which he was a 'Special Department Head'. Erwin Bohr, newly appointed head of personnel in Central Office in place of the dismissed Konrad Haasemann, a Bormann agent, reported the row over the cabinet by telephone to Speer's sickroom suite. Speer ordered the cabinet opened and learned that it contained hostile dossiers on many key people in the ministry, prepared for party purposes by Dorsch, whose secret role was thus laid bare to his chief, and Haasemann, already exposed and neutralised. The documents showed how Speer's promotion of a senior official had been frustrated by the party agents and Bormann. Speer telephoned Goebbels and persuaded him to support the appointment of Dr Gerhard Fränk, whose loyalty to Speer was absolute, as party representative in the ministry.

Speer repeatedly complained by letter to Hitler about the machinations, the blocked promotion, the Dorsch clique, Sauckel's interference in the armaments workforce, obstructionism by the Gauleiters ... Three letters totalling twenty-three typewritten pages were prepared in four days and sent off in the first eight days of Speer's stay in hospital. The letters should not be dismissed as mere desperate reminders of his continued existence from a bedridden man or waning favourite (although they contained a strong element of pleading): ever since Bormann had breezily seen off the Goebbels-Speer ploy against the triumvirate round Hitler led by himself, writing to Hitler via Bormann had become the normal means of seeking the dictator's attention. In the last of the series (copied to Bormann) Speer told Hitler that he intended to sack Dorsch, an official whose seniority made any such move subject to the consent of the Führer – who did not give it. He simply failed to reply to his erstwhile favourite's whingeing by instalments.

Dorsch, an 'old guard' party man and also an engineer of outstanding ability, stayed on and was admitted into the inner circle of Hitler's advisers in the absence of Speer. He was now enjoying the worst of all worlds: still overworking as minister but cast into outer darkness by a Hitler for whom absence was often synonymous with non-existence, sick and exhausted but unable to rest, yet with more than enough time to brood and sink into depression. He cannot have been as unpopular with his 'unrequited love', Hitler, as he suspected at the time because the dictator had ordered all bulletins on Speer to be passed to him personally via Dr Morrell.[10] Hitler also telephoned a few times and even sent flowers (but with an unsigned typewritten note).

Immobilised for three weeks by the plaster cast on his leg, Speer was allowed back on his feet, only to experience severe pains in his chest and back. He was also feverish, gasping, turning blue and spitting blood. Refusing on this occasion to experiment, Dr Gebhardt prescribed ineffectual nostrums. Gretel Speer called in Dr Brandt, who sent Professor Friedrich Koch, an internal specialist, to Hohenlychen to give a second opinion. Eventually he diagnosed a pulmonary embolism, a blood clot in the lung. Gravely ill though he was, to the point of a 'near-death experience' (and by his own admission hallucinating), Speer detected a plot involving Gebhardt, Morrell, Himmler, Bormann, Göring, Ley and Sauckel, along with Dorsch and Saur from within the ministry, to name but nine.

One may certainly ascribe incompetence to the black-uniformed carers supplied by a concerned SS; one may with equal confidence assume that the top Nazis were behaving, as usual, like equally black carrion crows, hoping for a piece of Speer's empire if he died, or if possible while he was still merely incapacitated. Half-overheard remarks passed by Himmler and Gebhardt and imparted later to Speer led him to believe there had been a plot against his very life, as his memoirs make clear. If this was so, the SS private health service, to say nothing of its notoriously ruthless leadership, showed an uncharacteristic timidity in failing to execute, as they could so easily have done, their dastardly plot against the Führer's fading favourite. Product of paranoia or persecution, the alleged plot against Speer could well have been inflated by an oversized ego indubitably under unprecedented strain. A conspiracy of this nature, after all, would be an indication of Speer's exceptional importance. Even so, the patient bounced back remarkably quickly from the edge, in a matter of days: the fever was gone by 15 February.

Professor Koch recommended that Speer should withdraw from the damp climate of Hohenlychen in winter and move to the mountain air of Merano in the Italian South Tyrol, as soon as he was strong enough. This proved to be possible on 18 March, the eve of his thirty-ninth birthday. A small baroque palace near Salzburg provided a convenient staging post for five days, to be followed by six weeks in Merano. Gretel and the children were able to join him for the longest period he would ever spend with them all.

Speer kept in close touch with his work as soon as he was over the aftermath of the embolism. Personal assistants such as Wolters and Frau Kempf, and important visitors including Milch and Dönitz, paraded in and out of his room. Hitler himself chose to come down from the nearby Obersalzberg to visit his sick minister immediately on his arrival in the evening of the 18th, the same day as Gretel brought the children to link up with him for the first (Austrian) stage of the convalescence. Their reunion with the permanently distracted paterfamilias after ten weeks was thus delayed a little longer. Bormann and Keitel came too. Hitler made an untranslatable remark to them afterwards, to the effect that Speer would never be the same again (*Speer wird nicht mehr*). Speer in his memoirs accused Dr Gebhardt of spreading false rumours of his purported 'terminal heart disease' to such as Göring, Dorsch and General Zeitzler. Dr Koch however certified otherwise: his heart was normal and all X-rays satisfactory when he left Hohenlychen with an SS escort, including Gruppenführer Gebhardt.

Speer had a 'funny turn' of a different sort on seeing Hitler for the first time in ten weeks: 'I had an extraordinary sense of unfamiliarity ... It was his face: I looked at it and thought, "My God, how could I never have seen how ugly he is? This broad nose, this sallow skin. Who is this man?"' Hitler looked in a second time on 23 March as Speer was preparing to move on to Merano: 'Hitler came once again to pay a farewell visit, as if he sensed the estrangement which had taken place within me during my illness. And, in spite of his repeated evidences [*sic*] of the old cordiality, my feelings toward Hitler had altered by a distinctly perceptible nuance.'[11] In English this means that disenchantment had set in. Disillusion is too strong a word for this context since Speer was still to demonstrate, at any rate for public consumption, an abiding belief in final victory for some time yet. But relations with a Führer seen as fickle had changed: they would definitely never be the same again. Absence had made Speer's heart grow neither weaker nor fonder.

But Goyen Castle above Merano gave him what he described as the six loveliest weeks of his ministerial career. The machinations at court continued. Göring 'adopted' Saur and Dorsch, according to Speer, taking them under his wing and along to Führer conferences (but someone had to make reports on arms production and construction work, as these two key department heads respectively did).

During Speer's convalescence the row at a distance with construction engineer Dorsch reached a new peak. In summer 1943 Hitler had ordered half a dozen 'mushroom' aircraft factories (hardened plants invented by Dorsch). The technique was to build an enormous curved earthwork, pour six or seven metres of concrete over it, let the carapace harden and then remove the earth. The drawback in this bold and simple idea was the vast amount of concrete required; Germany was surprisingly rich in ready-made caves and other geological features that could be converted into sheltered facilities by excavation rather than using mountains of precious material. Speer had therefore delayed the mushroom programme. But Hitler received Göring and Dorsch on 14 April 1944, while Speer was still enjoying the Dolomites, to demand a progress report. Hitler ordered Dorsch to build ten mushrooms as soon as possible, announcing that the TO would also take over all future major construction inside the Reich as well as outside it. Speer was not consulted; he threatened to resign in another screed to Hitler dated 19 April – the eve of the Führer's fifty-fifth birthday. The visiting Walter Rohland, Speer's tank producer, talked him out of sending it, arguing that it was his duty to stay on in Germany's hour of need.

Hitler was not so indifferent to the growing sense of grievance of his architect and armourer that he was prepared to ignore it altogether. On his birthday at Berchtesgaden he called in Field Marshal Milch, a known friend of Speer, to mediate. Milch stoutly spoke up for Speer, whom he had visited several times, insisted on his behalf that Dorsch must remain under his ministerial authority and even dared to press Hitler for a reassuring message to take to the minister skulking in his schloss, to convince him that he had not been cast out. 'Tell Speer I love him,' Hitler finally barked impatiently.

In the early hours of the 21st a bitter Speer told Milch on hearing these words, 'The Führer can lick my arse.' The field marshal bluntly told his petulant friend that he simply was not big enough to send such a message to Hitler and refused to deliver it. The rift was papered over; Speer drafted a letter to Dorsch for Hitler to sign, telling him to build six mushrooms as originally planned. Dorsch officially became Speer's deputy for construction at the ministry while retaining his TO post as head of construction. But the quasi-friendship between Hitler and Speer was at an end. From now on Speer's own agenda would be paramount. His overweening ego was fully engaged – in a campaign for the preservation of Albert Speer.[12]

11

Fighters and Resistance

(1944)

DURING HIS LONG CONVALESCENCE Speer received an unusual compliment from an unexpected quarter – the enemy. The intellectually distinguished London Sunday newspaper, The *Observer*, published an extremely well-informed and perceptive profile on 9 April 1944, under the headline, 'Albert Speer – Dictator of Nazi Industry'. Unsigned as the classic newspaper profile should be, it was the work of Sebastian Haffner, a German journalist and refugee from Nazism who became a widely respected, London-based commentator and historian. After an impressively accurate *curriculum vitae*, including an assessment Haffner had managed to acquire of Speer's character by his academic mentor, Professor Tessenow ('gifted ... rather cocksure ... [a] modest, pliable but enterprising young man'), Haffner concluded that Speer was by no means a typical Nazi; but as chauffeur of the war machine he was more important to the Nazis even than Hitler. Speer was 'the very epitome of the "managerial revolution" ... [who] might have joined any other political party which gave him a job':

He rather symbolises a type which is becoming increasingly important in all belligerent countries: the pure technician, the classless bright young man without background, with no other original aim than to make his way in the world and no other means than his technical and managerial ability.

It is the lack of psychological and spiritual ballast, and the ease with which he handles the terrifying technical and organisational machinery of our age which makes this slight type go extremely far nowadays [emphasis added].

The fate of nearly all these young men is circumscribed by the fact that they first find it very difficult to earn a living and then find it very easy to run the world. This is their age; the Hitlers and the Himmlers we may get rid of, but the Speers, whatever happens to this particular specimen will long be with us.

Speer soon heard of this not altogether backhanded compliment and clearly appreciated it enough to put it to prompt use. He claimed in his memoirs that it was to pre-empt Bormann that he personally handed a complete translation of the 1,500-word article to Hitler and made jocular remarks as Hitler read it, apparently with close attention: he seemed impressed but made no comment.[1] From the context of the recollection of the article in his memoirs, however, Speer must have saved it for showing to Hitler in mid-May, about five weeks after it appeared, which surely indicates that he attached exceptional import-ance to it (but also that Bormann had not exactly rushed to get his blow in first, suggesting that he either knew nothing of it or did not think it worth mentioning). The profile appeared just when Speer was feeling disenchanted with Hitler, at the height of the row about Dorsch, after a prolonged separation from the source of his prestige and power. The *Observer* appraisal must have stuck a special chord and remained near the forefront of his mind for weeks on end. Indeed it is reasonable to deduce that he came to see it as heaven-sent as it became increasingly clear to him that the war was lost and a terrible day of reckoning was approaching.

The Haffner article is the first known presentation of Speer as the quintessential manager and organiser, the apolitical technocrat who, by an unforced extension of Haffner's analysis, was arguably prevented by his own industriousness and absorption in his work from registering the extent and moral implications of the policies of his employer and his Nazi colleagues. We can be sure that Haffner had no intention of offering excuses for Speer, on the contrary; but the timing and conse-quent impact of his article allow us to infer that it served as the foundation-stone, if not the very inspiration, of his defence at Nur-emberg. His own earliest known echo of this handy evaluation of his role was in a memorandum to Hitler of 20 September 1944, which happened to be the first exhibit produced in his defence at Nuremberg: 'The task that I have to fulfil is an unpolitical [one]. I have felt very happy in my work so long as I personally, and also my work, was judged solely according to technical performance.'[2]

Speer came down from his mountain in the latter part of April 1944, somewhat earlier than intended. He was writing yet again to Hitler with second thoughts about the new arrangements concerning Dorsch. He now wanted Dorsch to be answerable to Hitler directly rather than through himself, in case anything went wrong with the mushrooms or with any other construction project that might be adversely affected by their competing (and huge) demands for materials and labour. Speer tore up the letter, having decided this was something better handled face to face. Dr Gebhardt was against him flying over the Alps to Obersalzberg; Professor Koch's second opinion differed. Gebhardt consulted Himmler, who agreed to Speer making the flight on the unmedical condition that he called on the Reichsführer-SS before seeing Hitler. Himmler warned Speer against making more trouble over Dorsch as it had already been agreed among Göring, Bormann and himself that the TO construction chief would indeed take charge of a new umbrella authority outside the Speer empire.

No sooner had Speer entered his house on the Obersalzberg for the first time in four months on the afternoon of 24 April than Hitler's invitation to tea arrived. Speer told the adjutant who delivered it that he had come to seek a formal audience with the Führer. For the first time in their relationship Hitler received Speer in ceremonial manner, in uniform on the steps of the Berghof, and ushered him inside like some visiting head of state. Construction was not to be removed from Speer's purview after all, he promised. What was more, no action would be taken against three of Speer's heads of department who had incurred the displeasure of Himmler and Bormann with their allegedly lukewarm enthusiasm for the regime – Willy Liebel of Central Office, Walter Schieber of supply and General Kurt Waeger of armaments (Himmler had gone further than vague threats on 14 March, when he had the rocket engineer Wernher von Braun and two assistants arrested for allegedly wasting time on peacetime projects, a direct blow against Speer's prestige as overlord of the SS-managed V2 programme. Speer successfully pleaded for a reluctant Hitler's intercession when the latter came to Salzburg on 18 March). Relieved by Hitler's concessionary mood and believing he had scored a victory over his main rivals, Bormann and Himmler, Speer stayed on for one of the dictator's notoriously unexciting evenings round the fireplace with the same old courtiers.

He was back at the Berghof on the 25th to see the seal set on his victory over Dorsch, whom he now formally presented to Hitler as the new overall head, under his ministerial authority, of construction with effect from 1 May (i.e. in both the TO and the ministry and also for the Luftwaffe); Speer even appointed Dorsch as his construction representative for the Four-Year Plan without bothering to consult Göring, who swallowed the impertinence whole. Himmler kept his own counsel; Bormann exuded a new cordiality, Speer noted with satisfaction.[3] He returned to Merano by overnight train, leaving the Tyrolean resort altogether at the end of the first week of May to attend his father's eighty-first birthday party in Heidelberg; he was back in his office in Berlin on Monday, 8 May.[4]

His departure from Merano put an end to the plotting and man-oeuvring, real and imagined, against him during his illness, whether by the 'big three' or Sauckel and the Gauleiters or indeed the black-clad doctors. That the medical component of these so-called machinations was founded on paranoia rather than fact is indicated by

Gebhardt's letter to Himmler of 21 February 1944, in which he reports that Speer had actually pressed the SS doctor and the Gebhardt family to accompany him into convalescence to help him adjust.[5] And if the preceding Hohenlychen experience had been so threatening, Speer surely had no need to stretch the bounds of insincerity so far as to go to the trouble of organising a high-powered farewell concert there, complete with the illustrious pianist Wilhelm Kempff, as a gesture of thanks to the caring SS staff. It seems no less odd that Gebhardt wrote to Speer on 28 April to mark the latter's departure, expressing his deep gratitude for Speer's kindness and friendship to his family and himself at Merano. And it could hardly have been mere flattery when Speer wrote fulsomely to congratulate Gebhardt on receiving a high award in June 1944 – or when he sent his ministerial colleague and friend, Jean Bichelonne, to Gebhardt at Hohenlychen for a knee operation in October 1944 (curiously enough the Frenchman died just weeks later – from a pulmonary embolism).[6]

Dorsch's role as Speer's construction supremo gave him control of Luftwaffe building also, as we saw – logical because the mushroom factories would be used to make fighters. This reflected another shift in control of arms production that took place during and immediately after Speer's illness: the transfer of air-force armament, including aircraft, from Göring's ministry to Speer's, thus completing his absorption of all munitions production for all the forces. The idea came from his old friend and colleague, Field Marshal Milch, who proposed during a visit to Hohenlychen late in February 1944 that a Fighter Staff (Jägerstab) be formed, on the analogy of the Ruhr Staff – a special organisational task-force for a top strategic and industrial priority. Göring naturally was opposed to what was really no more than a formalisation of the *de facto* partnership of Milch and Speer in Central Planning. Speer therefore went over Göring's head to Hitler.

But he overreached himself by once again nominating Karl Hanke, one of his few Gauleiter friends, who had been standing in for the sick Liebel, as fighter-production chief. Ironically, Hitler cited his own appointment of Sauckel (instead of Hanke as proposed by Speer) to Labour Deployment as evidence of the unwisdom of giving such posts to Gauleiters. Hitler announced that he would instead give the job to another Karl – Saur, Speer's technical lieutenant who, like Dorsch, had been encouraged to let his ambition emerge during the minister's illness.

Milch approved, so Speer did not try to undermine the choice. Saur thus became a chief of staff under Speer and Milch, charged with limiting the constant damage to fighter production caused by Allied bombing. A consummate crisis manager like his minister, Saur formed an instant think-tank of experts in aircraft production, planning, tooling, construction and all other aspects of making fighters. Special commissioners were attached to each factory as 'fixers' to keep it going and restore production whenever it was interrupted by whatever cause, while a representative of each plane-maker joined the Fighter Staff in Berlin to coordinate the new manufacturing and repair effort. Saur held an informal conference every morning at ten to discuss the developments of the preceding twenty-four hours. Even in the rapidly deteriorating circumstances of this stage of the war, the results were remarkable. In March 1944 some 2,200 fighters were added or returned to the order of battle, including 1,670 new ones, compared with an average of 1,100 per month for the preceding seven months. These were the kind of statistics Saur was proud to report to Hitler, who responded with enthusiasm, favouring Saur with attention and arousing more jealousy in Speer.

It was obviously now only a matter of time before all Luftwaffe armaments passed to the Speer ministry. Speer felt confident enough to request this of a compliant Hitler outright at Berchtesgaden on 4 June. He was told to visit Göring, who was also at Obersalzberg at the time, to sort matters out. As a sop to his dignity, Göring himself was allowed to issue the necessary decree. The Fighter Staff continued its invaluable work separately until the last consolidation of Speer's powers as master of all munitions production was decreed by Hitler himself on 1 August: the formation of the Armament Staff (Rüstungsstab), which set out to do for the entire field of munitions what the Jägerstab had briefly done for fighters alone. War production in general reached its peak in July 1944 but began to tail off dramatically after September. The Rüstungsstab was thus set up just in time to flog a dying horse; now everything had priority, which meant no real priority at all. It was the last great reform of the German war economy, now so battered that the Arms Staff, like the Fighter Staff before it, based itself in a train, the better to avoid interruption by bombing.

By this time administrative reform and efficiency drives within and by Speer's ministry were losing their relevance and their power to affect the war effort, which was lurching from crisis to crisis thanks to Allied *force majeure* – in the first instance, before the converging armies overran Germany, from the western Allies' incessant aerial bombardment. Speer told American debriefers immediately after the German surrender that the Allies had spent too much time and effort bombing the mouth of German war production rather than its source. In 1943 the British Dambusters did not bust enough strategic dams, and the almost crippling American attack on the ball-bearings industry had not been followed up hard enough or soon enough; in February 1944 bombers had attacked the German aircraft industry but targeted the dispersable aircraft-frame factories instead of the much more important (and unavoidably integrated) engine plants.[7] But in spring 1944 the bombing had reached such a pitch that its cumulative effects were palpable all over Germany; and on 12 May 1944, when the Americans launched a mass attack on both the German synthetic oil plants and the real-oil fields of Romania, Speer, just back in his office after a four-month absence, concluded that 'the technological war was decided'.

We have observed Hitler's lack of interest in defensive measures against bombing (other than anti-aircraft guns, whose proliferation affected anti-tank capability), such as pursuit-fighters and ground-to-air missiles; and also his whimsical approach to armament production, leading to sudden changes in priorities and over-concentration on the vengeance weapons, especially the V2. The latter is by common agreement the most important example of Hitler, this time supported by Speer, putting too many eggs in the wrong basket. But if there is one error of the opposite kind – failing to put enough eggs in the right basket – that stands out, it is Hitler's decision (and his alone) to throw away Germany's narrow but technically decisive lead in jet aircraft, just as the bombing began to have a strategic effect.

Willy Messerschmitt, son of a wine wholesaler from Frankfurt-am-Main, was only twenty-five years old when he founded an aircraft design company in Augsburg, Bavaria, producing his first all-metal aircraft, the M18, in 1926 and gaining the unusually early distinction of a professorship from Munich Technical University in 1930, when he was thirty-two. He later acquired control of the Bavarian Aircraft Works (Bayrische Flugzeugwerke, source of the initials 'Bf' on his earlier production models) with plants in Munich and Bamberg. At that time Messerschmitt was to aviation what Ferdinand Porsche was to cars, and as the latter laboured on designing the Volkswagen 'Beetle' in 1934, so the former was hard at work on the prototype of Germany's most successful fighter ever, the Messerschmitt Bf 109. It flew to universal acclaim in 1935 and two years later joined the Luftwaffe, which put it to devastating use in the Spanish Civil War and accumulated 1,000 of the type by 1939.

The 109 carried all before it until the Battle of Britain in summer 1940, when the RAF's Spitfire, also capable of well over 560 kilometres per hour, proved superior only in manoeuvrability and high-altitude performance (its main advantage being the world's first system of fighter control by radar); the 109 had the edge below 7,000 metres and when diving. Long series of variants of the two great rivals were built throughout the war. But one of the main weaknesses of German war production otherwise was the bewildering proliferation of aircraft types, sub-types and special applications. Not even Speer could cure this abiding symptom of the rule of military minds over manufacturing matters. The irresistible force of standardisation to increase production collided to the very end with the immovable object of operational requirements as conceived and stubbornly demanded by Wehrmacht commanders, not infrequently encouraged by Hitler. This tendency exacerbated Messerschmitt's difficulty in subordinating his genius as a designer to the down-to-earth requirements of wartime mass production. Yet more than 6,400 Bf 109Gs were made in 1943 and 14,200 in 1944; only in 1945 did the 'standardised' 109K go into belated production, taking total 109 output well past the 30,000 mark, compared with 20,000 for its even more formidable and versatile successor, the Focke-Wulf Fw 190.

Undeterred by his failures with the faulty Bf 110 and Me 210 heavy fighters and the lumbering Me 323 six-engined transport, the irrepressible Willy Messerschmitt went on to design the Me 163 rocket-powered interceptor, which could fly at 600 miles per hour but only for eight minutes – and his technical *tour de force*, the Me 262, the world's first operational jet aircraft. The design was completed in 1938 and the first airframe flew in 1941. But Göring and his deputy for Luftwaffe armament, Ernst Udet, incompetent predecessor of Erhard Milch who committed suicide in 1941, were not interested enough in jet propulsion to the put the world's first jet aircraft, the experimental model developed by Ernst Heinkel and flown in August 1939, into production. It became one of many victims of the innate conservatism of the First World War fighter aces who ran the Luftwaffe, as well as of general German over-confidence (and concomitant neglect of long-term research and in-depth preparation of the war economy) caused by the *Blitzkrieg* successes of 1939–41.

By the time the Me 262 revealed its potential, the mood had shifted, Heinkel had fallen out of favour and Messerschmitt was personally popular with the Nazi leadership, excluding Milch but including Hitler and Speer. Even so, the 262 design was not successfully married up to its power plant, the Junkers Jumo turbojet, until November 1943. But at this critical juncture, Hitler's obsession with vengeance, stoked up by the all-pervading Allied bombing, led him to concentrate on the V1 and V2, and to order in September 1943 that the Me 262 should not now go into priority production as planned by Milch, who did not allow his dislike of its inventor to cloud his admiration for the aircraft.[8]

In January 1944 Hitler changed his mind again, having read a report from the British press about the successful progress of the Gloster Meteor jet fighter, a prototype of which had first flown in March 1943 (the jet engine was invented in England by Frank Whittle in 1936, but as ever the British had been slow to recognise the potential of their own ingenious discovery). Hitler demanded all-out production of the 262 – but as a *bomber*. This only compounded the great error of massive over-commitment to the V2 rocket in particular (which *inter alia* reduced the resources available for the twin-engined jet). Speer, Milch, the Luftwaffe commanders and above all Adolf Galland, the thirty-one-year-old Inspector-General of fighters, protested in vain, recognising the possibilities of the jet as originally conceived – an uncatchable pursuit fighter, as much of a threat to the slower, Allied long-range fighter escorts as to the accursed bombers themselves.

Even Göring briefly joined Speer late in June 1944 in a protest against the misapplication of Messerschmitt's breakthrough. Fighters purportedly retained their absolute priority, at any rate among air weaponry, but the Me 262 fiasco can only, among many adverse side-effects, have interfered with the production of other fighters. Hitler meanwhile was simultaneously demanding all-out production of half a dozen new types of tank as if he had years rather then weeks to repel the inexorable Allied armies.

The Me 262A2, with improvised bomb-racks disfiguring its wings (and affecting its stability and speed), made its inordinately belated appearance at the front instead of over German cities and strategic installations – at the wrong time, in the wrong place and the wrong role to make a difference to the course of the war. It could carry one bomb on each side for a maximum bomb-load of 500 kilograms, or a mere two-thirds of the V2's unduly modest payload. Unable to exploit its maximum speed of 860 kilometres per hour with its bombs in place or do much damage to a protected target with its light payload and its primitive, spatchcocked bombsight, the world's first jet aircraft to go into production and battle was frittered away in penny-packets on ineffectual, short-range, tactical bombing raids. The latest Allied conventional fighters, fast enough to catch V1 flying bombs, did not have too much difficulty in shooting down more than 120 Me 262s, mostly in the misbegotten bomber mode, thus accounting for over half the total of 220 deployed in the war (although a total of 1,433 of both types – bomber and fighter – were completed, the war ended before enough pilots could be trained to man them).

The Me 262 was manufactured in three of Dorsch's 'mushroom' underground aircraft factories, designed in detail by Professor Franz Dischinger and ordered in May 1944. The first colossal installation was completed in November, hidden in a pine forest on the outskirts of Landsberg, the Bavarian town in whose fortress-prison Hitler had served his laughable sentence for the 'Beer-hall Putsch' and composed *Mein Kampf*. The Landsberg mushroom, its concrete roof covered by earth and transplanted trees, was built by 10,000 German artisans and an equal number of Jews, supplied by the SS from Hungary, Czechoslovakia and elsewhere. Speer visited the plant and associated labour camps in February 1945 and saw the appalling conditions in which the Jews worked, lived and all too frequently died.

It was a scene to challenge his doubtless suppressed memory of Dora, but on this occasion he seemed resigned to the unspeakable squalor and brutality of the SS system, merely telling a subordinate to contact Himmler's office about the Jews' condition.[9] This attitude was surely as much an indication of pessimism as of callousness at that stage of the war: with defeat looming, what conceivable economic benefit from a better-treated workforce was worth another row with the SS about its handling of slave labour? The enlightened self-interest which led him on earlier occasions to do something positive about the sufferings of forced labour for the benefit of productivity would have had little relevance in 1945.

By the time Speer went to the first Me 262 plant, Lieutenant-General Galland, ever mindful of the RAF's successful fighter-defence of Britain in 1940, had become a casualty of the battle over the deployment of the jets. Inevitably, Göring soon came round to accepting Hitler's strategic misjudgment in using them as bombers and, irritated beyond measure by Galland's protests, dismissed him for insubordination in January 1945. Hitler woke up to the 262's true potential far too late, ordering production to switch to the fighter-mode only on 22 March 1945. The Führer threw a contemptuous sop to Germany's most senior and distinguished fighter commander of the war by recalling him to the colours in a colonel's job, heading the newly formed Fighter Group 44 (equivalent to a British or US 'wing'), a quasi-kamikaze unit full of other disgraced 'delinquents'. The formation flew Me 262B fighters, giving Galland his chance to show what they could do, and what they might have done earlier – his last and most hair-raising taste of aerial combat in a very long personal war, begun over Spain in 1936. The result for his targets was devastating, but insignificant at this stage of the conflict: nothing could now make any difference to the continuing devastation of Germany from the air, which reached its peak with the gratuitous Anglo-American immolation of Dresden in February 1945. The world's most senior combat pilot was shot down by an American aircraft at the end of April, but was not seriously hurt.[10]

The errors over V2 and Me 262 were of commission and omission respectively; both were considerable contributions to Germany's defeat by the Nazi leaders themselves. Without such blunders, the Germans might conceivably have delayed the inevitable even longer than they did, thanks not least to the efforts of Speer, his subordinates and millions of German and foreign workers, to sustain the Wehrmacht. But events after the German surrenders at Stalingrad and in North Africa early in 1943 had turned the German military situation on all fronts in Europe into a vast rearguard action, sometimes conducted with brilliance despite increasingly common bursts of ineptitude by Commander-in-Chief Hitler. Even as the vast anti-Axis coalition with its hugely superior strength and resources ground towards victory, the Germans could hardly be written off. Swiftly producing the world's first cruise and ballistic missiles, jet aircraft and hydrodynamic sub-marines as well as new tanks and other army weapons, the Germans mounted a resolute defence of northern Italy, held off the avenging Red Army much longer than seemed possible after Stalingrad, defeated Montgomery's attempt to shorten the war by a thrust for the Rhine through the Netherlands (the Arnhem débâcle of September 1944), and even achieved strategic surprise with their last counter-attack in the Ardennes at the turn of 1944.

The odds against the Germans in the last phase of the European war, admittedly a much bigger affair, seem rather similar to those against the South in the final stages of the American Civil War, in which the overwhelming superiority of the North only asserted itself at a snail's pace against an ingenious and determined enemy who held out long after his cause had become hopeless. As the Americans and their British allies landed at Anzio in southern Italy in January 1944, the Russians at last raised the siege of Leningrad; and as the Germans abandoned their Italian fastness at Monte Cassino in May after one of the hardest-fought rearguard actions of the war, the Red Army recap-tured the Crimea on the southern sector of the German Eastern Front.

But the principal military event of 1944 came on 6 June, when the western Allies invaded Normandy. Stalin and a strongly vocal element in the American leadership had been calling for an assault on 'Fortress Europe' from the west for more than a year. The British, who were to provide the springboard and the naval cover plus large land and air forces, were more cautious. They preferred Churchill's 'soft underbelly' approach from the south; but, just as their flanking attack against a 'weak' Turkey in 1915 had been held off by an unexpectedly tough enemy at the Dardanelles, so the Germans' 'Gothic Line', still holding out and being strengthened in August 1944, had prevented a swift 'rolling up' of the map of Italy.

The Americans remained committed to a frontal assault on the main force of the main enemy, relying on superior firepower and resources. In so doing they were following the advice of the Prussian strategist Clausewitz (and the example of General Ulysses S. Grant, architect of victory in the Civil War). British circumspection had to a large degree been justified by events both before and after the brilliantly executed invasion of Normandy. The Americans were even less ready than Britain to take on the world's best army in 1943: hugely outnumbered and starved of supplies, the Germans held on in North Africa for six months after the American landing in November 1942 and then exacted a very high price for southern and central Italy in 1944. And just six days after the American, British and Canadian divisions landed in France, the first V1 flying bomb landed on London, opening the 'second Blitz' on the suffering British capital in the fifth year of the war. It was nothing like as extensive as the first, and the devastation caused by the two vengeance weapons was a fraction of Berlin's bomb damage; but the psychological effect of a new and eerie, even more unpredictable threat from the sky just as victory seemed to be in sight was enormous. The dismay was redoubled when the first V2 struck on 8 September.

When General Eisenhower gave the order to invade at dawn on 6 June, Hitler and his entourage were at the Berghof, his 'Eagle's Nest' on the Obersalzberg, while his 'Wolf's Lair' headquarters at Rastenburg was being strengthened yet again with another ocean of concrete. The first reaction from the Führer no less than his acolytes (who decided to let him sleep on after they got the flash message from Normandy) was that the landing must be a feint. For weeks beforehand, Allied bombers had been gumming up German coastal radar by dropping 'window' all along the coast of Fortress Europe (I can remember the strips of shiny metal tape raining down on my home town of Alkmaar in north-west Holland). Reconnaissance aircraft had been hyperactive also, and Allied intelligence services had been putting out all manner of disinformation, some of it crude, some of it very subtle. Long strings of apparent gibberish were being broadcast to secret agents and resistance groups all over occupied western Europe by the BBC, to the amusement, bewilderment and frustration of the German eavesdroppers.

The irony of the reaction to Operation Overlord was that Hitler had originally forecast Normandy as the target area. But Nazi Germany boasted no fewer than seven intelligence-gathering services, run respectively by the Foreign Office, the OKW or Wehrmacht High Command (the Abwehr), the three armed services, Göring's Research Bureau and the SS (RSHA or Reich main security office). Thus the potential for conflicting advice from fiercely competing agencies was rich indeed. According to Speer,[11] Hitler took the not unreasonable course of rejecting their conflicting predictions in favour of a new guess of his own – the Pas de Calais, not least because this area was closest to Britain and also accommodated fifty-five V1 launching sites (already the subject of crushing RAF attention). He therefore made the fateful error of preventing the German army, led in the west by Field Marshal Gerd von Rundstedt, from committing its local strategic reserve, two Panzer divisions, until well after daylight on 7 June, by which time they were vulnerable to ground attack by vastly superior Allied tactical airpower.

By then the Allied armies had established their bridgehead on the Normandy coast and the counter-thrust was blunted. Hitler clung to his belief that the Normandy assault, the largest of its kind in history, even though it coincided with the Americans' not much smaller amphibious Operation Forager in the central Pacific (against the Marianas and the Vulcan Islands, the largest in the theatre so far), was only a diversionary hors d'oeuvre. As the Allied forces poured ashore to join the heavy battle for the Norman city of Caen, Hitler kept the entire 15th Army idle at Calais, allowing Allied air forces to box it in by destroying the bridges on local main roads. Less than three weeks after D-day, three-quarters of a million Allied troops had come ashore in Normandy.

Hitler's insistence that the whole thing was a diversion doubtless explains the absence of special tension at the Berghof in the reaction to the return to north-west France of an Allied expeditionary force exactly four years after the last one was sent packing. Speer's sense of drama and of history in the making was notoriously deficient, even with the benefit of hindsight, as witness his need for prompting to include the *Reichskristallnacht* in his memoirs; but chapter twenty-four of *Inside the Third Reich* is extraordinarily downbeat about D-day. The reader can only deduce that Hitler's reaction to the reopening of the Western Front was indeed a pale shadow of his response to the Anglo-French declaration of war in 1939.

The V1 'Doodlebugs' meanwhile were causing pandemonium out of all proportion to their numbers as they buzzed and swooped over London. Of the first salvo of ten, launched overnight on 12–13 June, six misfired or fell in the sea, four managed to reach England and one killed six Londoners. But on 18 June, a V1 landed on the Guards' Chapel at Wellington Barracks near Buckingham Palace, killing 119 soldiers and civilians during a service and injuring 102. The previous day Hitler made a brief visit to one of his command bunkers, near Soissons in France (built for him in 1940 to superintend an invasion of Britain), for a briefing which rapidly became an argument with Rundstedt (C-in-C West) and Rommel (commanding Army Group B), who wanted to withdraw from the coastal area, under constant and massive British naval bombardment, to regroup and counter-attack in force. Hitler predictably refused, bemoaning their 'defeatism' and promising relief in the form of Me 262 jets (the first experimental wing of bomber-variants was formed at the end of the month). Shortly after the marshals, two of Germany's greatest generals, left empty-handed, Hitler and his bunker rocked to a direct hit on the thick, concrete roof – from a rogue V1 just launched nearby. Hitler returned to Berchtesgaden that evening; Speer was still there.

By then two 'Mulberry' artificial harbours were in place off Arromanches and St Laurent, enabling the Allies to dispense with conventional supply ports for the time being, and the U-boats had abandoned their French bases. On 22 June, the third anniversary of Barbarossa, the Russians hurled 1.2 million troops against the central sector of the German Eastern Front in the Soviet Union, where the Wehrmacht suddenly found itself outnumbered three to one. But on the same day the Luftwaffe showed it still had teeth by sending seventy-five aircraft to attack a Soviet airbase at Poltava, Ukraine. A group of B 17 Bombers of the US Army's Eighth Air Force, based in England, had landed there after another strategically damaging, long-range raid on a German synthetic oil plant which lay beyond the bombers' maximum radius, so that they could not fly back to Britain. Forty-seven Flying Fortresses were destroyed and another twenty-six badly damaged on the ground when a large fuel dump exploded. What would have been a blow of strategic proportions two and a half years earlier, when a Japanese attack on thirty-four grounded B 17s and some sixty smaller aircraft in the Philippines gave them local air superiority, was a minor setback to the Americans as they mustered overwhelming stockpiles for massive simultaneous operations in two theatres 10,000 miles apart.

Rundstedt, Rommel (both soon to be sacked) and Speer were among those who now fully understood what Hitler had done in taking on such a coalition of enemies: 'one part of my consciousness certainly acknowledged that now everything must be approaching the end.'[12] The fact that the V1s killed 2,000 Londoners in their first three weeks, provoking a second evacuation of the capital, made not a whit of strategic difference – except perhaps to harden the determination of British troops in the field.

Hitler however was far from alone in invoking the hope that secret weapons would enable Germany to paralyse the jaws of the great Allied pincer movement from east and west. He also ordered a quintupling of anti-aircraft gun production by December 1945 instead of concentrating on fighters, whose manufacture was to cease altogether and forthwith. Speer and Saur persuaded him to halve the unrealisable cannon target, more for the sake of argument than anything else, and agreed between themselves to ignore the moratorium on fighters, the indirect result of Galland's last stand against Hitler. 'That was the first command from Hitler that neither Saur nor I obeyed.'[13] They went on

churning out fighters at the spanking rate of more than 2,300 a month
for the last six months of 1944.

In his notorious visit to the Gauleiters at Posen in October 1943,
Speer had more than hinted that new miracle weapons would turn
the tide for Germany. Goebbels believed, at least for public con-
sumption – or, like Hitler, persuaded himself to believe – that the V1
and V2 would transform the deteriorating situation. Speer did nothing
to dampen his enthusiasm, presenting the Reich's leading cinema buff
with spectacular film of experimental V2 launches (actually the same
one photographed from many different angles). Goebbels rushed into
print in July 1944 with euphoric promises of unspecified technological
deliverance; they had the opposite of the desired effect on morale when
the bombers kept on coming and no such miracle transpired.

Speer was still talking up victory in August 1944, both at a meeting
with ministry staff on the first of the month, when he inveighed against
defeatism, and in an address to arms industry leaders on the 31st,
when he reminded them of what was coming: jet planes, new fast
submarines, vengeance weapons ... It was only in November 1944
that Speer wrote to Goebbels to say it was unrealistic to go on telling
the people to place their faith in salvation by miracle weapons because
this was deceiving them with false promises. But such new-found
scepticism did not stop him from urging his staff, industrialists and
workers, even soldiers when he met them, to carry on working flat
out for victory.

It was only in January 1945 that Speer publicly damped down
speculation about secret weapons for the first time, denying that
he had ever been responsible for such misleading propaganda.[14] He
conveniently forgot all this when debriefed by Allied interrogators in
May and June 1945, telling them that he had known by spring 1943
that the war was lost and blaming Hitler and Goebbels for hawking
the chimera of victory by miracle beyond all reason. We may safely
deduce that he was sufficiently in touch with reality early in 1943 to
see in his head, and probably in his heart as well, that his predecessor's
diagnosis an entire year earlier of an unwinnable war had been
justified, even well before the Stalingrad disaster. But it is surely
beginning to emerge from the story of Speer's life that he had a well-
developed capacity for psychological denial, the ability to evade the
truth by suppressing it.

In terms of desperation in the last year of the war the Germans did
not quite match their Japanese allies. There was no Nazi kamikaze
corps: Adolf Galland was at least given a formidable new weapon with
which to make his last stand rather than the wooden aircraft with
built-in suicide bombs flown at warships by Japanese pilots (although
Himmler wanted to send suicide pilots in rocket planes against the

bombers). But Germany deployed an extraordinary array of last-ditch armament in 1944 and 1945, very little of which was under Speer's productive control. Dönitz ordered one-man submarines in April 1944; the army ordered robot mini-tanks filled with explosives; great hopes were attached to the *Panzerfaust*, copied from the American bazooka, a hand-fired anti-tank rocket-launcher, of which three and a half million were made in the three months from 1 November 1944. These were to replace anti-tank guns, which would have been made in much greater numbers but for Hitler's endless demands for anti-aircraft guns which used the same barrels, a diversion of production made necessary by his own misuse of German fighter strength. But the point-blank *Panzerfaust*, even in infinite numbers, was no substitute for the high muzzle-velocity, armour-piercing shells of an accurate cannon fired at a safe distance.

Hitler suddenly remembered his own nasty experience at the end of the First World War and in autumn 1944 ordered mass production of masks, against the possibility of gas attacks by an enemy that could not now be repaid in kind without danger to the German population in the battle zones as they began to take in Reich territory. It was just as likely that Hitler was toying with the idea of using gas against the invaders, especially the downwind Russians, and ordered the masks to protect Germans from the effects; there is no concrete evidence of such intent. Remarkably for a war which brought an unprecedented and fiendish application of poison gas in the death camps and saw increasingly uninhibited, indiscriminate attacks on civilians, neither side deployed gas on the battlefield or in air-raids. It had been a two-edged sword when introduced by the Germans in April 1915, especially when the wind changed back to the prevailing south-west, but each side stockpiled gas weapons from 1939 in case the other used them. The Germans made 3,100 tons of mustard gas and 1,000 tons of deadly Tabun (nerve gas) per month for five years until summer 1944, when Allied attacks on the German chemical industry caused strategic disruption. Tabun production ceased altogether at the end of October 1944, while mustard-gas manufacture was cut by three-quarters, both for lack of the necessary constituents.[15] Speer said he ignored countermanding orders from Keitel of OKW and reallocated the chemicals as he saw fit.

Summer 1944 also brought all but terminal disruption to the German road and rail transport systems. The Ruhr had been embroiled in what amounted to a regional gridlock for six weeks by mid-November 1944. Coal was therefore short both within and outside the German region which produced more of it than any other. Discipline broke down as such coal trains as could be moved failed to reach their destinations and were looted by local party officials. Prolonged power cuts and domestic and industrial fuel shortages bit ever harder as an unusually cold winter set in early. The constant attacks on the synthetic-fuel plants and the Balkan oilfields compounded the transport crisis. The arms industry could now continue working only on the strength of its own stockpiles of materials and parts – which however proved remarkably large, despite all earlier strictures and threats of dire punishment for hoarding. This was the basis of Nazi Germany's last push in armaments production for which Hitler pointedly looked to Saur rather than Speer at the end of 1944.[16] By this time the latter was clearly not displeased to have the buck taken out of his hand and passed to his ambitious deputy for technical matters, who could conveniently shoulder the blame when things went wrong.

Like the gambler he had always been, Hitler resolved to stake everything on a last card, a counter-attack in the west. His mind was made up in the first few days of October 1944, as he confided to Speer on condition of absolute secrecy on the 12th. Two months before the event, Speer was told to assemble a special task-force of motorised Todt Organisation construction workers to back a counter-attack in the Ardennes and a drive on Antwerp, selected by the Allies for their principal supply port. The American army was to be pushed back and the British army encircled and driven into the sea as it had been in 1940. But the Russians were pressing in much greater numbers, already threatening the industrial zone of Silesia, second in importance only to the Ruhr for the German war economy. Inevitably rumours of a German counter-thrust began to spread – but the logical assumption by those not as privileged as Speer was that it would be against the Russians, whose greater numbers and lust for vengeance made them the greater threat.

The Ardennes offensive of 16 December 1944, leading to the 'Battle of the Bulge' (the salient the Germans created in the Allied line), proved to be a remarkably potent threat. It caught the Americans on the hop as they began to wind down for Christmas, and it was all the more remarkable in the light of increasing chaos and shortages in Germany caused by Allied bombing. But even the startling if temporary triumph over mounting difficulty behind the front looks insignificant in retrospect when compared with the high morale of Field Marshal Walter Model's troops – less than five months after the German army had been riven by the one serious plot made by Germans against Hitler's life.

The Normandy breakout and the Soviet assault of June 1944 at last convinced a small and mostly aristocratic coterie of German army officers that all was lost and something must be done against Hitler. The courage of Colonel Claus von Stauffenberg is not to be questioned here, any more than that of Hans and Sophie Scholl, the Munich students who shamed all contemporary Germans by protesting against the Nazis eighteen months before the army officers acted.

The main complaint history is entitled to raise against the German resistance to Hitler is that it was too little, too late. There was never very much of it, however brave individual resisters undoubtedly were and however great the risks they faced. If there is one overriding trend in the historiography of the Second World War, it is that anti-Nazi resistance is generally exaggerated (a form of inflation surpassed only by pilots reporting bomb damage and the like). This tendency is as pronounced in Germany as it is in France and other erstwhile occupied countries. It also applies in a different way to unoccupied Britain, where the questionable record (extreme heroism by individual agents notwithstanding) of the Special Operations Executive, which for example was tricked by the Abwehr into sending dozens of agents into captivity in the Netherlands despite warnings, was transmuted into a myth of unalloyed glory which has seldom been challenged. Suffice it to say that the German resistance to Hitler had a lot to be modest about.

The paucity and tardiness of the resistance is an obvious corollary of the fact that more Germans came to vote for Hitler than for any other party when they had the choice, and that still more Germans, clearly a comfortably absolute majority of the population, went along with most of what he proclaimed and, in the final analysis, what he did.

Ineffectual military putsch plots however had come to nothing in 1938, thanks to Hitler's diplomatic triumph at Munich, in November 1939, and again in January 1943 as defeat loomed at Stalingrad. Two further conspiracies by officers failed in March. Count von Stauffenberg was made of sterner stuff and took the lead among serious military conspirators in February 1944, which was also when one of Germany's most famous soldiers, Field Marshal Erwin Rommel, finally lost patience with Hitler's military incompetence (one may still wonder what took him so long and why he remained equivocal) and signalled his sympathy with retired General Ludwig Beck, leader of the disaffected officers.

Stauffenberg, born in 1907, was chief of staff to Colonel-General Friedrich Fromm, C-in-C of the Reserve Army, and as such often attended Führer conferences alongside or on behalf of his general. He came from a noble Bavarian family with strong monarchist, conservative and Catholic leanings. Strikingly handsome, even with an eye-patch and all too obvious wounds, he was known as the 'Bamberg Knight' because he so closely resembled the medieval statue of that anonymous hero in Bamberg cathedral. Stauffenberg joined a Bavarian cavalry regiment as a career officer and distinguished himself in the *Blitzkrieg* phase of the war and in North Africa, where he was machine-gunned by an Allied fighter in 1943. He emerged from hospital with one eye, one arm, half of one hand and a pronounced limp, and was appointed chief of staff at Army Ordnance.

Having had time, like his social and moral inferior Speer, to think while confined to hospital for months, Stauffenberg, who had in any case been moving leftward from his arch-conservative inheritance for some years, decided during his convalescence that something serious had to be done about Hitler. Hitherto he had suppressed his fastidious distaste for the upstart and taken the attitude of so many of his contemporaries at all levels in the army: 'my country, right or wrong'. Now he saw the Führer as the Antichrist and decided to take a leading role in the resistance. He joined the Kreisauer Kreis (Kreisau Circle) of Christian academics, aristocrats, diplomats, officers and professional men led by Helmuth Count von Moltke (whose estate was at Kreisau, now Krzyzowa, in Silesia). Stauffenberg by sheer force of personality became the head of what was now an active conspiracy rather than a talking shop, a 'when' rather than an 'if', extending well beyond Kreisau and the pockets of dissidence on the general staff to embrace churchmen, senior police officials, lawyers and politicians – the very people who should have acted in 1933 – and such egregious individuals as the Bonhoeffer brothers (theologian and lawyer) and Admiral Wilhelm Canaris, head of the Abwehr (OKW intelligence).

Stauffenberg and friends acquired from a plentiful captured stock a British time-bomb of the kind supplied to resistance forces and concealed it in the briefcase he always had with him at the conferences he attended with or for Fromm. With his two remaining fingers he carried the infernal machine into the daily situation conference at headquarters in Rastenburg, East Prussia, at 10 a.m. on 20 July 1944. He was scheduled to make a report on the state of the Home Army in the context of Operation Valkyrie, the plan to mobilise the reserves in defence of the homeland which had been under discussion all the way up to Führer level, and which the plotters intended to use as cover for a coup. Stauffenberg put his briefcase on the floor under the broad map-table around which the twenty-four participants were standing and then calmly excused himself 'to make a telephone call'. Colonel Heinz Brandt, the army's deputy chief of staff (operations), stumbled against the bag and impatiently kicked it away. It came to rest on the far side of a massive table support, by the near side of which Hitler happened to be standing.

The heavy wooden prop or, if you will, the Providence even he frequently spoke of, saw to it that Hitler's time did not then come. He was at the epicentre of the explosion at 12.50 p.m. and his face and clothing were scorched and blackened. But, thanks to a table leg, the Führer got away remarkably lightly from the blast. It wrecked the wooden guard barracks built by Speer's men and temporarily in use for meetings while work on extending and strengthening the Rastenburg bunker, arranged by Speer on Hitler's orders, was completed. One man was killed outright and three others, including Brandt, died of their wounds. Hitler's right (saluting) arm was partly paralysed, his hair caught fire and he was temporarily deafened by damage to his ear-drums. Some of the injured were blown bodily through the windows.

By the time his bomb went off, Lieutenant-Colonel Claus Schenk Count von Stauffenberg had left Rastenburg's fortified inner compound and been driven to the airstrip; he was already in the air bound for Berlin and phase two of the plot. At that moment Speer should have been sitting down to lunch at OKW headquarters in the Bendlerstrasse with Stauffenberg's chief, General Fromm, a friend of long standing. The invitation was delivered personally by his chief of staff on the 17th; Speer however had a genuine previous engagement – yet another presentation to a meeting of some 200 fellow-ministers and senior government officials with key industrialists at the Goebbels ministry about armament production problems. He declined, even when the crippled colonel insisted on the special importance of the occasion.

The Chronicle for 20 July 1944 is one of the few sources outside Speer's own writings for his actions on and around that bathetic day in German history. It is also laconic, in the historic present tense so favoured by German chroniclers: 'The 20th of July is at first a working day like any other. On the invitation of Reichsminister Dr Goebbels the Minister speaks before the members of the Reich Government in the Propaganda Ministry. He shows on slides the increase in performance of German armament [industries] ...' Speer made his usual appeal for total mobilisation on the home front and the meeting adjourned for lunch after a few words from Goebbels, who then led Speer and Funk, Minister of Economics, to his huge office (or else had them summoned there shortly afterwards, according to the Chronicle). The loudspeaker on his desk squawked an announcement from his secretary that Dr Otto Dietrich, as chief government press spokesman a key figure in the propaganda ministry, was on the telephone from Rastenburg and could not wait. Goebbels said he would take the call, pressing a button so that only his side of the ensuing brief conversation could be heard. But Speer was able to deduce that there had been an attempt on Hitler's life, that he had survived an explosion in the Speer Barracks at Rastenburg – and that Hitler suspected the hundreds of Todt Organisation men working on his bunker.[17]

Not surprisingly on this occasion, the egocentric Speer immediately thought of himself and his own position (his memoirs ring very true here): Speer's barracks, Speer's TO bunker task-force, whose chaotic presence Goebbels apparently saw as a massive breach of security at Rastenburg ... Speer none the less kept his late-lunch appointment with Colonel Gerhard Engel, who had recently exchanged an adjutant's post with Hitler for the fresh air of a field command. Speer wanted to discuss with this officer, seasoned by both front-line experience and top-level staff work, his draft memorandum, fortuitously dated 20 July, calling for a drive against the Wehrmacht's Byzantine and bottom-heavy structure, which saw to it that for every two men at the front there was a 'tail' or no fewer than nine support troops. Six major headquarters – the three armed forces, the Waffen-SS, the TO and the Labour Service – replicated autonomously and on a huge scale ancillary services which should be combined and radically reduced in numbers, freeing millions of extra men for both combat and industrial work, to say nothing of material and equipment.

After lunch Speer returned to his own office for talks with Minister Clodius, the German envoy to the Romanian satellite state, about restoring and protecting oil supplies after the recent raids from Italy by the US army's Fifteenth Air Force. Because of these raids, the aerial sowing of mines in the River Danube and the general shortage of railway tanker-wagons, exacerbated by RAF and Eighth US Army Air Force attacks on German transport, an underground pipeline was to be built from Ploesti to Germany. The discussion was interrupted by a personal call from Goebbels to Speer: would he kindly come to the propaganda minister's residence forthwith, for reasons he could not discuss over the telephone.

Goebbels's official apartments were close to the south side of the Brandenburg Gate, in the heart of the government quarter which was now sealed off by large numbers of Reserve Army troops. According to Speer, Goebbels wanted his cool head as a check on the measures he was proposing to take in order to nip a burgeoning military coup in the bud. Goebbels had already talked with Hitler by telephone, a fact he did not immediately disclose. Once again Speer convincingly conceded in his memoirs that he was primarily concerned with his own position, rapidly going over in his mind recent conversations with various generals, including his closest friends on the general staff, the outspoken Guderian, the thoughtful Zeitzler – and Fromm, already arrested at 6 p.m. on the 20th at Hitler's order and replaced as C-in-C of the Reserve by an ever-ready Himmler. These and other officers had freely exchanged criticisms of Hitler's military leadership with Speer.

His memoirs also make it plain that Speer was not merely exposed but actually accustomed to discussing with his highly placed military friends such dangerous and forbidden topics as Germany's increasingly hopeless position in the war, the overwhelming strength of its encircling enemies, the fuel and transport double crisis and even Hitler's incompetence and his offensive attitude to so many subordinates. By the paranoid standards of the Nazi regime this was treason. If deadly subjects such as these were not taboo in his circle, the reader of Speer's writings must find it very difficult indeed to accept his constant assertion that he was never involved in the kind of conversations that must have made him fully aware of the scale of Nazi crimes against humanity, if not of the detail that the regime tried so hard to conceal. We are asked to accept that doubt of final victory and disrespect for Hitler were all but commonplace in Speer's circle by summer 1944 whereas no noteworthy reference was made to the treatment of prisoners of war, concentration-camp inmates, foreign forced labour, 'subhuman' Slavs and Jews, of which categories so many worked at Speer's behest in plants that he controlled. The very idea of such a selective silence is unbelievable.

Speer wrote that his response to Goebbels's appeal for support was instantaneous and positive: 'I regarded a putsch in the present state of affairs as an utter disaster. I did not perceive the morality of it.'[18] So he stood at Dr Goebbels's window and looked down on the Potsdamerplatz as units of heavily armed, steel-helmeted troops surrounded the government quarter and set up road blocks everywhere in sight. He could see that grey-clad soldiers were blocking the door of Goebbels's own building; the Minister of Propaganda repaired to his bedroom and emerged with a handful of Nazi standard-issue cyanide pills 'just in case'. The propaganda minister established by telephone that troops of the Reserve were also on the march from Potsdam, the German army's historic garrison town south-west of Berlin, and other outlying areas towards the capital.

Hard as it is to credit, the would-be putschists against Adolf Hitler seem to have made no attempt to seize the usual installations targeted by modern revolutionaries: the communications facilities – radio stations, telephones and telegraphs, military signals headquarters and the like, let alone such resourceful loyalists as Goebbels who might be expected to move against them. Most probably, having set Operation Valkyrie in motion as per timetable before the bomb went off, the plotters were understandably paralysed by the news that it had failed. The fact that large numbers of troops were mobilised attests directly to the seriousness of the July Plot but by the same token indirectly suggests that previous alleged conspiracies by the military were insubstantial. Yet there was no sign of the only countervailing force that might by firm action have pre-empted, frustrated or ultimately opposed the army with weapons – the Waffen-SS, headed by Himmler, who as Minister of the Interior and chief of all the police forces of the Reich should have been in the forefront of the defence of the regime. Goebbels could not locate him, any more than Speer, absenting himself from Goebbels's study, could reach his friend Fromm by telephone at the Bendlerstrasse (unbeknown to him, the wavering general, unmanned by the news that Hitler had survived, had been placed under close arrest by the co-conspirators).

So, just as in 1938, when he had orchestrated the *Reichskristallnacht* which revealed the Nazis' real intentions against the Jews, Goebbels appointed himself the prime mover for the task of improvising the salvation of the regime from a disillusioned officer corps. He had made energetic telephone inquiries about the commander of the unit surrounding the government district, Major Otto Ernst Remer, aged thirty-two, who turned out to be a convinced Nazi, and on whom Hitler had personally conferred the Knight's Cross with Oakleaves, one of the rarest bravery awards. He led the élite 'Greater Germany' Guard Battalion, a unit of 500 men specially trained to defend Berlin against riot and revolt, in particular a rising by foreign workers. Speer was recalled by Goebbels to witness the exchange between the principal apologist of Nazism and the mere field officer commanding a few hundred of the Wehrmacht's millions of men who, did he but know it, could now sink or save the Third Reich. Thinking on his feet, Goebbels quickly primed Hitler and had him wait by the telephone at Rastenburg.

As soon as a nervous Major Remer marched in, the diminutive and equally tense propaganda minister reminded him of his oath to Hitler. The major replied that on the tragic death of the Führer he owed his immediate loyalty to the City Commandant, Major-General Paul von Haase (in fact one of the conspirators). 'But Hitler is alive!' Goebbels cried; and after a short harangue, with his well-practised sense of drama he reached for the telephone already connected to Rastenburg.

Hitler came on the line at once and after a few remarks Goebbels handed the receiver to the major, who sprang to attention as the familiar voice in his ear left Remer in no doubt that his beloved Führer was indeed alive. Hitler said he was promoting the major to major-general, a rise of four ranks in one leap, and told Remer to relieve Haase as commandant and to obey the orders of Goebbels (still Gauleiter of Berlin). The coup was soon broken as Remer, now supported by a loyal Panzer brigade which had rolled into the centre of the city, acted with the resolve so manifestly lacking among the coup leaders, devastated by the news that Hitler lived. Stauffenberg, who alone had directly risked his life for the plot, might have galvanised them into taking control of the levers of power, but he was arrested before he could act.

Remer, unaware of the Home Army commander's role in the conspiracy, freed the frightened Fromm, who now tried to save himself by pointing the guards towards the four conspirators present at the Bendlerstrasse, including Stauffenberg, his own chief of staff, and General Friedrich Olbricht, his deputy. Having thus turned his coat with bewildering speed a second time in one day, Fromm successfully urged Beck to commit suicide (having failed to kill himself with a pistol at the second attempt, the old general was dispatched by a sergeant) and then had the four detained officers arraigned before a drumhead court-martial and executed by firing squad in the headquarters yard late on the evening of the 20th.

Speer managed to speak to Fromm when the two men met in the Bendlerstrasse amid the milling troops that evening but failed to persuade him to stay his hand. The summary dispatch of the quartet turned out to be an unintentional act of mercy. Hitler's revenge was bestial. Nearly 200 men, including officers, members of the Kreisau Circle and other prominent dissidents, were subjected to Gestapo torture and then grotesque trials in Roland Freisler's People's Court, followed in many cases by strangulation or hanging from meathooks by piano wire in front of a movie camera. The hunt for traitors went on for the rest of the war; Fromm himself was arrested again the very night of the plot by order of Goebbels but was tried much later and executed only in March 1945.

The man who took personal charge of the remorseless machine of vengeance was Ernst Kaltenbrunner, Austrian head of the Reich Main Security Office and ex-officio overlord under Himmler of the Gestapo. Kaltenbrunner was at Rastenburg when Speer flew there with other ministers at Hitler's invitation on 21 July for a reception to congratulate him on his escape. To Speer's unease Dorsch and Saur, his two principal subordinates, were also invited (unlike other ministers' deputies); Speer jealously complained in his memoirs that they were much more cordially received than he was, none too subtly filching a corner of the plotters' postwar mantle of glory by indicating that the reason for the snub was widespread suspicion of his involvement with them.

12

Total War

(1944–45)

THE FROIDEUR BETWEEN FÜHRER AND MINISTER lasted only a day. On 22 July, Hitler chaired a meeting of Speer, Bormann, Keitel, Goebbels and Himmler (who had mysteriously shown up in Berlin at midnight on the 20th, after the coup had been suppressed). The Führer announced that he had decided to appoint Goebbels 'General Plenipotentiary for Waging Total War'. In his memoirs Speer complained that he was not credited with this idea, which he had most recently mentioned in a memorandum to Hitler early in July. There can be no doubt of his longstanding advocacy of such a measure, but the idea originally came from Goebbels, who now faced the challenge of making it work. Speer doubtless felt he should have got the job himself.

He was back in Berlin on the 24th when Kaltenbrunner, the saturnine secret-police chief with his pockmarked horse-face, turned up unannounced at his office. Interestingly, Speer was prostrate on a couch at the time, having had another attack of the leg trouble that was obviously a sign of acute stress in him. Without beating about the bush, Kaltenbrunner produced the July plotters' provisional cabinet list, a copy of which had conveniently been left in a safe at the Bendlerstrasse (researchers never cease to be amazed by the Nazi-German passion for keeping copies of very nearly everything, a foible which was to be of as much value to the Nuremberg prosecutors as it had been to the Gestapo). Beck was to have been provisional head of state and Carl Friedrich Goerdeler, the upright former Lord Mayor of Leipzig, was named acting Chancellor. Against the word Armaments stood the name 'Speer'. Had he known, asked Kaltenbrunner equably? Speer's horrified reaction apparently convinced the Reich's chief inquisitor, who at no time raised his voice and politely took his leave shortly afterwards. Speer needed the rest of the year to shake off the suspicion that attached to him thanks to this acutely embarrassing and momentarily terrifying discovery. Probably more persuasive for Kaltenbrunner than Speer's histrionic response was the remark 'if possible?' pencilled against his name. 'Minister's neck saved by question-mark' would have made a suitable headline; clearly the plotters had not approached Speer, let alone got his permission, before putting him on their list as indispensable. They obviously did not trust him enough to take him into their confidence before the coup but regarded him as a Vicar of Bray figure, likely to accept a change of regime with equanimity. They were right:

> Judging by all I know today about the individuals and the motives of the conspiracy, collaboration with them would within a short time have cured me of my loyalty to Hitler. They would quickly have won me over to their cause. But that in itself would have made my remaining in the government, doubtful enough for superficial reasons, impossible for psychological reasons. For if I had come to a moral understanding of the nature of the [Nazi] regime and of the part that I had played in it, I would have been forced to recognise that it was no longer conceivable for me to hold any position of leadership in a post-Hitler Germany.[1]

This did not prevent Speer from staying on under the shortlived government of Grand-Admiral Dönitz, or indeed from preparing to work on the postwar reconstruction of Germany under the Allies, whom he also confidently expected to regard him as indispensable.

Speer may have had his doubts of final victory and Hitler's ability to cope with Germany's crisis by this time, but he was not about to confide them to his staff at such a delicate and dangerous juncture. About 200 of the most senior gathered on the 24th to listen to him describe the failed coup as 'a turning-point in our fateful struggle ... towards a victorious outcome'. He even ended his address with 'Heil Hitler', the aggressively grovelling Nazi practice he had seldom if ever followed. Speer's effusive loyalty at this period suggests an attempt to counter rumours of his sympathy with the plotters. One rumour said he had been arrested (probably an extrapolation from Kaltenbrunner's visit). Yet there can be no gainsaying that Speer did put his head above the parapet after the event, to protest the innocence of a dozen or more leading industrial and other associates of his and also to intercede for at least two suspected generals, and with success. His appeals on behalf of his closest friends on the general staff, Fromm and Zeitzler, however, fell on deaf ears. He even offered, in vain, to appear in court as a character witness for Fromm. These uncharacteristically committed interventions help to explain why it was still necessary for Speer to write a comprehensive letter of denial to Kaltenbrunner on 29 December 1944.

Ironically, one reason for the persistent rumours was the fact that his suggestions about total mobilisation for the war effort early in July had been encapsulated in yet another draft decree on the concentration of war production dated 19 July, the eve of the coup attempt, and promulgated on the 22nd, two days after it. That Speer should be seeking even more power over the crucial period, that he was regarded as essential by the plotters and that he had persistently interceded for many suspects clearly raised a question-mark at Gestapo headquarters as equivocal as the one pencilled in the margin of the conspirators' cabinet list. That the benefit of the doubt ultimately went to Speer may have been a reflection of his abiding importance to Hitler personally or to the war effort or both.[2]

But the appointment of Goebbels as Total War Commissioner on 23 July was rounded out by a Führer order of the 25th, making Göring, as chairman of the Reich Defence Council, responsible for mobilising the public sector for total war and instructing Bormann as overlord of the Gauleiters to cooperate with Goebbels (they were soon given the right to be informed about economic measures in their areas, which entailed a new level of interference in the war economy just when it was least wanted). The realities of war saw to it that Sauckel's role as principal impresser of labour now faded away as the scope for forced recruitment of foreign workers dwindled with the territory still under German control. He was sidelined. Himmler was given the task on 2 August of looking for manpower economies in the Wehrmacht, Waffen-SS and police, the Todt Organisation and the Labour Front, in line with Speer's appeal to Hitler to streamline the forces in his 20 July memorandum (which was clearly completed in the small hours). Considerable inroads were thus made into Speer's empire and autonomy by Bormann, Goebbels, Himmler and (in theory, because he was ineffectual now) Göring, on the orders of Hitler in the immediate aftermath of the July Plot. Speer's stock must therefore have been in decline at headquarters. But all this fiddling while Berlin burned made no real difference to the course of the war.

Speer's faithful chronicler, Dr Wolters, was in no doubt that the failure of the coup was good news: 'The blame for the lousy weeks and months was shifted on to the hidden abscess [the July Plot]. Within the vigorous, the flame burned bright again.' This gung-ho entry in the Chronicle for 27 July 1944 appears only in the uncensored text. Something that was left out of either version is a note sent on 24 August to the chronicler, a squib which he decided to ignore:[3] 'Dr Wolters: the participation of our Minister in the unravelling of "July 20" was so active that it must be recorded in the Chronicle – what do you think of that? (the "passive" participation as well).' The sardonic note was, wisely one may feel, unsigned.

*

The Chronicle for August records the creation of the Armament Staff on the 1st. The new grouping included the commissioners for aircraft (Saur), U-boats (Merker), tanks (Rohland), weapons, ammunition, vehicles, locomotives and vengeance weapons, plus commissioners responsible for repairs. This vertical representation was as usual complemented by the horizontal one of those in charge of concerns common to all programmes, such as raw materials, parts, labour, energy, construction, delivery, transport and the like. The OKW and the three services were also represented at the Armament Staff daily meeting at 10 a.m. Mondays were devoted to aircraft, which were also reviewed briefly on the other days; Tuesdays went to tanks and tank guns; Wednesdays to either the navy or locomotives and V-weapons; Thursdays to weapons; and Fridays to ammunition. A new 'Commissioner for Performance-Recognition' was added to the staff to raise productivity by incentives for workers.

One of the first considerations of the Armament Staff was to minimise the damage, depredation and disruption caused by the Soviet advance, which now, *inter alia*, threatened the important industrial area of Upper Silesia. The two crucial chemical complexes of Blechhammer and Heydebreck were under threat; and the Chronicle solemnly warned of the danger represented by the 140,000 slave workers at the manufacturing facility at Auschwitz, 'who are a great danger in the rear as the enemy [draws] near'. There is no indication that this was meant ironically (unusually for a convinced German right-winger, Dr Wolters had a well-developed sense of irony and some of it leaks into the Chronicle; on balance, not here).

Auschwitz was the unnamed subject of a conversation in high summer 1944 between Speer and his old party comrade and friend, Karl Hanke, Gauleiter of Lower Silesia, a man he admired for his 'sympathy and directness'. Hanke, just returned from the neighbouring Gau of Upper Silesia, had often called by in the past to discuss his latest experiences with Speer:

This time, sitting in the green leather easy chair in my office, he seemed confused and spoke falteringly, with many breaks. He advised me never to accept an invitation to inspect a concentration camp in Upper Silesia. Never, under any circumstances. He had seen something there which he was not permitted to describe and moreover could not describe.

I did not query him, I did not query Himmler, I did not query Hitler, I did not speak with personal friends. I did not investigate – for I did not want to know what was happening there. Hanke must have been speaking of Auschwitz. During those few seconds, while Hanke was warning me, the whole responsibility had become a reality again.

This Awful Warning lay immediately behind Speer's acceptance at Nuremberg of his share of the overall responsibility for Nazi crimes, he wrote. In averting his eyes from the truth haltingly presented to him by his friend, he incurred indelible guilt. 'Because I failed at that time, I still feel, to this day, responsible for Auschwitz in a wholly personal sense.'[4]

In this disingenuous and sanctimonious passage Speer tried to suggest that he did not know about the death camp before Hanke's undated 'revelation' of summer 1944, less than a year before the war ended. What destroys this pretence to earlier ignorance is the word 'again' at the end of the passage quoted above: 'the whole responsibility had become a reality *again*.' The only 'responsibility' referred to in the broad context of this revealing adverb is Speer's own avowed share of the blame for Nazi atrocities of which, thanks to Hanke, he was reminded *again* – which in plain English (or German) means not for the first time. By his own admission here, Speer already knew of Auschwitz-Birkenau and its purpose. Hanke's unsettling account (of what must have been an unspeakably gruesome tour) told him nothing he did not know already. Speer was, as he wrote, hearing it *again*.

Hanke hankered after becoming a war hero. Having risen meteorically to state secretary in Goebbels's ministry, he rather fell out of favour when he provided consolation in kind to Magda Goebbels for her husband's sexual adventures and joined a tank unit on the outbreak of war. Restored to favour as Gauleiter in Breslau in February 1941, he told Speer in January 1945 that he would defend the handsome city to the (as distinct from his) death. The Russians, he declared over Speer's protest, would never get their hands on party headquarters, a neo-classical masterpiece by Speer's architectural role-model, Schinkel. The city duly all but died and Hanke had its mayor publicly hanged for trying to save it from the Russians; but the Gauleiter himself escaped southward to the Czech Sudetenland from his besieged and broken capital in one of the first operational helicopters. He was caught in SS uniform and incarcerated by Czech partisans in the last days of the war, only to be shot and then beaten to death in June 1945 while trying to escape from a column of German prisoners of war.

Hanke's helicopter rather spoiled the image he tried to present to Speer of himself as a latter-day Samson, determined to take a few Philistines with him in the wreckage of the party's Breslau temple. Like many another leading Nazi staring defeat in the face, he adopted the attitude of the dog in the manger, determined that nobody else, least of all the returning rightful owners, should benefit from what he himself now had no use for and must abandon. It was in this nihilistic spirit that some of the Dutch dikes were breached by retreating

Germans, and that Hitler ordered the destruction of Paris, ignored by General Choltitz, the city commandant, who surrendered it intact.

Adolf Hitler however, unlike most of his minions, fully intended to follow Samson's example by pulling the ruins of Germany down upon his head without trying to save himself. He issued his notorious 'scorched earth' decree only on 19 March 1945, ordering the destruction of anything on Reich territory likely to be of value to the enemy 'immediately or in the foreseeable future for the prosecution of the war'. But there is more than enough evidence of Hitler's commitment to such a policy from, at the very latest, the moment the Red Army began to reclaim the Wehrmacht's gains in the Soviet Union, during which the Russians had executed a scorched-earth policy of their own, thereby gaining Hitler's reluctant respect.

As noted, Hitler recognised at the beginning of 1943, after the Anglo-American Casablanca Conference and as the Stalingrad disaster loomed, that his regime had passed the point of no return ('burned its bridges' as he put it). On 26 June 1944 at the Obersalzberg, Hitler at Speer's request addressed 100 leading industrialists worried by the 'state socialism by stealth' of so much of the war economy, commanded as it was by the regime, and about a decidedly unrosy future. If the exercise was intended to be reassuring, a tired Hitler's rambling remarks had the opposite effect: 'There is no doubt that if we were to lose this war, German private business would not survive. Rather, with the destruction of the entire German nation, business would naturally be wiped out as well,' he said matter-of-factly.

On 13 July 1944, as the Allies closed in from west and east, Hitler issued two decrees on the defence of Reich territory, one on the chain of command and the other on cooperation between party and Wehrmacht authorities. On the 19th Keitel as chief of staff of the Wehrmacht High Command issued a complementary order on the defence of the Reich, in which the military was made responsible for 'dispersal, evacuation, obstruction and demolition' in operational areas and the Reich Defence Commissioners (i.e. the Gauleiters) for organising, at the behest of the relevant ministries (including Speer's), the same four tasks in areas behind the front. Immediately after the July Plot, Hitler had told his entourage: 'If the German nation is now defeated in this struggle, it will have been too weak. That will mean it has not stood up to the test of history and was fated for nothing except doom.'

On 7 September 1944 the main party newspaper, the *Völkischer Beobachter*, carried an editorial instigated by Hitler personally and calling on Germans to ensure that the enemy found 'every footbridge destroyed, every road blocked – nothing but death, annihilation and hate will meet him.' Hitler was also coming round to the view, crystallised orally for a shaken Speer on the latter's fortieth birthday in March 1945, that there was no point in worrying about what Germany would live on after the war; the German people did not deserve to survive the defeat he blamed on them (and anyone or everyone but himself): 'If the war is lost, the people will be lost also ... For the nation has proved to be the weaker, and the future belongs to the stronger eastern nation. In any case only the inferior will survive this struggle since the good have already been killed.'

The International Military Tribunal gave Speer credit in its judgment on the main Nazi war criminals for resisting Hitler's scorched-earth policy, in the occupied western countries as well as Germany, 'at considerable personal danger to himself'. Initially he did it by using Hitler's own promises that all enemy advances would soon be hurled back to argue that it would be counter-productive to destroy facilities which would quickly return to German hands. Speer was instrumental in preserving a large slice of French industry in August 1944 by persuading Hitler to accept its immobilisation rather than destruction as the Allies advanced across northern France. He achieved the same result for coal and steel in Alsace-Lorraine, the French region bordering Germany, which was about to change hands for the fourth time in sixty-four years. Although some French mines were dependent on electricity from the German Saar region, the current was not cut off and the all-important water-pumps preserved the viability of the pits.

German industrialists were naturally opposed to the destruction of their plant for political or military reasons; fortunately, so were at least some of the Gauleiters, who as Defence Commissioners were responsible for such demolition behind the lines but fully understood the implications for an area and its people. As the prospect of recovering lost ground diminished, so Speer shifted his argument from future to immediate need: it would be a self-inflicted wound, he argued, to destroy factories near to the front but capable of supplying its German defenders with ammunition and other necessities to the very last minute. If power stations were demolished in the face of the enemy, the troops trying to keep him out would lose their telephone lines. Speer was entitled as minister to direct the Gauleiters on these matters and ordered them not to destroy but only to immobilise threatened plants. But Speer failed to persuade Hitler to issue a general decree preferring paralysing to destroying and had to work, not always successfully, on a case-by-case basis.

Speer made two lengthy visits to the Western Front in the middle and at the very end of September 1944, on each occasion visiting Field Marshal Walter Model, who had taken over Army Group B from Rommel (dead by his own hand at Hitler's invitation on account of his alleged sympathy for the July Plot). Although he had identified the

Allied raids on the chemical and synthetic-fuel industries as the knell of doom for the German war economy, Speer did all he could to encourage, and where possible augment, munitions production in the areas immediately adjacent to the front, for supply direct to the defending troops. This was consistent with the efforts of his Ruhr Staff to keep the key industries of Germany's most important manufacturing area, now alarmingly close to the land front as well as under unrelenting aerial bombardment, at work as long and productively as possible, even after the transport necessary for the wider distribution of its output seized up under the bombing.

On 11 November he promised Hitler in a memorandum to do everything in his power to help win the 'battle for the Ruhr, decisive for the fate of our Reich'. Speer was in and out of the threatened industrial heartland for the rest of the year and beyond, switching scarce fuel, manpower and material reserves to it as far as possible, as well as anti-aircraft guns and fighters, and abandoning construction of defensive strongpoints in favour of constant road and runway repairs. The enormous, last-gasp effort to save (and at the same time to exploit) the Ruhr petered out only on 5 January 1945. Speer was trying to have his cake and eat it: he was unquestionably doing his best to save Ruhr industry, but he was prolonging and stiffening the hopeless German defensive struggle in the process, thus increasing the very damage he recognised as pointless in the light of an enemy onslaught inescapably destined to be victorious. By resisting chaos he was only increasing it.

The other irony in his rising defiance was that Speer could circumvent Hitler's scorched-earth policy only by virtue of enjoying the sentimental benevolence of a waning dictator determined to take much of Europe with him as a blazing backdrop to his personal *Götterdämmerung*. In vain did Speer try to persuade Hitler to visit the area threatened by the advance from the west. All Speer could do was to send a stream of teleprinter messages undermining 'scorched earth' by ordering immobilisation rather than destruction of endangered factories, power stations and other economic assets. Even Bormann concurred in this disobedience, telling his Gauleiters to obey Speer.[5]

For Speer the long illness at the beginning of 1944 had brought disenchantment with Hitler personally. This was closely allied to a general disillusion that was patchy (interspersed as it was with theatrical declarations of loyalty and calls for one last push to win a war he knew was already lost) but grew stronger as reality crowded in. Next came active disobedience, in the form of Speer's well-attested, effective resistance to Hitler's scorched-earth policy, accompanied by open dissent as he sent Hitler challenging memoranda and abdicated his day-to-day responsibility for arms production to Saur. Less well attested, but not unsupported, is the last wartime stage of Speer's disengagement from Hitler: positive disloyalty. The phrase may seem feeble for what Speer presented to American interrogators and later an astounded Nuremberg Tribunal as his intention to assassinate the Führer, but the 'plot' was even feebler, justifying some hesitation before calling it treason.

Speer describes in chapter twenty-eight of his memoirs how he was visited in February 1945, precisely three months before Germany surrendered, by Dr Friedrich Lüschen, then aged seventy, head of research and development at the giant Siemens company and his principal adviser on electrics. They talked in Speer's modest official flat at the back of the main ministry building on the Pariserplatz in Berlin. Lüschen produced two quotations from *Mein Kampf* in which Hitler had written not only that everything had to be done for the preservation and against the destruction of the nation, but also that the people should rise in revolt if their government was leading them to their doom (this is precisely what army and navy conscripts and Social Democrat politicians did in 1918, which Hitler presented elsewhere as the great 'stab in the back'; but *Mein Kampf* resembles the Bible in one important respect: it can be used in support of both sides of the same argument).

> Here was Hitler himself saying what I had been trying to get across during these past months. Only the conclusion remained to be drawn: Hitler himself – measured by the standards of his own political programme – was deliberately committing high treason against his own people, which had made vast sacrifices for his cause and to which he owed everything. Certainly more than I owed to Hitler.
>
> That night I came to the decision to eliminate Hitler. *My preparations, to be sure, went no further than the initial stages and therefore have a touch of the ridiculous about them* [emphasis added].

The motive was thus self-explanatory. The opportunity was readily available, more so than to almost anyone else other than Hitler's personal staff, to the man who was still Hitler's architect (even at this stage of the war they occasionally took refuge from reality by discussing postwar building plans in the small hours in the Berlin bunker). The means, Speer decided, would be to introduce into the air-supply system of Hitler's Berlin bunker the highly effective German nerve gas Tabun, stockpiled in huge quantities but never used in battle. To acquire some, Speer turned to a man whose fervent gratitude he had just earned by successfully interceding with the Gestapo, which suspected him of treasonable defeatism thanks to some incautiously realistic remarks he had made. He was the industrialist Dietrich Stahl, head of Speer's Main Committee on Munitions and the special committee for tracer bullets.

As they sheltered from yet another air-raid in the ministry bunker, Speer asked him if he could lay his hands on some Tabun. Stahl apparently could, but pointed out its disadvantages. The gas, an organic compound of phosphorus, was so dangerous that it was made of two separate solids which only came together when the shell containing them exploded on impact. This made Tabun rather difficult to introduce clandestinely into an air shaft; but sufficiently lethal 'traditional' poison gases were also available. Speer said he next turned to the Chancellery's chief engineer, a man called Henschel, whom he had known since he built the place, and told him the air filters of the ventilation system must need renewing after such prolonged use; the Führer had complained repeatedly of the poor underground air to Speer, the man who had designed building and bunker alike. All too promptly for an as yet unprepared Speer, Henschel removed the filters, leaving the system unprotected.

Finding a pretext for a reconnaissance of the earth-covered bunker roof in the Chancellery garden one evening, Speer wrote that he was 'stunned' to find a new and heavily armed SS guard detachment on the spot, new security searchlights – and a brand-new, steel chimney rising over three metres above the air intake where there had only been a cover at ground level before. It was no more than a coincidence: 'Hitler, temporarily blinded by poison gas during the First World War, had ordered the building of this chimney because poison gas is heavier than air,' Speer wrote.[6] In other words, if a gas shell went off on top of the bunker, the poisonous cloud would cling to the ground and not reach the top of the chimney.

Careful consideration leads to the conclusion that this 'gas the Führer plot' was no more than bunker bunkum. Was there only one air intake for a vast bunker when the blast and debris from a single high-explosive bomb or shell might so easily block it? Was the new chimney made of armour-plate so thick and heavy that it could not be shifted, broken off or breached? Had Germany run out of ladders? Hitler did not in any event take up permanent residence in his last redoubt under Berlin until the middle of March 1945, using the overground Chancellery whenever the bombers were not overhead.

In chapter nine the following item was noted from the minutes of a Speer conference with Hitler in February 1943: 'The Führer concurs with the proposal of Colonel Claus so to develop the design of the ventilation fittings that [poison gases] injected [into them will] run out again downwards.' Exactly two years before he allegedly planned to kill Hitler (and Bormann, Goebbels and Ley, he hoped) by introducing poison gas into the bunker ventilation system, Speer sanctioned precautions that made the whole harebrained scheme impossible in any event, tall chimney, searchlights, SS patrols or not. Perhaps he forgot. At any rate, 'the whole idea of assassination vanished from my considerations as quickly as it had come.' Speer recognised that he was not the type who could pull a pistol on Hitler and shoot him (he had a small automatic as part of his uniform and did practise using it for his own protection towards the end of the war). So it was back to sabotaging scorched earth with even greater zeal. But the assassination fantasy came in handy at Nuremberg, supported as it was by independent evidence from Stahl.

There were even less practicable dream-schemes in Speer's mind during the last weeks and days of the Second World War which he had done so much to prolong in Europe. One depended upon Colonel Werner Baumbach, master dive-bomber turned disaffected commander in the Galland mould. Baumbach had access to the long-range flying-boat used for supplying the German weather outpost in Greenland from northern Norway. He suggested taking refuge with a few chosen friends in Greenland until the war was over and possibly flying from there to England to surrender. Speer planned to take a lot of books, documents and writing paper with him to start work on his memoirs. He revealed this wheeze, codenamed 'Winnetou' (hero of Karl May's romantic Westerns so loved by Hitler), to his old friend Milch in the latter part of April 1945; the Luftwaffe field marshal recalled later that Speer's intention as stated to him was to return after a couple of months to take over the government of Germany.[7]

Baumbach was joined by Galland in discussions with Speer (who did not name the initiator) of a scheme to round up the likes of Bormann, Goebbels and Himmler at night when they were driven from the Chancellery bunker, after a hard day helping Hitler lose the war, to their respective refuges in untargeted villages well away from Berlin. Apparently their habit was to take cover off the road whenever the British pathfinders dropped their flares to direct the main bomber forces towards the capital. It would be easy, Speer and his airmen friends thought, to follow each small motorcade and mimic the RAF with Wehrmacht signal flares (stored for the purpose at Speer's house). Carefully chosen, heavily armed Luftwaffe troops would then overpower the scattering escorts and the VIPs. The underlying idea was to prevent the targeted Nazi leaders from evading justice by committing suicide. Dietrich Stahl (of the abortive 'gas in the air-duct' plot) was privy to this idea which, as he told US intelligence after the war, was the chosen substitute for an attack on the impregnable bunker. Not surprisingly, Speer was easily dissuaded when he confided the idea to

General Wolfgang Thomale, Panzer chief of staff, who advised that the fate of the leaders be left to God.

At this time four veteran, frontline officers mysteriously turned up uninvited at Speer's house in Berlin-Schlachtensee to act as his body-guard. He found out later that General Thomale had ordered this protection. Meanwhile his old friend and Panzer mastermind Heinz Guderian, who had succeeded a compromised Zeitzler as army chief of staff after the July Plot, had been dismissed on 28 March 1945, for urging a separate peace with the western Allies, excluding the Russians. His offence was not to suggest trying to split Stalin's 'Anti-Fascist Coalition' at its weakest join but the implication that the war was lost.[8]

Speer's last visit to the slowly crumbling German Western Front ended in the early hours of New Year's Eve. After supper with Colonel-General Sepp Dietrich, commander of the 6th SS Panzer Army, Speer drove with Major Manfred von Poser, his general staff liaison officer and a specially trusted aide since his assignment to Speer in May 1944, to Hitler's temporary headquarters for the Ardennes offensive near Bad Nauheim in the Eifel Mountains. Speer's third attempt as a minister to wish Hitler a Happy New Year in person failed again, by two hours: Poser and he had needed twenty-two hours to cover barely 300 kilometres. Hitler was full of optimism and kept it up for the best part of a week, even when Goebbels proposed, and Speer opposed (for reasons of even more industrial disruption) a *levée en masse* as a last throw for final victory. Hitler made it plain he would rather listen to the ritually optimistic Karl Saur than to Speer on the subject of arms production, which was now disintegrating, though still remarkably buoyant in some areas, even very close to the fronts.

When the great Soviet offensive of 12 January began to drive all before it, Speer decided, with the Ruhr now cut off from the rest of Germany, that he should make a tour of the other key economic zone of Upper Silesia with its coal belt and heavy industry. He reminded Hitler on 16 January of the importance of the directly threatened 'Magistrale' rail route from Oppeln in Upper Silesia to Gotenhafen (now Polish Gdynia) on the Baltic coast for Germany's coal supply. More generally, Speer told Hitler by teleprinter on the 21st, if the whole area was lost, economic collapse would follow. He urged handing up to half of local war production directly to the army group defending the tottering Eastern Front.

Meanwhile Guderian, urged on by Speer, was trying to persuade Hitler to reinforce the east with everything available as the last chance to hold the Russians while reaching an accommodation in the west. Speer was driving his official car when it hit a truck on the icy road to the regional capital of Kattowitz (now Polish Katowice); Poser was unhurt but Speer's chest was badly bruised by the steering wheel. Speer passed through Breslau (now Polish Wroclaw) for his last meeting with Gauleiter Hanke, as mentioned above, on his way back to report to Hitler. In Berlin Speer made his vain appeal for Guderian's strategy of concentration in the east, backed by photographs he had taken of columns of German refugees marching westward. Instead, Hitler railed against such defeatism, calling it treason and threatening all and sundry who succumbed to it; a silent Kaltenbrunner took to attending the daily *Lage* (situation conference).

As if he did not have enough to do, Speer somehow managed at this fraught period at the end of January 1945 to draw up a *Rechenschaftsbericht*, an account of his stewardship of the ministry, addressed to his 300 most senior associates and dated 27 January. This enormous report would probably run to 10,000 words in verbatim English translation and contains a mass of production statistics upon which Speer's reputation as an economic miracle-worker and consummate crisis-manager largely rests. As with so many other aspects of his work for Hitler and of his life-story as told by himself and others, Speer is the main if not the only source, sometimes borne out by other evidence but all too often uncorroborated. The principal claims in this summary of his work as Hitler's armourer have already been covered above, and the minutely detailed statistics in the body of the report are at best tedious if correct and a misleading waste of space if not. But the ending is interesting for making it clear that the report was intended as a farewell thank-you to a highly successful group of colleagues who could no longer be called together because of the chaos of the war. The *envoi*, just 100 days before Germany's unconditional surrender, shows the self-contradictory state of Speer's mind at this cataclysmic time:

> I ask you, my colleagues, in these gravest hours of our nation: be aware of your duty to sustain this battle for the fate of our nation with all [your] strength, always and without reservation in every situation. [You must] all help, united even further in comradeship [and] trusting in a higher justice, to master destiny, so as to preserve for our nation the preconditions for its survival.

Three days later Speer, an indefatigable generator of documents despite his oft-professed loathing of bureaucracy, sent Hitler another memorandum, copied to six leading generals such as Guderian, urging him to put the wellbeing of the people above munitions production, which was now a waste of resources and effort. Upper Silesia had fallen and Germany's last coal was lost; there was nothing soldiers could do to offset the consequent crippling of the German armaments industry. Hitler, flanked by a ritually optimistic Saur, coldly forbade Speer to repeat such a defeatist exercise or to show it to anyone else. It was the day of Hitler's last radio address, a bitter message of no surrender.

Leaving Saur in charge of armaments production, such as it now was, Speer devoted himself in the last months of the war, in consultation with his many industrialist friends and colleagues, to preserving as much as possible of Germany's manufacturing base. He flew into the blockaded Ruhr and persuaded the Wehrmacht not to destroy the bridges, railways and other installations or encourage the enemy to destroy them by using them as defensive positions. Field Marshal Model went so far as to ask the British to spare the Bayer plant at Leverkusen, then the largest in Germany and to this day one of the world's leading chemical companies, guaranteeing that he would not defend it or place his artillery in it.

On 19 March 1945 Albert Speer turned forty. His obsequious wish to his mentor was for a signed photograph, which Hitler, his right hand permanently atremble ever since the bomb plot, granted with a shaky dedication and autograph. Speer's 'present' to Hitler on his arrival at the Chancellery late on the evening of the 18th was another long memorandum, on coal supplies, which rapidly moved on to its author's urgent theme of the moment, making preparations to sustain life in a Reich whose infrastructure was shattered and whose territory was about to be overrun and occupied.

Each man, dictator and protégé, was in two minds about the other. Hitler was angered by Speer's constant 'pessimism' but insisted that his own chauffeur, Erich Kempka, should drive his esteemed arms minister and architect on his ever more perilous journeys to the front. Speer opposed Hitler's nihilistic last stand but wanted a memento of him to treasure. As soon as he had granted Speer's wish and bidden him farewell for another fraught trip with Kempka, Hitler appended his signature to the notorious 'scorched-earth decree' of the 19th, mentioned above. Responsibility for its execution, regardless of the interests or wellbeing of the civil population (which was to be evacuated from the fighting zone, a recipe for total chaos) was given to the military and the Gauleiters as Defence Commissioners. Hitherto such decisions had been left to Speer's ministry, which had thus been able to immobilise or paralyse rather than destroy. Hitler's decision to bypass it was a major blow to Speer's power and prestige.

Speer spent one day visiting the Western Front once more and another on a fleeting detour to Heidelberg, to give his parents the belated chance to congratulate him on his milestone birthday. He took the opportunity to ask the local Gauleiter and military commander to ignore the scorched-earth and evacuation orders from Berlin; they seemed only too ready to comply. On reaching Field Marshal Model's current headquarters in the Westerwald forest 200 kilometres of back roads to the north, Speer was handed a teleprinter message with the text of the 19 March decree. To a man who was always the centre of his own universe it read like a line-by-line rejection of his appeal of 18 March, although Hitler meant it for a rather wider audience.

Back at the Chancellery on the afternoon of the 21st, Speer detected a distinct coolness towards him on all sides. Four junior officers had just been executed for failing to blow up the railway bridge at Remagen, which the Americans had used to make the first enemy crossing of the Rhine; Hitler also personally ordered the execution of General Fromm at this juncture for his part in the July Plot, despite a plea for clemency from Speer.

On the 24th Speer made one last trip to the Ruhr, meeting Walter Rohland at the headquarters of the tireless Ruhr Staff which he led. They made plans to prevent the three Gauleiters of the region carrying out the destruction orders by hiding explosives (and also works of art) in coal mines, withholding transport and fuel while posting armed workers to guard vital installations; efforts to persuade party functionaries to ignore the insane evacuation order met with only limited success. On the 25th he was back in Heidelberg for another quick visit to his parents at the house on Schloss-Wolfsbrunnenweg; it was the last time he saw or spoke to either of them. He persuaded the local general, a Waffen-SS man, to declare Heidelberg an open city, thus preserving it from American artillery bombardment; the famous bridge over the River Neckar was the only major local landmark to be destroyed during the occupation of the area. On his roundabout way back to Berlin, Speer also talked the relevant Gauleiter out of finally destroying the battered ball-bearing factory at Schweinfurt which the American bombers had tried so hard, but ultimately failed, to knock out.

By the time he was back in Berlin on the 27th, Hitler had placed Kammler, the SS labour chief, in charge of fighter as well as rocket production, ending Speer's brief command over aviation. On the 28th, Hitler sent the fearlessly argumentative Guderian on 'sick leave'; it was meant and understood as a one-way ticket.

He wanted to do the same with Speer, who however refused to take leave unless dismissed. He had heard that Hitler intended to displace him altogether by making Himmler Inspector-General for War Production. Once again there was no recorded witness to their meeting late on 28 March, when Hitler purportedly presented his erstwhile favourite with an ultimatum: 'You have twenty-four hours to think over your answer. Tomorrow let me know whether you hope that the war can still be won.'[9]

Speer decided to respond by letter, only to be told by Hitler's secretary that a written answer was not acceptable: he had to return to the Chancellery and reply in person. Just before midnight on the 29th, Speer was ushered in to Hitler, who said, 'Well?' Speer says he replied: 'My Führer, I stand unreservedly behind you.' The confrontation promptly softened into a mawkishly sentimental occasion. They shook hands; Hitler's eyes filled with tears: 'Then all is well,' he declared. Speer wrote: 'I too was shaken for a moment by his unforeseen rush of feeling. Once again something of the old relationship could be felt between us.'

Speer seized the opportunity presented by this fragile reconciliation to draft a decree for Hitler to sign, modifying his drastic edict of 19 March. It had the effect of putting Speer back in charge of decisions on the demolition of strategic industrial plant and enabling destruction orders to be stayed for tactical reasons before they were executed – by the Ministry of Armaments. The option of immobilising rather than destroying was restored in what amounted to a renewed licence to Speer to do as he pleased. The concessions, however, officially applied only to industry; transport, communications and bridges were not spared. But at least Hitler conceded, if only orally, that scorched-earth was more appropriate in the vast spaces of Russia than amid the dense population and intricate infrastructure of Germany.

Speer set about organising local stockpiles of food and other essentials in Berlin and elsewhere, persuading many individual commanders and officials to refrain from an orgy of destruction, not only in Germany but also in the Netherlands, Czechoslovakia and Poland. Speer devoted all his efforts to saving everything he could, ignoring Hitler's order to limit himself to industry. But for him, thousands of bridges of all kinds, waterways, telegraphic and power facilities would have been blown up; life in bomb-blasted Berlin would have become well-nigh impossible had the order to destroy its bridges been carried out. The promoted Lieutenant-Colonel von Poser was able to tell him on a daily basis from military intelligence which areas of Germany would be occupied next, as a corrective to the increasingly unreal situation conferences in the bunker. The sheer output of self-contradictory orders about the destruction, immobilisation, strictly temporary preservation or total demolition of various economic assets from 19 March to 7 April was in itself a considerable contribution to the frustration of Adolf Hitler's determination to drag Germany down with him.

On 6 April, Speer sent his wife and six children to the Baltic coast of Schleswig-Holstein, a military backwater where Dr Robert Frank, a friend of his parents, had an estate at Kappeln; they were under strict orders to use a false surname. The Allied plan to divide Germany into four zones of occupation was already common knowledge, and the calculating Speer was determined to place his family in the British north-west. The zone allocated to the Americans (later subdivided between them and the French) was by definition more attractive than the Soviet one but was being heavily fought over, whereas occupied Scandinavia, the northern Netherlands (where thousands died of starvation in this 'Hunger Winter') and the north-west corner of Germany were sidelined, despite the presence of hundreds of thousands of German troops.

Dr Brandt, Speer's friend in the SS health service, similarly placed his wife, Gretel's best friend, and their child in Thuringia, in south-central Germany, which was taken by the Americans (but later handed to the Russians as agreed). Brandt, arrested for this treasonable act, was accused by Bormann of dealing with the enemy and eventually sentenced to death on Hitler's personal recommendation by a court-martial hastily convened in the bunker. Bormann regarded Brandt as an ally of his principal rival for Hitler's attention, Speer, and had already exploited the post-coup atmosphere of general suspicion to have the evil doctor dismissed from his post as one of Hitler's personal physicians. Mindful of this and his own exposure to a treason charge if his own family's whereabouts got out, Speer felt very uneasy when he heard of Brandt's plight. Himmler managed to delay the execution until the war was over, and the Americans 'rescued' Brandt from his SS guards. But he was condemned a second time at the Nuremberg 'Doctors' Trial' in 1947 for his diabolical experiments on prisoners and belatedly hanged in 1948.

The Russians were poised from the beginning of April to launch their long-awaited drive on Berlin (it began on the 16th). Speer, having received in September 1944 an open invitation from Goebbels's ministry to exhort the German people by radio to work harder for victory, decided that this was the time to take up the offer – to dissuade people from pointless destruction. He was about to record the speech on the 11th when he was ordered by Hitler to let him see it first. He emasculated it and Speer cancelled the broadcast. The next day Hitler was euphoric, regarding the death of President Roosevelt as the last-minute miracle that would save him.

Speer meanwhile was attending the last wartime concert of the Berlin Philharmonic orchestra. He had just saved the musicians from conscription into Goebbels's levée en masse by the simple expedient of having their call-up papers spirited away and destroyed. Highlight of the packed matinee concert by the all-Aryan orchestra (long since purged of its Jewish players) was the fourth ('Romantic') symphony by the Austrian Anton Bruckner. Speer saw to it that the lighting, if not the heating, in the concert hall remained on during power-cut hours for the Reich's last gala. Other items on the unabashedly Germanic programme, requested by Speer himself, included Beethoven's Violin Concerto and two mighty blasts of Wagner – Brünnhilde's last aria and the finale from *Götterdämmerung*. As if the emotional sledgehammer of a message from this unsubtly apocalyptic programme were not enough, somebody unknown had arranged for uniformed Hitler Youths to be standing at the exits of the undamaged Philharmonic Hall with baskets of free cyanide tablets. It seems mildly surprising that anybody failed to swallow one on the spot after such an orgy of sentimental romanticism.

Still in the grip of Wagnerian heroic emotion on 14 April, Speer, manifestly unaware of his old friend's burgeoning interest in helicopters, wrote a flowery letter to Karl Hanke congratulating him on his epic choice of a hero's death in besieged Breslau. Speer was driving to and fro in the narrowing band of northern German territory still controlled by the Nazis, dissuading army officers from unnecessary and pointless demolitions. As the Russians began their last advance on the 16th, he rewrote his radio speech, planning to have it broadcast when one of the main transmitters outside Berlin came under army battlezone control as the Red Army drew near.

On 18 April another friend among the Gauleiters, Kaufmann of Hamburg, managed to get a message to Speer requesting his urgent presence in the ruined city, where the navy was about to blow up the port. Kaufmann and Speer took the lead at a hastily convened conference of local officials, harbour, shipyard and industrial representatives as well as naval officers, who all agreed to destroy nothing. Speer then drove back to Berlin with his constant companion, Poser, to appeal to Hitler on the 19th to leave what was left of Hamburg alone. It was the eve of the Führer's fifty-sixth birthday. Speer was among the entourage that lined up to shake his trembling hand as Hitler made a brief last appearance above ground in the glass-strewn Chancellery; he handed out Iron Crosses to boy soldiers amid the debris of the garden for a last 'photo opportunity'.

After the ensuing situation conference the Nazi leadership broke up. Göring fled south to Berchtesgaden, Himmler to the far north; both were putting out ineffectual feelers towards the western Allies. Dönitz had already gone north on Hitler's order, to take command there before Germany's encircling enemies split up the Reich. Speer had decided to evacuate to the same area, near the naval academy at Plön and Lake Eutin in Schleswig-Holstein. His family was already in the area and ministry officials had commandeered two Reichsbahn caravans for him in a wood by the lake. First however he returned to Kaufmann in

Hamburg, who helped him organise the recording at last of the twice-deferred radio address to the German nation, which the Gauleiter was to look after until the moment came to broadcast it.

On 22 April Soviet troops crossed the eastern boundary of the sprawling city of Berlin. The hollow booming of heavy artillery, the crump of mortar bombs and the rattle of machine-guns could soon be heard all over the city. A section of Speer's broad east–west axis, the westerly extension of Unter den Linden from the Brandenburg Gate to the Victory Monument (today styled June 17 Street in honour of the East German workers' uprising of 1953), was closed to motor traffic and pressed into service as an airstrip.

Speer landed on it in a tiny Fieseler 'Storch' (stork) reconnaissance aircraft on 23 April. He had come against his better judgment for a last and personal farewell to Adolf Hitler. He tried to make the journey by car from Hamburg, but on encountering total traffic chaos some ninety kilometres north of Berlin, he turned back and drove to an airbase in Mecklenburg. From there he flew with the faithful Poser in a trainer escorted by a squadron of fighters to the Luftwaffe airfield at Gatow on the western edge of Berlin, which was as yet not cut off from that side. Two Storks took Speer and Poser to the centre in a ten-minute flight in the late afternoon.

By this time the Chancellery was already within 'lucky strike' range of the heaviest Soviet artillery pieces and was trembling to their barrages. The building was already a shambles, although the main structure still stood. Speer found a senior adjutant of Hitler's, SS-General Julius Schaub, drinking brandy with some others in the sitting room. Speer had radioed ahead that he was coming, yet the Chancellery staff were amazed to see him. But as he descended the four flights of concrete steps into the dank bunker he had little idea of what to expect. His memoirs do not say so, but one of the reasons he had returned to Berlin, apart from his declared wish to say goodbye to his mentor, was a teleprinter message from Bormann to all Gauleiters (including Kaufmann) of the day before, containing the ominous, unexplained question: 'Where is Speer?'

On arrival in the underground anteroom Speer was his usual cool, laid-back self, reacting to the astonishment of the secretaries by remarking: 'I dare say you did not expect to see me again.' Bormann appeared and, to Speer's admitted relief, was exceptionally polite, urging Speer to use his influence with Hitler to persuade him to fly to Berchtesgaden in the Obersalzberg to take over command in the south.[10]

Once more there is no witness other than Speer to what happened when he met Hitler for their last conversation. The Führer was tired and impassive. Hitler sought Speer's opinion of Dönitz, which was and remained favourable, without saying why. Hitler revealed that he planned to stay in Berlin and die by his own hand, with Eva Braun and his dog Blondi. Speer wrote that he then confessed to having ignored the scorched-earth decree. Once again Hitler's 'eyes filled with tears. But he did not react.' They were interrupted by the usual 'situation conference', now a risible shadow of its former self; all the leading henchmen had dispersed, and the map on the huge table showed Greater Berlin and environs only. When the brief session ended, Speer was dismissed with the rest but without a handshake. He went to see Magda Goebbels, fully aware that her fanatical husband was bent on murdering his family and killing himself alongside Hitler. Later he encountered Bormann, on his way to Hitler with a message from Göring indicating that he was about to take over under the decree of 19 June 1941 making him Hitler's deputy and heir. Hitler promptly ordered him stripped of all offices and indulged his infamous, spluttering temper one more time.

On his prolonged farewell tour of the bunker, Speer also took his leave of Eva Braun, whose composure he found admirable and moving. They shared champagne and cake and talked from before midnight until about 3 a.m. An exhausted Speer said goodbye and sought out Hitler for a third and last encounter:

> I was afraid that I would not be able to control myself at our parting. Trembling, the prematurely aged man stood before me for the last time; the man to whom I had dedicated my life twelve years before. I was both moved and confused. For his part, he showed no emotion when we confronted one another. His words were as cold as his hand: 'So, you're leaving? Good. *Auf Wiedersehen.*' No regards to my family; no wishes, no thanks, no farewell. For a moment I lost my composure, said something about coming back. But he could easily see that it was a white lie, and turned his attention to something else. I was dismissed.[11]

Returning to the surface of the earth, Speer paused in the courtyard of his Chancellery, the Court of Honour. An eerie silence, punctuated only by the occasional distant Soviet shellburst, had descended. Speer and Poser took to the air again from the city-centre airstrip and flew back to Rechlin in Mecklenburg before dawn on the 24th. Learning there that Himmler was staying in the very rooms that Speer had occupied at the Hohenlychen clinic forty kilometres away, he took off again to visit the SS chief. Himmler offered him a post in the government he was feverishly plotting to put together after coming to terms with the western allies.

Speer flew on to Hamburg, where Kaufmann was still holding his recorded radio speech, that evening and to his temporary base by Lake

Eutin the next day. From there he kept in touch with Grand Admiral Dönitz at Plön. The apotheosis of the submariner as the second and last ruler of the Third Reich was signalled by Bormann on 30 April, the day Hitler committed suicide in his bunker. On 1 May, Bormann's second telegram arrived, telling of Hitler's death and naming Dönitz as Reich President and Supreme Commander in accordance with the late Führer's last will and political testament (which, *inter alia*, named Saur as Speer's successor and appointed Hanke chief of police in place of the dismissed Himmler). Because Bormann's follow-up message named Goebbels as Prime Minister and Bormann as Party Minister, Dönitz suppressed it.

Speer immediately attached himself to the new head of state and moved temporarily from his caravan at Lake Eutin to a room in Dönitz's headquarters, where he effectively appointed himself the admiral's principal adviser. Dönitz's main preoccupation in the preceding days and weeks had been to evacuate as many Germans from north-east Germany as he could, before the Russians established themselves there; some two million people moved westward. On 2 May, Speer flew to Hamburg with a signed order from Dönitz authorising Kaufmann to hand the city over to the British army without a fight. He also made a live broadcast, abandoning his much reworked, recorded previous text in favour of a general exhortation against any demolition. Speer found Himmler waiting for him as he left the radio station, but the Reichsführer's attempts to claim a place in the Dönitz regime were firmly rejected (Himmler was eventually arrested by British troops and committed suicide in custody).

Speer was named Minister of Economics and Production in what he himself described as the new 'operetta government' of the Reich. Dönitz moved, with his government and within a week, to the more spacious naval school at Mürwik outside Flensburg, also taking over the liner *Patria* (an ironic choice; the Latin means 'fatherland') as temporary seat of government. Speer on 10 May took up stately residence at Glücksburg Castle a few miles away, at the invitation of the Duke of Mecklenburg and Holstein (prompted by some of Speer's staff, who had joined him in the north). From there the reappointed minister had himself driven to Flensburg for the daily 10 a.m. 'cabinet meeting' with Dönitz, who agreed to a ceasefire in the north on 4 May and then an unconditional surrender on all fronts on 7 May, to take effect the next day.

The British had raced across the lightly populated area of north Germany east of the Elbe as far as Magdeburg, in case the power vacuum that would otherwise have existed in the region proved irresistible to the Russians. For more than two weeks the British conquerors seemed to be too busy to take any notice of the 'government' solemnly discussing the administration of a prostrate and ruined Germany on a ship off the Baltic coast near Flensburg. A British liaison office moved on to the *Patria* and Allied reporters appeared. So did British and American intelligence officers, who wandered around the modest facilities of the last Reich government, informally questioning those they found.

On 15 May 1945 an American lieutenant appeared in Speer's room at Glücksburg Castle. 'Do you know where Speer is?' he asked. He identified himself and the young officer asked if he was willing to cooperate with the United States Strategic Bombing Survey, which was already hard at work collecting information on the effect of the air war, not least because Japan was still fighting on. On the 16th, a US Army Air Force general came by; three days of general discussion of the Allied bombing campaign ensued, in which the American visitors were struck by Speer's enormously detailed yet sweeping knowledge of the German war effort.

On the 19th, a heavyweight team of interrogators arrived to begin a serious and prolonged debriefing of Speer. They included George Ball, Dr John Kenneth Galbraith, Paul Nitze and several other extremely gifted young Americans who would distinguish themselves in their country's postwar service in many capacities. Speer was able to visit his family several times at their country hideaway only forty kilometres from Glücksburg. But on the 21st the British ceased to be nonchalant and confiscated his car. Speer was driven back to Flensburg and placed under armed guard overnight before being taken back to the castle. On 23 May 1945 British troops surrounded Glücksburg. A sergeant walked into his bedroom and placed him under arrest, whereupon he was driven to Flensburg to join the rest of the Dönitz government, which had been rounded up at the same time. The grandees of the Third Reich were strip-searched and processed by military police.

The bizarre interregnum was over. Albert Speer had become a prisoner.

PART THREE

Apologist

Put to the Question

(1945–46)

FIRST LIEUTENANT WOLFGANG G. SKLARZ, United States army, was one among hundreds of Americans of German origin (many were Jewish) who rendered invaluable service to Allied intelligence during the Second World War and the occupation of Germany which ensued. Sklarz, assisted by Technical Sergeant Harold E. Fassberg of similar background, began the first interrogation of Albert Speer on behalf of the 'spearhead team' of the United States Strategic Bombing Survey (USSBS) at Schloss Glücksburg, near Flensburg, on 15 May 1945 at 1.30 p.m. It lasted for three and a quarter hours and was the first of a unique and prolonged series of 'debriefings' of Hitler's Minister of Armaments and War Production. From Speer's point of view they merged seamlessly into pre-trial interrogations over a period of six months between his arrest and the opening of the main Nuremberg war-crimes case. No leading participant in a crucial historical event has been so thoroughly questioned about his part in it before or since. The resulting records are a major contribution to historiography for two reasons. Speer must have been constrained by the knowledge that this detailed protocol existed when preparing his memoirs for publication from 1966. Second, at least some of his interrogators were sceptical (though not enough; SHAEF G2 – the intelligence section of Supreme Headquarters, Allied Expeditionary Force – even set up a Speer Steering Committee in June 1945, to supervise and exploit the mass of material extracted from him and his minions by the SBS and others, but there are times when it is not clear from the records who was steering whom).

The interrogations form a substantial archive in themselves, even without the mound of documentation which Speer had the foresight to spirit out of Berlin and into a Hamburg bank to buttress his recollections of the Third Reich and, first of all, his defence. His draft memoirs, written in prison without access to archives, differed from them hardly at all, a testament to a memory which seems to have been of photographic quality in the short term and capable of well-nigh total recall (except for certain sensitive subjects).

The interrogations were literally innumerable. On some days he was questioned at three or even more sessions, some no more than continuations after a break but others often involving different personnel from different agencies or even countries raising different subjects. It is therefore impossible to arrive at a definitive total for the interrogations of Speer. He also wrote, sometimes at the request of his interrogators and sometimes on his own initiative, a number of papers on the Nazi regime, his role in it and various related topics. The calibre of the questioners was sometimes extraordinarily high, embracing not only the brilliant young Americans of the USSBS but also such intellectual luminaries of postwar Britain as Hugh Trevor-Roper, historian turned intelligence officer, and Nicholas Kaldor, Hungarian refugee and future economic guru. They came from American, British and joint intelligence agencies of many kinds; the British had their own Strategic Bombing Survey but it was a much more modest and limited exercise than the American, which had a huge budget, an unlimited remit and a talented team which recruited Britons as well as Americans (the poet W.H. Auden was enlisted to study German civilian morale).

The voluminous interrogation records on both sides of the Atlantic, whether of the invaluable USSBS or the eclectic Nuremberg prosecution, serve up an alphabet soup of agencies – OSS, FIAT, SHAEF, BIOS, CIOS, OCCPAC – that fell over themselves to examine Speer above all. The USSBS did a remarkable job with what it learned from this principal and many another source; its final report, written by Galbraith, showed that the effect of the bombing of Germany, while considerable at the end, had been outrageously overstated (a lesson ignored by the Americans in Korea and Vietnam). The first impression Speer made on a mere lieutenant was lasting, but no more striking than his effect on much older and more experienced interlocutors. Sklarz reported:

> Speer showed himself extremely co-operative. He is without a doubt a man of very unusual ability and has a complete picture of the German war effort. His memory, especially in regard to questions of armament production, both technically and economically, is astounding. He shows great pride in the results achieved by German production while under his control.

George Ball, founder-member of the USSBS set up in November 1944, arrived in Flensburg on 16 May for his first session, leading the questioning for three days; John Kenneth Galbraith, whom he recruited from economic journalism to the Overall Effects Division, arrived on the 19th, and eventually spent about a week with Speer. The American intellectuals, having far outstripped the US army's logistical reach (they were, after all, in the British zone), were obliged to conscript Annemarie Kempf, Speer's loyal principal secretary, to take notes from the running translation of a sergeant interpreter. The proceedings were interrupted when Speer failed to turn up for one session: he had been arrested by the OSS (the forerunner of the American Central Intelligence Agency). Small wonder that Speer's first reaction to the debriefing circus was to dismiss it variously as comic opera or a B-picture.

In his own memoirs, Galbraith is equally scathing about Speer's claims to have frustrated Hitler's scorched-earth decree almost single-handed and to have plotted to gas him and his henchmen. These stories, Galbraith thought, had gained much in the telling and contained 'major elements of fantasy'. So, he felt, did Speer's claims about the German war economy, whose exponential growth had been from a very small base and did not surpass a smaller Britain's until 1944. All this, and Speer's carefully nuanced candour, were part and parcel of his 'well-devised strategy of self-vindication and survival' – a conclusion reached by Galbraith not in his memoirs thirty-five years later but as early as autumn 1945, before the Nuremberg trials, in an article written with George Ball for *Life* magazine.[1]

The stories so crucial for Speer's later reputation emerged for the first time in a session which began at Glücksburg on the afternoon of 22 May, moved to a requisitioned villa in Flensburg and, judiciously lubricated by a bottle of whisky, lasted until just before dawn. That morning, the Dönitz 'government' including Speer was rounded up on the *Patria* and driven away to captivity in a convoy of trucks escorted by dozens of armoured vehicles.

The Reich government was flown from a local airfield to, of all places, Luxembourg City aerodrome, where hundreds of heavily armed American troops surrounded the two Douglas DC3 aircraft. Another convoy took the captives to the spa town of Mondorf-les-Bains and the undamaged, five-star Palace Hotel. The sprawling hostelry, stripped of most of its peacetime fripperies, was already heavily occupied by guards and Nazi leaders taken earlier, most notably Hermann Göring, a platoon of field marshals and generals and old friends such as Dr Karl Brandt. The VIP prisoner-collection centre was contemptuously codenamed Ashcan by the Americans and was soon besieged by angry Luxembourgers. Concentration-camp survivors had just begun to return home from such places as Dachau to the area and they and their families were incensed by the lavish nature of the Nazi leaders' accommodation. Prince Felix, consort of the Grand Duchess who was the constitutional ruler of the western European statelet, was called to address and pacify the crowd. A few protesters were shown round to prove that luxury had been dispensed with.

Most top Nazis remained there until mid-August, when their spartan lodgings in the prison attached to the Palace of Justice in Nuremberg were ready. But Speer was taken from Mondorf in the middle of June 1945 in a large staff car and driven via Paris to Versailles and the headquarters, in the grounds of the great palace, of General Dwight D. Eisenhower, the Supreme Allied Commander, Europe. Speer was assigned to a small room high up in the subsidiary palace of Chesnay. He soon discovered that his fellow-prisoners, with whom he was at first forbidden to communicate, were technocrats and the like. Many of them, such as Saur, Fränk, Heinkel and Dorpmüller, had worked under Speer and within a week he was allowed to mix with them between American and British interrogations. A British major even took him for a relaxing day's drive to Paris.

When Eisenhower moved his headquarters to Frankfurt, the prisoners were also moved, via an overnight stop at Mannheim, to the nearby Taunus Forest and the castle of Kransberg, where the endless technical and economic debriefings continued. Speer remembered refurbishing and extending this Schloss as a headquarters for Göring in 1939, when Hitler had one built for himself at nearby Bad Nauheim. The prisoners were quartered in the servants' annex added by Speer, but the atmosphere was relaxed, the American army rations cornucopian and the wooded surroundings secluded and pleasant. The British commandant ran a mild regime in the camp, wryly given a British translation of Ashcan as its codename – Dustbin. Scores of Speer's closest colleagues, industrial collaborators, staff members and associates such as Wernher von Braun, the rocket engineer, were assembled for longer or shorter periods at Kransberg, where the question-and-answer sessions pursued their desultory course. The interrogators undoubtedly worked hard (the output of paper proves it) but could only handle so many interviews per day, which meant that the élite prisoners spent most of their time at Dustbin awaiting the pleasure of their overworked captors. Meanwhile they organised their own keep-fit classes, sports, lectures, literary readings and even a cabaret.

Speer, depressed by all this idleness after years of intense work, was asked to write papers on his view of Germany's future in Europe, on Hitler's principal henchmen and, prompted by questions, on his own key subordinates (he took the opportunity to be positive all round except in two cases – the allegedly disloyal Saur and Dorsch). A British intelligence captain with a German background called Hoeffding made it his business to get as close to Speer as possible, partly to keep him occupied with requests for papers and other distractions but partly also, for sure, to squeeze him informally for more information.

Some time in September 1945 Speer was awakened by one of his former staff and told that the 6 a.m. news on the radio, controlled by the Allies, was reporting that he and Hjalmar Schacht would be principal defendants at Nuremberg in the first war-crimes trial, known to be in preparation. None the less, the British commandant once took Speer for a drive, walk and picnic without other escort in the Taunus Forest. Soon afterwards, at the end of September, a US army Jeep took Speer from Dustbin.

The Americans were in charge of the next stop which, fortunately for him, was for one night only: Oberursel, a former Nazi interrogation camp near Frankfurt at which, among others, captured Allied airmen and recaptured escapees from prisoner-of-war camps had been none too gently put to the question. The next day Speer and other VIP prisoners were herded into US army trucks and driven to Nuremberg. There he soon saw a familiar face: that of Colonel Burton C. Andrus, the US cavalry officer who had been in charge of security at Ashcan in Mondorf and became commandant of the war-criminals' prison at Nuremberg on 12 August 1945. The wheels of victors' justice were beginning to turn.[2]

The entire concept of putting war criminals on trial remains controversial to this day, revived by the atrocities perpetrated in former Yugoslavia in the 1990s but also by a steady stream of cases in Germany, Israel, France and other countries immediately after the war and for many years afterwards. Ageing Nazis were located, charged and tried for crimes about which the frail surviving victims found it almost impossible to speak half a century later. Britain got round to passing a law enabling such charges to be brought in its courts fifty years after the war ended. Even then there was much controversy.

In 1945 there was no real precedent, even though prosecutors could point to a string of international pacts broken by the Nazis. But there was no tariff of sanctions. 'Crimes against humanity' were a coinage of the Treaty of Versailles, which had also sweepingly blamed Germany alone for the First World War, a victors' verdict directly conducive, among other factors, to the rise of Hitler as we have seen. Efforts were made to put Kaiser Wilhelm II and other German war leaders on trial but the Netherlands to which he had fled refused to give him up. In the early Weimar Republic, the Reich Supreme Court at Leipzig reluctantly responded to Allied and American pressure, trying 901 blacklisted perpetrators of alleged breaches of international conventions governing conduct in war by 1922. Of these, 888 were acquitted or given an absolute discharge; the remaining thirteen received sentences ranging from the lenient to the derisory. The Germans were in no mood for what they regarded as undue process and not a few wrote to congratulate the prison warders when some of the convicted men escaped.

But in 1945 the mood was different. The Allies had made a war aim of their determination to punish the criminals responsible for a catalogue of unspeakable atrocities whose scale was unprecedented in the history of civilisation and of warfare. The Japanese had matched the Germans with such specific horrors as the massacre at Nanking as well as in medical experiments and maltreatment of 'racially inferior' captives. But they had openly subscribed to an uncompromising if also inhuman code which outlawed nothing except mercy (to their own people as well as the enemy) in waging war. The Germans, however, had signed many conventions, utopian or not, seeking to apply the spirit of boxing's Queensberry Rules to warfare. And although war has always been accompanied by atrocities, the Nazis' unprecedented campaign against European civilisation had genocide as its main aim, introducing the bureaucracy of massacre and the mechanised Holocaust to the conduct of aggressive war. The equivalent of the combined contemporary population of London, Paris and Berlin was systematically murdered by citizens of one of the most civilised and advanced nations on earth, for ideological reasons and without a vestige of military justification.

Representatives of the governments-in-exile of nine German-occupied countries in Europe therefore signed the St James's Declaration as early as January 1942, making a war aim of the punishment of Axis war criminals. The three principal Allies, America, Britain and Russia, concurred.

Seventeen countries set up a United Nations War Crimes Commission in London in 1943 to open dossiers on individual cases. It failed to amass much of the kind of evidence a war-crimes court would need and proved generally ineffectual. Then as now, United Nations institutions were as good as members allowed them to be. The Russians were not among the seventeen and the British were lukewarm; the idealistic and legalistic Americans were keenest. But the Moscow Declaration of November foreshadowed joint Allied action against war criminals, and the Allied summit conference at Teheran endorsed the idea. Public pressure mounted in the democracies when their troops found evidence of Nazi crimes in the advance on Germany. Americans were enraged when the Waffen-SS massacred seventy US army captives in the Ardennes offensive in December 1944; the British felt similarly about the Gestapo massacre of fifty RAF escapers from Stalag Luft III prisoner-of-war camp in March 1944.

Hitler's suicide on 30 April 1945 removed the biggest headache for those in the democracies who had considered all the ramifications of punishment and cringed at the possibility of Nazi- or Soviet-style show trials such as the recent treatment of the 20 July plotters. For Hitler there had been a possible precedent in the shape of Napoleon, sent without trial into exile at the other end of the earth, where he duly died; but Napoleon's effort to unite Europe had not included the planned slaughter of entire ethnic groups.

A US War Department memorandum in September 1944 proposed putting the leading Nazis on trial together with their principal institutions, such as the cabinet (an irrelevance as it had not sat as a body since 1937) and the SS. An Anglo-American summit conference in Quebec in September leaked a rumour that Churchill and Roosevelt favoured executing the top Nazis out of hand: at Teheran, Stalin 'jokingly' proposed shooting 50,000 leading Germans. Goebbels exploited such evidence of Allied vengefulness to urge the German people to fight to the bitter end because there was nothing to be gained by surrender. The British were opposed to a trial but Roosevelt and Stalin managed to agree on one at the Yalta Conference in February 1945, despite Churchill's disapproval. The moribund Roosevelt however was nothing like as keen as his successor, Harry Truman. The Russians and the French joined him in pressing the British to agree. The British cabinet reluctantly gave its formal consent to Truman's demand on 30 May 1945, but only to prevent their allies from going ahead without them.

Truman had already appointed an American chief prosecutor for the United Nations. Justice Robert H. Jackson of the United States Supreme Court, Chief of Counsel for the Prosecution of Axis Criminality from 26 April 1945, was a self-made advocate who learned his job by doing it, becoming a master of rhetoric and language in the old-fashioned American manner. His only formal legal education was one year at the law school at Albany, New York. A Democrat like Roosevelt, that other denizen of upstate New York, Jackson's local legal success won him political attention and federal government posts. He was Roosevelt's Solicitor-General in 1938 and Attorney-General two years later, rising to the Supreme Court bench after only eighteen months, in July 1941. Jackson was supported by a battery of legal talent, including Major-General William J. Donovan, head of the Office of Strategic Services.

The British decided to send their Attorney-General as their principal prosecuting counsel. Under what passes for the British constitution (said to be 'unwritten' but in fact an uncodified jumble of statutes in the middle of which lurks the black hole of 'royal prerogative') the role of the Attorney-General is uniquely ambiguous. He (there has been no she so far) has to be a Queen's (or King's) Counsel, a senior advocate, and is the government's chief legal representative; sometimes, though nowadays hardly ever, he appears in court as leading counsel in an important or politically sensitive case. But he is also very much a practising politician and member of the cabinet and is automatically given a knighthood on appointment. At Nuremberg, however, there would be no conflict of interest between the two roles once Churchill's coalition cabinet endorsed the trial.

So on 29 May 1945 His Majesty's Attorney-General, Sir David Maxwell-Fyfe, KC, MP, a Conservative politician, was appointed British chief prosecutor. But the general election of July 1945 stunned the world by unseating Churchill, symbol of British defiance, and giving the Labour Party a landslide victory. The new Prime Minister, Clement Attlee, appointed his own Attorney-General, Sir Hartley Shawcross, KC, MP, to lead for Britain at Nuremberg. Maxwell-Fyfe however stayed on as his deputy, in charge of the British case on a day-to-day basis.

The French prosecution team was led after the opening proceedings by Auguste Champetier de Ribes, a former cabinet minister who resisted the Nazis before and during the war. The Soviet prosecution was led by Major-General Roman Rudenko, the chief prosecutor of Ukraine.

Each of the 'Big Four' appointed two judges, one senior and one junior, to the Nuremberg bench. The President of the International Military Tribunal (IMT) was Lord Justice Lawrence, an appeal judge; the other senior judges were Justice Francis Biddle, Jackson's recently replaced successor as US Attorney-General; Major-General I.T. Nikit-chenko; and Professor Henri Donnedieu de Vabres.

The diplomatic, political and legal wrangling among the four powers about the charter, constitution and jurisdiction of the court, the accused, the charges, the indictment, the venue, the rules of procedure and almost every other aspect of a unique departure in international law need not detain us. What Stalin had realistically been wont to call 'the Anti-Fascist Coalition' was already breaking up, even before Japan surrendered. But as a sop to the Russians, who had wanted to try the top Nazis in the ruins of Berlin, the IMT was formally based there. Yet the court would sit in Nuremberg, a no less appropriate venue, where the huge justice facilities happened to be virtually intact amid the rubble of the erstwhile home of the Nazi Party Congress, ninety per cent destroyed by bombardment. The arrangements were settled at last after long negotiations in the British capital, leading to the London Agreement of August 1945.

The result was inevitably an untidy compromise. The French and the Russians (to say nothing of the German defendants and their lawyers) were steeped in variants of the Continental or Napoleonic legal system, which is inquisitorial: essentially, all present – bench, prosecution, defence – work together to probe the truth or otherwise of a lengthy indictment stating the case against the defendant in

Hitler and Speer take a stroll near the Fuhrer's temporary headquarters in the Ukraine, summer 1942.

Fat man, thin man: Hermann Göring with the newly appointed Reichsminister Speer, now sporting a Todt Organisation armband as its *ex officio* chief.

Seeing for himself: Speer at the controls of a tracked 'motor-cycle' built for the Russian mud in 1942.

Speer at Berchtesgaden sharing one of the cars he loved with five of his children: Albert Jr. and Hilde are in the front; Fritz (rear), Arnold and Margret are in the back. The absent youngest, Ernst, was born around the time this picture was taken in 1943.

Speer and the local Gauleiter chat with slave-workers from nearby Mauthausen concentration-camp at a steelworks near Linz, Austria, in 1944 (Speer was at the camp itself, the only one he visited, a year earlier).

The end of an architect's dream: the hall of Speer's 1938 Reich Chancellery, in 1945.

Under arrest: Speer with Dönitz (centre) and Keitel in northern Germany in May 1945.

Defendant Speer makes his final statement to the International Military Tribunal in Nuremberg, August 1946.

A snatched picture of Speer at work in the garden of Spandau prison in the early 1960s.

Speer with his wife, Margarete (Gretel), on his release from prison in 1966 at midnight on the night of September 30 to October 1.

Old age: Speer shortly before his death in 1981.

Legacy: the only realised element of Speer's grandiose plans for Berlin is a double row of these elegant twin streetlamps along Strasse des 17. Juni.

detail. The system inherited by the Americans from English law is confrontational: prosecution and defence argue over the briefest possible statement of charges before a lay jury, with the judge as referee. The Continental system has the advantage of apparent detachment but can look like a cosy if procedurally rigid lawyers' conference, in which the accused seems well-nigh irrelevant; the Anglo-Saxons have their quintessentially democratic jury system, but the outcome of a trial is at least as likely to depend on an advocate's skill as on the evidence.

The parameters within which the IMT would operate were laid down in its charter, of which Article 8 set out the most important 'Nuremberg Principle': the unacceptability of 'I was only obeying orders' as an excuse or defence (although it could be considered in mitigation of sentence). This was not new; even the German soldier's paybook ordered him not to obey an illegal command. In fact obedience to orders is a reasonable excuse at all but the highest level of responsibility if the alternative is torture or death; even in a democracy the power of the state is overwhelming if not infinite when compared with the power of the individual to resist it on moral grounds, as many a conscientious objector could confirm.

But this was not a problem for the tribunal or the prosecution. Their main need was readily accessible, court-quality evidence. The USSBS and intelligence agencies were told to look out for evidence of war crimes as they roamed across a prostrate Germany. We have noted the German predilection for recording almost everything on paper, even the most incriminating material. There was no shortage of records: the trick for the prosecutors was to find the nuggets of specifically incriminating material among the mountains of paper, in what proved to be a hopelessly short period for such a gigantic task. The German navy alone had stashed away 60,000 files in northern Bavaria, handed over intact by order of Dönitz and shipped to Britain. The German army's records were much bulkier and were shipped bodily to the United States, where they were carelessly dumped in various storehouses: one warehouse in Alexandria, Virginia, just across the river from Washington, was filled with packing cases of German papers that lay untouched for ten years after the war, and were only briefly thrown open to scholars before being returned to the West German government along with many other seized collections, including the naval papers from Britain. All this material went to the Federal German Archive in Koblenz or its military archive in Freiburg. The Nazi Party membership index of many millions of cards was discovered in a mound of rubble outside Munich; the German Foreign Office had deposited its entire main archive, weighing 485 tons, in the Harz Mountains.[3]

Speer's ministry had availed itself of the natural and manmade caves in the same central German repository of so many secrets. Together with large quantities of other documents, the top copy of Dr Wolters's Chronicle with its supporting papers was sent to Osterode in the Harz, whence it disappeared; another copy was sent to the ministry's reserve document store at a building company in Höxter, Westphalia, conveniently close to Wolters's home town. Many tons of ministry papers eventually found their way to Koblenz from dumps in several parts of Germany. Speer was able to add to them considerably himself, having had the foresight to store a judicious and general selection of documents from his private office (but no Chronicle) in the vaults of a Hamburg bank. He found them of enormous value for his defence: they helped to save his life.

The Americans, who put rather more lawyers and supporting staff into the Nuremberg process (thirteen trials in all, of which the case against the surviving leadership was the first) than the three other powers combined, also had overall responsibility for the prosecution as a whole. The accused faced four counts; each power took special responsibility for the investigation and presentation of one. Thus the Americans were in charge of Count I, conspiracy to commit the other three. The British handled Count II, crimes against peace; the French covered III and IV, war crimes and crimes against humanity respectively, in western Europe, and the Russians the same on the Eastern Front.

The Anglo-Saxon concept of conspiracy, a catch-all, bureaucrat's charge, caused particular difficulty during the haggling that preceded the trial. It was and remains alien to the Continental legal tradition, which contents itself with more concrete charges such as membership of a criminal organisation. There was no shortage of the latter; the prosecution asked the court to declare as criminal the main Nazi institutions – the cabinet (actually defunct), the party leadership, the SS, the SD and Gestapo (both controlled by the SS), the SA (superseded by the SS since 1934), the general staff (defunct since 1919) and the OKW (High Command of the Wehrmacht). This list of organisations was sloppily formulated, the first visible evidence of a lack of grasp by the prosecution, especially the American (which did the most work), of its admittedly indigestible and ferociously complicated, eclectic brief. The purpose behind the request to declare the organisations criminal was to facilitate the prosecution of the accused and of many others, who would be subject to conviction if their membership was proved.

The indictment proper consisted of twenty-seven closely printed, foolscap pages with a further sixteen for three appendices. It is a hybrid document, including charges briefly formulated in the Anglo-Saxon way and a discursive, general summary of the case against the accused in the Continental manner. It turned out to bear much the same relation to the judgment as the 1918 Armistice bore to the Treaty of Versailles.

There were twenty-four accused. Of these, one, Robert Ley, Minister of Labour, overwhelmed by an indictment which he equated with a judgment, committed suicide in Nuremberg before trial. One, Gustav Krupp, titular head of the arms conglomerate, was too senile to stand trial (another example of prosecution ignorance); his son Alfred, who ran the firm, was tried later and got away with three years served. And one, Martin Bormann, never found (he probably died in Berlin on 1 May 1945; his skull was located there in 1975) was tried *in absentia*. Twenty-one stood trial. They were Göring; Hess (flown in from the Tower of London); Ribbentrop (Foreign Minister); Field Marshal Keitel; Kaltenbrunner; Rosenberg (Minister for Occupied Eastern Territories); Hans Frank (Governor-General of Poland); Wilhelm Frick (Interior Minister); Julius Streicher (publisher of the anti-Semitic *Der Stürmer*); Walter Funk (Minister of Economics); Schacht (former Reichsbank President – acquitted); Dönitz; Grand-Admiral Erich Raeder; Baldur von Schirach (Reich Youth Leader and Gauleiter of Vienna); Sauckel; Colonel-General Alfred Jodl; Franz von Papen (briefly Hitler's Vice-Chancellor – acquitted); Arthur Seyss-Inquart (Commissioner for the Netherlands); Speer; Constantin von Neurath (Protector of Bohemia and Moravia); Hans Fritzsche (head of radio propaganda – acquitted). Not all were accused on all counts.

The indictment began with a long statement of justification for Count I, incorporating an exposition of how the Nazi Party acquired and extended its control of all aspects of German life and then of most of Europe, presenting the whole as a giant conspiracy. Count II, crimes against peace, was little more than a list of countries against which Germany waged war. Count III, war crimes, listed hundreds of atrocities country by country; other allegations included slave and forced labour, maltreatment of prisoners of war, killing of hostages, plundering and wanton destruction. Count IV, crimes against humanity, covered maltreatment of civilians in concentration and death camps, general persecution – and the genocide of the Jews.

Appendix A summarised the charges against each defendant one by one; B did the same for the criminal organisations; and C listed all twenty-six treaties, conventions and agreements violated by the Nazis.

The specific allegation against Speer said in full:

The defendant Speer between 1932–1945 was a member of the Nazi Party, Reichsleiter, member of the Reichstag, Minister for Armament and Munitions, Chief of the Organisation Todt, General Plenipotentiary for Armaments in the Office of the Four-Year Plan and Chairman of the Armaments Council. The defendant Speer used the foregoing positions and his personal influence in such a manner that he participated in the military and economic planning and preparation of the Nazi conspirators for wars of aggression and wars in violation of international treaties, agreements and assurances set forth in counts one and two of the indictment; and he authorised, directed and participated in the war crimes set forth in count three of the indictment and the crimes against humanity set forth in count four of the indictment, including more particularly the abuse and exploitation of human beings for forced labour in the conduct of aggressive war.

A copy of the indictment, in German translation, was served on each of the prisoners individually, in his cell at the jail behind the court and administrative complex of the Nuremberg Justice Buildings. The documents were distributed on 20 October by Major Airey Neave, a German speaker and the first Briton to get home from Colditz, a prisoner-of-war camp for persistent escapers; he qualified as an advocate while recuperating and then joined Military Intelligence. Sent to Germany to prepare the case against the Krupps, Neave stayed on as liaison officer to the accused, advising them of their rights to a full defence and supplying a list of German lawyers for those who could not nominate or locate their own advocates.

The heavy, late nineteenth-century justice complex, still in use today and looking much as it did originally, is about a kilometre west of Nuremberg's lovingly restored, historic centre, which lay in ruins in 1945 after countless aerial and artillery bombardments. SS units had made a last stand at the justice buildings but they were massively constructed in sandstone and were quickly restored to usable condition by captured SS labour. The self-contained complex, easily sealed off from the rest of the city, faces south on the Fürtherstrasse, with the courthouse (added in 1916) standing as the eastern appendage of the larger administrative blocks. To the north of those, behind a high wall, stands the prison, consisting of four main, three-tier blocks arranged like an open fan, pointing west, north-west, north-east and east. The defendants were placed in the latter (pulled down and rebuilt in the 1980s), which was closest to the court and connected to it by an underground passage with a lift at the end, whereby prisoners were conveyed to the courtroom on the second floor.

Witnesses were kept in a separate block and the complex was surrounded by American tanks, artillery, anti-aircraft units and infantry, with fighter support on call at Fürth airfield nearby. The perimeter was protected by barbed wire, sandbags and machine-gun nests and the complex swarmed with troops and heavily armed military police inside and out. Rumours of a Nazi uprising and concealed SS units abounded. Cleaning and other chores were assigned to German prisoners of war in uniform, who slept in their own separate prison block.

By his own admission Neave, then aged twenty-nine, was shattered to be given, on 18 October 1945, less than forty-eight hours' notice of his assignment to serve the indictments on the accused; he put on his best uniform with its chestful of gallantry medals and swallowed his stage fright. He was accompanied by Harold B. Willey, General Secretary of the IMT and former Chief Clerk of the US Supreme Court, Colonel Andrus as head of security, an American Lutheran pastor, two soldiers carrying the indictments and a US Military Police escort chewing gum and swinging blackjacks. The clutter of personnel and the clatter of boots lurched from one small cell to the next. The prisoners were moved around from time to time, but Speer spent most of his time at Nuremberg in cell number seventeen, east wing.

The accused had already been through Continental-style, pre-trial examinations but the trial proper would, as described above, be run on Anglo-Saxon lines. The indictment summarised the pre-trial findings but the brief charges added to the text gave at least one confused defendant the impression that they were findings of guilt: Robert Ley killed himself on the 25th. 'I did not realise that day how many of these defendants regarded the service of the indictment as the moment of doom. It was as if I had come to read the death-sentences,' Neave wrote.

Never the most reflective of men or the most fluent of writers, Neave also found Speer to be 'a gifted and compelling man ... who made Nazism acceptable to the arts and sciences ... his greatest crime'. Noting a certain repellent smoothness in the man, Neave wrote: 'Speer was the strongest in character and most genuinely courageous of all the prisoners at Nuremberg. Yet he was a man I could never trust.' He waited 'with a nervous smile' for his copy of the indictment:

> Speer was an impressive figure among the broken-down street politicians of the Nazi Party. His appearance was striking, even in his prison clothes. He was tall and dark with a strong, intelligent face. His manner was persuasive and he seemed like an athletic university professor who had turned to public administration. His eyes were very large and thoughtful. He was, I felt, a man of very considerable distinction ... [His] charm and apparent integrity seemed to shine in that sordid place...
>
> Why had this polite and intellectual person become so close a confidant of Hitler? ... He seemed the one civilised man I had met that afternoon.[4]

Tagging along with the milling indictment-serving party was Captain G.M. Gilbert, a German-speaking, American intelligence officer with a PhD in psychology, his profession in civilian life. Dr Gilbert, who had arrived in Nuremberg only that day, was left free to play an extraordinary if shadowy role among the prisoners in the background to the trial, manipulating them, studying their reactions under the extraordinary stress of the trial and evaluating their personalities. Two US army psychiatrist MDs were on hand at all times, but it is from Dr Gilbert that the historical record derives the main information about the mental state of the leaders of the Third Reich. He had his own copy of the indictment and he asked each prisoner to autograph it under Gilbert's note of his reaction to being served. Only Raeder and a shattered Ley refused to comment. Speer said: 'This trial is necessary. There is a common responsibility for such horrible crimes, even in an authoritarian system.' Gilbert noted that only Frank and von Schirach showed obvious remorse: 'Speer, the tall, shaggy-browed Armaments Minister of the Hitler war-machine, attracted little attention at first, but appeared to have a more sincere and less demonstrative conception of the Nazi guilt than anyone else.'[5]

One of Gilbert's initiatives was to subject the prisoners to a test of their intelligence quotients. Hjalmar Schacht, the central banker, came closest to a genius rating with an IQ of 143. Göring and Dönitz both got 138 and the already distrait Hess, apparently the least stable of the prisoners, managed 120. Streicher, rabidly anti-Semitic and sex-obsessed, came last with 106. Speer scored 126 (but revealingly claimed to Gitta Sereny that he had not tried, because he thought it was nonsense!).

Because of Ley's suicide (and that of a secondary detainee, one of the perverted SS medical officers arrested for a later doctors' trial at Nuremberg), the prisoners, one to a cell, were constantly watched by a military policeman standing with eyes clapped to the door aperture round the clock. A bright light shone all day in each cell and a dim one at night; the only place from which a prisoner could not be seen was when he was sitting on the lavatory just inside the door.

The overwhelming guard at Nuremberg proved powerless to prevent leaks of information to the outside world. The US forces' daily newspaper *Stars and Stripes* soon published detailed accounts of the indictment procedure, including quotations in response from individual defendants. Neave was admonished for not imparting to the prisoners the date the trial was due to start – 20 November 1946. He had not been told himself until after his tour was over, whereupon he made another brief visit to each cell with the information. On the following day he made a third visit, to take down the names of the lawyers chosen by the prisoners. He then caused searches to be made all over Germany for some of them. They all proved willing to serve; American rations were famously superior to the very short commons of the German people, who were mostly living on the edge of starvation.

Behind the scenes the preparations for the trial teetered on the brink of chaos and sometimes fell over the edge. Justice Jackson was nobody's idea of an administrator, and the 700 Americans working for the prosecution almost drowned in oceans of paperwork, which they processed only very slowly. With four prosecution teams and nearly two dozen defendants the numbers of copies required were astronomical. There was a chronic shortage of secretaries, stenographers and interpreters (the Soviet team arrived with none) and of forensically qualified German speakers capable of conducting the pre-trial examinations. These were largely done in haste in the early part of October, before the IMT met in its first formal pre-trial session on the 18th. The opening date was fixed at that meeting in the teeth of French and Russian prosecutors' demands for more time to prepare. The Anglo-Saxons were keen to get started before impetus and impact were lost; their efficiency improved on the appointment of an American brigadier-general as secretary of the IMT and of a British colonel as its quartermaster.

There was a health scare on 18 November, two days before the trial was due to begin, when Kaltenbrunner, the erstwhile head of the Reich Security Main Office, fell ill with suspected meningitis. Had the diagnosis been confirmed, all the prisoners and those dealing with them would have had to be quarantined for weeks; but the former Gestapo chief turned out to have had a mild cranial haemorrhage. He made his first appearance in court on 10 December, but shortly afterwards had another such episode.

It was not only among the prisoners that tension reached all but unbearable heights; rumours circulated of a plot to set them free, and the huge American military presence was in a permanent state of jitters. IMT officials, staff and journalists – mostly American with a sprinkling of British and French – based at or near the palatial Grand Hotel Fürstenhof held wild parties and heroic drinking sessions, sometimes entertained by the same lugubrious German songstress as had so recently sung there for local Nazis. The Russians lived apart in commandeered suburban villas where they held even wilder parties. The prisoners, except when summoned for examination by one or another prosecutor, sank into a general lethargy not untypical of any kind of prison. During the day the IMT met behind closed doors to hear pre-trial submissions. The last of these was hastily cobbled together by the gathering cloud of defence lawyers, who tried to stop the trial by persuading the judges that the entire process was null and void. It was based, they argued, on an IMT charter which had been agreed retrospectively, rather than on laws existing before the alleged crimes had been committed; the whole procedure was one-sided and unfair. But after all the wrangling, compromises and administrative difficulties endured by the IMT in preparing the trial, this move stood no chance of success. It was rejected two days later, after the proceedings had begun, but with a promise that the defence would have its chance to pursue the question of the validity of the proceedings later.

The courtroom was and remains a sombre affair with walls and coffered ceiling lined with dark wood panelling. The doorways have dark green marble surrounds. For the trial the windows high up in one wall were covered in dark green curtaining. The lighting was not only artificial but extremely harsh as it had to be bright enough for the newsreels and the official cameras recording the entire proceedings, which with breaks lasted more than ten months. Rare patches of colour were provided by the flags of the four powers behind the eight judges, who sat in pairs on a dais along the western wall. By common consent the judges, after taking turns for the pre-trial proceedings, agreed to let the English Lord Justice Lawrence preside permanently. Observers, including the Russians, were unanimous in their praise for his conduct of the trial; even the Germans recognised his fairness. He and the other western judges wore black gowns; the two Russians wore military uniform. An unexpected fleck of brightness was provided by the German defence lawyers, some of whom wore the coloured robes of their differing qualifications or regional courts; one wore a naval captain's uniform with rank markings. The US army's formal undress uniform of the time was dark brown tunic and tan trousers; the military police wore olive drab battledress with bright white helmets, belts and billyclubs but no firearms. Colonel Andrus alone carried a pistol, in a shoulder holster under his uniform.

The prisoners were attired in grey, brown or blue suits and dull shirts and ties or else in uniforms devoid of markings. They sat in two rows on the east side of the court, facing the bench. Their lawyers sat in front, facing the secretariat across the well of the court. The witness stand was in front and to the right of the bench and the stand for the lawyer speaking at the time was in front and to the left. The four groups of prosecutors and their assistants each had a separate cluster of desks along the north side, to the left of the bench and the right of the dock. The middle of the south wall featured a white screen for filmed evidence. To the right of that and the left of the dock were the glassed-in booths built for the world's first simultaneous-translation service in four languages.

At the opposite end of the court with its rare ornate touches of chandeliers, rendered superfluous by the hot floodlights, and a baroque clock, the north wall had been knocked down and rebuilt further back to lengthen the chamber and provide space for 150 reporters and, over their heads, a gallery for 250 visitors; this two-tier observers' section had plush, cinema-style folding seats and generous legroom. Under the hot lights the entire place reeked of new wood, varnish and paint. Among the reporters was the outstanding British writer Rebecca West, whose eloquent anti-Fascism had earned her a place on the Gestapo blacklist of those to be rounded up after the invasion of Britain. In her introduction to Airey Neave's book on the trial she wrote, in an uncharacteristically tortured way, that those responsible for the Allied thinking behind the Nuremberg trial 'wished not only that Germany might not do again what it had done; but that they need not do again what they had had to do in self-defence against the Germans.'

The evidence of one prominent aspect of what they had felt it necessary to do – indiscriminate bombing of cities – was to be seen in the desolation of rubble all round the judicial fortress. No mention was made, either in the general indictment or in the charges against Göring, of the bombing by the Luftwaffe of London, Rotterdam or Warsaw. Had the victor's shoe been on the other foot, Air Chief Marshal Sir Arthur Harris of RAF Bomber Command and General Carl Spaatz, USAAF, would doubtless have been afforded front-row seats in the dock.

The President of the court, Lord Justice Lawrence, introduced the only serious contender (despite many subsequent pretenders) for the title of Trial of the Century, and perhaps of all time, at 10 a.m. on Tuesday, 20 November 1945: 'This trial is unique in the history of the jurisprudence of the world and of supreme importance to millions of people all over the globe.' The rest of the first day was taken up with the reading of the indictment and the recital by each prosecuting team of the count or part-counts on which it would lead the presentation. The defendants wore the earphones of the simultaneous translation service but chatted among themselves from time to time; Hess read a paperback book. The second day was taken up with the pleas of each defendant to each charge; all pleaded Not Guilty to everything, including Speer. Speeches by the defendants were not allowed at this stage. Only Göring issued a bombastic, not to say rash, statement through his lawyers to the press at the time of the pleas, saying: 'I accept the political responsibility for all my own actions or for actions carried out on my orders.' Speer merely said, 'Not Guilty.'

If the keynote of Lawrence's short opening address had been dignity, his American judicial colleague turned chief prosecutor, Justice Jackson, chose a tone partly portentous, partly emotive, unnaturally slow and emphatic (later in the trial the interpreters would ask him to speak more slowly; on this occasion it was as if he were trying to make it easy for them). The result was generally admired for its passion, persuasiveness and honesty in facing the difficulties the trial raised:

> Either the victor must judge the vanquished or we must leave the defeated
> to judge themselves ... They might be the first national leaders of a
> defeated nation to be prosecuted, but they are also the first to be given
> the chance to plead in the name of the law ... Judicial action always
> comes after the event.

Jackson was even prepared to grasp the nettle of the Allied bombing, arguing that it was both a predictable response to the original Nazi aggression and a legitimate way to defeat it. War had in effect been rendered illegal by the treaties the Nazis had broken; and their atrocities were the very opposite of accidental lapses: they had been planned in detail.

The effect of a sonorous speech which lasted the best part of a day was devastating. Any forced levity or pretended insouciance among the defendants was long gone. Most others present thought the statement magnificent. Jackson's American juniors then summarised the evidence for the first, all-embracing charge, the count of conspiracy to wage aggressive war. Already at this very early stage of a trial which was to take up 246 days in court, the tedium which descends on even the most profoundly significant legal proceedings was beginning to show, hard though this may be to believe for those who have not attended a lengthy major trial. Rebecca West wrote of it; I remember my former colleague on *The Times* of London, Basil Gingell, who covered Nuremberg from start to finish, talking of it; and I have often experienced it myself in such contexts as South African treason trials, German concentration-camp, espionage and Baader-Meinhof terrorism cases and sensational murder hearings at the Old Bailey or libel suits at the Law Courts in London. Heads began to nod and jerk back to fitful alertness in the heat from the floodlights. Even the defendants on trial for their lives succumbed to the prevailing torpor, which would only be dispersed, usually briefly, by a new sensation.

One such was provided on an afternoon in the second week of the trial at the end of November, when the lights were dimmed, to general relief, and a projector began to whirr at the northern end of the court. On the screen at the southern end, flickering images of what this trial was really about engendered a deathly silence in court. For security reasons spotlights picked out the defendants as they watched or in most cases turned their heads away from the screen. Many observers and court personnel preferred to watch them rather than the appalling sights on the silent screen, of human beings reduced to matchstick figures, of mounds of corpses, of all those scenes of torture and massacre which never quite became commonplace in the rest of the century, whose absolute moral nadir this was. Brief newsreels of Allied troops liberating various camps had already been shown round the world;

but this was a compendious compilation, four hours in all, of footage put together by the Americans as part of the case for the prosecution of those who had led the regime responsible for the world's worst atrocities. Scenes of the British army's arrival at Belsen were particularly ghastly.

One riveting section covered the People's Court summary trial of the plotters of 20 July 1944, showing a group of broken men deprived of spectacles, false teeth and other props to their dignity and holding up oversized trousers, maliciously selected by the Gestapo, to stop them falling down; they were allowed no lawyers, and whenever they tried to speak they were screamed at by Judge Roland Freisler (who would undoubtedly have been in the dock at Nuremberg had an American bomb not killed him in the middle of one of his notorious treason trials in February 1945). The contrast between his kangaroo court and the Nuremberg proceeding could only redound to the benefit of the latter, which was presumably why the footage was included. Streicher watched it all uncritically, not to say avidly; Hess said he did not believe it but was hushed by an unusually subdued Göring. Some spectators cried out in shock; others fainted.

Nevertheless the tedium soon returned; the next sensation was the histrionic amnesia of Rudolf Hess, unlike his co-defendants back in a kind of limelight for the first time after four and a half years in British captivity. After a while he admitted he had been malingering and went so far as to accept responsibility for what he had done or signed; he seemed pleased by the interest he had aroused – pleased enough to 'try it on' in various ways many more times in a long and useless afterlife. Shortly afterwards the American prosecution completed its presentation.

Next up in the lawyers' 'pulpit' on 4 December was the spare, elegant figure of Sir Hartley Shawcross. He may have been the Attorney-General in the new British Labour government but he was born in Giessen, Germany, in 1902 and attended Dulwich College, an exclusive London 'public' school, before qualifying as a barrister in 1925. He spoke for five hours in the urbane, understated tones of the British establishment, the rapier to Jackson's battleaxe as he presented the case for the British count, crimes against peace. His forensic skill was overwhelming and the effect of his lucid argument all the more deadly for being so measured. One other difference between his performance and Jackson's was the Englishman's absolute mastery of his brief, something the American, to his later cost, could not begin to match.

Shawcross coldly shredded the defence of 'I was only obeying orders' before it was offered, and such connoisseurs of jurisprudence as Sir Norman Birkett, the British alternate judge, thought it was the best address of its kind they had ever heard, or heard of. Shawcross's opening and closing speeches at Nuremberg constituted the finest hour of a life which spanned very nearly the whole of the century but never quite matched the glittering promise of 1946; yet as finest hours go, his was unique – a distilled and refined condemnation of Nazism built on irresistible logic and muted passion and delivered for all the world to hear. As a working member of the cabinet, he had to return to London after part one of his *tour de force*, leaving his political predecessor and now prosecuting deputy, Sir David Maxwell-Fyfe, a master of cross-examination, in charge for Britain.

Sensations were few and far between as the quadruple case for the prosecution continued with the French and Russian presentations. Just before the Christmas recess the Americans produced grisly relics – parchment made of human skin, a shrunken head – from the big concentration camp at Buchenwald, a suburb of Weimar, historic centre of Germany's culture and of its first, failed attempt at democracy.

A rare frisson of excitement passed through the court in the first week of 1946, when SS-General Otto Ohlendorf, head of Einsatzgruppe D, one of the four extermination task-forces in Russia, went into the witness box (he was to be condemned at the later death-squad trial). After admitting the murder of 90,000 Jews on Himmler's orders, Ohlendorf came under unexpected cross-examination from a lawyer standing in for Dr Hans Flächsner, leading the defence of Albert Speer. Was the witness aware that his client had plotted not only the assassination of Hitler but also the arrest of Himmler in order to hand him over to the Allies? The witness was not; but at the adjournment shortly afterwards Göring lunged across the dock and hissed 'Traitor!' at Speer: how dare he break up the 'united front' of the prisoners, he roared. The other defendants were staggered, gazing at each other in astonishment as Göring fumed and seethed audibly. Henceforward the two men were bitter enemies. Göring saw Speer as the only other defendant in a position to hog the limelight which he planned to monopolise for himself. The burgeoning dispute and struggle for leadership of the accused was closely observed (and manipulated) by a fascinated Dr Gilbert, who spent a lot of time with both men in the prison complex away from the court – at meal-breaks, in the evenings and on days when the tribunal was not sitting or else working behind closed doors.[6] The explosion of the 'conspiracy' grenade was not pursued for the time being; but it obviously would be in due course.

Otherwise the prosecution dragged on with few noteworthy incidents until the middle of March 1946. The news media all but forgot Nuremberg until Hermann Göring, lean and mean by his expansive standards and obviously benefiting from his American 'cold turkey' anti-drug treatment, went into the witness box on 13 March – and promptly took charge of the proceedings. 'I do not intend to hide behind the Führer's order,' he declared, adopting a declamatory tone more suited to a Nuremberg rally than a Nuremberg trial. But his four days in the box soon had the court in thrall as he revealed the long-neglected gifts which had made him so influential and popular, and Hitler's heir-apparent, in the early days of Nazism before he so spectacularly went to seed. His bravura performance also showed undeniable personal courage. Breezily comparing the totalitarian command system of the Hitler regime with Stalin's Soviet Union and the Roman Catholic Church, Göring concluded by cheekily citing Winston Churchill as having said that there was no legality in a life-and-death struggle. A reluctantly admiring *Times* noted in London on 16 March that 'Göring, even in the dock, is not beyond an attempt to divide the Allies.'

The quality of his performance was thrown into even higher relief by the abject failure of Justice Jackson in cross-examination, as he fumbled and drowned in a sea of undigested paperwork which his quick-witted opponent, his mind doubtless concentrated by the prospect of hanging, had completely mastered for his own defence. To the American's exasperation, the British President allowed the German principal defendant to wipe the floor with the prosecution. Lawrence would not stop the flow or help the distraught Jackson out of the hole he was digging for himself. He all but resigned, complaining bitterly to the US judges in private about Lawrence. What was perhaps worse, Jackson was shown up a second time by his own side, when Maxwell-Fyfe rose to cross-examine the now over-confident defendant about the massacre of the fifty RAF men at Stalag Luft III, a Luftwaffe camp. Now it was Göring's turn to lose control; rattled, he let himself be manoeuvred by the incisive and brilliant Maxwell-Fyfe into defending the completely untenable position that neither he nor Hitler had done anything wrong or known of any crime whatsoever. Göring had so reverted to type that he had absurdly overreached himself, making a major contribution to his own death-sentence.

The general tedium of the long trial was enhanced by the routine into which all the participants soon lapsed. The American 'snowdrops' (their military police wore white helmets) lounged against the walls of the court. Some of them chewed gum. The press and the visitors came and went as they pleased and some were always in place before ten, when the hearing usually began. At the start of each open-court day, the defendants always entered first in bunches of three or four (governed by the capacity of the lift, within which was a wire screen to separate the prisoners from their guards). It might be Göring plus two more prisoners or else a group of four.

Before they entered the lift Colonel Andrus checked their drab clothes like an anxious parent before a school prizegiving. Each morning the prisoners, after being shaved by a military barber, were handed trouser belts or braces, ties and shoelaces; all had to be returned at the end of each day's proceedings as a precaution against suicide. After the prisoners came the teams of lawyers of prosecution and defence; and last of all the judges, whereupon the court was called to order and made to stand until the President was seated and had rapped his gavel (soon traded in for a less noisy pen). The court would sit from ten until one with a ten-minute break in mid-morning and an hour for lunch. The afternoon session lasted from two to five, also with a ten-minute break. Speer took to drawing landscapes on a large sketch-pad to while away his time in the dock; he used the results to decorate his cell.

When the lawyer planted the seed of the so-called assassination plot, Speer, as we saw, was all but assaulted by a seething Göring. He said to Dr Gilbert at the end of the day's proceedings: 'Damn that stupid fool! How could he stoop so low as to do such a rotten thing to save his lousy neck?' Gilbert, who was already working on Speer and Schirach to get them to denounce the Nazi regime from the witness box, now took it upon himself to loosen Göring's hold over the prisoners. He had the big buccaneer moved to a cell away from the rest and, working closely with Colonel Andrus, stopped him brow-beating others by having the prisoners kept separate from one another even when walking round the exercise yard. In so doing, Gilbert was actually following the advice of Speer, who had complained to him a month earlier how easy it was for Göring to influence others in such free and easy conditions of association. Certainly Speer could not hope to win support for his strategy of admitting shared, while denying specifically personal, responsibility for Nazi excesses with Göring on the loose.

At the colonel's invitation Gilbert reorganised the seating arrange-ments for lunch at court, dividing the twenty-one among five rooms in groups of four – with an extra room for Göring alone. Speer was assigned to what was nicknamed the 'youth room' with Fritzsche, Funk and von Schirach. Gilbert decided who sat where, his main concern being to terminate Göring's 'terrorising' influence and to break up the prisoners in such a way that those prepared to renounce and denounce might influence others to condemn the regime they had all served. Speer told Gilbert that he found the new arrangements much more helpful for the preparation of his defence, free of pressure to conform and support Göring's 'hang together' strategy.

*

In addition to the documents paraded by the prosecution, and the films (the Russians had shown one of their own, which included Auschwitz and matched the American epic in every harrowing aspect), there were also real, live (though only just in some cases) witnesses; the defence made a successful general objection to evidence by affidavit. SS men from the highest, such as Ohlendorf, to the lowest camp guards confirmed the nuts and bolts of genocide against Jews and Slavs; so did a handful of survivors from such places as Dachau.

14

Escaping the Noose

(1946)

THE CASE FOR THE DEFENCE of the twenty-one accused in the main trial at Nuremberg opened on Friday, 8 March 1946, after a three-day break. A request for a three-week adjournment to enable lawyers to complete their preparations amid an overwhelming mass of documentation was rejected. The lawyers laboured under an exacerbated version of the normal disadvantages of the defence at any multiple criminal trial. The prosecution had massively superior resources. Göring's campaign for a common front notwithstanding, different accused had different objectives and arguments. Defence lawyers had to be in court all day and every day in case something affecting their client's interests came up without warning, but were not even allowed to lunch with their clients; the various prosecutors could safely absent themselves for much of the proceedings. Prisoners' consultations with their lawyers took place in room fifty-five of the justice complex, in thinly partitioned booths with wire mesh between the interlocutors; when the mesh was replaced by glass during the trial, they had to shout, which led to pandemonium and protests. Intelligent dispersal and maximum use of the space available eased the problem.

Almost any document required by the defence had to be supplied by the prosecution, which thus had the chance to study it first; the same applied to any witness whose presence was requested, and who could be interrogated by the prosecution first. On this basis the defence could spring no surprises: all such applications had to be made in open court, giving the prosecution the chance to contest their admissibility.

On the other hand, while the prosecution often seemed to be blundering about blindly in a forest of paper, the defenders usually knew where they were going, armed with a map provided by their clients, who knew where to look for what (and often where it was best not to look). They could choose to fight on a narrow front of their own choosing whereas the prosecution felt obliged to sift through everything; even so it manifestly failed in many instances to grasp how Nazi Germany had functioned. The defence also enjoyed the considerable advantage of the native German speaker over the many prosecutors who knew little or nothing of a difficult language, let alone its jargon for jurisprudence, war and genocide. The documents of whose daunting extent everyone complained were, after all, in German. The world's first multilingual interpreting service worked remarkably well under the circumstances; but anyone commanding two or more languages who has tested the system in the European Union or the United Nations by comparing a speech with its interpretation will surely confirm that absolutely everything loses in translation.

Many defence lawyers served their clients badly, however, with ploys that were bound to fail. Instead of seeking to rebut the charges as they affected their clients, they often lapsed into the *tu quoque* (you too) defence. It was not only Germany that had raped and taken over half of Poland and occupied or attacked third countries but also the Soviet Union. It was not only Germany that signed the Nazi-Soviet Pact. It was not only Germany that had invaded Norway but also Britain; the Germans happened to win the ensuing tug of war. The Treaty of Versailles, universally loathed by Germans, which had served Hitler so well, might well have been unjust but would have been better left unmentioned as it was one of the very agreements whose breach the tribunal was trying. The most proficient defence lawyer, Captain Otto Kranzbühler (for Dönitz), who also stood out for wearing Kriegsmarine uniform, was on target when he challenged the tribunal's assumption that aggressive war was illegal: he even had the wit to persuade Fleet-Admiral Chester W. Nimitz, USN, to confirm in writing that his Pacific command had consistently waged unrestricted submarine warfare just like the U-boats.[1]

The case for the defence of each prisoner was presented separately by his lawyer, who would make an opening statement before putting his client in the witness box. After examination by his own advocate, the defendant faced cross-examination by one or more of the prosecutors handling the various counts. The defence of Albert Speer began on the afternoon of Wednesday, 19 June 1946.

We have noted the humiliation of Justice Jackson by Hermann Göring, the first to answer the charges, at the beginning of March. Having lost the duel ignominiously, the American lawyer then had to watch as Maxwell-Fyfe recovered some of the lost ground with his sharp, supplementary cross-examination. When it came to Speer's turn to be cross-examined by Jackson, the contrast was so striking that some commentators on the trial later alleged a private deal between him and Speer to save the latter's neck. To understand the reason for this speculation it is necessary to go back to Speer's pre-trial interrogations, before moving on to his defence, in which this background incident did not figure.

In the early days of November 1945 (the trial opened on the 20th) Speer was interrogated several times by US Army Major John J. Monigan, Jr, on behalf of Jackson's office. Like most of the other defendants, Speer did not have a lawyer with him, even though there were only days to go before the trial began (Dr Hans Flächsner was on his way). The tribunal did do the decent thing by allowing the accused to pick their own lawyers or, failing them, advocates from a reserve list. But the pre-trial examinations, which yielded much of the information used by the prosecution, pressed ahead regardless of whether the defendants had legal advice available. This aspect of the trial seems as questionable as the psychological manipulation, described above, of the prisoners during it, designed to change their attitudes to the Hitler regime and the indictment alike.

Speer had told Neave there were delicate issues, mentioned during his Dustbin interrogations, which he needed to discuss before they were raised in open court. This wish had been passed to Monigan, as the man assigned to question Speer immediately before the trial opened. The major asked for an explanation. Fearing that he might be abandoned to Soviet interrogators, Speer had pointed out at Dustbin, and emphasised again now, that he had information about the effects of bombing (especially its failures) that the Americans and British might not wish the Russians to know. To protect himself, Speer was playing the anti-Soviet card, a little more subtly perhaps but in the same way as other leading Nazis, including Hitler, Goebbels, Himmler and Göring, had done, especially in the last months of the war, exploiting the known strains between the Soviet Union and the Anglo-Americans, which duly swelled into the Cold War as soon as Germany fell. Although relations between the Russian judges and prosecutors on the one hand and the western judges and prosecution teams on the other were, in the circumstances, remarkably good despite the clashes behind the scenes over procedure (and later over sentencing), the court could not altogether cut itself off from the falling political temperature in the world outside.

Monigan asked Speer to write out the points he wished to make, in the form of a statement for forwarding to Jackson (an old-fashioned American conservative with no time for Communism). Speer wrote it on 15 November and handed it in the next day. It opened with the words, 'I am of the opinion that various items of knowledge about defence technology that I have should not become known to third parties.' He recalled that he and his colleagues had been interrogated from 1 June to the end of October 1945 by Anglo-American officers of FIAT (Field Intelligence Agency, Technical). He had thus unintentionally become aware of the main interests of the western Allies in German armament technology. 'I myself during this period not only gave all possible information but also, over and above that, quietly dispelled the misgivings of former colleagues against informing openly.'

Even before that, in May 1945, Speer wrote, he had given the US Strategic Bombing Survey detailed information about the Allied air offensive's effects on German war production, controlled by him. Errors were thus revealed whose elimination might well make the US bombardment of Japan more effective. 'I gave all this knowledge without reservation and, as far as I know, accurately. You can count on it that I carried out this work from conviction' and not for future advantage, Speer claimed. 'I would however regard myself as wretched if I were forced by third parties [i.e. Russians] to reveal this knowledge [to them].' In support of his claim to unique helpfulness on strategic bombing matters Speer gave the names of various interrogators at Glücksburg, Ashcan and Dustbin.[2]

The German revisionist historian, Werner Maser, wrote in his 1977 book 'Nuremberg – Tribunal of the Victors', translated into English in 1979 under the title, *Nuremberg – a Nation on Trial*, that Speer had secretly corresponded with Jackson and done a deal with him.[3] Speer, as he did so often after his release from prison, immediately took up his pen and burrowed into his voluminous personal archive to refute Maser's imputation in a German newspaper.[4] His case is fully supported by the American record of Speer's dealings with Monigan, cited above. In fact Speer had spoken in very similar terms as early as 17 May 1945, at his third interrogation session with the USSBS, when he made this statement before the questioning started:

> I think it is important for you to know that I am giving all information which I give here without reservation and in such a way that it can be of use to you. But, in order to prevent any false interpretation of my conduct from arising, I should like to make it clear that I have no need to assemble credits. The political side will be investigated by other agencies. I am giving this information so clearly because I regard it as necessary to act thus in the present [political] situation.[5]

Professor Galbraith's remark before the Nuremberg trial, quoted in the previous chapter, springs to mind here: from the outset, Speer had a 'well-devised strategy of self-vindication and survival'. Part of it was to play the anti-Soviet card, initially as a means of currying favour with the western powers and later at Nuremberg to attempt to split the prosecution and the bench alike, along what he had identified more readily than any other defendant as the principal fault-line in the hastily assembled, four-power machinery of justice.

*

Speer had half jokingly invited Galbraith's SBS colleague, George Ball, to act as his attorney, an honour the future adviser of US presidents declined. Eventually a German defender, Dr Hans Flächsner, born in Berlin in 1900 and thus five years older than his client, got the job. He had been approached as early as August 1945 by an American officer working for the tribunal because he had never been a member of the Nazi Party; on the contrary, he had a reputation as a liberal, even though as a very young man he had been retained out of the blue by Göring to defend him in civil actions for non-payment of medical bills after the 1923 Beer-hall Putsch. In the dark, immediate postwar days in Berlin Flächsner was on his uppers, trying to re-establish himself in a solo practice. He heard no more until the end of September, but at the second time of asking he agreed with alacrity to allow his name to go forward as a candidate for the legal defence team at Nuremberg. He had no idea to whom he would be assigned.

An American escort arrived early on the morning of 1 November to take Flächsner to Tempelhof airport in the American Zone of Berlin for the short flight to Fürth, a commandeered Luftwaffe airbase west of Nuremberg. From there a famished attorney was driven to the Grand Hotel for a breakfast which in those days was the stuff of dreams for most Germans. American rations were one of the main rewards for those Germans drafted in to serve the tribunal, whether as cleaners, secretaries, interpreters, handymen or lawyers. On arrival after break-fast at the justice complex, Flächsner was offered a choice of three 'clients': the brutal Kaltenbrunner of the Gestapo, the deranged Hess, once Hitler's party deputy, and Speer. He chose Speer at once. Speer was pleased to accept his services, finding the short, thin lawyer with the thick-lensed glasses agreeable in every sense. Friendly, unassuming, sensible, unhistrionic, circumspect and tactful were the adjectives Speer used about him; they became friends for life despite disagreements during the trial about the conduct and tactics of their defence strategy.[6] Sir Norman Birkett, the British alternate judge and one of the most gifted English barristers of the century, had a particularly low opinion of Flächsner, whom he regarded as the worst of a very bad bunch of German advocates for his bumbling slowness. But the judge, from an entirely different legal tradition and intolerant of fools, attached too much importance to matters of presentation and thus underestimated his mild-mannered, nitpicking bugbear.[7]

The need for careful preparation was underlined by the ferocity of American assistant prosecutor Thomas Dodd's presentation of the case against Speer in particular on 11 December 1945. Annemarie Kempf, still fiercely loyal to Speer and a woman of considerable initiative, managed early in December to get herself from Kransberg to Nuremberg and offered her services to the defence. Her main contribution at that stage was to commute several times between Dustbin and Nuremberg to smuggle documents requested by Flächsner from Speer's invaluable collection to bolster his defence.[8]

Attorney Dr Flächsner began by reminding the court that he would not be calling witnesses but relying on interrogation records; yet he had not received all the papers he had asked for. He then called on Speer to take the stand, where he raised his right hand and swore to tell the truth, the whole truth and nothing but the truth, and sat down.

Speer briefly outlined his life and career before Hitler made him a minister in February 1942. Describing his work as Hitler's architect, Speer said: 'Through Hitler's passion for his buildings I had a close personal contact with him. I belonged to a circle which was made up of other artists and of his personal staff of assistants. If Hitler had actually had friends, I would certainly have been one of his close friends.'

Flächsner might have been a windbag on occasion, but in his third question he swiftly disposed of Count I, the conspiracy: 'Did you ever take part in the planning and preparation of a war of invasion?'

No, as I was active as an architect until 1942, that cannot be said. All my buildings were prestige buildings for peaceful [purposes]. As an architect I made use of material, workers and monetary resources to a considerable extent for this purpose. After all, this material was lost to armament ... The execution of these great building plans of Hitler's were genuinely and in the main a hindrance to armament, psychologically also.

How had Speer become a minister? It was quite simple:

Hitler saw the main activity of Dr Todt up to then as building and therefore chose me as Todt's successor ... Immediately at the start of my activity it became clear that not building but stepping up Army weaponry was the most important part of my task, as the heavy material losses in the winter battles in Russia in 1941–2 had brought the heaviest losses [sic].

Todt had been responsible for army munitions but the Luftwaffe had enjoyed priority until then, so his ministry was not geared to expand army production, a shift of emphasis made by Speer. He had to read himself into a new field, prepare an organisation to carry out his new task and turn the downward trend in army munitions into a sharply rising one. 'As is generally known today, I succeeded,' said Speer without modesty. Flächsner, after establishing that Hitler told Speer his ministerial job would expire with the war, lost no time in introducing, courtesy of Annemarie Kempf's trawling at Kransberg, Speer's memorandum to Hitler of 20 September 1944 which handily opened with the words: 'The task that I have to fulfil is an unpolitical [one].' He had wanted nothing to do with party politics or bureaucracy but, as a non-expert, had surrounded himself with 6,000 experts from industry who worked for no pay, just like their American wartime counterparts.

He described how he had 2.6 million workers at his disposal for construction and army munitions at the outset. In spring 1943 the total rose to 3.2 million with responsibility for navy weaponry. In September it rose to twelve million when he took over much general production from the Ministry of Economics, and finally to fourteen million (within the Reich) on the takeover of aircraft production in August 1944. Speer denied responsibility for the working conditions of foreign, prisoner-of-war and concentration-camp labour. It was the Gauleiters as Defence Commissioners who had been responsible for coordinating the work of all state authorities concerned with the welfare of labour (which had never included his ministry); the SS had been a law unto itself. Labour Commissioner Sauckel had only been responsible for supplying the workers and to a limited extent for their conditions of work; he had tried to improve these, with Speer's support.

Flächsner now produced Hitler's order of March 1942 decreeing better nourishment and conditions for Russian workers, and another of May 1943 in similar vein. More rations had been given for heavy labour and concentration-camp workers had been included in extra handouts for good work. Working conditions in underground factories had been like those on the night shift in a normal factory; conditions had to be good for the production of the very latest, sophisticated weapons; and only a tenth of the planned three million square metres of such plant had been completed and put to use. He had seen nothing untoward during his visit to Mauthausen concentration camp in Austria in 1943. Bad working conditions militated against the high quality, high quantity production Speer was trying to achieve. It was enlightened self-interest to look after the workers. At the end of his first stint in the box, Speer denied forcing people to work; it was not possible to force fourteen million to produce satisfactorily by terror.

Resuming his examination-in-chief the next morning, the 20th, Flächsner turned from the use to the recruitment of labour, the other half of the main accusation against Speer. Speer admitted he had demanded new labour from Sauckel, that he knew foreigners were included and that many of them were working in Germany against their will. He had relied on Sauckel for much of his labour and was duly grateful to him for finding it.

There followed a long and wearisome march through the institutions and statistics of the Greater German war economy and those who worked for it, during which President Lawrence was moved to ask Flächsner what he was trying to prove as he seemed to be wandering far afield from the charges against Speer. But the lawyer eventually arrived at the no-go plants in occupied western Europe where labour working for Germany was protected by Speer from forced migration. Birkett doubtless approved heartily when his compatriot once again told Flächsner to stick to the point, before the mid-morning adjournment.

But he returned to the charge ten minutes later, inviting Speer to explain his arrangement with the Vichy-French Minister of Economics, Bichelonne, and spent the rest of the day hammering away at this and related questions about where Speer got his labour from, including concentration and prisoner-of-war camps, Russia and elsewhere. Speer took the opportunity to describe how he had stopped the execution of ten hostages in reprisal for sabotage in a French steelworks.

Another chance to emphasise the positive came when Flächsner raised the abortive plot of 20 July 1944 against Hitler and how Speer had been the only Nazi minister included in the conspirators' plans, though without his knowledge. He confirmed not only that he had no part in them but also that he would have opposed the assassination attempt at that time had he been consulted. The next topic – collective responsibility – gave Speer his opportunity, as planned, to 'own up', against his lawyer's advice. Did he limit his responsibility to his ministerial sphere? Flächsner asked.

> No. I have something fundamental to say on this. This war has brought an unimaginable catastrophe on the German nation and caused a world catastrophe. It is therefore my obvious duty to answer for this misfortune, including to the German nation. I have this duty all the more because the head of government has escaped his responsibility before the German nation and the world. As an important member of the leadership of the Reich I therefore share in the general responsibility from 1942 onwards. I shall present my arguments on this in my closing address ... Insofar as Hitler gave me orders and I carried them out, I bear the responsibility for them; besides, I did not carry out all orders.

Flächsner promptly turned to Hitler's scorched-earth policy and Speer's obstruction of it to round off his case. It would only take an hour, he assured the judges. In fact it took two, interrupted by the afternoon break, before the lawyer was able to tell the President, 'I am at the end of my examination of the accused Speer.'

The accused said he had bent all his efforts to keep Germany armed until January 1945, although he had realised well before then that the war was lost. There could have been no question of giving up while production was rising through most of 1944, when he produced enough to arm two million men – an output that would have been thirty per cent higher but for air attacks: the newest, potentially decisive weapons (jets, fast U-boats, missiles) were the worst affected. Speer had warned Hitler repeatedly of the effect of the bombing on key industries like chemicals and fuel. Hitler had deceived everyone with hints of negotiations with the enemy and his boasts of miracle weapons; meanwhile he had issued orders to destroy French, Belgian and Dutch industry as well as German, rather than let it fall into enemy hands.

However, Speer had persuaded army commanders in July 1944 not to do this. Hitler did not realise it until the liberated French press reported how quickly industry had been able to get back to work once the Germans had retreated over the border (Speer was able to dismiss this as enemy propaganda). Speer had also acted to preserve industry in Poland, Czechoslovakia and Austria. He had used Hitler's constant boasts that overrun territory would be recovered to argue that industry should therefore not be destroyed but only 'lamed', so that it would be available again straight after reconquest.

Just before the mid-afternoon break, Flächsner brought up the subject many had been waiting for: Speer's own personal assassination plan. He raised Dietrich Stahl's statement that Speer had asked the industrialist in February 1945 to get him some poison gas with which to attack Hitler, Bormann and Goebbels. Why?

> In my view there was no other way out. In my despair I wanted to take this step as I was certain from the beginning of February that Hitler wanted to continue the war by all means, regardless of his own people. It was clear to me that for him his own fate and the German people's were interchangeable if the war was lost, and that he saw the end of the German people in his own end. It was also clear that the war was so thoroughly lost that unconditional surrender would have to be accepted.

At this point, Speer became shy. Asked why his plan came to nothing, he said he did not want to go into detail, but he had 'had various technical difficulties'. President Lawrence pointedly observed: 'The court would much like to hear details about it, but after the adjournment.' Speer said on the resumption of the proceedings that he, as the architect of the bunker, knew its exact layout, including the ventilation system. He then described the difficulties: the gas needed an explosion to become active; a four-metre chimney had been installed suddenly over the vent. Flächsner, wisely perhaps, if against his natural inclination towards exhaustiveness, changed the subject as soon as he could.

He came back to the more credible matter of Speer's efforts at the bitter end of the war to defend Germany's ability to feed itself, at the expense of munitions production. The texts of his decrees proved it. He had diverted transport to distribute seed for the 1945 harvest, even though transport capacity had been reduced by up to eighty per cent. He admitted that such precautions were not so dangerous to carry out in the dying weeks of the war, when it was entirely possible to ignore orders with impunity. His last obstructive effort was to oppose, with considerable success, orders to destroy all bridges, especially in and around Berlin, as the army retreated from Eastern and Western Fronts. Speer quoted at length from his memoranda to Hitler, and Hitler's own orders in March 1945, including his ultimatum to Speer to withdraw his remark that 'the war is lost.'

From this useful material Flächsner departed once more with questions about Speer's 'plan' to arrest Himmler and others with the help of eight distinguished, highly decorated combat officers including Galland and Baumbach from the Luftwaffe. Speer then described his plans to broadcast to the nation a plea to preserve as much as possible and destroy nothing, foiled as it was by Goebbels and Hitler. What with all this defiance, why had he not resigned? Flächsner asked. 'From July 1944 I held it to be my duty to remain at my post.' He had broken his oath to Hitler because Hitler had finally proved disloyal to the German people.

Before facing cross-examination by the prosecution, Speer was questioned by lawyers for two of the other defendants. The first was Dr Robert Servatius for Fritz Sauckel, the man who had press-ganged millions from occupied Europe into serving the German war machine. Servatius established that Speer's representatives were sometimes present as Sauckel went trawling for labour in France, and that sometimes Speer's Todt Organisation had moved tens of thousands of Frenchmen into Germany for emergency works without consulting Sauckel. Speer said that at one time in 1943 Sauckel had brought more foreign workers into Germany than the armaments industry could use at the time, and that at the same time very large reserves of German labour, such as women, were left unused, as was proved when he managed to find two million extra workers inside Germany in 1944. Speer stated that he tried but failed to have Sauckel made directly answerable to him rather than Hitler; the Labour Commissioner always obtained permission to round up labour in occupied territory direct from Hitler, the only authority in such matters. When the court reconvened on the morning of 21 June it was the turn of Professor Herbert Kraus, deputy advocate for Hjalmar Schacht, the former Reichsbank President, to extract brief evidence from Speer about his client's open disagreements with Hitler on financial and economic policy, both in 1937 and 1944, when Hitler remarked that Schacht should have been shot before the war.

A few minutes into the morning session, Justice Jackson began his lengthy cross-examination. His first concern was to establish just what Speer had been responsible for. The American judge had no German (and very little understanding of the way Germany functioned) and was soon floundering among party titles. The smooth, question-and-answer record of the trial does not reveal how stilted it was when questions in another language were answered in German, especially when the questioner was not on familiar ground. The best efforts of the simultaneous interpreters could not prevent unnatural pauses between question and answer, especially when translating out of German, a language whose habit of placing clumps of verbs at the end of complex sentences can enervate quite rational people. Speer was also not above asking for a louder, repeat translation from time to time, a useful device for gaining time to think.

Having heard Speer deny that he had been a member of the SS since his earliest party days in 1932, Jackson gave an early example of his sloppy approach: 'You filled in an application once, or one was filled in for you, but it was, I believe, not accepted or something like that?' Speer explained that he had sidestepped the high honorary SS rank Himmler had offered him several times. He went on to admit that he had used concentration-camp labour in the arms industry and also threatened to send shirkers and malingerers to such camps. The threat was used to keep workers in line, but he had had no idea of the horrors being perpetrated, revealed to him at Nuremberg.

Jackson got Speer to concede that he knew about Nazi anti-Semitism and that 'the Jews were evacuated from Germany.' But he flatly denied involvement in the evacuations; one advantage from the pre-trial interrogations for the defendants was that they knew the likely thrust of the case against them from the documents used to challenge them (although the prosecution was always capable of springing a surprise). Speer must have been confident that the Wolters Chronicle had not been found when he made this flat and untrue denial. Jackson was genuinely trying to catch him out here because he immediately cited a 1943 letter saying Himmler had rounded up Jews working normally in France and put them in enclosed workplaces – with the concurrence of Sauckel and Speer. The latter returned this shot with ease, citing various individual documents, decrees and decisions on Jewish labour in munitions from his formidable memory for detail and emphasising that he had actually resisted the removal of Jews, especially skilled ones, from the industry because their loss was a blow to his production effort.

But he did not attempt to deny that he had actively concurred in the forced recruitment of labour in occupied countries to work in Germany and the arms industry without regard to legality. He had told Sauckel where workers were most needed but left it to him to find them. Only Russian prisoners of war (not protected by the Geneva Convention) and Italian military personnel interned after the surrender of Italy in September 1943 had been made to work in armaments. Goebbels and Ley, the Labour Minister, had suggested abandoning the Geneva Conventions in summer 1944 as part of total-war policy.

Goebbels wanted to use the February 1945 bombing of Dresden as an excuse not only to abrogate the conventions but also for resorting to poison gas. Speer said he had stopped production of the gases Tabun and Sarin in November 1944 by halting supplies of the necessary chemicals, including cyanide, which were needed for other purposes. The debate, such as it had been, about deploying gas had been a factor behind his own idea of using it to kill Hitler in the bunker, Speer confirmed at Jackson's invitation: with the war already lost, it was important that no breaches of international law should occur that would incriminate the German people.

Speer went on to admit that the V2 rocket had been an expensive mistake; the resources would have been better spent on fighters. Germany had also been one or two years away from achieving atomic fission during the war, and was so much behind thanks to the emigration of its (Jewish) leading nuclear scientists. Reports of secret and miracle weapons had been spread deliberately in the last phases of the war to encourage people and stiffen their resolve. Speer had visited some forty divisional sectors of the front from mid-1944 and been struck by the hopes placed in these purported wonders. He had objected to Hitler and Goebbels about this misleading propaganda. He had also done everything he could to limit wilful destruction of German assets in the last phase. Jackson's questions made it plain that he accepted in full Speer's version of his resistance to scorched earth.

The chief prosecutor's questioning was of a butterfly-minded nature, darting briefly from one topic, no matter how large or small, to another. Jackson clearly had a shopping list of issues he wanted to raise but did it in random order, returning more than once to topics from which he seemed to have moved on. After eliciting Speer's version of Hitler's bitter reaction to Göring's telegram claiming the leadership during Speer's last visit to the Berlin bunker, Jackson came back to the conspiracy issue a third time and did not hesitate to ask one leading question after another, a practice forbidden in Anglo-Saxon legal procedure; not a few of them enabled the defendant to present himself in the best possible light unchallenged: 'Is it not right that there was perhaps nobody at all in Hitler's entourage apart from yourself who had the courage to say to his face that the war was lost?' Speer did not find it unduly difficult to respond positively to such uninhibited blandness, like a tennis player dealing with a gentle lob.

Nor did he find Jackson's questioning about Krupp, Germany's leading arms maker based at Essen in the Ruhr district, exactly burdensome: 'I do not wish to suggest that you were personally responsible for the conditions but only to point out to you what the regime did, and I shall then ask you in what way these measures influenced your production efforts.' Speer had no knowledge, he said, of conditions and maltreatment of foreign workers at Krupp, of which stark evidence had been supplied during the prosecution case by a doctor, who had condemned the prolonged lack of basic facilities. Bad working conditions generally, said Speer, were often the result of bombing raids and lasted for a week or two.

Just how bad they could get Jackson chose to illustrate from a written statement by a tank builder, who had worked for Krupp at Essen, on how his colleague Löwenkamp treated foreign workers and stole their food:

> Every day he mishandled eastern workers, Russian PoWs, French, Italians and also other foreign civilians. He had a steel cage built that was so small, one could hardly stand up in it. In this cage he locked the foreigners, including females, up to forty-eight hours without giving the people anything to eat. They were not released to relieve themselves. Other people were forbidden to help or set free those locked up.

And so on. 'I regard the affidavit as a lie ... It is not possible here to drag the German people through the mud in this fashion,' said Speer indignantly. He did not believe the steel-cage story, obviously one of many exaggerations in postwar affidavits. Looking at a photograph of the cage, Speer identified it as just an ordinary clothes locker found in any factory. What about the eighty steel rods handed out to the guards at Krupp? 'That is nothing more than a substitute for a rubber truncheon. After all we had no rubber, and therefore the guard teams probably had something of that sort,' said Speer: police had to have something to carry, but that did not mean they used it all the time, or at all. 'That is the same conclusion as I drew from the document,' said an obliging Jackson.

And so, hand in hand metaphorically speaking, prosecutor and defendant wandered through the documentation of the horror of being a foreign worker at Krupp. The SS were to blame for the condition of slave workers at nearby concentration camps which supplied the firm with labour; the Allied air forces were to blame for the shocking conditions that prevailed after bombing; but Speer claimed the credit for improving the nourishment and working conditions of air-raid victims. A long list of other authorities was collectively responsible for working conditions, whereas Speer was responsible for improving them whenever he could, he told the court. Nor could he be expected to know what went on in Krupp's labour camps. Invited to expatiate on what he meant by accepting his share of responsibility for the Nazi regime, Speer said it was dual: specific responsibility for one's own sphere and collective responsibility for overall policy, though not for matters of detail in the spheres of others.

The Soviet deputy prosecutor, M.Y. Raginsky, was determined not to allow Speer such an easy ride; and for his part, Speer was not about to allow himself to be pushed around by a Russian who understood the Nazi apparatus rather better than Jackson. Raginsky asked almost at once whether Speer stood by his affirmative answer when asked by a Russian interrogator whether he agreed that Hitler had set out his anti-Soviet and other aims very clearly in *Mein Kampf*. No, he did not. Why not? Because he had been ashamed to admit at the time that he had not read it: 'I was fibbing.' If he was fibbing then, perhaps he was fibbing now, the Russian snapped. 'No.'

Speer had said on the day before that he was one of Hitler's friends. Did he now want the court to believe he had only heard of Hitler's plans from his book? He had indeed had close contact, Speer said, but nothing Hitler ever said indicated the real nature of his plans: 'I was particularly relieved in 1939 when the non-aggression pact with Russia was concluded; and after all, your diplomats must also have read *Mein Kampf*, yet even so they concluded the non-aggression pact. And they were certainly more intelligent than I, I mean in political matters.'

Raginsky let this aggressive answer go by. Instead, he and Speer next engaged in prolonged bickering about the role and political significance of various Nazi organisations such as Central Planning, and of various quotations from documents on the German war economy. The nitpicking got on Lawrence's nerves; more than once he asked General Raginsky what he was driving at. This turned out to be German plundering of occupied territory for raw materials. 'Then ask him directly about it,' said an irritated President. Speer objected to the word 'plundering' and on they went. He also took exception to one 'mistranslation' after another as the original German was filtered back to him via Russian and reinterpretation into German.

The judicial investigation of Germany's genocidal onslaught on European civilisation threatened to reduce itself to point-scoring about textual nuances in the documentation Speer himself had supplied to the court in his own defence, or else in papers produced on the spot by Raginsky, whose cross-examination petered out in peevishness on both sides.

As Speer had no military function in the Third Reich and had been an architect until the war was two and a half years old, the British were not interested in cross-examining him on their count, crimes against peace. Speer could regard himself as lucky that he was not exposed to a Maxwell-Fyfe cross-examination – which might have saved the world a great deal of argument about Speer decades later and made this book superfluous.

After brief re-examinations by Dr Servatius and Dr Flächsner and a few clarifying questions from the senior American judge, Francis Biddle, Speer was released from the witness box after two and a half days, the case for his defence was concluded and the court adjourned. His defence case was the eighteenth handled by the court. Perhaps the prosecution was flagging by then, but the record of the trial makes it clear beyond argument that Speer got off extraordinarily lightly in cross-examination, first by an American with no talent for it while benignly disposed towards him, then by a Russian who, while obviously hostile, could not see the wood for the trees and argued over detail with a witness who knew the material much better than he. Dr Gilbert was impressed. So was Birkett by Speer's long, carefully prepared critique of Hitler, which *The Times* of London thought made Speer sound like a crown witness who had turned state's evidence.

After the cases for Neurath and Fritzsche had been presented, each prisoner's leading defence lawyer was allocated a maximum of half a day for his closing speech, which the tribunal awarded itself the right to vet and have translated in advance. Even so, most of them were dreary, uninspired and rambling, with the notable exception of Kranzbühler for Dönitz; but then they faced an impossible task. The closing pleas, allowing for weekends and various extra adjournments, lasted from 4 to 25 July. Dr Flächsner spoke on Speer's behalf on the morning of the 23rd. It was an effort in what had by then become the finest tradition of the Nuremberg defence, so heavily disparaged by Sir Norman Birkett.

The conspiracy charge could not apply to his client, the advocate argued, because he had not exchanged his architect's post for a ministry until well into the war. Nor had he had anything to do with any crimes against peace.

Flächsner had not been happy about Speer's high-risk defence strategy of accepting general while denying specific responsibility for the actions of the Nazi regime. Nor had he approved the sensational intervention engineered by Speer, whereby he had Flächsner's stand-in raise the 'gas in the bunker' plot. He was now stuck with both, but he devoted his main effort to resisting the charges of war crimes and crimes against humanity which, in Speer's case, came down to the recruitment and deployment of PoW, forced and slave labour in the industries he controlled as the minister in charge of the Third Reich's war economy.

Economic warfare had been a top priority for both sides, as shown not only by German exploitation of occupied lands but also by the British naval blockade and the Allied bombing campaign, both of which had affected German territory indiscriminately. Each side tried to knock out the production capacity of the other, whether at the front or by bombing hundreds of miles behind the lines. Speer's job as minister was to resist this, and one method of dealing with the 'state of emergency' that thus arose was to make use of labour from occupied countries, Flächsner argued. But his client had increased production exponentially while expanding the munitions workforce only incrementally. His main instrument for raising production had been technical and organisational measures rather than extra labour. Given the choice, Speer preferred German workers and had cut the flow of labour from the west with his no-go factories, devoted to civil production while German plants concentrated on arms.

Besides, the import of foreign labour had been well established before Speer took over and he had assumed that the legal basis of this had been checked in Todt's time, said Flächsner innocently. Sauckel, directly responsible for such recruitment, had always insisted it was legal. Speer was like a technical director in a factory, who would hardly concern himself with the activities of the personnel director. It was not Speer's fault that Sauckel had regarded himself as Speer's agent. The two men had often fallen out, and Sauckel received requests for labour from elsewhere also. The Ministry of Labour and the Gauleiters played major parts in the deployment of labour, often against the wishes of Speer's ministry. Speer's key role in Central Planning in no sense gave him a monopoly over labour deployment as the prosecution had tried to argue.

The fact that Sauckel recruited workers in occupied territory against their will was an action entirely separate from the fact that Speer made use of such labour once it was in Germany, said Flächsner with breathtaking sophistry. The legal power to conscript and assign German labour had simply been extended to cover foreign workers in the Reich. The Hague Convention on Land Warfare did not specifically permit this, but it had not envisaged total economic warfare either. The message was clear: blame Sauckel, not Speer, whose responsibility was limited to the deployment of some of the foreign workers brought to Germany, not for their recruitment or deportation. When it came to the employment of prisoners of war, the Geneva Convention forbade their use in making or transporting war materials of all kinds or helping the war effort, such as by digging trenches. But in the case of

Speer, it all depended on how one defined the arms industry: whether for example it embraced steel or only the weapons made from it. Only about a third of all steel production had gone into armaments.

Flächsner was still on his feet when Lawrence adjourned for lunch, and after the break continued his densely argued, relentless exploration of the legal intricacies of deploying foreign civilian and military labour in wartime. He also looked at the treatment of concentration-camp prisoners; where Himmler sent them into Speer's arms factories their conditions dramatically improved, said his lawyer. But of course his client had enjoyed no control over the conditions of those kept by Himmler to make arms inside the camps for the Waffen-SS.

Speer had defied Hitler by insisting to his face that the war was lost, and had even visited his co-defendant Seyss-Inquart, Commissioner for the Netherlands, to persuade him to negotiate with an American emissary: 'this finally led to Holland's undestroyed handover to the Allies' (Holland was not destroyed in the narrowest, literal sense of the word, but the Dutch could be forgiven for regarding their condition on liberation – starving, frozen, flooded, their economic assets stolen or ruined – as a convincing imitation of destruction).

Evidence from Walter Rohland, Manfred von Poser and Annemarie Kempf, admittedly all loyal colleagues of Speer, supported the documents in proving how hard and long Speer had worked to frustrate Hitler's scorched-earth plans and preserve a great deal of industry, not only in Germany but also in France, Belgium and the Netherlands. At the very end he had conspired to bring down Hitler and his closest henchmen (Flächsner could hardly leave this out; but he gave it half a dozen lines in an enormous speech). His client had made his apolitical stance clear to Hitler in his memorandum of 20 September 1944; and he had been the only Nazi minister included on the cabinet list of the abortive military coup two months earlier. When Speer came to ministerial office at not quite thirty-seven, he found his country engaged in a life-and-death struggle. He could not evade his task, which appeared almost impossible. He was successful but had no illusions about the real state of affairs. He realised too late that Hitler was thinking of himself rather than his people at the end, even though he had written in *Mein Kampf* that a government should always remain aware of its people and should not leave it in the lurch in adversity; the government should step down at the right time to ensure the people's survival. Hitler did not apply this to his own government, and he decided that the German nation did not deserve to survive its failure to win the war.

Against this brutal egotism Speer preserved the feeling that he was a servant of his people and state. Without regard for his person, without thought of his own safety, Speer conducted himself as he held his duty to his nation to be.

Speer had to betray Hitler to maintain his loyalty to his people. Nobody will be able to withhold his respect for the tragedy that lies in such a fate.

The fourfold prosecution brought the proceedings to a close, the deliberations and decisions of the judges apart, with four withering final addresses. Jackson, in suit and bow tie and at his best on a set-piece occasion with plenty of time to hone his rhetoric in advance, once again surpassed himself, as he had done in his opening speech. This time his emotion was less evident and his approach more incisive: there was at least as much light as heat. Shawcross, back in Nuremberg for the penultimate drama, was once again on deadly form, cool yet abrasive and causing an early sensation by demanding the death penalty for every single defendant. The speech by Charles Dubost, the French replacement prosecutor, was notable not least for coining the word 'genocide'. The Soviet prosecutor, Roman Rudenko, was sober but as effective as the Frenchman; he too demanded the death sentence for all defendants. But it was the Jackson–Shawcross, warm–cold, emotional–intellectual double act which lingered in the memories of the observers.

August was occupied with the hearing of the case against the six Nazi organisations named in the indictment. This was an interlude of agonising uncertainty for the twenty-one accused, who were not recalled until the last day of the month, the 216th court day, to make their individual statements from the dock, limited to twenty minutes each. Most took rather less. As with the presentation of his defence, Speer came low down in the pecking order, according to his place on the indictment.

Hitler's dictatorship, he said, had been unique for exploiting modern technology to dominate the nation by radio, loudspeaker, telephone and teleprinter. The people had also been spied upon as never before and the whole intricate system had been made to express the will of one man. Technology enabled him also to dominate Europe; and technology had made huge advances in armaments possible on both sides – rockets, jets, submarines, atomic bombs and chemical warfare. A new war would now entail the destruction of human culture and civilisation. Meanwhile, Germany, which had contributed so much to world culture in the past, had been laid low, but could make a worthwhile contribution in the future if it rebuilt itself. 'A nation that believes in its future will not go under. God protect Germany and western culture.'

*

Fears of outbursts from the prisoners proved groundless, although one or two broke down in tears as they spoke, including Sauckel. President Lawrence had the grace to thank the German defence lawyers for their work; Jackson went so far as to confide to Dr Flächsner that his client was the only defendant he respected.[9] The Grand Hotel in Nuremberg was the scene of the ultimate Allied party that night; even some of the judges looked in. Their judgment however took longer than expected to formulate. The basic text was drawn up by Birkett, a feat he performed from memory, but arguments raged about the controversial conspiracy charge, the organisations, and by extension their many thousands of untried members, to be declared criminal (in the end only the SS, SD and Gestapo were so condemned), as well as the guilt of individual accused and the sentences. On 13 September judgment was deferred as the debate continued behind closed doors.

Meanwhile the regime in the prison behind its crenellated curtain wall was relaxed sufficiently to allow family visits to the accused as they awaited their fate. Speer had been sending occasional letters to his wife, Gretel, through his lawyer. Incoming letters had reached him by the same route, not only from her but also from at least one other correspondent: Rudolf Wolters, who had been following the trial from his home at Coesfeld, Westphalia, where he was already engaged as an architect in the reconstruction of public buildings. He wrote his first letter to 'Dear Speer' on 28 January 1946, in the spirit of 'there, but for the grace of God, go I' and telling of the postwar fates of mutual friends and colleagues. 'I stand by you in misfortune as in the good days. I believe as before in your lucky star.'[10]

As he awaited his fate in the closing stages of the trial, the recipient of this fervent protestation of loyalty and friendship decided to take its originator at his word. Quite clearly anticipating the death sentence, on 10 August 1946 Speer wrote a six-page literary last will and testament to the erstwhile chronicler of his ministry, asking Wolters to collect relevant documents and prepare a biography of his old chief:

> My dear friend Rudolf Wolters,
>
> You [the familiar *Du* is used] were one of the closest, and we know each other from early youth.
>
> I therefore have a request for you, to collect my work together for later ages and to recount much of my life. I think it will be honoured one day.

He was surely, he asserted, entitled to go down in history as 'different from all the repellent [Nazi] "bourgeois revolutionaries"'. Speer, as ever unburdened by false modesty, envisaged a biography in four parts: architecture, ministerial work, personal life and the memories he would be writing down in 'these last weeks', perhaps to be published separately decades later (he started this on the same day, producing a text amounting to just over 100 closely typed pages and entitled '[My] Activity as Minister', foreshadowing his 1969 memoirs.

Hindsight justifies us in giving special attention to the postscript to Wolters, in which Speer specifically invited him to edit and amend the various source texts, such as the Chronicle, as he saw fit: 'I know you will do it well. Perhaps it will even give you pleasure to complete thoroughly your activity as chronicler now.' Invoking the 'many happy memories' they shared, he signed off 'ever your friend, Albert Speer'.[11] He made no mention of his impending fate, but the letter as a whole can only be read as coming from a man setting his affairs in order while awaiting death. He had already prepared his brief statement from the dock.

Speer had almost nothing to say in the closing chapter of his memoirs about what must even for him have been a time of agonising tension, remarking only that he read *A Tale of Two Cities* by Charles Dickens (singularly ill-chosen as much of the story is set in the death cells of the Bastille). Flächsner said many years later that Speer was deeply depressed during this long waiting period.[12]

As 1,000 extra American troops reinforced the already massive steel barricade round the Nuremberg justice complex, the judges once again filed into a packed courtroom on the morning of Monday, 30 September 1946. The long recital of the judgment was broadcast live as the eight judges took turns to read it in short sections, beginning and ending with Lawrence. The biggest sensation of the day was the revelation that the Soviet judges were at odds with their western colleagues on the acquittals of the cabinet, the Wehrmacht High Command and the SA. The world had to wait another day for the verdicts and sentences on individual defendants.

On 1 October the accused were led into the dock one by one for sentence. Twelve, including the absent Bormann, were condemned to death, starting with Göring, guilty on all four counts (he killed himself two hours before he was due to hang). Three were acquitted (Schacht, Papen and Fritzsche) and three given life imprisonment, including Hess, the only one to serve it.

The nineteenth defendant, Albert Speer, was acquitted on counts one (conspiracy) and two (crimes against peace) and found guilty on counts three and four, war crimes and crimes against humanity. The nub of the case against him, the judges made clear, was his use of forced and slave labour. The man who met his requests for it, Fritz Sauckel, was obviously one of the 'repellent, petty-bourgeois revolutionaries' and was sentenced to death. Against the protests of the Soviet judges, who wanted him hanged, Speer, who had so impressed the Americans, and to a lesser degree the British, by 'owning up', was sentenced to twenty years. He condescended to say he thought this was fair, and did not appeal. He was the only defendant to bow to the judges on sentence.[13]

Avidly listening to the radio, Wolters swore he heard Speer sigh with relief when the sentence was announced.[14] His former chief was going to jail – but he had evaded the hangman's rope.

15

A Life-Support System

(1946–53)

THE NETWORK THAT SUSTAINED Albert Speer during his imprisonment began to form before verdict and sentence were pronounced. The first strand linked Dr Wolters, who had taken the initiative in contacting his old chief during the trial, with Gretel Speer in August 1946, in the fraught period of waiting for the judgment. The next connection was between Wolters, always the prime mover, and Annemarie Kempf, who had gone back to Kransberg to continue her work helping the Allies to interrogate leading Nazis for the twelve subsidiary trials at Nuremberg. He wrote to her on 13 November 1946:

> Meanwhile I have received via Dr Flächsner the letter from Father in which he commissions me to collect the material about his life and works and to write something suitable about them later. For me that is naturally an obligation which I shall most gladly fulfil ... I shall first attempt to put the material together as far as that is possible for me, and I still hope that one day I shall be able to hand over all the material to him personally so that he can write his memoirs [himself], because something like that has much greater documentary value. Should he rather have it otherwise, I would naturally undertake the work myself.[1]

The choice of the word 'father' to refer to Speer, still only forty-one years old, by a man two years his senior is most revealing about the relationship between Hitler's erstwhile 'whiz-kid' and those who worked for him. His all but impenetrable reserve, his aloof calm, his patrician manner and paternalism towards subordinates clearly put close associates in mind of a father-figure, despite such youthful qualities as dynamism, enthusiasm for work and ability to improvise which underlay his success as their boss. The degree of loyalty he could inspire, despite his persistent indifference to the concerns, needs and problems of others, would prove even more remarkable when he was locked away than it had been when he was physically present to manipulate them.

Wolters's letter to Frau Kempf crossed in the post with one from her dated four days earlier but which reached him later. She used the same expression, reporting that she was receiving letters from 'our Father'. She added that Wolters had been mentioned frequently by their 'father' during her visits to Speer at Nuremberg. She was allowed to leave Kransberg at Christmas and took up residence in one of the caravans in the forest by Lake Eutin in Schleswig-Holstein to which Speer had planned to withdraw before he was recruited into the Dönitz 'government'. She told Wolters in January 1947 that she would visit him as soon as she could to hand over papers relating to Speer and in her possession, in accordance with his wish that Wolters should collate them. This was uncommonly generous of her, as her personal circumstances at the time were desperate. She was a war widow; she had no home of her own, but she did have a mother with cancer, a brother invalided out of the army with lung trouble, a sister with multiple sclerosis and their respective dependants to look after. The extended family was allocated enough land for two houses in Eutin, but had to organise their construction for itself.[2]

Those condemned to die remained on the ground floor of the eastern cell block at Nuremberg prison; those condemned to live the greater part of their remaining lives in jail were ordered out of their cells on the same floor and moved up one storey. Ironically the three who were acquitted had to be given shelter in cells on the second floor until the hostile German crowd outside the justice complex had dispersed. The three groups were therefore together for the last time over lunch after the sentencing. It must have been one of the most extraordinary and distraught last repasts ever, but Speer's description of it is miserably sparse, as was so often the case with his written recollection of exceptional moments. Funk, Hess and Raeder had been awarded life sentences; Schirach and Speer twenty years; Neurath fifteen; Dönitz got ten. When Dr Gilbert made his round of their floor, Speer remarked: 'Fair enough; I can't complain.'[3] But he did so all the same, at the very start of his second book, the selectively rewritten, bestselling diary of his imprisonment, where he says of the three acquitted: 'So lies, smokescreens and dissembling statements have paid off after all.' In the light of Sauckel's impending doom, however, everything being relative, he could well have said the same of himself. His physical response to the stress of the occasion was heart palpitations, for which he was given aspirin. The hangings were carried out in the American manner, in the presence of eye-witnesses including eight reporters (among them Rebecca West), during the night of 15-16 October. The gallows chamber had been specially built at the eastern end of the east block and was razed after the trials were over to remove a potential shrine for sentimentalists.

Shortly after beginning his sentence, Speer had his 100-page memoir, misleadingly titled 'Activity as Minister' (described above; in fact it was rather broader), sent to his friend in 'Coburg'. The name stood for Coesfeld, to which Wolters had returned after the war – the first example of the childish, semi-transparent code Speer devised in jail. Gretel's post-judgment visit on 14 October was marked by the hammering from the gallows block. Three days later the seven survivors were made to clean out the cells of the executed – and their death-chamber. Otherwise they were isolated from one another. The regime was strict but not unkind; Speer was aware that the prisoners were faring rather better on US army rations than the half-starved German population. The prison however was unheated and he found himself reliant for warmth on a hooded winter jacket of the kind he had designed for the German troops when they encountered the Russian winter so arrogantly unprepared late in 1941. Now was his chance to find out for himself how inadequate Wehrmacht winter gear had been. In a letter to Gretel mailed by a chaplain he told her not to bother to try to send a Christmas parcel.

Ten days before the festival the seven were officially notified that they would be transferred to Berlin. In the particularly bitter winter of 1946–47 the shivering prisoners spent twenty-three hours per day in their cells. Fortunately books were readily available. One of the few interruptions to this deadening routine was the occasional call to give evidence or statements at succeeding Nuremberg trials. Other Nazi defendants were housed in the prison and Speer was able to renew many old acquaintanceships during exercise periods or in the showers. Rudolf Hess, late of Landsberg Castle and the Tower of London, was the only 'old lag' among the seven. He followed up his dramatic bout of 'amnesia' during the trial with delusions of grandeur after it. The guards told Speer he was handing out portfolios to a new 'cabinet'; but then megalomania was a besetting sin of the Nazis. As spring came there was still no news of the transfer to Berlin because the western Allies and the Russians could not agree on the details. Speer, who gave evidence for his friend Milch in February, was trying to sleep twelve hours a day instead of his customary six, a move which he calculated would mean he 'missed' a quarter of his term, at least in sentient mode. He refused to appear as a prosecution witness when the leading industrialists went on trial in spring 1947 but was not subjected to a subpoena.

While awake he was making desultory notes, with the idea of memoirs vaguely in mind, for the chaplain to forward to Gretel; the postal regime was remarkably relaxed at this earliest stage of his imprisonment. Letters were vetted but there was no limit on numbers written. How much of his time Speer expended on writing, except at specific periods, is well nigh impossible to determine, but an entry in December 1946 makes it clear that he recognised its importance to him very early on, long before the trickle became a flood. From the outset of his sentence, which took him from late youth to early old age, he was already writing at three levels. There were letters, intended for the eyes of their recipients; there were recollections, ultimately intended as exhaustive notes for his memoirs (unimportant in the first phase of imprisonment because he had already written what amounted to a 100-page précis); and there were diaries, which fell somewhere between the purposely private and the potentially public. The main thread running through them all was the past, particularly his own past and specifically what he had experienced in the period from 1933 to 1945, when he had been Hitler's architect and finally his armourer. That, in the end, was where he lived for the rest of his life.

Second only to that most exciting period as a constant theme was his extended family. If he was seen as 'our father' by the abidingly loyal personal staff of his heyday, he very much saw himself as an unavoidably absent but implacably conscientious paterfamilias in the Victorian manner, to his wife, their six children and his wayward elder brother, Hermann. Having forfeited to the fortunes of war his command of the German economy, his powerful appetite for control and manipulation was to be diverted to these two groups, his nascent life-support network and his family (which largely overlapped). As he considered and rationalised his past over a long period of enforced reflection, he had no compunction in exploiting his dramatically reduced but very real sphere of influence. It was as if they owed it to the prisoner to be at his disposal. The 20,000 scraps of paper he wrote on in jail show that he lost neither the arrogance of power nor the quality the Germans call *Besserwisserei* – I know best.

The first family event that intruded on his incarceration and brought its strict limitations home to him was the death, in his sleep, of his father at the age of eighty-four on 31 March 1947. The chaplain brought the news in the form of a telegram from his mother on 3 April, Good Friday. They had last met almost two years earlier. The demise of Albert Senior, an emotional milestone if ever there was one, typically gets short shrift in the diaries – all of ten lines in the published version. At least the old man had been diverted in his last months by the presence of his daughter-in-law and the six grandchildren: they had returned to Heidelberg from Schleswig-Holstein about a year after the end of the war – but not to the family home, which had been commandeered by the American army for a senior officer. The family used the small cottage in the grounds and for a while Gretel and the children stayed with her parents, the Webers. Speer and his father had not been close and had never expressed their personal feelings to each other. Like son, like father. Albert Junior, whether out of respect or depression or absence of new thought or events, wrote nothing for a fortnight; but when Milch drew a life sentence he rated thirty printed lines.

Speer was taking an interest in the progress (or regression) of Rudolf Hess in this uncertain spring of 1947, as the seven principal Nazi prisoners awaited the oft-deferred transfer to Berlin while hundreds of their former colleagues and subordinates in the Nuremberg jail were processed by the tribunal. Hess was decidedly eccentric and had clearly long since taken up residence in a world of his own. Now he was free to indulge the two sides of his personality, as Speer diagnosed it: 'the martyr and the buffoon'. He also detected symptoms of both megalomania and paranoia.

The next family manifestation was provided by Speer's elder and sole surviving brother, Hermann, who made a deceptively cheering visit to Nuremberg prison on 2 July 1947. Hermann had always represented a problem. He and Speer's younger brother, Ernst (lost at Stalingrad), had been the favourites, respectively, of their mother and their father, and had bullied the lonely middle sibling Albert. Hermann too had thrived at school, showing in his teens an aptitude for poetry, winning school prizes. He went, as few German children do, to a boarding school, where, according to Albert, he became even more eccentric. At the age of eighteen, Hermann was an enthusiastic member of the circle of admirers of the poet Stefan George, on whom Hermann had an adolescent crush. When the writer dropped Hermann, the youth was devastated and, again according to Albert, almost went mad. Eventually in the late 1920s he married a woman somewhat older than himself whose familiar name was Gustl (a diminutive form of Augusta), a plain, tough, outdoor type who impressed Albert. But Hermann was unable to apply himself to his studies or to settle down, and in 1933 he was the subject of a formal complaint to the police (for what offence is not known). Instead of being put on trial Hermann was sent to a psychiatric clinic for evaluation and occupational therapy was recommended, in the form of physical labour. Albert said he used his influence at the outset of his career with the Nazis to protect his brother.

At any rate Hermann joined the Labour Service, only to drift out of it after a while. He avoided military conscription, working variously for the Labour Front and the Ministry of Food. He passed across Albert's consciousness from time to time during the war, when others tried to use him to influence his powerful brother; on one occasion Hermann sought a larger allocation of iron for an industrialist. Since Albert Speer was incorruptible in this sense, Hermann soon ceased to be of interest to flatterers and manipulators and became something of a wastrel, largely dependent on handouts from his mother. Jealous of his famous brother, he consorted with Albert's enemies. They never could stand each other, but when Hermann came to visit, perhaps secretly pleased to see his almighty brother brought low at last, he managed to fill three hours with good cheer and optimism about the prisoner's future. They never got on so well before or after; but Hermann would cause Albert many a headache in the coming years.[4]

Whatever was wrong with his brother, Speer was well satisfied with himself in summer 1947. He could only agree when fellow-prisoner Raeder remarked that he, Speer, was adapting better than anyone else and was more balanced. In January he had been confiding to his burgeoning if fragmentary diary his 'real problem' – that everybody liked him, whether his teacher Tessenow, his mentor Hitler, prosecutor Jackson, the judges, the guards ... The complacency is breathtaking. No inroads were made on his insufferable vanity by an assessment of him from Dr Douglas Kelley, a prison psychiatrist at Nuremberg. Kelley thought Speer 'one of the most servile' but intelligent prisoners, a fine architect and a workaholic, inhibited but candid – 'a racehorse with blinkers'. This handily boosted Speer's assertion of ignorance of Nazi atrocities and his cultivated self-image as honourable for 'owning up' as well as exceptionally intelligent.

The seven prisoners were awakened by the clatter of a platoon's-worth of American army boots and the opening of their cell doors at 4 a.m. on 18 July 1947. They were given mere moments to pack their few belongings and escorted to a prison office for a cup of coffee. A shot rang out – but it was only a clumsy GI accidentally shooting himself in the foot. Each prisoner was handcuffed to a soldier and the group bundled into two heavily escorted military ambulances for transport to the airfield at Fürth. There they were transferred to a Dakota aircraft for the brief, unshackled flight to Berlin. Since the horizon of their world had been coterminous with the wall of the Nuremberg prison yard until then, the windows of the ambulance and plane afforded the prisoners their first exciting glimpses of the outside world for nearly two years. Speer in particular was fascinated by the bird's-eye view of the tidied-up wreckage of Berlin as the aircraft circled before landing at Tempelhof. Handcuffed again, they were herded into a bus with blacked-out windows for the westward drive to their new home. As there had for security reasons been no warning of the move, Speer missed a visit from Gretel, who was about to come to Nuremberg but could not afford to make the more expensive journey to Berlin.

Spandau prison was in the British Sector of occupied Berlin, on the western outskirts of the city and on the far side of the Olympic Stadium from the city centre. The British military authorities had their headquarters at the arena. The prison was thus well out of the way of city-centre traffic and conveniently close to the British Military Hospital. The jail, which stood on the Wilhelmstrasse (no connection with its 'Embassy Row' namesake in central Berlin), had been built with russet-coloured, hardened bricks of a kind widely used in the Germany of the late nineteenth century for public buildings – the exception which proves the rule that the Germans do not build in brick if they can avoid it. It was originally a military prison, constructed in the aftermath of the Franco–Prussian War of 1870, in the shape of a cross as if originally intended to be a church. In 1919 it was transferred to the civil sector but in 1939 it was used partly as a military prison once more, and partly as a transit stop for prisoners on their way to concentration camps. The execution chamber could function with guillotine or noose and was kept busy during the war (one source suggests there were 12,000 executions in six years). There were 132 cells, each with a flushing lavatory, a Death Row of five cells, and twelve dormitories, giving a total capacity of 600.

The four victorious Allies chose it for the exclusive use of those sentenced to imprisonment at the principal Nuremberg hearing while the trial was still on, but had then taken a year and a half to settle the modalities of four-power supervision of the 'Spandau Seven' in the British Zone. We may note here that the prison was pulled down with unseemly, even suspicious, haste by the British after the last prisoner, Rudolf Hess, was found dead in a garden hut on 17 August 1987 – when he was ninety-three. The old eccentric was reported to have garrotted himself with an electric flex attached to a window handle four and a half feet above the floor.

British army engineers prepared the jail for its new, highly political role, using German labour (the running costs were borne by the West Berlin civil administration from 1945 until demolition). The ground floor of the main cell block was turned into a self-contained unit; the rest of the solidly constructed prison, administrative facilities apart, was to be abandoned to the pigeons. The army cleared fields of fire all round the jail and raised an electrified fence topped with barbed wire round the curtain wall, to which they added five watchtowers. The guillotine was scrapped and the execution chamber turned into an emergency medical facility complete with operating table. The perimeter was guarded by the ostentatiously armed and inexpressibly bored troops of each of the four powers for one month at a time. Each power had a governor who also presided for one month in rotation. Prison warders from the four nations worked in three shifts, the nationality changing every twenty-four hours. In addition to these professional prison guards there were more than two dozen locally employed civilian personnel of several nationalities, such as medical orderlies, cooks and maintenance staff, who worked full-time in the jail.[5]

Having per hazard been the fifth of the prisoners to enter the building, Speer was assigned the number five, which he would bear for the next nineteen years, two months and thirteen days. The prisoners were stripped naked (and body-searched one by one out of sight of the others), for all the world as if they were being received into one of their own concentration camps, and were then issued with clothing left over from those very camps – not the infamous, black-and-white-striped 'pyjamas' but the rough, plain garb worn by labour forced to work outside the camps. Later they were given old, dyed British army battledress; later still they got brown corduroy suits. All uniforms bore the number of the prisoner on the back. After the medical inspection, Speer was taken to his cell – where he found five synthetic blankets stamped 'GBI' from his old General Building Inspectorate for Berlin; they would have been used by members of the Speer Construction Staff at barracks or work camps. As with his Wehrmacht winter parka at Nuremberg, he now learned for the first time that the blankets provided no real warmth.

The cell was four metres high with a floor area of 3 by 2.7 metres. The small, barred, high window was made of celluloid (an extreme precaution against wrist-slashing, but the gaolers had every reason to be on their guard against suicide attempts). Speer could see the top of a tree and a patch of sky. The walls were yellow and the ceiling white. Fittings including a table (but no chair) measuring eighty-one by forty-one centimetres and fixed to floor and wall at right angles to the short, narrow bed, a small, doorless cupboard with shelves, and a lavatory pan just inside the entrance (the only spot in the cell not visible from the spyhole in the steel door). Within the grounds of the prison was a large, overgrown and neglected garden of some 6,000 square metres. All the prisoners expressed themselves ready to work in it, even Hess; but they were on German civilian rations for the time being (in terms of quantity; the quality varied according to which power was 'in the chair' for the month) and these minimal amounts left them feeling hungry even without physical labour.

As in any institution, life soon settled into a routine with fourfold variations as guard, governor, warders and menus changed. Up at 6, wash and dress, breakfast at 6.30, a pipe of American tobacco; doors unlocked at 7.30, wash out cell and sweep corridor for fifteen minutes, then back behind the locked door at 7.45. The prisoners were initially allowed half an hour in the garden per day under a very strict regime, but lights-out came only at 10 p.m., giving plenty of time for reading. There was little else to do; visitors no longer came on an almost daily basis to examine one or other or several of them for other trials as at Nuremberg. Prisoners were allowed one visit of fifteen minutes by a family member, initially every two months, and to receive and to send one letter each per month. Speer all but gave up writing in the first few months, and Gretel could not afford the fare to see him. The inevitable general depression among the prisoners was soon countered however by occupational therapy: they were given permission to work in the garden, all day if they felt like it. This proved to be a saving grace.

Prisoner number five experienced a double improvement in his spirit and general morale three months after his arrival in Spandau. In just four days of mid-October 1947 his fortunes were transformed, courtesy of two young men from erstwhile Nazi-occupied countries who had found work at Spandau.

All the Spandau Seven were Protestant, at least nominally. Statistically, given the post-Reformation division of German Christianity, one would have expected at least two Roman Catholics, but they were all Evangelical Lutherans, the most numerous German denomination. Several prisoners protested in the early days over the absence of religious services or even a chaplain; both had been available at Nuremberg. The Soviet Union opted out of this problem and the Anglo-Americans could not produce a German-speaking Protestant minister from among their military chaplains. Ironically, therefore, it fell to the only officially Roman Catholic power of the four to produce a Protestant cleric: Georges Casalis, pastor of the Huguenot minority in the French Zone, then aged thirty, to serve as chaplain in Spandau. M. Casalis, who was married, had all the conscientious and industrious qualities of the Calvinists whose cruel and unwise expulsion from France in 1685 was of such benefit to all her neighbours; he had also been in the Resistance, a fact which won him the unanimous respect of the Allied military.

On 11 October, a Saturday, he led his first simple service in a chapel converted from a stark pair of cells with the dividing wall removed. His props were a wooden cross on a wall, a standard prison-issue table and a Bible. Only Hess (predictably) stayed away; he never attended. Casalis, formal in a black cassock, shook hands with each of the six members of his curious congregation, and then proceeded to deliver a sermon on the segregation of the lepers in biblical Israel. Not surprisingly, some of the prisoners, including the two admirals, took this personally and fulminated for days afterwards. Although Speer makes no mention of it and did not include the name of M. Casalis in the index of his book on Spandau, he spoke to the Frenchman after the service then and every week thereafter. The pastor became in effect his spiritual adviser for the three years he served in Berlin and at Spandau.[6]

Casalis soon had Speer reading the works of Professor Karl Barth, like Calvin himself a Swiss, who refreshed the theological and moral teachings of Calvinism (and returned home from Germany in 1935 rather than swear an oath of loyalty to Hitler). One of Barth's main themes was man's wickedness in pretending that he, rather than God, waß the centre of the universe. His published output was formidable in both quantity and quality; his main work was *Church Dogmatics*, whose German text exceeds 9,000 pages (which began to be published in 1932; he went on adding to it until his death in 1968).

We are not told what Speer got out of this colossus of a book, but the fact that he included it among the total of 5,000 works he said he read in twenty years in prison prompts a closer look at that claim. If we allow a total of 7,500 reading days (Nuremberg plus Spandau), then Speer read two titles every three days, perhaps 250 printed pages per day. Even if we allow that his way of working made him a fast reader, his sometimes furiously intense bouts of writing, gardening and other activities would have seriously reduced potential reading time, which had to be divided among heavy tomes such as Barth, architectural, travel or other non-fictional books and lighter matter (as well as newspapers in later years). He may have looked at these books, mostly loaned by Berlin public libraries, but he cannot have 'read' them all as reading is commonly understood. The claim looks suspiciously like another little piece of embroidery.

At any rate, Casalis seems to have got Speer thinking about the great issues of life and must have helped him adjust to prolonged incarceration, by which most people are said to be irretrievably changed if confined for more than about nine years. Since Speer undoubtedly emerged in full possession of his faculties and without obtrusive symptoms of 'jail fever', the early period under the tutelage of his French religious mentor must have been decisive for the process of adaptation. Whatever debt Speer owed Casalis, and he later acknowledged its magnitude to Gitta Sereny, he did not reciprocate. Speer was exceptionally proficient at dividing his life and thought into compartments: Casalis was there to be exploited for the spiritual advice and the useful training in the contemplative life which he offered, but not to be confided in about other matters, such as his writing plans and other distractions. The Frenchman was not a father-confessor.

Also of extreme value to Speer's programme of adjustment to semi-solitary confinement was the offer of a lifeline of an entirely different and completely practical sort: a permanent, secret, uncensored means of communicating with the outside world and the network already in place to support him. The opportunity came completely out of the blue on 14 October, when Speer was buttonholed by a Dutchman whom he disguised in his diaries under the pseudonym of Anton Vlaer. His real name was Toni Proost, born in Flushing in 1924, and he must have been a strange young man.

It turned out that he had been one of the millions who had worked for the Reich Minister for Armament and War Production in a Berlin munitions plant. He had been press-ganged in the middle of the war (he was only sixteen when the neutral Netherlands was overrun by the Germans in 1940). When Proost fell ill, as he confided to his former employer, he had gone into a Berlin hospital (constructed at Speer's behest for building workers before the war) and had been well treated; he was even temporarily 'adopted' by the family of the hospital's clinical chief, named in Speer's diaries as Dr Heinz. On recovery, Proost stayed on at the hospital for the rest of the war, qualifying as a medical orderly. He had been recruited for Spandau with an older Dutch colleague, Jan Boon: both men had decided to stay on in Berlin because they had married German girls, even so a most unusual decision for foreign ex-conscript workers, who usually could not wait to shake the dust of Germany off their feet and go home. Proost's wife Irmgard, née Unger, was the stronger of the two, as subsequent events would show. An apartment on prison premises came with the job.

Speer at first exploited his priceless new secret link with the world outside prison only sparingly, deriving more relief from knowing it was there than from overusing it in the first instance. But he was able to write his *Kassiber* (a word for a smuggled note which English could usefully adopt) on toilet paper and slip it to the Dutchman as he went on his rounds with his little medical bag. All the prisoners, even Hess, sooner or later acquired such secret channels and used them with ever-increasing boldness. After a while the Spandau Seven seldom seemed to go short of alcohol, some of it of the finest quality, even if it had to be delivered in medicine bottles and drunk from enamel mugs.

The arrangement between Speer and Proost, which was to endure for more than a decade, was his main conduit but was not exclusive. The resourceful Frau Kempf, who had thought nothing of passing herself off as a reporter on her first visit to Nuremberg, soon found her own means of getting messages to her surrogate father, and Speer, ever the prudent opportunist, did not commit all his precious reflections to the one messenger. Doing business was second nature to a Dutchman like Proost, and his relationship with Speer was mainly though not exclusively commercial. He had a wife who was even more interested in money, and a baby son, Bernd, to support in difficult circumstances.

Speer had no access to cash at this period and his wife was struggling; but there were family assets, such as the plot at 21 Kronprinzessinnenstrasse in Berlin-Schlachtensee, if he could ever realise on it. In any event he was in a position to make promises – and also practical arrangements in the 'black' letters to Gretel, which he could now send over and above the officially permitted, monthly letter to her. He also started to write secretly to the children, a series of cheery letters with drawings about his life in jail which he called by the punning codename, 'Spanish Illustrated'.

Life was slowly and hesitatingly improving in other small respects. Prisoners had to salute Allied officers and warders and were not supposed to speak, either with each other or with guards, unless spoken to. But French and (surprisingly) Russian personnel were soon ignoring this, while the more rigidly disciplined Anglophones were not above the odd informal exchange. Cell doors were often left open when the rules said they should be closed.

Just before the first Christmas in Spandau, an unexpected visit to his cell by a guard had caused Speer to panic; he threw his current notes and all his spare 'writing' paper into the lavatory and flushed them away. Speer's clandestine output was to be enormous, and the conditions in which it was written, in haste as well as in secret, did nothing for his handwriting. Fortunately he did not use the appalling 'Old German' script, which at least one commentator falsely accuses him of doing (the mistake is understandable on grounds of illegibility). But there were times when he might as well have done, squeezing as many cramped words as possible on to odd scraps of poor-quality paper in the early days, before the flow of writing materials swelled to match the flood of verbiage. Otherwise his was a conventional Continental hand, the letters tall and narrow and a little spiky. Wolters gladly handed over the problem of decipherment to his secretary, Marion Riesser, who in her capacity as chief 'translator' of the *Kassiber* output soon became as devoted to Speer as her employer and Frau Kempf. She economically transcribed the jottings on to both sides of precious onion-skin or blue airmail typing paper with the narrowest possible margins and single spacing. Thus the threat of a headache was just as real from reading her version as from poring over the crabbed original.

But Frau Riesser took the view that she owed her life to Albert Speer, a feeling which was probably not, or not very, exaggerated. She was Jewish on her father's side (he was a medical scientist who fled to Holland and spent the war in hiding there with friends); her Jewish grandmother, widow of a privy councillor, was sent to Theresienstadt concentration camp and never came back. The family house in Berlin was torn down on the orders of Speer as GBI, part of his eviction programme clearing the Jews out of the marble heart of Germania. But if there is one incontestable point in Speer's favour, it is that he took no notice of the racial, religious or political 'handicaps' (in Nazi eyes; Wolters called them *Webfehler*, flaws in the weave) of his staff, so long as they did their jobs properly. Marion Riesser was the senior of three secretarial staff in the office kept by Dr Wolters for his writing and presentational activities; her duties including typing the Chronicle (not once but twice, as will be seen). The considerable quantity of extra work Wolters assigned to her as a key member of the Speer life-support system became at least in part a labour of love. Her usual nickname in the fourth-form code of the black correspondence was Riesling, another feeble pun, or by extension from the wine grape, *Spätlese* (late vintage), whose characteristic is extra sweetness ... for Speer, women existed to be patronised.

But nobody noticed Speer's panicky early aborting of his writing material; it is astonishing that he was never caught in all his twenty years of often feverish scribbling in his cell, despite many lapses in security on his part. His first Spandau Christmas was otherwise noteworthy only because the prison regime allowed some music to be played (by Funk on a harmonium imported into the prison). No family parcels were allowed and Speer consoled himself with a little architectural draughtsmanship for the first time in years – a house.

The New Year of 1948 began auspiciously for the Spandau Seven with a sizable increase in food and fuel rations. Cells were noticeably less cold as the prisoners, in a short-lived experiment, were put to work making envelopes. Did he but know it, Speer's reviving interest in architecture was being monumentally snubbed at this time, as Wolters recorded. He had written to Dr Rudolf Pfister, the editor of the architectural journal *Baumeister*, applying for a subscription on Speer's behalf (Wolters's idea). Pfister snootily wrote back to say that the magazine was in short supply owing to paper rationing, and was genuinely needed by practising architects or students. It was not intended for the entertainment of people like Speer: 'I am of the opinion that Herr Speer has completely forfeited the right to carry on practising as an architect; further I have never regarded him as a good architect, which he also certainly is not.'[7]

By March 1948 Speer calculated he was twenty kilograms underweight at seventy kilograms, but he was working very hard in the garden which he above all, over a period of several years, helped to reshape, replant and turn into a miniature park. He was also reading for five hours a day, and drawing. Gretel had accumulated one hour's visiting allowance – now a year's entitlement of four quarterly quarter-hours – and planned to come to Berlin in May; but Speer asked Casalis to urge her not to come. The diaries do not immediately show whether she heeded this request; it is not until the end of August 1948 that she is even mentioned by name for the first time in the printed version, and then only in a reminiscence of prewar days. But Proost was being used as postman more and more often as Speer wrote down recollections whenever the mood took him. By this time the efficient Annemarie Kempf was acting as collator and clearing-house for Speer's growing correspondence, on his suggestion and that of Wolters, who was not yet in direct contact. She persuaded Gretel to forward everything she had received from Spandau to her, so that Speer's increasing requests and errands could be coordinated and passed on to the appropriate person for execution. She was soon able to organise the smuggling of requested documents into the prison; larger objects – books, bottles, even pots of Beluga caviar – soon ceased to present a challenge.

Inside the jail the prisoners failed to form close friendships. Funk, friendly and frail, got on well enough with Schirach and Raeder individually, but the latter and his erstwhile naval colleague, Dönitz, who had supplanted him, were constantly arguing about the conduct of the U-boat campaign which Dönitz had led. Eventually Speer came to like Neurath the most; they and the two admirals kept themselves busy while the other three, especially Hess, tended towards the passive. All were offered the chance to lunch as a group but declined, and they addressed each other as Herr plus surname. Titles were not used; but Third-Reich social precedence was observed (which led to friction between Dönitz, Hitler's successor, and Hess, Hitler's deputy). Fortunately the German language might have been designed for keeping others at a distance (or in their place).

The Berlin Blockade prevented Gretel's scheduled visit in February but it ended in May and she was able to come in mid-June 1949. Only at this juncture does the Spandau diary reveal that this was their first meeting in nearly three years, since the limbo period at Nuremberg when he was awaiting sentence. Speer was able to divert his mind from its habitual concentration on himself for long enough to become aware that the hour was an ordeal for her too, although she looked better than he remembered. She brought him a new pipe, a permitted luxury of which he was growing increasingly fond; he accumulated a large collection of expensive pipes, ordering specific designs of such costly brands as Dunhill and Petersen until new bouts of lung trouble persuaded him to give up smoking.

Meanwhile Wolters took an important step in Speer's interest on 1 September 1949, when he went to the Volksbank at Coesfeld and opened a special account in his own name, number 2390. Riesser, his beloved secretary of many years past and future, was authorised to administer it, pay in deposits and sign cheques. The two men were still not in direct communication, but Wolters applied considerable energy (and moral pressure) to the task of filling this 'school-money account', as he always called it from its original purpose, to support Speer's outsize family throughout their education and the man himself. Private schooling being all but unknown in Germany, the education of the six children would be free up to the age of nineteen (university however being funded by parents or state loans), but there would inevitably be associated expenses and Gretel always needed money.

As deposits accumulated, the *Schulgeldkonto* became the Albert Speer sustenance and benevolent fund, covering a wide variety of family expenses, payments to Proost and other messengers, holidays for Kempf, subventions and even bribes for people acting on Speer's behalf in legal matters or campaigns for his early release. He treated the money as if he had earned it and was entitled to spend it just as he liked. In the psychobabble of a generation later, Speer was a 'control-freak', and nowhere is this more clearly shown than in the ledgers and supporting correspondence relating to the school account, all conscientiously preserved for posterity by Wolters as part of his bequest to the German Archives. Speer used the initially modest account as an instrument for manipulating his family and others almost from the moment he knew of its existence.

Wolters funded the account by inviting or importuning Speer's former colleagues in architecture, industry and his ministry to make one-off contributions or preferably regular monthly payments by standing order, usually between ten and twenty marks. They were, after all, open to the argument that they owed him something for escaping the imprisonment which he, in a very real sense, was serving partly on their behalf. As early as December 1949, Speer's wife was receiving 200 marks a month, a handy sum in the new hard currency (whose introduction in 1948 had prompted the Soviet blockade of West Berlin; the resulting airlift by the western Allies had roared in and out over the prison for months on end).

In the outside world 1949 saw the foundation of the Federal Republic in West Germany in May and the German Democratic Republic in the Soviet East in October. Dr Konrad Adenauer, anti-Nazi former Mayor of Cologne and chairman of the conservative Christian Democratic Union, became the first postwar Chancellor at the head of a right-of-centre coalition. The dramatic further cooling in East–West relations which the formalised division of an already truncated Germany represented was seen by the prisoners as a direct threat to their interests. There was a rumour that in the event of a complete breakdown in East–West relations they would be handed back to whichever power had captured them. The crisis was also seen as a vindication of the belated Nazi attempt at divide and rule among the wartime allies towards the end of the conflict.

The outbreak of the Korean War in summer 1950 and the ensuing confrontation between the Communist and Western powers also sent a frisson through the jail, more among the prisoners than the guards, who managed to go about their business without coming to blows. Gretel was now visiting every three months, despite the fact that the meetings, under the eyes of the guards, were so lacking in spontaneous warmth that even the unspontaneous Speer noticed: he wrote down his not over-astute perception that his punishment was hers as well. He experienced another bout of heart palpitations after her visit in February 1950, even though the session had gone relatively well. Hess was playing up too, coming up with another attack, whether simulated or real nobody could tell, of amnesia, which lasted more than three months.

As the Federal Republic signed up with the Western Alliance against the Soviet bloc in the early 1950s, the second German democracy began to gain acceptance. Rearmament raced ahead on both sides of the intra-German border as it became clear that a third European conflict would be fought on German soil, which would meanwhile be used as the main forward base of the two opposed military groupings. But there were benefits too: Hilde Speer, his second-oldest and probably favourite child, born in 1936, was awarded a one-year scholarship to New England in the United States. Speer heard about this in March 1952; in June she was denied a visa because of her father, but a week later the Americans had the sense to relent, and she left in July.

Early in 1951 Rudolf Wolters, encouraged by frequent references to himself in Speer's letters to his wife, decided to send him a *Kassiber*, his first such initiative in five years. Wolters happened to believe that the whole Nuremberg judicial marathon had been misconceived and unjustified, that Hitler had not been given credit for those things – employment, public works – which he had got right, that reports of Nazi genocide were exaggerated by a factor of at least ten and that Germany had generally been harshly treated by the victors. On the other hand he had a lively sense of humour as well as an un-German feeling for irony. Wolters also, as his letters and other writings prove, had a way with words and a sound grasp of German culture, enabling him to write with breadth, depth and wit, much more readably than his mentor and long-term correspondent in Spandau. In his opening letter Wolters suggested that Speer go ahead with his memoirs, just as Speer himself was running through recollections in his head and beginning to write some of the resulting thoughts down.

The departure of Casalis in June 1950 passed unremarked in the diaries (a fact which, as so often noted, bore no relation to the importance to Speer of an emotionally significant event: he made a fetish of concealing his feelings). Insofar as he sought compensation or distraction for the departure of his spiritual guide, it was in gardening, to which he now devoted himself more enthusiastically and consistently than any other prisoner. He had also been forcing himself to take regular exercise – walking, mainly – since autumn 1949. Another variation on the tedium he invented in spring 1951 was a half-yearly 'holiday' – a fortnight of as much sleep as possible, aided by sleeping tablets. During this 'sleep cure' efforts by the network to gain support for an early release for Speer bore their first recorded fruit: Annemarie Kempf received a letter of sympathy from Paul Nitze, then Director of Policy Planning in the US State Department but six years earlier one of Speer's Strategic Bombing Survey interrogators.

Among those mobilised by Wolters to the same end was his lawyer, Werner Schütz, based in Düsseldorf, capital of North-Rhine-Westphalia, where Wolters kept an office because he was receiving a steady flow of architectural commissions from the state government. Schütz was a close political associate of Adenauer and later became Minister of Culture in the state, where he had helped to found the regional Christian Democratic Union. The immensely fat, immensely clever lawyer was retained by Wolters to act unofficially for Speer (who did not have the right to institute legal proceedings while in prison). He was offered a refund of his expenses from the school account but declined; for a while Wolters earmarked several thousand marks as an incentive to Schütz to intercede with Adenauer, who was indifferent, President Theodor Heuss, who refused, and his successor, Heinrich Lübke, who had worked on Speer's Construction Staff during the war but cited Soviet intransigence towards the Spandau Seven as his excuse for inaction. Schütz's honourable refusal to accept a single pfennig meant that the money could be diverted to Hilde Speer when she took up her father's cause while a student.

Speer's affairs were providing work for several attorneys in the early 1950s. Otto Kranzbühler, the gifted naval lawyer who had led the defence of Dönitz at Nuremberg, was masterminding legal moves for the remission of the admiral's and Speer's sentences in particular; he managed to take his case to Adenauer personally at the end of January 1952. General Hans Speidel, once Rommel's chief of staff and the first German general to be appointed to a senior Nato command, supported the early-release campaign both in Bonn and at Nato level.

Dr Flächsner, who had defended Speer, was working for him again from early in 1950, when denazification proceedings were instituted against his client. For the greater part of the ensuing decade and beyond Speer faced the prospect of being stripped of family assets as his contribution to atonement and reparation for Nazi crimes. This was a very real threat to Gretel and the children, and it meant even more supportive effort for Dr Wolters, who began in summer 1950 to collect affidavits on Speer's behalf. An ailing Professor Tessenow confirmed from his sick-bed in Berlin that Speer had shielded him during the war, and Professor Paul Bonatz confirmed from Hanover that Speer had protected him, like so many other politically suspect individuals, at the ministry. Another former ministry employee confirmed that Speer had acted to save works of art from the Russians by moving them westward out of Berlin in 1945. An old ministry hand confirmed Speer's dedicated opposition to 'scorched earth'. An American representing a 'Committee for International Justice' wrote to Gretel from New Jersey promising support for the release of all Germans still held for war crimes; *Time* magazine in June 1952 investigated this new, right-wing action group which Speer himself had rightly identified as a potential embarrassment to his cause.

An emotional Leni Riefenstahl, director of the most striking documentary films of the Nazi era, promised support in a letter from Rome dated 29 June 1952, perhaps influenced by the fact that she faced a similar process:

> I am so sorry about the frightful fate that has overtaken him, and I simply cannot believe that this man should have no more work. A miracle will save him one day; I know no personality that has impressed me as much as Speer, from the ethical [aspect] and as a genius. I still carry a picture of him with me – if only he has the strength to endure.

The recipient of this gushing commitment, Frau Kempf, had left Eutin, where she worked in child-care, to take up a post as secretary to a Bundestag deputy in Bonn from September 1950, a useful move for lobbying purposes. Meanwhile, as the affidavits flowed in, so did the money into the school fund – to such effect that Wolters raised Gretel's monthly stipend to 300 marks in October and again to 350 marks in November, with a Christmas bonus of 500 marks. The fund was also paying legal expenses – and giving 100 marks per month to Karl Cliever, a wartime assistant to Speer who had fallen on hard times.

While all the foregoing effort of the support network was expended on his behalf elsewhere, summer 1952 bore in on prisoner number five as a time of multiple family difficulties. The bad and then good news of Hilde's visa for the United States, a prospect that excited her father enormously, was followed twelve days later by sad news about his mother, Luise Mathilde Speer, who had died on 24 June. Even though he had been told of her stroke late in May, and even though the hard old lady had never shown any love for her middle son (but plenty of vicarious pride when he became famous), Speer regretted the fact that he had not seen her since April 1945. His distant relationship with her in childhood and later was undoubtedly a major factor underlying Speer's emotional remoteness and his manipulative charm alike. A depression followed. Speer's elder brother Hermann had been causing unspecified problems during the last months of their mother's life, as Kempf complained to Wolters: she described his behaviour as 'lack of moderation' but crossed out the adjective 'sadistic' which she had originally written in front of it. But Kempf reported a month later, in July 1952, that Gretel and Hermann had achieved a reconciliation after Frau Speer's death.[8]

Meanwhile Hilde was having a wonderful time on the other side of the Atlantic. She went in style on the liner *United States*, then the world's most luxurious, and was staying with a prosperous Quaker family in upper New York state. While there, she made her first *démarche* as envoy for her father: she contacted the man whose influence had seen to it that she got her visa for her American scholarship year, John J. McCloy. He had been US High Commissioner in West Germany from 1949 to 1952, when the Allied Control Commission, which he chaired, wound itself up and handed its residual powers of sovereignty to Bonn. McCloy then became chairman of a Boston bank. The McCloys entertained the fetching young Hilde to tea and were duly impressed; McCloy declared himself totally convinced that Speer should be given remission of his overlong sentence. Speer was vastly encouraged by the news from his daughter in autumn 1952, even though nothing concrete came of it. He was also availing himself of the postal services of an American prison guard, a sergeant whose first name was Frederick (the secret of his identity Speer took with him to the grave). The man's reward may have been a ranch-style house plan drawn by Speer and given by him to a 'friendly US sergeant'.

There was a small and deliciously ironic crisis in the prison early in April 1953, when the American director took it into his head to have the seven war criminals inducted into the secrets of basketwork. It will be remembered that there had been an early and brief experiment when the prisoners were recruited to make envelopes. They seem to have accepted that imposition without protest, but basket-weaving, the kind of occupational therapy commonly associated with mental hospitals, was too much. Speer confided to his diary on 2 April: 'To our minds that is ... incompatible with the Nuremberg sentences. *We were not sentenced ... to forced labour*' (author's italics). The seven agreed to form a united front. Speer asked Wolters to seek a legal opinion from Kranzbühler. He encouraged polite resistance on the grounds that it would sustain their status as 'gentlemen', which he regarded as vital to their prospects of an amnesty. The American director abandoned the idea of forced labour on baskets on 11 April, a rare victory.

Hilde kept her father fully informed about her doings in the United States, which included the remarkable coup, facilitated by John McCloy, of a meeting with Dean Acheson, Secretary of State from 1947 until 1953, on whom she also made a strongly positive impression. In May Speer wrote to her in fussy-father mode, reminding her to write thank-you letters to both State Department contacts from her host's home well before her scheduled return in July, in case they wished to give her a message to bring back.

For both Speer and his daughter, 1953 was a dramatic year to be out of circulation in Germany, whatever the reason. How out of touch the prisoners were was shown by their feverish excitement late in January over a fantastic 'plot' to free them and set up a new, post-Nazi government under Dönitz. The man said to be in charge was Otto Skorzeny, late SS colonel and Germany's most successful wartime commando leader, who had liberated both Mussolini and Horthy, the Hungarian Fascist leader, and staged a daring raid behind US lines in the Battle of the Ardennes. But Skorzeny, who had been acquitted of war crimes and then escaped from custody while awaiting trial on other charges, was safely running an import-export business in Spain and denied all knowledge of a helicopter assault on Spandau. The prisoners also hoped, vainly, that their lot would be eased when they heard of the death of Stalin in March. That this welcomed event was unlikely to affect the political tensions in the Eastern bloc or between East and West was shown by the tragically abortive workers' rising in East Germany in June, when Soviet tanks helped put down the revolt, as they were to do again in Poland, Hungary and Czechoslovakia in later years.

At this time also, Speer sought to sidestep the possible consequences of a denazification case (still on the stocks) going against him by reassigning his inheritance from his parents to the six children for their education in equal shares. About 60,000 marks was invested on behalf of each of them; he thought each might need an average of 30,000 marks to achieve a qualification and would then be left with the same amount as a reserve. Speer continued to let his family benefit from the school fund, although Gretel, back in the Heidelberg family home from December 1953, voluntarily halved her monthly subsidy from it, preferring to pay her own way by taking in lodgers. Hermann Speer, by contrast, was still being a nuisance and seemed set on frittering away his share of the inheritance, on the strength of which he had borrowed heavily before receipt. Speer was resigned to supporting his wastrel brother as early as August 1952; more than twenty years later, he was still doing so.[9]

16

Daddy's Girl

(1953–66)

O N HER SEVENTEENTH BIRTHDAY Hilde Speer presented her father with an awkward question. In a letter to him dated 17 April 1953 she asked:

> I can understand ... how [it was that] many intellectuals came to accept [Hitler], although in his book he had stated exactly what his aims were. What I cannot understand is how these educated people did not turn against him when he began persecuting the Jews; and after he had extended the borders of Germany ... I know that at the end you were no longer in agreement with him. But what I do not understand is why you did not break with him in 1940.

Speer's reply, dated 14 May, was of great length, showing that he took very seriously both such a question from such a source and the necessity of producing a convincing reply, upon which their future relations would depend. The huge importance Speer attached to his answer is proved by the fact that he later made a special point of showing it to his two previous biographers, William Hamsher and Gitta Sereny. He would, he wrote to Hilde, begin with the hardest part: 'There is no excuse ... There are things for which one has to carry the blame, even if purely factually one might find excuses.' He did not discuss this issue with his fellow-prisoners (or at all after Pastor Casalis left); and by avoiding self-justification he did not need to use the term 'guilt', he wrote. He had accepted Hitler's commands and must share the responsibility for their consequences, but 'I knew nothing of all the horrors' – a denial accepted at Nuremberg. He could have found out; instead he went along unthinkingly. Nuremberg had been necessary and the sentence was part of the price of his redemption.

Speer went on to cite an extraordinary 'analogy' which could have gone over his young daughter's head: the punishment of Oedipus for marrying his mother after killing his father, Laius, even though he had acted in ignorance of the identity of either at the time. 'Any contemporary court would have acquitted him,' he asserted, but ancient Greek morality had demanded punishment and Speer felt this was right, although he could not say why. It is actually quite easy to explain, whether in terms ancient or modern: Oedipus, even though his ignorance might have prevented his conviction for parricide and incest, was unquestionably guilty of homicide: after all, for no good reason he killed an apparent stranger met on the road. Speer misses the point of the legend and the tragic drama derived from it: a blinded Oedipus was cast out (though not executed) for what he had actually done. The punishment was decreed not by a court but by Apollo, who had warned him long in advance through the oracle at Delphi that he would kill his father and marry his mother (the god had also warned Laius against fathering a son). It was arguably open to Oedipus to avoid disaster by not killing at least an older man or marrying an older woman ...

The moral seems straightforward enough: we have to take the consequences, fair or not, of our own actions. Speer argues that Oedipus's ignorance of the identities of his parents should have won him a reprieve, and was akin to his own ignorance of the true horror of the Nazi regime, for which he was being unjustly punished – only because somebody had to take responsibility for what had actually been done (presumably his work for the regime is to be equated with the peccadillo of casually killing a stranger by the wayside).

But Speer went on to admit to his daughter that he had been in thrall to Hitler, who gave him his power as architect, minister and favourite and whom he reluctantly and belatedly opposed only when he intervened directly in Speer's area of responsibility with his scorched-earth policy. 'I have learned to understand that unfettered ambition can destroy one's innate awareness of ethical principles.'[1]

The inordinate length of the letter to Hilde, which she apparently found acceptable (to judge by her many years of subsequent hard work on her father's behalf), is all the more remarkable given its timing. Speer was keeping his two postmen busier than ever before in any case, because on Thursday, 8 January 1953, he sat down and wrote the first section of the draft of his memoirs. The transcription by Marion Riesser is seventeen single-spaced, typed sheets of A4 paper with the narrowest possible margins; in English there would have been room for 8,000 words or as much as can be readably printed on one page of a broadsheet newspaper without illustrations or headlines. The original was handwritten on fifteen metres of surplus lavatory paper. His starting point was the last few weeks of the war (he paid more attention to themes than to chronological order): 'scorched earth' and how he had undermined it, his oft-deferred radio broadcast and his last visit to Hitler. He noted hurriedly at the end, for Wolters's benefit:

> I attach no value to correcting it. I am quite content if the correct presentation is in your hands. I attach no value at all to making myself or the circumstances of the time [look] better than they were, in the leadership which ruined itself. That is always to be clearly distinguished from the decent heroism of the soldiers, of the civil population. The thought of them can only shame one. Despite that, despite all the 'sanitising' over recent years, *I would behave more or less exactly the same* [Speer's emphasis]. There was no choice. Where there is muck one gets dirty.

The first slab of memoirs was followed by a separate postscript to Wolters, dated 9 February, when the unprecedentedly large missive left the prison: 'Could not finish reading it last night. Hope you can read it ... Not satisfied with it. I need more time and rest for it. I have to keep one ear cocked, which is distracting.' Should he carry on? He asked Wolters not to show the draft to any outsider; he could understand now how hard it was to write.

By 7 March he had smuggled out two further lengthy extracts, as shown by a note to Wolters seeking his opinion and inviting him this time to canvass Gretel and one or two close friends for their views. Wolters thought already that Speer was being hard on Hitler but in the main held his fire until many years later so as not to discourage the writer. The blocks of memoirs became known in their private code as *Arien* (arias) while the diary notes were called *Späne* (literally and, one may suppose, metaphorically in this context, 'shavings', but also of course a pun on Spandau, like the *spanische Illustrierte* still being sent to the younger children). Production peaked on 21 March with an extract Frau Riesser needed forty-one typewritten pages to transcribe. On 9 January 1954, a year and a day after he began, Speer completed what would stand as the main draft of his memoirs, the basis of the book published in the English-speaking world under the title, *Inside the Third Reich*. He used some 1,100 pieces of writing paper to do it.

In his diaries, curiously enough, he gives the completion date of what might easily have amounted to half a million words in English as the end of December 1954, or well nigh a year later than was the case. The evidence of the correspondence in the Wolters Bequest is however conclusive: he finished his draft memoirs in a year and a day. It is a curious as well as elaborate transposition; whether it is dissimulation or a slip cannot be determined from the archival evidence.

Meanwhile Speer still found time for family concerns between bouts of scribbling. In August 1953 he asked Wolters to set up a pocket-money system for the children, specifying that the four eldest should have twelve marks and the two youngest six marks per week from 1 September, and that the school fund should also stump up the cash for account books, receipt books and even a textbook on book-keeping, so that they could be encouraged to look after the money properly. A year later the fund could be made to run to an extra fifty marks a month, with ten marks each going to the four eldest, seven to Arnold and just three extra to Ernst.

The failure of Albert, the eldest, in March 1955 to pass the *Abitur*, the matriculation examination usually taken at the age of nineteen with a view to higher education, drove a needlessly worried Speer into a particularly blatant manipulation of his children by money. Albert's disappointment at the age of twenty was a setback, because resitting the all-important examination was no easy matter for young people finished with school (or for mature students). But it was neither a disaster nor a sign of inadequacy: the young man had simply gone down with influenza in the middle of the ordeal. Having missed some schooling after the war and then served an apprenticeship as a carpenter, Albert had studied at night school to catch up. His father took advice through Wolters and had the young man sent to Bavaria, where the examination could be resat later in the year. He duly passed; and after studying architecture became a highly successful town-planner in Frankfurt, where he was living in the 1990s with his wife, a television presenter.

But the eldest son's educational hiccup prompted his father to set up a sliding scale of rewards for all the other children in April 1955. German school-test marks range from 1 (very good) to 6. Each child was to receive eighty marks for the former and four marks for a 4, the lowest pass mark; these rates were to be doubled for *Abitur* marks. On reflection, Speer halved the payments at the end of April because the school fund could not cope with the extra demand. In the letter to Wolters imposing the reduction, Speer mused: 'It is a real cross that I cannot live with the children. It is amazing that they are attached to me despite the ten years [in jail] and although they had nothing from me during the three years [as] Minister.'

But less than two months later he was telling Wolters of his anxiety about how the children were turning away. Hilde was growing up; Arnold found the decor of his father's prison more interesting than his father during his rare visit. But family contacts continued through thick and thin, once every three months or so: Hilde came in September 1953, to report in person on her American adventure, escorted by Albert; Ernst, the youngest and for his father always the most 'difficult', then aged ten, visited Spandau for the first time on 2 February 1954, first in a series of depressing encounters with the withdrawn boy, whom he had not seen since babyhood. Margret, the younger daughter, made a happier first visit to the prison on 2 May.

A four-power conference in March in Berlin about Spandau led to some improvements in conditions but no progress on remission: newspapers were allowed to the prisoners from May 1954; only stories relating to Spandau were censored. Speer's interest in architecture had revived sufficiently for him to request specialist magazines; its editor would doubtless have been miffed to learn that he was loaned the 1953 volume of *Baumeister* as part of the more relaxed regime.

Mortality began to intrude in September. Hess was never quite well, at least mentally; Raeder was in a slow decline. Then Neurath, also weakening, fell quite ill at the beginning of the month with heart trouble; and the diabetic Funk became the first prisoner to be taken out of the jail to the nearby British Military Hospital for a bladder operation in mid-month. (Neurath was set free on grounds of ill-health on 6 November; he died nearly two years later, in August 1956.) At the end of September there was a minor sensation when a French magazine published pages of 'inside Spandau' photographs. A French guard was sacked and black postal deliveries were suspended as a precaution by the illicit messengers.

On the last day of the month the obsessive Speer, who listed everything he 'read', wrote in his diary that he had walked round the prison garden, which he had done so much to improve, with a gait resembling that of a child taking its first steps. Having measured his shoe at thirty-one centimetres, he placed one foot in front of the other for a complete circuit of the main path round the garden and arrived at the conclusion that it measured 270 metres. Armed with this yardstick, he decided on about 20 September to go for a walk in his head from Berlin to Heidelberg, a distance of 626 kilometres. He recorded his daily, weekly and average progress in a table. It was the bemused Hess, wont to sit in the garden, who came up with a handy means of measuring circuits walked: he plucked thirty beans from the garden and told Speer to put them in his left pocket, transferring one bean to the right at the end of each circuit.

To calm himself down after the emotional upheaval of Neurath's release on compassionate grounds, Speer overdid things, walking more than twenty-four kilometres in a day; two days later his right knee swelled up, as had last occurred with the left five years before. This episode certainly had a plausible physical explanation, but since Speer had been walking some considerable distance daily for nearly two months and must have been used to it by then, there was probably a psychosomatic component as well. Neurath, after all, had been the most congenial fellow-prisoner and Speer, almost as much of a loner as Hess, felt a touch of loneliness all the same. Now they were six.

Speer was confined to bed with his knee, combating the pain with nothing more than aspirin every three hours; after a month of this he began spitting blood and experiencing chest pains. By mid-December Speer was in the throes of another lung crisis similar to his experience at the turn of 1943–44. The military doctor stuck to his diagnosis of bronchitis for the time being. He was transferred in mid-month to the infirmary, the former execution chamber, with a collapsed lung (pulmonary infarction) caused by a blood clot. He had to spend eight weeks lying on his front. On the 22nd Speer received a visit from his wife, bearing a recording of a J.S. Bach composition made by three of their children (Hilde on flute; Albert, 'cello; Margret, piano).

Having suggested in May using the school fund to buy the two girls a dog, delivered in October (as ever, Wolters did the organising) he included a sausage for the animal, a dachshund called simply Speer (his choice of name), among the presents funded from the same source and hung on the Christmas tree at Heidelberg on his behalf by Gretel. The sausage for the sausage-dog vastly amused the children; even grouchy Ernst thought it rather droll. He was specially favoured in Speer's gift budget, receiving fifty marks for a bicycle, whereas the five others received thirty marks apiece (but Arnold got a thirty-mark bonus for a school report in which all marks were above the 5 of failure). 'For the first time I have had some influence on the children's Christmas,' a satisfied Speer told his diary early in the New Year, on receiving their warm thank-you letter. But he had to be pushed to the chapel on a medical trolley for the Christmas Eve service and was only back in his cell, feeling very weak, at the end of the first week of January 1955. He was so noisily and uncharacteristically distressed by this premature return that sedatives were prescribed and precautions taken against a suicide attempt: his pills were doled out dose by dose and a warder made sure they actually went down his throat.

By this time Gretel Speer was doing well enough financially to be able to dispense with her monthly subvention from the school fund as from 1 January 1955 – or so her husband decided on her behalf in a letter to Wolters. The fund, Speer directed, should be reserved for paying fares for family visits to him, the children's pocket-money, summer holidays, Christmas extras, Annemarie Kempf's expenses and the payments to Proost. Speer advised Gretel directly not to sell the block of shares in the blooming Dortmunder Union brewery inherited from his parents but rather to sell off spare land round the Heidelberg house so as to keep the property without its becoming a burden.

Speer was fully recovered and in good spirits for his fiftieth birthday, 19 March 1955. The indefatigable Wolters had gone out of his way to mark this special occasion, the Germans attaching more importance to such rites of passage and milestones in life than most. He contacted many former colleagues and associates and asked them for greetings messages which he then assembled and dispatched in a secret bundle to Spandau on the 15th, for delivery on the day. Independently of each other, Speer and Wolters recollected that on the former's fortieth birthday, ten years before, Hitler had 'presented' Speer with his scorched-earth decree. Now, on his very birthday a decade later, Speer came to the end of his walk within the prison walls 'from Berlin to Heidelberg'. From his garden seat Hess encouraged him to carry on, south and east to Munich and beyond; this seems to have been the germination of the idea of extending his walk 'round the world', the most enduring and effective escape from reality that Speer discovered during his long imprisonment; it would help to see him through with remarkably little psychic damage. He drew up a meticulous and detailed programme of reading and reference to maps. He borrowed books in advance so as to read up on each section of his 'route' and the places to which it would take him, often sending an enthusiastic Wolters on errands to find out recondite facts about obscure corners of the world.

Another worry for Speer as he slowly recovered from his latest knee-lung double trouble was caused by his prime connection with the outside world, Toni Proost, or more precisely his little son, Bernd. Speer wrote to Wolters early in January, reporting that the boy had developed leukaemia and asking for a special payment of 200 marks to Proost if the school fund permitted. The boy showed no sign of improvement by March; a month later, Irmgard Proost wrote to Wolters to say the boy had gone down with jaundice. In June he needed ten transfusions. All the fresh blood did not prevent a severe throat infection as the boy's immune system gave way; in early August his kidneys, liver and spleen were affected and he died. Speer used the school fund to have red roses and forget-me-nots sent to the bereaved parents and money to pay for a gravestone. About a month later Irmgard safely gave birth to a daughter, Christiane, on 10 September. One week after this happy event brought a new resident to Spandau's staff accommodation, one of the old occupants of the prison block, Erich Raeder, was released on grounds of ill-health on the 17th (the unreconstructed Nazi admiral wrote two volumes of unrepentant memoirs and died in 1960). Then there were five.

Chancellor Adenauer's historic first visit to Moscow at the end of the month led to the release of thousands of German prisoners of war, but there was no concession over the Spandau five. An optimistic letter from General Speidel after a visit to Washington a few weeks later again raised Speer's hopes of release, to no avail. Visiting times were doubled in November 1955, but this only made an encounter with Fritz, perhaps the most gifted of the children and a first-class mathematician, all the more miserable; he was another 'difficult' boy as far as Speer was concerned. A visit by Gretel, accompanied by Ernst, went almost as badly a month later.

Illness struck from another direction at the end of 1955, when Frau Kempf had what it was then customary to call a nervous breakdown. Marion Riesser realised all was not well from the tone of her friend Annemarie's letters and Wolters offered her a holiday at Coesfeld, which she declined; she also sent back a cheque for 500 marks which Wolters had posted to her on Speer's suggestion for a skiing holiday. She had been working too hard, adding her unpaid and taxing role as clearing-house coordinator of the Speer correspondence to that of a full-time Bundestag secretary and taking no breaks. She may well also have had enough of being patronised and taken for granted; at any rate she got herself a new job, still working for a Bundestag deputy but in his constituency, well away from Bonn. She effectively dropped out of the Speer network for some six years without altogether losing touch. This meant more work for Wolters and Riesser, but they remained steadfast.

Speer, however, entered a period of mild but persistent depression in 1956, a classic case of the 'jail fever' which is a common ailment of long-term prisoners. He neglected his diary for weeks at a time and took long breaks from his walk 'round the world', but at least he continued with his mentally neutral work in the garden. Funk's new illness and the news of Neurath's death in August 1956 did not help.

Wolters was driven at the beginning of that year to chide Speer for missing what their code styled an 'astrological appointment' or later just an 'astrological' – the monthly prearranged exchange in which Wolters sent an omnibus letter containing points raised by various contacts and needing Speer's attention, while the latter sent an omnibus reply to various earlier messages. In the same long letter, Wolters raised an issue of much more serious moment for their extraordinary friendship. Mulling over Speer's draft memoirs and the reflections in his diaries in the context of his latest appeal for clemency, Wolters allowed himself to query his pen-friend's readiness to accept 'responsibility' for the Nazi regime's excesses. As we can deduce from his political stance described above, Wolters's main objection to this stratagem was his belief that Speer had nothing to apologise for; but on 13 January he made the point that if someone assumes responsibility he is seen to be signalling that he is guilty. It served Speer right therefore if he was taken at his word: 'One should be careful here and "admit" as little as possible ... I hope you give this up.'

Both Kempf and Riesser knew how strongly Wolters felt on this point, which he dutifully suppressed almost all the time so as not to upset Speer. It was a fundamental difference, the seed of the break between them fifteen years later; but Wolters did not allow the festering issue to interfere with his devotion to Speer's family, quite often to the detriment of his own. He acted as a generous uncle cum surrogate father to the children, all of whom he entertained at one time or another at Coesfeld; Gretel too became a friend of the Wolters family, on 'Du' terms with his wife Erika. In the same warning shot of a letter he discussed Margret's ambitions in interior design, revealing that he had conscientiously researched the field and learned that it was all but closed to women; and he offered Albert Junior, now studying at Munich like his father, a holiday job and even a bed in his Düsseldorf office so he could get some practice in architectural drawing.[2]

Just how close the two men – prisoner and confidential agent – were at this time is shown by their attempt at midnight on the immediately preceding New Year's Eve to 'get in touch' by telepathy. Each sheepishly admitted to the other that he had fallen asleep before midnight (Speer was consoling himself with *Sekt* in his cell; Wolters, a connoisseur of fine food and drink, made do with white wine).

As if to throw off his inertia and make some kind of a new start, Speer took it into his head in later summer 1956 to resume work on the doctoral thesis which he had barely begun after graduation nearly thirty years before, choosing Tessenow's assistantship and marriage instead. He also took up drawing again, never his strong suit but a rediscovered pleasure in the *spanische Illustrierte* for the children and now a more serious avocation. He became so enthusiastic that he was rebuked one evening for ignoring lights-out. *Fenster* (windows) joined the feebly codenamed flow from Spandau to Coesfeld as Speer reapplied himself to his 'History of the Window'. He had been doing a little reading from time to time on the subject over the preceding ten years but now threw himself into windows in something resembling the old, obsessive Speer manner. No longer so depressed, he was able to remember a great deal. Nor did he forget Gretel's impending fiftieth birthday, ahead of which he ordered the school fund to stump up money for a pair of gold earrings (once again Wolters did the work, paying 365 marks to Speer's chosen designer, Gerdy Troost, widow of the man he succeeded as Hitler's architect). A successful post-birthday visit by Gretel with Ernst early in September brought a further improvement in mood, as did another from Margret, who was about to follow her older sister's example and go to America for a year.

On 2 September Speer was formally notified that his case was coming up at the Berlin Denazification Tribunal, after a six-year wait. The notice was dated 18 August and the hearings, at which Dr Flächsner once again represented Speer, ground on in desultory fashion beyond the end of the year. Speer was bracing himself at this time for the next

Spandau milestone – the release of Dönitz at midnight on the night of 30 September, ten years to the day since they were sentenced at Nuremberg. He was the first prisoner to serve out his time. Their relations remained cool until the last – a brief exchange of courtesies as the prisoners turned in as usual at 10 p.m. Then, from midnight, there were four.

In an unsuccessful olive-branch of a letter to Annemarie Kempf in summer 1956, Wolters fretted over the denazification proceedings about which they had often corresponded: 'I am only anxious about the matter of the clearance of Jew-flats in Berlin. That could be a bullseye [against Speer]. And this is the point to which the defence should direct itself because it will come under discussion ...' Speer, Wolters wrote, hoped the case would not attract attention and was resigned to giving up the site of his Schlachtensee house in Berlin, his main asset after Werner Schütz had legally dispersed the bulk of his considerable inheritance from his mother to the children.[3] Flächsner tactlessly advised playing for even more time than had been allowed to pass already, implying to Speer's mind that his client had plenty of that commodity available. But even such a fretful occasion provided Speer with some emotionally undemanding company and conversation, for which he was grateful. In his diary for December 1956 he noted about this consultation: 'I could have gone on talking for hours. All I need is a subject.' He added the accurate self-perception: 'And my only subject is my past.'

The diaries became very sketchy again in the early months of 1957 when one of Speer's main themes is the rapid decline of Funk, deliberately exacerbating his diabetes by secretly gorging himself on sugar in the hope of an early release from his life sentence. He got his wish on 17 May 1957; he went home to Düsseldorf and died there three years later. Now there were three: Speer and Schirach, both more than halfway through their twenty-year sentences, and Rudolf Hess, who was there for life.

The revived window thesis was metaphorically defenestrated by Speer in March; with it went another tenuous link with his original profession. Also at this juncture, Speer asked Wolters to get him a book on contemporary etiquette, so that he could be fully prepared for a return to polite society in the event of remission. Links with the children were also hard to sustain during the drab days of 1957, as hopes of remission for the Spandau Three briefly rose and then fell. A visit from Ernst in August and an 'alienated' letter from Hilde in October only deepened Speer's melancholy; difficult Fritz, however, had gained an excellent *Abitur* the previous spring and was now studying chemistry at university.

The outside world impinged, briefly but enough to provoke a diary entry from time to time, as it had done in the double world crisis of autumn 1956 – Suez and Hungary. The first Soviet satellite, *Sputnik I*, reminded an anxious Speer in October 1957 of the excitement he felt over Wernher von Braun's experiments. Now here were the Russians with a notable scientific 'first' which did not bode well at a time of protracted East–West tension, in itself the opposite of good news for the prisoners. In the same month the Social Democrat Willy Brandt was elected Governing Mayor of West Berlin.

At the end of the year Speer lost his trusty Dutch messenger, Toni Proost, after a real-life drama to match any fictional spy novel set in divided Germany and its divided capital. At Christmas Toni and Irmgard and their baby daughter visited Irmgard's mother in East Berlin. They had a pleasant Christmas Eve, exchanging presents which included gifts bought from the school fund. But on the evening of Christmas Day two Russians knocked on the door and asked for help, saying one of them had broken his leg in a road accident. They asked Proost to drive them to their base at Karlshorst, just outside the city. Hard though it is to believe, Proost innocently complied. When they got there, the Russians inveigled Proost into a room, locked the door, addressed him by his full name, expressed their gratitude for the lift – and pressed the modest sum of fifteen marks in Western currency upon him. They then said that because he had always got on well with the Russians in Spandau, they wanted him to be their agent against the Western 'warmongers'. They made it clear it was an offer he would not be allowed to refuse and pressed him to sign a prepared letter in which he undertook to keep quiet about the arrangement. Two agents already in Spandau would be in touch to give him his first assignment on 5 January, his captors said.[4]

A terrified Proost agreed to everything but wisely reported the incident on his return to West Berlin. The Netherlands Consulate (he was still a citizen), the British Military Police and the British and American prison directors were unanimous in advising him to leave Spandau and Berlin at once. Irmgard appealed to Wolters for help with removal and travel expenses; she said they hoped to move to the Netherlands.

Wolters was able to enlist the aid of Kempf and Gretel Speer in resettling the Proosts. Toni left Berlin for his family in Flushing, calling at Coesfeld on the way. Wolters promised to try and find him a job on the border so that he could live in eastern Holland and work in West Germany and stored his effects in the meantime. Extricating the Proosts from Spandau cost nearly 2,000 marks. The school fund was overstretched at this period because Wolters was finding it increasingly difficult to sustain interest among Speer's dwindling circle of supporters, despite a special whip-round among the old faithfuls in January 1958.

The need to bail out Speer's pliable principal messenger – it was certainly his due for services rendered, but it was also prudent to keep him (and his determined wife) sweet – prompted Wolters to approach Gretel for the DM 2,000 instead. With her consent he organised the auction of some Speer family glassware with a reserve price of that amount. The sale yielded over 3,200 marks, which Wolters was finally able to forward to Gretel in summer 1958; this enabled her in turn to pay off the loan Kempf had been able to extract from her politician employer.

We may diverge here to note that Proost took a series of short-term jobs in Germany and by 1960 was living with his family in Eutin, Schleswig-Holstein, to which the versatile Annemarie Kempf had returned, to work once more with handicapped children. The school fund and the Speer family sent him money from time to time while he struggled to begin a new career as a builder's draughtsman. But the hapless former male nurse went into a decline and on 14 June 1962 died in his sleep after a long illness, aged only thirty-eight. His widow tried to tap Wolters for a loan of 3,000 marks for a building plot at Eutin in summer 1964 but the school fund could not run to this and Wolters regretfully turned her down.[5]

Proost had used a medical practitioner, Dr Erich Heins, of Charlottenburg, West Berlin (codenamed 'Heinerich' in the Wolters–Speer correspondence) as an intermediary for the mail he smuggled in and out of Spandau. After Proost's 'resignation' at the end of 1957, the intermission was brief and new West Berlin names and addresses began to appear in the postal chain, including an Irene Böttcher, who took deliveries of such items as bottles of wine and jars of caviar for forwarding to 'Uncle Alex' (Speer), and a young woman called Maria Wieden, née Herbst, who came recommended by Irmgard Proost and via whom Hilde was able to keep in touch with her father without needing to bother Wolters.

Hilde became her father's principal 'ambassador' in the campaign for his early release in autumn 1957, when she returned from her second year (this time between school and university) in the United States. She took with her a letter from Gretel to John J. McCloy, who was even more impressed by the striking young blonde the second time around.

The 'alienation' Speer detected in her letter to him of October 1957 from New England (she stayed with the same family) can only have been a passing mood because Hilde, who studied at Tübingen and Bonn universities (German and Latin initially; later sociology and education), threw herself more and more after her first two semesters as a student into the efforts to get her father out of prison. She was in touch with Werner Schütz, who had been ill, early in 1958, and began lobbying West German politicians shortly afterwards.

She managed to see at least one close adviser of Adenauer's and to have interviews with Foreign Minister Brentano, President Lübke and such leading figures in the Social Democratic Party as Carlo Schmid, Herbert Wehner and eventually Willy Brandt (an incorrigible ladies' man who was most taken with her). Karl Maria Hettlage, once Speer's head of ministerial finance, was state secretary in the West German Ministry of Finance by spring 1959; Hilde saw him too. Adenauer was 'Adèle' and Bretano was 'Brenner' in Speer's letters advising Wolters in summer 1958 on how to organise the campaign for his release and when or where to deploy Hilde. The associated press campaign had produced large articles in mass-circulation illustrated weeklies such as *Stern* and *Quick* earlier in the year; as a result, Speer received some 300 birthday cards. He wanted Hilde to tackle Franz Josef Strauss, right-wing leader of the Christian Social Union, the Bavarian sister-party of Adenauer's Christian Democrats. All these leading German politicians favoured the release of the Spandau Three; some said so in public.

Speer's manipulative outpourings from prison almost reached fever pitch as he sought to mobilise every conceivable source of support and sympathy in aid of his new appeal to all four powers with a say over Spandau. There was a German countess with British connections, one of whom knew Lord Kilmuir (the ennobled Sir David Maxwell-Fyfe of the British prosecution at Nuremberg). Speer made an interesting mistake about him: 'If it is possible, it would be best if this [British contact] were to speak with Lord Kilmour [*sic*], who, *although Jewish* [author's italics], showed sympathy for my attitude at Nuremberg.' Lord Kilmuir was not Jewish, but, like several other British politicians approached by Hilde towards the end of 1959, was indeed sympathetic. Even the Prime Minister, Harold Macmillan, sent her a warm letter, a fact Speer found amazing; it was however a substitute for action by a consummate politician. She also won over 'Cassandra' (Bill Connor), the respected columnist in the Socialist *Daily Mirror*, then enjoying Britain's largest daily circulation. Small wonder that Wolters wrote admiringly of Hilde in September 1958, his first letter since Proost's departure at the end of the previous year: 'She is the best horse in the stable.'

Wolters told Speer he had offered Schütz, now a Bonn cabinet minister, 3,000 marks 'in his hand' as soon as he was able to report he had seen Adenauer about Speer's case (handing German politicians bundles of 1,000-mark notes in brown envelopes was obviously already in vogue, although the practice seems to have peaked in the 1970s). Schütz refused (but did not break off relations), which meant the money could be diverted to Hilde for expenses and equipment such as tape-recorder, typewriter and telephone. The school fund was in healthy condition with a balance of 5,500 marks and 335 marks coming in monthly.

Hilde's efforts at lobbying in France, a much tougher proposition than America or Britain in this regard, at least produced news from reliable sources that Charles de Gaulle, just restored to power after thirteen years in the political wilderness, also thought that Spandau should be closed and its three remaining prisoners released. Speer advised Hilde against undertaking a lobbying trip to Moscow. Wolters thought her 'a first-class actress with great charm' and in 1960 he advised Speer to allow her to take a semester or two off so as to be free to devote herself full-time to the campaign. Speer rejected this idea (neither correspondent thought of consulting Hilde, now in her twenty-fourth year) and asked Wolters to advise her not to overdo her efforts. The climate for campaigning on such an issue ceased to be favourable when Adolf Eichmann was on trial in Israel in August. Besides, Hilde had met a student of German language and literature called Ulf Schramm at Tübingen and was in love.

The high-profile campaign for remission faded away with 1960; Bonn was losing interest and East–West relations were not propitious for any kind of four-power agreement. Hilde moved to Bonn University for the new semester in March 1960, useful for keeping in touch with the West German political establishment as and when it seemed appropriate; she continued to lobby for her father whenever an opportunity presented itself. Her eldest brother, Albert Junior, graduated with his father's qualification, a Diploma in Engineering for architecture, in November 1960. Hilde had got engaged in July 1961 (by which time Speer's walk round the world had brought him to 'Siberia') and married her Ulf in August (they eventually had two children), but carried on studying: she was awarded her Dr Phil in 1965. Ulf good-naturedly became a frequent correspondent with his father-in-law, who much admired his precocious wisdom.[6]

Any lingering hopes of a four-power consensus on closing Spandau were dashed in August 1961, when the East German regime, backed by the Russians, put up the Berlin Wall overnight as a desperate measure against the flood of illicit westward migration. The tension in the city, the worst since the war, was palpable inside the prison. Speer sank into another depression as the internal regime was tightened after a long period of laissez-faire; the Spandau Three were given a detailed programme of tedious household chores which for Speer meant less time for gardening and circumambulating the globe in his head. But the strict programme, instituted with rare accord by new American and Soviet governors, began to erode within weeks. Correspondence between Uncle Alex and his friend in 'Coburg' slackened in the latter part of 1961 because Wolters was suffering from hypertension and had to take a *Kur*, while the unfortunate 'translator' Marion Riesser, went into hospital with a duodenal ulcer.

There is no evidence to support such a theory, but the shared stress thus graphically illustrated is surely more likely than not to have been the result, at least in part, of the huge amount of voluntary extra work the pair were doing for Speer. Wolters's wife complained that he had been neglecting his own son and daughter (and herself) while devoting far too much time, effort and money to Speer's affairs and those of his wife and children. Fritz, whom Wolters regarded as the most mature of the Speer children, stayed for ten days at the end of summer; Margret also came for a few days (she was to marry in March 1962). Meanwhile Speer wrote in August to say that he had spent just three hours out of doors in the preceding eight months; this can hardly have been true as his walk round the world was still progressing, albeit for some time at a reduced rate of an average three kilometres a day: he could hardly have done this in his cell or the prison corridor.

By now Speer had served three-quarters of his sentence. The volume of diary output had slowed down and the pace of activity on his private network was also much gentler. The year 1962 produced little of recorded interest. On 28 January Speer confided a brief 'profession of faith' to his diary: 'I believe in a divine providence; I also believe in the wisdom and goodness of God; I trust in his ways ... It is not the powerful of the earth who decide the course of history. They think they are movers and they are moved.' It is an isolated entry with no clue as to what prompted it.

Later in the year Speer had a dream, of interest only because it was analysed by Professor Erich Fromm, the renowned German-American psychologist, co-originator of the theory of the authoritarian personality and analyst of nihilistic brutality. On 13 September Speer dreamed of himself sweeping up a factory before Hitler was due to inspect it. Afterwards he could not get his arm back into his sleeve while being transported in a car to a square with a memorial, where Hitler laid a wreath; then Hitler entered a grand building full of memorial plaques and laid an endless series of wreaths, emitting a sound like Gregorian chant the while. All this, said Fromm, showed Speer recognised Hitler as 'necrophilous', in love with death.[7] Speer ventured no self-analysis but let the dream speak for itself. The two men got to know each other after Speer's release.

The outside world intruded rudely again in October 1962, when world peace was threatened by the Cuba missile crisis and President John F. Kennedy, soon to visit beleaguered West Berlin, faced down Krushchev and Castro. Tension inside Spandau reflected the confrontation going on outside, in which Germany could have become a battleground for the assembled armies of East and West with their nuclear weaponry. 'The monotony of the past few weeks has been erased.' Speer's spirits sank even further when nineteen-year-old Ernst paid another of his grunt-filled, arm's-length visits; and briefly soared with the news the next day, 3 November, that Hilde had been to see Willy Brandt, who promised to work for an early release for her father. The appointment was of course arranged well in advance; its timing could hardly have been worse, given that nothing could be achieved without Soviet consent, and Moscow's policy remained that the prisoners must serve every minute of their sentences. It was a Soviet month at Spandau, and the Russians made life hard for the prisoners.

In May 1963, Speer gave up smoking; and in August, thanks to Margret, he became a grandfather; in October he learned that Wolf Jobst Siedler, distinguished director of the Ullstein publishing house and head of its Propyläen imprint (Berlin and Frankfurt), wanted to publish his memoirs after his release. Speer had this project very much in mind all year, as is shown by a note he wrote with his fountain-pen on a slip of light blue airmail paper on 6 March 1963. It states, first, that Hilde Speer alone, referred to in the third person, had the right to decide when, where, by whom, for how much and in what form his memoirs would be published at home and abroad. 'She is authorised to make any alteration she thinks is right.' Secondly, ten per cent of the advance was to be devoted to financing the preparation of the manuscript for publication. Third, from the balance, twenty per cent was to be divided between 'To and Mo' or their families (the Dutch and American messengers), in accordance with the proportion of the draft they smuggled out of the prison and delivered (Irmgard Proost would eventually benefit from this provision).

The note bears the date but no addressee, not even a 'to whom it may concern' line. The original and photocopies of it crop up in various places in the Wolters Bequest.[8] No wonder; it ran directly counter to Speer's letter from Nuremberg of 10 August 1946, appointing Wolters as his literary agent and executor. Here, as will be seen in the next chapter, was another seed of conflict between Speer and his true friend: time-bomb is not too strong a metaphor.

But more than a year and a half later (28 October 1964) Speer was writing to Wolters as if nothing had happened, setting out his latest thinking on the main segments of his book: his time as defendant and prisoner; armaments; architecture; documentation based on the Chronicle and record of Hitler conferences; discussion of the literature on the Third Reich; and his 'windows' thesis material. There would be no 'Persil' (i.e. whitewash; contemporary Germans referred to a denazification certificate as a *Persilschein*, a Persil pass). 'I am determined to make no money out of it as it would be a case of "dirty

money",' Speer wrote. There was no mention of Hilde, and the tone of
the letter is manifestly in keeping with the 'author–agent' relationship
Speer assigned to Wolters in 1946.

He made a point of saying, when he referred to his intention of
making use of the Chronicle as a source, that this would be done 'with
the compiler's suppression guaranteed'.[9] This prompted Wolters to dig
out the Chronicle from his voluminous archive, make a series of
deletions and have the hardworking Marion Riesser retype the entire
document thus sanitised. As Wolters recalled in 1980:

> In 1964, two years before Speer's return from Spandau, I read the
> Chronicle through again and decided on that occasion that it was
> necessary to retype the entire text, to remove grammatical and stylistic
> errors, to leave out a few unimportant and silly things, *but above all to
> delete certain parts on the basis of which Speer and one or another of his
> colleagues could have been prosecuted* [author's italics]. For the [West
> German] Ludwigsburg Central Office for 'war crimes' was still at work
> and an end of the persecution of National Socialists was not in sight.[10]

It will be necessary to return to this confession in later pages. But
before that, two other literary phenomena require attention. The first
is the doctoral thesis of Gregor Janssen, a student of the historian
Professor Walter Hubatsch of Bonn University. Through Schütz, who
knew Hubatsch, and Wolters, this thesis actually found its way to
Speer in Spandau some time in 1963 and, according to Wolters, was
'corrected at first hand', which can only mean by Speer (who later
remarked that it had been full of inaccuracies and preserved his notes
on it). The thesis became the basis of Dr Janssen's very useful published
book on the Speer ministry (see Bibliography) and is mentioned here
as the earliest example of Speer's manipulative readiness to assist, if
not steer, all those who approached him with intent to write about
him (which is not to say that they all, or always, fell for it). Discreetly,
Janssen's book, published by Ullstein in 1968, acknowledges the receipt
of 'written material' from Speer, among others.

But in his long letter to Wolters of 28 October 1964, cited above,
Speer also warns him off showing his draft memoirs to Hubatsch or
anyone else, for fear of a leak. In a rare display of displeasure with
his long-suffering correspondent, Speer expressed his annoyance that
Wolters had been discussing the memoirs project with Schütz, Hubatsch
and Janssen, as well as sounding out a publisher. On the advice of
Hilde, who had been in touch with Siedler in 1963 (presumably the
contact that prompted the note making her his literary agent), Speer
had already more or less made up his mind to do a deal with Ullstein-
Propyläen. Although he was ready to consider Hubatsch as his political

adviser after he left prison, he did not want anyone unnecessarily involved at this stage, when he had to act through intermediaries; as his release drew nearer, he also became more and more nervous of being caught by the prison staff with contraband correspondence.

The other literary matter that worried Speer as he prepared himself for release was raised in a letter from Wolters dated 17 February 1966, accompanied by photocopies of extracts from a new book. With his literary ambitions very much in mind, Speer had been keeping an eye on relevant publications, especially the recollections of his former fellow-inmates such as Raeder and Dönitz, whose respective memoirs he disparaged. But this latest book, on Hitler's 'miracle' weapons, was by an Englishman, even though he had written and published it exclusively in German. The author was David Irving, a highly contentious historian of the Third Reich and a man of marked, right-wing views who made his name as a revisionist, challenging the generally accepted quantification, as well as Hitler's knowledge, of the Nazis' crimes against humanity. Even Irving's most hostile critics, however, acknowledge his outstanding prowess and diligence as a researcher. His views undoubtedly made him a writer very much after Wolters's own heart (they corresponded cordially in later years). Speer's reaction on 8 March was anxious: ' "Miracle Weapons" extracts significant. Apparently there is still a copy of your Chronicle somewhere, as he quotes from it?? Can you ... check in the index? A copy of the literature named there, insofar as drawing on us, would interest me.'

Wolters replied on 1 April 1966:

> There is no index in Irving ... The Chronicle still exists from the time of the GBI in one further copy with Dr Lotz [a former colleague], who could never be persuaded to search it out again. Nowhere has it been cited as such, [or] as a named source. I assume that the Chronicle used in Irving could in certain circumstances be the Chronicle-material of Dr Goerner, which he willingly or unwillingly gave to the Americans.

Dr Goerner, another former colleague, had consistently been an important source of departmental information for the Chronicle, supplying Wolters regularly with his notes. He was even named in it as having stood in for Wolters in writing one monthly part: the document includes a note that the Chronicle for September 1943 had to be rewritten largely from memory by Goerner because the ministry's office at number 11 Viktoriastrasse in Berlin was destroyed by bombing on 22 November 1943.

Speer replied to Wolters on 10 April 1966: 'It is probably a case of Goerner's notes in Irving. One must track down more closely where they got to. I could have made very good use of them at Nuremberg!

Perhaps there is also a lot in them that would only have the effect today of spoiling [my case in] 1946?'

Wolters ended the exchange on 1 May by writing that he had 'never heard anything of Lotz. No idea if he is still alive.' With that, for the time being, both men let the matter drop.[11] Irving's discovery and legitimate citation of at least part of the Chronicle evoked no known comment or reaction anywhere other than at Spandau and Coesfeld. This gratifying silence must have made Speer over-confident, because less than four years later he made a mistake which almost ruined his reputation in his lifetime as an unimpeachable authority and unique source on the Nazi leadership and war economy – and destroys his claim to have repented.

That shock will be examined in due course, but the reader will have noted here that: Speer appointed Hilde over Wolters's head as his literary agent in March 1963; Speer told Wolters he had chosen a publisher for his memoirs in October 1964; Wolters was therefore prompted to 'clean up' the Chronicle in 1964; and both men knew early in 1966 that the secret of the Chronicle's existence had been laid bare because David Irving had quoted from its 1943 section. All these facts are confirmed beyond argument by documents in the Wolters Bequest to the German Archive. What the Bequest does *not* specifically tell us, however, is whether Speer told Wolters of the decision to supplant him as literary agent at the time he appointed Hilde; or whether Wolters told Speer of his cleansing of the Chronicle at the time he did it. But we are entitled to deduce that neither was the case, because Wolters did not comment when Speer continued to write to him as if he were still literary agent in 1964 and later; and Wolters, while not recording that he had told Speer of the clean-up when he did it in 1964, did note that he had reported it when he handed over *the rewritten version* to the released prisoner in October 1966.

It is as clear from Speer's diaries, whether unedited or in book form, as it is from the Wolters documentation that in the first nine months of 1966 he was obsessed with the prospect of his release at the stroke of midnight on the night of 30 September to 1 October; he had never been so obsessed since he thought he was going to hang twenty years before. He drove his network and his family to distraction with his stream of letters, redolent as they were of requests, attacks of panic, arrangements and rearrangements and his general absorption in himself down to the tiniest matters of detail. This is entirely under-standable: anyone, introverted, egotistical, 'control-freak' or not, was bound to be in a highly charged emotional state when facing the prospect of release into a dramatically transformed world at the age of sixty-one from a period of unremitting and unremitted incarceration begun at forty. He had suffered panic attacks after his sixtieth birthday in 1965, seeing himself almost as a broken old man; the demolition of what was left of his Chancellery building by the East Germans in July 1965 depressed him too. The only extant, physical manifestations of his work as an architect were now a row of lamp-posts on a West Berlin street and a couple of houses designed for an American sergeant and a US commandant, Colonel Eugene Bird. But on his release he was in remarkably good condition, with no sign of the knee and lung weaknesses which had prostrated him in three earlier crises. His main problem was anxiety.

Speer had given up on the idea of returning to architecture. Not only was he out of touch, but also the two former colleagues who had promised him work on his release, Otto Apel and Karl Piepenburg, had both died early in 1966; furthermore, in the preceding December Dipl. Ing. Albert Speer (Junior) had won a major architectural prize. Speer Senior rationalised his eventual decision to shy away from trying to re-establish himself as an architect by asserting that he did not want to spoil things for his son. Whatever the underlying reason, it was a wise decision.

The alternative was writing, and the signs were that it would be very lucrative. In July 1966 Wolters, still acting as literary representative, engaged a willing Professor Hubatsch as an adviser on Speer's memoirs and the editorial offers already pouring in. Journalistic cheque books were being waved from several quarters and a total well into six figures was on the table months before the doors of Spandau were due to creak open. *Der Spiegel*, the Hamburg news weekly, offered 50,000 marks for an exclusive first interview. It was not the highest bid, but Speer accepted it because the magazine was Germany's most influential medium for news (as distinct from opinion). Werner Schütz agreed to provide legal and political advice to Speer at Wolters's request. Speer meanwhile had an attack of nerves and stopped all incoming and outgoing illicit correspondence for fear of being caught at the last minute; the *Kassiber* blackout lasted from 1 June to 22 July.

On 1 September Gretel wrote to Wolters to report that she had found a secluded house to rent by the Kellersee in 'Holstein's Switzerland', the lakeland area of eastern Schleswig-Holstein to which Speer had planned to withdraw in April 1945 and where he sent his family at that time (Annemarie Kempf and later the Proosts had also taken refuge in this remote corner of Germany, where Eutin is the main centre of population).

As Wolters staged a final whip-round among the faithful supporters of the school fund in September, the two partners in a unique pen-friendship exchanged their last secret letters. On 2 August Wolters received congratulations for his sixty-fourth birthday in a telegram signed Alex. Speer was still 'walking round the world', abandoning the exercise only on 18 September, when he reckoned he had put 31,816 kilometres (just over three-quarters of the earth's circumference) behind him.

On 6 September, in his last letter to Spandau, Wolters suggested putting up fifteen of Speer's former architectural colleagues and financial supporters at a plush hotel near his home in Coesfeld so that they could be on hand for a 'welcome back' reception at his house. Speer replied in his last *Kassiber* to Wolters on 27 September with his programme, about which he had been in feverish correspondence separately with his family. He would give a short radio press conference (he had heard on his transistor radio that the reporters were already outside the jail with offers totalling 300,000 marks) and then be driven in a Mercedes-Benz with Gretel to a hotel in the wooded West Berlin suburb of Grunewald for one night. He would telephone Coesfeld as soon as he could that night. Then he would spend two weeks in the north with his wife and children – his 'quarantine' period, during which, however, he would telephone Wolters. After his first free fortnight he would visit Coesfeld. And so it was.

The prison routine of Spandau was no different on 30 September 1966 from the general pattern established over well nigh two decades. Speer, like Schirach who, also time-expired, would be leaving the jail a few seconds after him, took his leave of the forlorn Hess (he would stay on alone for an incredible twenty-one further years, the single pea in the fortified drum of Spandau, still solemnly guarded by the troops of four major armies in the bathetic farce which ended the process begun at Nuremberg forty-two years before).

A guard brought Speer the unlikely (but true) news that Willy Brandt had sent his daughter Hilde, long since resident in West Berlin, a congratulatory bunch of carnations on the eve of her father's release. Since the governing mayor was then in the throes of a federal election as a candidate for Chancellor, this was a remarkable gesture to a Nazi war-criminal's daughter (his wife would have been only a slightly less controversial choice) by a Social Democrat who had fled Hitler's Germany to escape persecution. It was not so much magnanimous as indiscreet; Brandt could never resist a pretty woman and had obviously never forgotten Hilde's ambassadorial appeal of a few years earlier. The real long-term benefit to Speer himself was that Brandt, who became Vice-Chancellor and Foreign Minister in Dr Kurt-Georg Kiesinger's Christian Democrat-led 'Grand Coalition' government, finally called a halt to the denazification proceedings that had hung over Speer for so long. No wonder that he voted SPD after his release.

A stilted farewell to the four governors and a brief encounter with Dr Flächsner and Gretel by the exit, whereupon all three got into a black Mercedes, were followed by the opening of the double gate at the stroke of midnight – and an electrical storm of television lights and photographic flashbulbs.

At 9.15 p.m. on the evening of 30 September 1966 an overnight-rate telegram was handed in at the post office at Tegel airport in the French sector of West Berlin – the last hurrah of a remarkably efficient, clandestine postal service. Addressed to 'Wolters, Beguinenstrasse 14, 4420 Coesfeld', it was received at Coesfeld post office at 6.56 a.m. on 1 October and passed on to the addressee by telephone at 7.03. The text read: 'Please collect me 35 km southward Guadalajara Mexico. Uncle Alex.' It was not a bad joke after twenty years.

Memoirs

(1966–70)

THE LAST WORD FROM SPANDAU reached Dr Rudolf Wolters after the first contact from the freed prisoner number five – the promised telephone call from Speer's Berlin hotel, at about 1 a.m. on 1 October 1966. But instead of bringing the long-anticipated joy to the released man's steadfast confidential agent, it managed to convey a brutal impression of what the long relationship really meant to its beneficiary. Speer made a series of calls that night, of which the one to Coesfeld was not the first. He coolly told Wolters that he had invited Ernst-Wolf Mommsen, the Düsseldorf industrialist who had been a member of Speer's wartime 'kindergarten' as well as a major fund-raiser and contributor to the school account, to join them at Wolters's house in Coesfeld – on 14 October, the very day he was due to arrive there after the protracted agony of the family reunion in Holstein.

It was an extraordinary tactless and unfeeling thing to do, even for a man looking forward to being the centre of attention for a while after twenty-one and a half years in captivity. Mommsen, who had laid on the Mercedes at Spandau, accepted the invitation with proper misgivings, feeling unable to refuse the freed man's first wishes. Wolters was devastated but, as he had done when faced with Speer's repeated disavowals in his writings of their former shared belief in Hitler and his repetitious *nostra culpa* mantra, he bit his lip and yet again let Speer take him for granted.[1] There was more of this to come, making certain that when the worm finally turned in Coesfeld, it would do so with vigour.

Speer had managed to get away with less than ten minutes in front of the press pack awaiting him at the hotel in leafy Grunewald. The clamouring questions were as uninspired as the answers, and before going upstairs to his suite, Speer announced that he hoped to return to his profession of architecture. He and Gretel managed to slip out of Berlin by air to Hamburg and thence to the hideaway for which the press vainly searched in the ensuing days.

A throng of a different sort awaited his arrival at the rented Kellersee holiday home: his six children, the two girls and the four boys, their respective spouses and assorted grandchildren. Everyone worked so hard at being relaxed that the return of the prodigal father – inevitably when its central figure was so lacking in spontaneity and just emerging from two decades of isolation – was thoroughly depressing for all concerned. As was to be the case for all but the last year of his life, Speer was utterly absorbed with himself and his past and took no more than a minimal, polite interest in the affairs of his huge, baffled and instantly alienated family. Henceforward he would walk backwards into the future, his eye unwaveringly fixed on his heyday as Hitler's architect and armourer until the very last.

Annemarie Kempf, whose local knowledge had helped in finding the secret rendezvous, was allowed to visit from Eutin after a few days and saw at once that Speer had changed surprisingly little in the twenty-one years since she had seen him last. She was therefore not at all surprised that the reunion had been a 'fiasco' from which the family never recovered.[2]

Waiting on tenterhooks at Coesfeld, Dr Wolters, ever the connoisseur and bon viveur, went down into his cellar to inspect the bottle of 1937 Fürst Metternich Schloss-Johannisberger Trockenbeerenauslese which he had been saving for the long-awaited reunion, fated in advance to be disappointing not only because of the Mommsen business but also because no such encounter could have lived up to the degree of emotion invested in it, if on one side only, in advance. An equally nervous Marion Riesser went over the bank statements of the school fund and arrived at a credit balance of 26,171 marks and three pfennigs, thanks to the final, pre-release push by Wolters and Mommsen.[3]

The two men, who had last seen each other in spring 1945 and had been in garrulous, written contact for the past fifteen years, kept their autumnal appointment on a Westphalian doorstep in 1966 with studied casualness. 'How goes it? It's been a long time,' said Speer, proffering his hand. As in that more celebrated, long-awaited encounter of the previous century which yielded the immortal banality, 'Dr Livingstone, I presume?', the reply of the man addressed is not recorded. The bottle of Johannisberger, the same vintage they had broached in 1937 on Speer's appointment as Inspector-General of Construction for the Reich Capital, was duly uncorked and savoured. In the same spirit of elaborate sentimentality, Wolters also produced a Westphalian smoked ham, from a pig of his born on the day Stalin died in March 1953, which he had hoped to have slaughtered and cured rather earlier. This too was as promised in a letter to Spandau.

On the first of the four days Speer spent with him, Wolters, 'in the presence of my assistant, Marion Riesser', handed over a tidy accumulation of papers. They included all the original *Kassiber* versions of Speer's *Arias* (memoir drafts), *Späne* (diary notes) and *Fenster* (window-thesis material) plus supplementary writings, together with a set of Riesser's transcriptions, copies of which had already been sent to Frau Kempf and Speer's family.

> As it was known to me that Speer wanted to publish his memoirs, already prepared in Spandau, as a book, after his release from prison at the end of 1966. I gave him the version of my Chronicle cleaned up by me for evaluation. I advised him at the time in summary form of slight alterations to the original version.

Wolters, showing how conscientiously he had carried out Speer's instructions in the latter's letter to him from Nuremburg in August 1946, also handed over copies of Speer's old building plans and Wolters's log of the 'walk round the world', which his livelier imagination had turned into a real cultural adventure for a prisoner pedestrian in every sense. The collection of mementoes also included photographs illicitly taken by Speer with a micro-camera smuggled to him in Spandau. He loaned Speer his file of the 'black' personal correspondence between them. Finally Marion Riesser presented him with a cheque for 25,000 marks against Speer's receipt formally discharging her from responsibility for the school fund (Speer used part of this generous final handout to buy an expensive sports car, raising more money shortly afterwards by selling the site of his Berlin house). The accounts showed that a remarkable total in excess of 158,000 marks had passed through the Volksbank at Coesfeld to the benefit of Speer and his family.[4]

On his last day there, Speer once again revealed his underlying arrogance towards the long-suffering Wolters, that of a master who took as of right from a servant who existed only to give. Having admired his loyal acolyte's modern filing cabinets, each with four drawers containing racks for hanging folders, he asked Wolters if he would kindly order five such for delivery to Heidelberg as soon as possible – not forgetting to ask for a twenty-five per cent discount. Wolters wrote to his supplier in Dortmund to fulfil this casual last request from his departing guest only two days after he had left. But he reflected later: 'I knew on the day of that first reunion, jolly though it was, that the Spandau friendship was over. As he stood there in person, in my mind I suddenly saw him quite differently from hitherto. It was somewhat like his first sight of Hitler after his long illness...'[5]

Like master, like servant. As Speer had been and become to Hitler in 1944, so Wolters had been and now became to Speer in 1966: the once purblind loyalist at the giving end of a one-way friendship who succumbed to bitter disillusion on reunion after a long parting. Had Speer ever had close friends, Wolters would surely have been one of them; Speer had now proved himself to be Wolters's unrequited love, although such cruel and thoughtless disregard would not lead to the final repudiation for another five years. It was all the worse when it came. Even so, Wolters could not allow a night to pass after his metaphorical 'father' had left before dictating to Marion a circular to outlying members of the network that had sustained Speer in Spandau.

Speer next went to Ratingen in the Ruhr for a brief call on Dr Walter Rohland, his wartime tank supremo, who wrote shortly afterwards to Wolters: 'I often had the feeling [during the visit] that it was too much for the homecomer. Nonetheless he survived it all well.' On leaving Rohland on 20 October, Speer posted separate letters to Wolters and his wife to thank them for their hospitality: the days in Coesfeld had been 'unforgettable' and 'wonderfully harmonious', he told Erika Wolters – a lovely start to real life after the exclusively familial days in Holstein. From Ratingen he went south, to the family home at Schloss-Wolfsbrunnenweg in Heidelberg.

Once installed there on the hillside overlooking Germany's beautiful intellectual capital, he lost no time in opening what was to become a vast correspondence with the outside world that turned almost nobody away. Having preserved his sanity and his brainpower by reading and writing in prison and having so notably failed to tune in to his family afterwards, Speer henceforward lived for and through his writing, whether as author or as indefatigable correspondent with all and sundry. One of the first addressees was Wolf-Jobst Siedler, his chosen publisher, suggesting a visit to Berlin to organise the commissioning of his memoirs. Siedler offered to come to Heidelberg but Speer insisted on returning to Berlin, before the end of the month in whose first minutes he had departed from Spandau.

Siedler, just turned forty and a power in the land of German publishing when Speer came out, told me he had been looking forward to the meeting since 1964, when he had met Hilde over lunch at a smart West Berlin restaurant after writing to her father via her mother early in 1963 to express his interest in Speer's memoirs. 'I had no sympathy for his past – I was "inside" under the Nazis. But I did feel some sympathy for him as a person and for his plight, as well as for his closing speech at Nuremberg.' Siedler was also intrigued by the central question about Speer: how someone with his background and gifts could have 'joined up with those crooks'.

Having heard from Hilde that a couple of dozen publishers had been in touch, including some of the mightiest in America and Britain,

Siedler wrote to Speer a second time just before his release, explaining that he was not interested in a mere personal apologia or in an auction for the book, which he proposed to bring out under Ullstein's artistic imprint, Propyläen. 'He insisted on coming to me, saying in his patrician, old-fashioned way that he had always understood a would-be author should call on a publisher and not the other way round. When we met, I addressed him as Herr Professor Speer and he corrected me, saying he had long since renounced the title bestowed on him by Hitler.'

Author-to-be and publisher conferred over lunch at the same exclusive restaurant. The talks went so well that Siedler had the draft contract brought to him at table, rather than escorting his guest back to the office. A modest advance was agreed, to tide Speer over while he did the writing. Royalties for the hardback were to be ten per cent for the first 50,000, eleven up to 100,000 and twelve up to 200,000 (this was not over-optimistic, far from it). Speer took everything on trust. Siedler was stunned when he suggested Speer should go to a quiet hotel, perhaps in Switzerland, to start work, only to be told that '10,000 pages' of notes already existed for Speer to draw upon.

Siedler also proposed enlisting Joachim Fest, journalist and author of *The Face of the Third Reich*, a highly perceptive analysis of archetypal Nazis (including Speer himself) published in 1963, as historical consultant and editorial adviser. *Lektor* was the word Siedler chose for Fest's role – publisher's reader and/or editor. Thus was established what Wolters later referred to by the Russian word *troika*, a span of three horses, author-publisher-editor, in which Speer was the 'shaft-horse'. They worked and reworked Speer's mass of raw material at intense sessions in out-of-the-way meeting-places in Switzerland, Italy, France and Bavaria. Speer would bring his draft material, listen to the advice he received and return to Heidelberg. 'Fest and I were the midwives,' said Siedler. The resulting memoirs appeared inside three years, in 1969; the same triumvirate worked on the follow-up volume, based on Speer's Spandau diaries, which appeared six years later.

The two midwives had to put in some hard work. Speer had devoted just one page to his farewell to Hitler on 23 April 1945, which Siedler reasonably felt to be totally inadequate coverage of a scene in which the author was taking leave of the man who had raised him to such a height and provided him with the greatest days of his life. 'I thought it had to be the most dramatic scene in the whole book.' The midwives developed a Socratic technique of endless questioning designed to draw out of Speer knowledge he did not realise he possessed. Siedler advised him against 'condemning himself every ten pages or so; two or three times in the book would be enough.' Ironically, it was the American publishers, Macmillan of New York, who demanded and got an extra leavening of such self-inculpations scattered throughout the book. The effect is false and unctuous.

Fest, whose greatest work, his biography of Hitler (still unsurpassed by any German) would appear in 1973, told me that his 'main job was to cut. I did it by marking the first draft, underlining the essential, putting a dotted line under the less important and leaving the dross unmarked.' The first typed manuscript ran to something between 1,600 and 1,800 pages, the second to 1,200 and the third to 700. 'Then I started editing and cleaning up the German. I suggested additions as well, such as *Reichskristallnacht*, which he had completely omitted, and lots of others.' Fest was bemused at the time by the fact that Speer apparently attached no importance to the 1938 pogrom, whose epicentre was Berlin where he had been at the time. Small wonder that the inserted passage, despite Fest's best advice, rings completely false: the author was patently uninterested and was paying lip-service when he included it. Hindsight enables us to recognise a clear symptom of psychological denial: Speer consciously suppressed, as has been made clear in this book, his eviction of Jews from Berlin, and in the light of that, it seems natural that he would instinctively pass over one of the main pointers to the escalating persecution in which he played a key early role.

Herr Fest, going further than Sebastian Haffner's *Observer* article of April 1944, had presented Speer as the quintessential 'amoral technocrat' in his thoughtful if slightly indulgent portrait of 1963. Recalling Speer as author thirty years later for my benefit, Fest said: 'He could not write as such, but he could produce a report with all the important facts in it. That he did very well. He was able to supply his thoughts when asked, and then it was very satisfactory, with a little editing. I had to ask him many times to write more about the genocide of the Jews. I think he had closed his mind to it. I told him many times that he had to say something or say more or say what he had thought, or, if he had not thought about it at the time, to say so.'

In the course of a long discussion of Speer, Fest spontaneously remembered his personal charm. 'He really was charming and also shy, or personally timid. I think he charmed Hitler too, although he had to pay a high price for it.' Speer had been, said Fest, using the English phrase, 'everybody's darling'. He had endured the entire Third Reich phenomenon, 'and all those crooks, untouched. But he was an artist, and artists incline towards anyone who enables them to practise their art. Hitler's offer was irresistible to the young architect. In that sense artists are predisposed to corruption. But Speer's life never recovered from the path he took in his late twenties. He never shed the burden of his past and I found there was always an air of melancholy about him.'

Speer's daughter, Dr Hilde Schramm, thought that both Siedler and Fest had exaggerated their role in preparing her father's memoirs for publication: 'He did all the hard work,' she told me. He had asked her to comment on early draft sections but she had been reluctant and did not help much. 'He would have liked me to carry on, but I didn't. I had my own life to lead,' she said. Herr Fest thought Hilde the strongest and least repressed of the Speer children but took the view that she had gone into radical politics (she won a seat on the 'Alternative List', allied to the Greens, in two successive elections for the West Berlin state legislature) by way of 'atonement' for her father. Had I been able to put this theory to her, I am sure she would have exploded; but she made it clear to me that a second interview on the subject of her father was not on offer (the first was no great shakes). That she underestimated the importance of Fest and Siedler to the success of Speer's published memoirs and diaries is shown by the miserable quality of his third book, on the SS economic empire (although Gitta Sereny will be seen to have another theory for its manifest inferiority). Hilde's protestation to me that it was written for the expert rather than the general reader does not alter the fact that *Infiltration* (the tome's unilluminating American title; the German, *Der Sklavenstaat*, and the British, *The Slave State*, is more transparent) comes across as unreadable.

We shall return to that last book at the proper time, but we should not leave the subject of Fest's unquestionably crucial role as Speer's editorial adviser from 1966 to 1975 without recording one other important view. Fest, for many years a senior editor on the arch-conservative *Frankfurter Allgemeine Zeitung*, is a humane liberal in matters of culture and history; his assessment of Speer, unchanged since 1963, is fair, thoughtful and even judiciously sympathetic. Wolters however was scathing about his influence: Speer, so far from availing himself of the advice of the 'best friend' to whom he was originally going to dedicate his book, 'subjected himself to the probing questions of Herr Fest, the representative of currently fashionable published opinion'.

The memoirs he had read piecemeal as they came out of Spandau had contained positive as well as negative points about the Hitler period; 'post Festum', all the positive judgments had been qualified by a 'yes, but ...' Wolters clearly relished the pun on the legal expression *post factum*, for in the long 1971 letter to Hermann Giesler, Speer's former architectural rival, from which the above passage comes, he uses it more than once:[6] the *Arias* had set out Speer's 'responsibility' for the Nazi past but, post Festum, the memoirs spoke of 'guilt' (as we have seen, not only had this overly repetitive breastbeating been injected at the behest of Speer's New York publisher rather than Fest;

but also it was Wolters's unshakable view that Speer had nothing to plead guilty about in the first place).

Speer 'came out' as an authoritative inside source, if not yet as a writer, on the inner life of Hitler's court and the governance of the Third Reich on 14 November 1966, six weeks after his release, in the Hamburg news weekly, *Der Spiegel*, which thereby enabled him to lay the foundations of his future role as leading German guru on the Nazi era. The paper is Germany's answer to the American *Time* magazine: where the US periodical has a red rim round its cover, the German favours orange. There is also little to choose between them when it comes to self-importance. The Hamburg paper has its own German dialect, convoluted, self-consciously trendy, staccato and nearly as smug as *The Economist* is in English. It goes in for all-knowing, fly-on-the-wall reporting of major events, has a huge staff and editorial budget and serves up a strong diet of scoops and old-fashioned, fearless, investigative journalism – virtues which, it must be said, far outweigh its weaknesses. Weekly magazines are much more important to news and current-affairs coverage in Germany than in Britain because the former has only a minimal Sunday press. *Der Spiegel* can and does rock governments, often making news in reporting it.

But its sensational, because (but only because) exclusive, interview with newly released Nazi war criminal Albert Speer, sixty-one, was a classic *Spiegel* combination of journalistic 'cop-out' and media arrogance. It was done at the Heidelberg house in the presence of a large tape-recorder, and took the form of a still typical *Spiegel–Gespräch* (interview), a very long, exhaustive and exhausting, question-and-answer article running to eighteen columns of text. This is to journalism as the laundry list is to poetry: it absolves the reporter from such tedious chores as sorting the wheat from the chaff, choosing the most enlightening presentation for the reader or adding significant items of background information, mood, tone, body-language and atmosphere. This important material is consigned to a short 'sidebar' report. All the 'reporter' needs to do with a 'Q & A' is to transcribe the tape, cutting out repetitions, sloppy syntax and unfinished sentences; all the editor needs to do is check the punctuation and spelling. The reporters (there are usually at least two present, collectively styled 'Spiegel' at the beginning of each question) can conveniently present themselves as having made all the right points but take no responsibility for evasive or misleading answers – even when they know the interviewee is not telling or facing the truth, a fact of which this format does not permit them to remind the inexpert reader. And having thus opted out, they invariably end every such exercise by awarding themselves the last word, with the infuriating formula, 'Herr Speer, we thank you for this interview.'

The sensation, worth every pfennig of 50,000 marks to the magazine in impact and free publicity from 'playbacks' round the world, lay in the fact rather than the content of the interview, which was thoroughly pedestrian, in keeping with the character of the subject. The most remarkable fact about it, viewed from three decades later, is how consistent it turned out to be, not only with Speer's defence at Nuremberg but also with everything he was to write, say in public and publish later.

Wolters read the article and chided Speer in a letter dated 30 November. He had fallen in with the *Spiegel* journalists' agenda, as revealed by their questions, and had provided answers exactly in line with current West German teaching on the Third Reich, Wolters complained. To blame Hitler, rather than Germany, for the war was to be wrong twice over, he wrote, partly because Germany had been behind him and partly because others, such as the Poles for provocation and the British for turning the invasion of Poland into a world conflict, had also been responsible. So were the Russians and the Americans, because the roots of the conflict went back well beyond Versailles to the nineteenth century. Wolters urged Speer to 'concentrate wholly on what really happened, leaving aside what the world thinks of it now'.

Leaving aside the overriding motive of self-preservation, the declared purpose behind Speer's acceptance of collective responsibility at Nuremberg was to shield the German people from the burden of guilt for Hitler. Wolters noted bitterly in this letter that Hitler had indeed been categorised as the devil – 'the basis of [West German] foreign policy' – and those who worked for him had been demonised as 'the devil's generals, the devil's doctors, the devil's architects etc'; but devil and under-devils were still German, a fact which led the victors to blame all Germans for Hitler. As a double generalisation, whether applied to the Germans or the victors or both, this is undeniably true. Wolters ended by expressing the hope that Speer's published memoirs would provide 'a truer and broader picture of the past' – but the reader senses that Wolters knew already they would do no such thing.[7]

Speer did not reply but continued to make use of Wolters during the period he was working up his memoirs into a book. He was back in Coesfeld briefly in January 1967, when Wolters, *inter alia*, laid on a reunion with Manfred von Poser, Speer's much appreciated liaison officer at the end of the war; he also got an introduction to some friends of Wolters in Portugal, where he was able to stay and work for a period.

In 1968 Gregor Janssen's book derived from his doctoral thesis, for a special printing of which Wolters had paid 500 marks in 1968, duly appeared. 'The Speer Ministry: Germany's Armament in the War', though never translated into English, remains the most thorough, published exploration of his period in charge of the German war economy and an indispensable source, more so than Zilbert's 1981 effort (see Bibliography). It was not a runaway bestseller, far from it; but it was a useful forerunner for Speer's own *Erinnerungen* (memoirs), which appeared in West Germany in September 1969.

An early sign of their staggering potential was a payment of 680,000 marks from *Die Welt*, the traditionally loss-making flagship of the Springer press empire, for serialisation. The timing was fortuitously well-nigh perfect. West Germany was in the throes of the election campaign which put an end to the series of right-of-centre governments led by the Christian Democrats for the first twenty years of German postwar democracy: Willy Brandt became Germany's first postwar Social Democrat Chancellor on 21 October. There had been a long series of major Nazi trials (they would continue for some years yet) in West Germany, where the wartime generation was going into retirement and its children were coming into their prime, both ready to read what 'really happened' under Hitler a quarter of a century after Germany's darkest hour.

A book, by someone best placed to know what really took place, which blamed Hitler and his leading henchmen (including the author) for Germany's shameful past and defeat was almost cathartic for many readers, and sales in Germany eventually approached the million mark. But for many older, more conservative readers Speer's memoirs were a double betrayal: of Hitler by his erstwhile favourite, and of themselves as loyal Germans, who were now being told by a German who had been at the heart of events that they had obeyed the orders of a criminal. Such people were to go to their graves believing that those few Germans who opposed Hitler before his death and those many who bad-mouthed him afterwards were traitors. The man who now became Chancellor, Willy Brandt, was particularly hated by such people; the intensity of this feeling was illustrated by a catcall from a right-ring deputy in the Bundestag, addressing Brandt as 'Herr Major' – a reference to the fact that he had returned from twelve years of political exile in the uniform of a Norwegian army major, to cover the Nuremberg trials for the Oslo press.

Speer's wartime associates were alienated in large measure, though Wolters doggedly kept up the connection (by this time it could hardly be described as a friendship any more) for a while yet. On receipt of a note from Gretel in November 1969 that Speer wanted to drop in at Coesfeld again in a few days, Wolters hurriedly completed a critique of the memoirs he had been working on and sent it to Heidelberg on the 14th with a covering note, both wry and sad, saying that if Speer now found he had a previous engagement and would be unable to come, Wolters would understand; but he would be happy to receive Speer on *Buss-und-Bettag* (a pointed reference to German Protestants' Day of Penance and Prayer on 19 November). The critique elaborates on Wolters's objections to the 1966 *Spiegel* interview. His respect, obviously reluctant, for Speer's readiness to admit guilt, not just responsibility as at Nuremberg, in his book and on television after its publication did not, Wolters wrote, affect his profound disagreement with the position thus adopted by his friend of forty years' standing:

> When one had read your book to the end, one is tempted to the conclusion that the author would henceforward, dressed in a hair-shirt, pass through the land as a preacher, scattering his wealth among the victims of National Socialism, renouncing all vanities and pleasures of life and living off locusts and wild honey. That is obviously not the case.

Wolters accused Speer of sacrificing principle for pragmatism in his memoirs. He had seen it coming in the Spandau correspondence but had suppressed his objections at the time. Now therefore their relations 'were in a fine mess'. The admission by Speer of his own weaknesses, so different from all other German postwar memoirs, was expressly disarming, said Wolters; he came within an ace of accusing Speer of hypocrisy in owning up not only to his own guilt, but also to 'much worse sins of other leaders of the Third Reich', as he had done with almost 'religious fervour' in his television interview.

Said interview was done, cosily one may think, by none other than Joachim Fest, then working as a television presenter. Wolters gave his scathing opinion post Festum in a letter to Annemarie Kempf on 11 November, remarking that Fest had taken Speer through his paces like 'an animal-tamer trained in liberty'. Speer had wildly exaggerated the significance of his rebellious memoranda to Hitler at the end of the war, for example: 'There is surely no doubt that a pragmatist like Albert was building himself up systematically for the postwar period, inter alia. Nobody can persuade me to the contrary; I know him too well for that.'[8]

The nature and content of Speer's memoirs have been summarised piecemeal in previous chapters, so only the briefest description is given here. It is a substantial volume, running to well over 500 pages in both German and English editions and consisting of an uncritical introduction by the American historian, Eugene Davidson, a short foreword in which the author promises to try to be honest, thirty-five digestibly brief chapters and a small afterword containing a few acknowledgments. Speer was well served by his English translators,

Richard and Clara Winston. The notes are commendably short at just over forty pages and the index is notable for giving no reference to any member of Speer's extended family – wife, parents, siblings, children. There are eleven references to 'Jews' and sixteen to 'guilt for Nazi crimes'.

The main weakness of the book is the contradiction between its intimate knowledge of the core of the Nazi regime, including Bormann, the doctors Brandt and Goebbels, Himmler and Hitler himself on the one hand, and the professed ignorance of their most evil crimes on the other. This gap is not covered by the admissions of wilful failure to inquire, or the readiness to accept the principle of the leadership's shared responsibility, *nostra maxima culpa*, or the acceptance after Nuremberg of shared *guilt* for using forced labour. All this should be apparent to the alert reader of the memoirs from internal evidence alone. But the indisputable fact that Speer took pains to conceal his *personal* guilt for the expulsion of Jews from Berlin emerged only after his death, and undermines (at the very least) his claim to ignorance of the regime's principal crimes.

Battalions of distinguished reviewers were recruited in Germany to give their opinions of Speer's memoirs and inevitably of the man himself and his place in history. Would they have anything to add, for example, to the 1947 assessment by Hugh Trevor-Roper of Speer as 'the real criminal of Nazi Germany', guilty of an especially heinous example of the *trahison des clercs* (but what about Dr Phil. Joseph Goebbels?); or to Joachim Fest's kinder 1963 portrayal of the 'amoral technocrat' who buried himself in his 'apolitical' work and awoke too late?[9]

As *Der Spiegel*, the country's ultimate news magazine, is to what Germany does, so that other Hamburg publication, *Die Zeit*, Europe's leading intellectual weekly, is to what Germany thinks. Its opinion therefore would be of immense importance to the book's fate, influencing other reviewers in less rarefied publications and thus ultimately the attitudes of potential readers who would never dream of looking at *Die Zeit*. Its reviewer, Waldemar Besson, began by hailing the first memoir from a leading Nazi that was actually readable and worth taking seriously. Speer presented himself as Hitler's quasi-friend who immersed himself in his work, ignored politics and served technology. But, Herr Besson astutely asked, was it only technology that Albert Speer served? He wrote of the stupefying boredom of Hitler's table at which he spent so many hours; so why did he stay there when that other great technician of the Third Reich, Fritz Todt, felt no need to? It could only have been ambition.

Speer promoted himself as representative of the higher technical intelligence only in retrospect. He aroused sympathy for himself by conceding that his punishment had been fair for serving as Hitler's supreme stage designer and props master. 'At the end of the memoirs there stands a picture of a historic figure who, hopelessly overtaxed as a person, succumbs to a dangerous temptation ... The moral burden that Albert Speer drags [round] with him is great and he does not seek to shake it off ... As historical source and as literary testament his memoirs stand far above the average.' If author and publisher did not break out the champagne on reading this balanced but in the end highly favourable review in the most important of places, they should have done.[10]

Golo Mann, one of the leading German postwar historians, found the book to be the most readable of all Nazi memoirs in his review for the *Süddeutsche Zeitung* of Munich, Germany's best-written and most thoughtful daily, but had no sympathy for the author as a person. Under the heading, 'The Devil's Architect', he wrote that Speer believed he had exchanged his old ego 'of an ambitious, arrogant youngster drunk on work, fame and power' for a new one, enabling him to analyse his old persona objectively. Mann acutely noted 'much self-criticism, [but] of remorse, *in the Christian sense of the word* [author's italics], hardly anything; perhaps he finds it unmanly.' The whole story was told in a monotone. 'On the murder of the Jews he says baldly, "I have no apology." He knew all about it; more precisely, he had an idea and could and should have got to know all about it.'

His friend Gauleiter Hanke described how he had been overcome by Auschwitz, but 'Speer did not ask; what the German conquerors did in Russia he mentions in one sentence, the horror in Poland and elsewhere not at all – and yet *calls himself "the second man in the state"* [author's italics].' This penetrating analysis appeared (at enormous length, the curse of German upmarket journalism; it would have been twice as devastating at half the wordage) within days of publication of the memoirs. Ironically, many of Mann's strictures on Speer's selective memory, split-mindedness about Hitler and blind obedience until just before the end will have struck chords among his older and more conservative readers, who might well have been prompted to go out and buy what even this hostile critic saw as 'among the peaks of political memoir-literature ... an extremely informative book'.[11]

Speer had intended to dedicate the book to his family and Dr Wolters, his friend, chronicler and agent while in prison, but decided to be neither invidious nor indiscreet and made no dedication at all. Wolters did not resent this or even his total absence from the text anything like as much as Speer's refusal to take his advice on the tone of the book, especially the 'Gregorian chant of *mea culpa*', as we have seen. As part of clearing his desk on completing his manuscript, however,

Speer, having suppressed his debt to Wolters, carelessly put himself and his unsung friend in jeopardy. He had done some research in a private room at the Federal Archive, checking his recollections against public records. In July 1969, two months before the results were published, he made a parcel of his copy of the Chronicle and sent it to the director, Dr Wolfgang Mommsen (as distinct from Ernst Wolf, Speer's industrialist friend) with a covering letter on 28 July 1969. But, as we noted above, his copy had been sanitised by Wolters, who had alerted him to the fact when he handed it over in October 1966: 'Unfortunately, Speer had nothing more pressing to do than to hand over this material – in keeping with German postwar custom – to Herr Mommsen, the President of the Federal Archive in Koblenz, without telling me in advance.'[12] Mommsen sent his thanks on 19 August, accepting the restrictions placed by Speer on its use (for serious historians only), but reasonably added a request: 'I should welcome it if you could arrange, by discussion with your former colleague, Dr Wolters, that he consign the original of the above-mentioned Chronicle in his possession to the Federal Archive, completely or at least temporarily for comparison with the typed copy on hand.'

Mommsen was aware of the discovery by British historian David Irving of the Chronicle for 1943 because the latter had cited it in his 1966 book on Hitler's 'miracle weapons' and given a copy to Koblenz. Speer made inquiries and finally enclosed extracts from the above letter with a panic-stricken one of his own to Wolters, dated 3 January 1970. It was written at a hotel in Selva di Val Gardena in the Italian South Tyrol, where he was on holiday with Gretel and her friend, Wolters's wife Erika, his son Arnold, and the latter's wife and children. He seems to have forgotten their correspondence just before his release in 1966 (cited earlier) about Irving's find:

> Now we are in a fine mess: in London while rummaging through the archives they [sic] have found one year of the Chronicle. They are searching hard for the remaining years, so the energetic writer David Irving tells me. I got Irving to send me a photocopy to compare it with the text you gave me. Happily there are only unimportant differences for the historiographer to discover, which I enclose for you. But all the same, would it not be better if we ourselves took the first step, and I replaced the typed copy of the Chronicle now stored in the Federal Archive with a photocopy of the original that is in your possession? In that case I would once again quickly establish where the differences exist and inform you in advance ... I hope you will allow me to adjust the obliterations [*Verwehungen*, lit. 'snowdrifts'] in the other years as well.[13]

Wolters replied on 10 January in a letter which he clearly enjoyed composing. It carried the heading 'Ref: fine mess' and began by explaining why and how he had organised the retyping and sim- ultaneous 'cleansing' of his copy of the Chronicle, of which he had informed Speer on handing over a carbon copy. He had thought his copy of the original the only one extant, had made small stylistic or grammatical corrections and deleted a very few 'pronounced inanities' plus minor matters of no historical import. As the author, he felt entitled to unimportant deletions:

> Mind you, I also regarded myself as obliged to take out a very few entries which unfortunately are not entirely unimportant for contemporary history. For example where it says: 'In the period from 18 October to 2 November (1941) in Berlin about 4,500 Jews were evacuated ...' These notes, repeated a few times, then peak in 1942 with a closing report by your friend Cl[ahes], from which is to be concluded that the number of resettled 'persons' came to 75,000 and that in all '23,765 Jewish flats were seized'. That is of course an achievement!

Wolters said he let these 'few but eloquent' notes 'fall under the table' for the time being, though he preserved his original intact. At the time he did it (1964) 'witch-hunts' had been in progress against 'deskbound delinquents' of the Nazi era. The widow Clahes survived with her children and had fought for years for a pension, and Speer himself was also still alive, and in Spandau to boot. The West German War-crimes Investigation Bureau at Ludwigsburg might have opened a new case against Speer because the Jewish evictions had not been included in the Nuremberg indictment against him.

Wolters now proposed asking Mommsen, 'to whom you prematurely gave a typed copy', to return it, so that the chronicler could restore the few omissions. Speer could see the original any time he liked, so long as he returned it intact. 'Handing it on, even in photocopy form, to Herr Mommsen, would not be pleasant for me, as one would be able to recognise the places deleted by pencil even after the most emphatic erasure [of the pencil strokes].' The proposed correction procedure could be represented to the archive as much cheaper and simpler than photocopying 800 pages of original. 'Or else simply tell them, "the fellow won't let go of the original" – I would happily give them my reasons.' Wolters concluded: 'By the way, you can rest easy: I have seen to it that the original will be made available to the public as soon as nobody can suffer damage from it any more (it is also possible that Marion [Riesser] will have destroyed the original first). And now, you decide, O great armourer (sorry).'

Speer, still in the Dolomites, left the date off his reply, in which he argued that his acceptance of shared responsibility for everything was 'all inclusive', and put forward his alternative solution to the Mommsen problem:

> I suggest: the relevant pages no longer exist. That means, contrary to your letter, no longer at all. A postponement to later historical times would be disadvantageous; who will answer for an adjusted presentation that is only enhanced by the fact of many years of suppression? It will be regarded as thoroughly legitimate that you left a few pages out of a series of documents ... Instead of a suspiciously clean copy, these archivists all too readily favour scraps and pages which, yellowed, stained by flecks of water, are almost no longer readable. *One should do them this favour* [author's italics].

It has to be said, if only in defence of the painstaking translation above (by the author), that this letter of Speer's contains the most convoluted German in all the outpourings of his that I read while researching this book. But it is indisputably clear that what he proposes is the deliberate suppression, by selective destruction and for ever, of the passages in the Chronicle (other than for 1943, already in the public domain at the time) which refer to his eviction of the Jews from Berlin. Wolters was responsible for the original sanitising, as he freely conceded, and was prepared to save his friend embarrassment by arranging the concealment of the original Chronicle until such time as nobody could be damaged by it; but the friend responded with the suggestion that the deletions be made permanent, in such a way that their previous existence would also be concealed. In other words, Speer planned to distort the historical record to preserve the place in history which he himself had sought to pre-empt with his bestselling memoirs, already being used as a 'horse's mouth' source by historians:

> Procedure: you send me (without 1943 and without the [cut] 'pages') year[s] 1941–1944 for read through and comparison. I send it (1) either back to you for you to forward to the Fed-Archive, or (2) directly to that place. I should regard the former as more appropriate. I hope, despite swathes of fog surrounding the building, that I have expressed myself clearly enough.

Speer signed off, 'Yours, Albert *felix minus*' (less happy).

Wolters did not tamper further with his original, leaving in place the deletions, the thick pencil strokes and the occasional, barely legible amendments in his very shaky hand. His next letter was dated 22 January and should have been written in ironic type:

> I have got round only today to answering your undated letter from Selva,

as not only I but also Marion have searched the whole time [for] where the original Chronicle could have got to. To come to the point: it has vanished without trace, it is gone, it is no longer there, it simply no longer exists.

Wolters thought this was 'a good thing too' as a second correction would have been impossible. He felt at ease about his deletions because he had been selective when writing the Chronicle and had every right to be so again when he came back to it. He could not come up with a third version now because of Irving's London discovery. But if there were problems, Speer was free to blame him and Marion – a more than generous offer in the circumstances.

Back in Heidelberg on 2 February, Speer thanked Wolters and promptly asked for another favour: could he rewrite the above letter 'in a form that I can forward to the Federal Archive? I believe that would be the end of the matter.' On the 10th, the long-suffering Wolters duly obliged, acknowledging the letter of the 4th in a covering note and enclosing the requested lie, addressed to 'Dear Speer' and marked: 'Ref: Chronicle':

> As I already told you by telephone, I have been unable to find the original of the Chronicle of your office among my papers any more. As I possessed only one copy of the Chronicle and this existed in part only in binders or individual sheets, I had the 800 or so pages retyped and additionally equipped with an index some time ago.

The fraudulent letter goes on to say that Wolters did tidy up grammar and style as well as removing very minor matters of no historical importance, and that as author of the Chronicle he felt he had every right to 'insignificant deletions', just as he had been selective when writing the original entries from a mass of raw material. He concluded: 'I regret I am unable to give you any further information.' Speer lost no time in forwarding the deliberately misleading letter to Dr Mommsen in Koblenz. His covering note, dated 13 February, regretted the receipt of a negative reply from his friend as per enclosure and added: 'I am sorry that I have not been more successful in this matter.' Speer reported the deed done in a letter to Wolters of the same date.[14]

At the end of this detailed documentation of Speer's attempt, successful for his lifetime, to cover up his direct role in the persecution of the Jews, two questions, admittedly rhetorical, seem to remain. The fraud was revealed by Wolters, partly in 1980 to the doctoral student, Matthias Schmidt, who published in 1982, and in full when his legacy reached the Federal Archive in 1983, including his copy of the original

Chronicle. Wolters had warned Speer that it would be 'rediscovered after my death'; Speer was thus lucky to die beforehand, in 1981.

The present author has no qualification in psychology to assist him with the first question, which may (or may not) answer itself: why did Speer, a man capable of well-nigh total recall and wholly committed to the lifesaving self-image he presented at Nuremberg, who knew of both the 'cleansing' of the Chronicle and Irving's London find, send the sanitised version to Koblenz at all: was this crass blunder really a Freudian slip indicating the guilty man's subconscious wish to be punished for his personal crime against the Jews – or was it just complacent arrogance?

The second question is, surely, what historical value can now attach to Speer's memoirs, or to the remorse for his share of general Nazi iniquity and concomitant denial of contemporaneous knowledge which they express *ad nauseam*, when we now know he was concealing his own specific crime as he wrote them?

18

One Jump Ahead

(1970–81)

A S PART OF THE STRATEGY to preserve his self-determined place in history, Speer never turned away any inquirer who wanted to consult him about his past, whether for an article, a thesis or a book. An endless stream of visitors, eventually including me, trekked up to his hated house in Heidelberg, to the bemusement and sometimes irritation of his wife and family; they knew better than anyone that he needed no such incentive to spend the vast majority of the fifteen years between his releases from prison and from life itself looking backwards.

He vetted Janssen's thesis while still in prison, as we saw; at and after the time his memoirs appeared in German in 1969 he made himself available to all comers; and again, only more so, when they came out in English a year later. He had also gone out of his way to help William Hamsher, a former correspondent in Germany of the London *Daily Express* who had covered Nuremberg, to prepare the first biography (as distinct from autobiography) of Speer, even when its subject knew that the journalist's book would coincide with the English translation of his own. The result, *Albert Speer – Victim of Nuremberg?* was worth the time and effort: the book, while not quite a hagiography, is both uncritical and a racy read, a useful external counterpoint to the memoirs and an elaborate exercise in mutual exploitation similar in motive, if not in scale, to my own little article on the English publication of Speer's diaries in 1976.

This policy of eternal availability endured to the last. Even Matthias Schmidt, the only visitor turned author on Speer apart from me who seems to have left Heidelberg as sceptical as he was on arrival, was allowed the favour of a prolonged interview in 1979, and again in 1980, even though Speer could tell he was unsympathetic. The all-time record is held by Gitta Sereny who interviewed him continuously, apparently *ad nauseam mutualem*, in 1978 for a long profile in the London *Sunday Times* and *Die Zeit* colour magazines, the genesis of her 1995 book. The interview lasted thirteen days (to follow the magazines) or three weeks (according to her book). That this constant stream of information-seekers was a strain at times is surely shown by the fact that Speer bought a remote farmhouse in the Bavarian Alps in 1973, where he did much of his later writing. He also regularly went into retreat during his last decade to the idyllically situated Benedictine abbey at Maria-Laach in the Rhineland, where the not overly religious Protestant came under the benign spiritual tutelage of the Catholic monk Father Athanasius. To see this as a form of voluntary solitary confinement out of nostalgia for the compulsory variety at Spandau may be facile but is also quite plausible. Among Speer's many correspondents, following upon his new fame as an author, was Pastor Casalis, his French interlocutor in the early days at Spandau, and Rabbi Raphael Geis, a German-Jewish contemporary who briefly became a close spiritual pen-friend from 1969 until his death in 1972.[1]

As the memoirs went into English and other foreign languages (eventually eighteen, including Serbo-Croat) in the year following the original German edition, the reviews continued to appear throughout 1970 and beyond, and interest in Speer as author and authority on Hitler was sustained by one article after another. The greatest of these was *Playboy*. The American journalist Eric Norden was the first interviewer to subject Speer to the kind of protracted grilling that he had last experienced in the Allied Ashcan and Dustbin debriefing centres and then Nuremberg in 1945–46. The resulting article, the longest ever written about him, appeared in 1971 in the American monthly, best known for its once groundbreaking centrefolds of pneumatic female nudes, but by then not above including more profound, verbal spreads on such topics as male cosmetics or the Holocaust. Mr Norden spent no fewer than ten days interviewing Speer for his question-and-answer piece, which sprawled across twenty-four pages (seventy columns of text, plus photographs and space for layout, headlines and advertisements). The article was remarkable not only for the magazine in which it appeared and its length but also for a few nuggets of revelation amid what was in the main a canter through the substance of the memoirs. Norden's marathon also had the significant if incidental side-effect of provoking Rudolf Wolters to break off relations with its subject in profound contempt when he saw translated extracts in the German illustrated weekly, *Quick*.

Mr Norden, who admitted that both he and his subject found their shared ordeal exhausting, was very perturbed by the fact that Speer spoke in a completely detached manner about terrible events. He used the same tranquil tone for offering cake and implicating himself in appalling crimes. 'I suspected, as some reviewers had, that the litany of his self-recrimination was in itself an evasion of ultimate responsibility.' Norden also quoted the British writers Geoffrey Barraclough and

Rebecca West, who challenged Speer's self-image variously as a distorted legend and a cynical whitewash.

Norden too was favoured with Speer's now familiar acknowledgment of how he had failed to take Hitler's threats against the Jews seriously or to register the fact that they were being fulfilled to the letter. Speer used an important word (which will come up again) to define the nature of his responsibility for Nazi crimes: *Billigung*, which can mean passive toleration/concurrence or active condonation/approval. Norden quoted Speer as saying: 'I just stood aside and said to myself that as long as I did not personally participate, it had nothing to do with me ... My toleration [*Billigung*] of the antisemitic campaign made me responsible for it.' There is only one way to interpret this revealing remark: passively tolerant or actively approving, *Billigung* means Speer *knew*. It is not possible either to tolerate or to approve something of which one is not aware. A dispute about how much or how little someone knew only serves to show he knew *something*. For *Playboy*, Speer went on to assert that 'I could not be blamed for not knowing what happened' because the Nazis had been so secretive, and to admit that 'If I did not see, it was because I did not want to see ... I stood at the pinnacle of power and I was intoxicated by the distant landscapes I saw – while all the time a charnel-house reeked at my feet.' But he *knew*.

Norden also used the quotation from Karl Maria Hettlage about Speer having been Hitler's 'unrequited love' and persuaded his subject to express, for the first time in public, his pride in his achievements as minister, followed by what Wolters identified as a 'post-Festum Yes, but':

> I cannot help feeling stirrings of pride ... I achieved things which many people predicted were impossible, and I suppose my ego still takes pleasure in those accomplishments. Then I think of all the cities destroyed, the soldiers killed, the Jews butchered between 1943 and 1945 – and my pride turns to sickness.

On Sauckel, the Labour Commissioner who found him slaves at his behest, Speer told Norden: 'I was his wholehearted collaborator on the forced-labour programme and I share his guilt.' Then he produced a sound simile: 'Our roles were rather like the captain of the slave-ship and the slave-owner who buys his cargo.' Norden quoted the Anglophile German newspaper correspondent, Willi Frischauer – 'I have come across nothing quite as repugnant as the tears Speer sheds' for the slave workers – a scathing dismissal which Speer could only accept, given what he had conceded earlier. At the end of this gargantuan interview Speer said he had pleaded Not Guilty at Nuremberg, despite his avowal of shared responsibility, because a plea of Guilty would have entailed 'an automatic death-sentence'.

Wolters had no English and never read the original of the foregoing, still less the catchphrase of the British Sunday columnist, Sir John Junor, to his secretary when faced with a case of extreme unction – 'pass the sickbag, Alice'. But that is undoubtedly how he felt when he saw the extracts in German in late May 1971 (by which time the June issue of *Playboy* was also available). He expressed his feelings on 24 May in a letter of unprecedented savagery: 'What on earth has got into you, that you don't stop condemning yourself as a criminal, time and again and ever more radically, after the acknowledgments of guilt in your memoirs?' Wolters pointed to the contrast between the repetitious *mea culpa* and the penitent's burgeoning lifestyle, 'of which *Playboy* or *Quick* readers naturally know nothing'. Speer had glibly written the leading Nazis off as totally corrupt criminals and casually dropped his old friends in the mire, such as the leading industrialists (unnamed) who paid bribes to Göring:

> In this letter, dear Albert, I'm saying everything I think. It is an awful imposition for me to reconcile your couple of pages [in *Quick*, about] the guilty criminal – colloquially, 'national rent-a-penitent' – with the other Albert Speer, his delight in successful tricks and his honestly admitted joy in *Geld und Geltung* [cash and cachet].

Wolters used the English word 'tricks' (what he meant by it will become clear in the Epilogue). His felicitous German pun, *Geld* (pronounced 'gelt') *und Geltung*, for once translates neatly into English. He hoped that one day Speer would not find it necessary to proclaim his guilt everywhere in order to render himself irreproachable. 'May I suggest,' Wolters's passionate and eloquent renunciation concluded, 'that we see each other again after the termination of this phase, i.e. only when you are no longer interested solely in your rehabilitation.'

Speer's reply was predictably distant. It was customary in civilised countries, he wrote coolly on 5 June, especially among friends, to question the offender before judgment. He would have had a lot to say about the *Playboy* article; 'today however, only this much: it was restructured and produced in a language [and] with crude formulations alien to me.' Wolters had known all about his attitude to guilt during the Spandau period. Speer particularly resented the gibe about his lifestyle, which he said he was enjoying all the more by virtue of having a clear conscience. Besides, after twenty years, he felt the need to catch up. 'By the way, a year ago I organised an alteration in my contract with Propyläen by which large parts of my receipts are diverted to good causes.' After tax he was getting about twelve per cent of the royalties [still a mighty sum], Speer said. 'In the light of the fact that industry and architects failed to concern themselves about a basis for my survival, I regard this unique, residual income from the book as necessary for securing my old age.' He left it to Wolters to decide whether or not to lift his embargo on their relationship. 'You will understand that from my side I cannot address myself to you again.'

Speer did indeed make substantial anonymous or indirect donations to charity from his massive royalties, including organisations in the United States and elsewhere which helped Jewish survivors of Nazi persecution. His publisher, Wolf Jobst Siedler, told me he would put it as high as eighty per cent, 'and he was a millionaire, or would have been.' Speer wanted the gifts to remain unsung for fear of rejection and of being called a hypocrite. Although they became known eventually, he cannot be accused of blowing his own trumpet about this personal reparation programme, which undoubtedly cost him many hundreds of thousands of marks, if not more. The gifts can legitimately be described in the circumstances as conscience money, but it is clear from Speer's casual largesse when a student that he was generous in cash and kind; when he had it, he gave it. What is more, he was tolerant of the views of other people, even if he took them for granted, as well as (by the same token, it can be argued) indifferent to their commitments, whether political, personal or professional.

But Wolters had crossed over this very high threshold by effectively calling him a hypocrite. Their friendship was mortally wounded and would never recover. Wolters could not bring himself to blow the whistle while both he and Speer were alive; but he made sure that his own protective cleansing of the Chronicle and Speer's plan to destroy the suppressed evidence of his crimes against the Jews, deceiving the Federal Archive and trying to rewrite history in his own interest, would inescapably become known. He originally promised his papers to the local state archives in Münster, Westphalia, warning Speer orally that the Chronicle would 'certainly be rediscovered after my death'.[2] In the end he bequeathed them to the Federal Archive. Subsequent events, to be described in their place, only stiffened the resolve of the apoplectic correspondent in Coesfeld to make sure the record would be corrected one day.

Frau Riesser was deeply upset by the break and wrote to Speer on her own account on 17 June 1971, saying she had long seen it coming, and while she shared her boss's misgivings about Speer's avowals of guilt, he would always have her best wishes: 'you can count on us if you ever need us again.' She signed it, 'your old pen-friend (involved for the past twenty years) – Marion.'

Speer's postbag was now enormous. We have seen that he turned nobody away and even acquired important new connections such as Rabbi Geis as a result of publishing his memoirs. One of the hundreds who wrote to him out of the blue was a teenage boy in Norway, who said he had found the memoirs fascinating. The boy was the eldest son of a retired pastor in the Norwegian state Lutheran Church and the upshot of his letter was an invitation to Speer from the father, Oeysten Hovden, to come north for a holiday some time in 1971. Intrigued, Speer accepted and eventually went for a fortnight; but not before being declared *persona non grata* by the Oslo government until it relented, as the newspaper *Stiftstidende* reported.[3] Mr Hovden however found his famous guest 'a very pleasant and interesting personality'. But he had been given a reminder that he was not 'everybody's darling' as Fest ironically described him; and there would be others.

The greatest alarum for Speer in 1971 came at the end of the year, on the publication of Professor Erich Goldhagen's sensational allegation that Speer had heard but suppressed Himmler's speech on the genocide programme to the Gauleiters at Posen on 6 October 1943, as described earlier. Speer buried himself in the archives at Koblenz looking for proof that he had not been in the hall when Himmler spoke the unspeakable, spelling out the meaning of the Final Solution. He spent the best part of eighteen months trying to bolster his claim that he had left by the time Himmler apostrophised him (in fairness, it is a common rhetorical ploy to address an absent person as if present: President Reagan did it in still divided Berlin in the late 1980s, challenging the last Soviet leader, 'Mr Gorbachev, open the Wall!'). The fact that Himmler had addressed Speer in the second person is no proof that he was there, but Speer was desperate to prove he was not. His undisproved presence was a permanent threat to the credibility of his postwar claims not to have known at the time of the Final Solution, the much vaunted central plank in the Nazis' ideological platform since 1922.

Not surprisingly, Speer was unable by his own efforts to prove the negative proposition that he had not been there when Himmler spoke that afternoon, an unfortunate fact for him which nevertheless cannot logically be taken as proof that he was present either. Speer wrote a long rebuttal in 1972, naturally and not unreasonably making an issue of the indefensible spoof 'quotation' aberrantly put into Himmler's mouth by Goldhagen himself, if only in a footnote (thus undermining its impact and credibility). Quotations from a plethora of documents, and of figures relating to Speer's employment of Jews in the armaments industry (whose living conditions and even lives were protected thereby), proved just how far and wide Speer had searched for an alibi. Fraudulently changing the comma in the Posen record to a full stop in the key quotation from Himmler – 'Of course that has absolutely nothing to do with Party-comrade Speer. You can [do] nothing about it' – Speer suggested that Himmler turned at that point (of time and punctuation) to address Sauckel, who was certainly there, rather than himself ... 'But even if it is assumed he meant me, that in no way proves that I was present,' Speer protested.

He was so obsessed with the irrepressible suspicion attaching to him that he supplemented his rebuttal five years later, proving that he had gone on digging in ever increasing circles. He now revealed that in his memoirs he had mixed up the departure arrangements after his two addresses to Gauleiters' meetings in Posen, on 6 October 1943 and 3 August 1944. He had indicated in his memoirs that he returned on the Gauleiters' special train in 1943 (hence the complaint about their riotous behaviour) and left by car in 1944; in fact it was the other way round! What was more, he could now prove he left early in 1943.

He had just happened, he said, to telephone his old friend Walter Rohland of the Ruhr steel industry (wartime tankbuilder-in-chief and subsequent exemplary subscriber to the school fund, the first man Speer visited after Wolters on his release) about another matter. Speer just happened to mention the niggling Posen controversy when 'Dr Rohland spontaneously declared to me that he remembered exactly our drive to Hitler's headquarters and an evening conversation with Hitler. An error was impossible as he had only been to Posen on this one occasion [6 October 1943], and further, the car journey with me had been unforgettable.' As if this inspired recollection were not enough, Dr Rohland was ready and able to gild the lily of his remembrance: he just happened, in the course of preparing his own memoirs, to have sworn an affidavit on this very matter as long ago as 6 July 1973! Four years before Speer produced his mark II rebuttal, Rohland had sworn: 'I wrote down this [account of the Posen trip] a year ago [i.e. 1972] without having taken up any kind of contact with Speer in advance about it.' No doubt Dr Rohland made his sworn statement, so convenient for Speer but of no conceivable use for Rohland, just in case it came in useful...

But not content with this helping hand from an old friend, Speer came up with another affidavit, dated 22 October 1975, by Herr Harry Siegmund, retired civil servant, the party official who had organised the Gauleiter conference at Posen in 1943. He remembered how he and a liaison officer in the local defence command, a leftover from a Ruritanian royal house who rejoiced in the title of Prince Reuss XXXVII, had compared the obnoxious Himmler speech with Speer's sober and businesslike presentation of the armament situation. Prince Reuss thereupon happened to mention that Speer had not been present for the Himmler speech. Over and above this hearsay evidence, Siegmund further swore that he himself happened to notice, when with

Himmler the next day, how thick his spectacle lenses were. 'It is therefore to be doubted whether Himmler could observe during his speech which individuals were present.' Besides, the lighting was bad in the hall!

Speer added that Field Marshal Milch, another old friend, had told the American revisionist historian John Toland that he (Speer) had not been there for the infamous speech. QED. The most lenient finding to which Speer is entitled on the basis of this belated concatenation of recollections is the questionable legal verdict, unique to Scots law, of Not Proven.[4]

By the time of the first rebuttal above, Speer was already preparing to follow up his memoirs with the much reworked text of what was published in 1975 as his Spandau diaries. The same troika laboured on this – Speer, advised by Fest and Siedler – as had produced the memoirs. The raw material was three cases of papers smuggled out of Spandau. Herr Fest told me that a great deal of work had to be done on arranging and selecting the entries, by no means all of which could be precisely dated. 'He often could not remember when he had an afterthought on an event. But he felt overall that the book was a good reflection of the development of his thinking while he was in Spandau.' This careful revamping and the eclectic nature of the entries make the book worthless as a historical and chronological record alike. But it was a unique if kaleidoscopic recollection of one prisoner's long years inside that melancholy, now vanished place, and of how he coped without losing his sanity, its main literary merit. As a spiritual auto-biography or supplementary reflection on the great events in which Speer had been involved, it is mostly superficial and banal.

He needed the best part of three years from early 1972 to prepare his second book; most of the period was spent researching and writing. Old cronies such as Annemarie Kempf and Theo Hupfauer tried in the early seventies to organise reunions of the Speer wartime staff in Munich and elsewhere, and a few were held. But they did not work well, because most who attended had led busy lives while Speer festered in jail; they were still working or had only just retired, whereas the guest of honour could only look backwards or else enthuse about his new status as the bestselling author of a book on that self-same past. Soon the thought of an evening with an introspective, egocentric and nostalgic former chief, completely out of touch with the present, began to lose its appeal and the fifty or so who first turned up dwindled to twenty before the idea was quietly dropped. Speer was a very lonely man in the last fifteen years of his life, another important reason why he welcomed letters and visits from all and sundry. In massaging his place in history by giving interviews and writing letters, he was also massaging his isolated ego, which his family could not touch (as more than one member confirmed to me).

On 25 July 1973 Hermann Speer chose in a letter to his younger brother to pour scorn on Albert's denials of anti-Semitism. Hermann had long since used up his inheritance from their parents' estate and had been tapping Albert for money since before his memoirs appeared. He was trying to get a commission for a book of his own about his brother yet was in dispute with him about family property in Mannheim. Hermann reportedly contacted Werner Maser, the German historian who had been highly critical of the memoirs (and was to claim in 1977 that Speer did a secret deal with the chief Nuremberg prosecutor, Justice Jackson) in the hope of enlisting his help with a book on 'My little brother Albert'.[5] Hermann accused his brother of going along 'with that stupid anti-Semitism'. In 1938, he claimed, Albert had suggested to Himmler the idea of forcing the inmates of Oranienburg concentration camp north of Berlin to make bricks for the capital's reconstruction. Hermann accused him of quipping at the time, 'After all, the Jews were already making bricks under the Pharaohs.'[6] Reporting the fraternal row of 1973 in 1975, Der Spiegel postulated cooperation between Maser, Hermann Speer and Rudolf Wolters in the alleged book project, which came to nothing after lawyers for Ullstein, Albert Speer's publishers, intervened. There is no trace of any correspondence at any time between Hermann Speer and Wolters in the latter's papers, although they include a number of cuttings and other references about the troublesome and troubled wastrel sibling.

In the middle of November 1973 Albert Speer was arrested at Heathrow Airport, London, on his arrival to give an interview to BBC Television for a programme about bombing in the Second World War. He had booked his seat under the pseudonym Reeps, a transparent jape reminiscent of the feeble codenames used in the illicit Spandau correspondence. British Immigration, notoriously deficient in the national sense of humour, took a dim view of this and detained Mr Reeps for eight hours before granting him entry for two days. The BBC's embarrassment was redoubled when Sir Arthur 'Bomber' Harris, late of RAF Bomber Command, flew into high dudgeon and refused to take part in any programme with Speer.[7] The latter's inability to say No to any approach was illustrated again in the same month, when Speer astoundingly agreed to a request from an American television-film company to return to Nuremberg and sit in his old seat in the dock, to promote, for a fat fee, a completely fictional thriller, The Tribunal, about a plot to free the war criminals during the trial.[8]

In March 1975, in good time for Speer's seventieth birthday on the 19th, Rudolf Wolters, who had been ill for much of the previous year, decided to extend an olive-branch. It took the form of a smoked Westphalian ham – and a length of toilet tissue with an execrable piece of doggerel typed on it by Marion Riesser (tremors made it pointless for Wolters to use his illegible handwriting for such a purpose). Speer replied in kind on another mock *Kassiber*, saying that Wolters's gesture had been his 'best birthday present'; even so, he casually left it to his old friend to decide whether to maintain the connection thus reopened: '*You* set the pace for once!' (Speer's emphasis). One wave from Wolters and he would come running, Speer wrote on 3 April. But that was precisely what Wolters had just done; no doubt shaking his head over his former master's ineptitude in human relations, he wrote again on 27 May, amiably suggesting an annual birthday exchange of Westphalian ham for Heidelberg honey. The letters passed haltingly to and fro for the rest of the year. But when Wolters sent a considered, five-page typed critique of the diaries, Speer was moved enough at last in July to send a seven-page apologia for his new book, making it clear it was a continuation to his defence of the memoirs six years earlier. As the arguments deployed by both were essentially the same as those of 1969, they need not be repeated here. Not surprisingly, neither man changed his view.[9]

But Wolters had refused in January 1975 to join in plans by former associates to organise a special commemoration for Speer's seventieth birthday. Wolters was not ready to meet him – and never did again. His disapproval of Speer's sackcloth-and-ashes act (he saw it as an act, and with reason, as will become clear) led him on 27 June 1975 to write to David Irving to congratulate him on the publication of his book on Hitler's generals, in which he challenged the usually accepted total of six million Jews murdered in the Final Solution. Wolters thought this total had one nought too many. Irving wrote back on 10 July, saluting Wolters as the author of the Chronicle he had cited for his 1966 book on V-weapons. The depth of Wolters's bitterness is revealed by a letter of 11 August to Arno Breker, the sculptor and architect, who won many commissions from Speer in the architectural and GBI days. Wolters thought it fortunate that Speer had taken only Germany's sins on his shoulders and not the entire world's, 'or he would have stolen the show from Jesus'. The sales of *Spandau* were therefore slightly lower than the Bible's. According to Siedler, the publisher, Speer had signed 60,000 copies; Wolters gleefully added that his local bookseller had told him this made the books worthless. These extracts from his huge correspondence show how obsessed with Speer he was, a fact which helped to make him the most revealing witness and source on Speer's general character as well as on the specific issue of his sincerity as a penitent.[10] His view was biased in later years; but it was also borne out by carefully collected and preserved evidence.

Speer meanwhile was reminded once more that he was not everybody's darling when a 'League of Democratic Academics' organised a (not very democratic) protest against Heidelberg University's invitation to him to participate in an inter-disciplinary symposium on the Nazi period. Speer returned home and stayed there after a Communist demonstration against his participation at the start of the proceedings early in April.

The diaries were not quite such a blockbuster in the bestseller lists as the memoirs, but they still outperformed nearly every other book by a German author since the end of the war. By August *Der Spiegel*, publisher of the country's main bestseller list, was reporting that 180,000 copies out of a print of 350,000 had been sold in hardback; *Die Welt* had paid 600,000 marks for serialisation and Macmillan of New York $350,000 for the English-language rights.

Despite his success and fame as an author after two such bestsellers, Speer maintained his policy of never turning historical inquirers away. He was approached during 1976 by Ernst A. Ostro, a historian based in Geneva but by origin a German Jew whose parents had been prescient and lucky enough to emigrate in 1933. Herr Ostro got his interview and was directed to Wolters for further information; he visited Coesfeld twice in 1977 but Wolters eventually dismissed him as being interested only in anecdotes. Ostro did not proceed to publish a biography and Wolters never heard from him again. Between his two visits, however, on 7 April 1977, Wolters wrote to him about Speer's character and how his 'charm' overcame Tessenow, their professor at Berlin, then Hitler and indeed everybody who became acquainted with him. But his real goal had been *Geld und Geltung* (see above; the phrase obviously pleased Wolters because he used it in several letters after coining it in 1975). But Speer also liked barbed practical jokes and was capable of making wounding remarks and subtly needling those who crossed him. Wolters said Speer's character had been altered not only by twenty years in prison but also by the distorted position he had taken at Nuremberg, where he had been disloyal to his fellow-accused.

His professed desire to protect ordinary Germans from condemnation had achieved the exact opposite, exonerating the enemy and, by blaming Hitler, also blaming the Germans who supported him (as witness the fact that there had been no real resistance to him). Speer 'generously takes responsibility for the killing of the Jews, of which he knew nothing' and made no mention of the mass of enemy soldiers and civilians who were killed by the weapons he made. Speer had remarked that he would have been Hitler's friend had he had any; the same applied to Wolters *vis à vis* Speer. As a pragmatist Speer was

'friendly only to those useful to him'.[11] The bitterness of Rudolf Wolters
was obviously maturing nicely.

So was Speer's continual refinement of his standing admission of
shared guilt for Nazi crimes. In April 1977 he received an unusual
request for help from the chairman of the Board of Deputies of South
African Jews. The board had initiated an action against local extreme
racists who, not content with the persecution of millions of 'non-
whites' under apartheid, had produced a pamphlet challenging Nazi
genocide under the title, 'Did six million die?' The board would be
grateful if Speer could kindly confirm that there had been a plan to
exterminate European Jewry, that he had heard of it and that it had
been carried out (and how he knew this was so). Speer responded with
a three-page affidavit, which helped to achieve the desired effect of a
court injunction against the offending publication. In it he averred:

> I still regard it as right today to take upon myself the responsibility, and
> with it the guilt, for everything that was undertaken by way of crime in
> the general sense after my entry into the Hitler government on 8 February
> 1942. [It is] not individual misdeeds, however great they may be, [that]
> incriminate me but rather my conduct in the leadership ... I still see my
> main guilt in connivance [*Billigung*] at the persecutions of the Jews and
> the murders of millions of them.[12]

This is a distilled version of what he had first admitted to *Playboy* in
1971, to the lasting fury of Wolters: that he had at the very least
tolerated, if not approved, the persecution of the Jews, an attitude
semantically and logically impossible for someone without knowledge.
Speer *knew*, and in addition to accepting his share of the Nazis' general
guilt, got round to admitting his contemporaneous knowledge of their
crimes at least three times in the last ten years of his life. But he is not
on record as having told the *whole* truth, which must include his
personal role in persecuting the Jews by evicting 75,000 of them from
their homes in Berlin.

When Gitta Sereny pressed Speer on whether he had known of the
Holocaust at the time it was happening, during her marathon interview
in February 1978, he dug the South African affidavit out of his files
and showed it to her – his way of indicating what he knew and when
(she can have had no knowledge at that time, or before Speer died, of
his personal role as recorded in the unexpurgated, but then still
undisclosed, Chronicle for 1941–42). Speer had telephoned Sereny the
previous year to commend her and my old friend and colleague, Lewis
Chester, for jointly performing a service to humanity by writing for the
Sunday Times a detailed rebuttal of Irving's hypothesis that Hitler had
not known of the Holocaust before Himmler's Posen speech of 6

October 1943. Sereny requested a meeting and thus started on the long trail which led to her 1995 book. According to *Die Zeit*'s version of her original interview (translated here by the present author), the following dialogue took place before he fetched the document:

Speer: I can say that I suspected.
Sereny: That you suspected what?
Speer: That something appalling was happening with the Jews...
Sereny: But if you 'suspected' it, then you must have heard something. One cannot suspect in a vacuum, without knowing something. You knew it.

Precisely. He had admitted as much with his *Billigung* concession to *Playboy* in 1971 and again in the affidavit he sent to Johannesburg in 1977, and now for the third time, as explicitly as he would ever say it, to Ms Sereny, to whom he also conceded in 1978 that such an outright admission now would change his position in the eyes of the public and in history: 'But it would be a relief.' He never told even her, however, about the eviction of the Berlin Jews ... Yet he did explain to *Die Zeit*'s colour magazine what he meant by the use of the word *Billigung* in the affidavit. Under the relevant third instalment of the Sereny series the journal reported: 'In a handwritten note for *Zeitmagazin* Speer explained the word *Billigung*: "connivance through looking away, not through knowledge of an order or of [its] execution. The first is as grave as the second." '[13]

Speer was rather more pleased about the appearance in 1978 of a lavishly illustrated volume about his architecture, edited by Georg G. Meerwein and published by Siedler's Propyläen, for which he wrote a brief introduction (dated 9 May) which soberly concludes: 'This volume here, a handful of photos, sketches, models, is all that is left of a lust for construction that knows no parallel in recent history.' Wolters, who had retired at the end of 1978, sent Speer a note of congratulation on the publication of the book on 2 January 1979; Speer acknowledged it briefly but warmly enough on the 28th. It was the last flicker of their friendship. A similar volume covering the same ground but with parallel English and French texts was edited by Leon Krier and published in Brussels in 1985.

In 1979 Adelbert Reif, who had edited and published in the previous year a collection of material about Speer including his Nuremberg defence, general articles about him and the main reviews of his memoirs and diaries, edited a volume entitled *Albert Speer – Technology and Power*. This unusual product is in fact a book-length, question-and-answer 'interview' in which Speer covers the themes suggested by the title in much the same terms as he had dealt with them in his own books. The short volume also contains the South African affidavit, complete with explanatory footnote on *Billigung*, but adds very little to the Speer *corpus*. By this time he was researching in the archives again.

Speer had planned to write a third book about German munitions in the Second World War but came across some Himmler papers at Koblenz. So, as he explained in the foreword, he chose as the theme for the whole of his third and last opus (rather than for just one chapter) the role of the SS in the economy of the Third Reich. It was to be published in 1981 in Germany and Britain as *The Slave State* and in America as *Infiltration*. Neither the book nor its English translation bears comparison with the previous two; post Festum, Speer's prose reverted to type – pedantic, pedestrian and ponderous.

Describing the SS as a state within the party within the state, Speer showed that Himmler's 'brutal and amateurish' methods failed out of sheer ignorance. The economic chief, SS-General Oswald Pohl, was as dim and inept as the early SS scheme for making weapons at Buchenwald camp (and later several others). Hitler's genocidal plans and SS inefficiency conspired to wreck both Himmler's economic ambitions and the war effort against Russia. Himmler wanted to have his cake and eat it by using slave labour and working it to death as part of the Final Solution (one deduces that SS brutality to slave labour was based on the arrogance of absolute power, on the assumption that there was always more where it had come from and on indifference to such factors as skill in the manufacture of weapons which was, in the limited time available, indispensable). Speer paints a detailed general picture of how Himmler, Pohl, Kammler and their cronies started and built up SS economic interests inside the Reich and to the east, both by using their own resources and muscling in on the interests of other departments, including Speer's (where Saur helped them a great deal). Chapter 17 describes how Speer, in the radio speech he wrote but never delivered, called for all Jews and political prisoners in the camps to be handed over to the advancing Allies without further ado. Then in part IV the book moves on to the fate of the Jews.

Here, in chapter 18, Speer endeavours to blame others for the deportation of the Jews from Berlin while further masking his own major contribution, which he never admitted, as we have seen. After he took over munitions in 1942, he wrote, the Armaments Inspectorate in Berlin tried to prevent the deportation of Jews working in the arms industry because they represented an important element in the skilled labour force. But in September 1942 Hitler ordered Labour Commissioner Sauckel to deport all such Jewish workers, whether from Berlin (where most of them were) or elsewhere, to the east (i.e. the slave-labour and extermination camps).

In fact such removals had already begun in October 1941; 8,000 had been expelled by 25 January 1942. A shortage of skilled men led to an interruption, although the remaining Jews were segregated for the convenience of later action. In autumn 1941, says Speer, without a hint of how his own GBI department was clearing Jewish apartment blocks for new construction and then more urgently for wounded soldiers and Aryans made homeless by bombing, there were still 75,000 Jews in Berlin, of whom 20,000 were at work in armaments and 10,000 in engineering (as the Chronicle proves, he had already caused large numbers to be evicted from their homes; many must therefore have been living in cramped, borrowed quarters with other Jews).

In May 1942 Goebbels, the local Gauleiter as well as Minister for Propaganda and unsurpassed anti-Semite, complained that there were still 40,000 Jews in Berlin (17,000 in war production) – one third of the total left in Germany, where there had been about 570,000 in 1933. In September, Speer wrote, Sauckel promised to replace the capital's residual Jewish labour force with Poles, who however had to be trained up. This process was far from complete by the next stage of the ethnic cleansing of Berlin and its arms factories: 11,000 more Jews were 'evacuated' in February 1943. But 4,000 slipped through the net, Speer noted, adding that an unidentified person in his ministry, unbeknown to him, was able to supply some of the Jews with special passes they could use to evade being rounded up. Speer claimed no credit, saying he made no such order. His account of these events was supported by the records at Koblenz.

Hitler, Sauckel and especially Goebbels (on the evidence of his own diaries) had major shares in the persecution of the Jews in Berlin and each had more to answer for than Speer and Dietrich Clahes, his chief bailiff for the eviction of the Jews, put together. But Speer's account is specious because he lies by the omission of his own involvement – his innermost secret, for which the grudging, step-by-step admission of connivance with the Nazis' greatest crime was the last line of defence – the final disarming concession designed to conceal his true guilt.

Speer continued to transfer large amounts from his royalties for the two earlier books to Jewish welfare organisations while he researched the third. In summer 1979 he began to raise a substantial sum for his own coffers by a sensational sale of sketches drawn by Hitler during their long architectural association.[14] The canny former court architect, it turned out, had saved the drawings the Führer tore out of his much-used sketchbook, entrusted them to an unidentified friend for safe keeping at the end of the war and unearthed them for auction when Hitler had receded sufficiently into the past for his mementoes to be marketable. The value of the uninspired drawings lay exclusively in their authorship, which meant that the market for them was dominated by Nazi sentimentalists and neo-Fascist collectors of 'militaria'. The sketches went back to 1934; Speer had started to collect them systematically in 1937 when he was appointed GBI. He delegated the task of preservation to Otto Apel, head of his architectural office at that time (and surely a strong candidate for the 'unidentified friend'; he died in 1966 before he could help Speer to return to architectural practice on his release). For authentication purposes the catalogue for the sale listed the items by date, subject and place drawn, and wherever possible Speer related each drawing to a reference in his memoirs.

They fetched 3,000–5,000 marks each in brisk trading, and in order not to undermine the market, Speer stopped selling for three months – when he learned to his annoyance that some of the drawings had already been resold in the United States for the same number of dollars as they had fetched in marks. Nazi souvenir hunters with deep pockets were, as ever, more plentiful, and freer with their money, in the United States than anywhere else (there are unduly large numbers in Britain also, but they tend to fiscal as well as intellectual poverty). Confirming the sales to *Stern* magazine of Hamburg, which wondered aloud why he had not presented the collection to the Federal Archive, Speer said he had given one or two to friends and that the proceeds were not noteworthy; nor were they being given to Jewish organisations, which continued to get royalty money from him anyway. It was another unedifying lapse of taste, to put alongside posing in the Nuremberg dock for the American television mini-series. This time he was coining money from the doodles of the man who made him famous but to whom he had already profitably ascribed the brunt of the crimes in connection with which he had proclaimed first his responsibility, then his guilt and finally his consent (but never, of course, his participation).

Following up his long interview with Albert Speer late in 1979, doctoral candidate Matthias Schmidt of the Friedrich Meinecke Institute for Historical Research in West Berlin paid a visit to the increasingly frail Dr Rudolf Wolters in Coesfeld in spring 1980; it was now Speer's habit, seemingly, to refer such inquiries to his old accomplice. Wolters, apparently impressed by the young man's ability and approach, extracted a promise that his visitor would publish nothing without express permission and then gave him a sight of his personal archive. Schmidt thus became the first person known to have seen the unexpurgated Chronicle after its author, its transcriber and its protagonist – Wolters, Riesser and Speer. He also saw evidence of the conspiracy, initiated by Speer, to cover up the cleansing of the Chronicle spontaneously undertaken by Wolters in 1964, five years before Speer rashly sent the expurgated version to Koblenz despite Irving's known discovery of one uncut year.

Recognising the significance of what he had been allowed to see,
Schmidt sought a follow-up interview with Speer shortly afterwards,
during which the latter expressly denied knowledge of the existence of
the unbowdlerised Chronicle and the deception of the Federal Archive.[15]

Soon after Schmidt's second interview with Speer, in April 1980,
Rudolf Wolters, a victim of chronic hypertension, was stunned to
receive a letter, dated the 14th, from Professor Dr Martin Löffler,
attorney at law of Stuttgart, asking him to acknowledge that copyright
in all the writings in his possession, whether originals or copies, by his
client, Albert Speer, was the exclusive property of said client. Löffler
had been a junior member under Flächsner of Speer's defence team at
Nuremberg. He asserted that the letter Speer sent to Wolters from his
cell on 10 August 1946 had been written under circumstances radically
different from those now prevailing, and had in any case been super-
seded by Speer's note of 6 March 1963 making Hilde rather than
Wolters his literary agent and/or executor. The addressee was not the
kind of man to tear up and throw away such a letter, as the reader
will be aware – his value, whether as a latter-day nuisance to Speer
or as a historical source, lay in his habit of keeping everything – but
he decided to ignore it.

The life-threatening rage of the trembling Wolters can only be
imagined when he opened Löffler's second letter of 2 May, in which
the lawyer complained that there had been no answer to his first –
and gave Wolters seven days to reply, on pain of legal action and costs.
The old man decided it was time to call in his own distinguished
lawyer, Dr Rudolf Lauscher of Düsseldorf, who sent a holding reply on
6 May, asking for a sight of Speer's power of attorney in favour of
Hilde.

That was irrelevant, Löffler loftily replied on the 23rd; the issue was
his client's basic rights to what he had written. With scarcely credible
arrogance and insensitivity, he claimed in well-nigh untranslatable,
legalistic German that what Wolters had done for Speer over the years
since the Nuremberg letter had been no more than the 'unremunerated
task of a friend'. So much for fifteen years and more of unremitting
and largely illegal activity as guardian of Speer's secret writings,
surrogate father and family adviser, all-purpose friend, indefatigable
campaigner, errand-boy and fundraiser-in-chief. The doddering but
mentally alert old man's apoplectic fury is not hard to envisage. Would
he kindly state, the letter concluded, what material he held and return
it to Speer, replying no later than 10 June?

Lauscher's reply of 6 June displayed righteous anger on behalf of his
client. The attempt to impose deadlines was as disgraceful as the
demand for costs when Speer was seeking something he had no right

to demand, the lawyer wrote. Eventually, on 11 July, Lauscher told Löffler that Wolters had handed over everything which was due to Speer when he came Coesfeld in October 1966 after his release. Only a few items, such as letters from Speer to his client, remained in the latter's possession.[16]

Wolters clearly took the view that as author of the Chronicle (the unmentioned bone of contention behind the unpleasant correspondence that buried the dead friendship), he had the absolute right to keep it, regardless of who had commissioned it. He hung on to it until just before his death on 7 January 1983, reportedly with the word 'Albert' on his lips. His bequest had already begun to arrive at the Federal Archive towards the end of 1982. Wolters was clearly aware that he had little time left and was determined to correct the historical record, as he had warned Speer he would. The legal battle looming between them came to nothing as a result of Speer's own death sixteen months earlier. Dr Schmidt took the view that Speer was trying to stop his successful thesis from being turned into the book it eventually became in 1982: *Albert Speer – the End of a Myth.*[17] It deserved a wider circulation than it had (and would probably have got had it not been published after rather than before its subject's sudden death). The last shot in the lawyers' undeclared war over the unexpurgated Chronicle took the form of an advertisement in the *Börsenblatt des deutschen Buchhandels* (the journal of the German book trade) in September 1980, headed 'Cancellation of power of attorney' and signed by Dr Löffler:

> During his imprisonment from May 1945 until October 1966 in Nuremberg and Spandau, my client, Albert Speer (Heidelberg), gave precautionary powers of attorney to third parties for possible access to, or use of, the copyright of his private and official writings.
>
> Although these powers of attorney were in any case for a limited period, my client has reason to believe that these powers are extinct and that his copyright at home and abroad will be wholly and exclusively exercised by him personally.

Schmidt had also taken legal advice and was confident that publication of his book could not have been affected, had Speer survived to bring what would surely have been a fascinating and sensational case. It would inevitably have been a disaster for his reputation as a historical source and author (and professional penitent) to have the double deception of the sanitised Chronicle and the conspiracy to cover up its existence revealed simultaneously, as they surely would have been. Indeed, the threat of exposure as a persecutor of the Jews, a liar, a fraud and a hypocrite would almost certainly have led to a settlement out of court; but the time-bomb represented by the Wolters original of

the Chronicle and the damning correspondence about the cheating of
the archive would inevitably have exploded no later than 1983, when
the material was examined at Koblenz. We can only conclude that
Speer, who had the luck to escape sharing Sauckel's appointment with
the hangman, was almost as lucky to die when he did, escaping the
multiple threat to his reputation posed by the resolute researcher
Schmidt, the alienated chronicler Wolters and the assorted lawyers
who were already well on the way to making matters worse, in one
of the time-honoured traditions of their profession.

It could also be argued that Albert Speer was no less lucky in the
manner of his dying as he was in its timing, whether the latter is seen
as a thirty-five-year stay of execution or as one merciful jump ahead
of the bailiffs of history closing in to take away his reputation.

At the turn of 1979 he received a letter from a reader in England
who had just come across the Spandau diaries and thought them the
best book she had ever read. That remarkable literary judgment derived
at least in part from the fact that this new correspondent and fan was
a German mother of two young children, married to an Englishman
and living in England; she found the book in some way cathartic for
herself as a German in exile.

Speer was naturally flattered and in his reply invited her to call
when she was next in Germany. So she did (my time in Germany
taught me that one does not emit invitations like 'we *must* do lunch'
in the insincere English manner, because a German so addressed will,
quite reasonably, produce a diary and ask when). *Mirabile dictu*, at the
age of seventy-five, Albert Speer immediately fell in passionate love for
the first time in his life with this tall, slender blonde half his age – and
she reciprocated. Although Speer was still working on the manuscript
of *The Slave State* (Sereny blames the liaison for its poor quality, but
Wolf Jobst Siedler rejected it because he thought even the best editor
would be hard put to make it readable) they lost no time in con-
summating the affair and took to meeting in a holiday house in the
south of France. Speer did not conceal his grand passion from his long-
suffering wife. Neither domestic embarrassment nor problems with the
last book (including the chore of finding a publisher) nor even the
ominous episode of a third pulmonary embolism in November 1980
deterred Speer from indulging his belated discovery of sexual passion
at the age of seventy-five.

So it was only natural that he should arrange another assignation
when he was due to go to England for only the second time in his
postwar life on 31 August 1981. The visit was for the same reason, a
television programme, and the host was once again the BBC. There
was no 'Mr Reeps' nonsense because Speer had taken care to confirm

that he was *persona grata* in the more indifferent Britain of the early 1980s. Even so this second fleeting visit was also to be marked by an arrest, albeit of a different sort altogether. He was to take part in a documentary on Nazi art for BBC television and was to be interviewed by Norman Stone, Professor of Modern History at Oxford, media star and scholar of the Third Reich. After a convivial and late working dinner with the professor, who thought he was in remarkable form, belying his age, he spent the one night of his visit at the Park Court Hotel in Bayswater. This smart area of inner west London, immediately north of Kensington Gardens, is very convenient for the BBC Television Centre at Wood Lane, a mile or so to the west; but then the BBC was paying the bill. He spent the first half of Tuesday, 1 September, at the studios.

He then returned to his hotel room for the assignation with his mistress. Just before 5 p.m. she rang reception in extreme agitation and called for help. Speer had suffered a stroke just before he was due to leave for Heathrow airport and was in a coma. An ambulance took him to St Mary's Hospital in nearby Paddington, where the best efforts of the 'crash' team could not prevent cardiac arrest. At about 9 p.m. Albert Speer died of a cerebral haemorrhage, without regaining consciousness.[18]

On 2 September Dr Irmhild Speer, physician and wife of Ernst, the youngest child of the deceased, flew from Frankfurt to London to make formal identification of the body in the mortuary at St Mary's. She arranged for its return by air and hearse to Heidelberg on the 4th for the obsequies.[19]

The Last Confession of Albert Speer

'**Y**OU WERE ALBERT'S FRIEND in his Spandau years, his only and best,' Margarete Speer wrote in her immaculate, well-brought-up girl's hand to Dr Rudolf Wolters on 29 September 1981, four weeks after her husband's death. 'This close attachment helped him to endure those years,' she continued. 'We all know what you did for us. I should like to say, also on behalf of our children, who asked me to do so, how painful it is for us that this friendship was broken off. For me there remains the memory of you as our helper in all the emergencies and sorrows of twenty-one years. It is also thanks to you that the children developed without a father into upright and effective people,' she concluded gracefully. She knew these were the sentiments which her late husband had owed to his most loyal friend but never really acknowledged. The frail Dr Wolters, who had lost no time in sending his generous, heartfelt condolences and regrets for the lost friendship on 2 September, had every right to regard them as well earned.

The Slave State appeared just a few weeks before Speer's death and the reviews were still coming in – all but unanimously bad. They merged into the obituaries, which were notably less harsh, tending overall to accept Speer's carefully cultivated self-image as the apolitical Nazi functionary who redeemed himself by owning up. Heinz Höhne, a senior journalist on *Der Spiegel* and an important historian of the Third Reich, astutely coined the ideal, neutral formulation on 7 September: 'His self-accusations brought him a reputation as Hitler's only repentant paladin.'

'I should certainly have been one of Hitler's close friends had he actually had any,' was Speer's apt summary of his other great bond, the only relationship in which he played second fiddle, as Wolters had done for him. The true life of Albert Speer thus boils down to a tale of two extraordinary friendships – and the deceit that destroyed both.

Speer's habit of rewriting history in his own interest is hardly unique. An anonymous observer once remarked of Churchill's history of the 1914–18 war that 'Winston has written an enormous book about himself and called it *The World Crisis.*' A combination of romanticism and arrogance led Speer to 'fine-tune' the facts of his life-story from the very opening of his memoirs: the birth put back to high noon, the thunderstorm brought forward, the peal of bells from the unbuilt church. He reckoned without the thoroughness of a Matthias Schmidt when telling these intrinsically harmless white lies; but once discovered, they must make the reader wonder what else had been tidied up. The story of his childhood is sparse but bleak, with scraps of affection from the lower orders, including Gretel's family, failing to make up for an indifferent father, a cold mother and two bullying brothers. The result was a calculating introvert who soon learned to use his considerable manipulative gifts to get his way without exposing himself emotionally.

Studiedly laid back and easy-going, Speer was also inhibited and obsessive, indifferent to the needs of subordinates and dependants and capable of malice, vengefulness and cruel practical jokes. While he probably learned to love his father when he was riding high and the old man had ceased to be a threat, to his own children he was the ultimate absentee father, not only when he had no choice in prison but throughout their formative youngest years, when he took refuge in work and preferred to spend Christmas with the Stakhanovites of the Todt Organisation in the snow rather than with his family in his passion-free private sphere.

Whenever possible Speer took firm charge of his personal environment, succumbing to panic attacks and significantly psychosomatic bouts of circulatory trouble when he felt threatened by forces too large for him to control. Paradoxically he took some mighty risks, whether driving at high speed, making rash delivery promises to Hitler, taking on stupendous tasks in unfamiliar fields and pitting himself against the likes of Göring, Himmler, Bormann and Hitler himself.

As a pragmatist and egocentric opportunist, Speer was as interested in office politics and party in-fighting (a matter of survival) as he was uninterested in ideology. But he was neither 'apolitical' nor a 'technocrat'; nor was he 'amoral' but rather immoral, having flouted rather than ignored morality in his dealings with the Jews. He was not a technocrat in the strict sense at all; he had no expert knowledge except of a professional field which he had 'chosen' at his father's behest in lieu of mathematics. His skill and output alike as Hitler's architect were indifferent at best and monstrous at worst; his most effective work was as a stage designer at Nuremberg. He could play politics for keeps when he had to: he threatened people with the SS and concentration camp, he ruined Lord Mayor Lippert of Berlin, he tried to do the same to his architectural rival, Hermann Giesler, and he manipulated Hitler himself by 'bombing' him with experts or presenting him with *faits accomplis.*

Yet he took over from the brilliant engineer and real technocrat Fritz Todt a portfolio of immense tasks, several of which should have had ministers of their own, and discharged them with aplomb. Speer's real talent was for organisation and improvisation. He worked wonders despite constant changes of mind and other interference by Hitler and his henchmen. He was at home with the 'big picture' and the details alike, mastering and remembering the most complicated and unfamiliar brief without visible effort. He had a talent for picking first-class subordinates whom he could inspire to huge effort and deep loyalty; to them he happily delegated enormous responsibilities, leaving them to their own devices even when he did not trust them personally. He did not hesitate to build on the acknowledged ideas of others, such as Todt.

He won the admiration not only of such a deeply cynical operator as Goebbels but also of conservative military professionals such as Milch, Dönitz and Guderian and leading industrialists, including Rohland, Porsche and Messerschmitt. All this amounts to a remarkable array of administrative and persuasive talent seldom found in a single personality. As an architect turned town-planner on a colossal scale, turned high-speed master-builder of huge and intricate projects such as a new Chancellery, Speer was not totally unprepared for what was thrown at him at the apex of his career.

By the time he took over responsibility for the war economy, Germany was fighting for its life and Speer in his element, as a crisis manager and supreme 'generalist', a problem-solver to his fingertips. But even he could not make up for Hitler's earlier, *Blitzkrieg*-based 'short-termism' and could only achieve too little, too late, even when building up production so spectacularly (if from a small base). He was also as responsible as Hitler himself for some immensely wasteful diversions of scarce resources, such as the V2 project, as well as for the suffering of the millions forced to work for him – and the tens of thousands of Jews he had directly caused to be thrown on to the streets of Berlin in the first stage of a journey that usually ended in murder.

His most significant act of rebellion, when he began to betray his declining mentor, was his wholesale subversion of the scorched-earth policy; the 'assassination plot' can be discounted as little more than thinking aloud when it belatedly became clear to him that all was lost. None the less he was proud of what he did achieve for Hitler, enabling him to stay in the war for another year or possibly two; and towards the end of his life he said as much, whether in his long interview for *Playboy* or in a drunken telephone call to Ms Sereny in his last year, described at the end of her book.

But the 'gas in the bunker' plot was enough to help save his neck when he returned as a prisoner to Nuremberg, scene of his most spectacular productions at gatherings of another kind. Göring's hiss of 'treason' at him on hearing of it was a backhanded seal of approval which clearly impressed chief prosecutor Jackson. And it heightened the contrast between the thug element in the dock and the personally modest, studious-looking, patrician Speer with his bold readiness to bow to the doctrine of collective responsibility for an evil regime known to have been dominated by the will of one man. Overlooking the fact that this concession was made under pressure, enough of the judges were impressed by Speer's self-deprecating self-incrimination to take his admission of shared responsibility, coupled with denial of commission or even knowledge of specific crimes, at its face value. They therefore spared him from the hangman to whom his slave-driving colleague, Fritz Sauckel, was consigned for meeting his requirements above all. Only the Russians, to whom he exhibited a degree of arrogance almost as risky as his *nostra culpa* ploy, did not accept Speer at his own valuation.

But then a prisoner on a capital charge can hardly be blamed for making the best possible case for himself, especially when the evidence against him is overwhelming. Perjury by the guilty is not only to be expected but is well-nigh unavoidable; lies are no less bound to be told in mitigation of punishment. Least of all can the accused be expected in such circumstances to own up to crimes with which he has not even been charged. Speer was accused and convicted of using forced and slave labour. He was not accused of evicting the Jews of Berlin from their homes because the prosecution had not found the Wolters Chronicle and did not know about it. Nor was he going to enlighten them, especially after the frightful courtroom shows of film from the death camps during the trial: he was neither suicidal nor a saint.

There was no occasion for surprise therefore when, after escaping execution but serving twenty years, enough to break the spirit of most people, Speer teasingly conceded, first that for the collective 'responsibility' he admitted at Nuremberg one could read shared 'guilt' and then that he had known rather more of 'what was happening with the Jews' than he ever acknowledged in court. Yet did he not stump the country after his release, owning up *ad nauseam*?

But this book, as no other, sets out in detail the evidence that Albert Speer was not an absent-minded, eyes-averted, amoral non-spectator of Nazi anti-Semitism but an active participant in ruining the lives, to put it no more strongly, of 75,000 Berlin Jews by having them evicted. Further, ever the opportunist, he sought to exploit the caution of Wolters in pruning the Chronicle of his wartime office by sending the sanitised version to the German Archive; when caught out, he sought to correct matters by deceit; and when he realised the implications of the Schmidt–Wolters connection, he threatened the scholar and the man who had so loyally discharged his 'unremunerated task for a friend' with legal action.

The eviction of the Jews does not put Speer on the bridge of the SS Holocaust or even in the engine room; but he was in the first-class saloon, driving steerage passengers out into the gathering storm. And he was in the captain's cabin when their subsequent fate was discussed over coffee and cake, as his memoirs deny but the diaries of Goebbels confirm. All the 'repentance' in the world cannot make up for the hypocrisy of Speer's claim to a share of the moral high ground on the basis of a 'confession' which throughout his life concealed his real crime by a lie of omission.

Of course he showed remorse. But remorse, regret for past actions, is not synonymous with contrition, true repentance deriving from knowledge of one's guilt and a desire to atone. There can be no repentance without remorse; but there can certainly be remorse without repentance. Anyone responsible for errors and omissions that earned him twenty years in jail would wish to have done otherwise. If Speer was sorry, it was for himself.

For absolution in the Christian sense, however, a full confession, true contrition and atonement by penance are required. On the historical evidence presented here, Albert Speer fulfilled only the last of these requirements. In the freely chosen role in his later life of public penitent number one, he did not tell the truth, certainly not the whole truth, and therefore he did not repent because he could not. In fact, on mature reflection, he thought he had done rather well in life after all. He therefore does not qualify for the absolution of history.

Should any doubts remain on the matter, there is a hitherto unpublished confession by Speer which is enough to see them off. He made it privately, within five years of his release from Spandau, to Dr Rudolf Wolters, his oldest friend who became the nemesis of his undeserved reputation as the repentant Nazi turned unique historical source. It is recorded in a long letter Wolters wrote to Speer's old enemy, the architect Hermann Giesler, on 21 May 1971, and it is to be found in file number forty-four of the Wolters Bequest at Koblenz.

It refers to Speer's memoirs which, Wolters wrote, once more reaching for his favourite phrase of the time, showed the author to have been no real Nazi but 'a man for whom the need for *Geld und Geltung* (cash and cachet) was decisive'. The outsider might find all his admissions of responsibility and failure to notice what was going on disarming but Wolters, once again reaching for an English word, went on to declare: *'er selbst nannte sie mir gegenüber seine "Tricks".'*

Albert Speer managed to prevent his personal war crime from

emerging in his lifetime and did everything he could to stop the inevitable revelation from ever being made. He admitted his personal share of collective responsibility for Nazi criminality. He vindicated the objection of his friend Wolters by accepting that such responsibility was indeed indistinguishable from guilt. He eventually admitted that he knew rather more about the Holocaust than he had let on at Nuremberg. He paraded his remorse on every possible occasion.

Until his death only Wolters (and his loyal assistant Marion Riesser) knew what Speer was really concealing, and to Wolters alone, in his own defence against his oldest friend's complaints, he confessed that the continual confession of guilt and the monotonous chant of repentance were only a sham:

He himself called them his 'tricks' to my face.

NOTES

1

Origins

(1905–18)

1 A copy of the certificate dated 4 August 1942 is included in file no. BDC 6055012165 RS, at the Berlin Documentation Center, where the Americans deposited Nazi Party records after the war. The suffix 'RS' denotes the Rasse- und Siedlungs-Hauptamt (RuSHA), the SS main office responsible for checking the racial purity of SS members.

This file contains many useful family details and was assembled by autumn 1942, when Speer was made an honorary SS member on the staff of SS-Reichsführer Heinrich Himmler without any action on Speer's part: this mark of distinction was commonly conferred on important people as a means of extending SS influence.

2 Albert Speer, *Inside the Third Reich* (Weidenfeld & Nicolson, 1970), p.4.

3 Matthias Schmidt, *Albert Speer – the End of a Myth* (Harrap, 1985), pp.23–4.

4 Gitta Sereny, *Albert Speer: his Battle with Truth* (Macmillan, 1995), p.41.

5 See file cited in note 1; Speer, *Third Reich*, chapter 1; William Hamsher, *Albert Speer – Victim of Nuremberg?* (Leslie Frewin, 1970) chapter 2; both *passim*.

6 Cited by Schmidt, op. cit., in his note 6 to chapter 2.

7 Hamsher, op. cit., chapter 2, *passim*.

8 Speer, *Third Reich*, p.5.

9 Gitta Sereny, article in *Zeitmagazin*, 20 October 1978 (originally in the *Sunday Times*, London).

10 Sereny, op. cit., p.42.

11 Speer, *Third Reich, p.5.*

12 *Ibid.*, p.4.

13 The foregoing necessarily brief outline of German history derives from broad reading over many years. For further information, Ryder's *Twentieth-Century Germany: from Bismarck to Brandt* and, for a German view, Golo

Mann's *The History of Germany since 1789* are recommended.

14 Albert Speer, *Technik und Macht* (Bechtle, 1979), p.149.

2

Enter Hitler

(1918–31)

1 Speer, *Third Reich*, pp.6–7; Hamsher, op. cit., chapter 3, *passim*.

2 Bundesarchiv (Federal Archive; BA), Nachlass Wolters (Wolters legacy, bequest no. NL 318), file no. 28 (BA-NL318/28): Mathilde Speer's memoir on Schloss-Wolfsbrunnenweg written in 1947 and sent to Wolters in 1951.

3 Hamsher, op. cit., chapter 2, *passim*.

4 Speer, *Third Reich*, pp.5–6.

5 Sereny, op. cit., p.50.

6 Speer, *Third Reich*, p.10.

7 Schmidt, op. cit., chapters 1 and 2, *passim*; countless refs in BA-NL318.

8 For accounts of Hitler and of Germany between the wars, see e.g. Alan Bullock, *Hitler – a Study in Tyranny* (Pelican, 1962); Joachim Fest, *Hitler* (Weidenfeld & Nicolson, 1974).

9 Quoted in Gerald Fleming, *Hitler and the Final Solution* (OUP, 1986) p.17.

10 Speer, *Third Reich*, pp.9–10.

11 See Christine Flon ed., *World Atlas of Architecture* (Mitchell Beazley, 1984), p.371.

12 Speer, *Third Reich*, chapter 1; Schmidt, op. cit., chapter 2.

13 Wolters, BA-NL318/29.

14 Do., NL318/44. Letter to Hermann Giesler, 21 May 1971.

15 Sereny, op. cit., p.73.

16 Schmidt, op. cit., pp.29–30.

17 *Der Angriff*, Goebbels's propaganda sheet for the Berlin Gau (party region), 5 December 1930.

3

Pillars of Light

(1931–33)

1 BDC 1110069306 PK, Speer's party record.

2 Speer, *Third Reich*, p.21.

3 Ibid., p.20.

4 Undated cutting in BA-NL 318/41 from *Jasmin* magazine (late 1969) by James P. O'Donnell, former *New York Times* correspondent in Germany. See also Speer, *Third Reich*, pp.133–4.

5 Speer, *Third Reich*, p.18.

6 *Ibid.*, pp.13–44.

7 BDC 2400029919 RKK, Speer's file as member of the Reichskulturkammer.

8 RKK file as above; Speer, *Third Reich*, pp.21–2.

9 Speer, *Third Reich*, p.22.

10 *Ibid.*, pp.23–4.

11 *Ibid.*, p.24.

12 For general developments in Germany at this time, see e.g. Bullock, op. cit.; Fest, *Hitler*; William L. Shirer, *The Rise and Fall of the Third Reich* (Simon & Schuster, 1960).

13 Speer, *Third Reich*, p.26.

14 *Ibid.*, p.27.

15 *Ibid.*, p.28.

16 Louis L. Snyder, *Encyclopaedia of the Third Reich* (McGraw Hill, 1976), p.254.

4

Supping with the Devil

(1933–37)

1 Speer, *Third Reich*, p.31.

2 For further reading on German and Nazi architecture, see (especially) Peter Adam, *Arts of the Third Reich* (Thames & Hudson, 1992); *The World Atlas of Architecture*; H.-J. Eitner, *Hitler's Deutsche – das Ende eines Tabus* (Casimir Katz, 1990).

3 *'Lumpenbarock'* is this bemused author's coinage for the baroque bunkers

built by King August the Strong and painstakingly restored after the Allied firebombing of Dresden in 1945. The king lacked the light touch; so did Semper.

4 Speer, *Third Reich*, chapter 4, *passim*.

5 The nice phrase was coined by Sir Nevile Henderson, British Ambassador to Berlin 1937–9.

6 Nuremberg City Archive, file no. C32/944.

7 BDC 1110069306 PK.

8 Speer, *Third Reich*, p.57 (footnote).

9 See Erich Fromm's *The Anatomy of Human Destructiveness* (Jonathan Cape, 1974), a seminal contribution to our understanding of Nazi atrocities.

10 Speer, *Third Reich*, chapter 5, *passim*.

11 Nuremberg City Archive, file C32/5.

12 Speer, *Third Reich*, pp.63–4.

13 Author's interviews with Siedler and Fest.

14 Adam, op. cit., chapter 11; Speer, *Third Reich*, chapter 5, both *passim*.

5

Redesigning Berlin

(1937–38)

1 Werner Durth's *Deutsche Architekten* (Friedrich Vieweg, 1987) is a detailed source on German architects, architecture and planning for the period 1900–70, including all Speer's leading contemporaries as well as the man himself and Rudolf Wolters.

The Speer–Lippert tussle is well documented in the Speer Collection at the Imperial War Museum, London (FD 3049/49 IV/133). See also references later in this chapter.

2 Speer, *Third Reich*, chapter 6, *passim*.

3 Wolters, NL 318/48. Durth, op. cit., pp.134–8.

4 NL 318/44, letter from Wolters to Hermann Giesler, 21.5.1971.

5 Leon Krier (ed.) *Albert Speer – Architecture* (Archives d'architecture moderne, 1985), pp.49ff, 121ff; Speer, *Third Reich*, chapter 10.

6 *Ibid.*, pp.197ff. The Beethoven joke is in a footnote to Speer, *Third Reich*, chapter 10; curiously, Speer records the anecdote without confirming or denying it.

7 Speer, *Third Reich*, chapter 7, *passim*. The Berghof was on the Obersalzberg

mountain near Berchtesgaden; the names are used interchangeably for Hitler's mountain lair, also styled the Eagle's Nest.

8 *Ibid.*

9 *Ibid.*, p.101.

10 The Chancellery is exhaustively described in Krier, op. cit. See Speer, *Third Reich*, p.133, for Speer Senior's remark.

11 Krier, op. cit., pp.125–61 (illustrations).

12 Speer, *Third Reich*, chapter 8, *passim*.

13 *Ibid.*

14 *Ibid.*, p.115.

6

Evicting the Jews

(1938–41)

1 Fest, interview with author, 17.11.1993.

2 Speer, *Third Reich*, pp.111–12.

3 *Ibid.*, pp.112–13.

4 Goebbels's Diary, 1 January 1939.

5 Durth, op. cit., pp.159–62; Wolters, NL 318/1, 'Chronik' (Chronicle) 1941 – the valuable, semi-official diary of Speer's private office – January, February and March.

6 Koblenz, BA R3/1503; presentations at discussions with the Führer. See also NL 318/1, Chronicle, January 1941.

7 *Ibid.* (both sources).

8 NL 318/44, Wolters's file on Speer and Giesler, *passim*.

9 Durth, op. cit., pp.159–62.

10 But see Hamsher, op. cit., chapter 11 and Elias Canetti's essay, 'Hitler, nach Speer' (Hitler according to Speer); see Bibliography.

11 Speer, *Third Reich*, pp.170–1.

12 NL 318/1, Chronicle, August 1941.

13 These three passages were of course among those excised by Wolters in 1964 for the sanitised version.

14 Speer, *Third Reich*, chapter 13, *passim*, and pp.189–92; also Speer interview with *Playboy* magazine, June 1971.

7

In Todt's Footsteps

(1942)

1 For an excellent summary of Todt's career, see Franz W. Seidler's profile in *Die Braune Elite* (Wissenschaftliche Buchgesellschaft, 1989) ed. Smelser and Zitelmann.

2 Todt's unpublished pessimism was noted by several contemporaries, including Walter Rohland (who helped run the steel industry for Todt and Speer and was interrogated by the US Strategic Bombing Survey), Wolters and Speer.

3 Churchill had the same quality. He once asked the Director of Naval Intelligence in the First World War why he was muttering, 'My name is Hall, my name is Hall,' during a midnight dispute. The director replied: 'Because if I listen to you much longer I shall be convinced it's Brown.' Only then did Churchill see that Captain Reginald Hall disagreed with him and would not give in.

4 Speer, *Third Reich*, chapter 14. See also NL 318/7, secret letter from Wolters to Speer about Todt, 16 March 1953.

5 Van der Vat, *The Atlantic Campaign* (Hodder & Stoughton, 1988), p.66.

6 Idem, *The Pacific Campaign*, (Simon & Schuster, 1991) chapter 1, *passim*.

7 R3/1501 contains Speer ministry copy of this memorandum.

8 See Gregor Janssen's *Das Ministerium Speer* (Ullstein, 1968), chapter 1, and Edward R. Zilbert's *Albert Speer and the Nazi Ministry of Arms* (Associated University Presses, 1981), chapters 2 and 3, for the economic background to German rearmament. Alan Milward's *The German Economy at War* (Athlone Press, 1965) also refers.

9 Speer concedes this in *Third Reich*, pp.208 and 210, referring to Rathenau as 'the great Jewish organiser', though what his race or religion had to do with anything is not explained. An interesting 'Freudian' slip.

10 NL 318/1, Chronicle (uncut), 1941, April.

11 Speer, *Third Reich*, p.199.

12 R3/1503–1511 contain the voluminous notes on these sessions.

13 Janssen, op. cit., chapter 4, *passim*.

14 Willi A. Boelcke's book, *Deutschlands Rüstung im Zweiten Weltkrieg* (Athenaion, 1969), contains many extracts from the Hitler conference records, with commentaries.

15 Janssen, op. cit., chapter 4, *passim*. See also Schmidt, op. cit., chapter 4, and notes.

16 *Die Zeit*, 2 November 1979.

8

Hard Labour

(1942–43)

1 NL318/2, Chronicle, April 1942. See also Janssen, op. cit., chapter 3, part 2; Speer, *Third Reich*, chapter 16, *passim*.

2 I owe this quotation to Sereny (p.310), who however seems to regard Sauckel as Speer's subordinate or even deputy, elsewhere. He was not, and proved it by cheerfully ignoring many of Speer's wishes.

3 Chronicle, March 1942.

4 Chronicle, either version, August 1943.

5 See Speer, *The Slave State* (Weidenfeld & Nicolson, 1981), for his account of the Mauthausen visit and its consequences, pp.42–5. See also Chronicle for March 1943.

6 See Schmidt, op. cit., p.190, for the first published account of this exchange.

7 Compare cut and uncut Chronicles at dates cited.

8 Uncut Chronicle at date cited.

9 For further reading on Germany and the bomb, see Bibliography for the books by Mark Walker and Thomas Powers, whose superbly argued defence of Heisenberg narrowly fails to rescue his reputation. See also Speer, *Third Reich*, pp.225–8.

10 See van der Vat's *Stealth at Sea* (Weidenfeld & Nicolson, 1994), and *Atlantic Campaign*, for full details of the Walter boats and construction programme.

11 The fullest account of the loss of Ernst Speer is in Sereny, op. cit., pp.364–6.

12 Chronicle, 1 September 1942.

13 *Ibid.*, September 15 (both versions).

9

Pinnacle of Power

(1943)

1 Speer, *Third Reich*, p.276.

2 See BA, NL 318/14, Speer's account of his 'Activity as Minister', part I,

section 3. This was written at Nuremberg while Speer awaited sentence. It has been described, by e.g. Sereny, as a first draft of his memoirs but was written as the last testament (and apologia) of a man expecting to hang.

3 Speer, *Third Reich*, chapter 18, *passim*.

4 Goebbels's Diary, 13 February 1943; NL 318/14 (cf. note 2), part I, section 6; Chronicle, 1 March 1943, referring to a 'fundamental political discussion' with Göring and Goebbels; Speer, *Third Reich*, pp.252–66. Hans Kehrl, head of planning at Speer's ministry, confirms in his memoirs that Speer saw himself as Hitler's successor – but their discussion took place in October 1943.

5 Höhne gives no sources in *Der Spiegel*, September 1981; see Sereny, op. cit., chapter 15, *passim*.

6 R3/1507, Führerbesprechungen, 6–7 February 1943.

7 US National Archive, Interrogation records of the Office of US Chief of Counsel for the Prosecution of Axis Criminality (OCCPAC), microfilm publication no. 1270, roll 29. See also Interrogation reports on Speer at Imperial War Museum, London, IWM/FDC 1, box S367, 28 May 1945.

8 Speer, *Third Reich*, p.274.

9 See Janssen, op. cit., chapter 13, *passim*, for an analysis of the breakdown in German transport.

10 See Speer, *Third Reich*, chapter 22, *passim*, esp. p.312.

11 Quoted in chapter 2 of Fleming, op. cit., one of the most important monographs on Nazi crimes ever written.

12 *Ibid.*, chapter 4; a useful summary is on pp.371–2 of Snyder, op. cit.

13 Text of Himmler's speech is in Koblenz file no. NS19 HR/10.

14 *Midstream* magazine, New York, October 1971.

15 See e.g. Sereny, op. cit., pp.393–4.

16 E.g. Speer, *Slave State* notes to chapter 20, p.362.

17 *Die Zeit*, 2 November 1979.

18 Chronicle, October 1943.

10

Production Peaks

(1943–44)

1 Speer wrote of this visit at length in *Third Reich*, chapter 25 and *Slave State*, chapter 16, both *passim*. See also Chronicle, December 1943; Sereny, op. cit., chapter 15; Schmidt, op. cit., chapter 12; and Jean Michel's memoir, *Dora* (Weidenfeld & Nicolson, 1979).

2 Speer, *Third Reich*, chapter 25, *passim*.

3 These figures are from Speer's summarising Report (Rechenschaftsbericht) for 1944, dated 27 January 1945 and distributed (300 copies) among his senior colleagues and subordinates. It is quoted in full in the Appendix to Janssen), op. cit., and is generally borne out by figures obtained after the war by the US Strategic Bombing Survey.

4 Speer, *Third Reich*, p.295.

5 *Ibid.*, p.303.

6 Chronicle, December 1943 (NL 318/4; BA R3/1738).

7 *Ibid.*

8 Speer, *Third Reich*, chapter 22, *passim*; chapter 23, p.327.

9 Schmidt, op. cit., chapter 6, *passim*.

10 *Ibid.*; see also Schmidt's source notes for evidence of his thorough researches on Speer's illness.

11 First quotation: Sereny, op. cit., p.422. Second: Speer, *Third Reich*, p.335.

12 See Schmidt's thoroughly researched reconstruction of Speer's 'resignation' crisis (chapter 6).

Speer's traditional insult is a quotation from Goethe (*Götz von Berlichingen*, line 4,713). Educated Germans have been known to refer police officers to this impeccable source. Literate officers charge them with 'insulting an official' regardless.

11

Fighters and Resistance

(1944)

1 Speer, *Third Reich*, pp.344–5.

2 Quoted at Nuremberg as Speer defence document no. 43 (International Military Tribunal, IMT, vol., XVI).

3 Speer, *Third Reich*, p.343.

4 Chronicle, May 1944.

5 Discovered by Sereny, op. cit., p.424.

6 See Schmidt, op. cit., chapter 6, and Sereny, op. cit., chapter 16, both *passim*.

7 Speer, *Third Reich*, p.336. See also US Strategic Bombing Survey (USSBS), European Survey, Interrogations of Albert Speer, 15 May 1945, in US National Archive.

8 Speer, *Third Reich*, pp.362–4, deals with Hitler's Me 262 blunder.

9 Sereny exhaustively researched Speer's visit to Landsberg in February 1945 and how it failed to register at Nuremberg and later; op. cit., pp.478–81 and 589 refer.

10 The *Guardian*, London, 14 February 1996: my obituary of Galland.

11 Speer, *Third Reich*, pp.354–7.

12 *Ibid.*, p.358.

13 *Ibid.*, p.409.

14 BA R3/1551–1556, Speer's speeches, closely analysed by Schmidt, op. cit., chapter 8, *passim*.

15 Speer, *Third Reich*, p.413, footnote.

16 *Ibid.*, p.415.

17 Chronicle, 20 July 1944 and after; Speer, *Third Reich*, chapter 26, *passim*. See also Schmidt, op. cit., chapter 7, *passim*.

18 Speer, *Third Reich*, p.383.

12

Total War

(1944–45)

1 Speer, *Third Reich*, p.392.

2 R3/1552, record of Speer's speech to department heads of 24 July 1944. See also Janssen, op. cit., chapter 15, part 2, for a sceptical review of his connection with the plot.

3 R3/1627, records of Speer's private office.

4 Speer, *Third Reich*, pp.375–6.

5 H.R. Trevor-Roper, *Hitler's War Directives* (Pan, 1966), section 58; Janssen, op. cit., chapter 18, part 1; Speer, *Third Reich*, pp.400–5.

6 Speer, *Third Reich*, pp.429–31.

7 *Ibid.*, p.494; Schmidt, op. cit., p.133, and note, p.239.

8 Speer, *Third Reich*, pp.466–7; USSBS, interrogations of Speer and Stahl, in Imperial War Museum Speer Collection, box 367, reels I and II.

9 Speer, *Third Reich*, chapter 30, *passim*.

10 The story of the war's end in Berlin is chaotic and in some respects incomplete or the subject of historical dispute, but is in general well known and available from many sources (e.g. H.R. Trevor-Roper's *The Last Days of Hitler* (Pan, 1983); Bullock, Shirer and Fest, all opp. cit.).

Speer's last decrees, including his 'stewardship' report, are well covered in Janssen, op. cit., chapter 18 *passim* and Appendix. Sereny, op. cit., supports Speer's account of the Wagnerian concert and the macabre poison-pills anecdote in her chapter 19.

11 Speer, *Third Reich*, p.485.

13

Put to the Question

(1945–46)

1 Galbraith did not however change his sceptical opinion. See *A Life in Our Times* (André Deutsch, 1981), chapter 14, 'Albert Speer and After', *passim*. See also his volume of essays, *A Contemporary Guide to Economics, Peace and Laughter* (New American Library, 1981), 'A Retrospect on Albert Speer'.

The Effects of Strategic Bombing on the German War Economy was published by the USSBS on 3 October 1945.

Records of interrogations of Speer are to be found in the Speer Collection at the Imperial War Museum, London (ref. FDC 1) and the National Archive, Washington (USSBS European Survey; and also the records of the Office of the US Chief of Counsel for the Prosecution of Axis Criminality – OCCPAC).

2 Speer is perfunctory in his memoirs about his detention and trial. Apart from the interrogation material cited above, the works listed in the Bibliography by Andrus, Gilbert, Neave, Taylor, Ann and John Tusa all contain largely overlapping material on the background, preparations and course of the Nuremberg trial. See also Sereny, op. cit., chapters 21 and 22, and Speer, *Third Reich*, Epilogue, both *passim*.

3 See Shirer, op. cit., Foreword.

4 Airey Neave, *Nuremberg* (Hodder & Stoughton, 1978), part II, *passim*.

5 G.M. Gilbert, *Nuremberg Diary* (Farrar Straus & Young, 1947), p.16.

6 *Ibid.*, chapter 3, *passim*.

14

Escaping the Noose

(1946)

1 For detailed general accounts of the Nuremberg prosecution, see the books by the Tusas, Telford Taylor, Neave, Gilbert and Andrus in the Bibliography.

2 US National Archive, microfilm document no. M1270, roll 20: OCCPAC interrogation transcripts.

3 *Tribunal der Sieger* was published by Econ Verlag, Düsseldorf; the translation by Scribner's, New York.

4 *Welt am Sonntag*, Hamburg, 31 October 1976.

5 USSBS, European Survey, Section 1, Interrogations of Albert Speer, 19 May 1945, third session.

6 Speer, *Third Reich*, p.511.

7 Telford Taylor, *The Anatomy of the Nuremberg Trials* (Bloomsbury, 1993), p.418.

8 Sereny, op. cit., pp.571–2.

9 Schmidt, op. cit., p.166.

10 Wolters Bequest, BA NL 318/40.

11 *Ibid.*, 42.

12 Interview with Sereny, op. cit., p.592.

13 This account of the trial is derived mainly from the official record, *Trials of the Major War Criminals before the International Military Tribunal* (Nuremberg, 1946, 42 vols). Volume IV contains the evidence against Speer and XVI his own evidence; XIX has Flächsner's closing speech and the proceedings proper end with XXII. Vol XLI contains the documents submitted by Speer and admitted in evidence by the tribunal (exhibits Speer 1–87). All translations from German are by the author.

14 NL 318064.

15

A Life-Support System

(1946–53)

1 Wolters, NL 318/28.

2 Sereny, op. cit., p.615.

3 Speer, *Spandau – the Secret Diaries* (Collins, 1976), pp.4 and 5. The original jottings from which *Spandau* was derived are at the Federal Archive in Koblenz.

4 Letter from Albert Speer to Wolters, 19 August 1952, in NL 318/29.

5 Tony Le Tissier, *Farewell to Spandau* (Ashford, Buchan & Enright, 1994), chapter 2, *passim*.

6 Sereny, op. cit., discovered the importance of the relationship. See her chapter 23.

7 NL 318/28, letter to Wolters, 16 February 1948.

8 *Ibid.*, network correspondence to 31 July 1952.

9 See note 4, above.

16

Daddy's Girl

(1953–66)

1 See Hamsher, op. cit., chapter 6, and Sereny, op. cit., chapter 23, both *passim*, for very lengthy textual extracts.

2 NL 318/24.

3 *Ibid.*, 30.

4 Ibid., letter from Irmgard Proost to Wolters, 30 December 1957.

5 NL 318/30 is dominated by the correspondence about the Proosts.

6 NL 318/26 and 27 contain many lengthy exchanges, about Hilde's work and related matters, between Wolters and Speer.

7 Fromm, op. cit., pp.443ff.

8 The original is in NL 318/42.

9 *Ibid.*

10 *Ibid.*

11 This correspondence is in NL 318/27.

17

Memoirs

(1966–70)

1 NL 318/39 and 40; Sereny, op. cit., chapter 25, *passim*.

2 Sereny, op. cit., p.664.

3 NL 318/42.

4 Ibid; and NL 318/64, Wolters's draft memoirs, also quoted, by permission of the Wolters family, in Sereny, op. cit., pp.667–8.

5 *Ibid.*; and NL 318/39.

6 NL 318/44.

7 *Ibid.*; quoted at length in Sereny, op. cit., p.671.

8 NL 318/41 and 43.

9 Trevor-Roper, *Last Days of Hitler* and Joachim Fest, *The Face of the Third Reich* (Weidenfeld & Nicolson, 1970) respectively.

10 *Die Zeit*, 10 October 1969.

11 *Süddeutsche Zeitung*, 20 September 1966.

12 NL 318/42.

13 NL 318/40.

14 *Ibid.*, where the entire foregoing correspondence is preserved.

18

One Jump Ahead

(1970–81)

1 Sereny, op. cit., pp.74ff. and 692ff.

2 NL 318/42, detailed but undated account by Wolters of the Chronicle affair.

3 The cutting in NL 318/44 is undated but from the context April 1971 looks likely.

4 The two rebuttals are reproduced in full in Adelbert Reif, *Albert Speer – Kontroversen um ein deutsches Phänomen* (Bernard und Graefe, 1978), pp.395–407.

5 *Der Spiegel*, 21 April 1975.

6 Sereny, op. cit., p.162.

7 Various articles in West German newspapers, mid-November 1973, in NL 318/44.

8 *Ibid.*

9 NL 318/40.

10 NL 318/45.

11 NL 318/46.

12 NL 318/48.

13 *Die Zeit-Magazin*, 20 October–3 November 1978.

14 *Stern* magazine, Hamburg, 19 July 1979.

15 Schmidt, op. cit., pp.205–6; NL 318/40 and 42.

16 NL 318/42.

17 Schmidt, op. cit., p.206.

18 Author's conversations with Wolf Jobst Siedler and Professor Norman Stone; Sereny, op. cit., Postscript, *passim*.

19 Contemporary cuttings in Speer Collection, Heidelberg City Archive.

ACKNOWLEDGMENTS

I should like to offer my best thanks to the following institutions and individuals for their help with this book. Any errors in it are mine alone.

The staffs of: the Berlin City Archive; the Berlin Documentation Center, including Dr David Marwell and Lon Dorsey; the Bundesarchiv (German Federal Archives), Koblenz, including Frau Tiefenbach and Frau Hermann; the German Embassy, London, including Margit Hosseini; the *Guardian*, London, including Desmond Christy, Helen Martin and colleagues, Deborah Orr and colleagues, Peter Preston and Alan Rusbridger; the Heidelberg City Archive; the Imperial War Museum, London, including Philip Reed; the Karlsruhe City Archive; the London Library; the Mannheim City Archive including Friedrich Teutsch; the Munich State and City archives; the National Archive, Washington DC; the Nuremberg State and City archives; the Public Record Office, Kew; Twickenham Public Library.

Joachim Fest; Hajo and Sybille Mohr; Professor Dr Karl-Heinz Niclauss; Klaus Platz; Andrea Rak; Dr Hilde Schramm; Wolf Jobst Siedler; Dipl.-Ing. Ernst Speer.

At Curtis Brown, London: Michael Shaw and Sophie Janson; at Curtis Brown, San Francisco: Peter Ginsberg; at Houghton Mifflin, Boston, MA: Christopher Carduff, Mindy Keskinen and Richard Todd; at Weidenfeld and Nicolson, London: Benjamin Buchan, Ion Trewin, Lord Weidenfeld and staff; Morag Lyall.

Grateful acknowledgment is made to the following publications, publishers and/or authors, their agents, heirs or assigns, for quotations from copyright works.

Deutsche Verlagsanstalt, Stuttgart, for *Der Sklavenstaat*; J.K. Galbraith and André Deutsch, London, for *A Life in Our Times*; G.M. Gilbert and Farrar, Straus and Young, New York, for *Nuremberg Diary*; *Midstream* magazine, New York, and Professor Erich Goldhagen for the critique of *Inside the Third Reich*, 1971; Airey Neave, Rebecca West and Hodder & Stoughton, London, for *Nuremberg* and its foreword; *Playboy* and Eric Norden, for the Albert Speer interview, June 1971; Adelbert Reif and

Bernard und Graefe, Munich, for *Albert Speer – Kontroversen um ein deutsches Phänomen*; Adelbert Reif and Bechtle Verlag, Esslingen, for *Albert Speer – Technik und Macht*; the *Observer* and Sebastian Haffner for the Albert Speer profile, 9 April 1944; Matthias Schmidt and Scherz Verlag, Berne and Munich, for *Albert Speer – der Tod eines Mythos*; Gitta Sereny and Macmillan, London, for *Albert Speer – his Battle with Truth*; *Der Spiegel* and Heinz Höhne, various articles; *Süddeutsche Zeitung* and Golo Mann for *Des Teufels Architekt* (review); Ullstein/Propyläen for Albert Speer's *Erinnerungen* (memoirs) and *Die Spandauer Tagebücher* (diaries); *Die Zeit* and Waldemar Besson, Lord Bullock and Gitta Sereny, various articles.

If there is any omission from the above lists, I offer my apologies – and the chance to correct matters in future editions.

SOURCES AND BIBLIOGRAPHY

I

Archives

The public documentation of Albert Speer's work as an administrator and minister is vast, notwithstanding the Third Reich's unconditional surrender followed by the Allied removal, and not always punctilious return, of mountains of German records. The sheer volume of this material tends to obscure the gaps, both in the official paperwork and in the documentation of other parts of Speer's life.

The most important official collection at the German Federal Archive (Bundesarchiv) at Koblenz is filed under the classification R3, the records of Speer's ministry. Also at Koblenz, R120 assembles the papers of the GBI (Inspector-General for Construction for Berlin). Records of the Inspectorates-General for Water and Energy and for German Highways under both Todt and Speer are in R4 and R65 respectively. R50/I covers the Todt Organisation and R50/II Todt's and Speer's transport units. Relevant collections of official printed papers at Koblenz include RD76 (information bulletins of Speer's office), RD77 (gazettes of Speer's ministry) and RD81a (bulletins of the Todt Organisation head office).

But by far the most revealing and interesting source of material on Speer is the Rudolf Wolters Legacy, also at Koblenz (Nachlass 318/Wolters, Rudolf). For access to all but the first few files in this collection, the 'Chronik' (Chronicle), the consent of the Wolters family is required.

Before tackling the foregoing principal archival sources on Speer, I took advantage of the presence in London of the Speer Collection at the Imperial War Museum, containing many British intelligence records on him. I also examined the papers of the United States Strategic Bombing Survey (USSBS), European Survey – records of interrogations of Albert Speer (and many others) in the US National Archive, Washington, DC. Also there are the often overlapping interrogation records of the Office of the US Chief of Counsel for the Prosecution of Axis Criminality (OCCPAC), taken at Nuremberg and elsewhere.

Also consulted were the Nazi Party records kept at the Berlin Documentation Center, run by the United States government until 1994, when they were handed over to the German federal government.

The record of the first and principal hearing at Nuremberg is to be found in the twenty-three volumes of *Trial of the Major War Criminals*, published without reservation of copyright by the Secretariat of the International Military Tribunal in English, French, German and Russian at Nuremberg in 1948.

Local records on Speer, mainly on architectural and planning matters, are kept at Berlin, Heidelberg, Karlsruhe, Munich (city and state archives) and Nuremberg (city and state archives), all of which I visited.

II

The Speer Corpus

(The main works by or about Speer)
(*indicates dependent on Speer: see Preface)

Boelcke, Willi A. (ed.): *Deutschlands Rüstung im Zweiten Weltkrieg – Hitlers Konferenzen mit Albert Speer* (Athenaion, Frankfurt-am-Main, 1969)*

Hamsher, William: *Albert Speer – Victim of Nuremberg?* (Leslie Frewin, London, 1970)*

Janssen, Gregor: *Das Ministerium Speer – Deutschlands Rüstung im Krieg* (Ullstein, Berlin, 1968)*

Krier, Leon (ed.): *Albert Speer – Architecture 1932–1942* (Archives d'architecture moderne, Brussels, 1985)*

Norden, Eric: Albert Speer Interview (*Playboy*, 6. 1971)

Reif, Adelbert (ed.): *Albert Speer – Kontroversen um ein deutsches Phänomen* (Bernard und Graefe, Munich, 1978)*

Schmidt, Matthias: *Albert Speer – the End of a Myth*, trans. Joachim Neugroschel (Harrap, London, 1985) (Originally published as *Albert Speer – der Tod eines Mythos*, by Scherz Verlag, Berne/Munich, 1982)

Sereny, Gitta: *Albert Speer – his Battle with Truth* (Macmillan, London, 1995)*

Speer, Albert: *Inside the Third Reich*, trans. Richard and Clara Winston (Weidenfeld & Nicolson, London, 1970)* (Originally published as *Erinnerungen*, by Ullstein, Berlin, 1969)

Speer, Albert: *Spandau – the Secret Diaries*, trans. Richard and Clara Winston (Collins, London, 1976)* (Originally published as *Spandauer Tagebücher*, by Ullstein, Berlin, 1975)

Speer, Albert: *Architektur – Arbeiten 1933–1942* (Propyläen, Frankfurt am Main, 1978)*

Speer, Albert: *The Slave State*, trans. Joachim Neugroschel (Weidenfeld & Nicolson, London, 1981)* (Originally published as *Der Sklavenstaat*, by Deutsche Verlagsanstalt, Stuttgart, 1981; US edition entitled *Infiltration*, Macmillan, New York, 1981)

'Speer, Albert': 'Die Bauten des Führers' (article attrib. to Speer in *Adolf Hitler –*

Bilder aus dem Leben des Führers, Cigaretten-Bilderdienst, Hamburg-Altona, 1936)

Speer, Albert (ed. Adelbert Reif): *Technik und Macht* (Bechtle, Esslingen, 1979)*

Wolters, Rudolf: *Neue deutsche Baukunst* (Volk und Reich, Berlin, 1941)*

Wolters, Rudolf: *Albert Speer* (Stalling, Oldenburg, 1943)*

Zilbert, Edward R: *Albert Speer and the Nazi Ministry of Arms* (Associated [US] University Presses, London, 1981)*

III

Other Works

Adam, Peter: *Arts of the Third Reich* (Thames & Hudson, London, 1992)

Bessel, Richard (ed.): *Life in the Third Reich* (Oxford UP, 1987)

Bloch, Michael: *Ribbentrop* (Bantam Press, London, 1994)

Bullock, Alan: *Hitler – a Study in Tyranny* (revised edition, Pelican, London, 1962)

Bullock, Alan: *Hitler and Stalin* (Harper Collins, London, 1991)

Calvocoressi, Peter: *Total War – the Causes and Courses of the Second World War: the Western Hemisphere* (second edition, Viking, London, 1989)

Canetti, Elias: *Das Gewissen der Worte – Essays* (Fischer Taschenbuch Verlag, Frankfurt am Main, 1988)

Dönitz, Karl: *Zehn Jahre und Zwanzig Tage* (Athenäum, Bonn, 1958)

Durth, Werner: *Deutsche Architekten – Biographische Verflechtungen 1900–1970* (Friedrich Vieweg & Sohn, Brunswick/Wiesbaden, revised edition, 1987)

Eitner, Hans-Jürgen: *Hitlers Deutsche – das Ende eines Tabus* (Casimir Katz, Gernsbach, 1990)

Ellis, John: *Brute Force – Allied Strategy and Tactics in the Second World War* (André Deutsch, London, 1990)

Fest, Joachim C.: *The Face of the Third Reich* (Weidenfeld & Nicolson, London, 1970)

Fest, Joachim C.: *Hitler* (Weidenfeld & Nicolson, London, 1974)

Fleming, Gerald: *Hitler and the Final Solution* (Oxford UP, 1986)

Flon, Christine (ed.): *The World Atlas of Architecture* (Mitchell Beazley, London, 1984)

Fromm, Erich: *The Anatomy of Human Destructiveness* (Jonathan Cape, London, 1974)

Galbraith, John Kenneth: *A Contemporary Guide to Economics, Peace and Laughter* (New American Library, New York, 1981)

Galbraith, John Kenneth: *A Life in Our Times – Memoirs* (André Deutsch, London, 1981)

Gesellschaft Für Literatur und Bildung (publ.): *Die Wehrmachtberichte 1939–1945* (three vols, Cologne, 1989)

Giesler, Hermann: *Ein anderer Hitler* (Druffel, Leoni/Bavaria, 1982)

Gilbert, G.M.: *Nuremberg Diary* (Farrar Straus & Young, New York, 1947)

Grunberger, Richard: *A Social History of the Third Reich* (Weidenfeld & Nicolson, London, 1971)

Hellman, Louis: *Architecture for Beginners* (Writers & Readers, New York, 1988)

Höhne, Heinz: *The Order of the Death's Head* (Secker & Warburg, London, 1969)

Kehrl, Hans: *Krisenmanager im Dritten Reich* (Droste, Düsseldorf, 1973)

Kershaw, Ian: *The 'Hitler Myth' – Image and Reality in the Third Reich* (Clarendon Press, Oxford, 1987)

Kitchen, Martin: *Nazi Germany at War* (Longman, London, 1995)

Le Tissier, Tony: *Farewell to Spandau* (Ashford, Buchan & Enright, Leatherhead, Surrey, 1994)

Mann, Golo: *The History of Germany since 1789*, trans. Marian Jackson (Chatto & Windus, London, 1968)

Mason, David: *Who's Who in World War II* (Weidenfeld & Nicolson, London, 1978)

Mercer, Derrik (ed.): *Chronicle of the Twentieth Century* (Longmans, London, 1988)

Mercer, Derrik (ed.): *Chronicle of the Second World War* (Longmans, London, 1990)

Michel, Jean: *Dora* (Weidenfeld & Nicolson, London, 1979)

Milward, Alan S.: *The German Economy at War* (Athlone Press, University of London, 1965)

Neave, Airey: *Nuremberg* (Hodder & Stoughton, London, 1978)

Overy, R.J.: *The Air War 1939–1945* (Europa, London, 1980)

Overy, R.J.: *Göring – the Iron Man* (Routledge & Kegan Paul, London, 1984)

Padfield, Peter: *Himmler* (Macmillan, London, 1990)

Powers, Thomas: *Heisenberg's War – the Secret History of the German Bomb* (Jonathan Cape, London, 1993)

Rössler, Eberhard: *The U-Boat*, trans. Harold Erenberg (Arms & Armour Press, London, 1981)

Rohland, Walter: *Bewegte Zeiten – Erinnerungen eines Eisenhütten-Mannes* (Seewald, Stuttgart, 1978)

Ryder, A.J.: *Twentieth Century Germany – from Bismarck to Brandt* (Macmillan, London, 1973)

Schneider, Rolf: *Prozess in Nürnberg* (Fischer Bücherei, Frankfurt am Main, 1968)

Shirer, William L.: *The Rise and Fall of the Third Reich* (Simon & Schuster, New York, 1960)

Simmons, Michael: *Berlin – the Dispossessed City* (Hamish Hamilton, London, 1988)

Smelser, Ronald, and Zitelmann, Rainer (eds): *Die Braune Elite – 22 Biographische Skizzen* (Wissenschaftliche Buchgesellschaft, Darmstadt, 1989)

Snyder, Dr Louis L.: *Encyclopaedia of the Third Reich* (McGraw Hill, New York, 1976)

Taylor, Fred (trans. and ed.): *The Goebbels Diaries 1939–1941* (Hamish Hamilton, London, 1982)

Taylor, Telford: *The Anatomy of the Nuremberg Trials* (Bloomsbury, London, 1993)

Terraine, John: *The Right of the Line* (Hodder & Stoughton, London, 1985)

Teut, Anna: *Architektur im Dritten Reich* (Ullstein, Berlin, 1967)

Trevor-Roper, H.R.: *The Last Days of Hitler* (fifth revised edition, Pan Books, London, 1983)

Trevor-Roper, H.R. (ed.): *Hitler's War Directives* (Pan Books, London, 1966)

Trevor-Roper, H.R. (ed.): *The Goebbels Diaries – the Last Days* (Secker & Warburg, London, 1978)

Tusa, Ann, and Tusa, John: *The Nuremberg Trial* (Macmillan, London, 1983)

van der Vat, Dan: *The Atlantic Campaign – the Great Struggle at Sea 1939–1945* (Hodder & Stoughton, London, 1988)

van der Vat, Dan: *The Pacific Campaign 1941–1945* (Simon & Schuster, New York, 1991)

van der Vat, Dan: *Stealth at Sea – the History of the Submarine* (Weidenfeld & Nicolson, London, 1994)

Vassiltchikov, Marie: *The Berlin Diaries 1940–1945* (Chatto & Windus, London, 1985)

Walker, Mark: *German National Socialism and the Quest for Nuclear Power 1939–1949* (Cambridge UP, 1989)

Wheal, Elizabeth-Anne, Pope, Stephen, and Taylor, James: *A Dictionary of the Second World War* (Grafton, London, 1989)

Wintle, Justin (ed.): *Dictionary of War Quotations* (Hodder & Stoughton, London, 1989)

Wistrich, Robert: *Wer war Wer im Dritten Reich* (Harnack, Munich, 1983)

INDEX

TEHANU

URSULA K. Le GUIN
TEHANU
The Last Book of Earthsea

A Jean Karl Book
ATHENEUM 1990 NEW YORK

Atheneum
Macmillan Publishing Company
866 Third Avenue, New York, NY 10022
Collier Macmillan Canada, Inc.
First Edition
Printed in the United States of America

10 9 8 7 6 5 4 3 2 1

Library of Congress Cataloging-in-Publication Data
Le Guin, Ursula K.
Tehanu : the last book of Earthsea / Ursula K. Le Guin.
—1st ed.   p.   cm.
"A Jean Karl book."
*Summary: When Sparrowhawk, the archmage of Earthsea, returns from the dark land stripped
of his magic powers, he finds refuge with the aging widow, Tenar, and a crippled girl who carries
an unknown destiny.*
ISBN 0–689–31595–3
[1. Fantasy.] I. Title.
PZ7.L45355Te 1990 [Fic]—dc20
89–32780 CIP AC

Only in silence the word,
only in dark the light,
only in dying life:
bright the hawk's flight
on the empty sky.

—The Creation of Éa

Contents

Kemay
Tutok Bay
Kedun
Oskres
Selt
Norvale
Up Norvale
Ten Alders
Medu
Lotin
Korry
Up Selt
Chodur
Desi Port
Ketoleko
Al
Toss
East Port
Var
Solwes
Ovark
Wiss
Tant
Beech Springs
Allage
Down Wiss
Essary
Lissu
Re Albi
Kahedanan
Kebas
Kaheda
Oak Village
Gont Port
Tettego
Etreke
Valmouth

Kameber

THE ISLAND OF GONT

Spevy

0   50   100

TEHANU

The Last Book of Earthsea

Lissu

R. Kaheda

Kahedanan

Re Albi

GONT PORT

• Oak Springs

Oak
Village

Sereva

Doly

Sodeva

Valmouth

R. Vale

Tettego

Etreke

A Bad Thing

After Farmer Flint of the Middle Valley died, his widow stayed on at the farmhouse. Her son had gone to sea and her daughter had married a merchant of Valmouth, so she lived alone at Oak Farm. People said she had been some kind of great person in the foreign land she came from, and indeed the mage Ogion used to stop by Oak Farm to see her; but that didn't count for much, since Ogion visited all sorts of nobodies.

She had a foreign name, but Flint had called her Goha, which is what they call a little white web-spinning spider on Gont. That name fit well enough, she being white-skinned and small and a good spinner of goat's-wool and sheep-fleece. So now she was Flint's widow, Goha, mistress of a flock of sheep and the land to pasture them, four fields, an orchard of pears, two tenants' cottages, the old stone farmhouse under the oaks, and the family graveyard over the hill where Flint lay, earth in his earth.

"I've generally lived near tombstones," she said to her daughter.

"Oh, mother, come live in town with us!" said Apple, but the widow would not leave her solitude.

"Maybe later, when there are babies and you'll need a hand," she said, looking with pleasure at her grey-eyed daughter. "But not now. You don't need me. And I like it here."

When Apple had gone back to her young husband, the widow closed the door and stood on the stone-flagged floor of the kitchen of the farmhouse. It was dusk, but she did not light the lamp, thinking of her own husband lighting the lamp: the hands, the spark, the intent, dark face in the catching glow. The house was silent.

"I used to live in a silent house, alone," she thought. "I will do so again." She lighted the lamp.

In a late afternoon of the first hot weather, the widow's old friend Lark came out from the village, hurrying along the dusty lane. "Goha," she said, seeing her weeding in the bean patch, "Goha, it's a bad thing. It's a very bad thing. Can you come?"

"Yes," the widow said. "What would the bad thing be?"

Lark caught her breath. She was a heavy, plain, middle-aged woman, whose name did not fit her body any more. But once she had been a slight and pretty girl, and she had befriended Goha, paying no attention to the villagers who gossiped about that white-faced Kargish witch Flint had brought home; and friends they had been ever since.

"A burned child," she said.

"Whose?"

"Tramps'."

Goha went to shut the farmhouse door, and they set off along the lane, Lark talking as they went. She was short of breath and sweating. Tiny seeds of the heavy grasses that lined the lane stuck to her cheeks and forehead, and she brushed at them as she talked. "They've been camped in the river meadows all the month. A man, passed himself off as a tinker, but he's a thief, and a woman with him. And another man, younger, hanging around with them most of the time. Not working, any of 'em. Filching and begging and living off the woman. Boys from downriver were bringing them farmstuff to get at her. You know how it is now, that kind of thing. And gangs on the roads and coming by farms. If I were you, I'd lock my door, these days. So this one, this younger fellow, comes into the village, and I was out in front of our house, and he says, 'The child's not well.' I'd barely seen a child with them, a little ferret of a thing, slipped out of sight so quick I wasn't sure it was there at all. So I said, 'Not well? A fever?' And the fellow says, 'She hurt herself, lighting the fire,' and then before I'd got myself ready to go with him he'd made off. Gone. And when I went out there by the river, the other pair was gone too. Cleared out. Nobody. All their traps and trash gone too. There was just their campfire, still smoldering, and just by it—partly in it—on the ground—"

Lark stopped talking for several steps. She looked straight ahead, not at Goha.

"They hadn't even put a blanket over her," she said.

She strode on.

"She'd been pushed into the fire while it was burning," she said. She swallowed, and brushed at the sticking seeds on her hot face. "I'd say maybe she fell, but if she'd been awake she'd have tried to save herself. They beat her and thought they'd killed her, I guess, and wanted to hide what they'd done to her, so they—"

She stopped again, went on again.

"Maybe it wasn't him. Maybe he pulled her out. He came to get help for her, after all. It must have been the father. I don't know. It doesn't matter. Who's to know? Who's to care? Who's to care for the child? Why do we do what we do?"

Goha asked in a low voice, "Will she live?"

"She might," Lark said. "She might well live."

After a while, as they neared the village, she said, "I don't know why I had to come to you. Ivy's there. There's nothing to be done."

"I could go to Valmouth, for Beech."

"Nothing he could do. It's beyond . . . beyond help. I got her warm. Ivy's given her a potion and a sleeping charm. I carried her home. She must be six or seven but she didn't weigh what a two-year-old would. She never really waked. But she makes a sort of gasping. . . . I know there isn't anything you can do. But I wanted you."

"I want to come," Goha said. But before they entered Lark's house, she shut her eyes and held her breath a moment in dread.

Lark's children had been sent outdoors, and the house was silent. The child lay unconscious on Lark's bed. The village witch, Ivy, had smeared an ointment of witch hazel and heal-all on the lesser burns, but had not touched the right side of the face and head and the right hand, which had been charred to the bone. She had drawn the rune Pirr above the bed, and left it at that.

"Can you do anything?" Lark asked in a whisper.

Goha stood looking down at the burned child. Her hands were still. She shook her head.

"You learned healing, up on the mountain, didn't you?" Pain and shame and rage spoke through Lark, begging for relief.

"Even Ogion couldn't heal this," the widow said.

Lark turned away, biting her lip, and wept. Goha held her, stroking her grey hair. They held each other.

The witch Ivy came in from the kitchen, scowling at the sight of Goha. Though the widow cast no charms and worked no spells, it was said that when she first came to

Gont she had lived at Re Albi as a ward of the mage, and that she knew the Archmage of Roke, and no doubt had foreign and uncanny powers. Jealous of her prerogative, the witch went to the bed and busied herself beside it, making a mound of something in a dish and setting it afire so that it smoked and reeked while she muttered a curing charm over and over. The rank herbal smoke made the burned child cough and half rouse, flinching and shuddering. She began to make a gasping noise, quick, short, scraping breaths. Her one eye seemed to look up at Goha.

Goha stepped forward and took the child's left hand in hers. She spoke in her own language. "I served them and I left them," she said. "I will not let them have you."

The child stared at her or at nothing, trying to breathe, and trying again to breathe, and trying again to breathe.

Going to the Falcon's Nest

It was more than a year later, in the hot and spacious days after the Long Dance, that a messenger came down the road from the north to Middle Valley asking for the widow Goha. People in the village put him on the path, and he came to Oak Farm late in the afternoon. He was a sharp-faced, quick-eyed man. He looked at Goha and at the sheep in the fold beyond her and said, "Fine lambs. The Mage of Re Albi sends for you."

"He sent you?" Goha inquired, disbelieving and amused. Ogion, when he wanted her, had quicker and finer messengers: an eagle calling, or only his own voice saying her name quietly—*Will you come?*

The man nodded. "He's sick," he said. "Will you be selling off any of the ewe lambs?"

"I might. You can talk to the shepherd if you like. Over by the fence there. Do you want supper? You can stay the night here if you want, but I'll be on my way."

"Tonight?"

This time there was no amusement in her look of mild scorn. "I won't be waiting about," she said. She spoke for a minute with the old shepherd, Clearbrook, and then turned away, going up to the house built into the hillside by the oak grove. The messenger followed her.

In the stone-floored kitchen, a child whom he looked at once and quickly looked away from served him milk, bread, cheese, and green onions, and then went off, never saying a word. She reappeared beside the woman, both shod for travel and carrying light leather packs. The messenger followed them out, and the widow locked the farmhouse door. They all set off together, he on his business, for the message from Ogion had been a mere favor added to the serious matter of buying a breeding ram for the Lord of Re Albi; and the woman and the burned child bade him farewell where the lane turned off to the village. They went on up the road he had come down, northward and then west into the foothills of Gont Mountain.

They walked until the long summer twilight began to darken. They left the narrow road then and made camp in a dell down by a stream that ran quick and quiet, reflecting the pale evening sky between thickets of scrub willow. Goha made a bed of dry grass and willow leaves, hidden among the thickets like a hare's form, and rolled the child up in a blanket on it. "Now," she said, "you're a cocoon. In the morning you'll be a butterfly and hatch out." She lighted no fire, but lay in her cloak beside the child and watched the stars shine one by one and listened to what the stream said quietly, until she slept.

When they woke in the cold before the dawn, she made a small fire and heated a pan of water to make oatmeal gruel for the child and herself. The little ruined butterfly came shivering from her cocoon, and Goha cooled the pan in the dewy grass so that the child could hold it and drink from it. The east was brightening above the high, dark shoulder of the mountain when they set off again.

They walked all day at the pace of a child who tired easily. The woman's heart yearned to make haste, but she walked slowly. She was not able to carry the child any long distance, and so to make the way easier for her she told her stories.

"We're going to see a man, an old man, called Ogion," she told her as they trudged along the narrow road that wound upward through the forests. "He's a wise man, and a wizard. Do you know what a wizard is, Therru?"

If the child had had a name, she did not know it or would not say it. Goha called her Therru.

She shook her head.

"Well, neither do I," said the woman. "But I know what they can do. When I was young—older than you, but young—Ogion was my father, the way I'm your mother now. He looked after me and tried to teach me what I needed to know. He stayed with me when he'd rather have been wandering by himself. He liked to walk, all along these roads like we're doing now, and in the forests, in the wild places. He went everywhere on the mountain, looking at things, listening. He always listened, so they called him the Silent. But he used to talk to me. He told me stories. Not only the great stories everybody learns, the heroes and the kings and the things that happened long ago and far away, but stories only he knew." She walked on a way before she went on. "I'll tell you one of those stories now.

"One of the things wizards can do is turn into something else—take another form. Shape-changing, they call it. An ordinary sorcerer can make himself look like somebody else, or like an animal, just so you don't know for a minute what you're seeing—as if he'd put on a mask. But the wizards and mages can do more than that. They can be the mask, they can truly change into another being. So a wizard, if he wanted to cross the sea and had no boat, might turn himself into a gull and fly across. But he has to be careful. If he stays a bird, he begins to think what a bird thinks and forget what a man thinks, and he might fly off and be a gull and never a man again. So they say there was a great wizard once who liked to turn himself into a bear, and did it too often, and became a bear, and killed his own little son; and they had to hunt him down and kill him. But Ogion used to joke about it, too. Once when the mice got into his pantry and ruined the cheese, he caught one with a tiny mousetrap spell, and he held the mouse up like this and looked it in the eye and said, 'I told you not to play mouse!' And for a minute I thought he meant it. . . .

"Well, this story is about something like shape-changing, but Ogion said it was beyond all shape-changing he knew, because it was about being two things, two beings, at once, and in the same form, and he said that this is beyond the power of wizards. But he met with it in a little village around on the northwest coast of Gont, a place called Kemay. There was a woman there, an old fisherwoman, not a witch, not learned; but she made songs. That's how Ogion came to hear of her. He was wandering there, the way he did, going along the coast, listening; and he heard somebody singing, mending a net or caulking a boat and singing as they worked:

> *Farther west than west*
> *beyond the land*
> *my people are dancing*
> *on the other wind.*

"It was the tune and the words both that Ogion heard, and he had never heard them before, so he asked where the song came from. And from one answer to another, he went along to where somebody said, 'Oh, that's one of the songs of the Woman of Kemay.' So he went on along to Kemay, the little fishing port where the woman lived, and he found her house down by the harbor. And he knocked on the door with his mage's staff. And she came and opened the door.

"Now you know, you remember when we talked about names, how children have child-names, and everybody has a use-name, and maybe a nickname too. Different people may call you differently. You're my Therru, but maybe you'll have a Hardic use-name when you get older. But also, when you come into your womanhood, you will, if all be rightly done, be given your true name. It will be given you by one of true power, a wizard or a mage, because that is their power, their art—naming. And that's the name you'll maybe never tell another person, because your own self is in your true name. It is your strength, your power; but to another it is risk and burden, only to be given in utmost need and trust. But a great mage, knowing all names, may know it without your telling him.

"So Ogion, who is a great mage, stood at the door of the little house there by the seawall, and the old woman opened the door. Then Ogion stepped back, and he held up his oak staff, and put up his hand, too, like this, as if trying to protect himself from the heat of a fire, and in his amazement and fear he said her true name aloud—'Dragon!'

"In that first moment, he told me, it was no woman he saw at all in the doorway, but a blaze and glory of fire, and a glitter of gold scales and talons, and the great eyes of a dragon. They say you must not look into a dragon's eyes.

"Then that was gone, and he saw no dragon, but an old woman standing there in the doorway, a bit stooped, a tall old fisherwoman with big hands. She looked at him as he did at her. And she said, 'Come in, Lord Ogion.'

"So he went in. She served him fish soup, and they ate, and then they talked by her fire. He thought that she must be a shape-changer, but he didn't know, you see, whether she was a woman who could change herself into a dragon, or a dragon who could change itself into a woman. So he asked her at last, 'Are you woman or dragon?' And she didn't say, but she said, 'I'll sing you a story I know.' "

Therru had a little stone in her shoe. They stopped to get that out, and went on, very slowly, for the road was climbing steeply between cut banks of stone overhung by thickets where the cicadas sang in the summer heat.

"So this is the story she sang to him, to Ogion.

"When Segoy raised the islands of the world from the sea in the beginning of time, the dragons were the first born of the land and the wind blowing over the land. So the Song of the Creation tells. But her song told also that then, in the beginning, dragon and human were all one. They were all one people, one race, winged, and speaking the True Language.

"They were beautiful, and strong, and wise, and free.

"But in time nothing can be without becoming. So among the dragon-people some became more and more in love with flight and wildness, and would have less and less to do with the works of making, or with study and learning, or with houses and cities. They wanted only to fly farther and farther, hunting and eating their kill, ignorant and uncaring, seeking more freedom and more.

"Others of the dragon-people came to care little for flight, but gathered up treasure, wealth, things made, things learned. They built houses, strongholds to keep their treasures in, so they could pass all they gained to their children, ever seeking more increase and more. And they came to fear the wild ones, who might come flying and destroy all their dear hoard, burn it up in a blast of flame out of mere carelessness and ferocity.

"The wild ones feared nothing. They learned nothing.

Because they were ignorant and fearless, they could not save themselves when the flightless ones trapped them as animals and killed them. But other wild ones would come flying and set the beautiful houses afire, and destroy, and kill. Those that were strongest, wild or wise, were those who killed each other first.

"Those who were most afraid, they hid from the fighting, and when there was no more hiding they ran from it. They used their skills of making and made boats and sailed east, away from the western isles where the great winged ones made war among the ruined towers.

"So those who had been both dragon and human changed, becoming two peoples—the dragons, always fewer and wilder, scattered by their endless, mindless greed and anger, in the far islands of the Western Reach; and the human folk, always more numerous in their rich towns and cities, filling up the Inner Isles and all the south and east. But among them there were some who saved the learning of the dragons—the True Language of the Making—and these are now the wizards.

"But also, the song said, there are those among us who know they once were dragons, and among the dragons there are some who know their kinship with us. And these say that when the one people were becoming two, some of them, still both human and dragon, still winged, went not east but west, on over the Open Sea, till they came to the other side of the world. There they live in peace, great winged beings both wild and wise, with human mind and dragon heart. And so she sang,

> Farther west than west
> beyond the land
> my people are dancing
> on the other wind.

"So that was the story told in the song of the Woman of Kemay, and it ended with those words.

"Then Ogion said to her, 'When I first saw you I saw your true being. This woman who sits across the hearth from me is no more than the dress she wears.'

"But she shook her head and laughed, and all she would say was, 'If only it were that simple!'

"So then after a while Ogion came back to Re Albi. And when he told me the story, he said to me, 'Ever since that day, I have wondered if anyone, man or dragon, has been farther west than west; and who we are, and where our wholeness lies.' . . . Are you getting hungry, Therru? There's a good sitting place, it looks like, up there where the road turns. Maybe from there we'll be able to see Gont Port, away down at the foot of the mountain. It's a big city, even bigger than Valmouth. We'll sit down when we get to the turn, and rest a bit."

From the high corner of the road they could indeed look down the vast slopes of forest and rocky meadow to the town on its bay, and see the crags that guarded the entrance to the bay, and the boats on the dark water like wood-chips or water beetles. Far ahead on their road and still somewhat above it, a cliff jutted out from the mountainside: the Overfell, on which was the village of Re Albi, the Falcon's Nest.

Therru made no complaints, but when presently Goha said, "Well, shall we go on?" the child, sitting there between the road and the gulfs of sky and sea, shook her head. The sun was warm, and they had walked a long way since their breakfast in the dell.

Goha brought out their water bottle, and they drank again; then she brought out a bag of raisins and walnuts and gave it to the child.

"We're in sight of where we're going," she said, "and I'd like to be there before dark, if we can. I'm anxious to see

Ogion. You'll be very tired, but we won't walk fast. And we'll be there safe and warm tonight. Keep the bag, tuck it in your belt. Raisins make your legs strong. Would you like a staff—like a wizard—to help you walk?''

Therru munched and nodded. Goha took out her knife and cut a strong shoot of hazel for the child, and then seeing an alder fallen above the road, broke off a branch of it and trimmed it to make herself a stout, light stick.

They set off again, and the child trudged along, beguiled by raisins. Goha sang to amuse them both, love songs and shepherd's songs and ballads she had learned in the Middle Valley; but all at once her voice hushed in the middle of a tune. She stopped, putting out her hand in a warning gesture.

The four men ahead of them on the road had seen her. There was no use trying to hide in the woods till they went on or went by.

"Travelers," she said quietly to Therru, and walked on. She took a good grip on her alder stick.

What Lark had said about gangs and thieves was not just the complaint each generation makes that things aren't what they used to be and the world's going to the dogs. In the last several years there had been a loss of peace and trust in the towns and countrysides of Gont. Young men behaved like strangers among their own people, abusing hospitality, stealing, selling what they stole. Beggary was common where it had been rare, and the unsatisfied beggar threatened violence. Women did not like to go alone in the streets and roads, nor did they like that loss of freedom. Some of the young women ran off to join the gangs of thieves and poachers. Often they came home within the year, sullen, bruised, and pregnant. And among village sorcerers and witches there was rumor of matters of their profession going amiss: charms that had always cured did not cure; spells of finding found nothing, or the wrong thing; love potions drove men into frenzies not of desire but of murderous jealousy. And worse than this, they said, people who knew nothing of the art of magic, the laws and limits of it and the dangers of breaking them, were calling themselves people of power, promising wonders of wealth and health to their followers, promising even immortality.

Ivy, the witch of Goha's village, had spoken darkly of this weakening of magic, and so had Beech, the sorcerer of Valmouth. He was a shrewd and modest man, who had come to help Ivy do what little could be done to lessen the pain and scarring of Therru's burns. He had said to Goha, "I think a time in which such things as this occur must be a time of ruining, the end of an age. How many hundred years since there was a king in Havnor? It can't go on so. We must turn to the center again or be lost, island against island, man against man, father against child. . . ." He had glanced at her, somewhat timidly, yet with his clear, shrewd look. "The Ring of Erreth-Akbe is restored to the Tower in Havnor," he said. "I know who brought it there. . . . That was the sign, surely, that was the sign of the new age to come! But we haven't acted on it. We have no king. We have no center. We must find our heart, our strength. Maybe the Archmage will act at last." And he added, with confidence, "After all, he is from Gont."

But no word of any deed of the Archmage, or any heir to the Throne in Havnor, had come; and things went badly on.

So it was with fear and a grim anger that Goha saw the four men on the road before her step two to each side, so that she and the child would have to pass between them.

As they went walking steadily forward, Therru kept very

close beside her, holding her head bent down, but she did not take her hand.

One of the men, a big-chested fellow with coarse black hairs on his upper lip drooping over his mouth, began to speak, grinning a little. "Hey, there," he said, but Goha spoke at the same time and louder. "Out of my way!" she said, raising her alder stick as if it were a wizard's staff—"I have business with Ogion!" She strode between the men and straight on, Therru trotting beside her. The men, mistaking effrontery for witchery, stood still. Ogion's name perhaps still held power. Or perhaps there was a power in Goha, or in the child. For when the two had gone by, one of the men said, "Did you see that?" and spat and made the sign to avert evil.

"Witch and her monster brat," another said. "Let 'em go!"

Another, a man in a leather cap and jerkin, stood staring for a moment while the others slouched on their way. His face looked sick and stricken, yet he seemed to be turning to follow the woman and child, when the hairy-lipped man called to him, "Come on, Handy!" and he obeyed.

Out of sight around the turn of the road, Goha had picked up Therru and hurried on with her until she had to set her down and stand gasping. The child asked no questions and made no delays. As soon as Goha could go on again, the child walked as fast as she could beside her, holding her hand.

"You're red," she said. "Like fire."

She spoke seldom, and not clearly, her voice being very hoarse; but Goha could understand her.

"I'm angry," Goha said with a kind of laugh. "When I'm angry I turn red. Like you people, you red people, you barbarians of the western lands. . . . Look, there's a town there ahead, that'll be Oak Springs. It's the only village on this road. We'll stop there and rest a little. Maybe we can get some milk. And then, if we can go on, if you think you can walk on up to the Falcon's Nest, we'll be there by nightfall, I hope."

The child nodded. She opened her bag of raisins and walnuts and ate a few. They trudged on.

The sun had long set when they came through the village and to Ogion's house on the cliff-top. The first stars glimmered above a dark mass of clouds in the west over the high horizon of the sea. The sea wind blew, bowing short grasses. A goat bleated in the pastures behind the low, small house. The one window shone dim yellow.

Goha stood her stick and Therru's against the wall by the door, and held the child's hand, and knocked once.

There was no answer.

She pushed the door open. The fire on the hearth was out, cinders and grey ashes, but an oil lamp on the table made a tiny seed of light, and from his mattress on the floor in the far corner of the room Ogion said, "Come in, Tenar."

Ogion

She bedded down the child on the cot in the western alcove. She built up the fire. She went and sat down beside Ogion's pallet, cross-legged on the floor.

"No one looking after you!"

"I sent 'em off," he whispered.

His face was as dark and hard as ever, but his hair was thin and white, and the dim lamp made no spark of light in his eyes.

"You could have died alone," she said, fierce.

"Help me do that," the old man said.

"Not yet," she pleaded, stooping, laying her forehead on his hand.

"Not tonight," he agreed. "Tomorrow."

He lifted his hand to stroke her hair once, having that much strength.

She sat up again. The fire had caught. Its light played on the walls and low ceiling and sent shadows to thicken in the corners of the long room.

"If Ged would come," the old man murmured.

"Have you sent to him?"

"Lost," Ogion said. "He's lost. A cloud. A mist over the lands. He went into the west. Carrying the branch of the rowan tree. Into the dark mist. I've lost my hawk."

"No, no, no," she whispered. "He'll come back."

They were silent. The fire's warmth began to penetrate them both, letting Ogion relax and drift in and out of sleep, letting Tenar find rest pleasant after the long day afoot. She rubbed her feet and her aching shoulders. She had carried Therru part of the last long climb, for the child had begun to gasp with weariness as she tried to keep up.

Tenar got up, heated water, and washed the dust of the road from her. She heated milk, and ate bread she found in Ogion's larder, and came back to sit by him. While he slept, she sat thinking, watching his face and the firelight and the shadows.

She thought how a girl had sat silent, thinking, in the night, a long time ago and far away, a girl in a windowless room, brought up to know herself only as the one who had been eaten, priestess and servant of the powers of the darkness of the earth. And there had been a woman who would sit up in the peaceful silence of a farmhouse when husband and children slept, to think, to be alone an hour. And there was the widow who had carried a burned child here, who sat by the side of the dying, who waited for a man to return. Like all women, any woman, doing what women do. But it was not by the names of the servant or the wife or the widow that Ogion had called her. Nor had Ged, in the darkness of the Tombs. Nor—longer ago, farther away than all—had her mother, the mother she remembered only as the warmth and lion-color of firelight, the mother who had given her her name.

"I am Tenar," she whispered. The fire, catching a dry branch of pine, leaped up in a bright yellow tongue of flame.

Ogion's breathing became troubled and he struggled for air. She helped him as she could till he found some ease.

They both slept for a while, she drowsing by his dazed and drifting silence, broken by strange words. Once in the deep night he said aloud, as if meeting a friend in the road, "Are you here, then? Have you seen him?" And again, when Tenar roused herself to build up the fire, he began to speak, but this time it seemed he spoke to someone in his memory of years long gone, for he said clearly as a child might, "I tried to help her, but the roof of the house fell down. It fell on them. It was the earthquake." Tenar listened. She too had seen earthquake. "I tried to help!" said the boy in the old man's voice, in pain. Then the gasping struggle to breathe began again.

At first light Tenar was wakened by a sound she thought at first was the sea. It was a great rushing of wings. A flock of birds was flying over, low, so many that their wings stormed and the window was darkened by their quick shadows. It seemed they circled the house once and then were gone. They made no call or cry, and she did not know what birds they were.

People came that morning from the village of Re Albi, which Ogion's house stood apart from to the north. A goat-girl came, and a woman for the milk of Ogion's goats, and others to ask what they might do for him. Moss, the village witch, fingered the alder stick and the hazel switch by the door and peered in hopefully, but not even she ventured to come in, and Ogion growled from his pallet, "Send 'em away! Send 'em all away!"

He seemed stronger and more comfortable. When little Therru woke, he spoke to her in the dry, kind, quiet way Tenar remembered. The child went out to play in the sun, and he said to Tenar, "What is the name you call her?"

He knew the True Language of the Making, but he had never learned any Kargish at all.

"Therru means burning, the flaming of fire," she said.

"Ah, ah," he said, and his eyes gleamed, and he frowned. He seemed to grope for words for a moment. "That one," he said, "That one—they will fear her."

"They fear her now," Tenar said bitterly.

The mage shook his head.

"Teach her, Tenar," he whispered. "Teach her all!—Not Roke. They are afraid— Why did I let you go? Why did you go? To bring her here—too late?"

"Be still, be still," she told him tenderly, for he struggled with words and breath and could find neither. He shook his head, and gasped, "Teach her!" and lay still.

He would not eat, and only drank a little water. In the middle of the day he slept. Waking in the late afternoon, he said, "Now, daughter," and sat up.

Tenar took his hand, smiling at him.

"Help me get up."

"No, no."

"Yes," he said. "Outside. I can't die indoors."

"Where would you go?"

"Anywhere. But if I could, the forest path," he said. "The beech above the meadow."

When she saw he was able to get up and determined to get outdoors, she helped him. Together they got to the door, where he stopped and looked around the one room of his house. In the dark corner to the right of the doorway his tall staff leaned against the wall, shining a little. Tenar reached out to give it to him, but he shook his head. "No," he said, "not that." He looked around again as if for something missing, forgotten. "Come on," he said at last.

When the bright wind from the west blew on his face and he looked out at the high horizon, he said, "That's good."

"Let me get some people from the village to make a litter

and carry you," she said. "They're all waiting to do something for you."

"I want to walk," the old man said.

Therru came around the house and watched solemnly as Ogion and Tenar went, step by step, and stopping every five or six steps for Ogion to gasp, across the tangled meadow towards the woods that climbed steep up the mountainside from the inner side of the cliff-top. The sun was hot and the wind cold. It took them a very long time to cross that meadow. Ogion's face was grey and his legs shook like the grass in the wind when they got at last to the foot of a big young beech tree just inside the forest, a few yards up the beginning of the mountain path. There he sank down between the roots of the tree, his back against its trunk. For a long time he could not move or speak, and his heart, pounding and faltering, shook his body. He nodded finally and whispered, "All right."

Therru had followed them at a distance. Tenar went to her and held her and talked to her a little. She came back to Ogion. "She's bringing a rug," she said.

"Not cold."

"*I'm* cold."

There was the flicker of a smile on her face.

The child came lugging a goat's-wool blanket. She whispered to Tenar and ran off again.

"Heather will let her help milk the goats, and look after her," Tenar said to Ogion. "So I can stay here with you."

"Never one thing, for you," he said in the hoarse whistling whisper that was all the voice he had left.

"No. Always at least two things, and usually more," she said. "But I am here."

He nodded.

For a long time he did not speak, but sat back against the

tree trunk, his eyes closed. Watching his face, Tenar saw it change as slowly as the light changed in the west.

He opened his eyes and gazed through a gap in the thickets at the western sky. He seemed to watch something, some act or deed, in that far, clear, golden space of light. He whispered once, hesitant, as if unsure, "The dragon—"

The sun was down, the wind fallen.

Ogion looked at Tenar.

"Over," he whispered with exultation. "All changed!— Changed, Tenar! Wait—wait here, for—" A shaking took his body, tossing him like the branch of a tree in a great wind. He gasped. His eyes closed and opened, gazing beyond her. He laid his hand on hers; she bent down to him; he spoke his name to her, so that after his death he might be truly known.

He gripped her hand and shut his eyes and began once more the struggle to breathe, until there was no more breath. He lay then like one of the roots of the tree, while the stars came out and shone through the leaves and branches of the forest.

Tenar sat with the dead man in the dusk and dark. A lantern gleamed like a firefly across the meadow. She had laid the woollen blanket across them both, but her hand that held his hand had grown cold, as if it held a stone. She touched her forehead to his hand once more. She stood up, stiff and dizzy, her body feeling strange to her, and went to meet and guide whoever was coming with the light.

That night his neighbors sat with Ogion, and he did not send them away.

The mansion house of the Lord of Re Albi stood on an outcrop of rocks on the mountainside above the Overfell. Early in the morning, long before the sun had cleared the mountain, the wizard in the service of that lord came down through the village; and very soon after, another wizard came toiling up the steep road from Gont Port, having set out in darkness. Word had come to them that Ogion was dying, or their power was such that they knew of the passing of a great mage.

The village of Re Albi had no sorcerer, only its mage, and a witchwoman to perform the lowly jobs of finding and mending and bonesetting, which people would not bother the mage with. Aunty Moss was a dour creature, unmarried, like most witches, and unwashed, with greying hair tied in curious charm-knots, and eyes red-rimmed from herb-smoke. It was she who had come across the meadow with the lantern, and with Tenar and the others she had watched the night by Ogion's body. She had set a wax candle in a glass shade, there in the forest, and had burned sweet oils in a dish of clay; she had said the words that should be said, and done what should be done. When it came to touching the body to prepare it for burial, she had looked once at Tenar as if for permission, and then had gone on with her offices. Village witches usually saw to the homing, as they called it, of the dead, and often to the burial.

When the wizard came down from the mansion house, a tall young man with a silvery staff of pinewood, and the other one came up from Gont Port, a stout middle-aged man with a short yew staff, Aunty Moss did not look at them with her bloodshot eyes, but ducked and bowed and drew back, gathering up her poor charms and witcheries.

When she had laid out the corpse as it should lie to be buried, on the left side with the knees bent, she had put in the upturned left hand a tiny charm-bundle, something wrapped in soft goatskin and tied with colored cord. The wizard of Re Albi flicked it away with the tip of his staff.

"Is the grave dug?" asked the wizard of Gont Port.

"Yes," said the wizard of Re Albi. "It is dug in the graveyard of my lord's house," and he pointed towards the mansion house up on the mountain.

"I see," said Gont Port. "I had thought our mage would be buried in all honor in the city he saved from earthquake."

"My lord desires the honor," said Re Albi.

"But it would seem—" Gont Port began, and stopped, not liking to argue, but not ready to give in to the young man's easy claim. He looked down at the dead man. "He must be buried nameless," he said with regret and bitterness. "I walked all night, but came too late. A great loss made greater!"

The young wizard said nothing.

"His name was Aihal," Tenar said. "His wish was to lie here, where he lies now."

Both men looked at her. The young man, seeing a middle-aged village woman, simply turned away. The man from Gont Port stared a moment and said, "Who are you?"

"I'm called Flint's widow, Goha," she said. "Who I am is your business to know, I think. But not mine to say."

At this, the wizard of Re Albi found her worthy of a brief stare. "Take care, woman, how you speak to men of power!"

"Wait, wait," said Gont Port, with a patting gesture, trying to calm Re Albi's indignation, and still gazing at Tenar. "You were—You were his ward, once?"

"And friend," Tenar said. Then she turned away her head and stood silent. She had heard the anger in her voice as she said that word, "friend." She looked down at her friend, a corpse ready for the ground, lost and still. They

stood over him, alive and full of power, offering no friend-
ship, only contempt, rivalry, anger.

"I'm sorry," she said. "It was a long night. I was with him
when he died."

"It is not—" the young wizard began, but unexpectedly
old Aunty Moss interrupted him, saying loudly, "She was.
Yes, she was. Nobody else but her. He sent for her. He sent
young Townsend the sheep-dealer to tell her come, clear
down round the mountain, and he waited his dying till she
did come and was with him, and then he died, and he died
where he would be buried, here."

"And," said the older man, "—and he told you—?"

"His name." Tenar looked at them, and do what she
would, the incredulity on the older man's face, the con-
tempt on the other's, brought out an answering disrespect
in her. "I said that name," she said. "Must I repeat it
to you?"

To her consternation she saw from their expressions that
in fact they had not heard the name, Ogion's true name;
they had not paid attention to her.

"Oh!" she said. "This is a bad time—a time when even
such a name can go unheard, can fall like a stone! Is listen-
ing not power? Listen, then: his name was Aihal. His name
in death is Aihal. In the songs he will be known as Aihal of
Gont. If there are songs to be made any more. He was a
silent man. Now he's very silent. Maybe there will be no
songs, only silence. I don't know. I'm very tired. I've lost
my father and dear friend." Her voice failed; her throat
closed on a sob. She turned to go. She saw on the forest path
the little charm-bundle Aunty Moss had made. She picked
it up, knelt down by the corpse, kissed the open palm of the
left hand, and laid the bundle on it. There on her knees she
looked up once more at the two men. She spoke quietly.

"Will you see to it," she said, "that his grave is dug here, where he desired it?"

First the older man, then the younger, nodded.

She got up, smoothing down her skirt, and started back across the meadow in the morning light.

Kalessin

"Wait," Ogion, who was Aihal now, had said to her, just before the wind of death had shaken him and torn him loose from living. "Over—all changed," he had whispered, and then, "Tenar, wait—" But he had not said what she should wait for. The change he had seen or known, perhaps; but what change? Was it his own death he meant, his own life that was over? He had spoken with joy, exulting. He had charged her to wait.

"What else have I to do?" she said to herself, sweeping the floor of his house. "What else have I ever done?" And, speaking to her memory of him, "Shall I wait here, in your house?"

"Yes," said Aihal the Silent, silently, smiling.

So she swept out the house and cleaned the hearth and aired the mattresses. She threw out some chipped crockery and a leaky pan, but she handled them gently. She even put her cheek against a cracked plate as she took it out to the midden, for it was evidence of the old mage's illness this past year. Austere he had been, living as plain as a poor farmer, but when his eyes were clear and his strength in him, he would never have used a broken plate or let a pan go unmended. These signs of his weakness grieved her, making her wish she had been with him to look after him.

"I would have liked that," she said to her memory of him, but he said nothing. He never would have anybody to look after him but himself. Would he have said to her, "You have better things to do?" She did not know. He was silent. But that she did right to stay here in his house, now, she was certain.

Shandy and her old husband, Clearbrook, who had been at the farm in Middle Valley longer than she herself had, would look after the flocks and the orchard; the other couple on the farm, Tiff and Sis, would get the field crops in. The rest would have to take care of itself for a while. Her raspberry canes would be picked by the neighborhood children. That was too bad; she loved raspberries. Up here on the Overfell, with the sea wind always blowing, it was too cold to grow raspberries. But Ogion's little old peach tree in the sheltered nook of the house wall facing south bore eighteen peaches, and Therru watched them like a mousing cat till the day she came in and said in her hoarse, unclear voice, "Two of the peaches are all red and yellow."

"Ah," said Tenar. They went together to the peach tree and picked the two first ripe peaches and ate them there, unpeeled. The juice ran down their chins. They licked their fingers.

"Can I plant it?" said Therru, looking at the wrinkled stone of her peach.

"Yes. This is a good place, near the old tree. But not too close. So they both have room for their roots and branches."

The child chose a place and dug the tiny grave. She laid the stone in it and covered it over. Tenar watched her. In the few days they had been living here, Therru had changed, she thought. She was still unresponsive, without anger, without joy; but since they had been here her awful vigilance, her immobility, had almost imperceptibly relaxed. She had desired the peaches. She had thought of planting the stone, of increasing the number of peaches in the world. At Oak Farm she was unafraid of two people only, Tenar and Lark; but here she had taken quite easily to Heather, the goatherd of Re Albi, a bawling-voiced, gentle lackwit of twenty, who treated the child very much as another goat, a lame kid. That was all right. And Aunty Moss was all right too, no matter what she smelled like.

When Tenar had first lived in Re Albi, twenty-five years ago, Moss had not been an old witch but a young one. She had ducked and bowed and grinned at "the young lady," "the White Lady," Ogion's ward and student, never speaking to her but with the utmost respect. Tenar had felt that respect to be false, a mask for an envy and dislike and distrust that were all too familiar to her from women over whom she had been placed in a position of superiority, women who saw themselves as common and her as uncommon, as privileged. Priestess of the Tombs of Atuan or foreign ward of the Mage of Gont, she was set apart, set above. Men had given her power, men had shared their power with her. Women looked at her from outside, sometimes rivalrous, often with a trace of ridicule.

She had felt herself the one left outside, shut out. She had fled from the Powers of the desert tombs, and then she had left the powers of learning and skill offered her by her guardian, Ogion. She had turned her back on all that, gone to the other side, the other room, where the women lived, to be one of them. A wife, a farmer's wife, a mother, a householder, undertaking the power that a woman was born to, the authority allotted her by the arrangements of mankind.

And there in the Middle Valley, Flint's wife, Goha, had

been welcome, all in all, among the women; a foreigner to be sure, white-skinned and talking a bit strange, but a notable housekeeper, an excellent spinner, with well-behaved, well-grown children and a prospering farm: respectable. And among men she was Flint's woman, doing what a woman should do: bed, breed, bake, cook, clean, spin, sew, serve. A good woman. They approved of her. Flint did well for himself after all, they said. I wonder what a white woman's like, white all over? their eyes said, looking at her, until she got older and they no longer saw her.

Here, now, it was all changed, there was none of all that. Since she and Moss had kept the vigil for Ogion together, the witch had made it plain that she would be her friend, follower, servant, whatever Tenar wanted her to be. Tenar was not at all sure what she wanted Aunty Moss to be, finding her unpredictable, unreliable, incomprehensible, passionate, ignorant, sly, and dirty. But Moss got on with the burned child. Perhaps it was Moss who was working this change, this slight easing, in Therru. With her, Therru behaved as with everyone—blank, unanswering, docile in the way an inanimate thing, a stone, is docile. But the old woman had kept at her, offering her little sweets and treasures, bribing, coaxing, wheedling. "Come with Aunty Moss now, dearie! Come along and Aunty Moss'll show you the prettiest sight you ever saw. . . ."

Moss's nose leaned out over her toothless jaws and thin lips; there was a wart on her cheek the size of a cherry pit; her hair was a grey-black tangle of charm-knots and wisps; and she had a smell as strong and broad and deep and complicated as the smell of a fox's den. "Come into the forest with me, dearie!" said the old witches in the tales told to the children of Gont. "Come with me and I'll show you such a pretty sight!" And then the witch shut the child in her oven and baked it brown and ate it, or dropped it into her well, where it hopped and croaked dismally forever, or put it to sleep for a hundred years inside a great stone, till the King's Son should come, the Mage Prince, to shatter the stone with a word, wake the maiden with a kiss, and slay the wicked witch. . . .

"Come with me, dearie!" And she took the child into the fields and showed her a lark's nest in the green hay, or into the marshes to gather white hallows, wild mint, and blueberries. She did not have to shut the child in an oven, or change her into a monster, or seal her in stone. That had all been done already.

She was kind to Therru, but it was a wheedling kindness, and when they were together it seemed that she talked to the child a great deal. Tenar did not know what Moss was telling or teaching her, whether she should let the witch fill the child's head with stuff. *Weak as woman's magic, wicked as woman's magic,* she had heard said a hundred times. And indeed she had seen that the witchery of such women as Moss or Ivy was often weak in sense and sometimes wicked in intent or through ignorance. Village witches, though they might know many spells and charms and some of the great songs, were never trained in the High Arts or the principles of magery. No woman was so trained. Wizardry was a man's work, a man's skill; magic was made by men. There had never been a woman mage. Though some few had called themselves wizard or sorceress, their power had been untrained, strength without art or knowledge, half frivolous, half dangerous.

The ordinary village witch, like Moss, lived on a few words of the True Speech handed down as great treasures from older witches or bought at high cost from sorcerers, and a supply of common spells of finding and mending, much meaningless ritual and mystery-making and jibberish, a solid experiential training in midwifery, bonesetting, and curing animal and human ailments, a good knowledge of herbs mixed with a mess of superstitions—all this built up on whatever native gift she might have of healing, chanting, changing, or spellcasting. Such a mixture might be a good one or a bad one. Some witches were fierce, bitter women, ready to do harm and knowing no reason not to do harm. Most were midwives and healers with a few love potions, fertility charms, and potency spells on the side, and a good deal of quiet cynicism about them. A few, having wisdom though no learning, used their gift purely for good, though they could not tell, as any prentice wizard could, the reason for what they did, and prate of the Balance and the Way of Power to justify their action or abstention. "I follow my heart," one of these women had said to Tenar when she was Ogion's ward and pupil. "Lord Ogion is a great mage. He does you great honor, teaching you. But look and see, child, if all he's taught you isn't finally to follow your heart."

Tenar had thought even then that the wise woman was right, and yet not altogether right; there was something left out of that. And she still thought so.

Watching Moss with Therru now, she thought Moss was following her heart, but it was a dark, wild, queer heart, like a crow, going its own ways on its own errands. And she thought that Moss might be drawn to Therru not only by kindness but by Therru's hurt, by the harm that had been done her: by violence, by fire.

Nothing Therru did or said, however, showed that she was learning anything from Aunty Moss except where the lark nested and the blueberries grew and how to make cat's cradles one-handed. Therru's right hand had been so eaten by fire that it had healed into a kind of club, the thumb usable only as a pincer, like a crab's claw. But Aunty Moss had an amazing set of cat's cradles for four fingers and a thumb, and rhymes to go with the figures—

Churn churn cherry all!
Burn burn bury all!
Come, dragon, come!

—and the string would form four triangles that flicked into a square. . . . Therru never sang aloud, but Tenar heard her whispering the chant under her breath as she made the figures, alone, sitting on the doorstep of the mage's house.

And, Tenar thought, what bond linked her, herself, to the child, beyond pity, beyond mere duty to the helpless? Lark would have kept her if Tenar had not taken her. But Tenar had taken her without ever asking herself why. Had she been following her heart? Ogion had asked nothing about the child, but he had said, "They will fear her." And Tenar had replied, "They do," and truly. Maybe she herself feared the child, as she feared cruelty, and rape, and fire. Was fear the bond that held her?

"Goha," Therru said, sitting on her heels under the peach tree, looking at the place in the hard summer dirt where she had planted the peach stone, "what are dragons?"

"Great creatures," Tenar said, "like lizards, but longer than a ship—bigger than a house. With wings, like birds. They breathe out fire."

"Do they come here?"

"No," Tenar said.

Therru asked no more.

"Has Aunty Moss been telling you about dragons?"

Therru shook her head. "You did," she said.

"Ah," said Tenar. And presently, "The peach you planted will need water to grow. Once a day, till the rains come."

Therru got up and trotted off around the corner of the house to the well. Her legs and feet were perfect, unhurt. Tenar liked to see her walk or run, the dark, dusty, pretty little feet on the earth. She came back with Ogion's watering-jug, struggling along with it, and tipped out a small flood over the new planting.

"So you remember the story about when people and dragons were all the same. . . . It told how the humans came here, eastward, but the dragons all stayed in the far western isles. A long, long way away."

Therru nodded. She did not seem to be paying attention, but when Tenar, saying "the western isles," pointed out to the sea, Therru turned her face to the high, bright horizon glimpsed between staked bean-plants and the milking shed.

A goat appeared on the roof of the milking shed and arranged itself in profile to them, its head nobly poised; apparently it considered itself to be a mountain goat.

"Sippy's got loose again," said Tenar.

"Hesssss! Hesssss!" went Therru, imitating Heather's goat call; and Heather herself appeared by the bean-patch fence, saying "Hesssss!" up at the goat, which ignored her, gazing thoughtfully down at the beans.

Tenar left the three of them to play the catching-Sippy game. She wandered on past the bean patch towards the edge of the cliff and along it. Ogion's house stood apart from the village and closer than any other house to the edge of the Overfell, here a steep, grassy slope broken by ledges and outcrops of rock, where goats could be pastured. As you went on north the drop grew ever steeper, till it began to fall sheer; and on the path the rock of the great ledge showed through the soil, till a mile or so north of the village the Overfell had narrowed to a shelf of reddish sandstone hanging above the sea that undercut its base two thousand feet below.

Nothing grew at that far end of the Overfell but lichens and rockworts and here and there a blue daisy, wind-stunted, like a button dropped on the rough, crumbling stone. Inland of the cliff's edge to the north and east, above a narrow strip of marshland the dark, tremendous side of Gont Mountain rose up, forested almost to the peak. The cliff stood so high above the bay that one must look down to see its outer shores and the vague lowlands of Essary. Beyond them, in all the south and west, there was nothing but the sky above the sea.

Tenar had liked to go there in the years she had lived in Re Albi. Ogion had loved the forests, but she, who had lived in a desert where the only trees for a hundred miles were a gnarled orchard of peach and apple, hand watered in the endless summers, where nothing grew green and moist and easy, where there was nothing but a mountain and a great plain and the sky—she liked the cliff's edge better than the enclosing woods. She liked having nothing at all over her head.

The lichens, the grey rockwort, the stemless daisies, she liked them too; they were familiar. She sat down on the shelving rock a few feet from the edge and looked out to sea as she had used to do. The sun was hot but the ceaseless wind cooled the sweat on her face and arms. She leaned back on her hands and thought of nothing, sun and wind and sky and sea filling her, making her transparent to sun, wind, sky, sea. But her left hand reminded her of its existence, and she looked round to see what was scratching the heel of her hand. It was a tiny thistle, crouched in a crack in the sandstone, barely lifting its colorless spikes into the light and wind. It nodded stiffly as the wind blew, resisting the wind, rooted in rock. She gazed at it for a long time.

When she looked out to sea again she saw, blue in the blue haze where sea met sky, the line of an island: Oranéa, easternmost of the Inner Isles.

She gazed at that faint dream-shape, dreaming, until a bird flying from the west over the sea drew her gaze. It was not a gull, for it flew steadily, and too high to be a pelican. Was it a wild goose, or an albatross, the great, rare voyager of the open sea, come among the islands? She watched the slow beat of the wings, far out and high in the dazzling air. Then she got to her feet, retreating a little from the cliff's edge, and stood motionless, her heart going hard and her breath caught in her throat, watching the sinuous, iron-dark body borne by long, webbed wings as red as fire, the outreaching claws, the coils of smoke fading behind it in the air.

Straight to Gont it flew, straight to the Overfell, straight to her. She saw the glitter of rust-black scales and the gleam of the long eye. She saw the red tongue that was a tongue of flame. The stink of burning filled the wind, as with a hissing roar the dragon, turning to land on the shelf of rock, breathed out a sigh of fire.

Its feet clashed on the rock. The thorny tail, writhing, rattled, and the wings, scarlet where the sun shone through them, stormed and rustled as they folded down to the mailed flanks. The head turned slowly. The dragon looked at the woman who stood there within reach of its scythe-blade talons. The woman looked at the dragon. She felt the heat of its body.

She had been told that men must not look into a dragon's eyes, but that was nothing to her. It gazed straight at her from yellow eyes under armored carapaces wide-set above the narrow nose and flaring, fuming nostrils. And her small, soft face and dark eyes gazed straight at it.

Neither of them spoke.

The dragon turned its head aside a little so that she was not destroyed when it did speak, or perhaps it laughed—a great "Hah!" of orange flame.

Then it lowered its body into a crouch and spoke, but not to her.

"*Ahivaraihe, Ged,*" it said, mildly enough, smokily, with a flicker of the burning tongue; and it lowered its head.

Tenar saw for the first time, then, the man astride its back. In the notch between two of the high sword-thorns that rose in a row down its spine he sat, just behind the neck and above the shoulders where the wings had root. His hands were clenched on the rust-dark mail of the dragon's neck and his head leaned against the base of the sword-thorn, as if he were asleep.

"*Ahi eheraihe, Ged!*" said the dragon, a little louder, its long mouth seeming always to smile, showing the teeth as long as Tenar's forearm, yellowish, with white, sharp tips.

The man did not stir.

The dragon turned its long head and looked again at Tenar.

"*Sobriost,*" it said, in a whisper of steel sliding over steel.

That word of the Language of the Making she knew. Ogion had taught her all she would learn of that tongue. Go up, the dragon said: mount! And she saw the steps to mount. The taloned foot, the crooked elbow, the shoulder-joint, the first musculature of the wing: four steps.

She too said, "Hah!" but not in a laugh, only trying to get her breath, which kept sticking in her throat; and she lowered her head a moment to stop her dizzy faintness.

Then she went forward, past the talons and the long lipless mouth and the long yellow eye, and mounted the shoulder of the dragon. She took the man's arm. He did not move, but surely he was not dead, for the dragon had brought him here and spoken to him. "Come on," she said, and then seeing his face as she loosened the clenched grip of his left hand, "Come on, Ged. Come on. . . ."

He raised his head a little. His eyes were open, but unseeing. She had to climb around him, scratching her legs on the hot, mailed hide of the dragon, and unclench his right hand from a horny knob at the base of the sword-thorn. She got him to take hold of her arms, and so could carry-drag him down those four strange stairs to earth.

He roused enough to try to hold on to her, but there was no strength in him. He sprawled off the dragon onto the rock like a sack unloaded, and lay there.

The dragon turned its immense head and in a completely animal gesture nosed and sniffed at the man's body.

It lifted its head, and its wings too half lifted with a vast, metallic sound. It shifted its feet away from Ged, closer to the edge of the cliff. Turning back the head on the thorned neck, it stared once more directly at Tenar, and its voice like the dry roar of a kiln-fire spoke: *"Thesse Kalessin."*

The sea wind whistled in the dragon's half-open wings.

"Thesse Tenar," the woman said in a clear, shaking voice.

The dragon looked away, westward, over the sea. It twitched its long body with a clink and clash of iron scales, then abruptly opened its wings, crouched, and leapt straight out from the cliff onto the wind. The dragging tail scored the sandstone as it passed. The red wings beat down, lifted, and beat down, and already Kalessin was far from land, flying straight, flying west.

Tenar watched it till it was no larger than a wild goose

or a gull. The air was cold. When the dragon had been there it had been hot, furnace-hot, with the dragon's inward fire. Tenar shivered. She sat down on the rock beside Ged and began to cry. She hid her face in her arms and wept aloud. "What can I do?" she cried. "What can I do now?"

Presently she wiped her eyes and nose on her sleeve, put back her hair with both hands, and turned to the man who lay beside her. He lay so still, so easy on the bare rock, as if he might lie there forever.

Tenar sighed. There was nothing she could do, but there was always the next thing to be done.

She could not carry him. She would have to get help. That meant leaving him alone. It seemed to her that he was too near the cliff's edge. If he tried to get up he might fall, weak and dizzy as he would be. How could she move him? He did not rouse at all when she spoke and touched him. She took him under the shoulders and tried to pull him, and to her surprise succeeded; dead weight as he was, the weight was not much. Resolute, she dragged him ten or fifteen feet inland, off the bare rock shelf onto a bit of dirt, where dry bunchgrass gave some illusion of shelter. There she had to leave him. She could not run, for her legs shook and her breath still came in sobs. She walked as fast as she could to Ogion's house, calling out as she approached it to Heather, Moss, and Therru.

The child appeared around the milking shed and stood, as her way was, obedient to Tenar's call but not coming forward to greet or be greeted.

"Therru, run into town and ask anyone to come—anybody strong— There's a man hurt on the cliff."

Therru stood there. She had never gone alone into the village. She was frozen between obedience and fear. Tenar saw that and said, "Is Aunty Moss here? Is Heather? The three of us can carry him. Only, quick, quick, Therru!'' She felt that if she let Ged lie unprotected there he would surely die. He would be gone when she came back—dead, fallen, taken by dragons. Anything could happen. She must hurry before it happened. Flint had died of a stroke in his fields and she had not been with him. He had died alone. The shepherd had found him lying by the gate. Ogion had died and she could not keep him from dying, she could not give him breath. Ged had come home to die and it was the end of everything, there was nothing left, nothing to be done, but she must do it. "Quick, Therru! Bring anyone!''

She started shakily towards the village herself, but saw old Moss hurrying across the pasture, stumping along with her thick hawthorn stick. "Did you call me, dearie?''

Moss's presence was an immediate relief. She began to get her breath and be able to think. Moss wasted no time in questions, but hearing there was a man hurt who must be moved, got the heavy canvas mattress-cover that Tenar had been airing, and lugged it out to the end of the Overfell. She and Tenar rolled Ged onto it and were dragging this conveyance laboriously homeward when Heather came trotting along, followed by Therru and Sippy. Heather was young and strong, and with her help they could lift the canvas like a litter and carry the man to the house.

Tenar and Therru slept in the alcove in the west wall of the long single room. There was only Ogion's bed at the far end, covered now with a heavy linen sheet. There they laid the man. Tenar put Ogion's blanket over him, while Moss muttered charms around the bed, and Heather and Therru stood and stared.

"Let him be now,'' said Tenar, leading them all to the front part of the house.

"Who is he?'' Heather asked.

"What was he doing on the Overfell?" Moss asked.

"You know him, Moss. He was Ogion's—Aihal's prentice, once."

The witch shook her head. "That was the lad from Ten Alders, dearie," she said. "The one that's Archmage in Roke, now."

Tenar nodded.

"No, dearie," said Moss. "This looks like him. But isn't him. This man's no mage. Not even a sorcerer."

Heather looked from one to the other, entertained. She did not understand most things people said, but she liked to hear them say them.

"But I know him, Moss. It's Sparrowhawk." Saying the name, Ged's use-name, released a tenderness in her, so that for the first time she thought and felt that this was he indeed, and that all the years since she had first seen him were their bond. She saw a light like a star in darkness, underground, long ago, and his face in the light. "I know him, Moss." She smiled, and then smiled more broadly. "He's the first man I ever saw," she said.

Moss mumbled and shifted. She did not like to contradict "Mistress Goha," but she was perfectly unconvinced. "There's tricks, disguises, transformations, changes," she said. "Better be careful, dearie. How did he get where you found him, away out there? Did any see him come through the village?"

"None of you—saw—?"

They stared at her. She tried to say "the dragon" and could not. Her lips and tongue would not form the word. But a word formed itself with them, making itself with her mouth and breath. "Kalessin," she said.

Therru was staring at her. A wave of warmth, heat, seemed to flow from the child, as if she were in fever. She said nothing, but moved her lips as if repeating the name, and that fever heat burned around her.

"Tricks!" Moss said. "Now that our mage is gone there'll be all kinds of tricksters coming round."

"I came from Atuan to Havnor, from Havnor to Gont, with Sparrowhawk, in an open boat," Tenar said drily. "You saw him when he brought me here, Moss. He wasn't archmage then. But he was the same, the same man. Are there other scars like those?"

Confronted, the older woman became still, collecting herself. She glanced at Therru. "No," she said. "But—"

"Do you think I wouldn't know him?"

Moss twisted her mouth, frowned, rubbed one thumb with the other, looking at her hands. "There's evil things in the world, mistress," she said. "A thing that takes a man's form and body, but his soul's gone—eaten—"

"The gebbeth?"

Moss cringed at the word spoken openly. She nodded. "They do say, once the mage Sparrowhawk came here, long ago, before you came with him. And a thing of darkness came with him—following him. Maybe it still does. Maybe—"

"The dragon who brought him here," Tenar said, "called him by his true name. And I know that name." Wrath at the witch's obstinate suspicion rang in her voice.

Moss stood mute. Her silence was better argument than her words.

"Maybe the shadow on him is his death," Tenar said. "Maybe he's dying. I don't know. If Ogion—"

At the thought of Ogion she was in tears again, thinking how Ged had come too late. She swallowed the tears and went to the woodbox for kindling for the fire. She gave Therru the kettle to fill, touching her face as she spoke to her. The seamed and slabby scars were hot to touch, but the child was not feverish. Tenar knelt to make the fire. Somebody in this fine household—a witch, a widow, a cripple, and a half-wit—had to do what must be done, and not frighten the child with weeping. But the dragon was gone, and was there nothing to come any more but death?

Bettering

He lay like the dead but was not dead. Where had he been? What had he come through? That night, in firelight, Tenar took the stained, worn, sweat-stiffened clothes off him. She washed him and let him lie naked between the linen sheet and the blanket of soft, heavy goat's-wool. Though a short, slight-built man, he had been compact, vigorous; now he was thin as if worn down to the bone, worn away, fragile. Even the scars that ridged his shoulder and the left side of his face from temple to jaw seemed lessened, silvery. And his hair was grey.

I'm sick of mourning, Tenar thought. Sick of mourning, sick of grief. I will not grieve for him! Didn't he come to me riding the dragon?

Once I meant to kill him, she thought. Now I'll make him live, if I can. She looked at him then with a challenge in her eye, and no pity.

"Which of us saved the other from the Labyrinth, Ged?"

Unhearing, unmoving, he slept. She was very tired. She bathed in the water she had heated to wash him with, and crept into bed beside the little, warm, silky silence that was Therru asleep. She slept, and her sleep opened out into a vast windy space hazy with rose and gold. She flew. Her voice called, "Kalessin!" A voice answered, calling from the gulfs of light.

When she woke, the birds were chirping in the fields and on the roof. Sitting up she saw the light of morning through the gnarled glass of the low window looking west. There was something in her, some seed or glimmer, too small to look at or think about, new. Therru was still asleep. Tenar sat by her looking out the small window at cloud and sunlight, thinking of her daughter Apple, trying to remember Apple as a baby. Only the faintest glimpse, vanishing as she turned to it—the small, fat body shaking with a laugh, the wispy, flying hair. . . . And the second baby, Spark he got called as a joke, because he'd been struck off Flint. She did not know his true name. He had been as sickly a child as Apple had been a sound one. Born early and very small, he had nearly died of the croup at two months, and for two years after that it had been like rearing a fledgling sparrow, you never knew if he would be alive in the morning. But he held on, the little spark wouldn't go out. And growing, he became a wiry boy, endlessly active, driven; no use on the farm; no patience with animals, plants, people; using words for his needs only, never for pleasure and the give and take of love and knowledge.

Ogion had come by on his wanderings when Apple was thirteen and Spark eleven. Ogion had named Apple then, in the springs of the Kaheda at the valley's head; beautiful she had walked in the green water, the woman-child, and he had given her her true name, Hayohe. He had stayed on at Oak Farm a day or two, and had asked the boy if he wanted to go wandering a little with him in the forests. Spark merely shook his head. "What would you do if you could?" the mage had asked him, and the boy said what he had never been able to say to father or mother: "Go to sea."

So after Beech gave him his true name, three years later, he shipped as a sailor aboard a merchantman trading from Valmouth to Oranéa and North Havnor. From time to time he would come to the farm, but not often and never for long, though at his father's death it would be his property. He was white-skinned like Tenar, but grew tall like Flint, with a narrow face. He had not told his parents his true name. There might never be anyone he told it to. Tenar had not seen him for three years now. He might or might not know of his father's death. He might be dead himself, drowned, but she thought not. He would carry that spark his life over the waters, through the storms.

That was what it was like in her now, a spark; like the bodily certainty of a conception; a change, a new thing. What it was she would not ask. You did not ask. You did not ask a true name. It was given you, or not.

She got up and dressed. Early as it was, it was warm, and she built no fire. She sat in the doorway to drink a cup of milk and watch the shadow of Gont Mountain draw inward from the sea. There was as little wind as there could be on this air-swept shelf of rock, and the breeze had a midsummer feel, soft and rich, smelling of the meadows. There was a sweetness in the air, a change.

"All changed!" the old man had whispered, dying, joyful. Laying his hand on hers, giving her the gift, his name, giving it away.

"Aihal!" she whispered. For answer a couple of goats bleated, out behind the milking shed, waiting for Heather to come. "Be-eh," one said, and the other, deeper, metallic, "Bla-ah! Bla-ah!" Trust a goat, Flint used to say, to spoil anything. Flint, a shepherd, had disliked goats. But Sparrowhawk had been a goatherd, here across the mountain, as a boy.

She went inside. She found Therru standing gazing at the

sleeping man. She put her arm around the child, and though Therru usually shrank from or was passive to touch or caress, this time she accepted it and perhaps even leaned a little to Tenar.

Ged lay in the same exhausted, overwhelmed sleep. His face was turned to expose the four white scars that marked it.

"Was he burned?" Therru whispered.

Tenar did not answer at once. She did not know what those scars were. She had asked him long ago, in the Painted Room of the Labyrinth of Atuan, jeering: "A dragon?" And he had answered seriously, "Not a dragon. One of the kinship of the Nameless Ones; but I learned his name. . . ." And that was all she knew. But she knew what "burned" meant to the child.

"Yes," she said.

Therru continued to gaze at him. She had cocked her head to bring her one seeing eye to bear, which made her look like a little bird, a sparrow or a finch.

"Come along, finchling, birdlet, sleep's what he needs, you need a peach. Is there a peach ripe this morning?"

Therru trotted out to see, and Tenar followed her.

Eating her peach, the child studied the place where she had planted the peach pit yesterday. She was evidently disappointed that no tree had grown there, but she said nothing.

"Water it," said Tenar.

Aunty Moss arrived in the midmorning. One of her skills as a witch-handywoman was basket making, using the rushes of Overfell Marsh, and Tenar had asked her to teach her the art. As a child in Atuan, Tenar had learned how to learn. As a stranger in Gont, she had found that people liked to teach. She had learned to be taught and so to be accepted, her foreignness forgiven.

Ogion had taught her his knowledge, and then Flint had taught her his. It was her habit of life, to learn. There seemed always to be a great deal to be learned, more than she would have believed when she was a prentice-priestess or the pupil of a mage.

The rushes had been soaking, and this morning they were to split them, an exacting but not a complicated business, leaving plenty of attention to spare.

"Aunty," said Tenar as they sat on the doorstep with the bowl of soaking rushes between them and a mat before them to lay the split ones on, "how do you tell if a man's a wizard or not?"

Moss's reply was circuitous, beginning with the usual gnomics and obscurities. "Deep knows deep," she said, deeply, and "What's born will speak," and she told a story about the ant that picked up a tiny end of hair from the floor of a palace and ran off to the ants' nest with it, and in the night the nest glowed underground like a star, for the hair was from the head of the great mage Brost. But only the wise could see the glowing anthill. To common eyes it was all dark.

"One needs training, then," said Tenar.

Maybe, maybe not, was the gist of Moss's dark reply. "Some are born with that gift," she said. "Even when they don't know it, it will be there. Like the hair of the mage in the hole in the ground, it will shine."

"Yes," said Tenar. "I've seen that." She split and resplit a reed cleanly and laid the splints on the mat. "How do you know, then, when a man is *not* a wizard?"

"It's not there," Moss said, "it's not there, dearie. The power. See now. If I've got eyes in my head I can see that you have eyes, can't I? And if you're blind I'll see that. And if you've only got one eye, like the little one, or if you've got three, I'll see 'em, won't I? But if I don't have an eye to see with, I won't know if you do till you tell me. But I do. I see, I know. The third eye!" She touched her forehead and gave a loud, dry chuckle, like a hen triumphant over an egg. She was pleased with having found the words to say what she wanted to say. A good deal of her obscurity and cant, Tenar had begun to realize, was mere ineptness with words and ideas. Nobody had ever taught her to think consecutively. Nobody had ever listened to what she said. All that was expected, all that was wanted of her was muddle, mystery, mumbling. She was a witchwoman. She had nothing to do with clear meaning.

"I understand," Tenar said. "Then—maybe this is a question you don't want to answer—then when you look at a person with your third eye, with your power, you see their power—or don't see it?"

"It's more a knowing," Moss said. "Seeing is just a way of saying it. 'Tisn't like I see you, I see this rush, I see the mountain there. It's a knowing. I know what's in you and not in that poor hollow-headed Heather. I know what's in the dear child and not in him in yonder. I know—" She could not get any farther with it. She mumbled and spat. "Any witch worth a hairpin knows another witch!" she said finally, plainly, impatiently.

"You recognize each other."

Moss nodded. "Aye, that's it. That's the word. Recognize."

"And a wizard would recognize your power, would know you for a sorceress—"

But Moss was grinning at her, a black cave of a grin in a cobweb of wrinkles.

"Dearie," she said, "a man, you mean, a wizardly man? What's a man of power to do with us?"

"But Ogion—"

"Lord Ogion was kind," Moss said, without irony.

They split rushes for a while in silence.

"Don't cut your thumb on 'em, dearie," Moss said.

"Ogion taught me. As if I weren't a girl. As if I'd been his prentice, like Sparrowhawk. He taught me the Language of the Making, Moss. What I asked him, he told me."

"There wasn't no other like him."

"It was I who wouldn't be taught. I left him. What did I want with his books? What good were they to me? I wanted to live, I wanted a man, I wanted my children, I wanted my life."

She split reeds neatly, quickly, with her nail.

"And I got it," she said.

"Take with the right hand, throw away with the left," the witch said. "Well, dearie mistress, who's to say? Who's to say? Wanting a man got me into awful troubles more than once. But wanting to get married, never! No, no. None of that for me."

"Why not?" Tenar demanded.

Taken aback, Moss said simply, "Why, what man'd marry a witch?" And then, with a sidelong chewing motion of her jaw, like a sheep shifting its cud, "And what witch'd marry a man?"

They split rushes.

"What's wrong with men?" Tenar inquired cautiously.

As cautiously, lowering her voice, Moss replied, "I don't know, my dearie. I've thought on it. Often I've thought on it. The best I can say it is like this. A man's in his skin, see, like a nut in its shell." She held up her long, bent, wet fingers as if holding a walnut. "It's hard and strong, that shell, and it's all full of him. Full of grand man-meat, manself. And that's all. That's all there is. It's all him and nothing else, inside."

Tenar pondered awhile and finally asked, "But if he's a wizard—"

"Then it's all his power, inside. His power's himself, see. That's how it is with him. And that's all. When his power goes, he's gone. Empty." She cracked the unseen walnut and tossed the shells away. "Nothing."

"And a woman, then?"

"Oh, well, dearie, a woman's a different thing entirely. Who knows where a woman begins and ends? Listen, mistress, I have roots, I have roots deeper than this island. Deeper than the sea, older than the raising of the lands. I go back into the dark." Moss's eyes shone with a weird brightness in their red rims and her voice sang like an instrument. "I go back into the dark! Before the moon I was. No one knows, no one knows, no one can say what I am, what a woman is, a woman of power, a woman's power, deeper than the roots of trees, deeper than the roots of islands, older than the Making, older than the moon. Who dares ask questions of the dark? Who'll ask the dark its name?"

The old woman was rocking, chanting, lost in her incantation; but Tenar sat upright, and split a reed down the center with her thumbnail.

"I will," she said.

She split another reed.

"I lived long enough in the dark," she said.

She looked in from time to time to see that Sparrowhawk was still sleeping. She did so now. When she sat down again with Moss, wanting not to return to what they had been saying, for the older woman looked dour and sullen, she said, "This morning when I woke up I felt, oh, as if a new wind were blowing. A change. Maybe just the weather. Did you feel that?"

But Moss would not say yes or no. "Many a wind blows here on the Overfell, some good, some ill. Some bears clouds and some fair weather, and some brings news to those who can hear it, but those who won't listen can't hear. Who am I to know, an old woman without mage-learning, without book-learning? All my learning's in the earth, in the dark earth. Under their feet, the proud ones. Under their feet, the proud lords and mages. Why should they look down, the learned ones? What does an old witch-woman know?"

She would be a formidable enemy, Tenar thought, and was a difficult friend.

"Aunty," she said, taking up a reed, "I grew up among women. Only women. In the Kargish lands, far east, in Atuan. I was taken from my family as a little child to be brought up a priestess in a place in the desert. I don't know what name it has, all we called it in our language was just that, the place. The only place I knew. There were a few soldiers guarding it, but they couldn't come inside the walls. And we couldn't go outside the walls. Only in a group, all women and girls, with eunuchs guarding us, keeping the men out of sight."

"What's those you said?"

"Eunuchs?" Tenar had used the Kargish word without thinking. "Gelded men," she said.

The witch stared, and said, *"Tsekh!"* and made the sign to avert evil. She sucked her lips. She had been startled out of her resentment.

"One of them was the nearest to a mother I had

there. . . . But do you see, Aunty, I never saw a man till I was a woman grown. Only girls and women. And yet I didn't know what women are, because women were all I did know. Like men who live among men, sailors, and soldiers, and mages on Roke—do they know what men are? How can they, if they never speak to a woman?"

"Do they take 'em and do 'em like rams and he-goats," said Moss, "like that, with a gelding knife?"

Horror, the macabre, and a gleam of vengeance had won out over both anger and reason. Moss didn't want to pursue any topic but that of eunuchs.

Tenar could not tell her much. She realized that she had never thought about the matter. When she was a girl in Atuan, there had been gelded men; and one of them had loved her tenderly, and she him; and she had killed him to escape from him. Then she had come to the Archipelago, where there were no eunuchs, and had forgotten them, sunk them in darkness with Manan's body.

"I suppose," she said, trying to satisfy Moss's craving for details, "that they took young boys, and—" But she stopped. Her hands stopped working.

"Like Therru," she said after a long pause. "What's a child for? What's it there for? To be used. To be raped, to be gelded— Listen, Moss. When I lived in the dark places, that was what they did there. And when I came here, I thought I'd come out into the light. I learned the true words. And I had my man, I bore my children, I lived well. In the broad daylight. And in the broad daylight, they did that—to the child. In the meadows by the river. The river that rises from the spring where Ogion named my daughter. In the sunlight. I am trying to find out where I can live, Moss. Do you know what I mean? What I'm trying to say?"

"Well, well," the older woman said; and after a while,

"Dearie, there's misery enough without going looking for it." And seeing Tenar's hands shake as she tried to split a stubborn reed, she said, again, "Don't cut your thumb on 'em, dearie."

It was not till the next day that Ged roused at all. Moss, who was very skillful though appallingly unclean as a nurse, had succeeded in spooning some meat-broth into him. "Starving," she said, "and dried up with thirst. Wherever he was, they didn't do much eating and drinking." And after appraising him again, "He'll be too far gone already, I think. They get weak, see, and can't even drink, though it's all they need. I've known a great strong man to die like that. All in a few days, shriveled to a shadow, like."

But through relentless patience she got a few spoonfuls of her brew of meat and herbs into him. "Now we'll see," she said. "Too late, I guess. He's slipping away." She spoke without regret, perhaps with relish. The man was nothing to her; a death was an event. Maybe she could bury this mage. They had not let her bury the old one.

Tenar was salving his hands, the next day, when he woke. He must have ridden long on Kalessin's back, for his fierce grip on the iron scales had scoured the skin off his palms, and the inner side of the fingers was cut and recut. Sleeping, he kept his hands clenched as if they would not let go the absent dragon. She had to force his fingers open gently to wash and salve the sores. As she did that, he cried out and started, reaching out, as if he felt himself falling. His eyes opened. She spoke quietly. He looked at her.

"Tenar," he said without smiling, in pure recognition beyond emotion. And it gave her pure pleasure, like a sweet flavor or a flower, that there was still one man living who knew her name, and that it was this man.

She leaned forward and kissed his cheek. "Lie still," she said. "Let me finish this." He obeyed, drifting back into sleep soon, this time with his hands open and relaxed.

Later, falling asleep beside Therru in the night, she thought, But I never kissed him before. And the thought shook her. At first she disbelieved it. Surely, in all the years— Not in the Tombs, but after, traveling together in the mountains— In *Lookfar,* when they sailed together to Havnor— When he brought her here to Gont—?

No. Nor had Ogion ever kissed her, or she him. He had called her daughter, and had loved her, but had not touched her; and she, brought up as a solitary, untouched priestess, a holy thing, had not sought touch, or had not known she sought it. She would lean her forehead or her cheek for a moment on Ogion's open hand, and he might stroke her hair, once, very lightly.

And Ged never even that.

Did I never *think* of it? she asked herself in a kind of incredulous awe.

She did not know. As she tried to think of it, a horror, a sense of transgression, came on her very strongly, and then died away, meaningless. Her lips knew the slightly rough, dry, cool skin of his cheek near the mouth on the right side, and only that knowledge had importance, was of weight.

She slept. She dreamed that a voice called her, "Tenar! Tenar!" and that she replied, crying like a seabird, flying in the light above the sea; but she did not know what name she called.

Sparrowhawk disappointed Aunty Moss. He stayed alive. After a day or two she gave him up for saved. She came and fed him her broth of goat's-meat and roots and herbs, propping him against her, surrounding him with the powerful smell of her body, spooning life into him, and grumbling. Although he had recognized her and called her by her use-name, and she could not deny that he seemed to be the man called Sparrowhawk, she wanted to deny it. She did not like him. He was all wrong, she said. Tenar respected the witch's sagacity enough that this troubled her, but she could not find any such suspicion in herself, only the pleasure of his being there and of his slow return to life. "When he's himself again, you'll see," she said to Moss.

"Himself!" Moss said, and she made that gesture with her fingers of breaking and dropping a nutshell.

He asked, pretty soon, about Ogion. Tenar had dreaded that question. She had told herself and nearly convinced herself that he would not ask, that he would know as mages knew, as even the wizards of Gont Port and Re Albi had known when Ogion died. But on the fourth morning he was lying awake when she came to him, and looking up at her, he said, "This is Ogion's house."

"Aihal's house," she said, as easily as she could; it still was not easy for her to speak the mage's true name. She did not know if Ged had known that name. Surely he had. Ogion would have told him, or had not needed to tell him.

For a while he did not react, and when he spoke it was without expression. "Then he is dead."

"Ten days ago."

He lay looking before him as if pondering, trying to think something out.

"When did I come here?"

She had to lean close to understand him.

"Four days ago, in the evening of the day."

"There was no one else in the mountains," he said. Then his body winced and shuddered as if in pain or the intolerable memory of pain. He shut his eyes, frowning, and took a deep breath.

As his strength returned little by little, that frown, the held breath and clenched hands, became familiar to Tenar. Strength returned to him but not ease, not health.

He sat on the doorstep of the house in the sunlight of the summer afternoon. It was the longest journey he had yet taken from the bed. He sat on the threshold, looking out into the day, and Tenar, coming around the house from the bean patch, looked at him. He still had an ashy, shadowy look to him. It was not the grey hair only, but some quality of skin and bone, and there was nothing much to him but that. There was no light in his eyes. Yet this shadow, this ashen man, was the same whose face she had seen first in the radiance of his own power, the strong face with hawk nose and fine mouth, a handsome man. He had always been a proud, handsome man.

She came on towards him.

"The sunlight's what you need," she said to him, and he nodded, but his hands were clenched as he sat in the flood of summer warmth.

He was so silent with her that she thought maybe it was her presence that troubled him. Maybe he could not be at ease with her as he had used to be. He was Archmage now, after all—she kept forgetting that. And it was twenty-five years since they had walked in the mountains of Atuan and sailed together in *Lookfar* across the eastern sea.

"Where is *Lookfar*?" she asked, suddenly, surprised by the thought of it, and then thought, But how stupid of me! All those years ago, and he's Archmage, he wouldn't have that little boat now.

"In Selidor," he answered, his face set in its steady and incomprehensible misery.

As long ago as forever, as far away as Selidor. . . .

"The farthest island," she said; it was half a question.
"The farthest west," he said.

They were sitting at table, having finished the evening meal. Therru had gone outside to play.

"It was from Selidor that you came, then, on Kalessin?"

When she spoke the dragon's name again it spoke itself, shaping her mouth to its shape and sound, making her breath soft fire.

At the name, he looked up at her, one intense glance, which made her realize that he did not usually meet her eyes at all. He nodded. Then, with a laborious honesty, he corrected his assent: "From Selidor to Roke. And then from Roke to Gont."

A thousand miles? Ten thousand miles? She had no idea. She had seen the great maps in the treasuries of Havnor, but no one had taught her numbers, distances. *As far away as Selidor . . .* And could the flight of a dragon be counted in miles?

"Ged," she said, using his true name since they were alone, "I know you've been in great pain and peril. And if you don't want, maybe you can't, maybe you shouldn't tell me—but if I knew, if I knew something of it, I'd be more help to you, maybe. I'd like to be. And they'll be coming soon from Roke for you, sending a ship for the Archmage, what do I know, sending a dragon for you! And you'll be gone again. And we'll never have talked." As she spoke she clenched her own hands at the falseness of her tone and words. To joke about the dragon—to whine like an accusing wife!

He was looking down at the table, sullen, enduring, like a farmer after a hard day in the fields faced with some domestic squall.

"Nobody will come from Roke, I think," he said, and it

cost him effort enough that it was a while before he went on. "Give me time."

She thought it was all he was going to say, and replied, "Yes, of course. I'm sorry," and was rising to clear the table when he said, still looking down, not clearly, "I have that, now."

Then he too got up, and brought his dish to the sink, and finished clearing the table. He washed the dishes while Tenar put the food away. And that interested her. She had been comparing him to Flint; but Flint had never washed a dish in his life. Women's work. But Ged and Ogion had lived here, bachelors, without women; everywhere Ged had lived, it was without women; so he did the "women's work" and thought nothing about it. It would be a pity, she thought, if he did think about it, if he started fearing that his dignity hung by a dishcloth.

Nobody came for him from Roke. When they spoke of it, there had scarcely been time for any ship but one with the magewind in her sails all the way; but the days went on, and still there was no message or sign to him. It seemed strange to her that they would let their archmage go untroubled so long. He must have forbidden them to send to him; or perhaps he had hidden himself here with his wizardry, so that they did not know where he was, and so that he could not be recognized. For the villagers paid curiously little attention to him still.

That no one had come down from the mansion of the Lord of Re Albi was less surprising. The lords of that house had never been on good terms with Ogion. Women of the house had been, so the village tales went, adepts of dark arts. One had married a northern lord, they said, who buried her alive under a stone; another had meddled with the unborn child in her womb, trying to make it a creature of power, and indeed it had spoken words as it was born, but it had no bones. "Like a little bag of skin," the midwife whispered in the village, "a little bag with eyes and a voice, and it never sucked, but it spoke in some strange tongue, and died. . . ." Whatever the truth of such tales, the Lords of Re Albi had always held aloof. Companion of the mage Sparrowhawk, ward of the mage Ogion, bringer of the Ring of Erreth-Akbe to Havnor, Tenar might have been asked to stay, it would seem, at the mansion house when she first came to Re Albi; but she had not. She had lived instead, to her own delight, alone in a tiny cottage that belonged to the village weaver, Fan, and she saw the people of the great house seldom and at a distance. There was now no lady of the house at all, Moss told her, only the old lord, very old, and his grandson, and the young wizard, called Aspen, whom they had hired from the School on Roke.

Since Ogion was buried, with Aunty Moss's talisman in his hand, under the beech tree by the mountain path, Tenar had not seen Aspen. Strange as it seemed, he did not know the Archmage of Earthsea was in his own village, or, if he knew it, for some reason kept away. And the wizard of Gont Port, who had also come to bury Ogion, had never come back either. Even if he did not know that Ged was here, surely he knew who she was, the White Lady, who had worn the Ring of Erreth-Akbe on her wrist, who had made whole the Rune of Peace— And how many years ago was that, old woman! she said to herself. Is your nose out of joint?

All the same, it was she who had told them Ogion's true name. It seemed some courtesy was owing.

But wizards, as such, had nothing to do with courtesy. They were men of power. It was only power that they dealt with. And what power had she now? What had she ever had? As a girl, a priestess, she had been a vessel: the power of the dark places had run through her, used her, left her empty, untouched. As a young woman she had been taught a powerful knowledge by a powerful man and had laid it aside, turned away from it, not touched it. As a woman she had chosen and had the powers of a woman, in their time, and the time was past; her wiving and mothering was done. There was nothing in her, no power, for anybody to recognize.

But a dragon had spoken to her. "I am Kalessin," it had said, and she had answered, "I am Tenar."

"What is a dragonlord?" she had asked Ged, in the dark place, the Labyrinth, trying to deny his power, trying to make him admit hers; and he had answered with the plain honesty that forever disarmed her, "A man dragons will talk to."

So she was a woman dragons would talk to. Was that the new thing, the folded knowledge, the light seed, that she felt in herself, waking beneath the small window that looked west?

A few days after that brief conversation at table, she was weeding Ogion's garden patch, rescuing the onions he had set out in spring from the weeds of summer. Ged let himself in the gate in the high fence that kept the goats out, and set to weeding at the other end of the row. He worked awhile and then sat back, looking down at his hands.

"Let them have time to heal," Tenar said mildly.

He nodded.

The tall staked bean-plants in the next row were flowering. Their scent was very sweet. He sat with his thin arms on his knees, staring into the sunlit tangle of vines and flowers and hanging beanpods. She spoke as she worked: "When Aihal died, he said, 'All changed. . . .' And since his death, I've mourned him, I've grieved, but something lifts up my grief. Something is coming to be born—has been set free. I know in my sleep and my first waking, something is changed."

"Yes," he said. "An evil ended. And . . ."

After a long silence he began again. He did not look at her, but his voice sounded for the first time like the voice she remembered, easy, quiet, with the dry Gontish accent.

"Do you remember, Tenar, when we came first to Havnor?"

Would I forget? her heart said, but she was silent for fear of driving him back into silence.

"We brought *Lookfar* in and came up onto the quai—the steps are marble. And the people, all the people—and you held up your arm to show them the Ring. . . ."

—And held your hand; I was terrified beyond terror: the faces, the voices, the colors, the towers and the flags and banners, the gold and silver and music, and all I knew was you—in the whole world all I knew was you, there by me as we walked. . . .

"The stewards of the King's House brought us to the foot of the Tower of Erreth-Akbe, through the streets full of people. And we went up the high steps, the two of us alone. Do you remember?"

She nodded. She laid her hands on the earth she had been weeding, feeling its grainy coolness.

"I opened the door. It was heavy, it stuck at first. And we went in. Do you remember?"

It was as if he asked for reassurance— Did it happen? Do I remember?

"It was a great, high hall," she said. "It made me think of my Hall, where I was eaten, but only because it was so high. The light came down from windows away up in the tower. Shafts of sunlight crossing like swords."

"And the throne," he said.

"The throne, yes, all gold and crimson. But empty. Like the throne in the Hall in Atuan."

"Not now," he said. He looked across the green shoots of onion at her. His face was strained, wistful, as if he named a joy he could not grasp. "There is a king in Havnor," he said, "at the center of the world. What was foretold has been fulfilled. The Rune is healed, and the world is whole. The days of peace have come. He—"

He stopped and looked down, clenching his hands.

"He carried me from death to life. Arren of Enlad. Lebannen of the songs to be sung. He has taken his true name, Lebannen, King of Earthsea."

"Is that it, then," she asked, kneeling, watching him— "the joy, the coming into light?"

He did not answer.

A king in Havnor, she thought, and said aloud, "A king in Havnor!"

The vision of the beautiful city was in her, the wide streets, the towers of marble, the tiled and bronze roofs, the white-sailed ships in harbor, the marvelous throne room where sunlight fell like swords, the wealth and dignity and harmony, the order that was kept there. From that bright center, she saw order going outward like the perfect rings on water, like the straightness of a paved street or a ship sailing before the wind: a going the way it should go, a bringing to peace.

"You did well, dear friend," she said.

He made a little gesture as if to stop her words, and then turned away, pressing his hand to his mouth. She could not bear to see his tears. She bent to her work. She pulled a weed, and another, and the tough root broke. She dug with her hands, trying to find the root of the weed in the harsh soil, in the dark of the earth.

"Goha," said Therru's weak, cracked voice at the gate, and Tenar looked round. The child's half-face looked straight at her from the seeing eye and the blinded eye. Tenar thought, Shall I tell her that there is a king in Havnor?

She got up and went to the gate to spare Therru from trying to make herself heard. When she lay in the fire unconscious, Beech said, the child had breathed in fire. "Her voice is burned away," he explained.

"I was watching Sippy," Therru whispered, "but she got out of the broom-pasture. I can't find her."

It was as long a speech as she had ever made. She was trembling from running and from trying not to cry. We can't all be weeping at once, Tenar said to herself—this is stupid, we can't have this!— "Sparrowhawk!" she said, turning, "there's a goat got out."

He stood up at once and came to the gate.

"Try the springhouse," he said.

He looked at Therru as if he did not see her hideous scars, as if he scarcely saw her at all: a child who had lost a goat, who needed to find a goat. It was the goat he saw. "Or she's off to join the village flock," he said.

Therru was already running to the springhouse.

"Is she your daughter?" he asked Tenar. He had never before said a word about the child, and all Tenar could think for a moment was how very strange men were.

"No, nor my granddaughter. But my child," she said. What was it that made her jeer at him, jibe at him, again?

He let himself out the gate, just as Sippy dashed toward them, a brown-and-white flash, followed far behind by Therru.

"Hi!" Ged shouted suddenly, and with a leap he blocked the goat's way, heading her directly to the open gate and Tenar's arms. She managed to grab Sippy's loose leather collar. The goat at once stood still, mild as any lamb, looking at Tenar with one yellow eye and at the onion-rows with the other.

"Out," said Tenar, leading her out of goat heaven and over to the stonier pasture where she was supposed to be.

Ged had sat down on the ground, as out of breath as Therru, or more so, for he gasped, and was evidently dizzy; but at least he was not in tears. Trust a goat to spoil anything.

"Heather shouldn't have told you to watch Sippy," Tenar said to Therru. "Nobody can watch Sippy. If she gets out again, tell Heather, and don't worry. All right?"

Therru nodded. She was looking at Ged. She seldom looked at people, and very seldom at men, for longer than a glance; but she was gazing at him steadily, her head cocked like a sparrow. Was a hero being born?

Worsening

It was well over a month since the solstice, but the evenings were still long up on the west-facing Overfell. Therru had come in late from an all-day herbal expedition with Aunty Moss, too tired to eat. Tenar put her to bed and sat with her, singing to her. When the child was overtired she could not sleep, but would crouch in the bed like a paralyzed animal, staring at hallucinations till she was in a nightmare state, neither sleeping nor waking, and unreachable. Tenar had found she could prevent this by holding her and singing her to sleep. When she ran out of the songs she had learned as a farmer's wife in Middle Valley, she sang interminable Kargish chants she had learned as a child priestess at the Tombs of Atuan, lulling Therru with the drone and sweet whine of offerings to the Nameless Powers and the Empty Throne that was now filled with the dust and ruin of earthquake. She felt no power in those songs but that of song itself; and she liked to sing in her own language, though she did not know the songs a mother would sing to a child in Atuan, the songs her mother had sung to her.

Therru was fast asleep at last. Tenar slipped her from her lap to the bed and waited a moment to be sure she slept on. Then, after a glance round to be sure she was alone, with an almost guilty quickness, yet with the ceremony of enjoyment, of great pleasure, she laid her narrow, light-skinned hand along the side of the child's face where eye and cheek had been eaten away by fire, leaving slabbed, bald scar. Under her touch all that was gone. The flesh was whole, a child's round, soft, sleeping face. It was as if her touch restored the truth.

Lightly, reluctantly, she lifted her palm, and saw the irremediable loss, the healing that would never be whole.

She bent down and kissed the scar, got up quietly, and went out of the house.

The sun was setting in a vast, pearly haze. No one was about. Sparrowhawk was probably off in the forest. He had begun to visit Ogion's grave, spending hours in that quiet place under the beech tree, and as he got more strength he took to wandering on up the forest paths that Ogion had loved. Food evidently had no savor to him; Tenar had to ask him to eat. Companionship he shunned, seeking only to be alone. Therru would have followed him anywhere, and being as silent as he was she did not trouble him, but he was restless, and presently would send the child home and go on by himself, farther, to what ends Tenar did not know. He would come in late, cast himself down to sleep, and often be gone again before she and the child woke. She would leave him bread and meat to take with him.

She saw him now coming along the meadow path that had been so long and hard when she had helped Ogion walk it for the last time. He came through the luminous air, the wind-bowed grasses, walking steadily, locked in his obstinate misery, hard as stone.

"Will you be about the house?" she asked him, across some distance. "Therru's asleep. I want to walk a little."

"Yes. Go on," he said, and she went on, pondering the indifference of a man towards the exigencies that ruled a woman: that someone must be not far from a sleeping child, that one's freedom meant another's unfreedom, unless some ever-changing, moving balance were reached, like the balance of a body moving forward, as she did now, on two legs, first one then the other, in the practice of that remarkable art, walking. . . . Then the deepening colors of the sky and the soft insistence of the wind replaced her thoughts. She went on walking, without metaphors, until she came to the sandstone cliffs. There she stopped and watched the sun be lost in the serene, rosy haze.

She knelt and found with her eyes and then with her fingertips a long, shallow, blurred groove in the rock, scored right out to the edge of the cliff: the track of Kalessin's tail. She followed it again and again with her fingers, gazing out into the gulfs of twilight, dreaming. She spoke once. The name was not fire in her mouth this time, but hissed and dragged softly out of her lips, "Kalessin. . . ."

She looked up to the east. The summits of Gont Mountain above the forests were red, catching the light that was gone here below. The color dimmed as she watched. She looked away and when she looked back the summit was grey, obscure, the forested slopes dark.

She waited for the evening star. When it shone above the haze, she walked slowly home.

Home, not home. Why was she here in Ogion's house not in her own farmhouse, looking after Ogion's goats and onions not her own orchards and flocks? "Wait," he had said, and she had waited; and the dragon had come; and Ged was well now—was well enough. She had done her part. She had kept the house. She was no longer needed. It was time she left.

Yet she could not think of leaving this high ledge, this hawk's nest, and going down into the lowlands again, the easy farmlands, the windless inlands, she could not think of that without her heart sinking and darkening. What of the dream she had here, under the small window looking west? What of the dragon who had come to her here?

The door of the house stood open as usual for light and air. Sparrowhawk was sitting without lamp or firelight on a low seat by the swept hearth. He often sat there. She thought it had been his place when he was a boy here, in his brief apprenticeship with Ogion. It had been her place, winter days, when she had been Ogion's pupil.

He looked at her entering, but his eyes had not been on the doorway but beside it to the right, the dark corner behind the door. Ogion's staff stood there, an oaken stick, heavy, worn smooth at the grip, the height of the man himself. Beside it Therru had set the hazel switch and the alder stick Tenar had cut for them when they were walking to Re Albi.

Tenar thought—His staff, his wizard's staff, yew-wood, Ogion gave it to him— Where is it?— And at the same time, Why have I not thought of that till now?

It was dark in the house, and seemed stuffy. She was oppressed. She had wished he would stay to talk with her, but now that he sat there she had nothing to say to him, nor he to her.

"I've been thinking," she said at last, setting straight the four dishes on the oaken sideboard, "that it's time I was getting back to my farm."

He said nothing. Possibly he nodded, but her back was turned.

She was tired all at once, wanting to go to bed; but he sat there in the front part of the house, and it was not yet entirely dark; she could not undress in front of him. Shame made her angry. She was about to ask him to go out for a while when he spoke, clearing his throat, hesitant.

"The books. Ogion's books. The Runes and the two Lore-books. Would you be taking them with you?"

"With me?"

"You were his last student."

She came over to the hearth and sat down across from him on Ogion's three-legged chair.

"I learned to write the runes of Hardic, but I've forgotten most of that, no doubt. He taught me some of the language the dragons speak. Some of that I remember. But nothing else. I didn't become an adept, a wizard. I got married, you know. Would Ogion have left his books of wisdom to a farmer's wife?"

After a pause he said without expression, "Did he not leave them to someone, then?"

"To you, surely."

Sparrowhawk said nothing.

"You were his last prentice, and his pride, and friend. He never said it, but of course they go to you."

"What am I to do with them?"

She stared at him through the dusk. The western window gleamed faint across the room. The dour, relentless, unexplaining rage in his voice roused her own anger.

"You the Archmage ask me? Why do you make a worse fool of me than I am, Ged?"

He got up then. His voice shook. "But don't you—can't you see—all that is over—is gone!"

She sat staring, trying to see his face.

"I have no power, nothing. I gave it—spent it—all I had. To close— So that— So it's done, done with."

She tried to deny what he said, but could not.

"Like pouring out a little water," he said, "a cup of water onto the sand. In the dry land. I had to do that. But now

I have nothing to drink. And what difference, what difference did it make, does it make, one cup of water in all the desert? Is the desert gone?—Ah! Listen!—It used to whisper that to me from behind the door there: Listen, listen! And I went into the dry land when I was young. And I met it there, I became it, I married my death. It gave me life. Water, the water of life. I was a fountain, a spring, flowing, giving. But the springs don't run, there. All I had in the end was one cup of water, and I had to pour it out on the sand, in the bed of the dry river, on the rocks in the dark. So it's gone. It's over. Done."

She knew enough, from Ogion and from Ged himself, to know what land he spoke of, and that though he spoke in images they were not masks of the truth but the truth itself as he had known it. She knew also that she must deny what he said, no matter if it was true. "You don't give yourself time, Ged," she said. "Coming back from death must be a long journey—even on the dragon's back. It will take time. Time and quiet, silence, stillness. You have been hurt. You will be healed."

For a long while he was silent, standing there. She thought she had said the right thing, and given him some comfort. But he spoke at last.

"Like the child?"

It was like a knife so sharp she did not feel it come into her body.

"I don't know," he said in the same soft, dry voice, "why you took her, knowing that she cannot be healed. Knowing what her life must be. I suppose it's a part of this time we have lived—a dark time, an age of ruin, an ending time. You took her, I suppose, as I went to meet my enemy, because it was all you could do. And so we must live on into the new age with the spoils of our victory over evil. You with your burned child, and I with nothing at all."

Despair speaks evenly, in a quiet voice.

Tenar turned to look at the mage's staff in the dark place to the right of the door, but there was no light in it. It was all dark, inside and out. Through the open doorway a couple of stars were visible, high and faint. She looked at them. She wanted to know what stars they were. She got up and went groping past the table to the door. The haze had risen and not many stars were visible. One of those she had seen from indoors was the white summer star that they called, in Atuan, in her own language, Tehanu. She did not know the other one. She did not know what they called Tehanu here, in Hardic, or what its true name was, what the dragons called it. She knew only what her mother would have called it, Tehanu, Tehanu. Tenar, Tenar . . .

"Ged," she said from the doorway, not turning, "who brought you up, when you were a child?"

He came to stand near her, also looking out at the misty horizon of the sea, the stars, the dark bulk of the mountain above them.

"Nobody much," he said. "My mother died when I was a baby. There were some older brothers. I don't remember them. There was my father the smith. And my mother's sister. She was the witch of Ten Alders."

"Aunty Moss," Tenar said.

"Younger. She had some power."

"What was her name?"

He was silent.

"I cannot remember," he said slowly.

After a while he said, "She taught me the names. Falcon, pilgrim falcon, eagle, osprey, goshawk, sparrowhawk. . . ."

"What do you call that star? The white one, up high."

"The Heart of the Swan," he said, looking up at it. "In Ten Alders they called it the Arrow."

But he did not say its name in the Language of the Making, nor the true names the witch had taught him of hawk, falcon, sparrowhawk.

"What I said—in there—was wrong," he said softly. "I shouldn't speak at all. Forgive me."

"If you won't speak, what can I do but leave you?" She turned to him. "Why do you think only of yourself? always of yourself? Go outside awhile," she told him, wrathful. "I want to go to bed."

Bewildered, muttering some apology, he went out; and she, going to the alcove, slipped out of her clothes and into the bed, and hid her face in the sweet warmth of Therru's silky nape.

"Knowing what her life must be . . ."

Her anger with him, her stupid denial of the truth of what he told her, rose from disappointment. Though Lark had said ten times over that nothing could be done, yet she had hoped that Tenar could heal the burns; and for all her saying that even Ogion could not have done it, Tenar had hoped that Ged could heal Therru—could lay his hand on the scar and it would be whole and well, the blind eye bright, the clawed hand soft, the ruined life intact.

"Knowing what her life must be . . ."

The averted faces, the signs against evil, the horror and curiosity, the sickly pity and the prying threat, for harm draws harm to it . . . And never a man's arms. Never anyone to hold her. Never anyone but Tenar. Oh, he was right, the child should have died, should be dead. They should have let her go into that dry land, she and Lark and Ivy, meddling old women, softhearted and cruel. He was right, he was always right. But then, the men who had used her for their needs and games, the woman who had suffered her to be used—they had been quite right to beat her unconscious and push her into the fire to burn to death. Only they had not been thorough. They had lost their nerve, they had left some life in her. That had been wrong. And everything she, Tenar, had done was wrong. She had been given to the dark powers as a child: she had been eaten by them, she had been suffered to be eaten. Did she think that by crossing the sea, by learning other languages, by being a man's wife, a mother of children, that by merely living her life, she could ever be anything but what she was—their servant, their food, theirs to use for their needs and games? Destroyed, she had drawn the destroyed to her, part of her own ruin, the body of her own evil.

The child's hair was fine, warm, sweet-smelling. She lay curled up in the warmth of Tenar's arms, dreaming. What wrong could she be? Wronged, wronged beyond all repair, but not wrong. Not lost, not lost, not lost. Tenar held her and lay still and set her mind on the light of her dreaming, the gulfs of bright air, the name of the dragon, the name of the star, Heart of the Swan, the Arrow, Tehanu.

She was combing the black goat for the fine underwool that she would spin and take to a weaver to make into cloth, the silky "fleecefell" of Gont Island. The old black goat had been combed a thousand times, and liked it, leaning into the dig and pull of the wire comb-teeth. The grey-black combings grew into a soft, dirty cloud, which Tenar at last stuffed into a net bag; she worked some burrs out of the fringes of the goat's ears by way of thanks, and slapped her barrel flank companionably. "Bah!" the goat said, and trotted off. Tenar let herself out of the fenced pasture and came around in front of the house, glancing over the meadow to make sure Therru was still playing there.

Moss had shown the child how to weave grass baskets, and clumsy as her crippled hand was, she had begun to get the trick of it. She sat there in the meadow grass with her work on her lap, but she was not working. She was watching Sparrowhawk.

He stood a good way off, nearer the cliff's edge. His back was turned, and he did not know anyone was watching him, for he was watching a bird, a young kestrel; and she in turn was watching some small prey she had glimpsed in the grass. She hung beating her wings, wanting to flush the vole or mouse, to panic it into a rush to its nest. The man stood, as intent, as hungry, gazing at the bird. Slowly he lifted his right hand, holding the forearm level, and he seemed to speak, though the wind bore his words away. The kestrel veered, crying her high, harsh, keening cry, and shot up and off toward the forests.

The man lowered his arm and stood still, watching the bird. The child and the woman were still. Only the bird flew, went free.

"He came to me once as a falcon, a pilgrim falcon," Ogion had said, by the fire, on a winter day. He had been telling her of the spells of Changing, of transformations, of the mage Bordger who had become a bear. "He flew to me, to my wrist, out of the north and west. I brought him in by the fire here. He could not speak. Because I knew him, I was able to help him; he could put off the falcon, and be a man again. But there was always some hawk in him. They called him Sparrowhawk in his village because the wild hawks would come to him, at his word. Who are we? What is it to be a man? Before he had his name, before he had knowledge, before he had power, the hawk was in him, and the man, and the mage, and more—he was what we cannot name. And so are we all."

The girl sitting at the hearth, gazing at the fire, listening, saw the hawk; saw the man; saw the birds come to him, come at his word, at his naming them, come beating their wings to hold his arm with their fierce talons; saw herself the hawk, the wild bird.

Mice

Townsend, the sheep-buyer who had brought Ogion's message to the farm in Middle Valley, came out one afternoon to the mage's house.

"Will you be selling the goats, now Lord Ogion's gone?"

"I might," Tenar said neutrally. She had in fact been wondering how, if she stayed in Re Albi, she would get on. Like any wizard, Ogion had been supported by the people his skills and powers served—in his case, anyone on Gont. He had only to ask and what he needed would be given gratefully, a good bargain for the goodwill of a mage; but he never had to ask. Rather he had to give away the excess of food and raiment and tools and livestock and all necessities and ornaments that were offered or simply left on his doorstep. "What shall I do with them?" he would demand, perplexed, standing with his arms full of indignant, squawking chickens, or yards of tapestry, or pots of pickled beets.

But Tenar had left her living in the Middle Valley. She had not thought when she left so suddenly of how long she might stay. She had not brought with her the seven pieces of ivory, Flint's hoard; nor would that money have been of use in the village except to buy land or livestock, or deal with some trader up from Gont Port peddling pellawi furs or silks of Lorbanery to the rich farmers and little lords of Gont. Flint's farm gave her all she and Therru needed to eat and wear; but Ogion's six goats and his beans and onions had been for his pleasure rather than his need. She had been living off his larder, the gifts of villagers who gave to her for his sake, and the generosity of Aunty Moss. Just yesterday the witch had said, "Dearie, my ringneck hen's brood's hatched out, and I'll bring you two-three chickies when they begin to scratch. The mage wouldn't keep 'em, too noisy and silly, he said, but what's a house without chickies at the door?"

Indeed her hens wandered in and out of Moss's door freely, and slept on her bed, and enriched the smells of the dark, smoky, reeking room beyond belief.

"There's a brown-and-white yearling nanny will make a fine milch goat," Tenar said to the sharp-faced man.

"I was thinking of the whole lot," he said. "Maybe. Only five or six of 'em, right?"

"Six. They're in the pasture up there if you want to have a look."

"I'll do that." But he didn't move. No eagerness, of course, was to be evinced on either side.

"Seen the great ship come in?" he asked.

Ogion's house looked west and north, and from it one could see only the rocky headlands at the mouth of the bay, the Armed Cliffs; but from the village itself at several places one could look down the steep back-and-forth road to Gont Port and see the docks and the whole harbor. Shipwatching was a regular pursuit in Re Albi. There were generally a couple of old men on the bench behind the smithy, which gave the best view, and though they might never in their lives have gone down the fifteen zigzag miles of that road to Gont Port, they watched the comings and goings of ships as a spectacle, strange yet familiar, provided for their entertainment.

"From Havnor, smith's boy said. He was down in Port bargaining for ingots. Come up yesterevening late. The great ship's from Havnor Great Port, he said."

He was probably talking to keep her mind off the price of goats, and the slyness of his look was probably simply the way his eyes were made. But Havnor Great Port traded little with Gont, a poor and remote island notable only for wizards, pirates, and goats; and something in the words, "the great ship," troubled or alarmed her, she did not know why.

"He said they say there's a king in Havnor now," the sheep-buyer went on, with a sidelong glance.

"That might be a good thing," said Tenar.

Townsend nodded. "Might keep the foreign riffraff out."

Tenar nodded her foreign head pleasantly.

"But there's those down in Port won't be pleased, maybe." He meant the pirate sea-captains of Gont, whose control of the northeastern seas had been increasing of late years to the point where many of the old trade-schedules with the central islands of the Archipelago had been disrupted or abandoned; this impoverished everyone on Gont except the pirates, but that did not prevent the pirates from being heroes in the eyes of most Gontishmen. For all she knew, Tenar's son was a sailor on a pirate ship. And safer, maybe, as such than on a steady merchantman. *Better shark than herring,* as they said.

"There's some who're never pleased no matter what," Tenar said, automatically following the rules of conversation, but impatient enough with them that she added, rising, "I'll show you the goats. You can have a look. I don't know if we'll sell all or any." And she took the man to the broom-pasture gate and left him. She did not like him. It wasn't his fault that he had brought her bad news once and maybe twice, but his eyes slid, and she did not like his company. She wouldn't sell him Ogion's goats. Not even Sippy.

After he had left, bargainless, she found herself uneasy. She had said to him, "I don't know if we'll sell," and that had been foolish, to say *we* instead of *I,* when he hadn't asked to speak to Sparrowhawk, hadn't even alluded to him, as a man bargaining with a woman was more than likely to do, especially when she was refusing his offer.

She did not know what they made of Sparrowhawk, of his presence and nonpresence, in the village. Ogion, aloof and silent and in some ways feared, had been their own mage and their fellow-villager. Sparrowhawk they might be proud of as a name, the archmage who had lived awhile in Re Albi and done wonderful things, fooling a dragon in the Ninety Isles, bringing the Ring of Erreth-Akbe back from somewhere or other; but they did not know him. Nor did he know them. He had not gone into the village since he came, only to the forest, the wilderness. She had not thought about it before, but he avoided the village as surely as Therru did.

They must have talked about him. It was a village, and people talked. But gossip about the doings of wizards and mages would not go far. The matter was too uncanny, the lives of men of power were too strange, too different from their own. "Let be," she had heard villagers in the Middle Valley say when somebody got to speculating too freely about a visiting weatherworker or their own wizard, Beech—"Let be. He goes his way, not ours."

As for herself, that she should have stayed on to nurse

and serve such a man of power would not seem a questionable matter to them; again it was a case of "Let be." She had not been very much in the village herself; they were neither friendly nor unfriendly to her. She had lived there once in Weaver Fan's cottage, she was the old mage's ward, he had sent Townsend down round the mountain for her; all that was very well. But then she had come with the child, terrible to look at, who'd walk about in daylight with it by choice? And what kind of woman would be a wizard's pupil, a wizard's nurse? Witchery there, sure enough, and foreign too. But all the same, she was wife to a rich farmer way down there in the Middle Valley; though he was dead and she a widow. Well, who could understand the ways of the witchfolk? Let be, better let be. . . .

She met the Archmage of Earthsea as he came past the garden fence. She said, "They say there's a ship in from the City of Havnor."

He stopped. He made a movement, quickly controlled, but it had been the beginning of a turn to run, to break and run like a mouse from a hawk.

"Ged!" she said. "What is it?"

"I can't," he said. "I can't face them."

"Who?"

"Men from him. From the king."

His face had gone greyish, as when he was first here, and he looked around for a place to hide.

His terror was so urgent and undefended that she thought only how to spare him. "You needn't see them. If anybody comes I'll send them away. Come back to the house now. You haven't eaten all day."

"There was a man there," he said.

"Townsend, pricing goats. I sent *him* away. Come on!"

He came with her, and when they were in the house she shut the door.

"They couldn't harm you, surely, Ged. Why would they want to?"

He sat down at the table and shook his head dully. "No, no."

"Do they know you're here?"

"I don't know."

"What is it you're afraid of?" she asked, not impatiently, but with some rational authority.

He put his hands across his face, rubbing his temples and forehead, looking down. "I was—" he said. "I'm not—"

It was all he could say.

She stopped him, saying, "All right, it's all right." She dared not touch him lest she worsen his humiliation by any semblance of pity. She was angry at him, and for him. "It's none of their business," she said, "where you are, or who you are, or what you choose to do or not to do! If they come prying they can leave curious." That was Lark's saying. She had a pang of longing for the company of an ordinary, sensible woman. "Anyhow, the ship may have nothing at all to do with you. They may be chasing pirates home. It'll be a good thing, too, when the king gets around to doing that. . . . I found some wine in the back of the cupboard, a couple of bottles, I wonder how long Ogion had it squirreled away there. I think we'd both do well with a glass of wine. And some bread and cheese. The little one's had her dinner and gone off with Heather to catch frogs. There may be frogs' legs for supper. But bread and cheese for now. And wine. I wonder where it's from, who brought it to Ogion, how old it is?" So she talked along, woman's babble, saving him from having to make any answer or misread any silence, until he had got over the crisis of shame, and eaten a little, and drunk a glass of the old, soft, red wine.

"It's best I go, Tenar," he said. "Till I learn to be what I am now."

"Go where?"

"Up on the mountain."

"Wandering—like Ogion?" She looked at him. She remembered walking with him on the roads of Atuan, deriding him: "Do wizards often beg?" And he had answered, "Yes, but they try to give something in exchange."

She asked cautiously, "Could you get on for a while as a weatherworker, or a finder?" She filled his glass full.

He shook his head. He drank wine, and looked away. "No," he said. "None of that. Nothing of that."

She did not believe him. She wanted to rebel, to deny, to say to him, How can it be, how can you say that—as if you'd forgotten all you know, all you learned from Ogion, and at Roke, and in your traveling! You can't have forgotten the words, the names, the acts of your art. You learned, you earned your power!—She kept herself from saying that, but she murmured, "I don't understand. How can it all . . ."

"A cup of water," he said, tipping his glass a little as if to pour it out. And after a while, "What I don't understand is why he brought me back. The kindness of the young is cruelty. . . . So I'm here, I have to get on with it, till I can go back."

She did not know clearly what he meant, but she heard a note of blame or complaint that, in him, shocked and angered her. She spoke stiffly: "It was Kalessin that brought you here."

It was dark in the house with the door closed and only the small western window letting in the late-afternoon light. She could not make out his expression; but presently he raised his glass to her with a shadowy smile, and drank.

"This wine," he said. "Some great merchant or pirate must have brought it to Ogion. I never drank its equal.

Even in Havnor." He turned the squat glass in his hands, looking down at it. "I'll call myself something," he said, "and go across the mountain, to Armouth and the East Forest country, where I came from. They'll be making hay. There's always work at haying and harvest."

She did not know how to answer. Fragile and ill-looking, he would be given such work only out of charity or brutality; and if he got it he would not be able to do it.

"The roads aren't like they used to be," she said. "These last years, there's thieves and gangs everywhere. Foreign riffraff, as my friend Townsend says. But it's not safe any more to go alone."

Looking at him in the dusky light to see how he took this, she wondered sharply for a moment what it must be like never to have feared a human being—what it would be like to have to learn to be afraid.

"Ogion still went—" he began, and then set his mouth; he had recalled that Ogion had been a mage.

"Down in the south part of the island," Tenar said, "there's a lot of herding. Sheep, goats, cattle. They drive them up into the hills before the Long Dance, and pasture them there until the rains. They're always needing herders." She drank a mouthful of the wine. It was like the dragon's name in her mouth. "But why can't you just stay here?"

"Not in Ogion's house. The first place they'll come."

"Well, what if they do come? What will they want of you?"

"To be what I was."

The desolation of his voice chilled her.

She was silent, trying to remember what it was like to have been powerful, to be the Eaten One, the One Priestess of the Tombs of Atuan, and then to lose that, throw it away, become only Tenar, only herself. She thought about how it was to have been a woman in the prime of life, with children and a man, and then to lose all that, becoming old and a widow, powerless. But even so she did not feel she understood his shame, his agony of humiliation. Perhaps only a man could feel so. A woman got used to shame.

Or maybe Aunty Moss was right, and when the meat was out the shell was empty.

Witch-thoughts, she thought. And to turn his mind and her own, and because the soft, fiery wine made her wits and tongue quick, she said, "Do you know, I've thought— about Ogion teaching me, and I wouldn't go on, but went and found myself my farmer and married him—I thought, when I did that, I thought on my wedding day, Ged will be angry when he hears of this!" She laughed as she spoke.

"I was," he said.

She waited.

He said, "I was disappointed."

"Angry," she said.

"Angry," he said.

He poured her glass full.

"I had the power to know power, then," he said. "And you—you shone, in that terrible place, the Labyrinth, that darkness. . . ."

"Well, then, tell me: what should I have done with my power, and the knowledge Ogion tried to teach me?"

"Use it."

"How?"

"As the Art Magic is used."

"By whom?"

"Wizards," he said, a little painfully.

"Magic means the skills, the arts of wizards, of mages?"

"What else would it mean?"

"Is that all it could ever mean?"

He pondered, glancing up at her once or twice.

"When Ogion taught me," she said, "here—at the hearth there—the words of the Old Speech, they were as easy and as hard in my mouth as in his. That was like learning the language I spoke before I was born. But the rest—the lore, the runes of power, the spells, the rules, the raising of the forces—that was all dead to me. Somebody else's language. I used to think, I could be dressed up as a warrior, with a lance and a sword and a plume and all, but it wouldn't fit, would it? What would I do with the sword? Would it make me a hero? I'd be myself in clothes that didn't fit, is all, hardly able to walk."

She sipped her wine.

"So I took it all off," she said, "and put on my own clothes."

"What did Ogion say when you left him?"

"What did Ogion usually say?"

That roused the shadowy smile again. He said nothing. She nodded.

After a while, she went on more softly, "He took me because you brought me to him. He wanted no prentice after you, and he never would have taken a girl but from you, at your asking. But he loved me. He did me honor. And I loved and honored him. But he couldn't give me what I wanted, and I couldn't take what he had to give me. He knew that. But, Ged, it was a different matter when he saw Therru. The day before he died. You say, and Moss says, that power knows power. I don't know what he saw in her, but he said, 'Teach her!' And he said . . ."

Ged waited.

"He said, 'They will fear her.' And he said, 'Teach her all! Not Roke.' I don't know what he meant. How can I know? If I had stayed here with him I might know, I might be able to teach her. But I thought, Ged will come, he'll know. He'll know what to teach her, what she needs to know, my wronged one."

"I do not know," he said, speaking very low. "I saw— In the child I see only—the wrong done. The evil."

He drank off his wine.

"I have nothing to give her," he said.

There was a little scraping knock at the door. He started up instantly with that same helpless turn of the body, looking for a place to hide.

Tenar went to the door, opened it a crack, and smelled Moss before she saw her.

"Men in the village," the old woman whispered dramatically. "All kind of fine folk come up from the Port, from the great ship that's in from Havnor City, they say. Come after the Archmage, they say."

"He doesn't want to see them," Tenar said weakly. She had no idea what to do.

"I dare say not," said the witch. And after an expectant pause, "Where is he, then?"

"Here," said Sparrowhawk, coming to the door and opening it wider. Moss eyed him and said nothing.

"Do they know where I am?"

"Not from me," Moss said.

"If they come here," said Tenar, "all you have to do is send them away—after all, you are the Archmage—"

Neither he nor Moss was paying attention to her.

"They won't come to *my* house," Moss said. "Come on, if you like."

He followed her, with a glance but no word to Tenar.

"But what am I to tell them?" she demanded.

"Nothing, dearie," said the witch.

◆◆◆◆◆◆◆

Heather and Therru came back from the marshes with seven dead frogs in a net bag, and Tenar busied herself cutting off and skinning the legs for the hunters' supper. She was just finishing when she heard voices outside, and looking up at the open door saw people standing at it—men in hats, a twist of gold, a glitter— "Mistress Goha?" said a civil voice.

"Come in!" she said.

They came in: five men, seeming twice as many in the low-ceilinged room, and tall, and grand. They looked about them, and she saw what they saw.

They saw a woman standing at a table, holding a long, sharp knife. On the table was a chopping board and on that, to one side, a little heap of naked greenish-white legs; to the other, a heap of fat, bloody, dead frogs. In the shadow behind the door something lurked—a child, but a child deformed, mismade, half-faced, claw-handed. On a bed in an alcove beneath the single window sat a big, bony young woman, staring at them with her mouth wide open. Her hands were bloody and muddy and her dank skirt smelled of marsh-water. When she saw them look at her, she tried to hide her face with her skirt, baring her legs to the thigh.

They looked away from her, and from the child, and there was no one else to look at but the woman with the dead frogs.

"Mistress Goha," one of them repeated.

"So I'm called," she said.

"We come from Havnor, from the King," said the civil voice. She could not see his face clearly against the light. "We seek the Archmage, Sparrowhawk of Gont. King Lebannen is to be crowned at the turn of autumn, and he seeks to have the Archmage, his lord and friend, with him to make ready for the coronation, and to crown him, if he will."

The man spoke steadily and formally, as to a lady in a palace. He wore sober breeches of leather and a linen shirt dusty from the climb up from Gont Port, but it was fine cloth, with embroidery of gold thread at the throat.

"He's not here," Tenar said.

A couple of little boys from the village peered in at the door and drew back, peered again, fled shouting.

"Maybe you can tell us where he is, Mistress Goha," said the man.

"I cannot."

She looked at them all. The fear of them she had felt at first—caught from Sparrowhawk's panic, perhaps, or mere foolish fluster at seeing strangers—was subsiding. Here she stood in Ogion's house; and she knew well enough why Ogion had never been afraid of great people.

"You must be tired after that long road," she said. "Will you sit down? There's wine. Here, I must wash the glasses."

She carried the chopping board over to the sideboard, put the frogs' legs in the larder, scraped the rest into the swill-pail that Heather would carry to Weaver Fan's pigs, washed her hands and arms and the knife at the basin, poured fresh water, and rinsed out the two glasses she and Sparrowhawk had drunk from. There was one other glass in the cabinet, and two clay cups without handles. She set these on the table, and poured wine for the visitors; there was just enough left in the bottle to go round. They had exchanged glances, and had not sat down. The shortage of chairs excused that. The rules of hospitality, however, bound them to accept what she offered. Each man took glass or cup from her with a polite murmur. Saluting her, they drank.

"My word!" said one of them.

"Andrades—the Late Harvest," said another, with round eyes.

A third shook his head. "Andrades—the Dragon Year," he said solemnly.

The fourth nodded and sipped again, reverent.

The fifth, who was the first to have spoken, lifted his clay cup to Tenar again and said, "You honor us with a king's wine, mistress."

"It was Ogion's," she said. "This was Ogion's house. This is Aihal's house. You knew that, my lords?"

"We did, mistress. The king sent us to this house, believing that the archmage would come here; and, when word of the death of its master came to Roke and Havnor, yet more certain of it. But it was a dragon that bore the archmage from Roke. And no word or sending has come from him since then to Roke or to the king. And it is much in the king's heart, and much in the interest of us all, to know the archmage is here, and is well. Did he come here, mistress?"

"I cannot say," she said, but it was a poor equivocation, repeated, and she could see that the men thought so. She drew herself up, standing behind the table. "I mean that I will not say. I think if the archmage wishes to come, he will come. If he wishes not to be found, you will not find him. Surely you will not seek him out against his will."

The oldest of the men, and the tallest, said, "The king's will is ours."

The first speaker said more conciliatingly, "We are only messengers. What is between the king and the archmage of the Isles is between them. We seek only to bring the message, and the reply."

"If I can, I will see that your message reaches him."

"And the reply?" the oldest man demanded.

She said nothing, and the first speaker said, "We'll be here some few days at the house of the Lord of Re Albi, who, hearing of our ship's arrival, offered us his hospitality."

She felt a sense of a trap laid or a noose tightening, though she did not know why. Sparrowhawk's vulnerability, his sense of his own weakness, had infected her. Distraught, she used the defense of her appearance, her seeming to be a mere goodwife, a middle-aged housekeeper—but was it seeming? It was also truth, and these matters were more subtle even than the guises and shape-changes of wizards.— She ducked her head and said, "That will be more befitting your lordships' comfort. You see we live very plain here, as the old mage did."

"And drink Andrades wine," said the one who had identified the vintage, a bright-eyed, handsome man with a winning smile. She, playing her part, kept her head down. But as they took their leave and filed out, she knew that, seem what she might and be what she might, if they did not know now that she was Tenar of the Ring they would know it soon enough; and so would know that she herself knew the archmage and was indeed their way to him, if they were determined to seek him out.

When they were gone, she heaved a great sigh. Heather did so too, and then finally shut her mouth, which had hung open all the time they were there.

"I never," she said, in a tone of deep, replete satisfaction, and went to see where the goats had got to.

Therru came out from the dark place behind the door, where she had barricaded herself from the strangers with Ogion's staff and Tenar's alder stick and her own hazel switch. She moved in the tight, sidling way she had mostly abandoned since they had been here, not looking up, the ruined half of her face bent down towards the shoulder.

Tenar went to her and knelt to hold her in her arms. "Therru," she said, "they won't hurt you. They mean no harm."

The child would not look at her. She let Tenar hold her like a block of wood.

"If you say so, I won't let them in the house again."

After a while the child moved a little and asked in her hoarse, thick voice, "What will they do to Sparrowhawk?"

"Nothing," Tenar said. "No harm! They come—they mean to do him honor."

But she had begun to see what their attempt to do him honor would do to him—denying his loss, denying him his grief for what he had lost, forcing him to act the part of what he was no longer.

When she let the child go, Therru went to the closet and fetched out Ogion's broom. She laboriously swept the floor where the men from Havnor had stood, sweeping away their footprints, sweeping the dust of their feet out the door, off the doorstep.

Watching her, Tenar made up her mind.

She went to the shelf where Ogion's three great books stood, and rummaged there. She found several goose quills and a half-dried-up bottle of ink, but not a scrap of paper or parchment. She set her jaw, hating to do damage to anything so sacred as a book, and scored and tore out a thin strip of paper from the blank endsheet of the Book of Runes. She sat at the table and dipped the pen and wrote. Neither the ink nor the words came easy. She had scarcely written anything since she had sat at this same table a quarter of a century ago, with Ogion looking over her shoulder, teaching her the runes of Hardic and the Great Runes of Power. She wrote:

go oak farm in midl valy to clerbrook
say goha sent to look to garden & sheep

It took her nearly as long to read it over as it had to write it. By now Therru had finished her sweeping and was watching her, intent.

She added one word:

to-night

"Where's Heather?" she asked the child, as she folded the paper on itself once and twice. "I want her to take this to Aunty Moss's house."

She longed to go herself, to see Sparrowhawk, but dared not be seen going, lest they were watching her to lead them to him.

"I'll go," Therru whispered.

Tenar looked at her sharply.

"You'll have to go alone, Therru. Past the village."

The child nodded.

"Give it only to him!"

She nodded again.

Tenar tucked the paper into the child's pocket, held her, kissed her, let her go. Therru went, not crouching and sidling now but running freely, flying, Tenar thought, seeing her vanish in the evening light beyond the dark doorframe, flying like a bird, a dragon, a child, free.

Hawks

Therru was back soon with Sparrowhawk's reply: "He said he'll leave tonight."

Tenar heard this with satisfaction, relieved that he had accepted her plan, that he would get clear away from these messengers and messages he dreaded. It was not till she had fed Heather and Therru their frog-leg feast, and put Therru to bed and sung to her, and was sitting up alone without lamp or firelight, that her heart began to sink. He was gone. He was not strong, he was bewildered and uncertain, he needed friends; and she had sent him away from those who were and those who wished to be his friends. He was gone, and she must stay, to keep the hounds from his trail, to learn at least whether they stayed in Gont or sailed back to Havnor.

His panic and her obedience to it began to seem so unreasonable to her that she thought it equally unreasonable, improbable, that he would in fact go. He would use his wits and simply hide in Moss's house, which was the last place in all Earthsea that a king would look for an archmage. It would be much better if he stayed there till the king's men left. Then he could come back here to Ogion's house, where he belonged. And it would go on as before, she looking after him until he had his strength back, and he giving her his dear companionship.

A shadow against the stars in the doorway: "Hsssst! Awake?" Aunty Moss came in. "Well, he's off," she said, conspiratorial, jubilant. "Went the old forest road. Says he'll cut down to the Middle Valley way, along past Oak Springs, tomorrow."

"Good," said Tenar.

Bolder than usual, Moss sat down uninvited. "I gave him a loaf and a bit of cheese for the way."

"Thank you, Moss. That was kind."

"Mistress Goha." Moss's voice in the darkness took on the singsong resonance of her chanting and spellcasting. "There's a thing I was wanting to say to you, dearie, without going beyond what I can know, for I know you've lived among great folks and been one of 'em yourself, and that seals my mouth when I think of it. And yet there's things I know that you've had no way of knowing, for all the learning of the runes, and the Old Speech, and all you've learned from the wise, and in the foreign lands."

"That's so, Moss."

"Aye, well, then. So when we talked about how witch knows witch, and power knows power, and I said—of him who's gone now—that he was no mage now, whatever he had been, and still you would deny it—But I was right, wasn't I?"

"Yes."

"Aye. I was."

"He said so himself."

"O' course he did. He don't lie nor say this is that and that's this till you don't know which end's up, I'll say that for him. He's not one tries to drive the cart without the ox, either. But I'll say flat out I'm glad he's gone, for it wouldn't do, it wouldn't do any longer, being a different matter with him now, and all."

Tenar had no idea what she was talking about, except for her image of trying to drive the cart without the ox. "I don't know why he's so afraid," she said. "Well, I know in part, but I don't understand it, why he feels such shame. But I know he thinks that he should have died. And I know that all I understand about living is having your work to do, and being able to do it. That's the pleasure, and the glory, and all. And if you can't do the work, or it's taken from you, then what's any good? You have to have something. . . ."

Moss listened and nodded as at words of wisdom, but after a slight pause she said, "It's a queer thing for an old man to be a boy of fifteen, no doubt!"

Tenar almost said, "What are you talking about, Moss?"—but something prevented her. She realized that she had been listening for Ged to come into the house from his roaming on the mountainside, that she was listening for the sound of his voice, that her body denied his absence. She glanced suddenly over at the witch, a shapeless lump of black perched on Ogion's chair by the empty hearth.

"Ah!" she said, a great many thoughts suddenly coming into her mind all at once.

"That's why," she said. *"That's* why I never—"

After a quite long silence, she said, "Do they—do wizards—is it a spell?"

"Surely, surely, dearie," said Moss. "They witch 'emselves. Some'll tell you they make a trade-off, like a marriage turned backward, with vows and all, and so get their power then. But to me that's got a wrong sound to it, like a dealing with the Old Powers more than what a true witch deals with. And the old mage, he told me they did no such thing. Though I've known some woman witches do it, and come to no great harm by it."

"The ones who brought me up did that, promising virginity."

"Oh, aye, no men, you told me, and them yurnix. Terrible!"

"But why, but why—why did I never *think*—"

The witch laughed aloud. "Because that's the power of 'em, dearie. You don't think! You can't! And nor do they, once they've set their spell. How could they? Given their power? It wouldn't do, would it, it wouldn't do. You don't get without you give as much. That's true for all, surely. So they know that, the witch men, the men of power, they know that better than any. But then, you know, it's an uneasy thing for a man not to be a man, no matter if he can call the sun down from the sky. And so they put it right out of mind, with their spells of binding. And truly so. Even in these bad times we've been having, with the spells going wrong and all, I haven't yet heard of a wizard breaking those spells, seeking to use his power for his body's lust. Even the worst would fear to. O' course, there's those will work illusions, but they only fool 'emselves. And there's witch men of little account, witch-tinkers and the like, some of them'll try their own spells of beguilement on country women, but for all I can see, those spells don't amount to much. What it is, is the one power's as great as the other, and each goes its own way. That's how I see it."

Tenar sat thinking, absorbed. At last she said, "They set themselves apart."

"Aye. A wizard has to do that."

"But you don't."

"Me? I'm only an old witchwoman, dearie."

"How old?"

After a minute Moss's voice in the darkness said, with a hint of laughter in it, "Old enough to keep out of trouble."

"But you said . . . You haven't been celibate."

"What's that, dearie?"

"Like the wizards."

"Oh, no. No, no! Never was anything to look at, but there was a way I could look at them . . . not witching, you know, dearie, you know what I mean . . . there's a way to look, and he'd come round, sure as a crow will caw, in a day or two or three he'd come around my place—'I need a cure for my dog's mange,' 'I need a tea for my sick granny,' —but I knew what it was they needed, and if I liked 'em well enough maybe they got it. And for love, for love—I'm not one o' them, you know, though maybe some witches are, but they dishonor the art, I say. I do my art for pay but I take my pleasure for love, that's what I say. Not that it's all pleasure, all that. I was crazy for a man here for a long time, years, a good-looking man he was, but a hard, cold heart. He's long dead. Father to that Townsend who's come back here to live, you know him. Oh, I was so heartset on that man I did use my art, I spent many a charm on him, but 'twas all wasted. All for nothing. No blood in a turnip. . . . And I came up here to Re Albi in the first place when I was a girl because I was in trouble with a man in Gont Port. But I can't talk of that, for they were rich, great folks. 'Twas they had the power, not I! They didn't want their son tangled with a common girl like me, foul slut they called me, and they'd have had me put out of the way, like killing a cat, if I hadn't run off up here. But oh, I did like that lad, with his round, smooth arms and legs and his big, dark eyes, I can see him plain as plain after all these years. . . ."

They sat a long while silent in the darkness.

"When you had a man, Moss, did you have to give up your power?"

"Not a bit of it," the witch said, complacent.

"But you said you don't get unless you give. Is it different, then, for men and for women?"

"What isn't, dearie?"

"I don't know," Tenar said. "It seems to me we make up most of the differences, and then complain about 'em. I don't see why the Art Magic, why power, should be different for a man witch and a woman witch. Unless the power *itself* is different. Or the art."

"A man gives out, dearie. A woman takes in."

Tenar sat silent but unsatisfied.

"Ours is only a little power, seems like, next to theirs," Moss said. "But it goes down deep. It's all roots. It's like an old blackberry thicket. And a wizard's power's like a fir tree, maybe, great and tall and grand, but it'll blow right down in a storm. Nothing kills a blackberry bramble." She gave her hen-chuckle, pleased with her comparison. "Well, then!" she said briskly. "So as I said, it's maybe just as well he's on his way and out o' the way, lest people in the town begin to talk."

"To talk?"

"You're a respectable woman, dearie, and her reputation is a woman's wealth."

"Her wealth," Tenar repeated in the same blank way; then she said it again: "Her wealth. Her treasure. Her hoard. Her value. . . ." She stood up, unable to sit still, stretching her back and arms. "Like the dragons who found caves, who built fortresses for their treasure, for their hoard, to be safe, to sleep on their treasure, to be their treasure. Take in, take in, and never give out!"

"You'll know the value of a good reputation," Moss said drily, "when you've lost it. 'Tisn't everything. But it's hard to fill the place of."

"Would you give up being a witch to be respectable, Moss?"

"I don't know," Moss said after a while, thoughtfully. "I

don't know as I'd know how. I have the one gift, maybe, but not the other."

Tenar went to her and took her hands. Surprised at the gesture, Moss got up, drawing away a little; but Tenar drew her forward and kissed her cheek.

The older woman put up one hand and timidly touched Tenar's hair, one caress, as Ogion had used to do. Then she pulled away and muttered about having to go home, and started to leave, and asked at the door, "Or would you rather I stayed, with them foreigners about?"

"Go on," Tenar said. "I'm used to foreigners."

That night as she lay going to sleep she entered again into the vast gulfs of wind and light, but the light was smoky, red and orange-red and amber, as if the air itself were fire. In this element she was and was not; flying on the wind and being the wind, the blowing of the wind, the force that went free; and no voice called to her.

In the morning she sat on the doorstep brushing out her hair. She was not fair to blondness, like many Kargish people; her skin was pale, but her hair dark. It was still dark, hardly a thread of grey in it. She had washed it, using some of the water that was heating to wash clothes in, for she had decided the laundry would be her day's work, Ged being gone, and her respectability secure. She dried her hair in the sun, brushing it. In the hot, windy morning, sparks followed the brush and crackled from the flying ends of her hair.

Therru came to stand behind her, watching. Tenar turned and saw her so intent she was almost trembling.

"What is it, birdlet?"

"The fire flying out," the child said, with fear or exultation. "All over the sky!"

"It's just the sparks from my hair," Tenar said, a little taken aback. Therru was smiling, and she did not know if she had ever seen the child smile before. Therru reached out both her hands, the whole one and the burned, as if to touch and follow the flight of something around Tenar's loose, floating hair. "The fires, all flying out," she repeated, and she laughed.

At that moment Tenar first asked herself how Therru saw her—saw the world—and knew she did not know: that she could not know what one saw with an eye that had been burned away. And Ogion's words, *They will fear her,* returned to her; but she felt no fear of the child. Instead, she brushed her hair again, vigorously, so the sparks would fly, and once again she heard the little husky laugh of delight.

She washed the sheets, the dishcloths, her shifts and spare dress, and Therru's dresses, and laid them out (after making sure the goats were in the fenced pasture) in the meadow to dry on the dry grass, weighting down the things with stones, for the wind was gusty, with a late-summer wildness in it.

Therru had been growing. She was still very small and thin for her age, which must be about eight, but in the last couple of months, with her injuries healed at last and free of pain, she had begun to run about more and to eat more. She was fast outgrowing her clothes, hand-me-downs from Lark's youngest, a girl of five.

Tenar thought she might walk into the village and visit with Weaver Fan and see if he might have an end or two of cloth to give in exchange for the swill she had been sending for his pigs. She would like to sew something for Therru. And she would like to visit with old Fan, too. Ogion's death and Ged's illness had kept her from the village and the people she had known there. They had pulled her away, as ever, from what she knew, what she knew how to do, the world she had chosen to live in—a world not of kings and queens, great powers and dominions, high arts and journeys and adventures (she thought as she made sure Therru was with Heather, and set off into town), but of common people doing common things, such as marrying, and bringing up children, and farming, and sewing, and doing the wash. She thought this with a kind of vengefulness, as if she were thinking it at Ged, now no doubt halfway to Middle Valley. She imagined him on the road, near the dell where she and Therru had slept. She imagined the slight, ashen-haired man going along alone and silently, with half a loaf of the witch's bread in his pocket, and a load of misery in his heart.

"It's time you found out, maybe," she thought to him. "Time you learned that you didn't learn everything on Roke!" As she harangued him thus in her mind, another image came into it: she saw near Ged one of the men who had stood waiting for her and Therru on that road. Involuntarily she said, "Ged, be careful!"—fearing for him, for he did not carry even a stick. It was not the big fellow with hairy lips that she saw, but another of them, a youngish man with a leather cap, the one who had stared hard at Therru.

She looked up to see the little cottage next to Fan's house, where she had lived when she lived here. Between it and her a man was passing. It was the man she had been remembering, imagining, the man with a leather cap. He was going past the cottage, past the weaver's house; he had not seen her. She watched him walk on up the village street without stopping. He was going either to the turning of the hill road or to the mansion house.

Without pausing to think why, Tenar followed him at a distance until she saw which turn he took. He went on up the hill to the domain of the Lord of Re Albi, not down the road that Ged had gone.

She turned back then, and made her visit to old Fan.

Though almost a recluse, like many weavers, Fan had been kind in his shy way to the Kargish girl, and vigilant. How many people, she thought, had protected her respectability! Now nearly blind, Fan had an apprentice who did most of the weaving. He was glad to have a visitor. He sat as if in state in an old carved chair under the object from which his use-name came: a very large painted fan, the treasure of his family—the gift, so the story went, of a generous sea-pirate to his grandfather for some speedy sailmaking in time of need. It was displayed open on the wall. The delicately painted men and women in their gorgeous robes of rose and jade and azure, the towers and bridges and banners of Havnor Great Port, were all familiar to Tenar as soon as she saw the fan again. Visitors to Re Albi were often brought to see it. It was the finest thing, all agreed, in the village.

She admired it, knowing it would please the old man, and because it was indeed very beautiful, and he said, "You've not seen much to equal that, in all your travels, eh?"

"No, no. Nothing like it in Middle Valley at all," said she.

"When you was here, in my cottage, did I ever show you the other side of it?"

"The other side? No," she said, and nothing would do then but he must get the fan down; only she had to climb up and do it, carefully untacking it, since he could not see well enough and could not climb up on the chair. He directed her anxiously. She laid it in his hands, and he peered with his dim eyes at it, half closed it to make sure the ribs played freely, then closed it all the way, turned it over, and handed it to her.

"Open it slow," he said.

She did so. Dragons moved as the folds of the fan moved. Painted faint and fine on the yellowed silk, dragons of pale red, blue, green moved and grouped, as the figures on the other side were grouped, among clouds and mountain peaks.

"Hold it up to the light," said old Fan.

She did so, and saw the two sides, the two paintings, made one by the light flowing through the silk, so that the clouds and peaks were the towers of the city, and the men and women were winged, and the dragons looked with human eyes.

"You see?"

"I see," she murmured.

"I can't, now, but it's in my mind's eye. I don't show many that."

"It is very wonderful."

"I meant to show it to the old mage," Fan said, "but with one thing and another I never did."

Tenar turned the fan once more before the light, then remounted it as it had been, the dragons hidden in darkness, the men and women walking in the light of day.

Fan took her out next to see his pigs, a fine pair, fattening nicely towards autumn sausages. They discussed Heather's shortcomings as a swill-carrier. Tenar told him that she fancied a scrap of cloth for a child's dress, and he was delighted, pulling out a full width of fine linen sheeting for her, while the young woman who was his apprentice, and who seemed to have taken up his unsociability as well as his craft, clacked away at the broad loom, steady and scowling.

Walking home, Tenar thought of Therru sitting at that loom. It would be a decent living. The bulk of the work was dull, always the same over, but weaving was an honorable trade and in some hands a noble art. And people expected weavers to be a bit shy, often to be unmarried, shut away at their work as they were; yet they were respected. And working indoors at a loom, Therru would not have to show her face. But the claw hand? Could that hand throw the shuttle, warp the loom?

And was she to hide all her life?

But what was she to do? "Knowing what her life must be . . ."

Tenar set herself to think of something else. Of the dress she would make. Lark's daughter's dresses were coarse homespun, plain as mud. She could dye half this width, yellow maybe, or with red madder from the marsh; and then a full apron or overdress of white, with a ruffle to it. Was the child to be hidden at a loom in the dark and never have a ruffle to her skirt? And that would still leave enough for a shift, and a second apron if she cut out carefully.

"Therru!" she called as she approached the house. Heather and Therru had been in the broom-pasture when she left. She called again, wanting to show Therru the material and tell her about the dress. Heather came gawking around from the springhouse, hauling Sippy on a rope.

"Where's Therru?"

"With you," Heather replied so serenely that Tenar looked around for the child before she understood that Heather had no idea where she was and had simply stated what she wished to be true.

"Where did you leave her?"

Heather had no idea. She had never let Tenar down before; she had seemed to understand that Therru had to be kept more or less in sight, like a goat. But maybe it was Therru all along who had understood that, and had kept herself in sight? So Tenar thought, as having no comprehensible guidance from Heather, she began to look and call for the child, receiving no response.

She kept away from the cliff's edge as long as she could. Their first day there, she had explained to Therru that she must never go alone down the steep fields below the house or along the sheer edge north of it, because one-eyed vision cannot judge distance or depth with certainty. The child had obeyed. She always obeyed. But children forget. But she would not forget. But she might get close to the edge without knowing it. But surely she had gone to Moss's house. That was it—having been there alone, last night, she would go again. That was it, of course.

She was not there. Moss had not seen her.

"I'll find her, I'll find her, dearie," she assured Tenar; but instead of going up the forest path to look for her as Tenar had hoped she would, Moss began to knot up her hair in preparation for casting a spell of finding.

Tenar ran back to Ogion's house, calling again and again. And this time she looked down the steep fields below the house, hoping to see the little figure crouched playing among the boulders. But all she saw was the sea, wrinkled and dark, at the end of those falling fields, and she grew dizzy and sick-hearted.

She went to Ogion's grave and a short way past it up the forest path, calling. As she came back through the meadow, the kestrel was hunting in the same spot where Ged had watched it hunt. This time it stooped, and struck, and rose with some little creature in its talons. It flew fast to the forest. She's feeding her young, Tenar thought. All kinds of thoughts went through her mind very vivid and precise, as she passed the laundry laid out on the grass, dry now, she must take it up before evening. She must search around the house, the springhouse, the milking shed, more carefully. This was her fault. She had caused it to happen by thinking of making Therru into a weaver, shutting her away in the dark to work, to be respectable. When Ogion had said

"Teach her, teach her all, Tenar!" When she knew that a wrong that cannot be repaired must be transcended. When she knew that the child had been given her and she had failed in her charge, failed her trust, lost her, lost the one great gift.

She went into the house, having searched every corner of the other buildings, and looked again in the alcove and round the other bed. She poured herself water, for her mouth was dry as sand.

Behind the door the three sticks of wood, Ogion's staff and the walking sticks, moved in the shadows, and one of them said, "Here."

The child was crouched in that dark corner, drawn into her own body so that she seemed no bigger than a little dog, head bent down to the shoulder, arms and legs pulled tight in, the one eye shut.

"Little bird, little sparrow, little flame, what is wrong? What happened? What have they done to you now?"

Tenar held the small body, closed and stiff as stone, rocking it in her arms. "How could you frighten me so? How could you hide from me? Oh, I was so angry!"

She wept, and her tears fell on the child's face.

"Oh Therru, Therru, Therru, don't hide away from me!"

A shudder went through the knotted limbs, and slowly they loosened. Therru moved, and all at once clung to Tenar, pushing her face into the hollow between Tenar's breast and shoulder, clinging tighter, till she was clutching desperately. She did not weep. She never wept; her tears had been burned out of her, maybe; she had none. But she made a long, moaning, sobbing sound.

Tenar held her, rocking her, rocking her. Very, very slowly the desperate grip relaxed. The head lay pillowed on Tenar's breast.

"Tell me," the woman murmured, and the child answered in her faint, hoarse whisper, "He came here."

Tenar's first thought was of Ged, and her mind, still moving with the quickness of fear, caught that, saw who "he" was to her, and gave it a wry grin in passing, but passed on, hunting. "Who came here?"

No answer but a kind of internal shuddering.

"A man," Tenar said quietly, "a man in a leather cap."

Therru nodded once.

"We saw him on the road, coming here."

No response.

"The four men—the ones I was angry at, do you remember? He was one of them."

But she recalled how Therru had held her head down, hiding the burned side, not looking up, as she had always done among strangers.

"Do you know him, Therru?"

"Yes."

"From—from when you lived in the camp by the river?"

One nod.

Tenar's arms tightened around her.

"He came here?" she said, and all the fear she had felt turned as she spoke into anger, a rage that burned in her the length of her body like a rod of fire. She gave a kind of laugh—"Hah!"—and remembered in that moment Kalessin, how Kalessin had laughed.

But it was not so simple for a human and a woman. The fire must be contained. And the child must be comforted.

"Did he see you?"

"I hid."

Presently Tenar said, stroking Therru's hair, "He will never touch you, Therru. Understand me and believe me: he will never touch you again. He'll never see you again unless I'm with you, and then he must deal with me. Do you understand, my dear, my precious, my beautiful? You need not fear him. You must not fear him. He wants you to fear him. He feeds on your fear. We will starve him, Therru. We'll starve him till he eats himself. Till he chokes gnawing on the bones of his own hands. . . . Ah, ah, ah, don't listen to me now, I'm only angry, only angry. . . . Am I red? Am I red like a Gontishwoman, now? Like a dragon, am I red?" She tried to joke; and Therru, lifting her head, looked up into her face from her own crumpled, tremulous, fire-eaten face and said, "Yes. You are a red dragon."

The idea of the man's coming to the house, being in the house, coming around to look at his handiwork, maybe thinking of improving on it, that idea whenever it recurred to Tenar came less as a thought than as a queasy fit, a need to vomit. But the nausea burned itself out against the anger.

They got up and washed, and Tenar decided that what she felt most of all just now was hunger. "I am hollow," she said to Therru, and set them out a substantial meal of bread and cheese, cold beans in oil and herbs, a sliced onion, and dry sausage. Therru ate a good deal, and Tenar ate a great deal.

As they cleared up, she said, "For the present, Therru, I won't leave you at all, and you won't leave me. Right? And we should both go now to Aunty Moss's house. She was making a spell to find you, and she needn't bother to go on with it, but she might not know that."

Therru stopped moving. She glanced once at the open doorway, and shrank away from it.

"We need to bring in the laundry, too. On our way back. And when we're back, I'll show you the cloth I got today. For a dress. For a new dress, for you. A red dress."

The child stood, drawing in to herself.

"If we hide, Therru, we feed him. We will eat. And we will starve him. Come with me."

The difficulty, the barrier of that doorway to the outside was tremendous to Therru. She shrank from it, she hid her face, she trembled, stumbled, it was cruel to force her to cross it, cruel to drive her out of hiding, but Tenar was without pity. "Come!" she said, and the child came.

They walked hand-in-hand across the fields to Moss's house. Once or twice Therru managed to look up.

Moss was not surprised to see them, but she had a queer, wary look about her. She told Therru to run inside her house to see the ringneck hen's new chicks and choose which two might be hers; and Therru disappeared at once into that refuge.

"She was in the house all along," Tenar said. "Hiding."

"Well she might," said Moss.

"Why?" Tenar asked harshly. She was not in the hiding vein.

"There's—there's beings about," the witch said, not portentously but uneasily.

"There's scoundrels about!" said Tenar, and Moss looked at her and drew back a little.

"Eh, now," she said. "Eh, dearie. You have a fire around you, a shining of fire all about your head. I cast the spell to find the child, but it didn't go right. It went its own way somehow, and I don't know yet if it's ended. I'm bewildered. I saw great beings. I sought the little girl but I saw them, flying in the mountains, flying in the clouds. And now you have that about you, like your hair was afire. What's amiss, what's wrong?"

"A man in a leather cap," Tenar said. "A youngish man. Well enough looking. The shoulder seam of his vest's torn. Have you seen him round?"

Moss nodded. "They took him on for the haying at the mansion house."

"I told you that she"—Tenar glanced at the house—"was with a woman and two men? He's one of them."

"You mean, one of them that—"

"Yes."

Moss stood like a wood carving of an old woman, rigid, a block. "I don't know," she said at last. "I thought I knew enough. But I don't. What— What would— Would he come to—to *see* her?"

"If he's the father, maybe he's come to claim her."

"Claim her?"

"She's his property."

Tenar spoke evenly. She looked up at the heights of Gont Mountain as she spoke.

"But I think it's not the father. I think this is the other one. The one that came and told my friend in the village that the child had 'hurt herself.' "

Moss was still bewildered, still frightened by her own conjurations and visions, by Tenar's fierceness, by the presence of abominable evil. She shook her head, desolate. "I don't know," she said. "I thought I knew enough. How could he come back?"

"To eat," Tenar said. "To eat. I won't be leaving her alone again. But tomorrow, Moss, I might ask you to keep her here an hour or so, early in the day. Would you do that, while I go up to the manor house?"

"Aye, dearie. Of course. I could put a hiding spell on her, if you like. But . . . But they're up there, the great men from the King's City. . . ."

"Why, then, they can see how life is among the common folk," said Tenar, and Moss drew back again as if from a rush of sparks blown her way from a fire in the wind.

Finding Words

They were making hay in the lord's long meadow, strung out across the slope in the bright shadows of morning. Three of the mowers were women, and of the two men one was a boy, as Tenar could make out from some distance, and the other was stooped and grizzled. She came up along the mown rows and asked one of the women about the man with the leather cap.

"Him from down by Valmouth, ah," said the mower. "Don't know where he's got to." The others came along the row, glad of a break. None of them knew where the man from Middle Valley was or why he wasn't mowing with them. "That kind don't stay," the grizzled man said. "Shiftless. You know him, miss's?"

"Not by choice," said Tenar. "He came lurking about my place—frightened the child. I don't know what he's called, even."

"Calls himself Handy," the boy volunteered. The others looked at her or looked away and said nothing. They were beginning to piece out who she must be, the Kargish woman in the old mage's house. They were tenants of the Lord of Re Albi, suspicious of the villagers, leery of anything to do with Ogion. They whetted their scythes, turned away, strung out again, fell to work. Tenar walked down from the hillside field, past a row of walnut trees, to the road.

On it a man stood waiting. Her heart leapt. She strode on to meet him.

It was Aspen, the wizard of the mansion house. He stood gracefully leaning on his tall pine staff in the shade of a roadside tree. As she came out onto the road he said, "Are you looking for work?"

"No."

"My lord needs field hands. This hot weather's on the turn, the hay must be got in."

To Goha, Flint's widow, what he said was appropriate, and Goha answered him politely, "No doubt your skill can turn the rain from the fields till the hay's in." But he knew she was the woman to whom Ogion dying had spoken his true name, and, given that knowledge, what he said was so insulting and deliberately false as to serve as a clear warning. She had been about to ask him if he knew where the man Handy was. Instead, she said, "I came to say to the overseer here that a man he took on for the haymaking left my village as a thief and worse, not one he'd choose to have about the place. But it seems the man's moved on."

She gazed calmly at Aspen until he answered, with an effort, "I know nothing about these people."

She had thought him, on the morning of Ogion's death, to be a young man, a tall, handsome youth with a grey cloak and a silvery staff. He did not look as young as she had thought him, or he was young but somehow dried and withered. His stare and his voice were now openly contemptuous, and she answered him in Goha's voice: "To be sure. I beg your pardon." She wanted no trouble with him. She made to go on her way back to the village, but Aspen said, "Wait!"

She waited.

" 'A thief and worse,' you say, but slander's cheap, and a woman's tongue worse than any thief. You come up here to make bad blood among the field hands, casting calumny and lies, the dragonseed every witch sows behind her. Did you think I did not know you for a witch? When I saw that foul imp that clings to you, do you think I did not know how it was begotten, and for what purposes? The man did well who tried to destroy that creature, but the job should be completed. You defied me once, across the body of the old wizard, and I forbore to punish you then, for his sake and in the presence of others. But now you've come too far, and I warn you, woman! I will not have you set foot on this domain. And if you cross my will or dare so much as speak to me again, I will have you driven from Re Albi, and off the Overfell, with the dogs at your heels. Have you understood me?"

"No," Tenar said. "I have never understood men like you."

She turned and set off down the road.

Something like a stroking touch went up her spine, and her hair lifted up on her head. She turned sharp round to see the wizard reach out his staff towards her, and the dark lightnings gather round it, and his lips part to speak. She thought in that moment, *Because Ged has lost his magery, I thought all men had, but I was wrong!*—And a civil voice said, "Well, well. What have we here?"

Two of the men from Havnor had come out onto the road from the cherry orchards on the other side of it. They looked from Aspen to Tenar with bland and courtly expressions, as if regretting the necessity of preventing a wizard from laying a curse on a middle-aged widow, but really, really, it would not do.

"Mistress Goha," said the man with the gold-embroidered shirt, and bowed to her.

The other, the bright-eyed one, saluted her also, smiling. "Mistress Goha," he said, "is one who, like the King, bears her true name openly, I think, and unafraid. Living in Gont, she may prefer that we use her Gontish name. But knowing her deeds, I ask to do her honor; for she wore the Ring that no woman wore since Elfarran." He dropped to one knee as if it were the most natural thing in the world, took Tenar's right hand very lightly and quickly, and touched his forehead to her wrist. He released her and stood up, smiling that kind, collusive smile.

"Ah," said Tenar, flustered and warmed right through— "there's all kinds of power in the world!—Thank you."

The wizard stood motionless, staring. He had closed his mouth on the curse and drawn back his staff, but there was still a visible darkness about it and about his eyes.

She did not know whether he had known or had just now learned that she was Tenar of the Ring. It did not matter. He could not hate her more. To be a woman was her fault. Nothing could worsen or amend it, in his eyes; no punishment was enough. He had looked at what had been done to Therru, and approved.

"Sir," she said now to the older man, "anything less than honesty and openness seems dishonor to the king, for whom you speak—and act, as now. I'd like to honor the king, and his messengers. But my own honor lies in silence, until my friend releases me. I—I'm sure, my lords, that he'll send some word to you, in time. Only give him time, I pray you."

"Surely," said the one, and the other, "As much time as he wants. And your trust, my lady, honors us above all."

She went on down the road to Re Albi at last, shaken by

the shock and change of things, the wizard's flaying hatred, her own angry contempt, her terror at the sudden knowledge of his will and power to do her harm, the sudden end of that terror in the refuge offered by the envoys of the king—the men who had come in the white-sailed ship from the haven itself, the Tower of the Sword and the Throne, the center of right and order. Her heart lifted up in gratitude. There was indeed a king upon that throne, and in his crown the chiefest jewel would be the Rune of Peace.

She liked the younger man's face, clever and kindly, and the way he had knelt to her as to a queen, and his smile that had a wink hidden in it. She turned to look back. The two envoys were walking up the road to the mansion house with the wizard Aspen. They seemed to be conversing with him amicably, as if nothing had happened.

That sank her surge of hopeful trust a bit. To be sure, they were courtiers. It wasn't their business to quarrel, or to judge and disapprove. And he was a wizard, and their host's wizard. Still, she thought, they needn't have walked and talked with him quite so comfortably.

The men from Havnor stayed several days with the Lord of Re Albi, perhaps hoping that the archmage would change his mind and come to them, but they did not seek him, nor press Tenar about where he might be. When they left at last, Tenar told herself that she must make up her mind what to do. There was no real reason for her to stay here, and two strong reasons for leaving: Aspen and Handy, neither of whom could she trust to let her and Therru alone.

Yet she found it hard to make up her mind, because it was hard to think of going. In leaving Re Albi now she left Ogion, lost him, as she had not lost him while she kept his house and weeded his onions. And she thought, "I will never dream of the sky, down there." Here, where Kalessin had come, she was Tenar, she thought. Down in Middle Valley she would only be Goha again. She delayed. She said to herself, "Am I to fear those scoundrels, to run from them? That's what they want me to do. Are they to make me come and go at their will?" She said to herself, "I'll just finish the cheese-making." She kept Therru always with her. And the days went by.

Moss came with a tale to tell. Tenar had asked her about the wizard Aspen, not telling her the whole story but saying that he had threatened her—which, in fact, might well be all he had meant to do. Moss usually kept clear of the old lord's domain, but she was curious about what went on there, and not unwilling to find the chance to chat with some acquaintances there, a woman from whom she had learned midwifery and others whom she had attended as healer or finder. She got them talking about the doings at the mansion house. They all hated Aspen and so were quite ready to talk about him, but their tales must be heard as half spite and fear. Still, there would be facts among the fancies. Moss herself attested that until Aspen came three years ago, the younger lord, the grandson, had been fit and well, though a shy, sullen man, "scared-like," she said. Then about the time the young lord's mother died, the old lord had sent to Roke for a wizard— "What for? With Lord Ogion not a mile away? And they're all witchfolk themselves in the mansion."

But Aspen had come. He had paid his respects and no more to Ogion, and always, Moss said, stayed up at the mansion. Since then, less and less had been seen of the grandson, and it was said now that he lay day and night in bed, "like a sick baby, all shriveled up," said one of the women who had been into the house on some errand. But the old lord, "a hundred years old, or near, or more," Moss insisted—she had no fear of numbers and no respect for them—the old lord was flourishing, "full of juice," they said. And one of the men, for they would have only men wait on them in the mansion, had told one of the women that the old lord had hired the wizard to make him live forever, and that the wizard was doing that, feeding him, the man said, off the grandson's life. And the man saw no harm in it, saying, "Who wouldn't want to live forever?"

"Well," Tenar said, taken aback. "That's an ugly story. Don't they talk about all this in the village?"

Moss shrugged. It was a matter of "Let be" again. The doings of the powerful were not to be judged by the powerless. And there was the dim, blind loyalty, the rootedness in place: the old man was *their* lord, Lord of Re Albi, nobody else's business what he did. . . . Moss evidently felt this herself. "Risky," she said, "bound to go wrong, such a trick," but she did not say it was wicked.

No sign of the man Handy had been seen up at the mansion. Longing to be sure that he had left the Overfell, Tenar asked an acquaintance or two in the village if they had seen such a man, but she got unwilling and equivocal replies. They wanted no part of her affairs. "Let be. . . ." Only old Fan treated her as a friend and fellow-villager. And that might be because his eyes were so dim he could not clearly see Therru.

She took the child with her now when she went into the village, or any distance at all from the house.

Therru did not find this bondage wearisome. She stayed close by Tenar as a much younger child would do, working with her or playing. Her play was with cat's cradle, basket making, and with a couple of bone figures that Tenar had found in a little grass bag on one of Ogion's shelves. There was an animal that might be a dog or a sheep, a figure that might be a woman or a man. To Tenar they had no sense of power or danger about them, and Moss said, "Just toys." To Therru they were a great magic. She moved them about in the patterns of some silent story for hours at a time; she did not speak as she played. Sometimes she built houses for the person and the animal, stone cairns, huts of mud and straw. They were always in her pocket in their grass bag. She was learning to spin; she could hold the distaff in the burned hand and twist the drop-spindle with the other. They had combed the goats regularly since they had been there, and by now had a good sackful of silky goathair to be spun.

"But I should be teaching her," Tenar thought, distressed. "Teach her *all,* Ogion said, and what am I teaching her? Cooking and spinning?" Then another part of her mind said in Goha's voice, "And are those not true arts, needful and noble? Is wisdom all words?"

Still she worried over the matter, and one afternoon while Therru was pulling the goathair to clean and loosen it and she was carding it, in the shade of the peach tree, she said, "Therru, maybe it's time you began to learn the true names of things. There is a language in which all things bear their true names, and deed and word are one. By speaking that tongue Segoy raised the islands from the deeps. It is the language dragons speak."

The child listened, silent.

Tenar laid down her carding combs and picked up a small stone from the ground. "In that tongue," she said, "this is *tolk.* "

Therru watched what she did and repeated the word, *tolk,* but without voice, only forming it with her lips, which were drawn back a little on the right side by the scarring.

The stone lay on Tenar's palm, a stone. They were both silent.

"Not yet," Tenar said. "That's not what I have to teach you now." She let the stone fall to the ground, and picked up her combs and a handful of cloudy grey wool Therru had prepared for carding. "Maybe when you have your true name, maybe that will be the time. Not now. Now, listen. Now is the time for stories, for you to begin to learn the stories. I can tell you stories of the Archipelago and of the Kargad Lands. I told you a story I learned from my friend Aihal the Silent. Now I'll tell you one I learned from my friend Lark when she told it to her children and mine. This is the story of Andaur and Avad. As long ago as forever, as far away as Selidor, there lived a man called Andaur, a woodcutter, who went up in the hills alone. One day, deep in the forest, he cut a great oak tree down. As it fell it cried out to him in a human voice. . . ."

It was a pleasant afternoon for them both.

But that night as she lay by the sleeping child, Tenar could not sleep. She was restless, concerned with one petty anxiety after another—did I fasten the pasture gate, does my hand ache from carding or is it arthritis beginning, and so on. Then she became very uneasy, thinking she heard noises outside the house. Why haven't I got me a dog? she thought. Stupid, not to have a dog. A woman and child living alone ought to have a dog these days. But this is Ogion's house! Nobody would come here to do evil. But Ogion is dead, dead, buried at the roots of the tree at the forest's edge. And no one will come. Sparrowhawk's gone, run away. Not even Sparrowhawk anymore, a shadow man, no good to anyone, a dead man forced to be alive. And I have no strength, there's no good in me. I say the word of the Making and it dies in my mouth, it is meaningless. A stone. I am a woman, an old woman, weak, stupid. All I do is wrong. All I touch turns to ashes, shadow, stone. I am the creature of darkness, swollen with darkness. Only fire can cleanse me. Only fire can eat me, eat me away like—

She sat up and cried out aloud in her own language, "The curse be turned, and turn!"—and brought her right arm out and down, pointing straight to the closed door. Then leaping out of bed, she went to the door, flung it open, and said into the cloudy night, "You come too late, Aspen. I was eaten long ago. Go clean your own house!"

There was no answer, no sound, but a faint, sour, vile smell of burning—singed cloth or hair.

She shut the door, set Ogion's staff against it, and looked to see that Therru still slept. She did not sleep herself, that night.

In the morning she took Therru into the village to ask Fan if he would want the yarn they had been spinning. It was an excuse to get away from the house and to be for a little while among people. The old man said he would be glad to weave the yarn, and they talked for a few minutes, under the great painted fan, while the apprentice scowled and clacked away grimly at the loom. As Tenar and Therru left Fan's house, somebody dodged around the corner of the little cottage where she had lived. Something, wasps or bees, were stinging Tenar's neck and head, and there was a patter of rain all round, a thundershower, but there were no clouds— Stones. She saw the pebbles strike the ground. Therru had stopped, startled and puzzled, looking around. A couple of boys ran from behind the cottage, half hiding, half showing themselves, calling out to each other, laughing.

"Come along," Tenar said steadily, and they walked to Ogion's house.

Tenar was shaking, and the shaking got worse as they walked. She tried to conceal it from Therru, who looked troubled but not frightened, not having understood what had happened.

As soon as they entered the house, Tenar knew someone had been there while they were in the village. It smelled of burned meat and hair. The coverlet of their bed had been disarranged.

When she tried to think what to do, she knew there was a spell on her. It had been laid waiting for her. She could not stop shaking, and her mind was confused, slow, unable to decide. She could not think. She had said the word, the true name of the stone, and it had been flung at her, in her face—in the face of evil, the hideous face— She had dared speak— She could not speak—

She thought, in her own language, *I cannot think in Hardic. I must not.*

She could think, in Kargish. Not quickly. It was as if she had to ask the girl Arha, who she had been long ago, to come out of the darkness and think for her. To help her. As she had helped her last night, turning the wizard's curse back on him. Arha had not known a great deal of what Tenar and Goha knew, but she had known how to curse, and how to live in the dark, and how to be silent.

It was hard to do that, to be silent. She wanted to cry out. She wanted to talk—to go to Moss and tell her what had happened, why she must go, to say good-bye at least. She tried to say to Heather, "The goats are yours now, Heather," and she managed to say that in Hardic, so that Heather would understand, but Heather did not understand. She stared and laughed. "Oh, they're Lord Ogion's goats!" she said.

"Then—you—" Tenar tried to say "go on keeping them for him," but a deadly sickness came into her and she heard her voice saying shrilly, "fool, halfwit, imbecile, woman!" Heather stared and stopped laughing. Tenar covered her own mouth with her hand. She took Heather and turned her to look at the cheeses ripening in the milking shed, and pointed to them and to Heather, back and forth, until Heather nodded vaguely and laughed again because she was acting so queer.

Tenar nodded to Therru—come!—and went into the house, where the foul smell was stronger, making Therru cower.

Tenar fetched out their packs and their travel shoes. In her pack she put her spare dress and shifts, Therru's two old dresses and the half-made new one and the spare cloth; the spindle whorls she had carved for herself and Therru; and a little food and a clay bottle of water for the way. In Therru's pack went Therru's best baskets, the bone person and the bone animal in their grass bag, some feathers, a little maze-mat Moss had given her, and a bag of nuts and raisins.

She wanted to say, "Go water the peach tree," but dared not. She took the child out and showed her. Therru watered the tiny shoot carefully.

They swept and straightened up the house, working fast, in silence.

Tenar set a jug back on the shelf and saw on the other end of the shelf the three great books, Ogion's books.

Arha saw them and they were nothing to her, big leather boxes full of paper.

But Tenar stared at them and bit her knuckle, frowning with the effort to decide, to know what to do, and to know how to carry them. She could not carry them. But she must. They could not stay here in the desecrated house, the house where hatred had come in. They were his. Ogion's. Ged's.

Hers. The knowledge. Teach her all! She emptied their wool and yarn from the sack she had meant to carry it in and put the books in, one atop the other, and tied the neck of the bag with a leather strap with a loop to hold it by. Then she said, "We must go now, Therru." She spoke in Kargish, but the child's name was the same, it was a Kargish word, flame, flaming; and she came, asking no questions, carrying her little hoard in the pack on her back.

They took up their walking sticks, the hazel shoot and the alder branch. They left Ogion's staff beside the door in the dark corner. They left the door of the house wide open to the wind from the sea.

An animal sense guided Tenar away from the fields and away from the hill road she had come by. She took a short-cut down the steep-falling pastures, holding Therru's hand, to the wagon road that zigzagged down to Gont Port. She knew that if she met Aspen she was lost, and thought he might be waiting for her on the way. But not, maybe, on this way.

After a mile or so of the descent she began to be able to think. What she thought first was that she had taken the right road. For the Hardic words were coming back to her, and after a while, the true words, so that she stooped and picked up a stone and held it in her hand, saying in her mind, *tolk;* and she put that stone in her pocket. She looked out into the vast levels of air and cloud and said in her mind, once, *Kalessin.* And her mind cleared, as that air was clear.

They came into a long cutting shadowed by high, grassy banks and outcrops of rock, where she was a little uneasy. As they came out onto the turn they saw the dark-blue bay below them, and coming into it between the Armed Cliffs a beautiful ship under full sail. Tenar had feared the last such ship, but not this one. She wanted to run down the road to meet it.

That she could not do. They went at Therru's pace. It was a better pace than it had been two months ago, and going downhill made it easy, too. But the ship ran to meet them. There was a magewind in her sails; she came across the bay like a flying swan. She was in port before Tenar and Therru were halfway down the next long turning of the road.

Towns of any size at all were very strange places to Tenar. She had not lived in them. She had seen the greatest city in Earthsea, Havnor, once, for a while; and she had sailed into Gont Port with Ged, years ago, but they had climbed on up the road to the Overfell without pausing in the streets. The only other town she knew was Valmouth, where her daughter lived, a sleepy, sunny little harbor town where a ship trading from the Andrades was a great event, and most of the conversation of the inhabitants concerned dried fish.

She and the child came into the streets of Gont Port when the sun was still well above the western sea. Therru had walked fifteen miles without complaint and without being worn out, though certainly she was very tired. Tenar was tired too, having not slept the night before, and having been much distressed; and also Ogion's books had been a heavy burden. Halfway down the road she had put them into the backpack, and the food and clothing into the woolsack, which was better, but not all that much better. So they came trudging among outlying houses to the landgate of the city, where the road, coming between two carved stone dragons, turned into a street. There a man, the guard of the gate, eyed them. Therru bent her burned face down towards the shoulder and hid her burned hand under the apron of her dress.

"Will you be going to a house in town, mistress?" the guard asked, peering at the child.

Tenar did not know what to say. She did not know there were guards at city gates. She had nothing to pay a toll-keeper or an innkeeper. She did not know a soul in Gont Port—except, she thought now, the wizard, the one who had come up to bury Ogion, what was he called? But she did not know what he was called. She stood there with her mouth open, like Heather.

"Go on, go on," the guard said, bored, and turned away.

She wanted to ask him where she would find the road south across the headlands, the coast road to Valmouth; but she dared not waken his interest again, lest he decide she was after all a vagrant or a witch or whatever he and the stone dragons were supposed to keep out of Gont Port. So they went on between the dragons—Therru looked up, a little, to see them—and tramped along on cobblestones, more and more amazed, bewildered, and abashed. It did not seem to Tenar that anybody or anything in the world had been kept out of Gont Port. It was all here. Tall houses of stone, wagons, drays, carts, cattle, donkeys, market-places, shops, crowds, people, people—the farther they went the more people there were. Therru clung to Tenar's hand, sidling, hiding her face with her hair. Tenar clung to Therru's hand.

She did not see how they could stay here, so the only thing to do was get started south and go till nightfall—all too soon now—hoping to camp in the woods. Tenar picked out a broad woman in a broad white apron who was closing the shutters of a shop, and crossed the street, resolved to ask her for the road south out of the city. The woman's firm, red face looked pleasant enough, but as Tenar was getting up her courage to speak to her, Therru clutched her hard as if trying to hide herself against her, and looking up she saw coming down the street towards her the man with the leather cap. He saw her at the same instant. He stopped.

Tenar seized Therru's arm and half dragged, half swung her round. "Come!" she said, and strode straight on past the man. Once she had put him behind her she walked faster, going downhill towards the flare and dark of the sunset water and the docks and quais at the foot of the steep street. Therru ran with her, gasping as she had gasped after she was burned.

Tall masts rocked against the red and yellow sky. The ship, sails furled, lay against the stone pier, beyond an oared galley.

Tenar looked back. The man was following them, close behind. He was not hurrying.

She ran out onto the pier, but after a way Therru stumbled and could not go on, unable to get her breath. Tenar picked her up, and the child held to her, hiding her face in Tenar's shoulder. But Tenar could scarcely move, thus laden. Her legs shook under her. She took a step, and another, and another. She came to the little wooden bridge they had laid from the pier to the ship's deck. She laid her hand on its rail.

A sailor on deck, a bald, wiry fellow, looked her over. "What's wrong, miss's?" he said.

"Is—Is the ship from Havnor?"

"From the King's City, sure."

"Let me aboard!"

"Well, I can't do that," the man said, grinning, but his eyes shifted; he was looking at the man who had come to stand beside Tenar.

"You don't have to run away," Handy said to her. "I don't mean you any harm. I don't want to hurt you. You don't understand. I was the one got help for her, wasn't I? I was really sorry, what happened. I want to help you with her." He put out his hand as if drawn irresistibly to touch Therru. Tenar could not move. She had promised Therru that he would never touch her again. She saw the hand touch the child's bare, flinching arm.

"What do you want with her?" said another voice. Another sailor had taken the place of the bald one: a young man. Tenar thought he was her son.

Handy was quick to speak. "She's got—she took my kid. My niece. It's mine. She witched it, she run off with it, see—"

She could not speak at all. The words were gone from her again, taken from her. The young sailor was not her son. His face was thin and stern, with clear eyes. Looking at him, she found the words: "Let me come aboard. Please!"

The young man held out his hand. She took it, and he brought her across the gangway onto the deck of the ship.

"Wait there," he said to Handy, and to her, "Come with me."

But her legs would not hold her up. She sank down in a heap on the deck of the ship from Havnor, dropping the heavy sack but clinging to the child. "Don't let him take her, oh, don't let them have her, not again, not again, not again!"

The Dolphin

She would not let go the child, she would not give the child to them. They were all men aboard the ship. Only after a long time did she begin to be able to take into her mind what they said, what had been done, what was happening. When she understood who the young man was, the one she had thought was her son, it seemed as if she had understood it all along, only she had not been able to think it. She had not been able to think anything.

He had come back onto the ship from the docks and now stood talking to a grey-haired man, the ship's master by the look of him, near the gangplank. He glanced over at Tenar, whom they had let stay crouching with Therru in a corner of the deck between the railing and a great windlass. The long day's weariness had won out over Therru's fear; she was fast asleep, close against Tenar, with her little pack for a pillow and her cloak for a blanket.

Tenar got up slowly, and the young man came to her at once. She straightened her skirts and tried to smooth her hair back. "I am Tenar of Atuan," she said. He stood still. She said, "I think you are the king."

He was very young, younger than her son, Spark. He could hardly be twenty yet. But there was a look to him that was not young at all, something in his eyes that made her think: He has been through the fire.

"My name is Lebannen of Enlad, my lady," he said, and he was about to bow or even kneel to her. She caught his hands so that they stood there face to face. "Not to me," she said, "nor I to you!"

He laughed in surprise, and held her hands while he stared at her frankly. "How did you know I sought you? Were you coming to me, when that man—?"

"No, no. I was running away—from him—from—from ruffians— I was trying to go home, that's all."

"To Atuan?"

"Oh, no! To my farm. In Middle Valley. On Gont, here." She laughed too, a laugh with tears in it. The tears could be wept now, and would be wept. She let go the king's hands so that she could wipe her eyes.

"Where is it, Middle Valley?" he asked.

"South and east, around the headlands there. Valmouth is the port."

"We'll take you there," he said, with delight in being able to offer it, to do it.

She smiled and wiped her eyes, nodding acceptance.

"A glass of wine. Some food, some rest," he said, "and a bed for your child." The ship's master, listening discreetly, gave orders. The bald sailor she remembered from what seemed a long time ago came forward. He was going to pick up Therru. Tenar stood between him and the child. She could not let him touch her. "I'll carry her," she said, her voice strained high.

"There's the stairs there, miss's. I'll do it," said the sailor, and she knew he was kind, but she could not let him touch Therru.

"Let me," the young man, the king, said, and with a

glance at her for permission, he knelt, gathered up the sleeping child, and carried her to the hatchway and carefully down the ladder-stairs. Tenar followed.

He laid her on a bunk in a tiny cabin, awkwardly, tenderly. He tucked the cloak around her. Tenar let him do so.

In a larger cabin that ran across the stern of the ship, with a long window looking out over the twilit bay, he asked her to sit at the oaken table. He took a tray from the sailor boy that brought it, poured out red wine in goblets of heavy glass, offered her fruit and cakes.

She tasted the wine.

"It's very good, but not the Dragon Year," she said.

He looked at her in unguarded surprise, like any boy.

"From Enlad, not the Andrades," he said meekly.

"It's very fine," she assured him, drinking again. She took a cake. It was shortbread, very rich, not sweet. The green and amber grapes were sweet and tart. The vivid tastes of the food and wine were like the ropes that moored the ship, they moored her to the world, to her mind again.

"I was very frightened," she said by way of apology. "I think I'll be myself again soon. Yesterday—no, today, this morning—there was a—a spell—" It was almost impossible to say the word, she stammered at it: "A c-curse—laid on me. It took my speech, and my wits, I think. And we ran from that, but we ran right to the man, the man who—" She looked up despairingly at the young man listening to her. His grave eyes let her say what must be said. "He was one of the people who crippled the child. He and her parents. They raped her and beat her and burned her; these things happen, my lord. These things happen to children. And he keeps following her, to get at her. And—"

She stopped herself, and drank wine, making herself taste its flavor.

"And so from him I ran to you. To the haven." She looked about at the low, carved beams of the cabin, the polished table, the silver tray, the thin, quiet face of the young man. His hair was dark and soft, his skin a clear bronze-red; he was dressed well and plainly, with no chain or ring or outward mark of authority. But he looked the way a king should look, she thought.

"I'm sorry I let the man go," he said. "But he can be found again. Who was it laid the spell on you?"

"A wizard." She would not say the name. She did not want to think about all that. She wanted them all behind her. No retribution, no pursuit. Leave them to their hatreds, put them behind her, forget.

Lebannen did not press, but he asked, "Will you be safe from these men on your farm?"

"I think so. If I hadn't been so tired, so confused by the—by the—so confused in my mind, so that I couldn't think, I wouldn't have been afraid of Handy. What could he have done? With all the people about, in the street? I shouldn't have run from him. But all I could feel was her fear. She's so little, all she can do is fear him. She'll have to learn not to fear him. I have to teach her that . . ." She was wandering. Thoughts came into her head in Kargish. Had she been talking in Kargish? He would think she was mad, an old mad woman babbling. She glanced up at him furtively. His dark eyes were not on her; he gazed at the flame of the glass lamp that hung low over the table, a little, still, clear flame. His face was too sad for a young man's face.

"You came to find him," she said. "The archmage. Sparrowhawk."

"Ged," he said, looking at her with a faint smile. "You, and he, and I go by our true names."

"You and I, yes. But he, only to you and me."

He nodded.

"He's in danger from envious men, men of ill will, and he has no—no defense, now. You know that?"

She could not bring herself to be plainer, but Lebannen said, "He told me that his power as a mage was gone. Spent in the act that saved me, and all of us. But it was hard to believe. I wanted not to believe him."

"I too. But it is so. And so he—" Again she hesitated. "He wants to be alone until his hurts are healed," she said at last, cautiously.

Lebannen said, "He and I were in the dark land, the dry land, together. We died together. Together we crossed the mountains there. You can come back across the mountains. There is a way. He knew it. But the name of the mountains is Pain. The stones . . . The stones cut, and the cuts are long to heal."

He looked down at his hands. She thought of Ged's hands, scored and gashed, clenched on their wounds. Holding the cuts close, closed.

Her own hand closed on the small stone in her pocket, the word she had picked up on the steep road.

"Why does he hide from me?" the young man cried in grief. Then, quietly, "I hoped indeed to see him. But if he doesn't wish it, that's the end of it, of course." She recognized the courtliness, the civility, the dignity of the messengers from Havnor, and appreciated it; she knew its worth. But she loved him for his grief.

"Surely he'll come to you. Only give him time. He was so badly hurt—everything taken from him— But when he spoke of you, when he said your name, oh, then I saw him for a moment as he was—as he will be again— All pride!"

"Pride?" Lebannen repeated, as if startled.

"Yes. Of course, pride. Who should be proud, if not he?"

"I always thought of him as— He was so patient," Leban-nen said, and then laughed at the inadequacy of his description.

"Now he has no patience," she said, "and is hard on himself beyond all reason. There's nothing we can do for him, I think, except let him go his own way and find himself at the end of his tether, as they say on Gont. . . ." All at once she was at the end of her own tether, so weary she felt ill. "I think I must rest now," she said.

He rose at once. "Lady Tenar, you say you fled from one enemy and found another; but I came seeking a friend, and found another." She smiled at his wit and kindness. What a nice boy he is, she thought.

The ship was all astir when she woke: creaking and groaning of timbers, thud of running feet overhead, rattle of canvas, sailors' shouts. Therru was hard to waken and woke dull, perhaps feverish, though she was always so warm that Tenar found it hard to judge her fevers. Remorseful for having dragged the fragile child fifteen miles on foot and for all that had happened yesterday, Tenar tried to cheer her by telling her that they were in a ship, and that there was a real king on the ship, and that the little room they were in was the king's own room; that the ship was taking them home, to the farm, and Aunty Lark would be waiting for them at home, and maybe Sparrowhawk would be there too. Not even that roused Therru's interest. She was blank, inert, mute.

On her small, thin arm Tenar saw a mark—four fingers, red, like a brand, as from a bruising grip. But Handy had not gripped her, he had only touched her. Tenar had told her, had promised her that he would never touch her again. The promise had been broken. Her word meant nothing. What word meant anything, against deaf violence?

She bent down and kissed the marks on Therru's arm.

"I wish I'd had time to finish your red dress," she said. "The king would probably like to see it. But then, I suppose people don't wear their best clothes on a ship, even kings."

Therru sat on the bunk, her head bent down, and did not answer. Tenar brushed her hair. It was growing out thick at last, a silky black curtain over the burned parts of the scalp. "Are you hungry, birdlet? You didn't have any supper last night. Maybe the king will give us breakfast. He gave me cakes and grapes last night."

No response.

When Tenar said it was time to leave the room, she obeyed. Up on deck she stood with her head bent to her shoulder. She did not look up at the white sails full of the morning wind, nor at the sparkling water, nor back at Gont Mountain rearing its bulk and majesty of forest, cliff, and peak into the sky. She did not look up when Lebannen spoke to her.

"Therru," Tenar said softly, kneeling by her, "when a king speaks to you, you answer."

She was silent.

The expression of Lebannen's face as he looked at her was unreadable. A mask perhaps, a civil mask for revulsion, shock. But his dark eyes were steady. He touched the child's arm very lightly, saying, "It must be strange for you, to wake up in the middle of the sea."

She would eat only a little fruit. When Tenar asked her if she wanted to go back to the cabin, she nodded. Reluctant, Tenar left her curled up in the bunk and went back up on deck.

The ship was passing between the Armed Cliffs, towering grim walls that seemed to lean above the sails. Bowmen on guard in little forts like mud-swallows' nests high on the cliffs looked down at them on deck, and the sailors yelled cheerfully up at them. "Way for the king!" they shouted, and the reply came down not much louder than the calling of swallows from the heights, "The king!"

Lebannen stood at the high prow with the ship's master and an elderly, lean, narrow-eyed man in the grey cloak of a mage of Roke Island. Ged had worn such a cloak, a clean, fine one, on the day he and she brought the Ring of Erreth-Akbe to the Tower of the Sword; an old one, stained and dirty and travelworn, had been all his blanket on the cold stone of the Tombs of Atuan, and on the dirt of the desert mountains when they had crossed those mountains together. She was thinking of that as the foam flew by the ship's sides and the high cliffs fell away behind.

When the ship was out past the last reefs and had begun to swing eastward, the three men came to her. Lebannen said, "My lady, this is the Master Windkey of Roke Island."

The mage bowed, looking at her with praise in his keen eyes, and curiosity also; a man who liked to know which way the wind blew, she thought.

"Now I needn't hope the fair weather will hold, but can count on it," she said to him.

"I'm only cargo on a day like this," said the mage. "Besides, with a sailor like Master Serrathen handling the ship, who needs a weatherworker?"

We are so polite, she thought, all Ladies and Lords and Masters, all bows and compliments. She glanced at the young king. He was looking at her, smiling but reserved.

She felt as she had felt in Havnor as a girl: a barbarian, uncouth among their smoothnesses. But because she was not a girl now, she was not awed, but only wondered at how men ordered their world into this dance of masks, and how easily a woman might learn to dance it.

It would take them only the day, they told her, to sail to Valmouth. They would make port there by late afternoon, with this fair wind in the sails.

Still very weary from the long distress and strain of the day before, she was content to sit in the seat the bald sailor contrived for her out of a straw mattress and a piece of sailcloth, and watch the waves and the gulls, and see the outline of Gont Mountain, blue and dreamy in the noon light, changing as they skirted its steep shores only a mile or two out from land. She brought Therru up to be in the sunshine, and the child lay beside her, watching and dozing.

A sailor, a very dark man, toothless, came on bare feet with soles like hooves and hideously gnarled toes, and put something down on the canvas near Therru. "For the little girl," he said hoarsely, and went off at once, though not far off. He looked around hopefully now and then from his work to see if she liked his gift and then pretended he had not looked around. Therru would not touch the little cloth-wrapped packet. Tenar had to open it. It was an exquisite carving of a dolphin, in bone or ivory, the length of her thumb.

"It can live in your grass bag," Tenar said, "with the others, the bone people."

At that Therru came to life enough to fetch out her grass bag and put the dolphin in it. But Tenar had to go thank the humble giver. Therru would not look at him or speak. After a while she asked to go back to the cabin, and Tenar left her there with the bone person, the bone animal, and the dolphin for company.

It's so easy, she thought with rage, it's so easy for Handy

to take the sunlight from her, take the ship and the king and her childhood from her, and it's so hard to give them back! A year I've spent trying to give them back to her, and with one touch he takes them and throws them away. And what good does it do him—what's his prize, his power? Is power that—an emptiness?

She joined the king and the mage at the ship's railing. The sun was well to the west now, and the ship drove through a glory of light that made her think of her dream of flying with the dragons.

"Lady Tenar," the king said, "I give you no message for our friend. It seems to me that to do so is to lay a burden on you, and also to encroach upon his freedom; and I don't want to do either. I am to be crowned within the month. If it were he that held the crown, my reign would begin as my heart desires. But whether he's there or not, he brought me to my kingdom. He made me king. I will not forget it."

"I know you will not forget it," she said gently. He was so intense, so serious, armored in the formality of his rank and yet vulnerable in his honesty, the purity of his will. Her heart yearned to him. He thought he had learned pain, but he would learn it again and again, all his life, and forget none of it.

And therefore he would not, like Handy, do the easy thing to do.

"I'll bear a message willingly," she said. "It's no burden. Whether he'd hear it is up to him."

The Master Windkey grinned. "It always was," he said. "Whatever he did was up to him."

"You've known him a long time?"

"Even longer than you, my lady. Taught him," said the mage. "What I could. . . . He came to the School on Roke, you know, as a boy, with a letter from Ogion telling us that he had great power. But the first time I had him out in a boat, to learn how to speak to the wind, you know, he raised up a waterspout. I saw then what we were in for. I thought, Either he'll be drowned before he's sixteen, or he'll be archmage before he's forty. . . . Or I like to think I thought it.''

"Is he still archmage?" Tenar asked. The question seemed baldly ignorant, and when it was greeted by a silence, she feared it had been worse than ignorant.

The mage said finally, "There is now no Archmage of Roke." His tone was exceedingly cautious and precise.

She dared not ask what he meant.

"I think," said the king, "that the Healer of the Rune of Peace may be part of any council of this realm; don't you think so, sir?"

After another pause and evidently with a little struggle, the mage said, "Certainly."

The king waited, but he said no more.

Lebannen looked out at the bright water and spoke as if he began a tale: "When he and I came to Roke from the farthest west, borne by the dragon . . ." He paused, and the dragon's name spoke itself in Tenar's mind, *Kalessin,* like a struck gong.

"The dragon left me there, but bore him away. The keeper of the door of the House of Roke said then, 'He has done with doing. He goes home.' And before that—on the beach of Selidor—he bade me leave his staff, saying he was no mage now. So the Masters of Roke took counsel to choose a new archmage.

"They took me among them, that I might learn what it might be well for a king to know about the Council of the Wise. And also I was one of them to replace one of their number: Thorion, the Summoner, whose art was turned against him by that great evil which my lord Sparrowhawk found and ended. When we were there, in the dry land, between the wall and the mountains, I saw Thorion. My lord spoke to him, telling him the way back to life across the wall. But he did not take it. He did not come back."

The young man's strong, fine hands held hard to the ship's rail. He still gazed at the sea as he spoke. He was silent for a minute and then took up his story.

"So I made out the number, nine, who meet to choose the new archmage.

"They are . . . they are wise men," he said, with a glance at Tenar. "Not only learned in their art, but knowledgeable men. They use their differences, as I had seen before, to make their decision strong. But this time . . ."

"The fact is," said the master windkey, seeing Lebannen unwilling to seem to criticize the Masters of Roke, "we were all difference and no decision. We could come to no agreement. Because the archmage wasn't dead—was alive, you see, and yet no mage—and yet still a dragonlord, it seemed. . . . And because our Changer was still shaken from the turning of his own art on him, and believed that the Summoner would return from death, and begged us to wait for him. . . . And because the Master Patterner would not speak at all. He is a Karg, my lady, like yourself; did you know that? He came to us from Karego-At." His keen eyes watched her: which way does the wind blow? "So because of all that, we found ourselves at a loss. When the Doorkeeper asked for the names of those from whom we would choose, not a name was spoken. Everybody looked at everybody else. . . ."

"I looked at the ground," Lebannen said.

"So at last we looked to the one who knows the names: the Master Namer. And he was watching the Patterner, who hadn't said a word, but sat there among his trees like a stump. It's in the Grove we meet, you know, among those trees whose roots are deeper than the islands. It was late in the evening by then. Sometimes there's a light among those trees, but not that night. It was dark, no starlight, a cloudy sky above the leaves. And the Patterner stood up and spoke then—but in his own language, not in the Old Speech, nor in Hardic, but in Kargish. Few of us knew it or even knew what tongue it was, and we didn't know what to think. But the Namer told us what the Patterner had said. He said: *A woman on Gont.*"

He stopped. He was no longer looking at her. After a bit she said, "Nothing more?"

"Not a word more. When we pressed him, he stared at us and couldn't answer; for he'd been in the vision, you see—he'd been seeing the shape of things, the pattern; and it's little of that can ever be put in words, and less into ideas. He knew no more what to think of what he'd said than the rest of us. But it was all we had."

The Masters of Roke were teachers, after all, and the Windkey was a very good teacher; he couldn't help but make his story clear. Clearer perhaps than he wanted. He glanced once again at Tenar, and away.

"So, you see, it seemed we should come to Gont. But for what? Seeking whom? 'A woman'—not much to go on! Evidently this woman is to guide us, show us the way, somehow, to our archmage. And at once, as you may think, my lady, you were spoken of—for what other woman on Gont had we ever heard of? It is no great island, but yours is a great fame. Then one of us said, 'She would lead us to Ogion.' But we all knew that Ogion had long ago refused to be archmage, and surely would not accept now that he was old and ill. And indeed Ogion was dying as we spoke,

I think. Then another said, 'But she'd lead us also to Sparrow-hawk!' And then we were truly in the dark."

"Truly," Lebannen said. "For it began to rain, there among the trees." He smiled. "I had thought I'd never hear rain fall again. It was a great joy to me."

"Nine of us wet," said the Windkey, "and one of us happy."

Tenar laughed. She could not help but like the man. If he was so wary of her, it behooved her to be wary of him; but to Lebannen, and in Lebannen's presence, only candor would do.

"Your 'woman on Gont' can't be me, then, for I will not lead you to Sparrowhawk."

"It was my opinion," the mage said with apparent and perhaps real candor of his own, "that it couldn't be you, my lady. For one thing, he would have said your name, surely, in the vision. Very few are those who bear their true names openly! But I am charged by the Council of Roke to ask you if you know of any woman on this isle who might be the one we seek—sister or mother to a man of power, or even his teacher; for there are witches very wise in their way. Maybe Ogion knew such a woman? They say he knew every soul on this island, for all he lived alone and wandered in the wilderness. I wish he were alive to aid us now!"

She had thought already of the fisherwoman of Ogion's story. But that woman had been old when Ogion knew her, years ago, and must be dead by now. Though dragons, she thought, lived very long lives, it was said.

She said nothing for a while, and then only, "I know no one of that sort."

She could feel the mage's controlled impatience with her. What's she holding out for? What is it she wants? he was thinking, no doubt. And she wondered why it was she could not tell him. His deafness silenced her. She could not even tell him he was deaf.

"So," she said at last, "there is no archmage of Earthsea. But there is a king."

"In whom our hope and trust are well founded," the mage said with a warmth that became him well. Lebannen, watching and listening, smiled.

"In these past years," Tenar said, hesitant, "there have been many troubles, many miseries. My—the little girl— Such things have been all too common. And I have heard men and women of power speak of the waning, or the changing, of their power."

"That one whom the archmage and my lord defeated in the dry land, that Cob, caused untold harm and ruin. We shall be repairing our art, healing our wizards and our wizardry, for a long time yet," the mage said, decisively.

"I wonder if there might be more to be done than repairing and healing," she said, "though that too, of course— But I wonder, could it be that . . . that one such as Cob could have such power because things were already altering . . . and that a change, a great change, has been taking place, has taken place? And that it's because of that change that we have a king again in Earthsea—perhaps a king rather than an archmage?"

The Windkey looked at her as if he saw a very distant storm cloud on the uttermost horizon. He even raised his right hand in the hint, the first sketch, of a windbinding spell, and then lowered it again. He smiled. "Don't be afraid, my lady," he said. "Roke, and the Art Magic, will endure. Our treasure is well guarded!"

"Tell Kalessin that," she said, suddenly unable to endure the utter unconsciousness of his disrespect. It made him stare, of course. He heard the dragon's name. But it did not make him hear her. How could he, who had never listened to a woman since his mother sang him his last cradle song, hear her?

"Indeed," said Lebannen, "Kalessin came to Roke, which is said to be defended utterly from dragons; and not through any spell of my lord's, for he had no magery then. . . . But I don't think, Master Windkey, that Lady Tenar was afraid for herself."

The mage made an earnest effort to amend his offense. "I'm sorry, my lady," he said, "I spoke as to an ordinary woman."

She almost laughed. She could have shaken him. She said only, indifferently, "My fears are ordinary fears." It was no use; he could not hear her.

But the young king was silent, listening.

A sailor boy up in the dizzy, swaying world of the masts and sails and rigging overhead called out clear and sweet, "Town there round the point!" And in a minute those down on deck saw the little huddle of slate roofs, the spires of blue smoke, a few glass windows catching the westering sun, and the docks and piers of Valmouth on its bay of satiny blue water.

"Shall I take her in or will you talk her in, my lord?" asked the calm ship's-master, and the Windkey replied, "Sail her in, master. I don't want to have to deal with all that flotsam!"—waving his hand at the dozens of fishing craft that littered the bay. So the king's ship, like a swan among ducklings, came tacking slowly in, hailed by every boat she passed.

Tenar looked along the docks, but there was no other seagoing vessel.

"I have a sailor son," she said to Lebannen. "I thought his ship might be in."

"What is his ship?"

"He was third mate aboard the *Gull of Eskel,* but that was more than two years ago. He may have changed ships. He's a restless man." She smiled. "When I first saw you, I thought you were my son. You're nothing alike, only in being tall, and thin, and young. And I was confused, frightened. . . . Ordinary fears."

The mage had gone up on the master's station in the prow, and she and Lebannen stood alone.

"There is too much ordinary fear," he said.

It was her only chance to speak to him alone, and the words came out hurried and uncertain—"I wanted to say— but there was no use—but couldn't it be that there's a woman on Gont, I don't know who, I have no idea, but it could be that there is, or will be, or may be, a woman, and that they seek—that they need—her. Is it impossible?"

He listened. He was not deaf. But he frowned, intent, as if trying to understand a foreign language. And he said only, under his breath, "It may be."

A fisherwoman in her tiny dinghy bawled up, "Where from?" and the boy in the rigging called back like a crowing cock, "From the King's City!"

"What is this ship's name?" Tenar asked. "My son will ask what ship I sailed on."

"*Dolphin,*" Lebannen answered, smiling at her. My son, my king, my dear boy, she thought. How I'd like to keep you nearby!

"I must go get my little one," she said.

"How will you get home?"

"Afoot. It's only a few miles up the valley." She pointed past the town, inland, where Middle Valley lay broad and sunlit between two arms of the mountain, like a lap. "The village is on the river, and my farm's a half mile from the village. It's a pretty corner of your kingdom."

"But will you be safe?"

"Oh, yes. I'll spend tonight with my daughter here in Valmouth. And in the village they're all to be depended on. I won't be alone."

Their eyes met for a moment, but neither spoke the name they both thought.

"Will they be coming again, from Roke?" she asked. "Looking for the 'woman on Gont'—or for him?"

"Not for him. That, if they propose again, I will forbid," Lebannen said, not realizing how much he told her in those three words. "But as for their search for a new archmage, or for the woman of the Patterner's vision, yes, that may bring them here. And perhaps to you."

"They'll be welcome at Oak Farm," she said. "Though not as welcome as you would be."

"I will come when I can," he said, a little sternly; and a little wistfully, "if I can."

Home

Most of the people of Valmouth came down to the docks to see the ship from Havnor, when they heard that the king was aboard, the new king, the young king that the new songs were about. They didn't know the new songs yet, but they knew the old ones, and old Relli came with his harp and sang a piece of the *Deed of Morred,* for a king of Earthsea would be the heir of Morred for certain. Presently the king himself came on deck, as young and tall and handsome as could be, and with him a mage of Roke, and a woman and a little girl in old cloaks not much better than beggars, but he treated them as if they were a queen and a princess, so maybe that's what they were. "Maybe it's his mother," said Shinny, trying to see over the heads of the men in front of her, and then her friend Apple clutched her arm and said in a kind of whispered shriek, "It is—it's mother!"

"Whose mother?" said Shinny, and Apple said, "Mine. And that's Therru." But she did not push forward in the crowd, even when an officer of the ship came ashore to invite old Relli aboard to play for the king. She waited with the others. She saw the king receive the notables of Valmouth, and heard Relli sing for him. She watched him bid his guests farewell, for the ship was going to stand out to sea again, people said, before night fell, and be on her way home to Havnor. The last to come across the gangplank were Therru and Tenar. To each the king gave the formal embrace, laying cheek to cheek, kneeling to embrace Therru. "Ah!" said the crowd on the dock. The sun was setting in a mist of gold, laying a great gold track across the bay, as the two came down the railed gangplank. Tenar lugged a heavy pack and bag; Therru's face was bent down and hidden by her hair. The gangplank was run in, and the sailors leapt to the rigging, and the officers shouted, and the ship *Dolphin* turned on her way. Then Apple made her way through the crowd at last.

"Hello, mother," she said, and Tenar said, "Hello, daughter." They kissed, and Apple picked up Therru and said, "How you've grown! You're twice the girl you were. Come on, come on home with me."

But Apple was a little shy with her mother, that evening, in the pleasant house of her young merchant husband. She gazed at her several times with a thoughtful, almost a wary look. "It never meant a thing to me, you know, mother," she said at the door of Tenar's bedroom—"all that—the Rune of Peace—and you bringing the Ring to Havnor. It was just like one of the songs. A thousand years ago! But it really was you, wasn't it?"

"It was a girl from Atuan," Tenar said. "A thousand years ago. I think I could sleep for a thousand years, just now."

"Go to bed, then." Apple turned away, then turned back, lamp in hand. "King-kisser," she said.

"Get along with you," said Tenar.

Apple and her husband kept Tenar a couple of days, but after that she was determined to go to the farm. So Apple walked with her and Therru up along the placid, silvery

Kaheda. Summer was turning to autumn. The sun was still hot, but the wind was cool. The foliage of trees had a weary, dusty look to it, and the fields were cut or in harvest.

Apple spoke of how much stronger Therru was, and how sturdily she walked now.

"I wish you'd seen her at Re Albi," Tenar said, "before—" and stopped. She had decided not to worry her daughter with all that.

"What did happen?" Apple asked, so clearly resolved to know that Tenar gave in and answered in a low voice, "One of *them*."

Therru was a few yards ahead of them, long-legged in her outgrown dress, hunting blackberries in the hedgerows as she walked.

"Her father?" Apple asked, sickened at the thought.

"Lark said the one that seems to be the father called himself Hake. This one's younger. He's the one that came to Lark to tell her. He's called Handy. He was . . . hanging around at Re Albi. And then by ill luck we ran into him in Gont Port. But the king sent him off. And now I'm here and he's there, and all that's done with."

"But Therru was frightened," Apple said, a bit grimly. Tenar nodded.

"But why did you go to Gont Port?"

"Oh, well, this man Handy was working for a man . . . a wizard at the lord's house in Re Albi, who took a dislike to me. . . ." She tried to think of the wizard's use-name and could not; all she could think of was *Tuaho,* a Kargish word for a kind of tree, she could not remember what tree.

"So?"

"Well, so, it seemed better just to come on home."

"But what did this wizard dislike you for?"

"For being a woman, mostly."

"Bah," said Apple. "Old cheese rind."

"Young cheese rind, in this case."

"Worse yet. Well, nobody around here that I know of has seen the parents, if that's the word for 'em. But if they're still hanging about, I don't like your being alone in the farmhouse."

It is pleasant to be mothered by a daughter, and to behave as a daughter to one's daughter. Tenar said impatiently, "I'll be perfectly all right!"

"You could at least get a dog."

"I've thought of that. Somebody in the village might have a pup. We'll ask Lark when we stop by there."

"Not a puppy, mother. A dog."

"But a young one—one Therru could play with," she pleaded.

"A nice puppy that will come and kiss the burglars," said Apple, stepping along buxom and grey-eyed, laughing at her mother.

They came to the village about midday. Lark welcomed Tenar and Therru with a festivity of embraces, kisses, questions, and things to eat. Lark's quiet husband and other villagers stopped by to greet Tenar. She felt the happiness of homecoming.

Lark and the two youngest of her seven children, a boy and a girl, accompanied them out to the farm. The children had known Therru since Lark first brought her home, of course, and were used to her, though two months' separation made them shy at first. With them, even with Lark, she remained withdrawn, passive, as in the bad old days.

"She's worn out, confused by all this traveling. She'll get over it. She's come along wonderfully," Tenar said to Lark, but Apple would not let her get out of it so easily. "One of *them* turned up and terrified her and mother both," said Apple. And little by little, between them, the daughter and the friend got the story out of Tenar that afternoon, as they opened up the cold, stuffy, dusty house, put it to rights, aired the bedding, shook their heads over sprouted onions, laid in a bit of food in the pantry, and set a large kettle of soup on for supper. What they got came a word at a time. Tenar could not seem to tell them what the wizard had done; a spell, she said vaguely, or maybe it was that he had sent Handy after her. But when she came to talk about the king, the words came tumbling out.

"And then there he was—the king!—like a swordblade— And Handy shrinking and shrivelling back from him— And I thought he was Spark! I did, I really did for a moment, I was so—so beside myself—"

"Well," said Apple, "that's all right, because Shinny thought you were his mother. When we were on the docks watching you come sailing in in your glory. She kissed him, you know, Aunty Lark. Kissed the king—just like that. I thought next thing she'd kiss that mage. But she didn't."

"I should think not, what an idea. What mage?" said Lark, with her head in a cupboard. "Where's your flour bin, Goha?"

"Your hand's on it. A Roke mage, come looking for a new archmage."

"Here?"

"Why not?" said Apple. "The last one was from Gont, wasn't he? But they didn't spend much time looking. They sailed straight back to Havnor, once they'd got rid of mother."

"How you do talk."

"He was looking for a woman, he said," Tenar told them. " 'A woman on Gont.' But he didn't seem too happy about it."

"A wizard looking for a woman? Well, that's something new," said Lark. "I'd have thought this'd be weevilly by now, but it's perfectly good. I'll bake up a bannock or two, shall I? Where's the oil?"

"I'll need to draw some from the crock in the cool-room. Oh, Shandy! There you are! How are you? How's Clearbrook? How's everything been? Did you sell the ram lambs?"

They sat down nine to supper. In the soft yellow light of the evening in the stone-floored kitchen, at the long farm table, Therru began to lift her head a little, and spoke a few times to the other children; but there was still a cowering in her, and as it grew darker outside she sat so that her seeing eye could watch the window.

Not until Lark and her children had gone home in the twilight, and Apple was singing Therru to sleep, and she was washing up the dishes with Shandy, did Tenar ask about Ged. Somehow she had not wanted to while Lark and Apple were listening; there would have been so many explanations. She had forgotten to mention his being at Re Albi at all. And she did not want to talk about Re Albi any more. Her mind seemed to darken when she tried to think of it.

"Did a man come here last month from me—to help out with the work?"

"Oh, I clean forgot!" cried Shandy. "Hawk, you mean—him with the scars on his face?"

"Yes," Tenar said. "Hawk."

"Oh, aye, well, he'll be away up on Hot Springs Mountain, above Lissu, up there with the sheep, with Serry's sheep, I believe. He come here and says how you sent him, and there wasn't a lick o' work for him here, you know, with Clearbrook and me looking after the sheep and I been dairying and old Tiff and Sis helping me out when needed, and I racked my brains, but Clearbrook he says, 'Go ask Serry's man, Farmer Serry's overseer up by Kahedanan, do they need herders in the high pastures,' he said, and that Hawk went off and did that, and got took on, and was off next day. 'Go ask Serry's man,' Clearbrook told him, and that's what he done, and got took right on. So he'll be back down with the flocks come fall, no doubt. Up there on the Long Fells above Lissu, in the high pastures. I think maybe it was goats they wanted him for. Nice-spoken fellow. Sheep or goats, I don't remember which. I hope it's all right with you that we didn't keep him on here, Goha, but it's the truth there wasn't a lick o' work for him what with me and Clearbrook and old Tiff, and Sis got the flax in. And he said he'd been a goatherd over there where he come from, away round the mountain, some place above Armouth he said, though he said he'd never herded sheep. Maybe it'll be goats they've got him with up there."

"Maybe," said Tenar. She was much relieved and much disappointed. She had wanted to know him safe and well, but she had wanted also to find him here.

But it was enough, she told herself, simply to be home—and maybe better that he was not here, that none of all that was here, all the griefs and dreams and wizardries and terrors of Re Albi left behind, for good. She was here, now, and this was home, these stone floors and walls, these small-paned windows, outside which the oaks stood dark in star-light, these quiet, orderly rooms. She lay awake awhile that night. Her daughter slept in the next room, the children's room, with Therru, and Tenar lay in her own bed, her husband's bed, alone.

She slept. She woke, remembering no dream.

After a few days at the farm she scarcely gave a thought to the summer passed on the Overfell. It was long ago and far away. Despite Shandy's insistence on there not being a lick o' work to be done about the farm, she found plenty that needed doing: all that had been left undone over the summer and all that had to be done in the season of harvest in the fields and dairy. She worked from daybreak till nightfall, and if by chance she had an hour to sit down, she spun, or sewed for Therru. The red dress was finished at last, and a pretty dress it was, with a white apron for fancy wear and an orangey-brown one for everyday. "Now, then, you look beautiful!" said Tenar in her seamstress's pride, when Therru first tried it on.

Therru turned her face away.

"You are beautiful," Tenar said in a different tone. "Listen to me, Therru. Come here. You have scars, ugly scars, because an ugly, evil thing was done to you. People see the scars. But they see you, too, and you aren't the scars. You aren't ugly. You aren't evil. You are Therru, and beautiful. You are Therru who can work, and walk, and run, and dance, beautifully, in a red dress."

The child listened, the soft, unhurt side of her face as expressionless as the rigid, scar-masked side.

She looked down at Tenar's hands, and presently touched them with her small fingers. "It is a beautiful dress," she said in her faint, hoarse voice.

When Tenar was alone, folding up the scraps of red material, tears came stinging into her eyes. She felt rebuked. She had done right to make the dress, and she had spoken the truth to the child. But it was not enough, the right and the truth. There was a gap, a void, a gulf, on beyond the right and the truth. Love, her love for Therru and Therru's for her, made a bridge across that gap, a bridge of spider web, but love did not fill or close it. Nothing did that. And the child knew it better than she.

The day of the equinox came, a bright sun of autumn

burning through the mist. The first bronze was in the leaves of the oaks. As she scrubbed cream pans in the dairy with the window and door wide open to the sweet air, Tenar thought that her young king was being crowned this day in Havnor. The lords and ladies would walk in their clothes of blue and green and crimson, but he would wear white, she thought. He would climb up the steps to the Tower of the Sword, the steps she and Ged had climbed. The crown of Morred would be placed on his head. He would turn as the trumpets sounded and seat himself on the throne that had been empty so many years, and look at his kingdom with those dark eyes that knew what pain was, what fear was. "Rule well, rule long," she thought, "poor boy!" And she thought, "It should have been Ged there putting the crown on his head. He should have gone."

But Ged was herding the rich man's sheep, or maybe goats, up in the high pastures. It was a fair, dry, golden autumn, and they would not be bringing the flocks down till the snow fell up there on the heights.

When she went into the village, Tenar made a point of going by Ivy's cottage at the end of Mill Lane. Getting to know Moss at Re Albi had made her wish to know Ivy better, if she could once get past the witch's suspicion and jealousy. She missed Moss, even though she had Lark here; she had learned from her and had come to love her, and Moss had given both her and Therru something they needed. She hoped to find a replacement of that here. But Ivy, though a great deal cleaner and more reliable than Moss, had no intention of giving up her dislike of Tenar. She treated her overtures of friendship with the contempt that, Tenar admitted, they perhaps deserved. "You go your way, I go mine," the witch told her in everything but words; and Tenar obeyed, though she continued to treat

Ivy with marked respect when they met. She had, she thought, slighted her too often and too long, and owed her reparation. Evidently agreeing, the witch accepted her due with unbending ire.

In mid-autumn the sorcerer Beech came up the valley, called by a rich farmer to treat his gout. He stayed on awhile in the Middle Valley villages as he usually did, and passed one afternoon at Oak Farm, checking up on Therru and talking with Tenar. He wanted to know anything she would tell him of Ogion's last days. He was the pupil of a pupil of Ogion's and a devout admirer of the mage of Gont. Tenar found it was not so hard to talk about Ogion as about other people of Re Albi, and told him all she could. When she had done he asked a little cautiously, "And the archmage—did he come?"

"Yes," Tenar said.

Beech, a smooth-skinned, mild-looking man in his forties, tending a little to fat, with dark half-circles under his eyes that belied the blandness of his face, glanced at her, and asked nothing.

"He came after Ogion's death. And left," she said. And presently, "He's not archmage now. You knew that?"

Beech nodded.

"Is there any word of their choosing a new archmage?"

The sorcerer shook his head. "There was a ship in from the Enlades not long ago, but no word from her crew of anything but the coronation. They were full of that! And it sounds as if all auspices and events were fortunate. If the goodwill of mages is valuable, then this young king of ours is a rich man. . . . And an active one, it seems. There's an order come overland from Gont Port just before I left Valmouth, for the nobles and merchants and the mayor and his council to meet together and see to it that the bailiffs of the district be worthy and accountable men, for they're the king's officers now, and are to do his will and enact his law. Well, you can imagine how Lord Heno greeted that!" Heno was a notable patron of pirates, who had long kept most of the bailiffs and sea-sheriffs of South Gont in his pocket. "But there were men willing to face up to Heno, with the king standing behind them. They dismissed the old lot then and there, and named fifteen new bailiffs, decent men, paid out of the mayor's funds. Heno stormed off swearing destruction. It's a new day! Not all at once, of course, but it's coming. I wish Master Ogion had lived to see it."

"He did," Tenar said. "As he was dying, he smiled, and he said, 'All changed. . . .' "

Beech took this in his sober way, nodding slowly. "All changed," he repeated.

After a while he said, "The little one's doing very well."

"Well enough. . . . Sometimes I think not well enough."

"Mistress Goha," said the sorcerer, "if I or any sorcerer or witch or I daresay wizard had kept her, and used all the power of healing of the Art Magic for her all these months since she was injured, she wouldn't be better off. Maybe not as well as she is. You have done *all* that can be done, mistress. You have done a wonder."

She was touched by his earnest praise, and yet it made her sad; and she told him why. "It isn't enough," she said. "I can't heal her. She is . . . What is she to do? What will become of her?" She ran off the thread she had been spinning onto the spindle-shank, and said, "I am afraid."

"For her," Beech said, half querying.

"Afraid because her fear draws to it, to her, the cause of her fear. Afraid because—"

But she could not find the words for it.

"If she lives in fear, she will do harm," she said at last. "I'm afraid of that."

The sorcerer pondered. "I've thought," he said at last in his diffident way, "that maybe, if she has the gift, as I think she does, she might be trained a bit in the Art. And, as a witch, her . . . appearance wouldn't be so much against her—possibly." He cleared his throat. "There are witches who do very creditable work," he said.

Tenar ran a little of the thread she had spun between her fingers, testing it for evenness and strength. "Ogion told me to teach her. 'Teach her all,' he said, and then, 'Not Roke.' I don't know what he meant."

Beech had no difficulty with it. "He meant that the learning of Roke—the High Arts—wouldn't be suitable for a girl," he explained. "Let alone one so handicapped. But if he said to teach her all but that lore, it would seem that he too saw her way might well be the witches' way." He pondered again, more cheerfully, having got the weight of Ogion's opinion on his side. "In a year or two, when she's quite strong, and grown a bit more, you might think of asking Ivy to begin teaching her a bit. Not too much, of course, even of that kind of thing, till she has her true name."

Tenar felt a strong, immediate resistance to the suggestion. She said nothing, but Beech was a sensitive man. "Ivy's dour," he said. "But what she knows, she does honestly. Which can't be said of all witches. *Weak as women's magic,* you know, and *wicked as women's magic!* But I've known witches with real healing power. Healing befits a woman. It comes natural to her. And the child might be drawn to that—having been so hurt herself."

His kindness was, Tenar thought, innocent.

She thanked him, saying that she would think carefully about what he had said. And indeed she did so.

◆◆◆◆◆◆

Before the month was out, the villages of Middle Valley had met at the Round Barn of Sodeva to appoint their own bailiffs and officers of the peace and to levy a tax upon themselves to pay the bailiffs' wages with. Such were the king's orders, brought to the mayors and elders of the villages, and readily obeyed, for there were as many sturdy beggars and thieves on the roads as ever, and the villagers and farmers were eager to have order and safety. Some ugly rumors went about, such as that Lord Heno had formed a Council of Scoundrels and was enlisting all the black-guards in the countryside to go about in gangs breaking the heads of the king's bailies; but most people said, "Just let 'em try!" and went home telling each other that now an honest man could sleep safe abed at night, and what went wrong the king was setting right, though the taxes were beyond all reason and they'd all be poor men for-ever trying to pay them.

Tenar was glad to hear of all this from Lark, but did not pay it much heed. She was working very hard; and since she had got home she had, almost without being aware of it, resolved not to let the thought of Handy or any such ruffian rule her life or Therru's. She could not keep the child with her every moment, renewing her terrors, forever remind-ing her of what she could not remember and live. The child must be free and know herself to be free, to grow in grace.

She had gradually lost the shrinking, fearful manner, and by now went all about the farm and the byways and even into the village by herself. Tenar said no word of caution to her, even when she had to prevent herself from doing so. Therru was safe on the farm, safe in the village, no one was going to hurt her: that must be taken as unquestionable. And indeed Tenar did not often question it. With herself and Shandy and Clearbrook around the place, and Sis and Tiff down in the lower house, and Lark's family all over the village, in the sweet autumn of the Middle Valley, what harm was going to come to the child?

She'd get a dog, too, when she heard of one she wanted: one of the big grey Gontish sheep-guards, with their wise, curly heads.

Now and then she thought, as she had at Re Albi, "I must be teaching the child! Ogion said so." But somehow nothing seemed to get taught to her but farm work, and stories, in the evening, as the nights drew in and they began to sit by the kitchen fire after supper before they went to bed. Maybe Beech was right, and Therru should be sent to a witch to learn what witches knew. It was better than apprenticing her to a weaver, as Tenar had thought of doing. But not all that much better. And she was still not very big; and was very ignorant for her age, for she had been taught nothing before she came to Oak Farm. She had been like a little animal, barely knowing human speech, and no human skills. She learned quickly and was twice as obedient and diligent as Lark's unruly girls and laughing, lazy boys. She could clean and serve and spin, cook a little, sew a little, look after poultry, fetch the cows, and do excellent work in the dairy. A proper farm-lassie, old Tiff called her, fawning a bit. Tenar had also seen him make the sign to avert evil, surreptitiously, when Therru passed him. Like most people, Tiff believed that you are what happens to you. The rich and strong must have virtue; one to whom evil has been done must be bad, and may rightly be punished.

In which case it would not help much if Therru became the properest farm-lassie in Gont. Not even prosperity would diminish the visible brand of what had been done to her. So Beech had thought of her being a witch, accepting, making use, of the brand. Was that what Ogion had meant, when he said "Not Roke"—when he said "They will fear her"? Was that all?

One day when a managed chance brought them together in the village street, Tenar said to Ivy, "There's a question I want to ask you, Mistress Ivy. A matter of your profession."

The witch eyed her. She had a scathing eye.

"My profession, is it?"

Tenar nodded, steady.

"Come on, then," Ivy said with a shrug, leading off down Mill Lane to her little house.

It was not a den of infamy and chickens, like Moss's house, but it was a witch-house, the beams hung thick with dried and drying herbs, the fire banked under grey ash with one tiny coal winking like a red eye, a lithe, fat, black cat with one white mustache sleeping up on a shelf, and everywhere a profusion of little boxes, pots, ewers, trays, and stoppered bottles, all aromatic, pungent or sweet or strange.

"What can I do for you, Mistress Goha?" Ivy asked, very dry, when they were inside.

"Tell me, if you will, if you think my ward, Therru, has any gift for your art—any power in her."

"She? Of course!" said the witch.

Tenar was a bit floored by the prompt and contemptuous answer. "Well," she said. "Beech seemed to think so."

"A blind bat in a cave could see it," said Ivy. "Is that all?"

"No. I want your advice. When I've asked my question, you can tell me the price of the answer. Fair?"

"Fair."

"Should I prentice Therru for a witch, when she's a bit older?"

Ivy was silent for a minute, deciding on her fee, Tenar thought. Instead, she answered the question. "I would not take her," she said.

"Why?"

"I'd be afraid to," the witch answered, with a sudden fierce stare at Tenar.

"Afraid? Of what?"

"Of her! What is she?"

"A child. An ill-used child!"

"That's not all she is."

Dark anger came into Tenar and she said, "Must a prentice witch be a virgin, then?"

Ivy stared. She said after a moment, "I didn't mean that."

"What did you mean?"

"I mean I don't know what she is. I mean when she looks at me with that one eye seeing and one eye blind I don't know what she sees. I see you go about with her like she was any child, and I think, What are they? What's the strength of that woman, for she's not a fool, to hold a fire by the hand, to spin thread with the whirlwind? They say, mistress, that you lived as a child yourself with the Old Ones, the Dark Ones, the Ones Underfoot, and that you were queen and servant of those powers. Maybe that's why you're not afraid of this one. What power she is, I don't know, I don't say. But it's beyond my teaching, I know that—or Beech's, or any witch or wizard I ever knew! I'll give you my advice, mistress, free and feeless. It's this: Beware. Beware her, the day she finds her strength! That's all."

"I thank you, Mistress Ivy," Tenar said with all the formality of the Priestess of the Tombs of Atuan, and went out of the warm room into the thin, biting wind of the end of autumn.

She was still angry. Nobody would help her, she thought. She knew the job was beyond her, they didn't have to tell her that—but none of them would help her. Ogion had died, and old Moss ranted, and Ivy warned, and Beech kept clear, and Ged—the one who might really have helped— Ged ran away. Ran off like a whipped dog, and never sent sign or word to her, never gave a thought to her or Therru, but only to his own precious shame. That was his child, his nurseling. That was all he cared about. He had never cared or thought about her, only about power—her power, his power, how he could use it, how he could make more power of it. Putting the broken Ring together, making the Rune, putting a king on the throne. And when his power was gone, still it was all he could think about: that it was gone, lost, leaving him only himself, his shame, his emptiness.

You aren't being fair, Goha said to Tenar.

Fair! said Tenar. Did he play fair?

Yes, said Goha. He did. Or tried to.

Well, then, he can play fair with the goats he's herding; it's nothing to me, said Tenar, trudging homeward in the wind and the first, sparse, cold rain.

"Snow tonight, maybe," said her tenant Tiff, meeting her on the road beside the meadows of the Kaheda.

"Snow so soon? I hope not."

"Freeze, anyway, for sure."

And it froze when the sun was down: rain puddles and watering troughs skimming over, then opaqued with ice; the reeds by the Kaheda stilled, bound in ice; the wind itself stilled as if frozen, unable to move.

Beside the fire—a sweeter fire than Ivy's, for the wood was that of an old apple that had been taken down in the orchard last spring—Tenar and Therru sat to spin and talk after supper was cleared away.

"Tell the story about the cat ghosts," Therru said in her husky voice as she started the wheel to spin a mass of dark, silky goat's-wool into fleecefell yarn.

"That's a summer story."

Therru cocked her head.

"In winter the stories should be the great stories. In winter you learn the *Creation of Éa,* so that you can sing it at the Long Dance when summer comes. In winter you learn the Winter Carol and the *Deed of the Young King,* and at the Festival of Sunreturn, when the sun turns north to bring the spring, you can sing them."

"I can't sing," the girl whispered.

Tenar was winding spun yarn off the distaff into a ball, her hands deft and rhythmic.

"Not only the voice sings," she said. "The mind sings. The prettiest voice in the world's no good if the mind doesn't know the songs." She untied the last bit of yarn, which had been the first spun. "You have strength, Therru, and strength that is ignorant is dangerous."

"Like the ones who wouldn't learn," Therru said. "The wild ones." Tenar did not know what she meant, and looked her question. "The ones that stayed in the west," Therru said.

"Ah—the dragons—in the song of the Woman of Kemay. Yes. Exactly. So: which will we start with—how the islands were raised from the sea, or how King Morred drove back the Black Ships?"

"The islands," Therru whispered. Tenar had rather hoped she would choose the *Deed of the Young King,* for she saw Lebannen's face as Morred's; but the child's choice was the right one. "Very well," she said. She glanced up at Ogion's great Lore-books on the mantel, encouraging herself that if she forgot, she could find the words there; and drew breath; and began.

By her bedtime Therru knew how Segoy had raised the first of the islands from the depths of Time. Instead of singing to her, Tenar sat on the bed after tucking her in, and they recited together, softly, the first stanza of the song of the Making.

Tenar carried the little oil lamp back to the kitchen, listening to the absolute silence. The frost had bound the world, locked it. No star showed. Blackness pressed at the single window of the kitchen. Cold lay on the stone floors.

She went back to the fire, for she was not sleepy yet. The great words of the song had stirred her spirit, and there was still anger and unrest in her from her talk with Ivy. She took the poker to rouse up a little flame from the backlog. As she struck the log, there was an echo of the sound in the back of the house.

She straightened up and stood listening.

Again: a soft, dull thump or thud—outside the house—at the dairy window?

The poker still in her hand, Tenar went down the dark hall to the door that gave on the cool-room. Beyond the cool-room was the dairy. The house was built against a low hill, and both those rooms ran back into the hill like cellars, though on a level with the rest of the house. The cool-room had only air-vents; the dairy had a door and a window, low and wide like the kitchen window, in its one outside wall. Standing at the cool-room door, she could hear that window being pried or jimmied, and men's voices whispering.

Flint had been a methodical householder. Every door but one of his house had a bar-bolt on each side of it, a stout length of cast iron set in slides. All were kept clean and oiled; none were ever locked.

She slipped the bolt across the cool-room door. It slid into place without a sound, fitting snug into the heavy iron slot on the doorjamb.

She heard the outer door of the dairy opened. One of them had finally thought to try it, before they broke the window, and found it wasn't locked. She heard the mutter of voices again. Then silence, long enough that she heard her heartbeat drumming in her ears so loud she feared she could not hear any sound over it. She felt her legs trembling and trembling, and felt the cold of the floor creep up under her skirt like a hand.

"It's open," a man's voice whispered near her, and her heart leapt painfully. She put her hand on the bolt, thinking it was open—she had unlocked not locked it— She had almost slid it back when she heard the door between the cool-room and the dairy creak, opening. She knew that creak of the upper hinge. She knew the voice that had spoken, too, but in a different way of knowing. "It's a storeroom," Handy said, and then, as the door she stood against rattled against the bolt, "This one's locked." It rattled again. A thin blade of light, like a knife blade, flicked between the door and the jamb. It touched her breast, and she drew back as if it had cut her.

The door rattled again, but not much. It was solid, solidly hinged, and the bolt was firm.

They muttered together on the other side of the door. She knew they were planning to come around and try the front of the house. She found herself at the front door, bolting it, not knowing how she came there. Maybe this was a nightmare. She had had this dream, that they were trying to get into the house, that they drove thin knives through the cracks of the doors. The doors—was there any other door they could get in? The windows—the shutters of the bedroom windows— Her breath came so short she thought she could not get to Therru's room, but she was there, she brought the heavy wooden shutters across the glass. The hinges were stiff, and they came together with a bang. Now they knew. Now they were coming. They would come to the window of the next room, her room. They would be there before she could close the shutters. And they were.

She saw the faces, blurs moving in the darkness outside, as she tried to free the left-hand shutter from its hasp. It was stuck. She could not make it move. A hand touched the glass, flattening white against it.

"There she is."

"Let us in. We won't hurt you."

"We just want to talk to you."

"He just wants to see his little girl."

She got the shutter free and dragged it across the window. But if they broke the glass they would be able to push the shutters open from the outside. The fastening was only a hook that would pull out of the wood if forced.

"Let us in and we won't hurt you," one of the voices said.

She heard their feet on the frozen ground, crackling in the fallen leaves. Was Therru awake? The crash of the shutters closing might have wakened her, but she had made no sound. Tenar stood in the doorway between her room and Therru's. It was pitch-dark, silent. She was afraid to touch the child and waken her. She must stay in the room with her. She must fight for her. She had had the poker in her hand, where had she put it? She had put it down to close the shutters. She could not find it. She groped for it in the blackness of the room that seemed to have no walls.

The front door, which led into the kitchen, rattled, shaken in its frame.

If she could find the poker she would stay in here, she would fight them.

"Here!" one of them called, and she knew what he had found. He was looking up at the kitchen window, broad, unshuttered, easy to reach.

She went, very slowly it seemed, groping, to the door of the room. It was Therru's room now. It had been her children's room. The nursery. That was why there was no lock on the inner side of the door. So the children could not lock themselves in and be frightened if the bolt stuck.

Around back of the hill, through the orchard, Clearbrook and Shandy would be asleep in their cottage. If she called, maybe Shandy would hear. If she opened the bedroom window and called—or if she waked Therru and they climbed out the window and ran through the orchard—but the men were there, right there, waiting.

It was more than she could bear. The frozen terror that had bound her broke, and in rage she ran into the kitchen that was all red light in her eyes, grabbed up the long, sharp butcher knife from the block, flung back the door-bolt, and stood in the doorway. "Come on, then!" she said.

As she spoke there was a howl and a sucking gasp, and a man yelled, "Look out!" Another shouted, "Here! Here!"

Then there was silence.

Light from the open doorway shot across the black ice of puddles, glittered on the black branches of the oaks and on fallen silver leaves, and as her eyes cleared she saw that something was crawling towards her on the path, a dark mass or heap crawling towards her, making a high, sobbing wail. Behind the light a black shape ran and darted, and long blades shone.

"Tenar!"

"Stop there," she said, raising the knife.

"Tenar! It's me—Hawk, Sparrowhawk!"

"Stay there," she said.

The darting black shape stood still next to the black mass lying on the path. The light from the doorway shone dim on a body, a face, a long-tined pitchfork held upright, like a wizard's staff, she thought. "Is that you?" she said.

He was kneeling now by the black thing on the path.

"I killed him, I think," he said. He looked over his shoulder, stood up. There was no sign or sound of the other men.

"Where are they?"

"Ran. Give me a hand, Tenar."

She held the knife in one hand. With the other she took hold of the arm of the man that lay huddled up on the path. Ged took him under the shoulder and they dragged him up the step and into the house. He lay on the stone floor of the kitchen, and blood ran out of his chest and belly like water from a pitcher. His upper lip was drawn back from his teeth, and only the whites of his eyes showed.

"Lock the door," Ged said, and she locked the door.

"Linens in the press," she said, and he got a sheet and tore it for bandages, which she bound round and round the man's belly and breast, into which three of the four tines of the pitchfork had driven full force, making three ragged springs of blood that dripped and squirted as Ged supported the man's torso so that she could wrap the bandages.

"What are you doing here? Did you come with them?"

"Yes. But they didn't know it. That's about all you can do, Tenar." He let the man's body sag down, and sat back, breathing hard, wiping his face with the back of his bloody hand. "I think I killed him," he said again.

"Maybe you did." Tenar watched the bright red spots spread slowly on the heavy linen that wrapped the man's thin, hairy chest and belly. She stood up, and swayed, very dizzy. "Get by the fire," she said. "You must be perishing."

She did not know how she had known him in the dark outside. By his voice, maybe. He wore a bulky shepherd's winter coat of cut fleece with the leather side out, and a shepherd's knit watch cap pulled down; his face was lined and weathered, his hair long and iron-grey. He smelled like woodsmoke, and frost, and sheep. He was shivering, his whole body shaking. "Get by the fire," she said again. "Put wood on it."

He did so. Tenar filled the kettle and swung it out on its iron arm over the blaze.

There was blood on her skirt, and she used an end of linen soaked in cold water to clean it. She gave the cloth to Ged to clean the blood off his hands. "What do you mean," she said, "you came with them but they didn't know it?"

"I was coming down. From the mountain. On the road from the springs of the Kaheda." He spoke in a flat voice as if out of breath, and his shivering made his speech slur. "Heard men behind me, and I went aside. Into the woods. Didn't feel like talking. I don't know. Something about them. I was afraid of them."

She nodded impatiently and sat down across the hearth from him, leaning forward to listen, her hands clenched tight in her lap. Her damp skirt was cold against her legs.

"I heard one of them say 'Oak Farm' as they went by. After that I followed them. One of them kept talking. About the child."

"What did he say?"

He was silent. He said finally, "That he was going to get her back. Punish her, he said. And get back at you. For stealing her, he said. He said—" He stopped.

"That he'd punish me, too."

"They all talked. About, about that."

"That one isn't Handy." She nodded toward the man on the floor. "Is it the . . ."

"He said she was his." Ged looked at the man too, and back at the fire. "He's dying. We should get help."

"He won't die," Tenar said. "I'll send for Ivy in the morning. The others are still out there—how many of them?"

"Two."

"If he dies he dies, if he lives he lives. Neither of us is going out." She got to her feet, in a spasm of fear. "Did you bring in the pitchfork, Ged!"

He pointed to it, the four long tines shining as it leaned against the wall beside the door.

She sat down in the hearthseat again, but now she was shaking, trembling from head to foot, as he had done. He reached across the hearth to touch her arm. "It's all right," he said.

"What if they're still out there?"

"They ran."

"They could come back."

"Two against two? And we've got the pitchfork."

She lowered her voice to a bare whisper to say, in terror, "The pruning hook and the scythes are in the barn lean-to."

He shook his head. "They ran. They saw—him—and you in the door."

"What did you do?"

"He came at me. So I came at him."

"I mean, before. On the road."

"They got cold, walking. It started to rain, and they got cold, and started talking about coming here. Before that it was only this one, talking about the child and you, about teaching—teaching lessons—" His voice dried up. "I'm thirsty," he said.

"So am I. The kettle's not boiling yet. Go on."

He took breath and tried to tell his story coherently. "The other two didn't listen to him much. Heard it all before, maybe. They were in a hurry to get on. To get to

Valmouth. As if they were running from somebody. Getting away. But it got cold, and he went on about Oak Farm, and the one with the cap said, 'Well, why not just go there and spend the night with—' "

"With the widow, yes."

Ged put his face in his hands. She waited.

He looked into the fire, and went on steadily. "Then I lost them for a while. The road came out level into the valley, and I couldn't follow along the way I'd been doing, in the woods, just behind them. I had to go aside, through the fields, keeping out of their sight. I don't know the country here, only the road. I was afraid if I cut across the fields I'd get lost, miss the house. And it was getting dark. I thought I'd missed the house, overshot it. I came back to the road, and almost ran into them—at the turn there. They'd seen the old man go by. They decided to wait till it was dark and they were sure nobody else was coming. They waited in the barn. I stayed outside. Just through the wall from them."

"You must be frozen," Tenar said dully.

"It was cold." He held his hands to the fire as if the thought of it had chilled him again. "I found the pitchfork by the lean-to door. They went around to the back of the house when they came out. I could have come to the front door then to warn you, it's what I should have done, but all I could think of was to take them by surprise—I thought it was my only advantage, chance. . . . I thought the house would be locked and they'd have to break in. But then I heard them going in, at the back, there. I went in—into the dairy—after them. I only just got out, when they came to the locked door." He gave a kind of laugh. "They went right by me in the dark. I could have tripped them. . . . One of them had a flint and steel, he'd burn a little tinder when they wanted to see a lock. They came around front. I heard you putting up the shutters; I knew you'd heard them. They talked about smashing the window they'd seen you at. Then the one with the cap saw the window—that window—" He nodded toward the kitchen window, with its deep, broad inner sill. "He said, 'Get me a rock, I'll smash that right open,' and they came to where he was, and they were about to hoist him up to the sill. So I let out a yell, and he dropped down, and one of them—this one—came running right at me."

"Ah, ah," gasped the man lying on the floor, as if telling Ged's tale for him. Ged got up and bent over him.

"He's dying, I think."

"No, he's not," Tenar said. She could not stop shaking entirely, but it was only an inward tremor now. The kettle was singing. She made a pot of tea, and laid her hands on the thick pottery sides of the teapot while it steeped. She poured out two cups, then a third, into which she put a little cold water. "It's too hot to drink," she told Ged, "hold it a minute first. I'll see if this'll go into him." She sat down on the floor by the man's head, lifted it on one arm, put the cup of cooled tea to his mouth, pushed the rim between the bared teeth. The warm stuff ran into his mouth; he swallowed. "He won't die," she said. "The floor's like ice. Help me move him nearer the fire."

Ged started to take the rug from a bench that ran along the wall between the chimney and the hall. "Don't use that, it's a good piece of weaving," Tenar said, and she went to the closet and brought out a worn-out felt cloak, which she spread out as a bed for the man. They hauled the inert body onto it, lapped it over him. The soaked red spots on the bandages had grown no larger.

Tenar stood up, and stood motionless.

"Therru," she said.

Ged looked round, but the child was not there. Tenar went hurriedly out of the room.

The children's room, the child's room, was perfectly dark and quiet. She felt her way to the bed, and laid her hand on the warm curve of the blanket over Therru's shoulder.

"Therru?"

The child's breathing was peaceful. She had not waked. Tenar could feel the heat of her body, like a radiance in the cold room.

As she went out, Tenar ran her hand across the chest of drawers and touched cold metal: the poker she had laid down when she closed the shutters. She brought it back to the kitchen, stepped over the man's body, and hung the poker on its hook on the chimney. She stood looking down at the fire.

"I couldn't do anything," she said. "What should I have done? Run out—right away—shouted, and run to Clearbrook and Shandy. They wouldn't have had time to hurt Therru."

"They would have been in the house with her, and you outside it, with the old man and woman. Or they could have picked her up and gone clear away with her. You did what you could. What you did was right. Timed right. The light from the house, and you coming out with the knife, and me there—they could see the pitchfork then—and him down. So they ran."

"Those that could," said Tenar. She turned and stirred the man's leg a little with the toe of her shoe, as if he were an object she was a little curious about, a little repelled by, like a dead viper. *"You* did the right thing," she said.

"I don't think he even saw it. He ran right onto it. It was like—" He did not say what it was like. He said, "Drink your tea," and poured himself more from the pot keeping warm on the hearthbricks. "It's good. Sit down," he said, and she did so.

"When I was a boy," he said after a time, "the Kargs raided my village. They had lances—long, with feathers tied to the shaft—"

She nodded. "Warriors of the God-Brothers," she said.

"I made a . . . a fog-spell. To confuse them. But they came on, some of them. I saw one of them run right onto a pitchfork—like him. Only it went clear through him. Below the waist."

"You hit a rib," Tenar said.

He nodded.

"It was the only mistake you made," she said. Her teeth were chattering now. She drank her tea. "Ged," she said, "what if they come back?"

"They won't."

"They could set fire to the house."

"This house?" He looked around at the stone walls.

"The haybarn—"

"They won't be back," he said, doggedly.

"No."

They held their cups with care, warming their hands on them.

"She slept through it."

"It's well she did."

"But she'll see him—here—in the morning—"

They stared at each other.

"If I'd killed him—if he'd die!" Ged said with rage. "I could drag him out and bury him—"

"Do it."

He merely shook his head angrily.

"What does it matter, why, why can't we do it!" Tenar demanded.

"I don't know."

"As soon as it gets light—"

"I'll get him out of the house. Wheelbarrow. The old man can help me."

"He can't lift anything any more. I'll help you."

"However I can do it, I'll cart him off to the village. There's a healer of some kind there?"

"A witch, Ivy."

She felt all at once abysmally, infinitely weary. She could scarcely hold the cup in her hand.

"There's more tea," she said, thick-tongued.

He poured himself another cupful.

The fire danced in her eyes. The flames swam, flared up, sank away, brightened again against the sooty stone, against the dark sky, against the pale sky, the gulfs of evening, the depths of air and light beyond the world. Flames of yellow, orange, orange-red, red tongues of flame, flame-tongues, the words she could not speak.

"Tenar."

"We call the star Tehanu," she said.

"Tenar, my dear. Come on. Come with me."

They were not at the fire. They were in the dark—in the dark hall. The dark passage. They had been there before, leading each other, following each other, in the darkness underneath the earth.

"This is the way," she said.

Winter

She was waking, not wanting to waken. Faint grey shone at the window in thin slits through the shutters. Why was the window shuttered? She got up hurriedly and went down the hall to the kitchen. No one sat by the fire, no one lay on the floor. There was no sign of anyone, anything. Except the teapot and three cups on the counter.

Therru got up about sunrise, and they breakfasted as usual; clearing up, the girl asked, "What happened?" She lifted a corner of wet linen from the soaking-tub in the pantry. The water in the tub was veined and clouded with brownish red.

"Oh, my period came on early," Tenar said, startled at the lie as she spoke it.

Therru stood a moment motionless, her nostrils flared and her head still, like an animal getting a scent. Then she dropped the sheeting back into the water, and went out to feed the chickens.

Tenar felt ill; her bones ached. The weather was still cold, and she stayed indoors as much as she could. She tried to keep Therru in, but when the sun came out with a keen, bright wind, Therru wanted to be out in it.

"Stay with Shandy in the orchard," Tenar said.

Therru said nothing as she slipped out.

The burned and deformed side of her face was made rigid by the destruction of muscles and the thickness of the scar-surface, but as the scars got older and as Tenar learned by long usage not to look away from it as deformity but to see it as face, it had expressions of its own. When Therru was frightened, the burned and darkened side "closed in," as Tenar thought, drawing together, hardening. When she was excited or intent, even the blind eye socket seemed to gaze, and the scars reddened and were hot to touch. Now, as she went out, there was a queer look to her, as if her face were not human at all, an animal, some strange horny-skinned wild creature with one bright eye, silent, escaping.

And Tenar knew that as she had lied to her for the first time, Therru for the first time was going to disobey her. The first but not the last time.

She sat down at the fireside with a weary sigh, and did nothing at all for a while.

A rap at the door: Clearbrook and Ged—no, Hawk she must call him—Hawk standing on the doorstep. Old Clearbrook was full of talk and importance, Ged dark and quiet and bulky in his grimy sheepskin coat. "Come in," she said. "Have some tea. What's the news?"

"Tried to get away, down to Valmouth, but the men from Kahedanan, the bailies, come down and 'twas in Cherry's outhouse they found 'em," Clearbrook announced, waving his fist.

"He escaped?" Horror caught at her.

"The other two," Ged said. "Not him."

"See, they found the body up in the old shambles on Round Hill, all beat to pieces like, up in the old shambles there, by Kahedanan, so ten, twelve of 'em 'pointed their-selves bailies then and there and come after them. And there was a search all through the villages last night, and this morning before 'twas hardly light they found 'em hiding out in Cherry's outhouse. Half-froze they was."

"He's dead, then?" she asked, bewildered.

Ged had shucked off the heavy coat and was now sitting on the cane-bottom chair by the door to undo his leather gaiters. *"He's* alive," he said in his quiet voice. "Ivy has him. I took him in this morning on the muck-cart. There were people out on the road before daylight, hunting for all three of them. They'd killed a woman, up in the hills."

"What woman?" Tenar whispered.

Her eyes were on Ged's. He nodded slightly.

Clearbrook wanted the story to be his, and took it up loudly: "I talked with some o' them from up there and they told me they'd all four of 'em been traipsing and camping and vagranting about near Kahedanan, and the woman would come into the village to beg, all beat about and burns and bruises all over her. They'd send her in, the men would, see, like that to beg, and then she'd go back to 'em, and she told people if she went back with nothing they'd beat her more, so they said why go back? But if she didn't they'd come after her, she said, see, and she'd always go with 'em. But then they finally went too far and beat her to death, and they took and left her body in the old shambles there where there's still some o' the stink left, you know, maybe thinking that was hiding what they done. And they came away then, down here, just last night. And why didn't you shout and call last night, Goha? Hawk says they was right here, sneaking about the house, when he come on 'em. I surely would have heard, or Shandy would, her ears might be sharper than mine. Did you tell her yet?"

Tenar shook her head.

"I'll just go tell her," said the old man, delighted to be first with the news, and he clumped off across the yard. He turned back halfway. "Never would have picked you as useful with a pitchfork!" he shouted to Ged, and slapped his thigh, laughing, and went on.

Ged slipped off the heavy gaiters, took off his muddy shoes and set them on the doorstep, and came over to the fire in his stocking feet. Trousers and jerkin and shirt of homespun wool: a Gontish goatherd, with a canny face, a hawk nose, and clear, dark eyes.

"There'll be people out soon," he said. "To tell you all about it, and hear what happened here again. They've got the two that ran off shut up now in a wine cellar with no wine in it, and fifteen or twenty men guarding them, and twenty or thirty boys trying to get a peek. . . ." He yawned, shook his shoulders and arms to loosen them, and with a glance at Tenar asked permission to sit down at the fire.

She gestured to the hearthseat. "You must be worn out," she whispered.

"I slept a little, here, last night. Couldn't stay awake." He yawned again. He looked up at her, gauging, seeing how she was.

"It was Therru's mother," she said. Her voice would not go above a whisper.

He nodded. He sat leaning forward a bit, his arms on his knees, as Flint had used to sit, gazing into the fire. They were very alike and entirely unlike, as unlike as a buried stone and a soaring bird. Her heart ached, and her bones ached, and her mind was bewildered among foreboding and grief and remembered fear and a troubled lightness.

"The witch has got our man," he said. "Tied down in case he feels lively. With the holes in him stuffed full of spiderwebs and blood-stanching spells. She says he'll live to hang."

"To hang."

"It's up to the King's Courts of Law, now that they're meeting again. Hanged or set to slave-labor."

She shook her head, frowning.

"You wouldn't just let him go, Tenar," he said gently, watching her.

"No."

"They must be punished," he said, still watching her.

" 'Punished.' That's what *he* said. Punish the child. She's bad. She must be punished. Punish me, for taking her. For being—" She struggled to speak. "I don't want punishment! — It should not have happened. — I wish you'd killed him!"

"I did my best," Ged said.

After a good while she laughed, rather shakily. "You certainly did."

"Think how easy it would have been," he said, looking into the coals again, "when I was a wizard. I could have set a binding spell on them, up there on the road, before they knew it. I could have marched them right down to Valmouth like a flock of sheep. Or last night, here, think of the fireworks I could have set off! They'd never have known what hit them."

"They still don't," she said.

He glanced at her. There was in his eye the faintest, irrepressible gleam of triumph.

"No," he said. "They don't."

"Useful with a pitchfork," she murmured.

He yawned enormously.

"Why don't you go in and get some sleep? The second room down the hall. Unless you want to entertain company. I see Lark and Daisy coming, and some of the children." She had got up, hearing voices, to look out the window.

"I'll do that," he said, and slipped away.

❖❖❖❖❖❖❖

Lark and her husband, Daisy the blacksmith's wife, and other friends from the village came by all day long to tell and be told all, as Ged had said. She found that their company revived her, carried her away from the constant presence of last night's terror, little by little, till she could begin to look back on it as something that had happened, not something that was happening, that must always be happening to her.

That was also what Therru had to learn to do, she thought, but not with one night: with her life.

She said to Lark when the others had gone, "What makes me rage at myself is how stupid I was."

"I did tell you you ought to keep the house locked."

"No—Maybe—That's just it."

"I know," said Lark.

"But I meant, when they were here—I could have run out and fetched Shandy and Clearbrook—maybe I could have taken Therru. Or I could have gone to the lean-to and got the pitchfork myself. Or the apple-pruner. It's seven feet long with a blade like a razor; I keep it the way Flint kept it. Why didn't I do that? Why didn't I do something? Why did I just lock myself in—when it wasn't any good trying to? If he— If Hawk hadn't been here— All I did was trap myself and Therru. I did finally go to the door with the butcher knife, and I shouted at them. I was half crazy. But that wouldn't have scared them off."

"I don't know," Lark said. "It was crazy, but maybe . . . I don't know. What could you do but lock the doors? But it's like we're all our lives locking the doors. It's the house we live in."

They looked around at the stone walls, the stone floors, the stone chimney, the sunny window of the kitchen of Oak Farm, Farmer Flint's house.

"That girl, that woman they murdered," Lark said, looking shrewdly at Tenar. "She was the same one."

Tenar nodded.

"One of them told me she was pregnant. Four, five months along."

They were both silent.

"Trapped," Tenar said.

Lark sat back, her hands on the skirt on her heavy thighs, her back straight, her handsome face set. "Fear," she said. "What are we so afraid of? Why do we let 'em tell us we're afraid? What is it *they're* afraid of?" She picked up the stocking she had been darning, turned it in her hands, was silent awhile; finally she said, "What are they afraid of us for?"

Tenar spun and did not answer.

Therru came running in, and Lark greeted her: "There's my honey! Come give me a hug, my honey girl!"

Therru hugged her hastily. "Who are the men they caught?" she demanded in her hoarse, toneless voice, looking from Lark to Tenar.

Tenar stopped her wheel. She spoke slowly.

"One was Handy. One was a man called Shag. The one that was hurt is called Hake." She kept her eyes on Therru's face; she saw the fire, the scar reddening. "The woman they killed was called Senny, I think."

"Senini," the child whispered.

Tenar nodded.

"Did they kill her dead?"

She nodded again.

"Tadpole says they were *here.*"

She nodded again.

The child looked around the room, as the women had done; but her look was utterly unacceptant, seeing no walls.

"Will you kill them?"

"They may be hanged."

"Dead?"

"Yes."

Therru nodded, half indifferently. She went out again, rejoining Lark's children by the well-house.

The two women said nothing. They spun and mended, silent, by the fire, in Flint's house.

After a long time Lark said, "What's become of the fellow, the shepherd, that followed 'em here? Hawk, you said he's called?"

"He's asleep in there," said Tenar, nodding to the back of the house.

"Ah," said Lark. The wheel purred. "I knew him before last night."

"Ah. Up at Re Albi, did you?"

Tenar nodded. The wheel purred.

"To follow those three, and take 'em on in the dark with a pitchfork, that took a bit of courage, now. Not a young man, is he?"

"No." After a while she went on, "He'd been ill, and needed work. So I sent him over the mountain to tell Clearbrook to take him on here. But Clearbrook thinks he can still do it all himself, so he sent him up above the Springs for the summer herding. He was coming back from that."

"Think you'll keep him on here, then?"

"If he likes," said Tenar.

Another group came out to Oak Farm from the village, wanting to hear Goha's story and tell her their part in the great capture of the murderers, and look at the pitchfork and compare its four long tines to the three bloody spots on the bandages of the man called Hake, and talk it all over again. Tenar was glad to see the evening come, and call Therru in, and shut the door.

She raised her hand to latch it. She lowered her hand and

forced herself to turn from it, leaving it unlocked.

"Sparrowhawk's in your room," Therru informed her, coming back to the kitchen with eggs from the cool-room.

"I meant to tell you he was here—I'm sorry."

"I know him," Therru said, washing her face and hands in the pantry. And when Ged came in, heavy-eyed and unkempt, she went straight to him and put up her arms.

"Therru," he said, and took her up and held her. She clung to him briefly, then broke free.

"I know the beginning part of the *Creation*," she told him.

"Will you sing it to me?" Again glancing at Tenar for permission, he sat down in his place at the hearth.

"I can only say it."

He nodded and waited, his face rather stern. The child said:

> *The making from the unmaking,*
> *The ending from the beginning,*
> *Who shall know surely?*
> *What we know is the doorway between them*
> *that we enter departing.*
> *Among all beings ever returning,*
> *the eldest, the Doorkeeper, Segoy. . . .*

The child's voice was like a metal brush drawn across metal, like dry leaves, like the hiss of fire burning. She spoke to the end of the first stanza:

> *Then from the foam bright Éa broke.*

Ged nodded brief, firm approval. "Good," he said.

"Last night," Tenar said. "Last night she learned it. It seems a year ago."

"I can learn more," said Therru.

"You will," Ged told her.

"Now finish cleaning the squash, please," said Tenar, and the child obeyed.

"What shall I do?" Ged asked. Tenar paused, looking at him.

"I need that kettle filled and heated."

He nodded, and took the kettle to the pump.

They made and ate their supper and cleared it away.

"Say the *Making* again as far as you know it," Ged said to Therru, at the hearth, "and we'll go on from there."

She said the second stanza once with him, once with Tenar, once by herself.

"Bed," said Tenar.

"You didn't tell Sparrowhawk about the king."

"You tell him," Tenar said, amused at this pretext for delay.

Therru turned to Ged. Her face, scarred and whole, seeing and blind, was intent, fiery. "The king came in a ship. He had a sword. He gave me the bone dolphin. His ship was flying, but I was sick, because Handy touched me. But the king touched me there and the mark went away." She showed her round, thin arm. Tenar stared. She had forgotten the mark.

"Some day I want to fly to where he lives," Therru told Ged. He nodded. "I will do that," she said. "Do you know him?"

"Yes. I know him. I went on a long journey with him."

"Where?"

"To where the sun doesn't rise and the stars don't set. And back from that place."

"Did you fly?"

He shook his head. "I can only walk," he said.

The child pondered, and then as if satisfied said, "Good night," and went off to her room. Tenar followed her; but Therru did not want to be sung to sleep. "I can say the *Making* in the dark," she said. *"Both* stanzas."

Tenar came back to the kitchen and sat down again across the hearth from Ged.

"How she's changing!" she said. "I can't keep up with her. I'm old to be bringing up a child. And she . . . She obeys me, but only because she wants to."

"It's the only justification for obedience," Ged observed.

"But when she does take it into her head to disobey me, what can I do? There's a wildness in her. Sometimes she's my Therru, sometimes she's something else, out of reach. I asked Ivy if she'd think of training her. Beech suggested it. Ivy said no. 'Why not?' I said. 'I'm afraid of her!' she said. . . . But you're not afraid of her. Nor she of you. You and Lebannen are the only men she's let touch her. *I* let that—that Handy—I can't talk about it. Oh, I'm tired! I don't understand anything. . . ."

Ged laid a knot on the fire to burn small and slow, and they both watched the leap and flutter of the flames.

"I'd like you to stay here, Ged," she said. "If you like."

He did not answer at once. She said, "Maybe you're going on to Havnor—"

"No, no. I have nowhere to go. I was looking for work."

"Well, there's plenty to be done here. Clearbrook won't admit it, but his arthritis has about finished him for anything but gardening. I've been wanting help ever since I came back. I could have told the old blockhead what I thought of him for sending you off up the mountain that way, but it's no use. He wouldn't listen."

"It was a good thing for me," Ged said. "It was the time I needed."

"You were herding sheep?"

"Goats. Right up at the top of the grazings. A boy they had took sick, and Serry took me on, sent me up there the first day. They keep 'em up there high and late, so the underwool grows thick. This last month I had the mountain pretty much to myself. Serry sent me up that coat and some supplies, and said to keep the herd up as high as I could as long as I could. So I did. It was fine, up there."

"Lonely," she said.

He nodded, half smiling.

"You always have been alone."

"Yes, I have."

She said nothing. He looked at her.

"I'd like to work here," he said.

"That's settled, then," she said. After a while she added, "For the winter, anyway."

The frost was harder tonight. Their world was perfectly silent except for the whisper of the fire. The silence was like a presence between them. She lifted her head and looked at him.

"Well," she said, "which bed shall I sleep in, Ged? The child's, or yours?"

He drew breath. He spoke low. "Mine, if you will."

"I will."

The silence held him. She could see the effort he made to break from it. "If you'll be patient with me," he said.

"I have been patient with you for twenty-five years," she said. She looked at him and began to laugh. "Come—come on, my dear—Better late than never! I'm only an old woman. . . . Nothing is wasted, nothing is ever wasted. You taught me that." She stood up, and he stood; she put out her hands, and he took them. They embraced, and their embrace became close. They held each other so fiercely, so dearly, that they stopped knowing anything but each other. It did not matter which bed they meant to sleep in. They lay that night on the hearthstones, and there she taught Ged the mystery that the wisest man could not teach him.

He built up the fire once, and fetched the good weaving off the bench. Tenar made no objection this time. Her cloak and his sheepskin coat were their blankets.

They woke again at dawn. A faint silvery light lay on the dark, half-leafless branches of the oaks outside the window. Tenar stretched out full length to feel his warmth against her. After a while she murmured, "He was lying here. Hake. Right under us. . . ."

Ged made a small noise of protest.

"Now you're a man indeed," she said. "Stuck another man full of holes, first, and lain with a woman, second. That's the proper order, I suppose."

"Hush," he murmured, turning to her, laying his head on her shoulder. "Don't."

"I will, Ged. Poor man! There's no mercy in me, only justice. I wasn't trained to mercy. Love is the only grace I have. Oh, Ged, don't fear me! You were a man when I first saw you! It's not a weapon or a woman can make a man, or magery either, or any power, anything but himself."

They lay in warmth and sweet silence.

"Tell me something."

He murmured assent sleepily.

"How did you happen to hear what they were saying? Hake and Handy and the other one. How did you happen to be just there, just then?"

He raised himself up on one elbow so he could look at her face. His own face was so open and vulnerable in its ease and fulfillment and tenderness that she had to reach up and touch his mouth, there where she had kissed it first, months ago, which led to his taking her into his arms again, and the conversation was not continued in words.

There were formalities to be got through. The chief of them was to tell Clearbrook and the other tenants of Oak Farm that she had replaced "the old master" with a hired hand. She did so promptly and bluntly. They could not do anything about it, nor did it entail any threat to them. A widow's tenure of her husband's property was contingent on there being no male heir or claimant. Flint's son the seaman was the heir, and Flint's widow was merely holding the farm for him. If she died, it would go to Clearbrook to hold for the heir; if Spark never claimed it, it would go to a distant cousin of Flint's in Kahedanan. The two couples who did not own the land but held a life interest in the work and profit of the farming, as was common on Gont, could not be dislodged by any man the widow took up with, even if she married him; but she feared they might resent her lack of fidelity to Flint, whom they had after all known longer than she had. To her relief they made no objections at all. "Hawk" had won their approval with one jab of a pitchfork. Besides, it was only good sense in a woman to want a man in the house to protect her. If she took him into her bed, well, the appetites of widows were proverbial. And, after all, she was a foreigner.

The attitude of the villagers was much the same. A bit of whispering and sniggering, but little more. It seemed that being respectable was easier than Moss thought; or perhaps it was that used goods had little value.

She felt as soiled and diminished by their acceptance as she would have by their disapproval. Only Lark freed her from shame, by making no judgments at all, and using no words—man, woman, widow, foreigner—in place of what she saw, but simply looking, watching her and Hawk with interest, curiosity, envy, and generosity.

Because Lark did not see Hawk through the words herdsman, hired hand, widow's man, but looked at him himself, she saw a good deal that puzzled her. His dignity and simplicity were not greater than that of other men she had known, but were a little different in quality; there was a size to him, she thought, not height or girth, certainly, but soul and mind. She said to Ivy, "That man hasn't lived among goats all his life. He knows more about the world than he does about a farm."

"I'd say he's a sorcerer who's been accursed or lost his power some way," the witch said. "It happens."

"Ah," said Lark.

But the word "archmage" was too great and grand a word to bring from far-off pomps and palaces and fit to the dark-eyed, grey-haired man at Oak Farm, and she never did that. If she had, she could not have been as comfortable with him as she was. Even the idea of his having been a sorcerer made her a bit uneasy, the word getting in the way of the man, until she actually saw him again. He was up in one of the old apple trees in the orchard pruning out deadwood, and he called out a greeting to her as she came to the farm. His name fit him well, she thought, perched up there, and she waved at him, and smiled as she went on.

Tenar had not forgotten the question she had asked him on the hearthstones under the sheepskin coat. She asked it again, a few days or months later—time went along very sweet and easy for them in the stone house, on the winter-bound farm. "You never told me," she said, "how you came to hear them talking on the road."

"I told you, I think. I'd gone aside, hidden, when I heard men coming behind me."

"Why?"

"I was alone, and knew there were some gangs around."

"Yes, of course— But then just as they passed, Hake was talking about Therru?"

"He said 'Oak Farm,' I think."

"It's all perfectly possible. It just seems so convenient."

Knowing she did not disbelieve him, he lay back and waited.

"It's the kind of thing that happens to a wizard," she said.

"And others."

"Maybe."

"My dear, you're not trying to . . . reinstate me?"

"No. No, not at all. Would that be a sensible thing to do? If you were a wizard, would you be here?"

They were in the big oak-framed bed, well covered with sheepskins and feather-coverlets, for the room had no fireplace and the night was one of hard frost on fallen snow.

"But what I want to know is this. Is there something besides what you call power—that comes before it, maybe? Or something that power is just one way of using? Like this. Ogion said of you once that before you'd had any learning or training as a wizard at all, you were a mage. Mage-born, he said. So I imagined that, to have power, one must first have room for the power. An emptiness to fill. And the greater the emptiness the more power can fill it. But if the power never was got, or was taken away, or was given away—still that would be there."

"That emptiness," he said.

"Emptiness is one word for it. Maybe not the right word."

"Potentiality?" he said, and shook his head. "What is able to be . . . to become."

"I think you were there on that road, just there just then,

because of that—because that is what happens to you. You
didn't make it happen. You didn't cause it. It wasn't because
of your 'power.' It happened to you. Because of your—
emptiness.''

After a while he said, "This isn't far from what I was
taught as a boy on Roke: that true magery lies in doing only
what you must do. But this would go further. Not to do,
but to be done to. . . .''

"I don't think that's quite it. It's more like what true
doing rises from. Didn't you come and save my life—didn't
you run a fork into Hake? That was 'doing,' all right, doing
what you must do. . . .''

He pondered again, and finally asked her, "Is this a wis-
dom taught you when you were Priestess of the Tombs?''

"No." She stretched a little, gazing into the darkness.
"Arha was taught that to be powerful she must sacrifice.
Sacrifice herself and others. A bargain: give, and so get.
And I cannot say that that's untrue. But my soul can't live
in that narrow place—this for that, tooth for tooth, death for
life. . . . There is a freedom beyond that. Beyond payment,
retribution, redemption—beyond all the bargains and the
balances, there is freedom.''

"The doorway between them," he said softly.

That night Tenar dreamed. She dreamed that she saw the
doorway of the *Creation of Éa.* It was a little window of
gnarled, clouded, heavy glass, set low in the west wall of an
old house above the sea. The window was locked. It had
been bolted shut. She wanted to open it, but there was a
word or a key, something she had forgotten, a word, a key,
a name, without which she could not open it. She sought for
it in rooms of stone that grew smaller and darker till she
found that Ged was holding her, trying to wake her and
comfort her, saying, "It's all right, dear love, it will be all
right!''

"I can't get free!" she cried, clinging to him.

He soothed her, stroking her hair; they lay back together, and he whispered, "Look."

The old moon had risen. Its white brilliance on the fallen snow was reflected into the room, for cold as it was Tenar would not have the shutters closed. All the air above them was luminous. They lay in shadow, but it seemed as if the ceiling were a mere veil between them and endless, silver, tranquil depths of light.

It was a winter of heavy snows on Gont, and a long winter. The harvest had been a good one. There was food for the animals and people, and not much to do but eat it and stay warm.

Therru knew the *Creation of Éa* all through. She spoke the Winter Carol and the *Deed of the Young King* on the day of Sunreturn. She knew how to handle a piecrust, how to spin on the wheel, and how to make soap. She knew the name and use of every plant that showed above the snow, and a good deal of other lore, herbal and verbal, that Ged had stowed away in his head from his short apprenticeship with Ogion and his long years at the School on Roke. But he had not taken down the Runes or the Lore-books from the mantelpiece, nor had he taught the child any word of the Language of the Making.

He and Tenar spoke of this. She told him how she had taught Therru the one word, *tolk,* and then had stopped, for it had not seemed right, though she did not know why.

"I thought perhaps it was because I'd never truly spoken that language, never used it in magery. I thought perhaps she should learn it from a true speaker of it."

"No man is that."

"No woman is half that."

"I meant that only the dragons speak it as their native tongue."

"Do they learn it?"

Struck by the question, he was slow to answer, evidently calling to mind all he had been told and knew of the dragons. "I don't know," he said at last. "What do we know about them? Would they teach as we do, mother to child, elder to younger? Or are they like the animals, teaching some things, but born knowing most of what they know? Even that we don't know. But my guess would be that the dragon and the speech of the dragon are one. One being."

"And they speak no other tongue."

He nodded. "They do not learn," he said. "They are."

Therru came through the kitchen. One of her tasks was to keep the kindling box filled, and she was busy at it, bundled up in a cut-down lambskin jacket and cap, trotting back and forth from the woodhouse to the kitchen. She dumped her load in the box by the chimney corner and set off again.

"What is it she sings?" Ged asked.

"Therru?"

"When she's alone."

"But she never sings. She can't."

"Her way of singing. 'Farther west than west . . .' "

"Ah!" said Tenar. "That story! Did Ogion never tell you about the Woman of Kemay?"

"No," he said, "tell me."

She told him the tale as she spun, and the purr and hush of the wheel went along with the words of the story. At the end of it she said, "When the Master Windkey told me how he'd come looking for 'a woman on Gont,' I thought of her. But she'd be dead by now, no doubt. And how would a fisherwoman who was a dragon be an archmage, anyhow!"

"Well, the Patterner didn't say that a woman on Gont was to be archmage," said Ged. He was mending a badly torn pair of breeches, sitting up in the window ledge to get what light the dark day afforded. It was a half-month after Sunreturn and the coldest time yet.

"What did he say, then?"

" 'A woman on Gont.' So you told me."

"But they were asking who was to be the next archmage."

"And got no answer to that question."

"Infinite are the arguments of mages," said Tenar rather drily.

Ged bit the thread off and rolled the unused length around two fingers.

"I learned to quibble a bit, on Roke," he admitted. "But this isn't a quibble, I think. 'A woman on Gont' can't become archmage. No woman can be archmage. She'd un-make what she became in becoming it. The Mages of Roke are men—their power is the power of men, their knowledge is the knowledge of men. Both manhood and magery are built on one rock: power belongs to men. If women had power, what would men be but women who can't bear children? And what would women be but men who can?"

"Hah!" went Tenar; and presently, with some cunning, she said, "Haven't there been queens? Weren't they women of power?"

"A queen's only a she-king," said Ged.

She snorted.

"I mean, men give her power. They let her use their power. But it isn't hers, is it? It isn't because she's a woman that she's powerful, but despite it."

She nodded. She stretched, sitting back from the spinning wheel. "What is a woman's power, then?" she asked.

"I don't think we know."

"When has a woman power because she's a woman? With her children, I suppose. For a while . . ."

"In her house, maybe."

She looked around the kitchen. "But the doors are shut," she said, "the doors are locked."

"Because you're valuable."

"Oh, yes. We're precious. So long as we're power-less. . . . I remember when I first learned that! Kossil threatened me—me, the One Priestess of the Tombs. And I realized that I was helpless. I had the honor; but she had the power, from the God-king, the man. Oh, it made me angry! And frightened me. . . . Lark and I talked about this once. She said, 'Why are men *afraid* of women?' "

"If your strength is only the other's weakness, you live in fear," Ged said.

"Yes; but women seem to fear their own strength, to be afraid of themselves."

"Are they ever taught to trust themselves?" Ged asked, and as he spoke Therru came in on her work again. His eyes and Tenar's met.

"No," she said. "Trust is not what we're taught." She watched the child stack the wood in the box. "If power were trust," she said. "I like that word. If it weren't all these arrangements—one above the other—kings and masters and mages and owners— It all seems so unnecessary. Real power, real freedom, would lie in trust, not force."

"As children trust their parents," he said.

They were both silent.

"As things are," he said, "even trust corrupts. The men on Roke trust themselves and one another. Their power is pure, nothing taints its purity, and so they take that purity for wisdom. They cannot imagine doing wrong."

She looked up at him. He had never spoken about Roke thus before, from wholly outside it, free of it.

"Maybe they need some women there to point that possibility out to them," she said, and he laughed.

She restarted the wheel. "I still don't see why, if there can be she-kings, there can't be she-archmages."

Therru was listening.

"Hot snow, dry water," said Ged, a Gontish saying. "Kings are given power by other men. A mage's power is his own—himself."

"And it's a male power. Because we don't even know what a woman's power is. All right. I see. But all the same, why can't they find an archmage—a he-archmage?"

Ged studied the tattered inseam of the breeches. "Well," he said, "if the Patterner wasn't answering their question, he was answering one they didn't ask. Maybe what they have to do is ask it."

"Is it a riddle?" Therru asked.

"Yes," said Tenar. "But we don't know the riddle. We only know the answer to it. The answer is: A woman on Gont."

"There's lots of them," Therru said after pondering a bit. Apparently satisfied by this, she went out for the next load of kindling.

Ged watched her go. " 'All changed,' " he said. "All . . . Sometimes I think, Tenar—I wonder if Lebannen's kingship is only a beginning. A doorway . . . And he the doorkeeper. Not to pass through."

"He seems so young," Tenar said, tenderly.

"Young as Morred was when he met the Black Ships. Young as I was when I . . ." He stopped, looking out the window at the grey, frozen fields through the leafless trees. "Or you, Tenar, in that dark place . . . What's youth or age?

I don't know. Sometimes I feel as if I'd been alive for a thousand years; sometimes I feel my life's been like a flying swallow seen through the chink of a wall. I have died and been reborn, both in the dry land and here under the sun, more than once. And the *Making* tells us that we have all returned and return forever to the source, and that the source is ceaseless. *Only in dying, life. . . .* I thought about that when I was up with the goats on the mountain, and a day went on forever and yet no time passed before the evening came, and morning again. . . . I learned goat wisdom. So I thought, What is this grief of mine for? What man am I mourning? Ged the archmage? Why is Hawk the goatherd sick with grief and shame for him? What have I done that I should be ashamed?"

"Nothing," Tenar said. "Nothing, ever!"

"Oh, yes," said Ged. "All the greatness of men is founded on shame, made out of it. So Hawk the goatherd wept for Ged the archmage. And looked after the goats, also, as well as a boy his age could be expected to do. . . ."

After a while Tenar smiled. She said, a little shyly, "Moss said you were about fifteen."

"That would be about right. Ogion named me in the autumn; and the next summer I was off to Roke. . . . Who was that boy? An emptiness . . . A freedom."

"Who is Therru, Ged?"

He did not answer until she thought he was not going to answer, and then he said, "So made—what freedom is there for her?"

"We are our freedom, then?"

"I think so."

"You seemed, in your power, as free as man can be. But at what cost? What made you free? And I . . . I was made, molded like clay, by the will of the women serving the Old Powers, or serving the men who made all services and ways and places, I no longer know which. Then I went free, with you, for a moment, and with Ogion. But it was not *my* freedom. Only it gave me choice; and I chose. I chose to mold myself like clay to the use of a farm and a farmer and our children. I made myself a vessel. I know its shape. But not the clay. Life danced me. I know the dances. But I don't know who the dancer is."

"And she," Ged said after a long silence, "if she should ever dance—"

"They will fear her," Tenar whispered. Then the child came back in, and the conversation turned to the bread dough raising in the box by the stove. They talked so, quietly and long, passing from one thing to another and round and back, for half the brief day, often, spinning and sewing their lives together with words, the years and the deeds and the thoughts they had not shared. Then again they would be silent, working and thinking and dreaming, and the silent child was with them.

So the winter passed, till lambing season was on them, and the work got very heavy for a while as the days lengthened and grew bright. Then the swallows came from the isles under the sun, from the South Reach, where the star Gobardon shines in the constellation of Ending; but all the swallows' talk with one another was about beginning.

The Master

Like the swallows, the ships began to fly among the islands with the return of spring. In the villages there was talk, secondhand from Valmouth, of the king's ships harrying the harriers, driving well-established pirates to ruin, confiscating their ships and fortunes. Lord Heno himself sent out his three finest, fastest ships, captained by the sorcerer-seawolf Tally, who was feared by every merchantman from Soléa to the Andrades; his fleet was to ambush the king's ships off Oranéa and destroy them. But it was one of the king's ships that came into Valmouth Bay with Tally in chains aboard, and under orders to escort Lord Heno to Gont Port to be tried for piracy and murder. Heno barricaded himself in his stone manor house in the hills behind Valmouth, but neglected to light a fire, it being warm spring weather; so five or six of the king's young soldiers dropped in on him by way of the chimney, and the whole troop walked him chained through the streets of Valmouth and carried him off to justice.

When he heard this, Ged said with love and pride, "All that a king can do, he will do well."

Handy and Shag had been taken promptly off on the north road to Gont Port, and when his wounds healed enough Hake was carried there by ship, to be tried for murder at the king's courts of law. The news of their sentence to the galleys caused much satisfaction and self-congratulation in Middle Valley, to which Tenar, and Therru beside her, listened in silence.

There came other ships bearing other men sent by the king, not all of them popular among the townsfolk and villagers of rude Gont: royal sheriffs, sent to report on the system of bailiffs and officers of the peace and to hear complaints and grievances from the common people; tax reporters and tax collectors; noble visitors to the little lords of Gont, inquiring politely as to their fealty to the Crown in Havnor; and wizardly men, who went here and there, seeming to do little and say less.

"I think they're hunting for a new archmage after all," said Tenar.

"Or looking for abuses of the art," Ged said—"sorcery gone wrong."

Tenar was going to say, "Then they should look in the manor house of Re Albi!" but her tongue stumbled on the words. What was I going to say? she thought. Did I ever tell Ged about— I'm getting forgetful. What was it I was going to tell Ged? Oh, that we'd better mend the lower pasture gate before the cows get out.

There was always something, a dozen things, in the front of her mind, business of the farm. "Never one thing, for you," Ogion had said. Even with Ged to help her, all her thoughts and days went into the business of the farm. He shared the housework with her as Flint had not; but Flint had been a farmer, and Ged was not. He learned fast, but there was a lot to learn. They worked. There was little time for talk, now. At the day's end there was supper together, and bed together, and sleep, and wake at dawn and back to work, and so round and so round, like the wheel of a water mill, rising full and emptying, the days like the bright water falling.

"Hello, mother," said the thin fellow at the farmyard gate. She thought it was Lark's eldest and said, "What brings you by, lad?" Then she looked back at him across the clucking chickens and the parading geese.

"Spark!" she cried, and scattered the poultry, running to him.

"Well, well," he said. "Don't carry on."

He let her embrace him and stroke his face. He came in and sat down in the kitchen, at the table.

"Have you eaten? Did you see Apple?"

"I could eat."

She rummaged in the well-stocked larder. "What ship are you on? Still the *Gull*?"

"No." A pause. "My ship's broke up."

She turned in horror—"Wrecked?"

"No." He smiled without humor. "Crew's broke up. King's men took her over."

"But—it wasn't a pirate ship—"

"No."

"Then why—?"

"Said the captain was running some goods they wanted," he said, unwillingly. He was as thin as ever, but looked older, tanned dark, lank-haired, with a long, narrow face like Flint's but still narrower, harder.

"Where's dad?" he said.

Tenar stood still.

"You didn't stop by your sister's."

"No," he said, indifferent.

"Flint died three years ago," she said. "Of a stroke. In the fields—on the path up from the lambing pens. Clearbrook found him. It was three years ago."

There was a silence. He did not know what to say, or had nothing to say.

She put food before him. He began to eat so hungrily that she set out more at once.

"When did you eat last?"

He shrugged, and ate.

She sat down across the table from him. Late-spring sunshine poured in the low window across the table and shone on the brass fender in the hearth.

He pushed the plate away at last.

"So who's been running the farm?" he asked.

"What's that to you, son?" she asked him, gently but drily.

"It's mine," he said, in a rather similar tone.

After a minute Tenar got up and cleared his dishes away. "So it is."

"You can stay, o' course," he said, very awkwardly, perhaps attempting to joke; but he was not a joking man. "Old Clearbrook still around?"

"They're all still here. And a man called Hawk, and a child I keep. Here. In the house. You'll have to sleep in the loft-room. I'll put the ladder up." She faced him again. "Are you here for a stay, then?"

"I might be."

So Flint had answered her questions for twenty years, denying her right to ask them by never answering yes or no, maintaining a freedom based on her ignorance; a poor, narrow sort of freedom, she thought.

"Poor lad," she said, "your crew broken up, and your father dead, and strangers in your house, all in a day. You'll want some time to get used to it all. I'm sorry, my son. But I'm glad you're here. I thought of you often, on the seas, in the storms, in winter."

He said nothing. He had nothing to offer, and was unable to accept. He pushed back his chair and was about to get up when Therru came in. He stared, half-risen—"What happened to her?" he said.

"She was burned. Here's my son I told you about, Therru, the sailor, Spark. Therru's your sister, Spark."

"Sister!"

"By adoption."

"Sister!" he said again, and looked around the kitchen as if for witness, and stared at his mother.

She stared back.

He went out, going wide of Therru, who stood motionless. He slammed the door behind him.

Tenar started to speak to Therru and could not.

"Don't cry," said the child who did not cry, coming to her, touching her arm. "Did he hurt you?"

"Oh Therru! Let me hold you!" She sat down at the table with Therru on her lap and in her arms, though the girl was getting big to be held, and had never learned how to do it easily. But Tenar held her and wept, and Therru bent her scarred face down against Tenar's, till it was wet with tears.

Ged and Spark came in at dusk from opposite ends of the farm. Spark had evidently talked with Clearbrook and thought the situation over, and Ged was evidently trying to size it up. Very little was said at supper, and that cautiously. Spark made no complaint about not having his own room back, but ran up the ladder to the storage-loft like the sailor he was, and was apparently satisfied with the bed his mother had made him there, for he did not come back down till late in the morning.

He wanted breakfast then, and expected it to be served to him. His father had always been waited on by mother, wife, daughter. Was he less a man than his father? Was she to prove it to him? She served him his meal and cleared it away for him, and went back to the orchard where she and Therru and Shandy were burning off a plague of tent caterpillars that threatened to destroy the new-set fruit.

Spark went off to join Clearbrook and Tiff. And he stayed mostly with them, as the days passed. The heavy work requiring muscle and the skilled work with crops and sheep was done by Ged, Shandy, and Tenar, while the two old men who had been there all their lives, his father's men, took him about and told him how they managed it all, and truly believed they were managing it all, and shared their belief with him.

Tenar became miserable in the house. Only outdoors, at the farmwork, did she have relief from the anger, the shame that Spark's presence brought her.

"My turn," she said to Ged, bitterly, in the starlit darkness of their room. "My turn to lose what I was proudest of."

"What have you lost?"

"My son. The son I did not bring up to be a man. I failed. I failed him." She bit her lip, gazing dry-eyed into the dark.

Ged did not try to argue with her or persuade her out of her grief. He asked, "Do you think he'll stay?"

"Yes. He's afraid to try and go back to sea. He didn't tell me the truth, or not all the truth, about his ship. He was second mate. I suppose he was involved in carrying stolen goods. Secondhand piracy. I don't care. Gontish sailors are all half-pirate. But he lies about it. He lies. He is jealous of you. A dishonest, envious man."

"Frightened, I think," Ged said. "Not wicked. And it is his farm."

"Then he can have it! And may it be as generous to him as—"

"No, dear love," Ged said, catching her with both voice

and hands—"don't speak—don't say the evil word!" He was so urgent, so passionately earnest, that her anger turned right about into the love that was its source, and she cried, "I wouldn't curse him, or this place! I didn't mean it! Only it makes me so sorry, so ashamed! I am so sorry, Ged!"

"No, no, no. My dear, I don't care what the boy thinks of me. But he's very hard on you."

"And Therru. He treats her like— He said, he said to me, 'What did she do, to look like that?' What did *she do*—!"

Ged stroked her hair, as he often did, with a light, slow, repeated caress that would make them both sleepy with loving pleasure.

"I could go off goat-herding again," he said at last. "It would make things easier for you here. Except for the work. . . ."

"I'd rather come with you."

He stroked her hair, and seemed to be considering. "I suppose we might," he said. "There were a couple of families up there sheep-herding, above Lissu. But then comes the winter. . . ."

"Maybe some farmer would take us on. I know the work—and sheep—and you know goats—and you're quick at everything—"

"Useful with pitchforks," he murmured, and got a little sob of a laugh from her.

The next morning Spark was up early to breakfast with them, for he was going fishing with old Tiff. He got up from the table, saying with a better grace than usual, "I'll bring a mess of fish for supper."

Tenar had made resolves overnight. She said, "Wait; you can clear off the table, Spark. Set the dishes in the sink and put water on 'em. They'll be washed with the supper things."

He stared a moment and said, "That's women's work," putting on his cap.

"It's anybody's work who eats in this kitchen."

"Not mine," he said flatly, and went out.

She followed him. She stood on the doorstep. "Hawk's, but not yours?" she demanded.

He merely nodded, going on across the yard.

"It's too late," she said, turning back to the kitchen. "Failed, failed." She could feel the lines in her face, stiff, beside the mouth, between the eyes. "You can water a stone," she said, "but it won't grow."

"You have to start when they're young and tender," Ged said. "Like me."

This time she couldn't laugh.

They came back to the house from the day's work and saw a man talking with Spark at the front gate.

"That's the fellow from Re Albi, isn't it?" said Ged, whose eyes were very good.

"Come along, Therru," Tenar said, for the child had stopped short. "What fellow?" She was rather nearsighted, and squinted across the yard. "Oh, it's what's his name, the sheep-dealer. Townsend. What's he back here for, the carrion crow!"

Her mood all day had been fierce, and Ged and Therru wisely said nothing.

She went to the men at the gate.

"Did you come about the ewe lambs, Townsend? You're a year late; but there's some of this year's yet in the fold."

"So the master's been telling me," said Townsend.

"Has he," said Tenar.

Spark's face went darker than ever at her tone.

"I won't interrupt you and the master, then," said she,

and was turning away when Townsend spoke: "I've got a message for you, Goha."

"Third time's the charm."

"The old witch, you know, old Moss, she's in a bad way. She said, since I was coming down to Middle Valley, she said, 'Tell Mistress Goha I'd like to see her before I die, if there's a chance of her coming.'"

Crow, carrion crow, Tenar thought, looking with hatred at the bearer of bad news.

"She's ill?"

"Sick to death," Townsend said, with a kind of smirk that might be intended for sympathy. "Took sick in the winter, and she's failing fast, and so she said to tell you she wants bad to see you, before she dies."

"Thank you for bringing the message," Tenar said soberly, and turned to go to the house. Townsend went on with Spark to the sheepfolds.

As they prepared dinner, Tenar said to Ged and Therru, "I must go."

"Of course," Ged said. "The three of us, if you like."

"Would you?" For the first time that day her face lightened, the storm cloud lifted. "Oh," she said, "that's—that's good—I didn't want to ask, I thought maybe— Therru, would you like to go back to the little house, Ogion's house, for a while?"

Therru stood still to think. "I could see my peach tree," she said.

"Yes, and Heather—and Sippy—and Moss—poor Moss! Oh, I have longed, I have longed to go back up there, but it didn't seem right. There was the farm to run—and all—"

It seemed to her that there was some other reason she had not gone back, had not let herself think of going back, had not even known till now that she yearned to go; but whatever the reason was it slipped away like a shadow, a word forgotten. "Has anyone looked after Moss, I wonder, did anyone send for a healer. She's the only healer on the Overfell, but there's people down in Gont Port who could help her, surely. Oh, poor Moss! I want to go— It's too late, but tomorrow, tomorrow early. And the master can make his own breakfast!"

"He'll learn," said Ged.

"No, he won't. He'll find some fool woman to do it for him. Ah!" She looked around the kitchen, her face bright and fierce. "I hate to leave her the twenty years I've scoured that table. I hope she appreciates it!"

Spark brought Townsend in for supper, but the sheep-dealer would not stay the night, though he was of course offered a bed in common hospitality. It would have been one of their beds, and Tenar did not like the thought. She was glad to see him go off to his hosts in the village in the blue twilight of the spring evening.

"We'll be off to Re Albi first thing tomorrow, son," she said to Spark. "Hawk and Therru and I."

He looked a little frightened.

"Just go off like that?"

"So you went; so you came," said his mother. "Now look here, Spark: this is your father's money-box. There's seven ivory pieces in it, and those credit counters from old Bridgeman, but he'll never pay, he hasn't got anything to pay with. These four Andradean pieces Flint got from selling sheepskins to the ship's outfitter in Valmouth four years running, back when you were a boy. These three Havnorian ones are what Tholy paid us for the High Creek farm. I had your father buy that farm, and I helped him clear it and sell it. I'll take those three pieces, for I've earned them. The rest, and the farm, is yours. You're the master."

The tall, thin young man stood there with his gaze on the money-box.

"Take it all. I don't want it," he said in a low voice.

"I don't need it. But I thank you, my son. Keep the four pieces. When you marry, call them my gift to your wife."

She put the box away in the place behind the big plate on the top shelf of the dresser, where Flint had always kept it. "Therru, get your things ready now, because we'll go very early."

"When are you coming back?" Spark asked, and the tone of his voice made Tenar think of the restless, frail child he had been. But she said only, "I don't know, my dear. If you need me, I'll come."

She busied herself getting out their travel shoes and packs. "Spark," she said, "you can do something for me."

He had sat down in the hearthseat, looking uncertain and morose. "What?"

"Go down to Valmouth, soon, and see your sister. And tell her that I've gone back to the Overfell. Tell her, if she wants me, just send word."

He nodded. He watched Ged, who had already packed his few belongings with the neatness and dispatch of one who had traveled much, and was now putting up the dishes to leave the kitchen in good order. That done, he sat down opposite Spark to run a new cord through the eyelets of his pack to close it at the top.

"There's a knot they use for that," Spark said. "Sailor's knot."

Ged silently handed the pack across the hearth, and watched as Spark silently demonstrated the knot.

"Slips up, see," he said, and Ged nodded.

They left the farm in the dark and cold of the morning. Sunlight comes late to the western side of Gont Mountain, and only walking kept them warm till at last the sun got round the great mass of the south peak and shone on their backs.

Therru was twice the walker she had been the summer before, but it was still a two days' journey for them. Along in the afternoon, Tenar asked, "Shall we try to get on to Oak Springs today? There's a sort of inn. We had a cup of milk there, remember, Therru?"

Ged was looking up the mountainside with a faraway expression. "There's a place I know. . . ."

"Fine," said Tenar.

A little before they came to the high corner of the road from which Gont Port could first be seen, Ged turned aside from the road into the forest that covered the steep slopes above it. The westering sun sent slanting red-gold rays into the darkness between the trunks and under the branches. They climbed half a mile or so, on no path Tenar could see, and came out on a little step or shelf of the mountainside, a meadow sheltered from the wind by the cliffs behind it and the trees about it. From there one could see the heights of the mountain to the north, and between the tops of great firs there was one clear view of the western sea. It was entirely silent there except when the wind breathed in the firs. One mountain lark sang long and sweet, away up in the sunlight, before dropping to her nest in the untrodden grass.

The three of them ate their bread and cheese. They watched darkness rise up the mountain from the sea. They made their bed of cloaks and slept, Therru next to Tenar next to Ged. In the deep night Tenar woke. An owl was calling nearby, a sweet repeated note like a bell, and far off up the mountain its mate replied like the ghost of a bell. Tenar thought, "I'll watch the stars set in the sea," but she fell asleep again at once in peace of heart.

She woke in the grey morning to see Ged sitting up beside her, his cloak pulled round his shoulders, looking out through the gap westward. His dark face was quite still, full of silence, as she had seen it once long ago on the beach of Atuan. His eyes were not downcast, as then; he looked into the illimitable west. Looking with him she saw the day coming, the glory of rose and gold reflected clear across the sky.

He turned to her, and she said to him, "I have loved you since I first saw you."

"Life-giver," he said and leaned forward, kissing her breast and mouth. She held him a moment. They got up, and waked Therru, and went on their way; but as they entered the trees Tenar looked back once at the little meadow as if charging it to keep faith with her happiness there.

The first day of the journey their goal had been journeying. This day they would come to Re Albi. So Tenar's mind was much on Aunty Moss, wondering what had befallen her and whether she was indeed dying. But as the day and the way went on her mind would not hold to the thought of Moss, or any thought. She was tired. She did not like walking this way again to death. They passed Oak Springs, and went down into the gorge, and started up again. By the last long uphill stretch to the Overfell, her legs were hard to lift, and her mind was stupid and confused, fastening upon one word or image until it became meaningless—the dish-cupboard in Ogion's house, or the words *bone dolphin*, which came into her head from seeing Therru's grass bag of toys, and repeated themselves endlessly.

Ged strode along at his easy traveler's gait, and Therru trudged right beside him, the same Therru who had worn out on this long climb less than a year ago, and had to be carried. But that had been after a longer day of walking. And the child had still been recovering from her punishment.

She was getting old, too old to walk so far so fast. It was so hard going uphill. An old woman should stay home by her fireside. The bone dolphin, the bone dolphin. Bone, bound, the binding spell. The bone man and the bone animal. There they went ahead. They were waiting for her. She was slow. She was tired. She toiled on up the last stretch of the hill and came up to them where the road came out on the level of the Overfell. To the left were the roofs of Re Albi slanting down towards the cliff's edge. To the right the road went up to the manor house. "This way," Tenar said.

"No," the child said, pointing left, to the village.

"This way," Tenar repeated, and set off on the right-hand way. Ged came with her.

They walked between the walnut orchards and the fields of grass. It was a warm late afternoon of early summer. Birds sang in the orchard trees near and far. He came walking down the road from the great house towards them, the one whose name she could not remember.

"Welcome!" he said, and stopped, smiling at them.

They stopped.

"What great personages have come to honor the house of the Lord of Re Albi," he said. Tuaho, that was not his name. The bone dolphin, the bone animal, the bone child.

"My Lord Archmage!" He bowed low, and Ged bowed to him.

"And my Lady Tenar of Atuan!" He bowed even lower to her, and she got down on her knees in the road. Her head sank down, till she put her hands in the dirt and crouched until her mouth too was on the dirt of the road.

"Now crawl," he said, and she began to crawl towards him.

"Stop," he said, and she stopped.

"Can you talk?" he asked. She said nothing, having no words that would come to her mouth, but Ged replied in his usual quiet voice, "Yes."

"Where's the monster?"

"I don't know."

"I thought the witch would bring her familiar with her. But she brought you instead. The Lord Archmage Sparrowhawk. What a splendid substitute! All I can do to witches and monsters is cleanse the world of them. But to you, who used at one time to be a man, I can talk; you are capable of rational speech, at least. And capable of understanding punishment. You thought you were safe, I suppose, with your king on the throne, and my master, our master, destroyed. You thought you'd had your will, and destroyed the promise of eternal life, didn't you?"

"No," said Ged's voice.

She could not see them. She could see only the dirt of the road, and taste it in her mouth. She heard Ged speak. He said, "In dying is life."

"Quack, quack, quote the Songs, Master of Roke—schoolmaster! What a funny sight to see, the great archmage all got up like a goatherd, and not an ounce of magic in him—not a word of power. Can you say a spell, archmage? Just a little spell—just a tiny charm of illusion? No? Not a word? My master defeated you. Now do you know it? You did not conquer him. His power lives! I might keep you alive here awhile, to see that power—my power. To see the old man I keep from death—and I might use your life for that if I need it—and to see your meddling king make a fool of himself, with his mincing lords and stupid wizards, looking for a woman! A woman to rule us! But the rule is here, the mastery is here, here, in this house. All this year I've been gathering others to me, men who know the true power. From Roke, some of them, from right under the noses of the schoolmasters. And from Havnor, from under the nose of that so-called Son of Morred, who wants a woman to rule him, your king who thinks he's so safe he can go by his true name. Do you know my name, archmage? Do you remember me, four years ago, when you were the great Master of Masters and I was a lowly student at Roke?"

"You were called Aspen," said the patient voice.

"And my true name?"

"I don't know your true name."

"What? You don't know it? Can't you find it? Don't mages know all names?"

"I'm not a mage."

"Oh, say it again."

"I'm not a mage."

"I like to hear you say it. Say it again."

"I'm not a mage."

"But I am!"

"Yes."

"Say it!"

"You are a mage."

"Ah! This is better than I hoped! I fished for the eel and caught the whale! Come on, then, come meet my friends. You can walk. She can crawl."

So they went up the road to the manor house of the Lord of Re Albi and went in, Tenar on hands and knees on the road, and on the marble steps up to the door, and on the marble pavements of the halls and rooms.

Inside the house it was dark. With the darkness came a darkness into Tenar's mind, so that she understood less and less of what was said. Only some words and voices came to her clearly. What Ged said she understood, and when he spoke she thought of his name, and clung to it in her mind. But he spoke very seldom, and only to answer the one whose name was not Tuaho. That one spoke to her now and then, calling her Bitch. "This is my new pet," he said to other men, several of them that were there in the darkness where candles made shadows. "See how well trained she is? Roll over, Bitch!" She rolled over, and the men laughed.

"She had a whelp," he said, "that I planned to finish punishing, since it was left half-burned. But she brought me a bird she'd caught instead, a sparrowhawk. Tomorrow we'll teach it to fly."

Other voices said words, but she did not understand words any more.

Something was fastened around her neck and she was made to crawl up more stairs and into a room that smelled of urine and rotting meat and sweet flowers. Voices spoke. A cold hand like a stone struck her head feebly while something laughed, "Eh, eh, eh," like an old door creaking back and forth. Then she was kicked and made to crawl down halls. She could not crawl fast enough, and was kicked in the breasts and in the mouth. Then there was a door that crashed, and silence, and the dark. She heard somebody crying and thought it was the child, her child. She wanted the child not to cry. At last it stopped.

Tehanu

The child turned left and went some way before she looked back, letting the blossoming hedgerow hide her.

The one called Aspen, whose name was Erisen, and whom she saw as a forked and writhing darkness, had bound her mother and father, with a thong through her tongue and a thong through his heart, and was leading them up toward the place where he hid. The smell of the place was sickening to her, but she followed a little way to see what he did. He led them in and shut the door behind them. It was a stone door. She could not enter there.

She needed to fly, but she could not fly; she was not one of the winged ones.

She ran as fast as she could across the fields, past Aunty Moss's house, past Ogion's house and the goats' house, onto the path along the cliff and to the edge of the cliff, where she was not to go because she could see it only with one eye. She was careful. She looked carefully with that eye. She stood on the edge. The water was far below, and the sun was setting far away. She looked into the west with the other eye, and called with the other voice the name she had heard in her mother's dream.

She did not wait for an answer, but turned round again and went back—first past Ogion's house to see if her peach tree had grown. The old tree stood bearing many small, green peaches, but there was no sign of the seedling. The goats had eaten it. Or it had died because she had not watered it. She stood a little while looking at the ground there, then drew a long breath and went on back across the fields to Aunty Moss's house.

Chickens going to roost squawked and fluttered, protesting her entrance. The little hut was dark and very full of smells. "Aunty Moss?" she said, in the voice she had for these people.

"Who's there?"

The old woman was in her bed, hiding. She was frightened, and tried to make stone around her to keep everyone away, but it didn't work; she was not strong enough.

"Who is it? Who's there? Oh dearie—oh dearie child, my little burned one, my pretty, what are you doing here? Where's she, where's she, your mother, oh, is she here? Did she come? Don't come in, don't come in, dearie, there's a curse on me, he cursed the old woman, don't come near me! Don't come near!"

She wept. The child put out her hand and touched her. "You're cold," she said.

"You're like fire, child, your hand burns me. Oh, don't look at me! He made my flesh rot, and shrivel, and rot again, but he won't let me die—he said I'd bring you here. I tried to die, I tried, but he held me, he held me living against my will, he won't let me die, oh, let me die!"

"You shouldn't die," the child said, frowning.

"Child," the old woman whispered, "dearie—call me by my name."

"Hatha," the child said.

"Ah. I knew. . . . Set me free, dearie!"

"I have to wait," the child said. "Till they come."

The witch lay easier, breathing without pain. "Till who come, dearie?" she whispered.

"My people."

The witch's big, cold hand lay like a bundle of sticks in hers. She held it firmly. It was as dark now outside the hut as inside it. Hatha, who was called Moss, slept; and presently the child, sitting on the floor beside her cot, with a hen perched nearby, slept also.

Men came when the light came. He said, "Up, Bitch! Up!" She got to her hands and knees. He laughed, saying, "All the way up! You're a clever bitch, you can walk on your hind legs, can't you? That's it. Pretend to be human! We have a way to go now. Come!" The strap was still around her neck, and he jerked it. She followed him.

"Here, you lead her," he said, and now it was that one, the one she loved, but she did not know his name any more, who held the strap.

They all came out of the dark place. Stone yawned to let them pass and ground together behind them.

He was always close beside her and the one who held the strap. Others came behind, three or four men.

The fields were grey with dew. The mountain was dark against a pale sky. Birds were beginning to sing in the orchards and hedgerows, louder and louder.

They came to the edge of the world and walked along it for a while until they came to where the ground was only rock and the edge was very narrow. There was a line in the rock, and she looked at that.

"He can push her," he said. "And then the hawk can fly, all by himself."

He unfastened the strap from around her neck.

"Go stand at the edge," he said. She followed the mark

in the stone out to the edge. The sea was below her, nothing else. The air was out beyond her.

"Now, Sparrowhawk will give her a push," he said. "But first, maybe she wants to say something. She has so much to say. Women always do. Isn't there anything you'd like to say to us, Lady Tenar?"

She could not speak, but she pointed to the sky above the sea.

"Albatross," he said.

She laughed aloud.

In the gulfs of light, from the doorway of the sky, the dragon flew, fire trailing behind the coiling, mailed body. Tenar spoke then.

"Kalessin!" she cried, and then turned, seizing Ged's arm, pulling him down to the rock, as the roar of fire went over them, the rattle of mail and the hiss of wind in upraised wings, the clash of the talons like scytheblades on the rock.

The wind blew from the sea. A tiny thistle growing in a cleft in the rock near her hand nodded and nodded in the wind from the sea.

Ged was beside her. They were crouched side by side, the sea behind them and the dragon before them.

It looked at them sidelong from one long, yellow eye.

Ged spoke in a hoarse, shaking voice, in the dragon's language. Tenar understood the words, which were only, "Our thanks, Eldest."

Looking at Tenar, Kalessin spoke, in the huge voice like a broom of metal dragged across a gong: *"Aro Tehanu?"*

"The child," Tenar said—"Therru!" She got to her feet to run, to seek her child. She saw her coming along the ledge of rock between the mountain and the sea, toward the dragon.

"Don't run, Therru!" she cried, but the child had seen

her and was running, running straight to her. They clung to each other.

The dragon turned its enormous, rust-dark head to watch them with both eyes. The nostril pits, big as kettles, were bright with fire, and wisps of smoke curled from them. The heat of the dragon's body beat through the cold sea wind.

"Tehanu," the dragon said.

The child turned to look at it.

"Kalessin," she said.

Then Ged, who had remained kneeling, stood up, though shakily, catching Tenar's arm to steady himself. He laughed. "Now I know who called thee, Eldest!" he said.

"I did," the child said. "I did not know what else to do, Segoy."

She still looked at the dragon, and she spoke in the language of the dragons, the words of the Making.

"It was well, child," the dragon said. "I have sought thee long."

"Shall we go there now?" the child asked. "Where the others are, on the other wind?"

"Would you leave these?"

"No," said the child. "Can they not come?"

"They cannot come. Their life is here."

"I will stay with them," she said, with a little catch of breath.

Kalessin turned aside to give that immense furnace-blast of laughter or contempt or delight or anger—"Hah!" Then, looking again at the child, "It is well. Thou hast work to do here."

"I know," the child said.

"I will come back for thee," Kalessin said, "in time." And, to Ged and Tenar, "I give you my child, as you will give me yours."

"In time," Tenar said.

Kalessin's great head bowed very slightly, and the long, sword-toothed mouth curled up at the corner.

Ged and Tenar drew aside with Therru as the dragon turned, dragging its armor across the ledge, placing its taloned feet carefully, gathering its black haunches like a cat, till it sprang aloft. The vaned wings shot up crimson in the new light, the spurred tail rang hissing on the rock, and it flew, it was gone—a gull, a swallow, a thought.

Where it had been lay scorched rags of cloth and leather, and other things.

"Come away," Ged said.

But the woman and the child stood and looked at those things.

"They are bone people," Therru said. She turned away then and set off. She went ahead of the man and woman along the narrow path.

"Her native tongue," Ged said. "Her mother tongue."

"Tehanu," said Tenar. "Her name is Tehanu."

"She has been given it by the giver of names."

"She has been Tehanu since the beginning. Always, she has been Tehanu."

"Come on!" the child said, looking back at them. "Aunty Moss is sick."

They were able to move Moss out into the light and air, to wash her sores, and to burn the foul linens of her bed, while Therru brought clean bedding from Ogion's house. She also brought Heather the goatgirl back with her. With Heather's help they got the old woman comfortable in her bed, with her chickens; and Heather promised to come back with something for them to eat.

"Someone must go down to Gont Port," Ged said, "for the wizard there. To look after Moss; she can be healed.

And to go to the manor house. The old man will die now. The grandson might live, if the house is made clean. . . ." He had sat down on the doorstep of Moss's house. He leaned his head back against the doorjamb, in the sunlight, and closed his eyes. "Why do we do what we do?" he said.

Tenar was washing her face and hands and arms in a basin of clear water she had drawn from the pump. She looked round when she was done. Utterly spent, Ged had fallen asleep, his face a little upturned to the morning light. She sat down beside him on the doorstep and laid her head against his shoulder. Are we spared? she thought. How is it we are spared?

She looked down at Ged's hand, relaxed and open on the earthen step. She thought of the thistle that nodded in the wind, and of the taloned foot of the dragon with its scales of red and gold. She was half-asleep when the child sat down beside her.

"Tehanu," she murmured.

"The little tree died," the child said.

After a while Tenar's weary, sleepy mind understood, and woke up enough to make a reply. "Are there peaches on the old tree?"

They spoke low, not to waken the sleeping man.

"Only little green ones."

"They'll ripen, after the Long Dance. Soon now."

"Can we plant one?"

"More than one, if you like. Is the house all right?"

"It's empty."

"Shall we live there?" She roused a little more, and put her arm around the child. "I have money," she said, "enough to buy a herd of goats, and Turby's winter-pasture, if it's still for sale. Ged knows where to take them up the mountain, summers. . . . I wonder if the wool we combed is still there?" So saying, she thought, We left the books, Ogion's books! On the mantel at Oak Farm—for Spark, poor boy, he can't read a word of them!

But it did not seem to matter. There were new things to be learned, no doubt. And she could send somebody for the books, if Ged wanted them. And for her spinning wheel. Or she could go down herself, come autumn, and see her son, and visit with Lark, and stay a while with Apple. They would have to replant Ogion's garden right away if they wanted any vegetables of their own this summer. She thought of the rows of beans and the scent of the bean flowers. She thought of the small window that looked west. "I think we can live there," she said.